MW01011419

"AN EXCELLENT FORTRESS FOR HIS
ARMIES, A REFUGE FOR THE PEOPLE"

"An Excellent Fortress for His Armies, a Refuge for the People"

Egyptological, Archaeological, and Biblical Studies in Honor of James K. Hoffmeier

EDITED BY RICHARD E. AVERBECK
AND K. LAWSON YOUNGER JR.

EISENBRAUNS | University Park, Pennsylvania

Library of Congress Cataloging-in-Publication Data

Names: Hoffmeier, James Karl, 1951– honouree. | Averbeck, Richard E., editor. | Younger,
    K. Lawson, Jr., editor.
Title: "An excellent fortress for his armies, a refuge for the people" : Egyptological, archaeo-
    logical, and biblical studies in honor of James K. Hoffmeier / edited by Richard E. Aver-
    beck and K. Lawson Younger, Jr.
Description: University Park, Pennsylvania : Eisenbrauns, [2020] | Includes bibliographical
    references and index.
Summary: "A collection of Egyptological, archaeological, and biblical studies papers deal-
    ing with the history, religion, and culture of the ancient Near East, assembled in honor of
    James K. Hoffmeier"—Provided by publisher.
Identifiers: LCCN 2019059728 | ISBN 9781575069944 (hardback)
Subjects: LCSH: Middle East—Antiquities. | Egypt—Antiquities. | LCGFT: Festschriften.
Classification: LCC DS56.A645 2020 | DDC 939.4—dc23
LC record available at https://lccn.loc.gov/2019059728

Eisenbrauns is an imprint of The Pennsylvania State University Press.

The Pennsylvania State University Press is a member of the Association of University
Presses.

It is the policy of The Pennsylvania State University Press to use acid-free paper. Publications on uncoated stock satisfy the minimum requirements of American National Standard for
Information Sciences—Permanence of Paper for Printed Library Material, ANSI Z39.48-1992.

CONTENTS

PREFACE

This volume honors our esteemed colleague, James K. Hoffmeier upon his retirement. Professor Hoffmeier has been Professor of Old Testament and ancient Near Eastern history and archaeology at Trinity Evangelical Divinity School of Trinity International University, Deerfield, Illinois from 1999 to 2019. These twenty years have been a true delight, and out of a deep appreciation for Jim's copious scholarship and wonderful friendship, the editors desired to make this volume a reality. His contributions to our department have been many, especially in the development and maintenance of a wonderful camaraderie. But it has undoubtedly been Professor Hoffmeier's impact on students that will be long-term. He has mentored many who now have successful academic careers, as well as others who will come along in the future.

The editors would like to express our most sincere gratitude to the Lanier Theological Library Foundation for its generous support in the subvention for this volume. We thank Jim Eisenbraun, who offered clear and helpful advice at all stages of the publication. We also thank Pennsylvania State University Press for its help at every stage in the publication of this volume.

Finally, we thank the thirty-three contributors—teachers, colleagues, and students of James K. Hoffmeier—from all over the world, who responded most enthusiastically to the editors' invitation to honor Professor Hoffmeier. The editors anticipate that the seminal essays in this volume will contribute in significant ways to three disciplines—Egyptology, archaeology and biblical studies—the areas of Jim's interests and his own publications.

The title for this volume, *"An Excellent Fortress for His Armies, a Refuge for the People,"* comes from the Gebel Barkal Stela of Thutmose III (line 7) and seems quite appropriate for honoring James K. Hoffmeier, given his significant excavations of the ancient fortress at Tell el-Borg.

Richard E. Averbeck
K. Lawson Younger, Jr.

ABBREVIATIONS

A¹P	Artzxerxes I Persepolis inscriptions
A²H	Artaxerxes II Hamadan inscriptions
A²S	Artaxerxes II Susa inscriptions
A³P	Artaxerxes III Persepolis inscriptions
ÄA	Ägyptologische Abhandlungen
AAS	*Annales Archéologiques de Syrie*, later *Annales Archéologiques Arabes Syriennes*
ÄAT	Ägypten und Altes Testament.
AB	Anchor (Yale) Bible
ABD	*Anchor Bible Dictionary*. Edited by David N. Freedman. 6 vols. Garden City, NY: Doubleday, 1992.
ABL	*Assyrian and Babylonian Letters Belonging to the Kouyunjik Collections of the British Museum*. Edited by Robert F. Harper. 14 vols. Chicago: University of Chicago, 1892–1914.
ABRL	Anchor (Yale) Bible Reference Library
ABS	Archaeology and Biblical Studies
AEL	*Ancient Egyptian Literature: A Book of Readings*. Miriam Lichtheim. 3 vols. Berkeley: University of California, 1973–1980.
AeL	*Ägypten und Levante*
AIL	Ancient Israel and Its Literature
A.J.	Josephus *Antiquitates judaicae*
AJA	*American Journal of Archaeology*
ALASP	Abhandlungen zur Literatur Alt-Syrien-Palästinas
AMI	Archäologische Mitteilungen aus Iran
AnOr	Analecta Orientalia
AnSt	*Anatolian Studies*
AOAT	Alter Orient und Altes Testament
AOS	American Oriental Society
ApOTC	Apollos Old Testament Commentary
ARM	Archives royales de Mari
AS	Assyriological Studies
ASAE	*Annales du Service des Antiquités de l'Égypte*

AuOr	*Aula Orientalis*
AUSS	*Andrews University Seminary Studies*
BA	*Biblical Archaeologist*
BACE	*The Bulletin of the Australian Centre for Egyptology*
BAR	*Biblical Archaeology Review*
BARIS	British Archaeological Report International Series
BASOR	*Bulletin of the American Schools of Oriental Research*
BBR	*Bulletin for Biblical Research*
BBRSup	Bulletin for Biblical Research Supplements
BECNT	Baker Exegetical Commentary on the New Testament
BETL	Bibliotheca Ephemeridum Theologicarum Lovaniensium
Bib	*Biblica*
BIFAO	*Bulletin de l'Institut français d'Archéologie orientale*
B.J.	Josephus *Bellum judaicum*
BN	*Biblische Notizen*
BNP	*Brill's New Pauly: Encyclopedia of the Ancient World*. Edited by Hubert Cancik, Helmuth Schneider, and Manfred Landfester. 22 vols. Leiden: Brill, 2003–2011.
BRev	*Bible Review*
BRLJ	Brill Reference Library of Judaism
Bryce	Bryce, Trevor R. *Kingdom of the Hittites*. New ed. Oxford: Oxford University Press, 2005.
BSac	*Bibliotheca Sacra*
BSFE	*Bulletin de la Société Française d'Égyptologie*
BTAVO	Beihefte zum Tübinger Atlas des Vorderen Orients
BZ	*Biblische Zeitschrift*
CAH	Cambridge Ancient History
CAL	Comprehensive Aramaic Lexicon (www.cal1.cn.huc.edu)
CHANE	Culture and History of the Ancient Near East
CHC	Cambridge History of Christianity
CHD	*The Hittite Dictionary of the Oriental Institute of the University of Chicago*. Edited by Hans G. Güterbock, Harry A. Hoffner Jr., and Theo P. J. van den Hout. Chicago: Oriental Institute of the University of Chicago, 1989–.
CHI	Cambridge History of Iran
CHJ	Cambridge History of Judaism
CHLI 1	*The Hieroglyphic Luwian Inscriptions of the Iron Age*. Vol. 1 of *Corpus of Hieroglyphic Luwian Inscriptions*. J. D. Hawkins. Untersuchungen zur indogermanischen Sprach- und Kulturwissenschaft 8.1. Berlin: de Gruyter, 2000.
CHLI 2	*Karatepe-Aslantaş. The Inscriptions: Facsimile Edition*. Vol. 2 of *Corpus of Hieroglyphic Luwian Inscriptions*. Halet Çambel; with a contribution by Wolfgang Röllig and tables by J. D. Hawkins. Untersuchungen zur indogermanischen Sprach- und Kulturwissenschaft 8.2. Berlin: de Gruyter, 1999.

COS	*The Context of Scripture.* Edited by William W. Hallo and K. Lawson Younger Jr. 4 vols. Leiden: Brill, 1997–2002, 2016.
CRAIBL	*Comptes rendus de l'Académie des inscriptions et belles lettres*
CRIPEL	*Cahiers de recherches de l'Institut de papyrologie et d'égyptologie de Lille*
CTH	*Catalogue des textes hittites.* Emmanuel Laroche. Paris: Klincksieck, 1971.
DAIK	Deutsches Archäologisches Institut, Abteilung Kairo
DB	Darius's Bisitun inscription
DBH	Dresdner Beiträge zur Hethitologie
DDD	*Dictionary of Deities and Demons.* Edited by Karel van der Toorn, Bob Becking, and Pieter W. van der Horst. Leiden: Brill, 1995. 2nd rev. ed. Grand Rapids: Eerdmans, 1999.
DH	Darius's Hamadan inscription
Dietrich	Dietrich, Manfried. "Salmanassar I. von Assyrien, Ibirānu (VI.) von Ugarit und Tudḫalija IV. von Hatti." *UF* 35 (2003): 103–39.
DLE	Leonard H. Lesko, ed. *A Dictionary of Late Egyptian.* 5 vols. Providence: B. C. Scribe, 1982–1990.
DNa–e	Darius's Naqsh-i Rustam inscriptions a–e
Dom.	Seutonius *Domitianus*
DP	Darius's Persepolis inscription
DS	Darius's Susa inscriptions
DZc	Darius's Suez inscription
EA	El Amarna letter
ENiM	*Équipe Égypte Nilotique et Méditerranéenne*
ErIsr	*Eretz Israel*
ExpTim	*Expository Times*
FAT	Forschungen zum Alten Testament
Flac.	Cicero *Pro Flacco*
Frahm	Frahm, Eckhart. "Assur 2001: Die Schriftfunde." *Mitteilungen der Deutschen Orient-Gesellschaft* 134 (2002): 47–86.
FSN	*Felsinschriften aus dem sudanesischen Nubien.* Fritz Hintze, Walter Friedrich Reineke, and Adelheid Burkhardt. Publikation der Nubien-Expedition 1961–1963 1. Berlin: Akademie, 1989.
GBS	Guides to Biblical Scholarship
Glassner	Glassner, Jean-Jacques. *Mesopotamian Chronicles.* WAW 19. Atlanta: Society of Biblical Literature, 2004.
GM	*Göttinger Miszellen: Beiträge zur ägyptologischen Diskussion*
Grayson	Grayson, A. K. *Assyrian Rulers of the Early First Millennium BC I (1114–859 BC).* Royal Inscriptions of Mesopotamia, Assyrian Periods 2. Toronto: University of Toronto Press, 1991.
HÄB	Hildesheimer ägyptologische Beiträge
HALOT	Koehler, Ludwig, Walter Baumgartner, and Johann J. Stamm. *The Hebrew and Aramaic Lexicon of the Old Testament.* Translated and edited under the supervision of Mervyn E. J. Richardson. 2 vols. Leiden: Brill, 2001.

Hannig	Hannig, Rainer. *Ägyptisches Wörterbuch II*. Mainz: von Zabern, 2006.
HdO	Handbuch der Orientalistik
HDT	*Hittite Diplomatic Texts*. Gary Beckman. Edited by Harry Hoffner. 2nd ed. WAW 7. Atlanta: Society of Biblical Literature, 1996.
Hist.	*Historiae*
HSM	Harvard Semitic Monographs
IBS	Innsbrucker Beiträge zur Sprachwissenschaft
IEJ	*Israel Exploration Journal*
ISBL	Indiana Studies in Biblical Literature
JAEI	*Journal of Ancient Egyptian Interconnections*
JANER	*Journal of Ancient Near Eastern Religions*
JANES	*Journal of the Ancient Near Eastern Society*
JARCE	*Journal of the American Research Center in Egypt*
JBL	*Journal of Biblical Literature*
JCAV	*Journal of the Classical Association of Victoria*
JCS	*Journal of Cuneiform Studies*
JEA	*Journal of Egyptian Archaeology*
JESHO	*Journal of the Economic and Social History of the Orient*
JETS	*Journal of the Evangelical Theological Society*
JHebS	*Journal of Hebrew Studies*
JNES	*Journal of Near Eastern Studies*
JNSL	*Journal of Northwest Semitic Languages*
JSNTSup	Journal for the Study of the New Testament Supplement Series
JPOS	*Journal of the Palestine Oriental Society*
JSOT	*Journal for the Study of the Old Testament*
JSOTSup	Journal for the Study of the Old Testament Supplement Series
JSSEA	*Journal of the Society for the Study of Egyptian Antiquity*
JTISup	Journal of Theological Interpretation Supplement
JTS	*Journal of Theological Studies*
KAI	*Kanaanäische und aramäische Inschriften*. H. Donner and Wolfgang Röllig. 3 vols. Wiesbaden: Harrassowitz, 1962–64, 2002.
KRI	*Ramesside Inscriptions: Historical and Biographical*. Kenneth A. Kitchen. Oxford: Blackwell, 1979–.
KTU	*The Cuneiform Alphabetic Texts from Ugarit, Ras Ibn Hani, and Other Places*. Manfried Dietrich, Oswald Loretz, and Joaquín Sanmartín. 2nd ed. ALASP 8. Münster: Ugarit-Verlag, 1995.
KUB	Keilschrifturkunden aus Boghazköi
LÄ	*Lexikon der Ägyptologie*. Edited by Wolfgang Helck et al. Wiesbaden: Harrassowitz, 1977–.
LAPO	Littératures anciennes du Proche-Orient
LHBOTS	Library of Hebrew Bible/Old Testament Studies
MDAIK	*Mitteilungen des Deutschen Archäologischen Instituts, Abteilung Kairo*
MIO	*Mitteilungen des Instituts für Orientforschung*

MSJ	*The Master's Seminary Journal*
NAC	New American Commentary
NEA	*Near Eastern Archaeology*
NIBC	New International Biblical Commentary
NICOT	New International Commentary on the Old Testament
NIVAC	NIV Application Commentary
NJPS	New Jewish Publication Society translation
NovTSup	Supplements to Novum Testamentum
NRSV	New Revised Standard Version
OAC	Orientis Antiqui Collectio
OBO	Orbis Biblicus et Orientalis
OBO.SA	Orbis Biblicus et Orientalis Series Archaeologica
OEAE	*The Oxford Encyclopedia of Ancient Egypt*. Edited by Donald Redford. 3 vols. New York: Oxford University Press, 2001.
OED	*Oxford English Dictionary*
OIMP	Oriental Institute Museum Publications
OIP	Oriental Institute Publications
OLA	Orientalia Lovaniensia Analecta
OLZ	*Orientalistische Literaturzeitung*
Or	*Orientalia* (NS)
OTL	Old Testament Library
OTS	Old Testament Studies
PAe	Probleme der Aegyptologie
PEQ	*Palestine Exploration Quarterly*
PIHANS	Publications de l'Institut historique-archéologique néerlandais de Stamboul
PT	Pyramid Text
RA	*Revue d'Assyriologie et d'archéologie orientale*
RBS	Resources for Biblical Study
RdÉ	*Revue d'Égyptologie*
RHA	*Revue hittite et asianique*
RITA	*Ramesside Inscriptions: Translated and Annotated/Notes and Comments*. Kenneth A. Kitchen. 6 volumes. Oxford: Blackwell, 1993–2013.
RS	Ras Shamra tablet
RSO	*Rivista degli Studi Orientali*
RSOu 4	*Les textes para-mythologiques de la 24e campagne (1961)*. Dennis Pardee. Publications de la Mission Française Archéologique de Ras Shamra-Ougarit 4. Paris: Éditions Recherche sur les Civilisations, 1988.
SAK	*Studien zur altägyptischen Kultur*
SAOC	Studies in Ancient Oriental Civilizations
Sasson	Sasson, Jack M. *From the Mari Archives: An Anthology of Old Babylonian Letters*. Winona Lake, IN: Eisenbrauns, 2015.
SBLSPS	*Society of Biblical Literature Seminar Papers Series*
SEL	*Studi epigrafici e linguistici*

SJOT	*Scandinavian Journal of the Old Testament*
SNTSMS	Society for New Testament Studies Monograph Series
STJ	*Stulos Theological Journal*
Strom.	Clement, *Stromateis*
SymS	Symposium Series
TA	*Tel Aviv*
Thureau-Dangin	Thureau-Dangin, F. *Recueil de tablettes Chaldéennes*. Paris: Leroux, 1903.
TJ	*Trinity Journal*
TLC	*Treaty, Law and Covenant in the Ancient Near East, Part 1: The Texts*. Kenneth A. Kitchen and Paul Lawrence. Wiesbaden: Harrasowitz, 2012.
Transeu	*Transeuphratène*
TSAJ	Texts and Studies in Ancient Judaism
UF	*Ugarit Forschungen*
Urk	*Urkunden des ägyptischen Altertums*. Edited by Georg Steindorf. Leipzig, 1905–1957.
VT	*Vetus Testamentum*
VTSup	Supplements to Vetus Testamentum
WAB	Thureau-Dangin, F. "Iasmaḫ-Adad," *RA* 34 (1937): 135–39.
WAW	Writings from the Ancient World
Wb.	*Wörterbuch der ägyptischen Sprache*. Edited by Adolf Erman and Hermann Grapow. 11 vols. Berlin: Akademie, 1926–1963.
WTJ	*Westminster Theological Journal*
WUNT	Wissenschaftliche Untersuchungen zum Neuen Testament
XE	Xerxes's Gandj Nameh/Elvend inscription
XPa–f	Xerxes's Persepolis inscriptions a–f
XPh	Daiva inscription
XV	Xerxes's Van inscription
YES	Yale Egyptological Studies
YNER	Yale Near Eastern Researches
ZÄS	*Zeitschrift für Ägyptische Sprache und Altertumskunde*
ZAW	*Zeitschrift für die Alttestamentliche Wissenschaft*
ZDPV	*Zeitschrift des Deutschen Palästina-Vereins*

CONTRIBUTORS

Richard E. Averbeck, Trinity Evangelical Divinity School
Joshua Berman, Bar Ilan University
Louise Bertini, The American Research Center in Egypt
Aaron A. Burke, University of California, Los Angeles
S. Cameron Coyle, Southwestern Baptist Theological Seminary
Pearce Paul Creasman, University of Arizona
Thomas W. Davis, Southwestern Baptist Theological Seminary
Joanna Dębowska-Ludwin, Jagiellonian University in Krakow, Poland
David A. Falk, University of British Columbia
Deirdre N. Fulton, Baylor University
Kaz Hayashi, Baylor University
Tomasz Herbich, Institute of Archaeology and Ethnology, Polish Academy of Sciences
Richard S. Hess, Denver Seminary
Hesham M. Hussein, Egyptian Ministry of Antiquities, North Sinai
Salima Ikram, American University in Cairo
Mark D. Janzen, Louisiana College
Jens Bruun Kofoed, Fjellhaug International University College
Ash Melika, California Baptist University
Edmund S. Meltzer, Pacifica Graduate Institute
Alan Millard, University of Liverpool
Ellen Morris, Barnard College
Greg Mumford, University of Alabama, Birmingham
Steve Ortiz, Southwestern Baptist Theological Seminary
Miller C. Prosser, University of Chicago
Donald B. Redford, Pennsylvania State University
Karolina Rosińska-Balik, Jagiellonian University in Krakow, Poland
Gary A. Rendsburg, Rutgers University
Nili Shupak, Haifa University
Stuart Tyson Smith, University of California, Santa Barbara
Eric J. Tully, Trinity Evangelical Divinity School
Carola Vogel, Johannes Gutenberg Universität, Mainz
Kei Yamamoto, University of Arizona
K. Lawson Younger Jr., Trinity Evangelical Divinity School

PERSONAL AND ACADEMIC BIOGRAPHY
OF JAMES K. HOFFMEIER

James Karl Hoffmeier was born in Cairo, Egypt on February 13, 1951. He was raised in a small village in central Egypt where his parents, Charles and Vivian Hoffmeier, served as missionary educators. It was here that his love for ancient Egyptian history first emerged. In 1967, he moved to Pennsylvania where he graduated from high school. In 1974, Jim married his college sweetheart, Cathy Tom. They have two children. Jessica is a graduate of Johns Hopkins University in Near Eastern Studies (BA) and Trinity (MA) in Near Eastern Archaeology; and did work on her PhD in Egyptology at Memphis. Jessica and her husband Paul are the proud parents of Danny, Peter, Nate and Gabe. Benjamin is a graduate (BA) of Centre College in Kentucky and holds his MA from Trinity in Theological Studies. He coached American football at Trinity College, Wheaton College, Houston Baptist University, and after getting married to Farren in July 2018, he began a new position as head football coach and Bible teacher at Brazos Christian School in Bryan, Texas.

Jim attended Pennsylvania State University, receiving in 1971 his AA in Letters, Arts, and Science. In 1973, he graduated from Wheaton College (Illinois) with a BA in Near Eastern Archaeology. He was awarded the MA in Egyptian Archaeology from the University of Toronto in 1975. From 1975 to 1977, Hoffmeier participated in excavations in Egypt with the Akhenaten Temple Project, based in Luxor and directed by Professor Donald Redford. It was during this time that Jim began to publish his first articles, many of which were devoted to studies of hunting and ancient Egyptian weaponry and warfare. While working on his dissertation, Wheaton College invited him to return and begin teaching Old Testament and Near Eastern history as well as build an MA archaeology program. In 1982, Hoffmeier earned his PhD from the University of Toronto in Near Eastern Religions, with a major in Egyptian Religion and a minor in Israelite Religion.

From 1980 to 1999, Jim was on the faculty of Wheaton College where he taught and mentored hundreds of students and chaired the Department of Biblical and Archaeological Studies for five years. During these years, he produced a substantial number of peer-reviewed articles and key publications. Especially noteworthy are his book, *"Sacred" in the Vocabulary of Ancient Egypt* (1985) and his widely read monograph, *Israel in Egypt: Evidence for the Authenticity of the Exodus Tradition* (1997; repr. 1999).

In 1999, Jim moved and became Professor of Old Testament and Ancient Near Eastern History and Archaeology at Trinity Evangelical Divinity School of Trinity International University, Deerfield, Illinois. He took a liking immediately to the international component of an academically oriented, graduate divinity school.

Having started the North Sinai Archaeological Project in 1994—devoted to researching and studying Egypt's frontier of the New Kingdom period—the move to Trinity enabled Hoffmeier to conduct thorough survey work in the region and concentrate on the excavations of Tell el-Borg during eight seasons from 1999 to 2008. Jim began to fulfill his vision as an educator, which included taking students out of the classroom and into the fields of Egypt to excavate. Thus, he brought numerous students and his family to help dig the site. One of Hoffmeier's methodological emphases in the excavation was to bring in and include experts in the various technical areas of Egyptian archaeology and to create a highly collaborative environment in order to gain as much understanding from the site as possible. While Jim has churned out many articles and essays based on the excavations, laudably, he has published both volumes of the final reports of the excavations at Tell el-Borg: *Tell el-Borg I: Excavations in North Sinai* (2014) and *Tell el-Borg II: Excavations in North Sinai* (2019).

Jim has also produced many significant articles and essays (see the list of publications below), but also important monographs like *Ancient Israel in Sinai: Evidence for the Authenticity of the Wilderness Tradition* (2005/2010), *The Archaeology of the Bible* (Oxford: Lion Hudson, 2008), available in German, Italian, Spanish, Dutch, Romanian, Norwegian, and Arabic. In 2009, he authored *The Immigrations Crisis: Immigrants, Aliens and the Bible*. He has edited *Abortion: A Christian Understanding and Response* (1987), *Faith, Tradition and History: Old Testament Historiography in its Near Eastern Context* (1994; re-released as a paperback in 2010), *The Future of Biblical Archaeology* (2004), and *Do Historical Matters Matter to Faith* (2012). Recently, he has authored the monograph, *Akhenaten, His Religion and the Origins of Monotheism* (2015), and *Genesis: History, Fiction, or Neither? Three Views on the Bible's Earliest Chapters* (with Gordon Wenham and Kenton Sparks, 2015).

Jim Hoffmeier has also appeared in a number of TV programs on Egypt and the Bible for the *Discovery Channel*, the *Learning Channel*, the *History Channel*, and *National Geographic*.

Although these contributions are undoubtedly important to Jim, it is clear that he places a higher emphasis on the people around him, and especially his students, who have experienced his generosity and his willingness to share his expertise. On the one hand, they know they must understand the various interpretive options that he has rigorously covered; yet, on the other hand, they must go where the evidence leads. His deep faith convictions born out of commitment to the historical reliability of the Old Testament is what has driven his detailed scholarship and his giving of himself in Christian selflessness for his students, colleagues, and others.

Dr. Hoffmeier has served as an elder at Crossroads Community Church (Carol Stream), and speaks at various conferences, and teaches and preaches in churches throughout America and around the world. He has taught in Mongolia, Taiwan, Hong Kong, Romania, and throughout the Middle East. During the 2018–2019 academic year, Jim did research for a book on the relationship between biblical views of creation and science, funded by a grant from the Templeton Foundation, administered by the Carl Henry Center at Trinity.

Jim retired from Trinity in 2018. However, there can be little doubt that his witty remarks, puns and wordplays, his gentle yet determined spirit, and his example of diligence and integrity will be forever etched in the minds of all those who sat under his teaching, worked alongside him on an excavation, traveled with him on a study tour, worked with him as a colleague, or known him through professional meetings. It is an honor and privilege to celebrate him with this volume.

Richard E. Averbeck and K. Lawson Younger, Jr.

PUBLICATIONS OF JAMES KARL HOFFMEIER

Books

"Sacred" in the Vocabulary of Ancient Egypt: The Term "ḎSR," with Special Reference to Dynasties I–XX. OBO 59. Fribourg: Universitätsverlag; Göttingen: Vandenhoeck & Ruprecht, 1985.

Israel in Egypt? The Evidence for the Authenticity of the Exodus Tradition. Oxford: Oxford University Press, 1997.

Israel in Egypt? The Evidence for the Authenticity of the Exodus Tradition. Paperback edition with revisions. Oxford: Oxford University Press, 1999.

Ancient Israel in Sinai: The Evidence for the Authenticity of the Wilderness Traditions. Oxford: Oxford University Press, 2005.

The Archaeology of the Bible. Oxford: Lion Hudson, 2008.

The Archaeology of the Bible (German, Italian, Spanish, Dutch and Romanian editions), 2008.

The Immigration Crisis: Immigrants, Aliens and the Bible. Wheaton: Crossway, 2009.

The Archaeology of the Bible (Norwegian edition), 2010.

Ancient Israel in Sinai: The Evidence for the Authenticity of the Wilderness Traditions. Paperback edition with revisions. Oxford: Oxford University Press, 2011.

Tell el-Borg I: Excavations in North Sinai; "The Dwelling of the Lion" on the Ways of Horus. Winona Lake, IN: Eisenbrauns, 2014.

Akhenaten and the Origins of Monotheism. Oxford: Oxford University Press, 2015.

Genesis: History, Fiction, or Neither? Three Views on the Bible's Earliest Chapters. Counterpoints: Bible and Theology. Grand Rapids: Zondervan, 2015. With Gordon Wenham and Kenton Sparks.

The Archaeology of the Bible (Arabic Edition). Dar el Kelama Press, 2016.

Tell el-Borg II: Excavations in North Sinai; "The Dwelling of the Lion" on the Ways of Horus. State College, PA: Eisenbrauns, 2019.

Recent Studies on North Sinai: Archaeological, Historical, Geological and Biblical. ÄAT 94. Münster: Zaphon, 2019.

In the Footsteps of the Prophets: A Survey of the Old Testament Prophetic Literature. Grand Rapids: Kregel, forthcoming.

Edited Works

Scripta Mediterranea: Bulletin of the Society for Mediterranean Studies, University of Toronto. (Founding Editor) 1980–1983.

Egyptological Miscellanies: A Tribute to Professor Ronald J. Williams. Ancient World 6.1–4. Chicago: Ares Publishers, 1983. With Edmund S. Meltzer.

Abortion: A Christian Understanding and Response. Grand Rapids: Baker, 1987.

A New Commentary on the Whole Bible Based on Jamieson, Fausset and Brown. Wheaton, IL: Tyndale House Publishers, 1990. With J. D. Douglas and Philip W. Comfort.

Faith, Tradition, History: Old Testament Historiography in its Near Eastern Context. Winona Lake, IN: Eisenbrauns, 1994. With Alan R. Millard and David W. Baker.

Future of Biblical Archaeology: Reassessing Methods and Assumptions. Grand Rapids: Eerdmans, 2004. With Alan R. Millard.

Do Historical Matters Matter to Faith: A Critical Appraisal of Modern and Postmodern Approaches to Scripture. Wheaton: Crossway, 2012. With Dennis R. Magary.

"Did I Not Bring Israel out of Egypt?" Biblical, Archaeological, and Egyptological Perspectives on the Exodus Narratives. BBRSup 13. Winona Lake, IN: Eisenbrauns, 2016. With Alan R. Millard and Gary A. Rendsburg.

Articles and Essays

"Hunting Desert Game with the Bow: A Brief Examination." *Society for the Study of Egyptian Antiquities Newsletter* 6.2 (1975): 8–13.

"The Hieroglyph ⯑ and the Egyptian Bowstring." *Society for the Study of Egyptian Antiquities Newsletter* 6.3 (1976): 6–11.

"Observations on the Evolving Chariot Wheel in the 18th Dynasty." *JARCE* 13 (1976): 43–45.

"Tents in Egypt and the Ancient Near East." *Society for the Study of Egyptian Antiquities Newsletter* 7.3 (1977): 13–28.

"Comments on an Unusual Hunt Scene from the New Kingdom." *JSSEA* 10.3 (1980): 195–200.

"Possible Origins of the Tent of Purification in the Egyptian Funerary Cult." *SÄK* 9 (1981): 167–77.

"A New Insight on Pharaoh Apries from Herodotus, Diodorus and Jeremiah 46:17." *JSSEA* 11 (1981): 165–70.

"Some Egyptian Motifs Related to Enemies and Warfare and Their Old Testament Counterparts." Pages 53–70 in *Egyptological Miscellanies: A Tribute to Professor Ronald J. Williams*. Edited by James K. Hoffmeier and Edmund S. Meltzer. Ancient World 6. Chicago: Ares, 1983.

"Some Thoughts on Genesis 1 and 2 and Egyptian Cosmology." *JANES* 15 (1983): 39–49.

"The Arm of God Versus the Arm of Pharaoh in the Exodus Narratives." *Bib* 67 (1986): 378–87.

"Moses." Pages 415–25 in vol. 3 of *International Standard Bible Encyclopedia*. Edited by Geoffrey W. Bromiley. Grand Rapids: Eerdmans, 1986.

"Mediterranean Sea." Page 306 in vol. 3 of *International Standard Bible Encyclopedia*. Edited by Geoffrey W. Bromiley. Grand Rapids: Eerdmans, 1986, 3:306.

"Further Evidence for Infant Sacrifice in the Ancient Near East." *BAR* 13.2 (1987): 60–61.

"Quiver"; "Shihor"; "(Pharaoh) So"; "Stiff-necked"; "Straw"; "Taskmaster"; "Weapons of War"; and "Zipporah." In vol. 4 of *International Standard Bible Encyclopedia*. Edited by Geoffrey W. Bromiley. Grand Rapids: Eerdmans, 1988.

"A Relief of 'the Chief of the Gang' from Deir el-Medineh at Wheaton College, Illinois." *JEA* 74: (1988): 217–20.

"Egypt as an Arm of Flesh: A Prophetic Response." Pages 79–97 in *Israel's Apostasy and Restoration: Essays in Honor of Roland K. Harrison*. Edited by Abraham Gileadi. Grand Rapids: Baker, 1988.

"The Chariot Scenes of Akhenaten at Karnak." Pages 35–45 in *Rwd-Mnw and Inscriptions*. Vol. 2 of *The Akhenaten Temple Project*. Edited by Donald B. Redford. Toronto: University of Toronto Press, 1988.

"Reconsidering Egypt's Part in the Termination of the Middle Bronze Age in Palestine." *Levant* 21 (1989): 181–93.

"Exodus." In *Evangelical Commentary on the Bible*. Edited by Walter Elwell. Grand Rapids: Baker, 1989.

"Some Thoughts on William G. Dever's 'Hyksos,' Egyptian Destructions, and the End of the Palestinian Middle Bronze Age.'" *Levant* 22 (1990): 83–89.

"James Weinstein's 'Egypt and the Middle Bronze IIC/Late Bronze IA': A Rejoinder." *Levant* 23 (1991): 117–24.

"The Aftermath of David's Triumph Over Goliath: The Text of 1 Samuel 17:54 in Light of Near Eastern Parallels." *Archaeology in the Biblical World* 1 (1991): 18–23.

"The Coffins of the Middle Kingdom: The Residence and the Regions." Pages 69–86 in *Middle Kingdom Studies*. Edited by Stephen Quirke. Surrey: Sia, 1991.

"Plagues of Egypt." *ABD* 5:374–78

"The Wives' Tales of Genesis 12, 20, and 26 and the Covenants at Beersheba." *Tyndale Bulletin* 43 (1992): 81–99.

"The Problem of 'History' in Egyptian Royal Inscriptions." Pages 291–99 in *VI. Congresso Internazionale di Egittologia Atti*. Edited by Silvio Curto et al. Torino: Societa italiana per il gas, 1993.

"The Use of Basalt on the Floors of Some Old Kingdom Pyramid Complexes." *JARCE* 30 (1993): 117–23.

"The Structure of Joshua 1–11 and the Annals of Thutmose III." Pages 165–79 in *Faith, Tradition, History: Old Testament Historiography in its Near Eastern Context*. Edited by Alan R. Millard, James K. Hoffmeier, and David W. Baker. Winona Lake, IN: Eisenbrauns, 1994.

"The Egyptians." Pages 251–90 in *Peoples of the Old Testament World*. Edited by Edwin Yamauchi, Gerald L. Mattingly and Alfred J. Hoerth. Grand Rapids: Baker, 1994.

"The King as God's Son in Egypt and Israel." *JSSEA* 24 (1994): 28–38.

"Of Minimalists and Maximalists." *BAR* 21.2 (1995): 20–22.

"The Recently Discovered Tell Dan Inscription: Controversy and Confirmation." *Archaeology in the Biblical World* 3 (1995): 12–15.

"The Archaeological Salvage Work in Northern Sinai." *Archaeology in the Biblical World* 3 (1995): 3–4.

"Are There Regionally Based Theological Differences in the Coffin Texts?" Pages 45–54 in *The World of the Coffin Texts: Proceedings of the Symposium Held on the Occasion of the 100th Birthday of Adriaan de Buck*. Edited by Harco Willems. Egyptologische Uitgaven. Leiden: Nederlands Institut voor het Nabije Oosten, 1996.

"Son of God from Pharaoh to Israel's Kings to Jesus." *BRev* (1997): 44–49, 54.

"King Lists, Historiography." *COS* 1:68–73.

"The Evangelical Contribution to Understanding the (Early) History of Ancient Israel in Recent Scholarship." *BBR* 7 (1997): 1–14.

"Once Again the 'Plumb Line' Vision of Amos: An Interpretive Clue from Egypt?" Pages 304–19 in *Boundaries of the Ancient Near Eastern World: A Tribute to Cyrus H. Gordon*. Edited by Meir Lubetski, Claire Gottlieb, and Sharon R. Keller. JSOTSup 273. Sheffield: Sheffield Academic, 1998.

"Egypt"; "Joseph"; "Plagues of Egypt"; "Reed"; "Fish, fishing"; "Flax linen." In *New International Dictionary of Old Testament Theology and Exegesis*. Edited by Willem Van Gemeren. Grand Rapids: Zondervan, 1999.

"Chariots." Pages 193–95 in *Encyclopedia of the Archaeology of Ancient Egypt*. Edited by Kathryn Bard. London: Routledge, 1999.

"The Heavens Declare the Glory of God: The Limits of General Revelation." *TJ* 21 (2000): 17–24.

"The Biography of Ahmose son of Ebana"; "The Annals of Thutmose III"; "The Gebel Barkal Stela of Thutmose III"; "The Armant Stela of Thutmose III"; "The Memphis and Karnak Stelae of Amenhotep II"; "The (Israel) Stela of Merneptah." *COS* 2:5–22, 40–41.

"Fate"; "Israel"; "Military, Materiel." *OEAE* 1:507–8; 2:194–96; 2:406–12.

"Understanding Hebrew and Egyptian Military Texts: A Contextual Approach." *COS* 3:xxi–xxvii.

"Tell el-Borg in North Sinai." *Egyptian Archaeology* 20 (2002): 18–20.

"Everyday Life in Ancient Egypt." Pages 327–51 in *Life and Culture in the Ancient Near East*. Edited by Richard E. Averbeck, Mark W. Chavalas and David S. Weisberg. Bethesda, MD: CDL, 2003.

"Egypt's Role in the Events of 701 B.C. in Jerusalem." Pages 219–34 in *Jerusalem in Bible and Archaeology: The First Temple Period*. Edited by Andrew G. Vaughn and Ann E. Killebrew. SymS. Atlanta: Society of Biblical Literature, 2003.

"Egypt's Role in the Events of 701 B.C.: A Rejoinder to J. J. M. Roberts." Pages 285–89 in *Jerusalem in Bible and Archaeology: The First Temple Period*. Edited by Andrew G. Vaughn and Ann E. Killebrew. SymS. Atlanta: Society of Biblical Literature, 2003.

"A New Military Site on 'the Ways of Horus'—Tell el-Borg 1999–2001: A Preliminary Report." *JEA* 89 (2003): 169–97. With Mohamed Abd el-Maksoud.

"Aspects of Egyptian Foreign Policy in the Eighteenth Dynasty in Western Asia and Nubia." Pages 121–41 in *Egypt, Israel, and the Ancient Mediterranean World: Studies in Honor of Donald B. Redford*. Edited by Gary Knoppers and Antoine Hirsch. PAe 20. Leiden; Brill, 2004.

"The North Sinai Archaeological Project's Excavations at Tell el-Borg (Sinai): An Example of the 'New' Biblical Archaeology?" Pages 53–68 in *Future of Biblical Archaeology: Reassessing Methods and Assumptions*. Edited by James K. Hoffmeier and Alan R. Millard. Grand Rapids: Eerdmans, 2004.

"Tell el-Borg on Egypt's Eastern Frontier: A Preliminary Report on the 2002 and 2004 Seasons." *JARCE* 41 (2004): 85–111.

"New Inscriptions Mentioning Tjaru from Tell el-Borg, North Sinai." *RdÉ* 56 (2005): 79–84. With R. D. Bull.

"A New Royal Chariot Scene from Tell el-Borg." *JSSEA* 32 (2005): 81–92. With Lyla Pinch-Brock.

"New Paleo-Environmental Evidence from North Sinai to Complement Manfred Bietak's Map of the Eastern Delta and Some Historical Implications." Pages 167–76 in vol. 2 of *Timelines: Studies in Honour of Manfred Bietak*. Edited by Ernst Czerny, Irmagard Hein, Hermann Hunger, Dagmar Melman, and Angela Schwab. 3 vols. OLA 149. Leuven: Peeters, 2006. With S. O. Moshier.

"Recent Excavations on the 'Ways of Horus': The 2005 and 2006 Seasons at Tell el-Borg." *ASAE* 80 (2006): 257–79.

"Sulla via di Horus." *Pharaon* 2.7–8 (2006): 6–13.

"'The Walls of the Ruler' in Egyptian Literature and the Archaeology Record: Investigating Egypt's Eastern Frontier in the Bronze Age." *BASOR* 343 (2006): 1–20.

"An Archaeological Context for the Exodus." *BAR* 33.1 (2007): 30–41, 71.

"Reshep and Astarte in North Sinai: A Recently Discovered Stela from Tell el-Borg." *AeL* 17 (2007): 127–36. With Kenneth Kitchen.

"Amarna Period Kings in Sinai." *Egyptian Archaeology* 31 (2007): 38–39. With Earl Ertman.

"What is the Biblical Date for the Exodus? A Response to Bryant Wood." *JETS* 50 (2007): 225–47.

"Ramesses of the Exodus Narratives Is the Thirteenth Century B.C. Royal Ramesside Residence." *TJ* 28 (2007): 281–89.

"A Report on the Trinity International University Project at Tell el-Borg: the 2005 Season." *ASAE* 4 (2007): 109–30. Arabic Edition.

"The Search for Migdol of the New Kingdom and Exodus 14:2: An Update." *Buried History* 44 (2008): 3–12.

"A New Fragmentary Relief of King Ankhkheperure from Tell el-Borg (Sinai)?" *JEA* 94 (2008): 296–302. With Earl Ertman.

"Major Geographical Issues in the Accounts of the Exodus." Pages 97–129 in *Israel: Ancient Kingdom or Late Invention*. Edited by Donald Block. Nashville: Broadman & Holman, 2008.

"Migdol auf der Spur." *Welt und Umwelt der Bibel* 54.4 (2009): 68.

"New Light on the Amarna Period from North Sinai." *JEA* 96 (2010): 191–205. With Jacobus van Dijk.

"David's Triumph Over Goliath: 1 Samuel 17:54 and Ancient Near Eastern Analogues." Pages 84–110 in *Egypt, Canaan and Israel: History, Imperialism and Ideology*. Edited by Dan'el Kahn and J. J. Shirley. CHANE 52. Leiden, Brill, 2011.

"The Gate of the Ramesside Period Fort at Tell el-Borg, North Sinai." Pages 207–17 in *Ramesside Studies in Honour of K. A. Kitchen*. Edited by Mark Collier and Steven R. Snape. Bolton: Rutherford, 2011.

"Deities of the Eastern Frontier." Pages 197–216 in *Scribe of Justice: Egyptological Studies in Honour of Shafik Allam*. Edited by Zahi A. Hawass, Khaled A. Daoud, and Ramadan B. Hussein. Supplement aux Annales du Service des Antiquités de l'Egypte 42. Cairo: Ministry of State for Antiquities, 2011.

"'These Things Happened': Why a Historical Exodus Is Essential for Theology." Pages 99–134 in *Do Historical Matters Matter to Faith: A Critical Appraisal of Modern and Postmodern Approaches to Scripture*. Edited by James K. Hoffmeier and Dennis R. Magary. Wheaton: Crossway, 2012.

"Sinai in Egyptian, Levantine and Hebrew (Biblical) Perspectives." Pages 104–24 in *The History of the Peoples of the Eastern Desert*. Edited by Hans Barnard and Kim Duistermaat. Monograph 73. Los Angeles: Cotsen Institute of Archaeology Press, 2012.

"Reconstructing Egypt's Eastern Frontier Defense Network in the New Kingdom (Late Bronze Age)." Pages 163–94 in *The Power of Walls: Fortifications in Ancient Northeastern Africa*. Edited by Friedrerike Jesse and Carole Vogel. Colloquium Africanum 5. Köln: Heinrich-Barth-Institut, 2013.

"'A Highway out of Egypt': The Main Road from Egypt to Canaan." Pages 485–510 in *Desert Road Archaeology in Ancient Egypt and Beyond*. Edited by Frank Förester and Heiko Riemer. Africa Praehistorica 27. Köln: Heinrich-Barth-Institut, 2013. With S. O. Moshier.

"'The Ways of Horus': Reconstructing Egypt's East Frontier Defense Network and the Military Road to Canaan in the New Kingdom Times." Pages 34–61 in *Tell el-Borg I: The Excavations in North Sinai; "The Dwelling of the Lion" on the Ways of Horus*. Edited by James K. Hoffmeier. Winona Lake, IN: Eisenbrauns, 2014.

"The Exodus and Wilderness Narratives." Pages 46–90 in *Ancient Israel's History: An Introduction to Issues and Sources*. Edited by Bill T. Arnold and Richard S. Hess. Grand Rapids, Baker Academic, 2014.

"Egyptologists and the Israelite Exodus from Egypt." Pages 197–208 in *Israel's Exodus in Transdisciplinary Perspective: Text, Archaeology, Culture, and Geoscience*. Edited by Thomas Levy, Thomas Schneider, William H. Propp, and Brad C. Sparks. New York: Springer, 2015.

"Which Way Out of Egypt? Physical Geography Related to the Exodus Itinerary." Pages 101–8 in *Israel's Exodus in Transdisciplinary Perspective: Text, Archaeology, Culture, and Geoscience*. Edited by Thomas Levy, Thomas Schneider, William H. Propp, and Brad C. Sparks. New York: Springer, 2015. With S. Moshier.

"The Genre of Genesis 1–11: History and Theology." Pages. 23–58, 98–100, 140–149 in *Genesis: History, Fiction, or Neither? Three Views on the Bible's Earliest Chapters*. Counterpoints: Bible and Theology. Grand Rapids: Zondervan, 2015. With Gordon Wenham and Kenton Sparks.

"The Great Hymns of the Aten: The Ultimate Expression of Atenism." *JSSEA* 42 (2015–2016): 43–55.

"Egyptian Religious Influences on the Early Hebrews." Pages 3–35 in *"Did I Not Bring Israel out of Egypt?" Biblical, Archaeological, and Egyptological Perspectives on the Exodus Narratives*. Edited by James K. Hoffmeier, Alan R. Millard, and Gary A. Rendsburg. BBRSup 13. Winona Lake, IN: Eisenbrauns, 2016.

"New Archaeological Evidence for Ancient Bedouin (Shasu) on Egypt's Eastern Frontier at Tell el-Borg." *AeL* 26 (2016): 285–311. With T. Davis and R. Hummel.

"Hebrew Gemstones in the Old Testament: A Lexical, Geological, and Archaeological Analysis." *BBR* 27 (2017): 1–52. With J. Harrell and K. Williams.

"A Possible Location in Northwest Sinai for the Sea and Land Battles Between the Sea Peoples and Ramesses III." *BASOR* 380 (2018): 1–25.

"The Presence and Absence of God in Jeremiah." Pages 190–202 in *Interpreting the Old Testament Theologically: Essays in Honor of Willem A. VanGemeren*. Edited by Andrew Abernathy. Grand Rapids: Zondervan, 2018.

"An Unusual New Kingdom Funerary Structure from Tell el-Borg, North Sinai: An Interpretive Clue from Giza." In *Zahi Hawass Festschrift*. Edited by M. Barta, S. Ikram, J. Kamrin, M. Lehner, and M. Megahed. Prague: Charles University, forthcoming.

"The Curious Phenomenon of Moving Military Sites on Egypt's Eastern Frontier." *JSSEA* 36 forthcoming.

Book Reviews

The Bible in Its World, by Kenneth A. Kitchen. *JSSEA* 8 (1977): 99–102.

City of the Dead: Thebes in Egypt, by Lise Manniche. *Near Archaeological Society Bulletin* 30 (1988): 107–9.

Fecundity Figures, by John Baines. *JEA* 75 (1988): 255–56.

The Egyptians, by Cyril Aldred; and *The World of the Pharaohs*, by Christine Hobson. *Biblical Archaeologist* 53.1 (1989): 41–43.

Beyond Roots: In Search of Blacks in the Bible, by William McKissic. *Archaeology in the Biblical World* 1 (1991): 56–59.

Popular Religion in Egypt During the New Kingdom, by Ashraf Iskander Sadek. *JEA* 78 (1992): 338–39.

Centuries of Darkness, by Peter James. *BAR* 19.6 (1993): 6–10.

Out of the Desert? Archaeology and the Exodus/Conquest Narratives, by William H. Steibing Jr. *Ashland Theological Journal* (1993): 132–35.

Les chevaux du nouvel empire égyptien: Origines, races, harnachement, by Catherine Rommelaere. *JARCE* 30 (1994): 228–29.

Stranger in the Valley of the Kings, by Ahmed Osman. *Archaeology in the Biblical World* 2.2 (1994): 52–53.

Where Can Wisdom be Found? The Sage's Language in the Bible and in Ancient Egyptian Literature, by Nili Shupak. *Hebrew Studies* 38 (1997): 159–62.

Texts from the Amarna Period in Egypt, by William J. Murnane. *JBL* 117 (1998): 337–39.

The Amarna Age: Western Asia, by Fredrick J. Giles. *Bibliotheca Orientalis* 47 (2000): 577–79.

What Did the Biblical Writers Know and When Did They Know It, by William Dever. *Hebrew Studies* 43 (2002): 247–50.

Studies in Archaeology of the Iron Age in Israel and Jordan, ed. Amihai Mazar. *BBR* 13 (2003): 290–94.

The Hyksos: New Historical and Archaeological Perspectives, ed. Eliezer Oren. *JEA* 90 (2004): 26–29.

Tell el-Dabʿa I: Tell el-Dabʿa and Qantir, by Labib Habachi. *Bibliotheca Orientalis* 52 (2005): 471–72.

The Wars in Syria and Palestine of Thutmose III, by Donald B. Redford. *Near East Archaeological Society Bulletin* 50 (2006): 50–53.

The Campaign of Pharaoh Shoshenq I into Palestine, by Kevin A. Wilson. *BASOR* 349 (2008): 88–91.

Of God and Gods: Egypt, Israel, and the Rise of Monotheism, by Jan Assman. *Review of Biblical Literature* 6 (2011).

A Companion to Ancient Egypt, ed. Alan B. Lloyd. *BASOR* 369 (2013): 252–54.

The Book of Hosea, by J. Andrew Dearman. *TJ* 35 (2014): 136–38.

Treaty, Law and Covenant in the Ancient Near East, by Kenneth A. Kitchen and Paul J. N. Lawrence. *TJ* 37 (2016): 264–66.

CHAPTER 1

The Tests of a Prophet

Richard E. Averbeck

THE KEY TORAH PASSAGES for tests to determine whether a prophet was a true or false prophet are Deut 13:2–6 [ET 1–5] and especially 18:9–22. Of course, other passages in the Torah and through the rest of the Old Testament and into the New Testament also contribute to biblical teaching on this complex and important matter, especially Jer 26–29. I am delighted to dedicate this essay to James Hoffmeier, a colleague and friend, who has devoted much time and effort to the book of Jeremiah. Because they are programmatic, Deut 13 and 18 will provide the framework for the study, but we will consider Jer 26–29 and other Old Testament passages within that framework. We will also reflect on relevant New Testament passages along the way.

Deuteronomy 16:18–18:22 sets forth the basic regulations for Israel's four most important institutions: judges, kings, priests, and finally prophets. There is good reason to believe that the prophetic institution was deemed to be the most authoritative of the four.[1] The prophet is the successor to Moses, the authoritative spokesman for the Lord. In the beginning, he even anointed the kings. Although we find this in neither the Hebrew text of the Exod 20 report of the words of the Lord at Sinai when the people backed away and asked that Moses be their mediator, nor do we read it in Moses's review of what happened at Sinai forty years later in Deut 5, here in Deut 18:17–20 Moses inserts more of the Lord's additional first-person instructions given at Sinai:

> [17] The LORD said to me: "What they say is good. [18] *I* will raise up for them a prophet like you from among their fellow Israelites, and *I* will put my words in his mouth. He will tell them everything *I* command him. [19] *I myself will call to account anyone who does not listen to my words that the prophet speaks in my name.* [20] But a prophet who presumes to speak in my name anything *I* have not commanded, or a prophet who speaks in the name of other gods, is to be put to death." (NIV emphasis added)

The point in 18:19 is especially important here: "I myself will call to account anyone who does not listen to my words that the prophet speaks in my name" (NIV). Nothing like this is said about judges, kings, or priests in Deut 17–18. After Abraham the prophet, the institution of prophecy developed in full force with the reliable and dependable Moses, and was to continue in likeness to Moses. To disobey such a

---

1. Jeffrey H. Tigay, *The JPS Torah Commentary: The Traditional Hebrew Text with the New JPS Translation; Deuteronomy* (Philadelphia: Jewish Publication Society, 1996), 172, 177.

prophet was to disobey God.[2] This, of course, "raises the stakes," so to speak, for the importance of tests for true versus false prophets in Israel. It was of the utmost importance that they be able to tell the difference between true and false prophets and prophecies. This was a serious concern in the Bible as well as in the ancient Near Eastern world of the day. This brings us to the comparisons and contrasts between prophecy in the Bible and the ancient Near East.

Background in the Ancient Near Eastern World

There are actually two main units in the regulations for prophets in Deut 18: Deut 18:9–14, the occult; and 18:15–22, the prophet. The first unit makes the background of prophesy in the ancient Near Eastern world relevant to the issue of true versus false prophecy in the passage. For our purposes here it is helpful to render the pivot between the two units in 18:14–15 in this more literal way:

> [14] For these nations that you are dispossessing, sorcerers and diviners *they obey*, but as for you, the Lord your God has not given you (permission to do) so. [15] A prophet from your midst, from your brothers, *like me*, the Lord your God will raise up for you. *You must obey him.* (my translation)[3]

This rendering is intended to capture the contextual syntactic relationship between 18:14 and 18:15. The people you are displacing in Canaan do this, but in Israel you must do the other instead. They *obey* these occult practitioners listed in 18:9–11 but, instead of that, you must *obey* prophets "like me," Moses.

There is not time here to treat all the different kinds of occult practices mentioned in 18:9–11, 14, and that is not the purpose of this essay in any case. Nevertheless, it is important to observe here that prophecy in Israel fit into the same basic concerns as these other such practices did among the surrounding peoples of Canaan and the ancient Near East at large. The reason we have the two units in the prophetic regulations in Deut 18 is to make a carefully defined and forceful distinction between Canaanite occult practices and prophecy. In the ancient Near East, *both* were part of the same repertoire of methods for prognostication. In Israel prophecy was distinguished as the exclusive form, aside from the high priest's Urim and Thummim (see, e.g., Exod 28:30; Lev 8:8; Num 27:21; Deut 33:8; 1 Sam 28:6; Ezra 2:63; Neh 7:65).

Although the distinction is not absolute in practice, there were two different kinds of legitimate prophetic activity in the Old Testament—mantic and classical prophecy.[4] The latter refers to prophets who brought messages to the people directly from the Lord without specific prompting from the people. Mantic prophecy, however, refers to the practice of going to a prophet to gain the Lord's guidance on a specific matter. The prophet could get a word from the Lord for the person or group in need. It was common, for example, for a king or leader of an army to ask for an oracle of divine

2. Ibid., 172, and other scholars.
3. Unless otherwise indicated, all translations are the author's.
4. See the discussion in Tigay, *Deuteronomy*, 178.

approval before going into battle. We see this in a number of passages in the Old Testament; for example, when Jehoshaphat asked "Is there no prophet of the LORD here, through whom we may inquire of the LORD?" (NIV) before going into battle against Mesha of Moab (2 Kgs 3:11; see similarly, e.g., 1 Sam 7:7–11; 13:8–14). The answer from the Lord was positive. On another occasion the wife of Jeroboam went to inquire from Ahijah, a prophet of the Lord, about whether her son would survive his illness. The answer was not good in this instance (1 Kgs 14:1–19). Examples could be multiplied.

The point here is that in the Old Testament the only legitimate source for such mantic guidance was an oracle from a legitimate prophet of the Lord. Occult divinatory practices were forbidden. Nevertheless, in their rebellion the ancient Israelites would regularly resort to these occult practices alongside of prophets. For example, before going into battle against the Philistines King Saul could not get an oracle from the Lord "by dreams or Urim or prophets" (1 Sam 28:6), legitimate means, so he pursued his guidance through illegitimate means: "Saul then said to his attendants, 'Find me a woman who is a medium, so I may go and inquire of her'" (28:7). Similarly, as Jeremiah puts it in Jer 27:9–10, "do not listen to your prophets, your diviners, your interpreters of dreams, your mediums or your sorcerers who tell you, 'You will not serve the king of Babylon.'¹⁰ They prophesy lies to you that will only serve to remove you far from your lands; I will banish you and you will perish" (NIV). Later on in the same passage he refers to all these simply as "prophets" when he says, "¹⁴ Do not listen to the words of the prophets who say to you, 'You will not serve the king of Babylon,' for they are prophesying lies to you. ¹⁵ 'I have not sent them,' declares the LORD. 'They are prophesying lies in my name." (27:14–15a NIV; see also Jer 29:8–9).

In general, the classical prophets functioned differently. They focused primarily on reforming the behavior of the people and the nation as a whole by calling them back to exclusive and heartfelt covenant loyalty and obedience to the Lord and his word already revealed. Jeremiah 26–29 recounts battles between the true Yahwistic prophet, Jeremiah, who preached that the people of Judah and Jerusalem should submit to the Babylonian exile, as opposed Hananiah and Shemaiah who were false Yahwistic prophets, whose message was that they would not be taken into exile and should resist the Babylonians. To the leadership in Jerusalem, for Jeremiah to preach this message was treason against the sovereign state of Israel. Jeremiah's prophetic message, nevertheless, would come true. We will discuss this passage further below.

We have a good deal of primary source material for prophets and prophecy extant from the ancient Near East from Mesopotamia down through the Levant and into Egypt.[5] A close connection between divination and prophecy can be seen, for example, in the prophetic oracle reports from centuries before Moses found among the cuneiform letters discovered at Mari. This was a very ancient city even before Abraham, located on the middle Euphrates River. The texts we are referring to here come from around the same time as Hammurabi's rule in Babylon, the founder of the Old Babylonian Empire.[6] The oracles derive originally from various kinds of oracular

5. See the helpful presentation and discussion of the texts in Martti Nissinen, *Prophets and Prophecy in the Ancient Near East*, WAW 12 (Atlanta: Society of Biblical Literature, 2003).

6. For a handy collection of the Mari prophetic texts see now Nissinen, *Prophets and Prophecy*, 13–77. See also the helpful discussions in Jack M. Sasson, *From the Mari Archives: An Anthology of Old Babylonian Letters* (Winona Lake, IN: Eisenbrauns, 2015), 271–93; and Jeffrey Stackert, *A Prophet Like Moses:*

functionaries and include both dreams and visions, much as we find mentioned in Num 12:6–8: "When there is a prophet among you, I, the LORD, reveal myself to them in *visions*, I speak to them in *dreams*. 7 But this is not true of my servant Moses; he is faithful in all my house. 8 With him I speak face to face" (NIV, emphasis added).

One of the points that stands out at Mari is that when prophetic visions or dreams were reported it was expected that they would need to be confirmed by divinatory methods, especially extispicy—the discerning of messages from the gods through reading the innards of slaughtered sheep, particularly the liver. We have numerous extant inscribed clay liver models from Mari to Ugarit to Hazor in northern Israel indicating the condition of a liver when an extispicy was taken and the diviner gave an interpretation. For example, the inscription on one such liver model from Mari reads, "If the enemy plots an attack against any town, yet the plan becomes known; this (liver) omen would look like this."[7] It was common for a *bārûm* priest, a haruspex (i.e., an examiner of entrails), or a diviner to perform multiple extispicies over a period of days in order to gain confidence in the answer.[8]

One year Zimri-Lim, the king of Mari, had almost five thousand sheep sacrificed for this purpose. The meat of the animals went to the palace residents.[9] Jack Sasson notes that the goal was not to predict the future as much as to "assess the auspiciousness of a contemplated activity in order to develop a strategy on how to proceed on it. The art had much to do with posing inquiry with skill before killing an animal and with ascertaining the usefulness of the answer by repeating the procedure with an inverse version of the same inquiry."[10] For example, one text gives the following set of interlocking queries: "[Zimri-Lim writes to his wife Shiptu] For now, inquire about Hammurabi of Babylon: 'Will this man die? Will he be honest with us? Will he battle against us? If I go north, will he besiege us? What?' Inquire about the man. Once you inquire, follow with another (round) of inquiries and send me a report about him on all you have found out by inquiring."[11]

With regard to prophetic oracles in particular, in one Mari prophetic text the prophet delivers an oracle from the god Dagan, saying, "How much longer will I not drink pure water? Write to your lord that he may provide me with pure water." The official, who sent the letter reporting the oracle to the king of Mari, then writes: "Now I have sent a

---

Prophecy, Law, and Israelite Religion (Oxford: Oxford University Press, 2014), 39–51. The literature on the topic is voluminous. Other important recent discussions can be found in Dominique Charpin, "Prophetism in the Near East According to the Mari Archives," in *Gods, Kings, and Merchants in Old Babylonian Mesopotamia* (Leuven: Peeters, 2015), 11–58; Jonathan Stökl, *Prophecy in the Ancient Near East: A Philological and Sociological Comparison*, CHANE 56 (Leiden: Brill, 2012); Shawn Zelig Aster, "Treaty and Prophecy: A Survey of Biblical Reactions to Neo-Assyrian Political Thought," in *The Southern Levant Under Assyrian Domination*, ed. Shawn Zelig Aster and Avraham Faust (University Park, PA: Eisenbrauns, 2018), 89–118; Herbert B. Huffmon, "A Company of Prophets: Mari, Assyria, Israel," in *Prophecy in Its Ancient Near Eastern Context: Mesopotamian, Biblical, and Arabian Perspectives*, ed. Martti Nissinen, SymS 13; Atlanta: Society of Biblical Literature, 2000), 47–69, and several chapters in the same volume; Martii Nissinen, "What Is Prophecy? An Ancient Near Eastern Perspective," in *Inspired Speech: Prophecy in the Ancient Near East; Essays in Honor of Herbert B. Huffmon*, ed. John Kaltner and Louis Stulman, JSOTSup 378 (London: T&T Clark, 2004), 17–37, and other chapters in the same volume.

7. Sasson, *From the Mari Archives*, 274.
8. Ibid., 273–77.
9. Ibid., 276 n. 119.
10. Ibid., 272 n. 114.
11. Ibid., 275–76.

lock of [the hair of] his head and his garment hem to my lord; let my lord perform the purification offering," which would probably include the performance of an extispicy to confirm the veracity of the prophetic message.[12] Another text contains a dream report from a female prophet. The official who sent the letter concluded it with the following: "By means of bird divination I inquired about her, and the dream was really seen. Now I send her hair and a fringe of her garment. Let my lord inquire about her."[13] The king would have likely "inquired" about her, as the text puts it, through extispicy to determine whether or not he should heed the dream. This understanding is supported by, among other evidence, a text that says, "About the lock (of hair) and (garment) fringes of the young man that you conveyed to me: I took omens over the lock and fringes, and they are favorable."[14] As this text suggests, they could also multiply different kinds of divination, such as watching and interpreting the flights of birds. There are approximately fifty prophetic letters from the Mari archive and fourteen of them refer to the sending of the hair and hem of the prophet along with the letter to the king.[15]

Cale Johnson has recently argued that the hair (Akk. *šārtum*) and the fringe (Akk. *sissiktum*) "pun on the terms for 'wind' (Akk. *šārum*) and 'little breeze' (Akk. *sissikum*). This was in order to recall the metaphysical underpinnings of the corresponding mantic or prophetic inspiration."[16] It is worth noting here that the Old Testament prophetic institution was closely associated with the work of the Spirit of God in the Old Testament. The term "S/spirit" (capital S or lower case s) in both the Old Testament (רוח) and New Testament (πνεῦμα) often refer to "wind" or "breath," not necessarily "spirit," and on occasion the relationship between the two is played on (see, e.g., Ezek 37:5–10, 15 with John 3:8). The point is that divine prophetic revelations were like "wind": powerful, meaningful, and to be taken seriously, but hard to discern and interpret. The prophetic work of the Lord in the Old Testament was not under the control of anyone but God; that is, if it was true and not false prophecy.

The main significance of this line of evidence is at least threefold. First, just as in the Old Testament, others in the ancient Near East were concerned about determining whether or not they could rely on a prophetic oracle as being authentic. They wanted to be sure before obeying it. Second, in the texts that we have from Mari, prophetic oracles were considered less reliable than other forms of prognostication. Such oracles needed to be checked by divination, most often multiple extispicies, which was considered to be the more reliable science of the day. Third, and related to the previous point, divination and other forms of prognostication were forbidden in Israel precisely because they did not go directly to Yahweh for guidance, but to other means of discerning the will of God, or the gods, believing that their will was written on the exta of animals, for example. In Israel, however, divination could not be used to confirm or disconfirm the truth of a prophetic oracle revelation from the Lord. Other means of

12. Nissinen, *Prophets and Prophecy*, 49–50.

13. Ibid., 60.

14. Sasson, *From the Mari Archives*, 277.

15. Jeffrey Stackert, "The Syntax of Deuteronomy 13:2–3 and the Conventions of Ancient Near Eastern Prophecy," *JANER* 10 (2010): 162–63.

16. J. Cale Johnson, "The Metaphysics of Mantic/Prophetic Authentication Devices in Old Babylonian Mari," in *Akkade is King: A Collection of Papers by Friends and Colleagues Presented to Aage Westenholz on the Occasion of His 70th Birthday 15th of May 2009*, ed. Gojko Barjamovic et al., PIHANS 118 (Leiden: Nederlands Instituut voor het Nabije Ooosten, 2011), 151.

determining the validity of a supposed prophetic revelation were called for; namely, tests of prophecy as they are found in Scripture.

The Problem of False Prophets and Prophecy

According to Deut 18:19, the Lord declared to Moses that, instead of obeying the oracles of occult practitioners like those listed above (18:9–14), "19 I myself will call to account anyone who does not listen to my words that the prophet speaks in my name" (18:19 NIV), referring to the prophet "like me," Moses (18:15).[17] This was the kind of prophet the Lord would raise up for them from among their fellow Israelites. As the Lord puts it, "I will put my words in his mouth. He will tell them everything I command him" (18:18b). Unfortunately, not all "prophets" would remain faithful to this calling (18:20). In the meantime, the Lord makes it perfectly clear that they must obey the words he speaks through his faithful prophet.

This, of course, brings up the problem of false prophets and the messages they proclaim in Deut 18:20:

אַךְ הַנָּבִיא אֲשֶׁר יָזִיד לְדַבֵּר דָּבָר בִּשְׁמִי אֵת אֲשֶׁר לֹא־צִוִּיתִיו לְדַבֵּר וַאֲשֶׁר יְדַבֵּר בְּשֵׁם אֱלֹהִים אֲחֵרִים
וּמֵת הַנָּבִיא הַהוּא:

But the prophet who presumes to speak a word *in my name* that I have not commanded him to speak, and the one who speaks *in the name of other gods*, that prophet shall die. (emphasis added).

This verse distinguishes between two types of false prophecy, both of which were punishable by the execution of the prophet.[18] First, there could be Yahwistic prophets who spoke oracles that they said came from the Lord, but which the Lord had not given them. This was presumptuous. The prophet was to be a spokesman for God, and must say only what God said. Even the non-Israelite prophet Balaam knew that. After forceful prompting from Balak to curse Israel, Baalam said, "Even if Balak gave

---

17. Daniel Block, *The Triumph of Grace: Literary and Theological Studies in Deuteronomy and Deuteronomic Themes* (Eugene, OR: Cascade, 2017), 349–73 argues against taking this in a messianic way, eventually applying to Jesus Christ. He raises important objections here. The expression "like me" (Deut 18:15; cf. 18:18), of course, is not limited to one prophet but to a sequence of them that the Lord would raise up to guide Israel by his word through them. There are, however, good reasons to believe that the New Testament cites or alludes to this passage in application to Christ as the ultimate prophet in the chain, beginning with John 1:19–21, when the priests and Levites asked John the Baptist whether he was the Messiah, the prophet Elijah, and then asked, "Are you the Prophet?" Once again John responded "no." More specifically, Acts 3:22–23 suggests that such New Testament prophetic application of Deut 18:15 "like me" to Jesus is appropriate and intentional. John B. Polhill, *Acts*, NAC 26 (Nashville: Broadman & Holman, 1992); and Darrell L. Bock, *Acts*, BECNT (Grand Rapids: Baker, 2007) both point to the intertestamental tradition and the Jewish New Testament reference to it.

18. Some of the important and recent discussions of false prophecy in the Old Testament are R. W. L. Moberly, *Prophecy and Discernment* (Cambridge: Cambridge University Press, 2006); Daniel I. Block, "What Has Delphi to Do with Samaria? Ambiguity and Delusion in Israelite Prophecy," in *Writings and Ancient Near Eastern Society: Papers in Honour of Alan R. Millard*, ed. Piotr Beinkowski, Christopher Mee, and Elizabeth Slater, LHBOTS 426 (London: T&T Clark, 2005), 189–216; Nan Kim, "The Complexity of False Prophecy," *STJ* 11 (2003): 21–39; James E. Brenneman, *Canons in Conflict: Negotiating Texts in True and False Prophecy* (Oxford: Oxford University Press, 1997).

me all the silver and gold in his palace, I could not do anything great or small to go beyond the command of the LORD my God" (Num 22:18). Second, any prophet who spoke "in the name of other gods" was, of course, a false prophet. The Israelites must listen only to the word of the Lord and obey his word exclusively.

Deuteronomy 13:2–3 [ET 1–2] and 18:20, False Prophets, and Prophetic Signs and Wonders

The stipulatory section of Deuteronomy begins in Deut 12:2–3 with prohibitions against any kind of worship of any other deities in the land: "² Destroy completely all the places on the high mountains, on the hills and under every spreading tree, where the nations you are dispossessing worship their gods. ³ Break down their altars, smash their sacred stones and burn their Asherah poles in the fire; cut down the idols of their gods and wipe out their names from those places" (NIV). It would violate their basic commitment to exclusive worship of Yahweh to worship and obey any of these other supposed deities. The same emphasis reappears at the end of the chapter in Deut 12:29–13:1, thus, forming something of an inclusion for chapter 12.

Deuteronomy 13 follows through with further specific regulations to highlight the prohibition against turning to other gods in Israel. It begins with a regulation against following a prophet or visionary dreamer who would entice the Israelites to worship other gods. The first two verses are awkward in Hebrew (Deut 13:2–3 [1–2]) and require careful analysis:[19]

2 כִּי־יָקוּם בְּקִרְבְּךָ נָבִיא אוֹ חֹלֵם חֲלוֹם וְנָתַן אֵלֶיךָ אוֹת אוֹ מוֹפֵת:

3 וּבָא הָאוֹת וְהַמּוֹפֵת אֲשֶׁר־דִּבֶּר אֵלֶיךָ לֵאמֹר נֵלְכָה אַחֲרֵי אֱלֹהִים אֲחֵרִים אֲשֶׁר לֹא־יְדַעְתָּם וְנָעָבְדֵם:

The NIV renders them, "¹ If a prophet, or one who foretells by dreams, appears among you and announces to you a sign or wonder, ² and if the sign or wonder spoken of takes place, and the prophet says, 'Let us follow other gods (gods you have not known) and let us worship them.'"[20]

Jeffrey Tigay suggests a different rendering based on some rearranging of the clauses: "If there appears among you a prophet or a dream-diviner saying, 'Let us follow and worship another god whom you have not experienced,' and he gives you a sign or a portent, even if the sign or portent that he named to you comes true," leading into the prohibition in 13:4 against obeying such a prophet. He is by definition a false prophet.[21] This rendering might be charted in the Hebrew text this way:

2 כִּי־יָקוּם בְּקִרְבְּךָ נָבִיא אוֹ חֹלֵם חֲלוֹם   וְנָתַן אֵלֶיךָ אוֹת אוֹ מוֹפֵת:

3 וּבָא הָאוֹת וְהַמּוֹפֵת אֲשֶׁר־דִּבֶּר אֵלֶיךָ ↑ **לֵאמֹר** נֵלְכָה אַחֲרֵי אֱלֹהִים אֲחֵרִים אֲשֶׁר לֹא־יְדַעְתָּם וְנָעָבְדֵם:

---

19. I do not propose to deal here with all the exegetical issues and suggested solutions for reading these two verses. For a more complete discussion, see Stackert, "Syntax of Deuteronomy 13:2," 159–71. His own proposal is on pp. 171–75 (see the discussion below).

20. Deut 13:2–3 in Hebrew is 13:1–2 in the English translations.

21. Tigay, *Deuteronomy*, 129.

According to this reading, the actual prophetic message introduced by לֵאמֹר in 13:3 would have been spoken right after the prophet or dreamer appeared in the first clause of 13:2, but it is placed in the position of what some would call an "afterthought" later in the sequence. Presumably, the clauses would have been arranged as they are in the MT both to put the actual message of the prophet just before the prohibition against worshiping other gods that follows in 13:4–6 [ET 3–5], and to put the issue of signs and wonders up front. Even if such a prophetic message was supported by an accompanying sign or wonder (13:2b–3a), they must not heed that prophet (13:4).[22] The determinative issue is the message the false prophet is preaching to follow after other gods (13:3b), not the sign (13:2b–3a).

Jeffrey Stackert offers a similar solution, but highlights other grammatical syntactic problems here, especially the relative clause at the end of 13:3a, אֲשֶׁר־דִּבֶּר אֵלֶיךָ, literally "which he spoke to you." He points out that elsewhere in the Hebrew Bible the verb דִּבֶּר followed by the infinitive construct of לֵאמֹר always introduces a direct quotation. If the normal grammar holds true here, the relative clause does not belong to the previous clause as in Tigay's translation, but introduces what follows. Of course, in this instance there is also a relative pronoun at the head of the clause, so the question becomes: what is the antecedent? According to Stackert, the antecedent of the relative clause is not the coming to pass of the sign or portent referred to just previously, at the beginning of 13:3, but the introduction of the false prophet in 13:2a. Like Tigay, Stackert relies on the parallel passage in 1 Kgs 13:1–3, where the message is proclaimed before the sign or portent is introduced into the sequence. He also draws upon the grammatical syntactic discussions of Moshe Goshen-Gottstein and, more recently, Robert Holmstedt, suggesting that the clause in question should be taken as an instance of the so-called "afterthought relative construction" or "relative clause extraposition."[23] Thus, according to Stackert, we have here an "absolute use of the relative" referring back to the prophet introduced in 13:2a and leading into the quotation of the original message of the prophet. The relative clause would be rendered, "one who spoke to you saying." This would suggest a rendering of 13:2–4a something like this: "If a prophet or dreamer arises in your midst and announces to you a sign or wonder, and the sign or wonder takes place—one who spoke to you saying, 'Let us go after other gods you have not known and let us worship them'—you must not obey the words of that prophet.'" In this case, one could chart the Hebrew text this way:

22. The term "wonder" (מוֹפֵת) carries the sense that a miraculous event would take place, as for example in splitting the altar apart in 1 Kgs 13:3, 5. "Sign" (אוֹת) can refer to such miraculous events, but often refers to such things as putting the blood on the doorframes as a "sign" to prevent the death of firstborn sons among the Israelites (Exod 12:13). They are sometimes used together to capture the whole repertoire of prophetic portents used to support prophetic messages from the Lord, as here in Deut 13:2–3 (see also, e.g., Exod 7:3; Deut 4:34; 6:22; 7:19).

23. Stackert, "Syntax of Deuteronomy 13:2–3," 171–75, referring to Moshe H. Goshen-Gottstein, "Afterthought and the Syntax of Relative Clauses in Biblical Hebrew," JBL 68 (1949): 35–47; and Robert D. Holmstedt, "Headlessness and Extraposition: Another Look at the Syntax of אשׁר," JNSL 27 (2001): 1–16. Neither Goshen-Gottstein nor Holmstedt in their articles cites Deut 13:2–3 as an example of this construction. In fact, Stackert admits that the extraposition of the relative clause in Deut 13:2–3 is more far removed from its antecedent than in any of the other examples given by Goshen-Gottstein and Holmstedt. Nevertheless, he argues that "the author of Deut 13:2–3 could justify the awkward syntax of his text on its resemblance to naturally occurring examples of extraposition" (Stackert, "Syntax of Deuteronomy 13:2–3," 174).

2 כִּי־יָקוּם בְּקִרְבְּךָ נָבִיא אוֹ חֹלֵם חֲלוֹם   וְנָתַן אֵלֶיךָ אוֹת אוֹ מוֹפֵת:

3 וּבָא הָאוֹת וְהַמּוֹפֵת   ↑ אֲשֶׁר־דִּבֶּר אֵלֶיךָ **לֵאמֹר** נֵלְכָה אַחֲרֵי אֱלֹהִים אֲחֵרִים אֲשֶׁר
לֹא־יְדַעְתָּם וְנָעָבְדֵם:

Rhetorically, the relative clause recalls the prophet or dreamer introduced in 13:2a. The text, however, inserts the sign or wonder part of the scenario before the prophetic message in order to emphasize that one must not obey such a prophet even if he or she performs a sign or wonder to support the authenticity of the message.

Again, as noted above, the syntax here is awkward. Some scholars, therefore, have gone so far as to argue that 13:2b–3a constitute a later interpolation.[24] The supposed original passage would have read: "If a prophet or dreamer arises in your midst saying, 'Let us go after other gods which you have not known, and let us worship them.'" The prohibition in 13:4 follows. This would eliminate the syntactic problem, but it ignores the common practice in the Bible and the ancient Near East to confirm prophetic oracles with various kinds of divination or signs in order to convince the hearers to obey the prophetic command (see above, and more on this below). One wonders if the original writer would have left this out of the regulation. The awkward syntax of the passage, therefore, may arise out of the need to take into consideration the practice of prophetic confirmation through a sign or wonder without weakening the focus on the false prophetic message itself. The author, therefore, inserted the note on a sign or wonder (13:2b) immediately after introducing the prophet or dream diviner (13:2a). He maintained the focus on the false prophetic message by resuming it after the insertion, starting with the extraposed relative pronoun and clause.

The primary concern all along was to prevent the Israelites from violating the exclusivity of their covenant commitment to Yahweh. As noted above, this is the thrust of Deut 12:2–3 (cited above) as well as the verses that come at the end of the chapter in Deut 12:29–13:1, leading into 13:2–6 and the whole rest of the chapter. The entire focus of the following verses in Deut 13 is on maintaining this exclusive commitment to Yahweh (13:7–19). With regard to the prophetic institution under consideration in Deut 13:2–6, the writer did not feel that he could leave out the problem of a false prophet performing a sign or wonder that could perhaps convince the Israelites to violate their exclusive covenant loyalty to Yahweh. He simply had to get this into the passage. What we have is the result. On the one hand, the false prophetic message is placed at the end in order to highlight and emphasize its primary importance for the prohibition that follows. On the other hand, in the meantime, the writer needed to address one of the reasons the Israelites might fall prey to such a message; namely, the support of a sign or wonder. Without the latter there would be less reason for them to even consider obeying such a prophet and his message.

In practice, as noted above, the prophet would have given his prophetic message before performing the sign or wonder to confirm its validity (see, e.g., 1 Kgs 13:1–3; Isa 38:4–8), but the sign or wonder would have been key to why the people might fall into the trap of obeying the false prophetic message. Thus, 13:2–3 in the Hebrew text have set up the dilemma that the people would be faced with in the situation envisioned here: We are supposed to obey prophets, and this prophet has even given us a sign to

---

24. See, e.g., the literature cited in Stackert, "Syntax of Deuteronomy 13:2–3," 159–60.

confirm his message, but the message is counter to our covenant loyalty to Yahweh. What to do?!? The answer is given in 13:4–6:

> [4] you must not listen to the words of that prophet or that dreamer for the LORD your God is testing you to know whether you really love him with all your heart and with all your soul. [5] It is the LORD your God you must follow after, it is him you must fear, it is his commandments you must keep commands, it his voice you must obey him, it is him you must serve, and to him you must hold fast. [6] That prophet or that dreamer shall be put to death because he has spoken falsehood against the LORD your God [*or*, "because he has spoken rebellion against the LORD your God"], who brought you out from the land of Egypt and redeemed you out from the house of slavery, to turn you aside from the way in which the LORD your God commanded you to go. So you must purge the evil from your midst.

In such a case there is a no toleration policy. They must completely and summarily rid themselves of this evil influence in their midst. There was no excuse for falling into such deception, since the Lord had already made it clear that they must maintain their exclusive covenant loyalty to him. There is to be no going against their commitment to exclusive covenant loyalty to Yahweh their God no matter what kind of smoke screen any false prophet throws up to confuse them.

The problem may be accentuated even further depending on how one takes כִּי־דִבֶּר־ סָרָה in 13:6, which could mean either "because he spoke falsehood" or "because he spoke rebellion" (see the parenthesis in the translation above). The term סָרָה could derive from the root סרר "to be deceitful, stubborn" or סור "to turn aside, rebel," respectively.[25] Tigay argues forcefully and at length that it means the prophet has "uttered falsehood about the Lord." More specifically, the prophet has used his Yahwistic prophetic office and the supporting practice of performing a sign or wonder to urge the Israelites to worship other deities, falsely saying that the message to do so was from the Lord himself. He was calling for syncretistic worship of Yahweh along with other deities and saying that this is the word of Yahweh himself.[26]

In favor of Tigay's interpretation is Jer 28:16, where Jeremiah spoke a word from the Lord against Hananiah because he "spoke falsely with regard to the LORD" (כִּי־סָרָה דִבַּרְתָּ אֶל־יְהוָה) when he broke the yoke off Jeremiah's neck and said in 28:10–11, "This is what the LORD says: 'In the same way I will break the yoke of Nebuchadnezzar king of Babylon off the neck of all the nations within two years'" (see also Jer 29:32 in its context).[27] And yet, Deut 13:2–6 does not actually say that the prophet

25. See *HALOT*, s.vv. "סָרָה"; "סור II"; "סרר". *HALOT*, s.v. "סָרָה II," 2 classifies Deut 13:6 under the meaning "falsehood."

26. Tigay, *Deuteronomy*, 130–31, 367 nn. 19–24, citing Maimonides and Ramban in support. Both Daniel I. Block, *Deuteronomy*, NIVAC (Grand Rapids: Zondervan, 2012), 330–31; and J. G. McConville, *Deuteronomy*, ApOTC 5 (Downers Grove, IL: InterVarsity Press, 2002), 234, 238 follow Tigay in this interpretation. Lundbom argues against this interpretation in support of the more common understanding that the prophet has simply called for rebellion against the Lord; Jack R. Lundbom, *Deuteronomy: A Commentary* (Grand Rapids: Eerdmans, 2013), 453–54.

27. There have been a number of recent studies focused on false prophecy in Jer 26–29: Seth B. Tarrer, *Reading with the Faithful: Interpretation of True and False Prophecy in the Book of Jeremiah from Ancient Times to Modern*, JTISup 6 (Winona Lake, IN: Eisenbrauns, 2013); Matthijs J. De Jong, "The Fallacy of

spoke his prophetic message "in the name of the LORD." Perhaps this is intentional and it is better to leave the interpretation open ended in this regard. This prophet could be speaking either in the name of the Lord or in the name of another god or other gods. Of course, Deut 18:20b (cited above) calls for the death penalty on any prophet who speaks in the name of any other gods.

In any case, this regulation in Deut 13:2–6 prohibits worship of other deities even if a prophet brings a message to do so and supports it with a sign or wonder. It details a particularly deceptive and subversive kind of false prophecy in ancient Israel. The prophet is a false prophet, but uses all the influence and accoutrements of his prophetic practice to deliver and reinforce a message that flies directly in the face of Israel's basic and exclusive covenant commitment to Yahweh. It violates the first two commandments of the law as it was originally given at Sinai (Exod 20:2–6; cf. Deut 5:6–10). Such a prophet intended to put the Israelites "between a rock and a hard place," so to speak: on the one hand, they must obey the word of Yahweh through the prophet the Lord sends to them (Deut 18:19) but, on the other hand, they must not worship and serve any other god(s) (Deut 12:2–3, 29–30; 13:7–19; 17:2–3; 18:20b). The Israelites were prone to idolatrous syncretism anyway, so this would have been naturally enticing to them. The Lord's solution was to pierce through the deception to the message that was clearly against what the Lord was calling for in his covenant relationship with the Israelites. The message was determinative no matter whom the prophet said he was speaking for and no matter how persuasive he was.

This provides background for why Jesus insisted that his message was not in contradiction to the teachings of the Law and the Prophets, for example, in Matt 5:17–20, although he was indeed speaking against the way many of his contemporaries were teaching it:[28]

> [17] Do not think that I have come to abolish the Law or the Prophets; I have not come to abolish them but to fulfill them. [18] For truly I tell you, until heaven and earth disappear, not the smallest letter, not the least stroke of a pen, will by any means disappear from the Law until everything is accomplished. [19] Therefore anyone who sets aside one of the least of these commands and teaches others accordingly will be called least in the kingdom of heaven, but whoever practices and teaches these commands will be called great in the kingdom of heaven. [20] For I tell you that unless your righteousness surpasses that of the Pharisees and the teachers of the law, you will certainly not enter the kingdom of heaven. (NIV)

Similarly, like Deut 13:2–6, in the New Testament 1 John 4:1–3 emphasizes the need to stay focused on the primary message in the midst of what could become a confusing mix of true and false prophetic proclamations:

'True and False' in Prophecy Illustrated by Jer 28:8–9," *JHebS* 12.10 (2012): 1–29; J. Todd Hibbard, "True and False Prophecy: Jeremiah's Revision of Deuteronomy," *JSOT* 35 (2011): 339–58; Carolyn J. Sharp, *Prophecy and Ideology in Jeremiah: Struggles for Authority in the Deutero–Jeremianic Prose*, OTS (London: T&T Clark, 2003).

28. See the extensive discussion of this matter in Richard E. Averbeck, "The Law and the Gospels, with Attention to the Relationship Between the Decalogue and the Sermon on the Mount/Plain," in *Oxford Handbook of Biblical Law*, ed. Pamela Barmash (Oxford, 2019), 409–24.

Dear friends, do not believe every spirit, but *test the spirits* to see whether they are from God, because many *false prophets* have gone out into the world. [2] This is how you can recognize the Spirit of God: *Every spirit that acknowledges that Jesus Christ has come in the flesh is from God*, [3] but every spirit that does not acknowledge Jesus is not from God. This is the spirit of the antichrist, which you have heard is coming and even now is already in the world. (NIV, emphasis added)

The message the prophet gave, therefore, was the first and most determinative criterion for discerning between true and false prophets and prophecy in the Hebrew Old Testament and in the Greek New Testament. It overruled even if the prophet performed a sign or wonder to support the message.

Nevertheless, prophetic signs and wonders were part of the prophetic institution in ancient Israel. They were a second test of the veracity of prophets and their prophetic messages. They fulfilled a similar role as divination did in Mari, where extispicy was commonly used to confirm the oracles of prophets or dreamers (see discussion earlier in this essay). For example, in 1 Kgs 13:1–5 a "man of God" (another term for prophets in the Old Testament) came to Jeroboam at Bethel (ca. 930 BCE) to predict the coming of King Josiah three hundred years later (ca. 630 BCE), and that he would sacrifice the priests of Bethel on the altar. To confirm the prophecy, which of course would not actually come to pass until centuries later, 13:3 says, "[3] On that day he gave [i.e., announced] a wonder [מוֹפֵת] saying, 'This is the wonder [הַמּוֹפֵת] that Yahweh has spoken, "Behold the altar will be split apart and the ashes that are on it will be poured out."'" After Jeroboam's objections and the shriveling of his hand, the text reports in 13:5, "Then the altar was split apart and the ashes from the altar were poured out, according to the wonder [הַמּוֹפֵת] that the man of God had given by the word of Yahweh."

Again, when God proclaimed to Hezekiah through Isaiah the prophet that he would add fifteen years to his life and would deliver Jerusalem from the hand of Sennacherib (Isa 38:1–6), Isaiah added in 38:7–8, "And this is the sign to you from Yahweh, that Yahweh will perform the word that he has spoken, 'I will now cause the shadow of the steps that has gone down on the stairway of Ahaz in the sun to turn back ten steps.' So the sun turned back ten steps on the stairway that it had gone down."

According to the New Testament, Jesus himself acted as a prophet when he performed many prophetic signs and wonders to confirm the message that he preached. The Gospel of John, for example, was written largely to report the signs so that people would believe in him and his message: "[30] Jesus performed many other signs in the presence of his disciples, which are not recorded in this book.[31] But these are written that you may believe that Jesus is the Messiah, the Son of God, and that by believing you may have life in his name" (John 20:30–31, NIV). Unfortunately, in some of the places where he did the most signs, most of the people still would not believe (Matt 11:20–24). For this reason, in some cases, he simply refused to do any further signs (see, e.g., Matt 12:38–39 and parallels). The point of the signs was not the signs themselves, but the prophetic message the people needed to believe and obey, as was also the case with true prophecy in the Old Testament.

In sum, the first and primary test of prophecy was whether or not the prophetic message that was given corresponded to the clear teaching already given in scripture, calling for exclusive covenant loyalty to Yahweh. This was an absolute test of true prophecy. Of course, not all false prophecies would necessarily be challenging this exclusively covenant loyalty to Yahweh, so this test would not always apply to the situation at hand. The second test of prophecy was not so absolute. Nevertheless, it was a common and approved practice for the prophet to perform a separate sign or wonder to confirm that the message the prophet was giving was true and, therefore, must be obeyed.

Given this, however, the Bible also makes it clear in both the Old Testament and the New Testament that signs could also be performed by other supernatural forces, or by deception for purposes of misleading the people of God. Consider, for example, the Egyptian magicians in Exod 7:8–13, and what Jesus says in Mark 13:22, "For false messiahs and false prophets will appear and perform signs and wonders to deceive, if possible, even the elect." This brings us to the third test of prophecy.

Deuteronomy 18:21–22 and Prophecy Coming True

The third test is anticipated by Deut 18:20a, "the prophet who presumes to speak a word in my name that I have not commanded him to speak." After forbidding any prophetic messages in the names of other gods (18:20b, see the discussion of Deut 13:2–6 above), the text returns in 18:21–22 to this problem of a prophet who speaks in the name of the Lord a word that he never commanded him to speak. Commentators regularly remark on how unhelpful the third test in Deut 18:21–22 appears to be on the surface. As J. G. McConville puts it, "The problem with such a test is that the proof might come too late!"[29] Deuteronomy 18:21–22 reads as follows:

21 וְכִי תֹאמַר בִּלְבָבֶךָ אֵיכָה נֵדַע אֶת־הַדָּבָר אֲשֶׁר לֹא־דִבְּרוֹ יְהוָה:

22 אֲשֶׁר יְדַבֵּר הַנָּבִיא בְּשֵׁם יְהוָה וְלֹא־יִהְיֶה הַדָּבָר וְלֹא יָבוֹא הוּא הַדָּבָר אֲשֶׁר לֹא־דִבְּרוֹ יְהוָה בְּזָדוֹן דִּבְּרוֹ הַנָּבִיא לֹא תָגוּר מִמֶּנּוּ:

> [21] If you in your heart should say, "How will we know the word that the LORD has not spoken?" That which the prophet speaks in the name of the LORD but the word does not happen and does not come true, that is the word that the LORD has not spoken. The prophet has spoken it presumptuously. You shall have no fear of him.

How were they supposed to know whether to obey a prophetic message if they did not know it was a true prophecy until after the message had already come true? It seems that the point of stating this test in this way was simply to make the point that true prophecy comes true. It is what Herbert Huffmon has dubbed the "time will tell" principle.[30] This is the "bottom line," so to speak.

29. McConville, *Deuteronomy*, 303; see similarly Tigay, *Deuteronomy*, 175–76; Lundbom, *Deuteronomy*, 560; Block, *Deuteronomy*, 441–42; Christopher J. H. Wright, *Deuteronomy*, NIBC 4 (Peabody MA: Hendrickson, 1996), 219; Peter C. Craigie, *The Book of Deuteronomy*, NICOT (Grand Rapids: Eerdmans, 1976), 263; and Eugene H. Merrill, *Deuteronomy*, NAC (Nashville: Broadman & Holman, 1994), 274.

30. Herbert B. Huffmon, "The Exclusivity of Divine Communication in Ancient Israel: False Prophecy in the Hebrew Bible and the Ancient Near East," in *Mediating Between Heaven and Earth: Communication*

There is more to it than this, however. One of the natural extensions of the principle stated here is that prophets could gain a reputation over time. This comes out, for example, in the statement about the reputation of the prophet Samuel in 1 Sam 3:19–20: "¹⁹ Samuel grew up, and the LORD was with Samuel and he did not let any of his words fall to the ground. ²⁰ So all Israel from Dan to Beersheba knew that Samuel was trustworthy as a prophet of the LORD." If Samuel said it, one must obey it, because everyone knew that his prophecies always came true. There had been enough occasions on which Samuel had already fulfilled the requirement of Deut 18:21–22. In other words, practically speaking, one would not have to wait on the fulfillment of another prophecy that Samuel gave to know whether or not it was from the Lord and that one must obey it. Samuel's reliability was a preestablished fact. He was a prophet "like me"; that is, like Moses (Deut 18:15, 18). Similarly, we have a text from Mari that tells us that the official who sent a dream oracle to the king did not include the hair and the hem of the prophet in that instance because that particular dreamer was known to be a reliable prophet. The letter concludes: "Because the man who told this dream is to make a *pagrûm*-offering to Dagan, I have not sent him to my lord. Moreover, because this man is reliable, I have not taken from his hair or (garment) fringe."[31]

The narrative of Jer 26–29 raises other related issues amid conflict between true and false prophets; most importantly, the reality that God might not follow through on a judgment prophecy if the people would repent. In Jer 26:2–3 the Lord tells Jeremiah to speak his judgment oracle against Judah in full force, not leaving anything out, so that "perhaps they will listen and turn back each man from his evil way and I will relent concerning the calamity that I am planning to do to them because of their evil practices." Even the summary of the message itself is stated conditionally (26:4–6).

Unfortunately, the priests, prophets, and people interpreted his message as treason, so they wanted to execute him. The officials, however, decided against execution because Jeremiah had spoken to them in the name of the Lord (26:16). Some of the elders supported this decision, referring to what happened over a century earlier when Micah spoke such a judgment oracle to Hezekiah the king and the people of Judah (26:17–19). They cited Mic 3:12, "Therefore because of you, Zion will be plowed like a field, Jerusalem will become a heap of rubble, and the temple mount a wooded high place." The elders reported that, in that earlier incident, because Hezekiah and the people repented, feared the Lord, and sought his favor, the Lord did indeed relent from bringing the disaster on them through Sennacherib, king of Assyria in that day. There is no indication of the repentance in the context of Mic 3:12, except perhaps the well-known salvation oracle that follows in Mic 4:1–5 (see also the same oracle delivered by his contemporary Isaiah in Isa 2:2–4). Nevertheless, these elders knew that Hezekiah and the people of Judah had repented in response this prophetic oracle in that earlier day.

Even if the judgment oracle was not stated in a contingent way like it was in Jer 26:3–6, repentance was generally the hoped for outcome, and if the people did repent

───────────

with the Divine in the Ancient Near East, ed. C. L. Crouch, Jonathan Stöck, and Anna Elise Zernecke, LHBOTS 566 (New York: Bloomsbury, 2014), 70.

31. Sasson, *From the Mari Archives*, 287–88 (ARMT 26 line 233; also in Nissinen, *Prophets and Prophecy*, 62–65 with notes).

the judgment oracle might not be fulfilled. God retained the prerogative to withdraw it. In this way there are occasions when the true oracles of true prophets might not come to pass. This may seem contrary to Deut 18:21–22, but it is actually a dynamic built into the very purpose of prophetic oracles as envisioned in Deuteronomy.[32] The primary goal of such prophecy was to call the people to faithful adherence to their covenant commitments to the Lord. Moreover, as Amos puts it, "⁷ Surely the Sovereign LORD does nothing without revealing his plan to his servants the prophets. ⁸ The lion has roared—who will not fear? The Sovereign LORD has spoken—who can but prophesy?" (NIV). The Lord works with his people through the prophets to announce messages that they must obey. If they obey there is blessing. They disobeyed at great cost: curses (Deut 28).

Other passages support the same understanding of how prophecy worked. Jonah 3–4 recounts Jonah's effective preaching of judgment to ancient Nineveh, their repentance, and the fact that God relented. According to Jonah 3:9, even the Ninevites relied on this possibility, "Who knows? God may yet relent and with compassion turn from his fierce anger so that we will not perish" (NIV). Jonah was aware that this was a possibility too, based on Jonah 4:2, "I knew that you are a gracious and compassionate God, slow to anger and abounding in love, a God who relents from sending calamity." He had hoped, however, that this result would not materialize in the case of the Ninevites.

The point is that this was the Lord's character proclaimed from his own lips in Exod 34:6, "The LORD, the LORD, the compassionate and gracious God, slow to anger, abounding in love and faithfulness" (NIV). It was this character of Israel's God that allowed them to recover from the golden calf debacle way back in Exod 32, and a good number of passages cite it accordingly, in appropriate contexts (see, e.g., Num 14:18; Pss 86:15; 103:8; Joel 2:13). Joel 2:13–14a is especially helpful here, "¹³ Rend your heart and not your garments. Return [שׁוּב] to the LORD your God, for he is gracious and compassionate, slow to anger and abounding in love, and he relents from sending calamity. ¹⁴ Who knows? He may turn [שׁוּב] and relent." If the people שׁוּב, the Lord himself might שׁוּב. Here is another instance where the people apparently did in fact repent. After the summary of the judgment oracle (2:15–17) we read without any preparation in 2:18, "Then the LORD was jealous for his land and took pity on his people."[33] It is readily apparent that between 2;17 and 18 the people did, in fact, respond to the

32. See the rather extensive discussion of this in Anthony Chinedu Osuji, *Where Is the Truth? Narrative Exegesis and the Question of True and False Prophecy in Jer 26–29 (MT)*, BETL 214 (Leuven: Peeters, 2010), see esp. the summary discussion on pp. 388–93, but also supported by detailed exegesis elsewhere in the volume. It is not within the purview of this essay to treat the issue of other kinds of "unfulfilled" prophetic predictions. See, e.g., Osuji, *Where Is the Truth?* 378 n. 20 and the literature cited there.

33. The second edition of the NIV translation has rightly reversed its earlier decision to translate the preterite verbs here in 2:18 as future tense "Then the Lord will be jealous for his land and take pity on his people." They put the past tense translation in the margin. The second edition has reversed this and put the past tense translation in the main text, "Then the Lord was jealous for his land and took pity on his people." They still maintain the future tense translation in the margin, however. See also the remarks in James L. Crenshaw, *Joel: A New Translation with Introduction and Commentary*, AB 24C (New York: Doubleday, 1995), 147–48; and John Barton, *Joel and Obadiah: A Commentary*, OTL (Louisville: Westminster John Knox, 2001), 86–88.

judgment oracle with repentance in that historical situation, so in 2:18 we get an abrupt shift to salvation oracles (see also Mal 3:16–18).

Conclusion

The "word of the LORD" was a serious matter in the Old Testament, and it still is. To be a person through whom God speaks his word to his people is a high and heavy responsibility, not to be undermined or trifled with. The first test of prophetic authenticity was whether or not the prophet spoke a message that betrayed the exclusive covenant commitment of the people to worship and serve the Lord their God alone (Deut 13:2–6), or spoke in the name of other gods (Deut 18:20b). An especially pernicious form of this would be when a prophet, whether speaking in the name of the Lord or of (an)other god(s) reinforced his idolatrous message with a sign or wonder to convince the hearers that they must obey the word he has given (Deut 13:2–6).

Performing such signs or wonders was one way authentic prophets regularly reinforced the truth of their prophetic word (see historical examples cited above). In fact, Jesus himself performed many such signs and wonders for this very purpose. Thus, the second test of prophecy was the performance of a sign or wonder to support the message delivered as the word of the Lord. The first test was absolute. The second was not. The latter, however, could reinforce belief in and obedience to a prophet and his or her prophetic message if the message itself did not violate the first test. This was especially useful if the fulfillment of the prophetic message would not be fulfilled for some time. This brings us to the third test of prophecy.

The third test was whether or not the message proclaimed as the word of the Lord actually proved to be true by coming to pass. As noted above, a sign or wonder was sometimes performed to support the coming fulfillment of the message, sometimes a long time later. The goal was to urge and convince people to believe the message even before it was fulfilled so that they would act on it. It is common to distinguish between "foretelling" and "forthtelling," but even with forthtelling the perspective was forward-looking toward ongoing obedience to God's word whether previously or newly revealed. As the apostle John puts it, "we know that when Christ appears, we shall be like him, for we shall see him as he is. [3] All who have this hope in him purify themselves, just as he is pure" (1 John 3:2b–3). Almost all of God's will for everyone who is in Christ has already been revealed to us. We do indeed walk by faith and not by sight (2 Cor 5:7), but we do not lack guidance on what it means to live godly in Christ Jesus right now.

The ancient Israelites were expected to live in the light of what God had already revealed to them, too. The world of prophets and prophetic oracles, however, could be confusing, as we can see, for example, from Jer 26–29. This is why God gave tests for the authenticity of prophets and their prophetic messages. Unfortunately, some of the same problems have continued through into the New Testament and up to our present day. The battle for truth was often difficult and harsh in ancient Israel, and the same was true in Jesus's day, as he himself said: [15] "Watch out for *false prophets*. They come to you in sheep's clothing, but inwardly they are ferocious wolves. [16] By their fruit you will recognize them" (Matt 7:15–16a; emphasis added). False prophetic would be betrayed by their own bad fruit. Moreover, not everyone who calls Jesus "Lord" actually belongs to him (7:21). They might even prophesy in his name, drive our demons, and even do attesting miracles (cf. Deut 13:2–3), but this is no guarantee that Jesus "knows" them (Matt 7:21–23). The real test is whether or not they "do the will" of the "Father in heaven" (7:21).[34]

People can do all sorts of religious things for religious purposes and for their own reasons, whether those reasons be academic, ecclesiastical, personal self-righteousness, or whatever. In all ages it takes courage and perseverance to engage in the battle of truth against the lies of the age. One of the tests of a true prophet in all ages has always been their way of life. Do they do the will of the Father in heaven according to the word, in which he has revealed his divine will? What kind of fruit do they bear? Ultimately, the real issue is whether the Lord really knows her or him as his (Matt 7:21–23). In the meantime, those who live for the Lord have the word of God revealed as their guide. We need to do all we can to stay faithful to God's purpose and plan according to his word even in spite of our many struggles and faults. This is the way, the truth, and the life, and what a tremendous way of life it is!

---

34. See the helpful discussion in Osuji, *Where Is the Truth?* 380–83.

Fishing for Fissures: The Literary Unity of the Kadesh Poem of Ramesses II and Its Implications for the Diachronic Study of the Hebrew Bible

Joshua Berman

IN THE SUMMER OF 2011 I attended the Old Testament Study Group at Tyndale House, Cambridge. I was the only Orthodox Jew in attendance; indeed, I may be the only Orthodox Jew ever to attend that forum. I had been in England for the International Meeting of the Society of Biblical Literature that summer in London, but I was keen to attend the gathering at Tyndale House as well. I wanted to see how top-notch scholars with conservative religious leanings plied their trade. I was looking, to use a Hasidic term, for a "rebbe"—a mentor for a specific area of spiritual growth. It was here that I met Jim Hoffmeier for the first time. I had always been told that the good scholar is the scholar that entirely bifurcates his spiritual life and his intellectual life. In our first talk, I remember Jim spoke about prayer, and how refreshing it felt to speak to a Bible scholar who wasn't ashamed to do so. In the years since I have learned from Jim what it means to push back against fundamentalists who cannot accept what evidence dictates. No less importantly, I have learned from Jim that the best criticism is often that which is leavened with the sensitivities found in our traditions. Far from an impediment to doing good scholarship, our traditions are sometimes the very key to getting the scholarship right. At the publication of this tribute to Jim—my rebbe—I bless him with the blessing of Moses to Jethro, "Please don't leave us. You know where we can camp in the wilderness, and you can be our guide."

Across a distinguished career, of course, Jim worked in two fields—Egyptology and Hebrew Bible—often discovering the nexus between them. This paper follows in his path. The question of how we can discern signs of diachronic development in the text of the Hebrew Bible is emerging as an increasingly difficult issue to answer.[1] As I have argued elsewhere, there is no intuitive way to determine what constitutes a fissure in a text from another period and another locale. These sensitivities must be learned, and acquired by careful study. When claims for revision rely on a perceived inconsistency or tension in the text and there is no external evidence to corroborate this perception, we may well be imposing modern canons of consistency on these ancient texts, effectively inventing the problem to which revision is the solution.[2]

---

1. A session devoted to the question was sponsored by the Pentateuch Section of the Society of Biblical Literature, at the Annual Meeting of the Society of Biblical Literature, Denver, 17–21 November 2018.

2. See generally Joshua Berman, *Inconsistency in the Torah: Ancient Literary Convention and the Limits of Source Criticism* (New York: Oxford University Press, 2017); see also Berman, "The Biblical Criticism of Ibn Hazm the Andalusian: A Medieval Control for Modern Diachronic Method," *JBL* 138 (2019): 377–90. See discussion in Raymond F. Person Jr. and Robert Rezetko, "Introduction: The Importance of Empirical

A survey of six primers for source-critical methodology reveals a telling lacuna: all offer detailed examples of how to identify inconsistencies, tensions, and contradictions within the texts of the Torah and as telltale signs of revision.[3] But all assume that the modern exegete will be able to correctly flag these on the basis of his or her own notion of consistency and literary unity. Not one of these primers suggests that competency in the writings of the ancient world is necessary in order to avoid anachronism. Not one cites even a single example of a seeming inconsistency, but one we know to overlook because of evidence from other ancient works. Source critics need to become aware of the situatedness of their own aesthetic senses of literary unity.

The problem is particularly acute with regard to the genre of narrative. We have fine studies that survey the poetics of narrative in biblical literature.[4] To date, however, no comparable work has been written for any of the cognate narrative corpora of the ancient Near East. There has been no survey of Egyptian narrative techniques, nor of the poetics of Mesopotamian narrative that would allow us to test the bounds of literary unity in narrative for these ancient writers. Suffice it to say, there has also been no monograph produced that sets out to compare biblical narrative technique with that of the surrounding cultures. Lacking a thorough knowledge of the ancient notions of literary unity, modern scholars, perforce, perform their diachronic work in the dark, arriving at conclusions derived exclusively from their own notions of textual cohesion.

Here, I examine the Kadesh poem of Ramesses II, a text universally recognized by Egyptologists to have been commissioned as a whole by the aforementioned pharaoh sometime following his return from the battle of Kadesh against his archenemy the Hittities in 1274 BCE. As we shall see, this composition displays precisely the types of textual fissures that diachronic scholars of the Hebrew Bible routinely identify as signs of textual growth and of the compositional nature of the biblical text. The nexus that I seek to draw between biblical studies and Egyptology is in two directions; the fields emerge as mutually fructifying. On the one hand, biblical studies has witnessed a great boon in the attention to literary artistry at work in the Hebrew Bible, and I shall marshal some of these insights to shed light on some of the textual difficulties we find in the Kadesh poem. Conversely, I shall take some of the textual data from the Kadesh poem as illustrative of the fact that what looks to modern eyes as clear signs of fissure

---

Models to Assess the Efficacy of Source and Redaction Criticism," in *Empirical Models Challenging Biblical Criticism*, ed. Raymond F. Person Jr. and Robert Rezetko, AIL 25 (Atlanta: SBL Press, 2016), 29–30.

3. Claus Westermann, *Genesis 1–11: A Commentary* (London: SPCK, 1984), 575–84; Odil Steck, *Old Testament Exegesis: A Guide to Methodology*, trans. James D. Nogalski, 2nd ed., RBS 39 (Atlanta: Scholars Press, 1998), 54–58; Suzanne Boorer, "Source and Redaction Criticism," in *Methods for Exodus*, ed. Thomas B. Dozeman (Cambridge: Cambridge University Press, 2010), 95–129; Alexander Rofé, *Introduction to the Literature of the Hebrew Bible* (Jerusalem: Simor, 2009), 166–213; Richard E. Friedman, *Who Wrote the Bible?* (New York: Harper & Row, 1987), 52–60. See also Norman Habel, *Literary Criticism of the Old Testament*, GBS (Philadelphia: Fortress, 1971). Habel pays lip service to this imperative: "The literary critic should also try to relate his literary findings to their historical context. To do this he will need to use all the pertinent information at his disposal about the language, culture, history, thought forms and religions of the ancient world" (p. 7). However, at no point, in his long primer does Habel adduce an example where such context corrects for the modern interpreter's anachronistic instincts of literary unity.

4. See, e.g., Robert Alter, *The Art of Biblical Narrative* (New York: Basic Books, 1981); Meir Sternberg, *The Poetics of Biblical Narrative: Ideological Literature and the Drama of Reading*, ISBL (Bloomington: Indiana University Press, 1985).

in the text, did not necessarily appear that way to those responsible for composing our control text, the Kadesh poem of Ramesses II.

The Kadesh Inscriptions of Ramesses II:
Conflicting Versions of a Single Story

The battle of Kadesh, in the fifth year of the reign of Ramesses II, pitted Egypt against the Hittite Empire for control of the states of the northern Levant. While the results of the battle are disputed, my interest here is not with what actually happened on the plain of Kadesh in 1274 BCE, but in how its results were projected post facto in Egypt.[5] Accounts of the battle of Kadesh are displayed in ten copies on public buildings, in five temples located at Abydos, Karnak, Luxor, Abu Simbel, and the king's mortuary temple, the Ramesseum. These compositions contain two separate literary accounts of the battle of Kadesh. The longer one, some 350 lines, is conventionally referred to as the poem, while the second account, conventionally called the bulletin, is about a third as long.[6] In all, we have evidence of seven carvings of the bulletin and eight of the poem as well as fragments of the poem on two hieratic papyri, p. Sallier III and p. Chester Beatty III. At most sites the accounts are also accompanied by bas-reliefs depicting the different stages of the battle—an innovation of Ramesside art—complete with captions.[7] At least three of these sites—Luxor, the Ramesseum, and Abydos—feature carvings of both the poem and the bulletin and the same may have been true at the temple at Karnak.[8] The accounts both tell of a common core event: As the pharaoh's troops approached Kadesh they were surprised by a large force of Hittite chariotry. Ramesses's own troops broke ranks and the king was left to face the Hittite confederacy alone. Undaunted, he charged into their lines, single-handedly defeating them. These events are recorded in each composition utilizing an array of identical stock phrases.[9] Numerous differences, however, distinguish the two texts: (1) the role of the deity in each; (2) scenes found in one are absent from the other; (3) the names of the nations that joined the Hittite confederation do not match; (4) finally, I note a series of stylistic differences between the two accounts. Some four-fifths of the poem is verse, while only about a quarter of the bulletin is verse.[10] The poem routinely alternates between first-person and third-person narration, while narration in the bulletin is nearly entirely reported in third-person. Complicating matters even further is the fact that a third and often divergent account of the battle is depicted in the bas-reliefs and their accompanying captions. Here we discover information not

5. For bibliography on the Kadesh Inscriptions see *RITA* 2:3–5.

6. Alan H. Gardiner, *The Kadesh Inscriptions of Ramesses II* (Oxford: Griffith Institute, 1960), 4–5; *AEL* 2:57.

7. *AEL* 2:57. While some scholars have seen the bulletin as an extended caption servicing the reliefs most scholars see the poem, the bulletin, and the reliefs as three separate accounts. See *AEL* 2:58; *RITA* 2:8.

8. Gardiner, *Kadesh Inscriptions of Ramesses II*, 3.

9. See discussion in Gardiner, *Kadesh Inscriptions of Ramesses II*, 46. A brief discussion of the thematic structures of the two compositions is found in Thomas von der Way, *Die Textüberlieferung Ramses' II. zur Qadeš-Schlacht: Analyse und Struktur*, HÄB 22; Hildesheim: Gerstenberg, 1984), 272–75.

10. *RITA* 2:8.

found in either the poem or the bulletin, information that, indeed, is antithetical to the spirit found in those two accounts.[11]

In accounting for these conflicting accounts Egyptologists are of one mind: no diachronic explanation for these differences can be offered. Scholars do, indeed, debate the date of composition of these texts. Some scholars believe that Ramesses commissioned the inscriptions upon his return from Kadesh, while others maintain that the inscriptions date from several decades later during his long reign, following the establishment of peaceful relations with the Hittite kingdom in 1258 BCE.[12] Yet all scholars maintain that these compositions were commissioned at one and the same time; the debate is solely over whether this was at an earlier or later date in the reign of Ramesses II.

Egyptologists have grappled to make sense of the presence of these deliberately juxtaposed conflicting accounts. Miriam Lichtheim writes that we may "assume that the Bulletin and the Poem were written by the same author." [13] Likewise, Alan Gardiner wrote that we may assume common authorship "with practical certainty."[14] By contrast, Anthony Spalinger questions whether there is in fact proof for single authorship.[15] Concerning the question of authorship, a sharpening of terms is in order, and we may make good use of a dichotomy from the field of authorship studies. In classical literature from ancient Rome, there is a distinction between *auctoritas* and *scriptor*. The *auctoritas* is the person who commissions a work and takes responsibility for it. The individual who executes the commissioned work, who puts the words together is the *scriptor*.[16] There is no recourse other than to conclude that the poem and the bulletin were commissioned for inscription at the same time, by one and the same *auctoritas*, Ramesses II.[17] Gardiner sums up the issue well: "I cannot help envisaging a command given by the king to the ablest experts of his time to display to his awe-stricken subjects his great military achievement in two mutually complementary forms."[18] In light of the fact that the two compositions are carved in juxtaposition in several monumental settings, no Egyptologist has proposed that the texts were intended for different audiences. We may not be able to reconstruct the precise purpose of each composition. It seems reasonable however, to conclude with Lichtheim that for the king and for his potential audiences, "the Bulletin and the Poem each had a

11. I take up these differences in Joshua Berman, "Juxtaposed Conflicting Compositions (Gen 1–2:4a; 2:4b–2:24; Exod 14–15, Judg 4–5): A New Kingdom Egyptian Parallel," *JNSL* 42 (2016), 1–13; and in greater depth in Berman, *Inconsistency in the Torah*, 17–34.

12. For the former view see Boyo Ockinga, "On the Interpretation of the Kadesh Record," *Chronique d'Egypte* 62 (1987): 43–46. For the latter view see Jan Assmann, "Krieg und Frieden im alten Aegypten: Rameses II und die Schlacht bei Kadesch," *Mannheimer Forum* 83–84 (1983): 175–217; von der Way, *Die Textüberlieferung Ramses' II,* 393–98.

13. *AEL* 2:59.

14. Gardiner, *Kadesh Inscriptions of Ramesses II*, 46.

15. Anthony J. Spalinger, *Aspects of the Military Documents of the Ancient Egyptians* (New Haven: Yale University Press, 1982), 185.

16. Atle Kittang, "Authors, Authorship, and Work: A Brief Theoretical Survey," in *Modes of Authorship in the Middle Ages*, ed. Slavica Rankovic, Papers in Mediaeval Studies 22 (Toronto: Pontifical Institute of Mediaeval Studies, 2012), 19.

17. See Scott Morschauser, "Observations on the Speeches of Ramesses II in the Literary Record of the Battle of Kadesh," in *Perspectives on the Battle of Kadesh*, ed. Hans Goedicke (Baltimore: Halgo, 1985), 206 n. 78: "Ramesses was the ultimate inspiration, if not the actual source."

18. Gardiner, *Kadesh Inscriptions of Ramesses II*, 47

purpose and complemented each other."[19] Each of the three accounts has a clear focus: The poem focuses on the miraculous divine aid bestowed upon the pharaoh by the god Amun. The bulletin makes virtually no mention of divine aid at all. It extols the bravery of the earthly king, who engages battle single-handedly. The reliefs, by contrast with both, make no mention of the gods, and only secondary mention of the king. Their focus is upon the heroic deeds of the Nearin brigade.

Modern historians read these accounts and try to sort out fact from fiction; they attempt to create a mélange of all three accounts, in the hopes of recreating what actually happened on the plains of Kadesh in 1274 BCE.[20] In all likelihood, though, ancient readers made no effort to sort "fact from fiction," cognitive categories distinct to the modern mindset. They made no attempt to integrate and combine that which had been presented separately. Rather they encountered the Kadesh Inscriptions at sites that trumpet the greatness of the pharaoh. The inscriptions were a communication—an exhortation—from Ramesses to his subjects. Here is where the king could communicate to his subject the vital lessons they needed to learn. Audiences of the Kadesh Inscriptions may not have been able to sort out the precise chronology of that battle. But they would have come away from reading the pharaoh's words with a greater sense of their indebtedness to Amun, the prowess of their monarch, and a sense of their own civic duties as soldiers in the pharaoh's army. These were the lessons to be learned from the deeds of the past, these compositions of exhortation.

Epigraphic remains of the Kadesh poem attest to just this function. In addition to the eight copies of the poem found carved at the monumental structures at Thebes, two hieratic versions survive, p. Sallier III and p. Chester Beatty III. The latter was found in the workmen's village of Deir el-Medina, located in the Valley of Kings. Several scholars have surmised that the existence of these hieratic copies suggests that they were published widely and were probably used for public celebration and cult of the king: for the sort of adoration of the king demanded by the Loyalist Instruction. They encapsulated an ideological statement of the relationship between king and god, and a political statement of the king's superior fitness for authority over his army and advisors.[21]

Internal Contradictions Within the Kadesh Poem of Ramesses II

The foregoing discussion well sets up a further investigation of inconsistency within the Kadesh poem itself. If we see that the conventions of the time display a predilection for tolerating inconsistency between juxtaposed texts for rhetorical and didactic

19. *AEL* 2:59.

20. See the survey of these various opinions in *RITA* 2:21–49.

21. Christopher J. Eyre, "Is Historical Literature 'Political' or 'Literary?,'" in *Ancient Egyptian Literature: History and Forms*, ed. Antonio Loprieno, PAe 10 (Leiden: Brill, 1996), 427; von der Way, *Die Textüberlieferung Ramses' II*, 39–43; Irene Shirun-Grumach, "Kadesh Inscriptions and Königsnovelle," in *Proceedings of the Seventh International Congress of Egyptologists: Cambridge, 3–9 September 1995*, ed. Christopher J. Eyre, OLA 82 (Leuven: Peeters, 1998), 1067; Anthony J. Spalinger, *The Transformation of an Ancient Egyptian Narrative: P. Sallier III and the Battle of Kadesh*, Göttinger Orientforschungen Ägypten 40 (Wiesbaden: Harrassowitz, 2002), 329; Donald B. Redford, *Pharaonic King-lists, Annals and Day-books: A Contribution to the Study of the Egyptian Sense of History*, SSEA Publication 4 (Mississuaga: Benben, 1986), 51–54.

purposes, we should not be surprised to find the same tendency between various episodes within a single composition such as the Kadesh poem. Here, I would like to
look at three literary phenomena in the text of the Kadesh poem. Each of them is of a
kind with the types of "fissure" that diachronic scholars of the Hebrew Bible routinely
identify as markers of textual growth. The unitary composition of the Kadesh poem,
however, gives us license—nay, mandate—to examine how the inconsistency contributes to the rhetorical and didactic aims of the specific passage at hand.

Shift in Narratorial Voice

Most egregious of all the inconsistencies in this composition is the shift from third-
person narration to first-person narration in line 88 of the poem:[22]

> (80) Then His Majesty set forth at a gallop, (81) he plunged into the midst of the
> forces of the Hittite foe, (82) he being entirely on his own, no-one else with him.
> (83) So His Majesty went to look around him; (84) he found 2,500 chariot-spans
> hemming him in, all around him, (85) even all the champion ("runners") of the
> Hittite foe, along with the numerous foreign countries who were with them—
> (86) from Arzawa, Masa and Pidassa; {from Gasgas, Arwanna and Qizzuwatna;
> from Aleppo, Ugarit Qadesh and Lukka;} (87) they were 3 men to a chariot-
> span, acting as a unit. (88) *But there was no high officer with me, no charioteer*
> (89) *no army-soldier, no shield bearer.* (90) *But my army and my chariotry*
> *melted away before them,* (91) *none could withstand them, to fight with them.*

Lines 88–90 organically advance the plot that had begun in line 25, detailing the
march northward through the engagement with the Hittite forces. From a narratological perspective, the entire scene is narrated in third-person until we reach these three
verses. If we didn't know that the poem is a unitary composition, these lines would
certainly arouse our suspicion that we are witness here to diachronic development,
as the shift in narratorial voice is jarring. Moreover, the information contained in lines
88–91 is superfluous, as the third-person narrator had already informed us in line 82
that the king was entirely alone in the face of the Hittite onslaught.

To better appreciate the rhetorical force of what has been achieved here, I would like
to make a structural observation about the poem as a whole. I open with some remarks
about the variation in narratorial voice generally in the Kadesh poem. In this regard, the
poem splits into three: (1) Lines 24–87: The march northward and the initial engagement with the Hittite forces. This is narrated entirely in the third-person. (2) Lines
88–332: This is the main section of narration, including the king's appeal to Amun,
his successful forays into the Hittite camp, his lectures to his troops, and the surrender
of the Hittite king. This section is narrated almost entirely in the first-person.[23] The
only exceptions to this are minor expositional introductions that help position the king
within the plot (lines 92a, 166, 208, 214, 220, 251–252), and an extended description of

---

22. All translations of the poem are taken from *RITA* 2:2–14 (emphasis added).
23. Some variants conclude first-person narration at line 330, others at 331.

the Hittite camp, which Ramesses could not have seen, and therefore could not have plausibly narrated (lines 143–153). (3) Lines 333–343: These lines chronicle the king's victorious march homeward and the crowning glory he receives upon his return. This is all narrated in the third-person. Put differently, the narration forms an enveloping structure with bookends. The march north and the victorious march south are narrated in the third-person. While at first blush, the first-person narration of lines 88–90 is incongruous with the third-person narration that precedes them, we see now that lines 88–91 lie at the narratological fulcrum of the entire composition: It is these lines that open the first-person narration that details the king's exploits across the main block of the work. The lines therefore confront us with a paradox: In terms of content they are part and parcel of account of the first engagement with the Hittite troops, and are set off in no way from that account. Yet, they are the lines that open the mode of narration that will dominate for the remainder of the composition.

What characterizes these lines and sets them off from the preceding narration is that they underscore the king's interiority; what he was experiencing and feeling. It is true that already in line 82 we learned that he was alone in his encounter with the Hittite chariotry. But those earlier lines (76–82) underscore that the king did not bat an eye-lash when he learned of the Hittite trap, and rushed out to battle. He may have done so with the assumption that his forces would follow closely behind his lead. Indeed, line 83 stresses that it was only when the king looked around that he fully comprehended the situation. Lines 88–90 do more than convey to us that the king was alone; they convey to us his sense of being alone; his sense of having been forsaken.

These lines are crucial because they mark a turning point: heretofore, Ramesses fought as a valorous king (lines 76–80). In lines 83–90 Ramesses recognizes that he is at once surrounded—by enemy forces—and abandoned by his own troops, at the same time. Put differently, the turning point of lines 88–91 is the moment at which he realizes he must turn to his god for help, because he cannot achieve victory alone. It is from the despair of having been forlorn that he turns to Amun in prayer in lines 92–120. Indeed, within the prayer itself, Ramesses highlights the existential crisis he experienced that led him to pray in the first place:

(110) I have called on you, O Amun,
(111) while I am amidst multitudes whom I know not.
(112) All the foreign countries have united against me,
I being (left) entirely alone, no one else with me.
(113) My regular troops have abandoned me,
(114) not one of them has looked for me, from my chariotry.
(115) When I kept on shouting out to them,
(116) none of them heeded me as I called out.
(117) Amun I found more help to me than millions of troops,
than hundred thousands of chariotry.

The fact that Ramesses was abandoned by his own troops and left all alone is a trope that the poem returns to again and again. Following his first victory, he rebukes his troops:

(169) Stand firm, be bold-hearted, my troops,

(170) see my triumph (all) on my own,

(171) with only Amun to be my protector,
his hand with me.

(172) And how cowardly are your hearts, my chariotry,

(173) it's no use trusting in you either.

(186) Now see—you did a rotten trick, all tougher as one:
Not a man of you stood firm to give me a hand as I fought.

Later his shield-bearer exclaims:

(208) My good Lord, (209) O mighty Ruler, great Protector of Egypt on the day
of the battle, (210) we stand alone in the midst of the foe! (211) see, the troops
and chariotry have abandoned us!

And later, the king again rebukes his troops:

(258) have I done no good to (even) one of you,

(259) (for) your abandoning me, alone amidst the strife?

(263) What will be said in gossip when it is heard of,

(264) your abandoning me, I being (left) alone without companion?

(265) And neither high-officer, chariot-warrior nor soldier came, to give me a
hand,

(266) as I fought!

The analysis of the structure of a text has been a central concern for biblicists for
quite some time now.[24] Here we can see the benefits of applying this same methodology to an Egyptian composition.

Inconsistency Concerning the Pharaoh's Isolation

For all of the importance of the trope of the king's isolation in the Kadesh poem, the
details of this "isolation" are manipulated in different ways in different passages of
the poem. The initial description of the king's isolation is found in lines 80–90, cited
above, particularly in lines 88–90: "there was no high officer with me, no charioteer
(89) no army-soldier, no shield bearer. (90) But my army and my chariotry melted
away before them." Yet, further on in the composition, we find two separate accounts
in which the king was said to fight while in the company of others. The first of these is
in lines 205–219, and here we find a dialogue between the king and his shield bearer,
Menna:

24. See Robert M. Polzin, *Biblical Structuralism: Method and Subjectivity in the Study of Ancient
Texts* (Philadelphia: Fortress, 1977); Jerome T. Walsh, *Style and Structure in Biblical Hebrew Narrative*
(Collegeville, MN: Liturgical Press, 2001).

(205) Now when Menna my shield-bearer saw (206) that a huge number of chariots hemmed me in, (207) then he was dismayed, his heart sank, and stark fear possessed his body. (208) Then he said to His Majesty: My good Lord, (209) O mighty Ruler, great protector of Egypt on the day of the battle, (210) we stand alone in the midst of the foe! (211) See, the troops and chariotry have abandoned us, (212) why do you stay to save them? (213) Let's get clear, save us, O Usimare Setepenre! (214) Then said His Majesty to his shield-bearer: (215) be firm, be bold-hearted, my shield-bearer! (216) I shall go into them like the pounce of a falcon, (217) killing, slaughtering, felling to the ground. (218) What are these effeminate weaklings to you (219) for millions of whom I care nothing.

Here we see a good example of how consistency of details is sacrificed for the sake of the rhetorical needs of each of the three passages. The earlier passage, lines 80–90 truly strives to create the strongest sense of the king's isolation. In contrast to the swarm of enemies surrounding him in lines 83–86, the poem stresses his solitary stance by underscoring the various personages that ought to be at his side but are entirely absent: high officers, charioteers, army soldiers, and shield bearers.

The dialogue with Menna (lines 205–219) is the opening scene of the king's victorious efforts on the battlefield, encompassing lines 205–222. It tells of a later stage of battle, and even references the fact when the king charges forward here (line 221) that it was for the sixth time in the war. The passage presents plot incongruities relative to the earlier scene. It makes no mention of Menna's arrival. If Menna had been at the king's side all along, then the king had not been all alone, as suggested in the earlier passages. And if Menna had now returned to his king's side, why is no mention made of the fact—which would certainly highlight his courage? This type of fissure in biblical studies would be marshaled as a sign of a seam in the text, that clearly different accounts had been assembled in a way that is plain for the eye to see.

The fact that the Kadesh poem is a literary unity points to the fact that painting a seamless coherent plot is not the goal of the poem. Rather, it tailors individual scenes to achieve specific rhetorical goals. In this section, Menna serves as a foil; his faint-heartedness, and especially his alarm that they alone face the entire Hittite force, serve to underscore the king's valor. Menna's presence also creates the artifice of a witness to the events, so that they may be told now. In fact, the king notes this fact in line 275. Because Menna serves here as a foil of fear for the king's bravery, there is no place, rhetorically speaking, to draw attention to the fact of his putative return. To do so would undercut the rhetorical logic of the passage.

We find in the poem yet a third passage describing the king's isolation as he faced the enemy, this one describing a third configuration of individuals. It is contained in the pharaoh's second rebuke of his troops:

(263) What will be said in gossip, when it is heard of, (264) your abandoning me, I being (left) alone, without companion? (265) And neither high officer, chariot-warrior nor soldier came, to give me a hand, (266) as I fought! I repulsed a million foreign lands, on my own, (267) with (only) Victory in Thebes and Mut is Content, my great chariot-steeds.... (272) It was they whom I found amidst

the strife, with the charioteer (273) Menna, my shield-bearer, (274) and with my household butlers who were at my side, (275) those who are my witnesses regarding the fighting. See—I found them!

According to this passage, the king entered battle with Menna, who is now called his charioteer (273)—contra his epithet as shield bearer earlier (205)—as well as his unnamed shield bearer, and an untold number of house butlers (274).

The details concerning who stood by the king's side in this summary rebuke of the troops (251–275) accords with neither of the scenes of isolation depicted earlier, nor with any other narrated in the poem. Were such incongruities discovered in a biblical text, a diachronic scholar would well suggest that the text bears witness to multiple traditions surrounding the king's isolation, that have now been melded into the final form of the text. But the text of the Kadesh poem was composed at once, and thus perforce, we must conclude that details are manipulated to serve maximum rhetorical benefit. To understand the points being underscored, we need to take a wider look at the rebuke. It is a rebuke, specifically, of his combat troops:

> (251) Then said His Majesty to his troops and his officers, (252) and likewise (to) his chariotry: (253) What's wrong with you, my officers, (254) my troops and my chariotry, who do not know how to fight?

The lengthy rebuke to these senior combat troops concludes by offering a roll call of those meeker, subordinate figures who nonetheless chose to remain by the king's side: horses (!), a charioteer, his shield bearer, and his house butlers. Listing these subordinate figures underscores their bravery. Their inclusion here is a necessary element of the description of the king's isolation here, as it brings further disgrace and dishonor to those who fled.

Inconsistent References to the Pharaoh's Steed

When the Hittite's first attack, we learn of Ramesses's chariot steed:

> (76) Then His Majesty appeared (gloriously) like his father Montu, (77) he took his panoply of war, and girded himself in his coat of mail; (78) he was like Baal in his hour. (79) The great (chariot)-span which bore His Majesty was (named) *Victory in Thebes*, of the great Stable of Usimare Setepenre.

Although this section heralds a lone steed, Victory in Thebes, the king's summary rebuke of his troops, which we just saw earlier, makes mention of two horses:

> (266) I repulsed a million foreign lands, on my own, (267) with (only) *Victory in Thebes* and *Mut is Content*, my great chariot-steeds. (268) It was they whom I found to help me, (269) when all alone I fought with multitudinous foreign lands! (270) I shall stoop to feeding them myself, personally, (271) every day that I am in the Palace.

Again, we can well imagine that were a diachronically inclined scholar to find such an incongruity within the text of the Hebrew Bible, he or she would conclude that there were two traditions concerning Ramesses's horses: one tradition that knew of only one horse, as per the earlier passage, Victory in Thebes, and another tradition that knew of two horses. Here, too, the rhetorical needs of the passage provide license to stray from full plot consistency. There is no earlier mention that Mut is Content had provided help to the king, as per line 268, for only Victory in Thebes is mentioned. In this latter passage, however, the author explores the concept of honor. This is explicit in one of the soliloquy's opening lines: "Does a man not make himself honoured in his city, at his return, when he has played the hero before his lord?" (255–256). The officers, troops, and chariotry displayed dishonor and indignity by deserting the king. The horses displayed dignity by carrying Ramesses into battle, in spite of the arrows being shot at them. On the surface of it, the image of Ramesses descending to the stable, sloshing through the manure as he personally feeds the horses would seem to be an undignified one: the king debasing himself and his high office, all to feed animals. But because the horses displayed honor on the battlefield, it is now a source of dignity even for the king to feed such meritorious beasts. The multiple number of noble horses fed here serves to make the contrast all the greater. The more noble horses to feed, the greater the dignity for the man who does so—even for the king himself.

CHAPTER 3

Food for the Forces: An Investigation of Military Subsistence Strategies in New Kingdom Border Regions

Louise Bertini and Salima Ikram

Introduction

The frontiers of ancient Egypt have played a multifaceted role in the discipline, control, and coordination of many socio-economic aspects of Egypt, including contact with merchants and caravans along trade routes, soldiers, and envoys. Although the Middle Kingdom (ca. 1974–1781 BC) fortresses in Nubia are quite well known (Williams 2012, 1999; Shinnie 1996; Reisner 1960), it is only recently that attention has been given to the string of New Kingdom (ca. 1549–1069 BC) fortresses along the borders of the western (Spencer 2017, 2008; Snape 2010; Snape and Wilson 2007; Thomas 2000) and eastern Nile Delta (Hoffmeier 2004, 2006, 2011, 2014; Hoffmeier and Abd el-Maksoud 2003; Abd el-Maksoud 1998; Abd el-Maksoud and Valbelle 2005; 2011). While the defensive nature of such fortresses may be clear, thus far little work has been carried out to understand how the forts themselves were provisioned, and the extent to which these sites may have been self-sufficient.

With the start of the New Kingdom (ca. 1549 BC), there was both a reestablishment of the southern border with Nubia (Edwards 2004) along with a new series of fortresses constructed (ca. 1380 BC) at Egypt's northeastern border along the Ways of Horus (Hoffmeier 2004, 2006, 2011; Hoffmeier and Abd el-Maksoud 2003; Abd el-Maksoud 1998; Abd el-Maksoud and Valbelle 2005; 2011). The earliest textual references of the Ways of Horus date to the Fifth Dynasty (ca. 2500–2350 BC), but are only referred to in titles, indicating that this location was more a region (Valbelle 1994), rather than a specific route (Gardiner 1920). No architectural structures along this route/region appear until the mid-Eighteenth Dynasty at sites such as Tell el-Borg (Hoffmeier 2014) and Tell Hebua (Abd el-Maksoud 1998).

While the Eighteenth Dynasty rulers showed a greater interest in the southern and eastern border regions, a change is seen in the Nineteenth Dynasty during the reign of Ramesses II (ca. 1279–1212 BC) with an additional focus on the western frontier (Snape 2003). During this time, a series of new military installations along the Mediterranean coast were constructed (Zawiyet Umm el-Rakham, el-Alamein, and el-Gharbaniyat), along with new exterior fortification walls around existing western delta settlements at sites such as Kom Firin and Tell Abqa'in (Snape 2003; Thomas 2000).[1] Clearly Ramesses

---

1. Although there is no confirmed architectural evidence at Kom Firin prior to the reign of Ramesses II, a foundation dating to the reign of Sety I (ca. 1296–1279 BC) is probable. Burials have also been found

was concerned not only with the Road to Qadesh, but also with the Mediterranean coast and Libyan border, as well as any issues with nomadic populations in these areas. Although it is not the goal of this paper to discuss why this change occurred, the interpretation of the faunal remains can provide insights on the subsistence strategies of the forts, and possibly on some of the activities that occurred therein.

Only a limited amount of work has been carried out on the economy of the New Kingdom in terms of faunal material, in part due to the paucity of excavated material from settlement contexts that has been analyzed. The few sites that have been examined include Amarna (Hecker 1984; Legge 2010, 2012), Malkata (Ikram 1995), the New Kingdom settlement at Abydos (Bertini, unpublished data), and a Ramesside domestic complex at Saïs (Bertini and Linseele 2011).

Although many animals, both domestic and wild, played a role in the ancient Egyptian economy, the most economically important were the domestic herd animals: cattle, ovicaprines, and pigs. They provided meat, secondary products, such as milk, labor, and raw materials, including gut, hide, and bones, to be crafted into other objects. By the New Kingdom, this group of domestic mammals overwhelmingly dominates faunal assemblages found at settlement sites such as the different parts of Amarna, Malkata, Kom Firin, and Saïs (fig. 3.1). However, the percentages of the three main domesticates vary from site to site (fig. 3.2). This is due to a combination of various environmental locations (the wet delta as opposed to the drier and less verdant areas of Upper Egypt), as well as economic choices, such as the degree to which the inhabitants of different areas were involved in wheat/barley agriculture as opposed to a focus on meat/milk production.

But what was going on at fortified settlement sites, such as Zawiyet Umm el-Rakham, Kom Firin, and Tell el-Borg (fig. 3.3), sites that were presumably, to some extent state supported? Since a comparative study of faunal remains from New Kingdom fort sites has never been made, this paper seeks to provide a baseline for future research in creating a model of the socio-economic infrastructure of New Kingdom fortresses, while also taking into account the environmental variability between sites, as well as possible trade contacts.

Materials and Methods

The data discussed in the paper derive from the sites of Kom Firin, Tell el-Borg, and Zawiyet Umm el-Rakham (table 3.1). We would like to thank the excavation directors, and the Egyptian Ministry of Antiquities for access to the material.[2]

Bones were identified using publications (Schmid 1992) and a reference collection provided by American University in Cairo's Ibrahim Helmy Memorial Bioarchaeology Laboratory. Sheep and goat differentiation was made when possible following established methodologies (Zeder and Lapham 2010; Boessneck 1970). A total of just

---

dating to the late Middle Kingdom/Second Intermediate Period (ca. 1900–1530 BC) in the vicinity, indicating an earlier settlement of the site (Spencer 2014).

2. Much appreciation is due to the directors including Dr. James Hoffmeier (Tell el-Borg), Dr. Neal Spencer (Kom Firin), and Dr. Steven Snape (Zawiyet Umm el-Rakham).

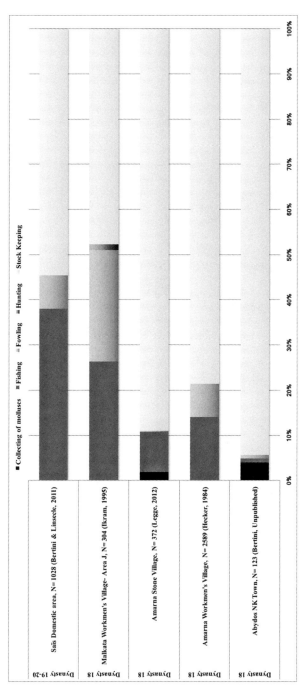

FIGURE 3.1. Relative importance of the different subsistence strategies at selected New Kingdom sites.

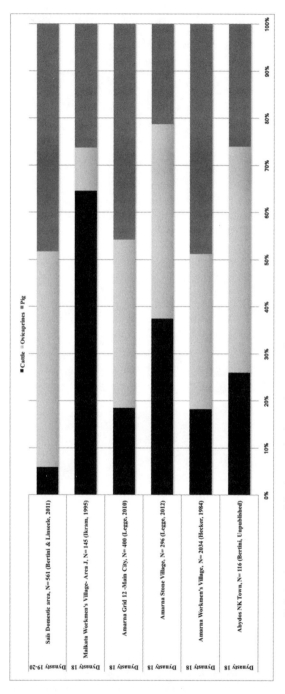

FIGURE 3.2. Relative importance of the three main domesticates at selected New Kingdom sites.

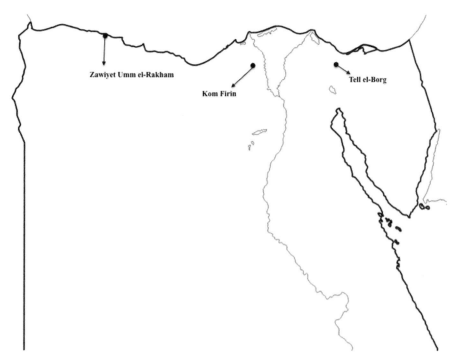

FIGURE 3.3. The location of each of the three New Kingdom fort sites.

over five thousand bones between the three site samples will be discussed in this paper (table 3.1). With the exception of the data from Field IV at Tell el-Borg, which comes from a vernacular residential area (Hoffmeier 2014), all contexts come from areas inside the fortification that are associated with potential provisioning activity (Hoffmeier 2014; Spencer 2017; Snape 2010).

The following information was recorded on all specimens: taxon, element, portion, side, age, butchery marks, gnawing, burning, erosion, and breakage patterns. Fragments of limb bones, ribs, and vertebrae that could not be identified to a specific taxon were identified only by their mammal size: large (e.g., cattle, horse), medium to large (e.g., young cattle, donkey), medium (e.g., ovicaprines, pig), and small mammals (e.g., hare). All bone fragments were counted, but not weighed (table 3.1).

Although there are various problems with different quantification methods (Gautier 1984), due to the various taphonomic issues associated with understanding a faunal assemblage (Reitz and Wing 2008), the number of individual specimens (NISP) is the quantification method that will be used in this paper. NISPs are the simplest to calculate, are readily available for comparative sites, and have the best results for both inter- and intrasite comparison (Gautier 1984).

Aging of bones was based on established methodologies (Silver 1969; Barone 1965; Grant 1982; Hambleton 2001; Payne 1973) that were applied to both limb bone fusion and tooth wear to construct age distributions. The age distributions were smoothed using the running mean and then converted into relative frequencies in order to allow for the different data sets to be directly compared. Mammal and bird measurements were taken when possible (following von den Driesch 1976).

On the whole, the faunal material for all three sites is generally well preserved, especially in the case for Kom Firin and Zawiyet Umm el-Rakham. At Tell el-Borg, however, the salty and wet environment of the north Sinai has resulted in large amounts of sand encrustation accreting on many bones, which consumed time and effort to remove in order to ensure identification, and whose removal was detrimental to the bone surface.

The Sites

Kom Firin is close to the western border of the delta. It was situated on a turtleback, with easy access to fresh water and land that could be used for grazing of smaller ungulates. The studied material comes from within the Ramesside enclosure area, specifically a group of excavated residential and storage units (Spencer 2017).

Tell el-Borg is located in the north Sinai, situated along the Ways of Horus, on the main military road connecting Egypt to Asia. In antiquity, the environment of Tell el-Borg consisted of wetlands and shallow ponds surrounded by a paleolagoon (Moshier 2014). All the bones come from areas inside the fortification that are associated with potential provisioning activity, save for the material from Field IV, which comes from a temporary residential area of reed huts (Hoffmeier 2014).

The fort of Zawiyet Umm el-Rakham is located on the Mediterranean Coast, far west of Alexandria. The environment of the area both in antiquity and today is a semi-arid, rocky, coastal plain. The faunal data discussed from the fort of Zawiyet Umm el-Rakham comes from both Area K (the residential complex) and Area S (partially excavated structure whose exact purpose is not known, but a series of limestone monoliths were excavated inside), both of which are inside the fortified area (Snape 2010).

Results

Table 3.1 is a summary of all the number of identified specimens from each site and area. The faunal results from these sites show a variety of exploitation strategies being used (table 3.2) that include: the collecting of mollusks, fishing, fowling, hunting, and stock keeping.

Collecting Mollusks

Kom Firin yielded mollusk remains, both gastropods and bivalves (Bertini 2014). The identified bivalves (N=10) were all freshwater clams that were probably consumed as food, after which the shells also could have served as small containers, such as those used by scribes for holding water or mixing ink, such as featured on the statue of Amenhotep Son of Hapu.[3] It was odd that the site yielded so few bivalves, given its location and the amount of water surrounding it. Clearly mollusks did not provide the site's inhabitants with any meaningful amount of food; for this they would have

---

3. Egyptian Museum, Cairo, JE 44861.

TABLE 3.1. Animal taxa from contexts associated with provisioning at Zawiyet Umm el-Rakham (ZUR), Tell el-Borg, and Kom Firin. Numbers refer to the amount of number of individual specimens (NISP).

Species	ZUR Area K	ZUR Area S	ZUR TOTAL	ZUR %	Tell el-Borg Field IV	Tell el-Borg Field V	Tell el-Borg Field VI	Tell el-Borg TOTAL	Tell el-Borg %	Kom Firin Ramesside Enclosure	Kom Firin %
Bivalvia (marine and fresh water mollusks)	0	0	0		0	0	0	0	0	10	27.8%
Gastropada (snails and slugs)	0	0	0		0	0	0	0	0	26	72.2%
Total identified mollusks	0	0	0		0	0	0	0	0	36	100.0%
Bagrus bajad (bagrus catfish)	0	0	0		0	0	0	0	0	2	1.5%
Clariidae (clariid catfish)	0	0	0		0	0	0	0	0	46	34.3%
Condrichthyes (shark-?)	0	0	0		0	0	0	0	0	3	2.2%
Hyperopisus bebe (elephant-snout fish)	0	0	0		0	0	0	0	0	1	0.7%
Lates niloticus (Nile perch)	0	0	0		0	0	0	0	0	3	2.2%
Myliobatoidei (rays)	0	0	0		0	0	0	0	0	12	9.0%
Sparus aurata (gilt-head bream)	0	0	0		0	0	0	0	0	7	5.2%
Synodontis sp. (synodontis catfish)	0	0	0		0	0	0	0	0	54	40.3%
Tilapiini (tilapia)	0	0	0		0	0	0	0	0	6	4.5%
Total identified fish	0	0	0		0	0	0	0	0	134	100.0%
Anas crecca (teal)	0	0	0	0.00%	0	22	0	22		0	0.0%
Anatinae (duck)	0	0	0	0.00%	0	0	0	0		69	93.20%
Anser sp. (goose)	0	0	0	0.00%	0	0	0	0		5	6.80%
Coturnix coturnix (common quail)	87	0	87	19.16%	0	0	0	0		0	0.0%
Passierform (perching bird)	4	0	4	0.88%	0	0	0	0		0	0.0%
Streptopelia turtur (turtle dove)	355	0	355	78.19%	0	0	0	0		0	0.0%
Struthio camelus- shell (ostrich shell)	8	0	8	1.76%	55	4	16	75		0	0.0%

TABLE 3.1. (cont'd) Animal taxa from contexts associated with provisioning at Zawiyet Umm el-Rakham (ZUR), Tell el-Borg, and Kom Firin. Numbers refer to the amount of number of individual specimens (NISP).

Species	ZUR Area K	ZUR Area S	ZUR TOTAL	ZUR %	Tell el-Borg Field IV	Tell el-Borg Field V	Tell el-Borg Field VI	Tell el-Borg TOTAL	Tell el-Borg %	Kom Firin Rameside Enclosure	Kom Firin %
Total identified Birds	**454**	**0**	**454**	**100.00%**	**55**	**26**	**16**	**97**		**74**	**100.0%**
Crocodilus niloticus (crocodile)	0	0	0	0.00%	1	8	8	17		0	0.0%
Testudo kleinmanni (tortoise)	31	0	31	100.00%	0	0	0	0		0	1.3%
Trionyx triunguis (softshell turtle)	0	0	0	0.00%	0	0	0	0		21	0.5%
Total identified reptiles	**31**	**0**	**31**	**100.00%**	**1**	**8**	**8**	**17**		**21**	1.2%
Bos taurus (cow)	11	4	15	5.10%	21	24	34	79	18.0%	40	5.3%
Chiroptera (bat)	0	0	0	0.00%	0	2	0	2	0.5%	0	0.0%
Canis familiaris (dog)	90	0	90	30.30%	1	6	12	19	4.3%	10	1.3%
Capra hircus (goat)	18	7	25	8.40%	0	2	0	2	0.5%	4	0.5%
Equus asinus (donkey)	2	0	2	0.70%	1	1	0	2	0.5%	9	1.2%
Equus caballus (horse)	0	0	0	0.00%	0	14	19	33	7.5%	15	2.0%
Equus (unidentified equid)	1	0	1	0.30%	3	69	12	84	19.1%	97	13%
Felis catus (cat)	0	0	0	0.00%	0	8	0	8	1.8%	2	0.3%
Gazella (gazelle)	1	0	1	0.30%	0	1	0	1	0.2%	0	0.0%
Ovis aries (sheep)	17	2	19	6.40%	3	3	0	6	1.4%	13	1.7%

TABLE 3.1. (*cont'd*) Animal taxa from contexts associated with provisioning at Zawiyet Umm el-Rakham (ZUR), Tell el-Borg, and Kom Firin. Numbers refer to the amount of number of individual specimens (NISP).

Species	ZUR Area K	ZUR Area S	ZUR TOTAL	ZUR %	Tell el-Borg Field IV	Tell el-Borg Field V	Tell el-Borg Field VI	Tell el-Borg TOTAL	Tell el-Borg %	Kom Firin Ramesside Enclosure	Kom Firin %
Ovis/Capra (sheep/goat)	118	22	140	47.10%	25	58	40	123	28.0%	45	6.0%
Rodentia sp. (rodent)	2	0	2	0.70%	2	33	3	38	8.6%	28	3.7%
Crocidura sp. (shrew)	0	0	0	0.00%	0	10	12	22	5.0%	0	0.0%
Sus scrofa (pig)	2	0	2	0.70%	5	3	13	21	4.8%	485	64.8%
Total identified mammals	**262**	**35**	**297**	**100.00%**	**61**	**234**	**145**	**440**	**100.0%**	**748**	**100.0%**
Large mammal	14	0	14		111	88	103	302		133	
Medium mammal	182	4	186		97	274	719	1090		531	
Medium–large mammal	41	0	41		2	20	58	80		10	
Small mammal	0	0	0		0	2	3	5		3	
Total identified mammals based on size	**237**	**4**	**241**		**210**	**384**	**883**	**1477**		**677**	
Unidentified fish	0	0	0		0	0	0	0		21	
Unidentified bird	402	3	405		6	37	18	61		0	
TOTAL ASSEMBLAGE	**1386**	**42**	**1428**		**333**	**689**	**1070**	**2092**		**1711**	

TABLE 3.2. Relative importance of different animal procurement strategies at
ZUR, Tell el-Borg, and Kom Firin.

	% ZUR	% Tell el-Borg	% Kom Firin
Collecting of mollusks	0.6	0.0	1
Fishing	0.0	0.0	17
Fowling	68.4	8.7	9
Hunting	0.2	0.4	0
Stock keeping	30.8	90.9	73
N	652	254	805

depended on domestic animals. The identified gastropods (N=26) come from topsoil
contexts, signaling a lack of human activity rather than consumption. No mollusks
were retrieved either at Zawiyet Umm el-Rakham or Tell el-Borg.[4] This is curious
as both sites, particularly the former, would have had access to a variety of shellfish
given their costal nature.

Fishing

Kom Firin has a relatively high fish NISP, which makes up 17.8 percent of the faunal
remains, and, by extension, the diet (tables 3.1, 3.2). Tell El-Borg also yielded a relatively large number of fish bones, but these have yet to be analyzed. The assemblages
of both Kom Firin and Tell el-Borg are in marked contrast with that of Zawiyet Umm
el-Rakham, which, despite being near the coast is surprisingly devoid of fish bones.[5]
This imbalance in the analyzed data unfortunately skews our understanding of the
subsistence strategy percentages (table 3.2), which will have to be addressed in the
future. Preliminary analysis of the Tell el-Borg sample includes large quantities of
freshwater fish including catfish (*Clariidae, Bagrus sp.,* and *Synodontis* sp.), Nile
perch (*Lates nilotocus*), and Tilapia (*Tilapiini*), most of which can survive in slightly
brackish water as well. No marine species have been identified as yet. The Kom Firin
fish sample consists mainly of catfish (*Clarriidae* and *Synodontis)* and other freshwater fish (table 3.1). There are, however, a few identified marine taxon including the gilt
head bream, stingray, and possibly shark (Bertini 2014).

Fowling

While bird remains at Kom Firin and Tell Borg are quite small, Zawiyet Umm
el-Rakham yielded a NISP of 454. These are more than 78 percent of the bones found
at the site, suggesting that fowling may have been the main subsistence strategy here
(table 3.2). At Zawiyet Umm el-Rakham, all of the identified bird bones came from a

---

4. Although the site of Tell el-Borg is currently about seventy kilometers from the coast, in the New
Kingdom the site would have been only about three to five kilometers from the coast. Moshier 2014.

5. A small number of fish bones are reported to have been collected (Snape 2010) but were not part of
the analyzed sample discussed here.

single midden deposit, consisting only of turtle dove (N=355) and quail (N=87) bones. A further 402 bird bones consisting of ribs, vertebrae, and limb bone fragments also came from the same deposit, and are likely either turtle dove or quail. Both of these birds are migratory, mostly obtained along the Mediterranean Sea, and are a highly esteemed article of food (Houlihan 1986). In fact, even today during autumn, most of the north coast is lined with nets for bird catching (Moreau 1927–1928), particularly for quail. These birds land on the Mediterranean coast after their long flight from Europe and are easily trapped here. It is also possible, given the limited species, that this midden assemblage reflects the deposit of a single autumnal event. In any case, it clearly demonstrates that collection of birds was a key part of the economy and diet of the inhabitants of Zawiyet Umm el-Rakham.

At Kom Firin and Tell el-Borg the more typical duck and goose assemblages of avian bones were identified. However, the NISPs of birds at these two sites are very low, indicating that birds played little or no part in their diet and subsistence. These two sites depended far more on stock animals.

The faunal assemblages of Zawiyet Umm el-Rakham and Tell el Borg yielded few bird bones, but they did contain fragments of ostrich eggshells. At Zawiyet Umm el-Rakham eight shell fragments and Tell el-Borg seventy-five ostrich eggshells were identified. No complete eggs were found. Although the eggshells at Tell el-Borg have not yet been measured, the Zawiyet Umm el-Rakham fragments range is size from 14.6 mm to 48.5 mm by 5.93 mm to 32.7 mm. The eggshells are all tan in color, and display no evidence of incised decoration or painting. The eggs might have been eaten, but it is more likely that they were used as vessels to transport water or other liquids.

Hunting

Although wild mammals are known from all three sites, they are clearly not the main source of food at any of them. Wild animals are represented by the gazelle, crocodile, softshell turtle (*Trionx triunguis*), and the tortoise (*Testudo kleinmanni*).[6] Gazelle are rare, with only one identified bone from both Zawiyet Umm el-Rakham and Tell el-Borg each. The softshell turtle is only identified at Kom Firin, with its more riverine environment in which this species thrives. While there is evidence that softshell turtles were consumed (Fischer 1968; Boessneck 1988; Bertini 2014), given that only carapace fragments were found, another option is object use, possibly as a protective shield (Fischer 1968, 13; Boessneck 1988; Bertini 2014), with examples of such shields still being made in Nubia and possibly the Sudan.[7] Interestingly enough, at Zawiyet Umm el-Rakham, a different type of Testudine was identified, the considerably smaller tortoise. While it is possibly that the carapace may have also been used as an object (Boessneck 1988; Anderson 1976; Hickmann 1949), postcranial bones made up a significant number of finds from the site, all coming from a known food production area (Snape 2010), supporting the idea that they were consumed. While there is evidence

6. The gazelle species identified are most likely *Gazella dorcas*, although *Gazella gazella* are also known from ancient Egypt. However, it is difficult to differential between the two species morphologically.

7. Ikram has seen these in an ethnographic collection in Asyut (no number) and in Cairo at the Agricultural Museum (no number available), as well as for sale in the *souk* in Aswan in the 1990s.

TABLE 3.3. Relative importance (%) of domestic cattle, sheep/goats and pigs at ZUR, Tell el-Borg, and Kom Firin.

	% ZUR	% Tell el-Borg	% Kom Firin
Cattle	0.6	34.2	6.8
Ovicaprines	91.5	56.7	10.6
Pig	1.0	9.1	82.6
N	201	231	587
Number of identified sheep	19	6	13
Number of identified goat	25	2	4
Number of nonidentifiable mammal bones	241	1477	1711

for the consumption of Testudines at both Zawiyet Umm el-Rakham and Kom Firin, Tell el-Borg offers evidence for the consumption of a different reptile: the crocodile.

Crocodiles were a source of food for the early inhabitants of the Nile Valley (Ikram 2010), with their remains found at early Predynastic settlements such as Maadi and Omari (Boessneck 1988). In addition to providing food, soldiers might also have hunted crocodiles for their skins and scales to be used in weaponry; a later example of Roman armor made of crocodile hide from Manfalut is in the British Museum.[8]

Stock Animals

Domestic animals provide the most numerous of the identified bone fragments. However, there is considerable variation in their relative proportions at each of the three sites (table 3.3).

Ovicaprines are by far the most commonly identified domestic animal at both Zawiyet Umm el-Rakham (N=184) and Tell el-Borg (N=131). Very few bones, however, could be further identified to the species level (table 3.3). Sheep and goat are recorded at all three sites, but again in different ratios. Goat appears to be more common at Zawiyet Umm el-Rakham, (with a sheep-to-goat ratio of 1:1.3), whereas sheep are more common at both Kom Firin and Tell el Borg (Kom Firin sheep-to-goat ratio is 3.3:1, while at Tell el-Borg it is 3:1).

Cattle remains are not as common at Zawiyet Umm el-Rakham and Kom Firin (table 3.3), as they are at Tell el-Borg (N=79), accounting for 34.2 percent of the three main domestic animals. While the percentage of cattle as compared to ovicaprines is only slightly less, cattle do provide more meat per unit of bone (Dahl and Hjort 1976), thus providing a major source of animal protein, yielding twice as much as sheep and goats. This suggests that the residents of Tell el-Borg were more reliant on cattle than on ovicaprines.

While pig remains are almost nonexistent in the samples coming from Zawiyet Umm el-Rakham (N=2), they are slightly more prevalent at Tell el-Borg (N=21), providing 9.1 percent of the domestic animals. At Kom Firin, however, they are by far the

8. Roman solider parade armor, British Museum Number: EA 5473, Registration number: 1846,0501.9.

most numerous (N=485), accounting for 82.6 percent of the domestic animals, indicating heavy reliance on these animals for food. In fact, the pig-rearing regime suggests that not only were there possibly mixed herds of domestic and wild pigs, but also the hunting of wild boar/feral pigs provided both food and sport at Kom Firin (Bertini and Cruz-Rivera 2014).

Discussion

Food Production

While the samples from these three sites are quite small, models can still be created that show that different methods of food procurement were used at each fort. Zawiyet Umm el-Rakham displays a subsistence strategy that is completely contrary to the other fort sites. While there is an extraordinary amount of fowl that was locally caught, domestic animals, particularly ovicaprines played a significant role in the diet there. Cattle, however, seem to have played a larger role at Tell el-Borg based on their NISP (79), accounting for 34.2 percent of the domestic mammals at the site. The mortality profiles of cattle at Tell el-Borg (fig. 3.4b) are actually quite similar to what is reported from the Giza Workmen's Village (Redding 1992), with 75.8 percent of the cattle being less than two years of age. Although cattle are less frequently found at Kom Firin, they are also being killed at an early age, with 92.5 percent being killed before two years. This age is also seen in cattle that are given as offerings (Ikram 1995, 237–96). Unfortunately, no sex estimations could be made at either of the sites. This does seem to point to cattle possible being provisioned at Tell el-Borg, and possibly at Kom Firin, based on comparisons with the Giza Workmen's Village. However, the sheep and goat ratios are quite different.

At Zawiyet Umm el-Rakham, goats are slightly more common than sheep (1:1.3). Comparative studies from Iran and Iraq (Redding 1981, 1984) have shown that when the ratio is this low, a mixed strategy of herding and farming is taking place. If goats and sheep are being maintained together, then the kill-off patterns of sheep and goat would differ (Redding 1992).

Figure 3.4a illustrates a comparative survivorship curve for all three sites based on both limb bone fusion and tooth wear. The Zawiyet Umm el-Rakham sample curve indicates two possible ages of slaughter: one peaking between one to two years, and the second ranging between four to eight years. While this might not offer information on which taxon is being slaughtered at a specific age, it does indicate that the majority of ovicaprines (about 45 percent), probably males, are being slaughtered at the selected age of one to two, with about 32 percent of the sample living between four and eight years and beyond. This supports a mixed herding regime, with some animals slaughtered at a later age, probably females, utilizing a strategy of maximizing meat, milk, possibly wool, and herd security (Redding 1981).

Given this intensive involvement on both fowling and the herding of ovicaprines, Zawiyet Umm el-Rakham exhibits the characteristics of self-sufficiency through locally exploited resources. Other locally available resources exploited at Zawiyet Umm el-Rakham including local limestone and mud-brick for construction, along

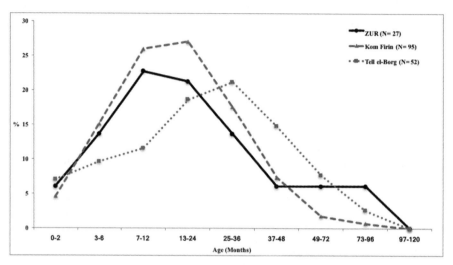

FIGURE 3.4a. Caprine survivorship based on limb bone fusion and tooth wear. Tooth wear estimates following Payne (1973) and limb bone fusion after Barone (1965).

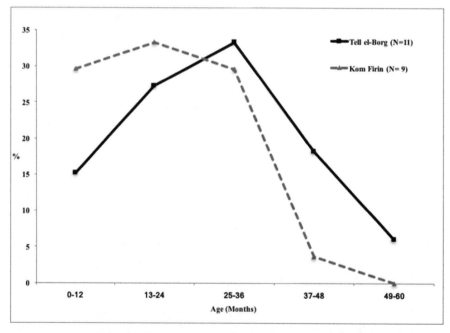

FIGURE 3.4b. Cattle survivorship based on limb bone fusion and tooth wear. Tooth wear estimates following Grant (1982) and limb bone fusion after Barone (1965).

with much-needed water through wells and local grain cultivation. There is, however, evidence of imported grain as well (Snape 2010). The high presence of ovicaprines along with a small percentage of cattle, does point to at least some degree of small-scale agriculture and livestock maintenance at the site that would have been used to supply the garrison.

At Tell el-Borg, while there also is a reliance on ovicaprines (table 3.3), sheep out-number goat, with a 3:1 ratio. This is, however, based on a small sample and should be viewed with caution. If this ratio holds true, it is a bit unusual given the high percentage of cattle at the site, as they are known to compete with sheep for food (Redding 1984). Still, sheep are more convenient "food bundles" than cattle; they can be easily slaughtered and used to feed smaller groups of people without worrying about meat preservation. Given the broad age of both the cattle and ovicaprines (fig. 3.4a, 3.4b), it is also likely that the people at Tell el-Borg were utilizing a mixed strategy of main-taining these animals, similar to that at Zawiyet Umm el-Rakham. Sheep and goats kept for milk, wool, and reproductive stock were likely kept/grazed further away from the site.

While Zawiyet Umm el-Rakham and Tell el-Borg appear to have heavy depen-dence on ovicaprines, the Kom Firin assemblage is dominated by pig remains. This is explained by the fact that the excavated remains originate from residential, nonelite dwellings (Spencer 2014), as pigs are an inexpensive, locally maintained resource that would be easy to keep, such as is seen at the Workmen's Village at Tell el-Amarna (Hecker 1982, 1984) and the less elite areas at Malkata (Ikram 1995, 207–10, 212–19). If the residents are rearing pigs on their own, does this mean that the state was not involved in provisioning the site and that Kom Firin was self-sufficient? However, as the environment is ideally situated for pig rearing, the choice to raise pigs is based not only on the possible lack of state involvement in provisioning, but also on envi-ronmental suitability for pig rearing. Perhaps pork served to augment what the state provided, and it is possible that, since Kom Firin was located in a more salubrious place, that the state provided less than it would to those located in more challenging landscapes.

While sites like Zawiyet Umm el-Rakham seem to have a high degree of planning with all necessary facilities (including large-scale, planned store rooms) inside the fortress, Kom Firin does not seem to have this degree of planning in storage facilities, which are comparatively smaller and irregularly organized (Spencer 2017). Could random arrangement of considerably smaller storage facilities reflect a centralized administrative takeover of food supplies? If this does reflect an administrative take-over of the site where the state became more involved with the food supplies and their storage when Ramesses II had the town enclosure wall constructed, then why are there so many pigs? What is even more curious at Kom Firin is not only the evidence for a population of domestic pigs, but multiple populations, possible including locally hunted wild boar/feral pigs (Bertini and Curz-Rivera 2014), and potentially either dif-ferent breeds or larger sows kept for reproductive purposes, supporting a very mixed swine herding regime. If the state did become involved in site provisioning, then the hunting of wild boar/feral pigs helps to eliminate potential competitors for the crops that are possible being planted, so that they do not destroy them.

Environmental Impact on Animals and Food Supply

Although one would assume that all three sites had some degree of state provisioning, the faunal material points to a different reality. Ovicaprines and pigs, as well as poultry and fish, can be acquired or reared independently by individuals or small groups, as is reflected in the variety of faunal material found at each site. It seems from the current evidence that each site's environment played a significant role in its provisioning, quite independent of the state.

The faunal assemblage at Kom Firin is different from that of Zawiyet Umm el-Rakham and Tell el-Borg, leaving the drastically different environment as the only possible explanation for this. The delta is a very wet, marshy landscape, and even the location of Kom Firin was between two now dried-up riverbeds: the Rosetta and Canopic branches of the Nile (Spencer 2017). This provided easy access to freshwater, and is ideal for pig rearing, and easy fishing.

Aside from the major pig-rearing regime in place at Kom Firin, the fishing industry was also notable (table 3.2). The fish assemblage predominately represents almost equal examples of freshwater species from shallow water (*Clarriidae* and *Tilapiini*, N=52) and open water (*Synodontis*, *Bagarus*, and *Lates*, N=59), with a few (N=22) marine species represented (gilt-head bream, ray, and shark). All of these marine species are known to enter estuarine areas and have also been identified at other nearby sites such as Saïs (Bertini and Linseele 2011).

While the marshy lagoon (Moshier 2014) that Tell el-Borg was situated on was ideal for many types of animal herding regimes, including the pig, the environment of Zawiyet Umm el-Rakham in conjunction with the local resident Libyan population that were quite likely resident at the site before the fort's construction (Snape 2003; O'Connor 1987) were more influential on subsistence strategies there. The economy of this group of local nomadic-pastoralists that were already in the region before the fort's construction was based primarily on the herding of sheep and goat supplemented by small-scale agriculture (Conwell 1987; Snape 2003). Though the presence of the fortress obviously implies an acquisition of the Libyan land, it can be assumed that the Egyptians took booty as well, probably in the forms of animals and also adopted the successful subsistence strategies already in practice. Later texts from the reign of Ramesses III (ca. 1185–1153 BC) even make specific reference to the large number of cattle, sheep, goats, and donkeys that were taken from the Libyans (Edgerton and Wilson 1936). While it makes economic sense to adapt to the ways and animals of a particular landscape when successful, which seems to be the overwhelming case at Zawiyet Umm el-Rakham, it is also true that the Egyptians may have brought practices and animals from the Nile Valley to this area—this might explain the presence of the pig in this inimical environment.

Trade and Impact on Subsistence

The forts at Zawiyet Umm el-Rakham and Tell el-Borg were located some distance away from the Nile Valley and had contacts to the west and east, respectively, creating a variety of cultural entanglements. These would no doubt affect the diet and economies of each site. While there may be some evidence for Libyans working within the fort at Zawiyet Umm el-Rakham or at least contributing to its economy (Snape 2010), it has also been suggested that the garrison was involved in trade, with merchants bringing in, among other things, ostrich eggs as containers or the eggs themselves (Snape 2010; Conwell 1987).

Uses of the ostrich egg vary from consumption (Bagnold 2011; Ikram 1995) to object use, including vessels (Houlihan 1986; Laufer 1926), and are shown being brought to Egypt by bearers from Libya (Garis Davies 1905), Punt (Garis Davies 1943; Naville 1898), Syria (Brack and Brack 1980), and Nubia (Davies 1936). While it has been previously suggested (Snape 2003, 2010) that the presence of ostrich eggs at Zawiyet Umm el-Rakham are potential indicators of Libyan imports either via intimidation, acquiescence, or active cooperation, the presence of an even larger number of egg-shells at Tell el-Borg offers another option.

Although the Libyans may very well have brought the eggs to Zawiyet Umm el-Rakham, the trade of ostrich eggs extended considerably and was important during the New Kingdom throughout the eastern Mediterranean (Laufer 1926; Conwell 1987). These objects theoretically could have come from anywhere in Africa. Adding to this, the large number of eggshells at Tell el-Borg comes from a slightly earlier context, the Eighteenth Dynasty (Hoffmeier 2014), whereas Zawiyet Umm el-Rakham has exclusively Nineteenth Dynasty contexts (Snape 2003, 2010). While the ostrich is supposed to have been present all over the country in the New Kingdom (Manlius 2001), because no bones of the birds were found, it indicates that, at least on this site, it was the eggs that played a role in the diet or, perhaps more likely, as raw materials. The presence of eggshell fragments at Tell el-Borg from an earlier date also supports the idea that they were traded from many places throughout the New Kingdom.

Conclusions

Each of the three sites discussed in this paper has its own distinctive subsistence economy and patterns of animal exploitation, especially of the three main domesticates: cattle, ovicaprines, and pigs (fig. 3.5). The occupants of Zawiyet Umm el-Rakham seem to have adopted a strategy that had already been successfully employed by the local nomadic pastoralists that were present in the area before the construction of the fort. Given the type of environment, limited access to water, and grazing land, there is an emphasis on sheep and goat, animals that thrive in such a landscape. The presence of a few pig bones at the site, an animal that has a high-water requirement, suggests that they might have come in as preserved meat, which is supported by the fact that all the identified pig bones come from fore and hind limbs. Only a limited number of cattle bones, the traditional form of state support (Redding 1992) aside from grain, have been found here.

Tell el-Borg was situated at a crucial location along the Ways of Horus, one which probably saw more troop (and trade) movement. The garrison itself might have been larger than that at Zawiyet Umm el-Rakham. Here, the number of cattle bones provides more evidence for regular state support, although the garrison did exploit ovicaprines, which, particularly the goats, could succeed in the area. At both Tell el-Borg and Zawiyet Umm el-Rakham hunting augmented the diet (and also probably

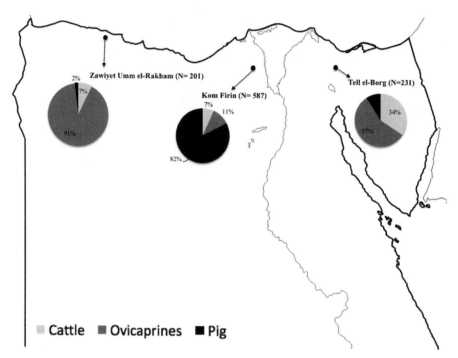

FIGURE 3.5. Map of the sites with the percentages of the three main domesticates.

provided an outlet for the soldiers' energy), reflecting the exploitation of the environment. At Kom Firin, there are few cattle remains, suggesting that this was not, at least in this aspect, a highly state-supported installation. Rather, its people were more self-sufficient, depending on the local environment between the two branches of the Nile, which provided huge numbers of fish and a fertile environment for pigs. Essentially the state did not need to provide for the inhabitants of Kom Firin, as they could provide for themselves.

While these are preliminary data and the picture can change at any time, the present evidence suggests that the state would provision institutions in a variety of ways, depending on their geographical location and function. This would make for a more efficient use of the state's resources, and not only devolve responsibility on each institution for its successful functioning, but also confer some degree of autonomy.

BIBLIOGRAPHY

Abd el-Maksoud, Mohamed. 1998. *Tell Heboua (1981–1991): Enquête archéologique sur la deuxième période intermédiaire et le nouvel empire à l'extrémité orientale du Delta.* Paris: Ministère des Affaires Étrangères.

Abd el-Maksoud, Mohamed, and Dominique Valbelle. 2005. "Tell Héboua-Tjarou: l'apport de l'épigraphie." *RdÉ* 56:1–43.

———. 2011. "Tell Héboua II: Rapport préliminaire sur le décor et l'épigraphie des éléments architectoniques découverts au cours des campagnes 2008–2009 dans la zone centrale de Khétem de Tjarou." *RdÉ* 62:1–39.

Anderson, Robert D. 1976. *Catalogue of Egyptian Antiquities in the British Museum, III: Musical Instruments*. London: British Museum Publications.

Bagnold, Ralph A. 2011. *Libyan Sands: Travel in a Dead World*. London: Eland.

Barone, Robert. 1965. *Anatomie comparée des mammifères domestiques*. Paris: Vigot.

Bertini, Louise C. 2014. "Faunal Remains at Kom Firin." Pages 306–11 in *Kom Firin II: The Urban Fabric and Landscape*. Edited by Neal Spencer. London: British Museum.

Bertini, Louise, and Edwin Cruz-Rivera. 2014. "The Size of Ancient Egyptian Pigs: A Biometrical Analysis Using Molar Width." *Bioarchaeology of the Near East* 8:83–107.

Bertini, Louise, and Veerle Linseele. 2011. "Appendix 7: Faunal Report." Pages 277–85 in *Sais I: The Ramesside-Third Intermediate Period at Kom Rebwa*. Edited by Penelope Wilson. EES Excavation Memoir 98. London: Egypt Exploration Society.

Boessneck, Joachim. 1970. "Osteological Differences Between Sheel (*Ovis Ariea Linné*) and Goats (*Capra Hircus Linné*)." Pages 331–58 in *Science in Archaeology*. Edited by Don Brothwell and Eric Higgs. New York: Praeger.

———. 1988. *Die Tierwelt des alten Ägypten: Untersucht anhand kulturgeschichtlicher und zoologischer Quellen*. Munich: Beck.

Brack, Annelies, and Artur Brack. 1980. *Das Grab Des Haremheb: Theben Nr. 78*. Mainz: von Zabern.

Conwell, David. 1987. "On Ostrich Eggs and Libyans." *Expedition* 29:25–34.

Dahl, Gudrun, and Anders Hjort. 1976. *Having Herds: Pastoral Growth and Household Economy*. Stockholm Studies in Social Anthropology 2. Stockholm: University of Stockholm.

Davies, Nina M. 1936. *Ancient Egyptian Paintings*. Chicago: University of Chicago Press.

Driesch, Angela von den. 1976. *A Guide to the Measurement of Animal Bones from Archaeological Sites*. Peabody Museum Bulletins 1. Boston: Havard University.

Edgerton, William F., and John A. Wilson. 1936. *Historical Records of Ramses III*. SAOC 12. Chicago: University of Chicago Press.

Edwards, David N. 2004. *The Nubian Past: An Archaeology of the Sudan*. New York: Routledge.

Fischer, Henry G. 1968. *Ancient Egyptian Representations of Turtles*. Metropolitan Museum of Art Papers 13. New York: Metropolitan Museum of Art.

Gardiner, Alan H. 1920. "The Ancient Military Road Between Egypt and Palestine." *JEA* 6:99–116.

Garis Davies, Norman de. 1905. *The Rock Tombs of El Amarna: The Tombs of Panehesy and Meryra*. Archaeological Survey of Egypt Memoir 14. London: Egypt Exploration Fund.

———. 1943. *The Tomb of Rekh-Mi-Rē at Thebes*. Publications of the Metropolitan Museum of Art Egyptian Expedition 11. New York: Metropolitan Museum of Art.

Gautier, Achilles. 1984. "How Do I Count You, Let Me Count the Ways: Problems of Archaeozoological Quantification." Pages 237–51 in *Animals and Archaeology 4: Husbandry in Europe*. Edited by Caroline Grigson and Juliet Clutton-Brock. BARIS 227. Oxford: British Archaeological Reports.

Grant, Annie. 1982. "The Use of Tooth Wear as a Guide to the Age of Domestic Ungulates." Pages 91–108 in *Ageing and Sexing Animal Bones from Archaeological Sites*. Edited by Bob Wilson, Caroline Grigson, and Sebastion Payne. BAR British Series 109. Oxford: British Archaeological Reports.

Hambleton, E. 2001. "A Method for Converting Grant Mandibular Wear Stages to Payne Style Wear Stages in Sheep, Cow, and Pig." Pages 103–8 in *Archaeological Sciences 1997 Proceedings of the Conference Held at University of Durham, 2nd–4th September 1997*. Edited by Andrew Millard. BARIS 939. Oxford: Archaeopress.

Hecker, Howard. 1982. "A Zooarchaeoogical Inquiry into Pork Consumption in Egypt From Prehistoric to New Kingdom Times." *JARCE* 19:59–71.

———. 1984. "Preliminary Report on the Faunal Remains from the Workmen's Village." Pages 154–64 in *Amarna Reports I*. Edited by Barry Kemp. London: Egypt Exploration Society.

Hickmann, Hans. 1949. *Catalogue général des antiquités égyptiennes du Musée de Caire: Nos. 69201-69852; Instruments de Musique*. Cairo: Institut français d'archéologie orientale.

Hoffmeier, James K. 2004. "Tell El-Borg on Egypt's Eastern Frontier: A Preliminary Report on the 2002 and 2004 Seasons." *JARCE* 41:85–111.

———. 2006. "'The Walls of the Ruler' in Egyptian Literature and the Archaeological Record: Investigating Egypt's Eastern Frontier in the Bronze Age." *BASOR* 343:1–20.

———. 2011. "The Gate of the Ramesside Fort at Tell El-Borg, North Sinai." Pages 207–17 in *Ramesside Studies in Honour of K. A. Kitchen*. Edited by Mark Collier and Steven R. Snape. Bolton: Rutherford.

———. 2014. *Tell El-Borg I: Excavations in North Sinai*. Winona Lake, IN: Eisenbrauns.

Hoffmeier, James K., and Mohamed Abd el-Maksoud. 2003. "A New Military Site on the Ways of Horus: Tell El-Borg 1999–2001: A Preliminary Report." *JEA* 89:169–97.

Houlihan, Patrick F. 1986. *The Birds of Ancient Egypt*. Cairo: American University in Cairo.

Ikram, Salima. 1995. *Choice Cuts: Meat Production in Ancient Egypt*. OLA 69. Leuven: Peeters.

———. 2010. "Crocodiles: Guardians of the Gateways." Pages 85–98 in *Thebes and Beyond: Studies in Honor of Kent R. Weeks*. Edited by Zahi Hawass and Salima Ikram. Cairo: Supreme Council of Antiquities.

Laufer, Berthold. 1926. *Ostrich Egg-Shell Cups of Mesopotamia and the Ostrich in Ancient and Modern Times*. Chicago: Field Museum of Natural History.

Legge, Anthony. 2010. "The Mammal Bones from Grid 12." Pages 445–52 in *Busy Lives at Amarna: Excavations in the Main City (Grid 12 and the House of Ranefer, N49.18); Volume 1; The Excavations, Architecture, and Environmental Remains*. Edited by Barry Kemp and Anna Stevens. EES Excavation Memoir 90. London: Egypt Exploration Society.

———. 2012. "Animal Remains at the Stone Village." Pages 9–13 in *Akhenaten's Workers: The Amarna Stone Village Survey, 2005–9; Volume II; The Faunal and Botanical Remains, and Objects*. Edited by Anna Stevens. EES Excavation Memoir 101. London: Egypt Exploration Society.

Manlius, Nicolas. 2001. "The Ostrich in Egypt: Past and Present." *Journal of Biogeography* 28:945–53.

Moreau, R. E. 1927–1928. "Quail." *Bulletin of the Zoological Society of Egypt* 1:6–13.

Moshier, Stephen O. 2014. "The Geological Setting of Tell El-Borg with Implications for Ancient Geography of Northwest Sinai." Pages 62–83 in *Tell El-Borg I: Excavations in North Sinai*. Edited by James K. Hoffmeier. Winona Lake, IN: Eisenbrauns.

Naville, Edouard. 1898. *The Temple of Deir El Bahari: Its Plan, Its Founders, and Its First Explorers*. Vol. 3. EES Excavation Memoir. London: Egypt Exploration Fund.

O'Connor, David. 1987. "Egyptians and Libyans in the New Kingdom." *Expedition* 29:35–37.

Payne, Sebastian. 1973. "Kill off Patterns in Sheep and Goats: The Mandibles from Asvan Kale." *AnSt* 23:281–303.

Redding, Richard. 1981. "Decision Making in Subsistence Herding of Sheep and Goats in the Middle East." PhD diss., University of Michigan.

———. 1984. "Theoretical Determinants of a Herder's Decisions: Modeling Variation in the Sheep/Goat Ratio." Pages 223–41 in *Animals and Archaeology: 3, Early Herders and Their Flocks*. Edited by Juliet Clutton-Brock and Caroline Grigson. BARIS 202. Oxford: British Archaeological Reports.

———. 1992. "Egyptian Old Kingdom Patterns of Animal Use and the Value of Faunal Data in Modeling Socioeconomic Systems." *Paléorient* 18:99–107.

Reisner, George A. 1960. "The Egyptian Forts from Halfa to Semna." *Kush* 8:11–24.

Reitz, Elizabeth, and Elizabeth Wing. 2008. *Zooarchaeology*. Cambridge Manuals in Archaeology. Cambridge: Cambridge University Press.

Schmid, Elisabeth. 1992. *Atlas of Animal Bones: For Prehistorians Archaeologists, and Quaternary Geologists*. New York: Elsevier.

Shinnie, Peter L. 1996. *Ancient Nubia*. London: Kegan Paul International.

Silver, I. A. 1969. "The Ageing of Domestic Animals." Pages 251–68 in *Science in Archaeology: A Survey of Progress and Re-research*. Edited by Don Brothwell and Eric Higgs. New York: Basic Books.

Snape, Steven. 2003. "The Emergence of Libya on the Horizon of Egypt." Pages 93–106 in *Mysterious Lands: Encounters with Ancient Egypt*. Edited by David O'Connor and Stephen Quirke. London: UCL Press.

———. 2010. "Vor der Kaserne: External Supply and Self-Sufficiency at Zawiyet Umm El-Rakham." Pages 271–88 in *Cities and Urbanism in Ancient Egypt: Papers From a Workshop in November 2006 at the Austrian Academy of Sciences*. Edited by Manfred Bietak, Ernst Czerny, and Irene Forstner-Müller. Denkschriften der Gesamtakakademie 60. Vienna: Österreicheschen Akademie der Wissenschaften.

Snape, Steven, and Penelope Wilson. 2007. *Zawiyet Umm El-Rakham I: The Temple and Chapels*. Bolton: Rutherford.

Spencer, Neal. 2008. *Kom Firin I: The Ramesside Temple and the Site Survey*. London: British Museum.

———. 2017. *Kom Firin II: The Urban Fabric and Landscape*. London: British Museum.

Thomas, Susanna. 2000. "Tell Abqa'in: A Fortified Settlement in the Western Delta; Preliminary Report of the 1997 Season." *MDAIK* 56:371–76.

Valbelle, Dominique. 1994. "La (les) route(s) d'horus." Pages 379–86 in *Hommages à Jean Leclant: Nubie, Soudan, Ethiopie*. Edited by Catherine Berger, Gisèle Clerc, and Nicolas Grimal. Cairo: Institut français d'archéologie orientale.

Williams, Bruce. 1999. "Serra East and the Mission of Middle Kingdom Fortresses in Nubia." Pages 435–53 in *Gold of Praise: Studies on Ancient Egypt in Honor of Edward F. Wente*. Edited by Emily Teeter and John A. Larson. SAOC 58. Chicago: Oriental Institute of the University of Chicago.

———. 2012. "Second Cataract Forts." Pages 340–47 in *Ancient Nubia: African Kingdoms on the Nile*. Edited by Marjorie M. Fischer, Peter Lacovara, Salima Ikram and Sue D'Auria. Cairo: American University in Cairo.

Zeder, Melinda A., and Heather A. Lapham. 2010. "Assessing the Reliability of Criteria Used to Identify Postcranial Bones in Sheep, *Ovis* and Goats, *Capra*." *Journal of Archaeological Science* 37:2887–905.

CHAPTER 4

Left Behind: New Kingdom Specialists at the End of Egyptian Empire and the Emergence of Israelite Scribalism

Aaron A. Burke

IT IS A PLEASURE to have this opportunity to dedicate this article to James Hoffmeier, with whom I began my studies in Egyptian archaeology and history. Never would I have imagined that these studies would have played such a pivotal role in the foundations of my research into the Egyptian Empire in Canaan during the New Kingdom, as explored during my excavations in Jaffa (from 2011 to 2014), nor into the broader questions of the influence of Egypt on the evolution of society and economy in the southern Levant. With this contribution I thank him for all of the opportunities he provided me to explore Egyptian history and archaeology over the years.

In this article I begin a broader study of the implications of the demise of Egyptian New Kingdom rule in Canaan, focusing here on likely vectors of the transmission of Egyptian and other foreign traditions after approximately 1125 BCE and examining their implications for emergent states in the southern Levant, notably, ancient Israel during the early Iron Age. To date, in both biblical studies and Levantine archaeology, emphasis has been placed upon population movements, principally migrations of one scale or another, from Egypt to Canaan during the New Kingdom that may lie behind the exodus tradition in the Hebrew Bible as the primary framework for considering the transfer of customs and practices to early Iron Age Israel. I suggest, however, that because of limited information concerning Egypt's empire in Canaan until more recent studies, we have overlooked a significant vector in the transmission of these customs and practices, namely that individuals negotiated their identities in the context of the changing social, political, and economic circumstances that accompanied the demise of Egyptian rule at the end of the New Kingdom. The starting point for this reappraisal is a review of the evidence, particularly concerning the chronology for this process, that is now available from Jaffa. From there I consider the range of specialists impacted by Egypt's decline and the likelihood of their absorption into emerging early states like Israel. In this context, it is not my aim to replace previous discussions concerning the origins of Egyptian influences and what they may owe to other population movements. Rather, I wish to open up consideration of the very significant influence that the Egyptian Empire, after more than 350 years of direct rule in Canaan, had upon a range of traditions, many of which appear among Israelite traditions in the Hebrew Bible.

This paper was originally presented under the title "Left Behind: The Decoupling of Specialists at the End of the Bronze Age and Its Implications for the Emergence of Iron Age States" in the colloquium "New Light on the Egyptian Origin of the Hebrew Alphabet," held at the Young Research Library at the University of California, Los Angeles on 2 December 2016.

The End of New Kingdom Rule and the Egyptian Fortress at *Yapu* (Jaffa)

Recent excavations in Jaffa provide the clearest evidence available to date for situating the discussion of the end of Egyptian imperial control of Canaan and the relationship of these circumstances to ensuing developments during the early Iron Age (Burke et al. 2017). While destructions at the end of the Late Bronze Age at sites such as Lachish and Megiddo, which exhibit some Egyptian presence, have served as the basis for suggesting around 1130 BCE for the end of Egyptian rule in Canaan, this date was arrived at via the simplistic assumption that the discovery of an Egyptian statue base of Ramesses VI found in a secondary context at Megiddo pointed to him as the last pharaoh to have maintained control of Canaan, and that a conventionally accepted date around 1130 for the end of his reign thereby marked it as a *terminus post quem* for Egyptian rule. The problems with this are many and do not warrant repeating here.[1] In stark contrast to this, the final phases of Jaffa's Egyptian garrison, which have yielded radiocarbon dates from two successive destructions, provide the first unequivocal basis for suggesting a date for the end of Egyptian rule and, thus, for evaluating the impact of resistance to it. This is because, in contrast to Megiddo or Lachish, Jaffa was a pillar of New Kingdom military control and administration, having been continuously occupied since the start of Egyptian Empire, which is traditionally identified with the reign of Thutmose III (Burke et al. 2017, 120–28). Furthermore, its coastal location and role as an Egyptian harbor permits the inference that Jaffa's eventual abandonment involved the figurative and literal "raising of the anchor" on Egypt's efforts to control Canaan. The lengthy history of the Egyptian fortress in Jaffa can be taken, therefore, as a bellwether of Egypt's control of Canaan, and a date for its final destruction therefore serves as a reasonable proxy for the terminus of Egyptian efforts to rule Canaan.

Radiocarbon dates for the penultimate and ultimate destructions of Jaffa's Egyptian garrison originate from the gate complexes of phases RG-4a and RG-3a, and they provide a *terminus post quem* for the final stage in the demise of Egyptian rule and the opening of a phase during which some individuals, formerly associated with Egyptian installations like Jaffa, sought new environs in which to practice their arts. Using C14 samples from seeds recovered during excavations between 2011 and 2014, OxCal Bayesian modeling places these destructions at around 1135 and 1125 BCE, respectively, (Burke et al. 2017, 118–20). Despite the application of Bayesian analysis to refine these dates, it must be noted, however, that the latter of these two dates, 1125 BCE, only serves a *terminus post quem* (i.e., the earliest reasonable approximation of a date) for the destruction of the final fortress. Consequently, any date as late as approximately 1067 BCE, the date for the end of the reign of Ramesses XI, remains possible based on the lower end of the range of unmodeled dates for the phase RG-3a gate destruction.[2] Irrespective of which date between 1125 and 1067 BCE may ultimately prove correct, it remains impossible for us to definitively conclude that the destruction of Jaffa's Egyptian garrison represents the final moment in Egyptian

1. For an extensive discussion, see Burke et al. (2017, 127).
2. In this work, dates for New Kingdom reigns follow Kenneth A. Kitchen (2000).

control or merely one moment in the protracted demise of Egyptian rule in Canaan. Nevertheless, for the first time, we possess scientific dates for a context that reveals the extent to which Egyptian imperial control had unraveled by the last quarter of the twelfth century BCE. This information, in light of a virtual dearth of radiocarbon-dated Iron I sites, also suggests that many transitional sites and contexts assigned to the Iron I period (traditionally dated ca. 1200–1000 BCE) based on their material culture may actually be dated within a period starting not earlier than 1125 BCE (and possibly later). Thus, Egyptian empire, in whatever tenuous and reduced state, remained a reality in Canaan until at least 1125 BCE, and the cultural, social, and political implications of this remain to be more closely studied.

Egyptian Specialists in Canaan, Circa 1300–1125 BCE

The primary focus of discussions of Egyptian cultural influences on the early Iron Age Israelite state, which emerged somewhere in the second half of the eleventh century BCE according to the chronology provided by the Hebrew Bible, has centered on identifying migration from Egypt during the New Kingdom as the principal vector of this transmission (e.g., Hoffmeier 1997, 2005; Friedman 2017), though other suggestions for an even earlier context like the Hyksos period have also been entertained (see Sarna and Shanks 2011, 51–52). Within this framework consideration of Egyptian influences has been primarily limited to specific areas of Israelite culture that appear to have been influenced by Egyptian practices, such as scribalism and cult. Studies of scribalism in ancient Israel, for example, have long observed a residue of "Egypt's role in early Levantine scribalism" as in Egyptian loanwords for writing technologies in Hebrew. Furthermore, these studies acknowledge the likelihood that the earliest known scribes in David and Solomon's courts originate with a figure whose identity, Shesh, was likely a "straightforward Hebraizing of the Egyptian word for scribe" (Schniedewind 2013, 56–60). This is in addition to the other observations concerning the relationship of early Canaanite writing to Egyptian practices (e.g., Goldwasser 2011). Similarly, ample reflection has been given to the associations between Egyptian connections and Israelite cult practice, ranging from studies of the locus of this transmission in Egypt, to terms for ritual accoutrements, and the corpus of Egyptian personal names (e.g., Hoffmeier 2005).

Another productive avenue that must be considered is the influences of the full range of personnel that were attached to Egyptian imperial efforts during approximately 350 years of its presence in Canaan. The suggested down-dating of the end of Egyptian imperial control, as demonstrated by the evidence from Jaffa, has significant implications, therefore, for understanding the timing of and means by which Egyptian customs, present in Canaan during the decline of Egypt's empire, surfaced among the traditions of early Iron Age cultures like Israel and its neighbors. Understanding the broader social implications of Egypt's withdrawal from Canaan is only possible, however, by accounting for both the full range of Egyptian personnel present in Canaan during the New Kingdom and the traditions they embodied.

Although usually assumed as a full withdrawal of Egypt's personnel at the closure of the New Kingdom, it remains very likely that these individuals were actually faced with the possibilities of either returning to Egypt or staying in Canaan where it seems many had developed significant, often kinship-based, ties with local communities. This is most evident with the record of ceramic, anthropoid sarcophagai in Canaan (Dothan 1979; Arensburg and Smith 2010; van den Brink et al. 2017).[3] This distinctly Egyptian practice, which was part of the evolution in sarcophagus design (Lapp and Niwiński 2001, 281–82; Mumford 2014, 78), reveals not only that Egyptian officers stationed in Canaan were buried there but, more importantly, that they intermarried with local Canaanite women, establishing families and new kin relations. Indeed, the choice to be buried in Canaan should not be taken for granted but would have been influenced primarily by these social entanglements. While the corpus of such burials is relatively small, exemplars are restricted principally to the thirteenth and twelfth centuries BCE (Killebrew 2005, 65–67), exposing the degree to which members of Egypt's regime were increasingly socially entangled with Canaan's non-Egyptian inhabitants, even as the empire was in decline.[4] These circumstances, which Michael Dietler describes as entanglement (Dietler 2010, 74), were as complex as any we can imagine, an observation much better provided by archaeological data than textual sources for this period. Interestingly, there are no indications of the primary capacity in which the individuals interred in these sarcophagi served the Egyptian Empire.

The full range of Egyptian personnel attached to the Egyptian imperial apparatus can be reconstructed from both archaeological and textual sources during the New Kingdom. Among these were Egyptian, but also Nubian, Sherden, and Meshwesh soldiers (e.g., *COS* 3:11), as well as Habiru and *maryannu* (possibly Hurrian) elements integrated into Egyptian operations (Spalinger 2005, 170–71). Generals like Djehuty, in the Tale of the Capture of Joppa, also reveal social stratification within Egypt's military ranks, the upper crest of whom apparently were able to bring their families to Canaan with them (Simpson 2003, 72–74). Egyptian administrators, commonly referred to as governors, are also attested (Singer 1983).

Scribes were also a central element within the Egyptian administration of Canaan. The Craft of the Scribe in Papyrus Anastasi I (*COS* 3:9–14) reveals the duties of the Egyptian military scribe, which ranged far beyond simply the ability to read and write, but included translation, administration, logistics, and knowledge of regional geography, social structures, political regimes, and customs. The presence of scribes in Canaan under Egyptian administration is made clear in the Amarna Letters in the mid-fourteenth century BCE, where as many as eighteen Akkadian-proficient scribes have been identified at that time (Millard 1999, 318). Egyptian scribes are also revealed through Hieratic inscriptions on vessels, which identify centers of tribute collection in Canaan that included at least "Lachish, Tel Seraʿ, Tel Haror, Tell el-Farʿah (S), and Beth Shemesh" (Wimmer 2010, 226) but possibly also Tell eṣ-Ṣafi/Gath (Wimmer

---

3. It is worth noting that earlier discussions of these coffins led to their association with Philistine burial practices (Wright 1959), but that this is now effectively discounted.

4. I would contend that further study of dates of this burial practice in Canaan will reveal its principal locus in the twelfth century BCE. This is the result of the fact that previous assignments of terminal Late Bronze Age dates presumed the thirteenth century as the end of Late Bronze Age material culture, rarely accounting for the possibility that New Kingdom presence and thirteenth century material remains are effectively indistinguishable from those of the twelfth century in the absence of radiocarbon-dated contexts. Burials have yet to produce such samples and thus the dating of their contexts depend on relative assignments for artifact styles, foremost of which are ceramics.

2017), as well as through the presence of Egyptian seals and sealings (Brandl 2010b) and an ivory pen case from Megiddo inscribed with the name of Ramesses III (Loud 1939, no. 377, 11–12), which was found in the destruction debris of Stratum VIIA, dated to the second half of the twelfth century (Harrison 2004, 11).

A Proto-Canaanite inscription from the destruction debris of Jaffa's Phase RG-4a gate dated to ca. 1135 BCE, and others from similar contexts in Canaan, may even directly implicate Egyptian scribes in the proliferation of alphabetic Proto-Canaanite. While a reading of the Jaffa ostracon is far from certain, William Schniedewind and Matthew Suriano identify it as Proto-Canaanite.[5] Nevertheless, most of the earliest alphabetic inscriptions appear during the LB IIB to LB III (thirteenth to twelfth centuries BCE) among Egyptian administrative centers in the coastal plain like Jaffa, Lachish, and Qubur al-Walayda (cf. Finkelstein and Sass 2013, 204). The distribution of the Proto-Canaanite inscriptions, originating in thirteenth to twelfth centuries BCE contexts at Egyptian sites throughout the coastal plain from Jaffa in the north to Lachish in the east (Tufnell, Inge, and Harding 1940, 49–54) and Qubur al-Walayda in the south (Nathaniel 2017), is revealing of the relationship between Egyptian scribalism at the end of the twelfth century and scribalism during the ensuing eleventh century BCE. A range of material artifacts therefore point to the presence of Egyptian scribes potentially working in at least two different scribal traditions in Canaan at the close of Egyptian Empire during the twelfth century BCE.

Archaeological remains also suggest a vibrant range of other craft specialists attached to the Egyptian New Kingdom imperial presence. While some artifacts reflect imports, even possibly the temporary presence of itinerant craft specialists from Egypt, the vast majority reveal the presence of a range of Egyptian crafts being practiced in places such as Jaffa and other Egyptian settlements, which ranged from garrison fortresses, to rural farmsteads, and temple estates. The artifacts associated with these crafts attest to the range of such craft specialists including ritual practitioners, scribes, architects, and various craftsmen including potters, stoneworkers, and metalsmiths. These include potters evidenced in locally produced Egyptian ceramics (Burke and Lords 2010, 19–25; Killebrew 2010; Martin 2011, 20–21), stone carvers who produced architectural monuments such as the portals of gates at Jaffa (Burke and Peilstöcker 2016) and stelae, statues, and cultic tables carved from local stone (Brandl 2010a). More recently, suggestions include the identification of Egyptian bronze-working traditions (Naama 2015). To these we can add Egyptian architects or foremen, who were behind the construction (and occasional rebuilding) of Egyptian fortifications like the gate complex at Jaffa and so-called governor's residences (Oren 1984). Egyptian architectural or mason marks even appear on stone pillar bases of the so-called Lion Temple in Area A in Jaffa (fig. 4.1), which is contemporaneous with the twelfth century Phase RG-4a gate (Burke et al. 2017, 126).

Egyptian ritual personnel were also attached to Egypt's New Kingdom presence in Canaan and are revealed among elements of cultic paraphernalia. Indeed, it would be surprising that Egyptian cultic personnel would not be present in Canaan during the New Kingdom, servicing Egyptian communities abroad (Wimmer 1998). Locally produced Egyptian cultic items in Canaan include well-known Qudshu plaque figurines,

---

5. Article to be published with the final excavation report for Jaffa's excavations, 1955–2014.

FIGURE 4.1. Stone pillar base (MHA 4332) with architectural marks from Lion Temple in Jaffa.

as also from Jaffa (Press 2017, 432, fig. 28.2.2, and bibliography therein), but also clay cobras as from Beth-Shean (Szpakowska 2015). The large quantity of scarabs associated with Amenhotep III and his wife, Tiy, as also found at Jaffa (Burke et al. 2017, 110, 12), may likewise point to an official cult in Canaan and its officiants. In sum, archaeology in combination with textual sources points, therefore, not only to general influences from the presence of Egyptian individuals, but concrete evidence for a wide range of personnel representing a spectrum of Egyptian-affiliated specialists who resided in Canaan during the New Kingdom.

Egyptians in Canaan After Empire, Circa 1125–950 BCE

But what evidence is there that the specialists behind these arts did not all return to Egypt or leave for other lands after the close of the New Kingdom empire in Canaan? The clues to this reality are limited, but they are, nonetheless, emerging from early Iron Age assemblages of the twelfth and eleventh centuries BCE as a wider recognition of the timing and scope of the transition from the Bronze Age to the Iron Age are reinvestigated. As might be expected, they consist of the many lines of material culture discussed above, albeit in muted quantities, which illustrate not only a persistence of Canaan's heterogeneous population but also the contribution of Egyptian craftspersons to emerging craft traditions during the early Iron Age (ca. 1125 to 950 BCE).

During the eleventh century, artifacts reveal the continuation of a range of activities from food preparation and consumption, to textile production, and cultic activities associated with Egyptians, presumably with individuals previously attached to the

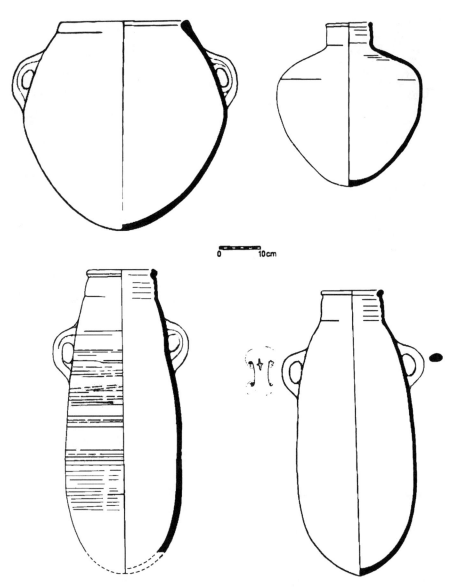

FIGURE 4.2. Egyptian ceramics from Tel Qasile, Stratum X (after Oren 2015).

Egyptian imperial apparatus who were still dwelling in Canaan during this period. If there is any doubt about the potential lines of evidence that directly support the identification of Egyptians still living in Canaan during the early Iron Age, vis-à-vis earlier categories of evidence, then examples drawn from the ceramic repertoire illuminate these circumstances (fig. 4.2). Ceramic spinning bowls, which are distinctive of Egyptian techniques in textile production as early as LB IIA (fourteenth century BCE), continue, for example, through the Iron I and persist until the seventh century (Martin 2011, 45–46). They are attested at Aphek in strata X12 (Gadot 2009, fig. 8.56.3) and X8 (Gadot 2009, figs. 8.84.2, 8.88.8, 8.82.19), during the LB III and Iron IIA, respectively. Cultic lamp and bowl deposits also continue, which were features of thirteenth to mid-eleventh centuries BCE contexts in the North Sinai such as Bir el-ʿAbd and Haruvit, and in Canaan at Deir el-Balah, Ashkelon, Jemmeh, Tell el-Hesi, Tell el-Farʿah (S), Seraʿ, Azekah, Maresha, Beth-Shemesh, Lachish, Ekron, and Pella (Bunimovitz and Zimhoni 1993).

Imported vessels at Tel Qasile in Stratum X also reveal the maintenance of trade relationships with Egypt, which likely delivered Egyptian delicacies catering to an Egyptian-influenced palette. Vessels of Egyptian form include storage jars, amphorae, jars, and bird bowls (Oren 2015). The jars likely transported Nile perch, dried meats, and other Egyptian delicacies. An assemblage of Egyptian ceramics, dated to approximately 1100–850 BCE, has now been identified at Tel Dor as well, consisting of imported store jars, jugs, juglets, possibly a cooking pot, and a few bowls (Waiman-Barak, Gilboa, and Goren 2014). More of these types will be identified as they receive greater attention, just as the assemblage of New Kingdom ceramics in Canaan was vastly expanded during its study in the past twenty years. They also fit neatly into a persistent, if radically reduced, relationship with Egypt as portrayed in the Tale of Wenamun, which is set in the eleventh century (e.g., Gilboa 2015).

Given the limited evidence for personal ornamentation and trade during the Iron I period, it is quite possible that the few Egyptian-style personal objects dated to this period originally belonged to Egyptian individuals or their descendants (fig. 4.3). Two recently published Egyptian finger-rings from Iron IB Ekron, which dated to the Nineteenth and Twentieth Dynasties (Brandl 2016b) are reasonable candidates for heirlooms passed on to family members, potentially descendants of earlier Egyptians. These artifacts find an interesting meaning perhaps in association with Egyptian statuary in Iron I contexts at Ekron, like an inscribed baboon statue of Thoth (Dothan and Regev 2016; Brandl 2016a), the patron god of scribes, that is hard to understand as a trophy or other traded item. Given Thoth's patronage of Egyptian scribes, perhaps it belonged to an Egyptian scribe or his progeny. The persistence of cult practices of an Egyptianizing type during the early Iron Age are further attested among a variety of other artifacts. The appearance of whole Qudshu-style figurines still in Aphek X9 (Guzowska and Yasur-Landau 2009, 390–91) suggest a continuation of personal cult practices from the Late Bronze Age as well. A large range of Egyptian amulets are also attested throughout Canaan after the Late Bronze Age (Herrmann 2016), and while they are frequently spoken of as trinkets and considered in the framework of trade, much room remains for contextual studies of them and the possibility that some actually belonged to the descendants of individuals formerly attached to the Egyptian imperial apparatus.

Although they comprise a relatively small corpus, a number of Proto-Canaanite inscriptions are also dated to this period based on archaeological or paleographic evidence (see Byrne 2007, 17–22). In light of the prevailing evidence for Egyptian and Akkadian scribal traditions before 1125 BCE, it is noteworthy that the corpus that followed was exclusively alphabetic. A number of abecedaries from the period, including ʿIzbet Sartah (Demsky 1986, and bibliography therein) and Tel Zayit (Tappy et al. 2006) point to this process. By the end of the eleventh century a shift from short inscriptions and abecedaries to longer texts is in evidence. The Khirbet Qeiyafa ostracon (Misgav, Garfinkel, and Ganor 2009), which may have been a list and perhaps functioned as a scribal exercise (Demsky 2012), might suggest the evolution of this

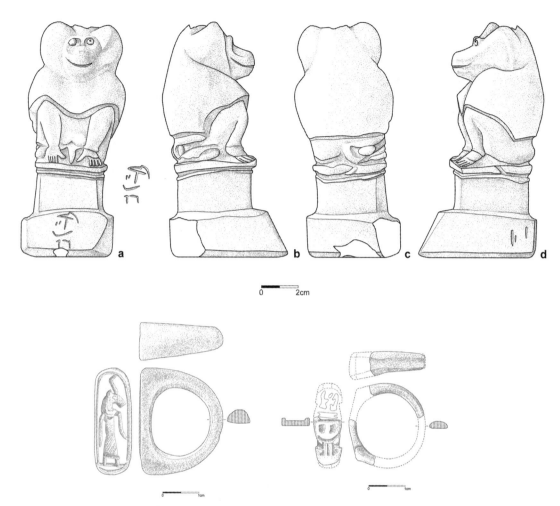

FIGURE 4.3. Egyptian personal items at Ekron during the Iron IB (after Brandl 2016a, 2016b).

process. The listing tradition is, however, certainly present on the Gezer Calendar, dated paleographically to the tenth century BCE (McCarter 2002).

Added to these inscriptions are a large collection of inscribed arrowheads, most of which lack any provenance, but are dated paleographically to this period. They include the el-Khadr arrowheads from the Judean Hills (Hamilton 2002), but also examples from the northern Levant (e.g., Starcky 1982). The inscriptions are very short and presumably identify their owners in the personal names inscribed on them, particularly given multiple occurrences of the same name and formula. While this is a maximalist reading of the data, by the eleventh century BCE the locus of scribal traditions had notably shifted eastward, away from the collapsed Egyptian nodes, like Jaffa and Aphek, and Canaanite centers to the Shephelah (see Finkelstein and Sass 2013), the new refuge of scribalism (Byrne 2007). The eleventh century BCE was, therefore, the critical moment for the transition from Proto-Canaanite experimentation to full-fledged employment of alphabetic Canaanite in an emerging scribal tradition.

We can end this discussion with a variety of biblical references to Egyptians and related identities in Canaan, such as Nubians and other non-Semitic groups, that are localized specifically to this period, noting that such groups appear principally in the biblical narratives set in the early Iron Age. Among these is an Egyptian slave of an Amalekite captured by David (1 Sam 30:11–15) and reference to a Kushite runner at David's court (2 Sam 18:21–32). Kushites, who were Nubians, are properly considered within the Egyptian context because of their extensive incorporation within the Egyptian army (Spalinger 2005, 171). The killing of an Egyptian warrior also plays an important role in the tradition associated with the rise of Benaiah son of Jehoiada, one of David's "heroes," who presided over the Cherethites and Pelethites (2 Sam 23:20–21; 8:18). These two groups are of ambiguous origins (Ehrlich 1992a, b), but should probably be identified as foreign military elements alongside Philistines, who of course receive pride of place as Israel's early enemy (Katzenstein 1992). Solomon's scribes, Elihoreth and Ahijah, sons of *Shisha* (lit. Egyptian "sons of scribes," i.e., members of the scribal guild), are mentioned in 1 Kgs 4:3 and point to the foundational role that Egyptian scribalism played in early Israelite scribalism. Perhaps in this context it is not surprising that a marriage to an Egyptian slave named Jarha, who belonged to Sheshan (another name constructed around the Egyptian word for scribe?), is also remembered within Judah's ancestry in later tradition (1 Chr 2:34–35). Aegean mercenaries, Egyptians, and Nubians, all of whom were the legacy of a lengthy imperial Egyptian presence, therefore made up not insignificant communities living among Israelites and Canaanites in this brave new world according to the biblical narratives.

A combination of archaeological and historical sources come together, therefore, to expose the eleventh century BCE, around 1125 to 950 BCE, as the crucial moment in the transition between Late Bronze and Iron Age traditions. The withdrawal of Egyptian Empire set in motion the recombination of social, political, and economic elements that are embodied in an array of conspicuous agents including warriors, scribes, and ritual practitioners. Because scribes were directly implicated in the production of textual sources, they are perhaps the most conspicuous among these individuals during this transition.

The Crucible of Scribalism: Scribes and Emerging States in the Eleventh Century BCE

Observations in recent years concerning evident continuities across a wide range of material culture from the end of the Late Bronze Age (until ca. 1125 BCE) through the early Iron Age (ca. 950 BCE) support our efforts to understand the influences of Egyptian culture on Iron I traditions, among them scribalism. The prevalence of finds during this period with strong correlations to Egyptian traditions after the end of Egyptian Empire center on scribalism, and biblical and linguistic studies have previously identified it as one of the major loci exhibiting Egyptian connections. It is during the eleventh century BCE in the realignment of the scribal art in Canaan that we may consider the role of Egyptian scribes, particularly as "independent specialists"—for a brief moment detached from the Egyptian imperial apparatus.

The first question that must be posed is: What good was a scribe in the largely atextual and mostly illiterate, courtless world after Egyptian withdrawal? In the first place, this characterization can be challenged since, based on the characterization in Egyptian literature, the scribe's value far exceeded his capability in the written arts. While this has remained the locus of discussion concerning efforts to trace the emergence of Iron Age scribalism (e.g., Byrne 2007), a list of the scribal arts should include, however, at least the following capabilities: technological (e.g., work with pen, palette, papyrus), linguistic (e.g., ability in Egyptian and Canaanite dialects), pedagogical (i.e., knowledge of teaching tools), mnemonic (i.e., keeper of traditions, wisdom, and memory), administrative (e.g., mathematical, logistical, legal), geographic (e.g., political, geography, biogeography), and relational (i.e., socially networked to other scribes and administrators). Although this list of the scribe's potential assets is not likely exhaustive, the scribe's familiarity with a wide range of practical knowledge would have meant that while technical aspects of the craft may have undergone substantial changes, the scribe's depth of knowledge on a range of subjects made him an indispensable element to emerging states and their rulers. By virtue of prior dependence upon them within the imperial apparatus of Egypt as well as within Canaanite courts, the social networks of scribes were essential assets to aspiring leaders during the early Iron Age.

Not only are a constellation of arts connected to the basic function of the scribe as recorder, the scribe embodied an even wider collection of wisdom that could be employed in the absence of or in an environment where the production, even the value, of writing was vastly diminished, as during the early Iron Age. As no other evident context existed for the regular transmission of such knowledge in Canaan during the Late Bronze Age, the scribe served, effectively, as a walking computer, a "Spock," "Data," or "C3PO" of sorts, permitting their new masters to navigate the changing world around them. Scribes, like other specialists, clearly constituted what Etienne Wenger identifies as a "community of practice" (Wenger 1998). As such, scribes possessed a shared repertoire of "routines, words, tools, ways of doing things, stories, gestures, symbols, genres, actions, or concepts" (Wenger 1998, 83). Their collective identity, a guild of sorts, would have been significant in navigating the transition of the scribal arts following the collapse of Egyptian rule; no single scribe was therefore responsible for this, but it was a collective process that was worked out gradually. "Community of practice" provides, therefore, a useful framework for this discussion, addressing a range of shared experiences and not just the practical or tactile aspects of the art within a community or guild. Everything from the material to the ideological, from tools to routines, stories, training, and symbols embody critical aspects of the "community of practice" among early Iron Age scribes.

In this context, to the extent that scribes were decoupled from Egyptian and Canaanite administrative contexts, they were likely not unattached for very long. Indeed, it has been argued that the boundaries between "attached" and "independent" specialists, as discrete categories, likely never existed so purely, but that specialists navigated between these extremes on a continuum (Costin 1998, 5), a situation that would well describe the transition between the Bronze and Iron Age contexts. Such flexibility served scribes well as they sought to realign with emerging leaders and their communities. It was, in fact, the social networks of scribes, the maintenance of communication with others in their "guild" who also now found themselves embedded in newly emerging states, that was perhaps their greatest value. It follows, then, that the scribal arts, for which connections can be reconstructed between Egyptian and Proto-Canaanite scribal traditions, experienced a realignment during the eleventh century BCE, and it was in this environment that changes in the technology of writing and a shift in the prevailing languages of communication occurred, away from Akkadian and Egyptian to local dialects.

The perpetuation of craft specializations during the eleventh century, especially scribalism, was embedded within specific "cultural domains," whether "economic, social, political," or "ritual" as Cathy Costin observes.

> Specialized craft producers are actors involved in the creation and maintenance of social networks, wealth, and social legitimacy. Artisans and consumers must accept, create or negotiate the social legitimacy of production and the conditions of production and distribution, usually defined in terms of social identity. The nature of that process defines the organization of production and the social relations of production that characterize the relationships between producers and consumers (Costin 1998, 3).

Indeed, their place within the social networks in which they had previously functioned no doubt largely shaped the relationships that scribes sought after the collapse of Egyptian rule. Some form of reattachment was the most likely outcome, even if it required an adaptation of one's existing skill set; a change in orthography and language was a relatively small part of the collective traditions embodied in the scribe's function, as observed above. Scribes would have been sought out, therefore, as useful for their mastery of the arts of communication, which was their inherent prestige. This prestige was enhanced by the extremely limited number of such individuals and we are likely speaking of a very limited number of individuals who remained in Canaan, perhaps fewer than even the eighteen Akkadian scribes estimated for Canaan in the Amarna period. The end of the Late Bronze Age not only brought about the demise of Egyptian administration, which had supported Egyptian scribal arts, but also of Canaanite palatial systems that supported Akkadian-based scribal programs, as the disappearance of Akkadian during the early Iron Age reveals. The decoupling of scribal traditions from both of these palatial and cultural support systems denied subsequent scribes access to a number of elements critical to the perpetuation of these scribal traditions in their previous incarnations. There were reductions in the availability of (1) inscribed materials, in either Egyptian or Akkadian, through which calligraphy could be perpetuated, (2) the tools of the trade (i.e., technologies), (3) linguistic influences that shaped scribalism in the Late Bronze Age (e.g., glossaries), and (4) access to sources of training that perpetuated "histories of learning" that defined scribes as a community of practice.

Scribes, however, embodied the knowledge and memory of their craft, relying more heavily on oral tradition and one-on-one transfers of their knowledge to do so. The perpetuation of a variety of duties associated with the role of the scribe necessitated flexibility and adaptation within the scribal arts and thus, unsurprisingly, it resulted in a craft replete with hybrid forms. Because their technical abilities within Egyptian and Akkadian circles were no longer supported, the orthographic systems they perpetuated were abandoned and new, simpler systems, as evidenced with Proto-Canaanite, took root and proliferated. Scribes therefore retained their value as purveyors of crucial information, permitting them the opportunity to adapt their technical skills to adopting and refining of a simplified hybrid writing system for Canaanite that borrowed materially and ideationally from Egyptian, while not altogether abandoning Akkadian contributions to the world of Levantine scribalism. Akkadian traditions, such as the rubrics of scribal training that included list making, letter writing, and tabulation were retained. Several lines of evidence, particularly evident and better preserved during the mature stages of this new scribal tradition in the later Iron II, reveal that various traditions from both Egyptian and Akkadian scribal customs were creatively adapted to accommodate training in this alphabetic tradition. Among these were the adoption of (1) writing media from Egyptian tradition including papyrus, pottery sherds (ostraca), the palette, and the reed pen; (2) an Egyptian-influenced orthography for the alphabet; (3) Egyptian hieratic numerals for tabulations, and (4) Akkadian list and glossary practices for training (Schniedewind 2013, 58–60). To be sure, while this process was already underway before the disappearance of the Egyptian Empire, it was hastened once these earlier traditions could no longer be supported, in much the same way that older, computer operating systems cease to be supported and are abandoned. So does this process intimate the coming together of independent scribes to redefine a community of practice? Seemingly. The origins, perpetuation, and success of hybrid, yet productive new alphabetic writing systems and the means by which their training was perpetuated are difficult to explain otherwise.

Conclusions

Two broad areas of culture transfer, ritual practice and scribalism, have been the primary focus of studies of the biblical text that have sought to identify strands of Egyptian influence among early Israelite traditions. However, as I have suggested in this work, greater consideration needs to be given to the context for cultural exchanges and the enduring influences of the protracted presence of Egyptian Empire in Canaan during the New Kingdom. Although largely neglected, increasing evidence of cultural continuity among a range of practices during the end of the Late Bronze Age and the early Iron Age suggests that the decoupling of specialists from both Egyptian and Canaanite contexts opened avenues for the transmission of cultural traditions among a range of arts, from scribalism and ritual practice, to warfare, ceramic production, and metallurgy. While our tendencies are to assume that Egyptian Empire contracted, taking all of its personnel with it, studies of analogous imperial contexts, such as the Roman periphery (Elton 1996), reveal the degrees to which such social boundaries were highly fluid and easily traversed during periods of political uncertainty.

BIBLIOGRAPHY

Arensburg, Baruch, and Patricia Smith. 2010. "Human Remains from the Cemetery." Pages 49–50 in *Deir el-Balah: Excavations in 1977–1982 in the Cemetery and Settlement I; Stratigraphy and Architecture*. Edited by Trude Dothan, and Baruch Brandl. Qedem 49. Jerusalem: Israel Exploration Society.

Brandl, Baruch. 2010a. "Four Amarna-Type Stone Supports for Bed Legs." Pages 229–31 in *Deir el-Balah: Excavations in 1977–1982 in the Cemetery and Settlement II; the Finds*. Edited by Trude Dothan, and Baruch Brandl. Qedem 50. Jerusalem: Israel Exploration Society.

———. 2010b. "Two Bullae, a Plaque, Four Scarabs and a Stamp Seal." Pages 207–23 in *Deir el-Balah: Excavations in 1977–1982 in the Cemetery and Settlement II; the Finds*. Edited by Trude Dothan, and Baruch Brandl. Qedem 50. Jerusalem: Israel Exploration Society.

———. 2016a. "The Thoth Baboon Statuette: The Inscription and Its Dating." Pages 467–68 in *Tel Miqne-Ekron Excavations 1985–1988, 1990, 1992–1995: Field IV Lower—The Elite Zone Part 1, The Iron Age I Early Philistine City*. Edited by Trude Dothan, Yosef Garfinkel, and Seymour Gitin. Tel Miqne-Ekron Final Field Report Series 9/1. Winona Lake, IN: Eisenbrauns.

———. 2016b. "Two Scarabs and Two Finger-Rings from Iron Age I Contexts." Pages 503–9, 595 in *Tel Miqne-Ekron Excavations 1985–1988, 1990, 1992–1995: Field IV Lower—The Elite Zone Part 1, The Iron Age I Early Philistine City*. Edited by Trude Dothan, Yosef Garfinkel, and Seymour Gitin. Tel Miqne-Ekron Final Field Report Series 9/1. Winona Lake, IN: Eisenbrauns.

Brink, Edwin C. M. van den, Ron Beeri, Dan Kirzner, Enno Bron, Anat Cohen-Weinberger, Elisheva Kamaisky, Tamar Gonen, Lilly Gershuny, Yossi Nagar, Daphna Ben-Tor, Naama Sukenik, Orit Shamir, Edward F. Maher, and David Reich. 2017. "A Late Bronze Age II Clay Coffin from Tel Shaddud in the Central Jezreel Valley, Israel: Context and Historical Implications." *Levant* 49:105–35.

Bunimovitz, Shlomo, and Orna Zimhoni. 1993. "'Lamp-and-Bowl' Foundation Deposits in Canaan." *IEJ* 43:99–125.

Burke, Aaron A., and Krystal V. Lords. 2010. "Egyptians in Jaffa: A Portrait of Egyptian Presence in Jaffa During the Late Bronze Age." *NEA* 73:2–30.

Burke, Aaron A., and Martin Peilstöcker. 2016. "Fragments of a Gateway Facade of Ramesses II." Pages 81–83 in *Pharaoh in Canaan: The Untold Story*. Edited by Daphna Ben-Tor. Jerusalem: Israel Museum.

Burke, Aaron A., Martin Peilstöcker, Amy Karoll, George A. Pierce, Krister Kowalski, Nadia Ben-Marzouk, Jacob Damm, Andrew Danielson, Heidi Dodgen Fessler, Brett Kaufman, Krystal V. L. Pierce, Felix Höflmayer, Brian N. Damiata, and Michael W. Dee. 2017. "Excavations of the New Kingdom Egyptian Fortress in Jaffa, 2011–2014: Traces of Resistance to Egyptian Rule in Canaan." *AJA* 121:85–133.

Byrne, Ryan. 2007. "The Refuge of Scribalism in Iron I Palestine." *BASOR* 345:1–31.

Costin, Cathy Lynne. 1998. "Craft and Social Identity." *Archeological Papers of the American Anthropological Association* 8:3–16.

Demsky, Aaron. 1986. "The 'Izbet Sartah Ostracon Ten Years Later." Pages 186–97 in *'Izbet Ṣarṭah: An Early Iron Age Site near Rosh Ha'ayin, Israel*. Edited by Israel Finkelstein. BARIS 299. Oxford: Archaeopress.

———. 2012. "An Iron Age IIA Alphabetic Writing Exercise from Khirbet Qeiyafa." *IEJ* 62:186–99.

Dietler, Michael. 2010. *Archaeologies of Colonialism: Consumption, Entanglement, and Violence in Ancient Mediterranean France*. Berkeley: University of California.

Dothan, Trude. 1979. *Excavations at the Cemetery of Deir el-Balah*. Qedem 10. Jerusalem: Hebrew University of Jerusalem.

Dothan, Trude, and Dalit Regev. 2016. "An Inscribed Thoth Baboon Statuette from Iron Age I Contexts." Pages 463–66, 590 in *Tel Miqne-Ekron Excavations 1985–1988, 1990, 1992–1995: Field IV Lower—The Elite Zone Part 1, The Iron Age I Early Philistine City*. Edited by Trude Dothan, Yosef Garfinkel, and Seymour Gitin. Tel Miqne-Ekron Final Field Report Series 9/1. Winona Lake, IN: Eisenbrauns.

Ehrlich, Carl S. 1992a. "Cherethites." *ABD* 1:898–99.

———. 1992b. "Pelethites." *ABD* 5:219.

Elton, Hugh. 1996. *Frontiers of the Roman Empire*. London: Batsford.

Finkelstein, Israel, and Benjamin Sass. 2013. "The West Semitic Alphabetic Inscriptions, Late Bronze II to Iron IIA: Archeological Context, Distribution and Chronology." *Hebrew Bible and Ancient Israel* 2:149–220.

Friedman, Richard Elliott. 2017. *The Exodus: How It Happened and Why It Matters*. New York: HarperOne.

Gadot, Yuval. 2009. "Late Bronze and Iron Age Pottery." Pages 182–341 in *Aphek-Antipatris II: The Remains on the Acropolis, the Moshe Kochavi and Pirhiya Beck Excavations*. Edited by Yuval Gadot, and Esther Yadin. Monograph Series of the Institute of Archaeology of Tel Aviv University 27. Tel Aviv: Yass Publications in Archaeology, Institute of Archaeology, Tel Aviv University.

Gilboa, Ayelet. 2015. "Dor and Egypt in the Early Iron Age: An Archaeological Perspective of (Part of) The Wenamun Report." *AeL* 25:247–74.

Goldwasser, Orly. 2011. "The Advantage of Cultural Periphery: The Invention of the Alphabet in Sinai (Circa 1840 B.C.E.)." Pages 255–321 in *Cultural Contacts and the Making of the Cultures: Papers in Homage to Itamar Even-Zohar*. Edited by Rakefet Sela-Sheffy, and Gideon Toury. Tel Aviv: Tel Aviv University.

Guzowska, Marta, and Assaf Yasur-Landau. 2009. "Anthropomorphic Figurines." Pages 387–95 in *Aphek-Antipatris II: The Remains on the Acropolis, the Moshe Kochavi and Pirhiya Beck Excavations*. Edited by Yuval Gadot, and Esther Yadin. Monograph Series of the Institute of Archaeology of Tel Aviv University 27. Tel Aviv: Yass Publications in Archaeology, Institute of Archaeology, Tel Aviv University.

Hamilton, Gordon J. 2002. "The el-Khadr Arrowheads (2.84)." *COS* 2:221–22.

Harrison, Timothy P., ed. 2004. *Megiddo 3: Final Report on the Stratum VI Excavations*. OIP 127. Chicago: Oriental Institute of the University of Chicago.

Herrmann, Christian. 2016. *Ägyptische Amulette aus Palästina/Israel IV: Von der Spätbronzezeit IIB bis in römische Zeit*. OBO.SA 38. Fribourg: Academic Press; Göttingen: Vandenhoeck & Ruprecht.

Hoffmeier, James K. 1997. *Israel in Egypt: The Evidence for the Authenticity of the Exodus Tradition*. New York: Oxford University.

———. 2005. *Ancient Israel in Sinai: The Evidence for the Authenticity of the Wilderness Tradition*. Oxford: Oxford University.

Katzenstein, H. J. 1992. "Philistines." *ABD* 5:326–28.

Killebrew, Ann E. 2005. *Biblical Peoples and Ethnicity: An Archaeological Study of Egyptians, Canaanites, Philistines, and Early Israel 1300–1100 B.C.E.* ABS 9. Atlanta: Society of Biblical Literature.

———. 2010. "The Kilns and Potters' Workshop." Pages 267–85 in *Deir el-Balah: Excavations in 1977–1982 in the Cemetery and Settlement I; Stratigraphy and Architecture*. Edited by Trude Dothan and Baruch Brandl. Qedem 49. Jerusalem: Israel Exploration Society.

Kitchen, Kenneth A. 2000. "Regnal and Genealogical Data of Ancient Egypt (Absolute Chronology I): The Historical Chronology of Ancient Egypt; a Current Assessment." Pages 39–52 in *The Synchronisation of Civilisations in the Eastern Mediterranean in the Second Millennium B.C.: Proceedings of an International Symposium at Schloss Haindorf, 15th–17th November 1996 and at the Austrian Academy, Vienna, 11th–12th of May 1998*. Edited by Manfred Bietak. Contributions to the Chronology of the Eastern Mediterranean 1. Vienna: Österreichische Akademie der Wissenschaften.

Lapp, Günther, and Andrzej Niwiński. 2001. "Coffins, Sarcophagi, and Cartonnages." *OEAE* 1:279–87.

Loud, Gordon. 1939. *The Megiddo Ivories*. OIP 52. Chicago: University of Chicago Press.

Martin, Mario A. S. 2011. *Egyptian-Type Pottery in the Late Bronze Age Southern Levant*. Contributions to the Chronology of the Eastern Mediterranean 29. Denkschriften der Gesamtakademie 69. Vienna: Österreichische Akademie der Wissenschaften.

McCarter, P. Kyle, Jr. 2002. "The Gezer Calendar (2.85)." *COS* 2:222.

Millard, Alan R. 1999. "The Knowledge of Writing in Late Bronze Age Palestine." Pages 317–26 in *Languages and Cultures in Contact: At the Crossroads of Civilizations in the*

Syro-Mesopotamian Realm, Proceedings of the 42nd RAI. Edited by Karel van Lerberghe, and Gabriela Voet. OLA 96. Leuven: Peeters.

Misgav, Haggai, Yosef Garfinkel, and Saar Ganor. 2009. "The Ostracon." Pages 243–57 in *Khirbet Qeiyafa 1: Excavation Report 2007–2008*. Edited by Yosef Garfinkel and Saar Ganor. Jerusalem: Israel Exploration Society; Institute of Archaeology, Hebrew University of Jerusalem.

Mumford, Gregory D. 2014. "Egypt and the Levant." Pages 69–89 in *The Oxford Handbook of the Archaeology of the Levant (c. 8000–332 BCE)*. Edited by Margreet L. Steiner, and Ann E. Killebrew. Oxford: Oxford University Press.

Naama, Yahalom-Mack. 2015. "Egyptian Bronzeworking Practices in Late Bronze Age Canaan." *BASOR* 374:103–14.

Nathaniel, E. Greene. 2017. "The Qubur al-Walaydah Bowl: New Images and Old Readings." *BASOR* 377:39–47.

Oren, Eliezer D. 1984. "'Governor's Residences' in Canaan Under the New Kingdom: A Case Study of Egyptian Administration." *JSSEA* 14:37–56.

———. 2015. "Iron Age IB–IIC Egyptian and Egyptian-Type Pottery." Pages 555–64 in vol. 2 of *The Ancient Pottery of Israel and Its Neighbors from the Iron Age Through the Hellenistic Period*. Edited by Seymour Gitin. 2 vols. Jerusalem: Israel Exploration Society; Albright Institute of Archaeological Research; Israel Antiquities Authority; American Schools of Oriental Research.

Press, Michael D. 2017. "Bronze and Iron Age Figurines and Zoomorphic Vessels from Jaffa, 1955–1974." Pages 429–38 in *The History and Archaeology of Jaffa 2*. Edited by Aaron A. Burke, Katherine Strange Burke, and Martin Peilstöcker. Jaffa Cultural Heritage Project 2. Monumenta Archaeologica 41. Los Angeles: Cotsen Institute of Archaeology Press.

Sarna, Nahum M., and Hershel Shanks. 2011. "Israel in Egypt: The Egyptian Sojourn and the Exodus." Pages 35–57 in *Ancient Israel: From Abraham to the Roman Destruction of the Temple*. Edited by Hershel Shanks. 3rd ed. Washington, DC: Biblical Archaeology Society.

Schniedewind, William M. 2013. *A Social History of Hebrew: Its Origins through the Rabbinic Period*. ABRL. New Haven: Yale University Press.

Simpson, William Kelly. 2003. *The Literature of Ancient Egypt: An Anthology of Stories, Instructions, Stelae, Autobiographies, and Poetry*. 3rd ed. New Haven: Yale University Press.

Singer, Itamar. 1983. "Takuhlinu and Haya: Two Governors in the Ugarit Letter from Tel Aphek." *TA* 10:3–25.

Spalinger, Anthony J. 2005. *War in Ancient Egypt: The New Kingdom*. Ancient World at War. Malden, MA: Blackwell.

Starcky, Jean. 1982. "La flèche de Zakarbaal roi d'Amurru." Pages 179–86 in *Archéologie au Levant: Recueil à la mémoire de Roger Saidah*. Collection de la Maison de l'Orient méditerranéen 12. Lyon: Maison de l'Orient.

Szpakowska, Kasia. 2015. "Snake Cults and Egyptian Military Bases." Pages 274–91 in *Walls of the Prince: Egyptian Interactions with Southwest Asia in Antiquity; Essays in Honour of John S. Holladay Jr*. Edited by Timothy Harrison, E. B. Banning, and Stanley Klassen. CHANE 77. Leiden: Brill.

Tappy, Ron E., P. Kyle McCarter, Marily J. Lundberg, and Bruce Zuckerman. 2006. "An Abecedary of the Mid-Tenth Century B.C.E. from the Judaean Shephelah." *BASOR* 344:5–46.

Tufnell, Olga, Charles H. Inge, and Lankester Harding. 1940. *Lachish II: The Fosse Temple*. Wellcome-Marston Archaeological Research Expedition to the Near East 2. London: Oxford University Press.

Waiman-Barak, Paula, Ayelet Gilboa, and Yuval Goren. 2014. "A Stratified Sequence of Early Iron Age Egyptian Ceramics at Tel Dor, Israel." *AeL* 24:315–42.

Wenger, Etienne. 1998. *Communities of Practice: Learning, Meaning, and Identity*. Cambridge: Cambridge University Press.

Wimmer, Stefan. 1998. "(No) More Egyptian Temples in Canaan and Sinai." Pages 87–123 in *Jerusalem Studies in Egyptology*. Edited by Irene Shirun-Grumach. ÄAT 40. Weisbaden: Harrassowitz.

———. 2010. "A Hieratic Inscription." Pages 225–28 in *Deir el-Balah: Excavations in 1977–1982 in the Cemetery and Settlement II; the Finds*. Edited by Trude Dothan, and Baruch Brandl. Qedem 49. Jerusalem: Israel Exploration Society.

———. 2017. "Fragments of Egyptian Writing from Tell es-Safi/Gath." *NEA* 80:298–99.

Wright, G. Ernest. 1959. "Philistine Coffins and Mercenaries." *BA* 22:53–66.

CHAPTER 5

The *Fiscus Judaicus* and the New Testament

Thomas W. Davis

E. P. SANDERS REMINDS US that "History is not in fact always composed of sequential developments which lead to terminal points" and this study of the *fiscus judaicus*, including its impact upon the last New Testament writings, exemplifies Sanders's characterization.[1] Details of the *fiscus judaicus* are lacking in our primary sources and conjecture must by necessity have a place in this discussion. Josephus records the implementation of the *fiscus* in a short notice in his presentation of the impacts of the great revolt. He reports that Vespasian "imposed a tax on all Jews everywhere, making them each pay two drachmae a year to the Capitoline, just as they had previously contributed to the Jerusalem Temple" (*B.J.* 7.6.6; author's translation). The Roman historian Cassius Dio informs us that "from then on the Jews who continued to observe their ancestral customs should pay an annual two drachma tax to the Capitoline" (*Hist.* 65.7.2; author's translation). The original name of the tax appears to be Dio's term, *denarii duo judaeorum*, "the two denarii of the Jews."[2] There is no mention of this tax in Suetonius's biography of Vespasian except to emphasize the assiduousness of Vespasian's rebuilding of the Capitoline temple. Suetonius does discuss the tax again in his biography of Vespasian's son, the Emperor Domitian. He records the rigorous implementation of the tax near the end of Domitian's reign and with a sympathetic eye, mentions seeing an elderly man of ninety stripped to determine if that gentleman was circumcised or not (*Dom.* 12.2).

Archaeology provides valuable documentation of the tax. Excavators from a joint Polish-French team working at the site of Apollinopolis Magna (Tell Edfu) in Upper Egypt from 1937–1939, recovered numerous receipts dealing with the tax from a

---

I first met Jim Hoffmeier through the auspices of Alfred Hoerth, an archaeology professor at Wheaton College, who taught us both. I graduated in 1979, one year before Jim began to teach at Wheaton, but Mr. Hoerth bridged the gap. Al cared deeply for his students and he went out of his way to ensure that Jim and I met each other, hoping the acquaintanceship would help us both in our budding careers. Over the years since, we developed a close friendship that was renewed annually at the ASOR meetings. When Jim began his major field project at Tell el Borg, he invited me to join him and I happily worked as a field director for all seven years of the project. I am deeply in his debt for his unstinting belief in my abilities and his constant prodding of me to remain involved in biblical archaeology, even when my professional life was far removed from that world. I would not hold my current position as a Professor of Archaeology at Southwestern Baptist Theological Seminary were it not for Jim. Accordingly, I am honored to be asked to contribute to this volume. Throughout his writings, Jim has used the cultural setting of the ancient world to provide insight into Scripture, a lesson he learned at Wheaton. I hope this article honors both Jim and Al, our joint mentor.

1. E. P. Sanders, *Paul and Palestinian Judaism: A Comparison of Patterns of Religion* (Philadelphia: Fortress, 1977), 22.

2. E. Mary Smallwood, *The Jews Under Roman Rule: From Pompey to Diocletian; A Study on Political Relations*, SJLA 20 (Leiden: Brill, 1981), 372.

concentrated area of the site.[3] Written in Greek, they detail tax payments made over a generation by residents in Egypt for a wide range of taxes including for police, guards, guard posts, dikes, baths, the poll tax, and the *fiscus judaicus*. The ostraca dated before the eighth year of Domitian call it τιμὴ δηνρίων δύο Ἰουδαίων, "the price of the two denarii of the Jews"; after this date the term Ἰουδαϊκόν τέλεσμα predominates; both terms clearly refer to the same tax.[4]

The *fiscus judaicus* replaced the original temple tax of a half shekel paid by all adult Jews, both in Palestine and in the diaspora, to the Jerusalem temple to maintain the fundamental requirement of sacrifice. This tax is well documented in contemporary literature (Cicero, Josephus, Philo); Jesus paid his tax (and Peter's tax bill) with a coin recovered from the mouth of a fish (Matt 17:24–27).[5] The tax was a tangible way for the diaspora to feel connected to the worship in the temple. The sacrifices were also literally on their behalf because of the payment of the tax.[6] Annually, the diaspora contributed a massive amount of money to the Jerusalem temple. This is best illustrated in a legal case brought against L. Valerius Flaccus in 59 BCE for maladministration of public funds when he was governor of Asia (Cicero, *Flac.* 66–9). The public funds included alleged temple tax funds from four cities: Apamea, Laodicea, Adramyttium, and Pergamum. This was a huge amount (in gold more than 120 pounds) almost certainly more than one year's taxes.[7] In the time of Augustus, diaspora communities sought explicit permission to gather taxes or administer their own finances. Augustus responded (according to Josephus) that the tax could be sent to Jerusalem and that this right was inviolable (*A.J.* 16:162–165).

The destruction of the temple in 70 CE was the catalyst for the change in the temple tax and its new implementation as the *fiscus judaicus*. Clearly, with the destruction of the temple, there was no longer any religious reason for a diaspora Jew to send money to maintain a ruin with no priesthood and no sacrifices. If the Roman government had not intervened, it is possible that some Jews would have continued to piously pay the tax, perhaps to their local leadership, in the hopes of a restoration of the temple at some future date when the stockpiled funds could be used to finance its rebuilding. However, Vespasian's decision to continue the tax but redirect it to rebuild the temple in Rome of Jupiter Capitolinus ended the possibility of any formal, legally recognized, continuation of the tax on an internal basis.

Vespasian and Titus

Josephus, in an excursus on the coup of Vespasian, describes the looting and burning of the temple of Jupiter Capitolinus in Rome (*B.J.* 4.649). The second century

3. Victor A. Tcherikover and Alexander Fuchs, eds., *Corpus Papyrorum Judaicarum Vol. II* (Cambridge: Harvard University Press, 1960), 108–77.

4. Tcherikover and Fuchs, *Corpus*, 112.

5. Garland argues that Matthew includes this story to provide "precise moral guidance" on the payment of the tax for Jewish Christians. David E. Garland, "Matthew's Understanding of the Temple Tax (Matt 17:24–27)," *Society of Biblical Literature 1987 Seminar Papers*, SBLSPS 23 (Atlanta: Scholars Press, 1987), 195.

6. Paul R. Trebilco, *Jewish Communities in Asia Minor*, SNTSMS 69 (Cambridge: Cambridge University Press, 1991), 16.

7. Trebilco, *Jewish Communities*, 14.

Roman historian Tacitus deplores the destruction as "the saddest and most shameful [*luctuosissimum foedissimumque*] crime that the Roman state had ever suffered since its foundation" (*Hist.* 3.62). He records the Roman Senate's decision to restore the temple; an opponent of Vespasian proposes that it should be restored at public expense and that Vespasian should assist in the work. The amendment regarding Vespasian's responsibility did not pass: "The more prudent senators passed [the proposal] over in silence and then allowed it to be forgotten" (*Hist* 4.9), but the pressure on Vespasian to provide assistance was clear. Tacitus tells how the temple was rebuilt on the same site since "the gods were unwilling to have the old plan changed" (*Hist* 4.53).

The financial motivation for Vespasian's decision to transfer the revenues is obvious. The new emperor's reputation for financial conservatism was a necessary virtue, because after years of military strife, the public purse was practically empty. The new source of revenue for the state addressed an immediate financial concern. The need to quickly rebuild the temple was paramount for Flavian propaganda to show that the new dynasty was actually a restoration of divinely approved governance, rather than a naked usurpation of power. "Vespasian had solved the Senate's problem of financing its reconstruction in his own way."[8]

There is a debate among scholars about additional motivations for the imposition of the *fiscus judaicus*. Martin Goodman, in a series of publications, has forcefully argued that the tax was deliberately designed as a punishment for the greater Jewish community.[9] The new tax symbolizes "the deliberate destruction not just of the free Jewish state but of the religion and society of Judaea before A.D. 66."[10] Paul Foster disagrees with Goodman saying that the increase of taxation under Vespasian was across the board, which undercuts the argument that the goal was the "deliberate destruction of the Jewish state."[11] In his argument, Goodman compares the Jewish revolt with the Boudicca revolt in Britain in 60 CE. Usually after a revolt has been put down, Rome restores a thoroughly romanized ruling class to keep the peace. This was the case in Britannia, but the opposite action happened in Judaea where Goodman blames the involvement of the ruling class in the revolt for the Roman intransigence. "Therefore both the religion and the ruling class were to be altogether expunged for the sake of the empire's security. Jews evidently could not live in the Roman world in

---

8. Miriam Griffin "The Flavians," in the *The High Empire, A.D. 70–192*, ed. Alan K. Bowman, Peter Garnsey, and Dominic Rathbone, 2nd ed., CAH 11 (Cambridge: Cambridge University Press, 2000), 27.

9. Martin Goodman, *The Ruling Class of Judaea: The Origins of the Jewish Revolt Against Rome AD 66–70* (Cambridge: Cambridge University Press, 1987); Goodman, "Diaspora Reactions to the Destruction of the Temple," in *Jews and Christians: The Parting of the Ways A.D. 70 to 135; The Second Durham Tübingen Research Symposium on Earliest Christianity and Judaism (Durham, September, 1989)*, ed. James D. G. Dunn, WUNT 66 (Tübingen: Mohr, 1992), 27–38; Goodman, *Mission and Conversion: Proselytizing in the Religious History of the Roman Empire* (Oxford: Clarendon, 1994); Goodman, "Judaea," in Bowman, *High Empire*, 664–78; Goodman, "Trajan and the Origins of the Bar-Kokhba War," in *The Bar-Kohkba War Reconsidered*, ed. Peter Schäfer, TSAJ 100 (Tubingen: Mohr Siebeck, 2003), 23–29; Goodman, "The *Fiscus Iudaicus* and Gentile Attitudes to Judaism in Flavian Rome," in *Flavius Josephus and Flavian Rome*, ed. Jonathan Edmondson, Steve Mason, and James Rives (Oxford: Oxford University Press, 2005) 167–77; Goodman, *Rome and Jerusalem: The Clash of Ancient Civilizations* (London: Penguin 2008).

10. Goodman, *Ruling Class*, 232.

11. Paul Foster, "Vespasian, Nerva, Jesus and the *Fiscus Judaicus*," in *Israel's God and Rebecca's Children: Christology and Community in Early Judaism and Christianity: Essays in Honor of Larry W. Hurtado and Alan F. Segal*, ed. David B. Capes, et al. (Waco: Baylor University Press, 2007), 307.

peace."[12] The closing of the "inoffensive" temple of the God of Israel at Leontopolis in 72 CE shows Roman approval of persecution of Jews.[13] With no surviving landed elite in Judaea, the redirection of the temple tax would insure that the financial ability for the Jewish community to rebuild the temple in Jerusalem would be compromised. For Goodman, this message is reinforced by Vespasian's issue of the famous Judeaea capta coins. This is in sharp contrast to the situation after the defeat of Boudicca in Britain, when Nero did not issue any commemorative coins.[14] Goodman's position on the *fiscus judaicus* as a collective punishment has gained widespread support.[15]

Mary Smallwood sees the tax through the lens of the full Roman response to the revolt. She notes that the status of Judaism as a *religio licta* is unchanged in both Judaea and the diaspora. "To deprive the Diaspora, who had played no part of any consequence in the war, of their religious liberty in the process of punishing the sins of Palestine would have been unjustifiable."[16] Dio records that neither Vespasian nor Titus added "Judaicus" to their formal titles though they celebrated a joint triumph (*Hist.* 66.7.2). Smallwood suggests this was not done by the victors because to embrace the title might have reflected discredit against the diasporan community who had not risen up against Rome in support of their coreligionists.[17] For Smallwood, the Jerusalem temple was destroyed because it was a center for military resistance, not for its religious role. "It did not symbolize any Roman intention of eliminating Judaism."[18] Rome's quarrel was with Jewish nationalism, not the Jewish faith. James Paget supports this interpretation. "Some of course might say that the imposition on all Jews of the so called *fiscus judaicus* contradicts that element of differentiation manifest in the actions of Titus [refusing to punish Alexandrian and Antiochene Jews for the first revolt]. This is true, although we should note that the empire-wide imposition of such a tax may simply have been an example of financial opportunism and a recognition of the fact that Jews in the Diaspora as well as Palestine were regular payers of the temple tax and had now to have their payment redirected." [19]

Smallwood recognizes the tax was a burden, "psychological as well as financial" on the diasporan community.[20] It may have been an economic burden, but it was not an *added* burden. The Jewish tax was already in place, and was from the Roman

12. Goodman, *Ruling Class*, 239.

13. Goodman, "Diaspora Reactions," 28. Goodman refines the chronology from 71 CE, used in this article, for the destruction of the Leontopolis temple in "Judaea": "Roman retaliation included the closure of the Jewish temple at Leontopolis in the Egyptian delta in A.D. 72 and its precincts in A.D. 73 even though the shrine had never been a center of unrest since its foundation in the mid-second century B.C.," 665.

14. Goodman, *Ruling Class*, 235.

15. Tessa Rajak, "The Jewish Diaspora," in *Origins to Constantine*, ed. Margaret M. Mitchell and Frances M. Young, CHC I (Cambridge: Cambridge University Press, 2006), 66; Menahem Mor, *The Second Jewish Revolt: The Bar Kokhba War, 132–136 CE*, BRLJ 50 (Leiden: Brill, 2016).

16. Smallwood, *Jews Under Roman Rule*, 344. Goodman finds diasporan attitudes to the revolt very difficult to determine; see "Diaspora Reactions."

17. Smallwood, *Jews Under Roman Rule*, 329. Griffin believes it was embarrassment at the presentation of a provincial revolt as an outside conquest that prevents using the title; Griffin "Flavians," 15.

18. Smallwood, *Jews Under Roman Rule*, 346. The destruction was accidental in that it was not planned. She emphasizes that there is no evidence that the rebuilding of the temple was ever forbidden between 70 CE and 135 CE. The relationship changes of course after the Bar Kokhba revolt.

19. James C. Paget, *Jews, Christians, and Jewish Christians in Antiquity*, WUNT 251 (Tübingen: Mohr Siebeck, 2010), 397.

20. Smallwood, *Jews Under Roman Rule*, 344.

perspective, a voluntary one. Pious Jews had paid the tax to the temple and by this action they were meeting the criteria of following the customs of their ancestors, so they would have been liable to continue to pay the new tax. Christians who did not live as Jews (in other words "maintain their ancestral customs"), would not have been liable to the tax.[21] The redirection of the revenue did not add to the fiscal burden of already paying Jews, but from the perspective of the entire community, the new iteration of the tax was an *expanded* burden. Vespasian widened the pool of individuals subject to the tax to be any Jew from the age of three to at least sixty-two for the women and possibly life for the men.[22]

Under the senior Flavians, the tax was self-defined. Vespasian announced the redirection of the tax and appears to have left the decision up to the individual whether they will openly be Jewish and pay the tax. The decision was governed by whether the potential taxpayers openly maintained "their ancestral customs." As already mentioned, it was a net gain for the Roman treasury no matter how few actually paid. The Edfu ostraca suggest that the tax was collected like any other government revenue; there is no clear evidence from the receipts that the Jewish community collected the tax themselves although specific tax collecting officers had responsibility for the tax.[23]

There is an undeniable religious aspect to the postrevolt tax. In its new iteration, the tax provides benefit to Jupiter Capitolinus, not the God of Israel. Morton Smith points out that religious scruples seem not to have been invoked by the Jewish community; the idea "that paying a tax which would go to a pagan temple was in effect committing idolatry, was probably never raised and never considered."[24] Smallwood acknowledges this religious aspect to Rome's response when she described Jupiter as "the god who in the Roman victory had triumphed over the God of Israel."[25] Smallwood believes the new version of the tax was the price that the Jews had to pay to remain a *religio licta* and retain their freedom to worship Yahweh and opt out of the imperial cult. Helmut Schweier understands the tax as one aspect of the Flavian campaign to transfer to Jupiter the attributes of the defeated god of the Jews. This divine triumph legitimizes the Flavian dynasty and requires the destruction of the temple and the end of the cult.[26]

There may be more at work here than has been so far recognized. Repeatedly in Josephus's writings he stresses that God is sovereign over history and that the Romans have their rule because it is his will that they do so (see *B.J.* 2.390; 5.367–69). In his appeal before the walls of Jerusalem Josephus makes this explicit. "You fight not only against the Romans but against God himself" (*B.J.* 5.379). As part of this process, God has relocated his presence in the earth. This extraordinary event is described by Josephus. "At the feast called Pentecost, the priests, on entering the inner court of the

21. Garland, "Matthew's Understanding," 201.

22. Smallwood, *Jews Under Roman Rule*, 345. The sources are unclear if the age cutoff applies to men as well.

23. Tcherikover and Fuchs, *Corpus*, 108–77.

24. Morton Smith, "The Troublemakers," in *The Early Roman Period*, ed. William Horbury, W. D. Davies, and John Sturdy, CHJ 3 (Cambridge: Cambridge University Press, 1999), 561.

25. Smallwood, *Jews Under Roman Rule*, 347.

26. Helmut Schwier, *Tempel und Tempelzerstörung: Untersuchungen zu den theologischen und ideologischen Faktoren im ersten jüdisch-römischen Krieg (66–74 n.Chr.)*, NTOA 11 (Göttingen: Vandenhoeck & Ruprecht; Fribourg: Universitätsverlag, 1989), 308–37.

temple by night as was their custom carrying out their service, reported that they heard a noise and after that the voice as of a multitude saying, 'We are departing hence'" (*B.J.* 6.300). Intriguingly, this is also recounted by the Roman historian Tacitus who reports that "of a sudden the doors of the shrine opened and a superhuman voice cried: 'the gods are departing' [*excedere deos*] at the same moment the mighty stir of their going was heard" (*Hist.* 5.14). Tacitus's account may witness to an independent Roman source for the story.[27] For Josephus the conclusion is clear and he tells the Jerusalemites, "God is fled out of his sanctuary and stands on the side of those against whom you fight" (*B.J.* 5.412).

Divine sanction is a very important element in Roman military ideology. Goodman reminds us that "the cults of defeated enemies were usually either wooed to Rome during the war to aid the Romans, or were worshipped at Rome in syncretistic guise within the cult of a Roman divinity, or, perhaps most common of all, were carried to Rome as one of the prizes of conquest."[28] The wooing referred to by Goodman is formally played out in the ritual of *evocatio*.[29] This Roman religious rite invites the deity of an enemy to come to take up residence in Rome and receive correct worship, not the incorrect rites of the Roman enemy. Livy records an incidence of this and an inscription recently discovered in Anatolia appears to refer to this rite in the first century BCE. No ancient source claims that the rite of evocation was formally carried out in respect to Jerusalem, probably because fundamentally, this was a revolt not a conquest. It is possible that the rite was invoked, but it is unlikely.[30] For Josephus, God is the prime mover, so he cannot be seen to be responding to an invitation from the Romans. However, this concept underlies the way Josephus tells the story.[31]

Where has God gone? He has moved to Rome. Goodman correctly recognizes that Josephus thought this "since he claimed that in effect, God had crossed over to Rome from Jerusalem and taken up residence on the Capitol."[32] This is the clear implication of Josephus's description of a dream he had where he tells God that he goes to Rome not as a deserter but as a follower (*B.J.* 3.354). The only scenario where Josephus remains a follower and not a deserter is if God has relocated to Rome. Of course, the only appropriate place for the God of the universe to dwell in Rome would be at the temple of Jupiter Best and Greatest on the Capitoline Hill. For Josephus, it is important to remind his readers that this temple burns down *before* the temple in Jerusalem. The destruction in Rome prefigures what will happen in Jerusalem, implying that these two sacred spaces are linked. The destruction of the Roman temple could be seen as a physical manifestation of divine "housecleaning"; the God of Israel has moved in and the new sanctuary will be his, despite the Roman belief that Jupiter is the main inhabitant.

27. T. D. Barnes, "The Sack of the Temple in Josephus and Tacitus," in Edmondson, *Flavius Josephus and Flavian Rome*, 129–44.

28. Goodman, *Ruling Class*, 235.

29. Hendrik Versnel, "Evocatio," *BNP* A5:252; Goodman mentions this rite in a footnote, *Ruling Class*, 235 n. 7.

30. James Rives, "Flavian Religious Policy and the Destruction of the Jerusalem Temple," in Edmondson, *Flavius Josephus and Flavian Rome*, 149. Rives rejects the possibility.

31. Marcel Simon, "Jupiter-Yahvé: Sur un essai de théologie pagano-juive," *Numen* 23 (1976): 56.

32. Goodman, *Ruling Class*, 235.

Goodman dismisses any possibility of a rapprochement between the recently dislocated Jewish God and Rome. Goodman acknowledges that the decision by Vespasian to use the tax for the rebuilding of Jupiter Capitolinus was a religiously conscious decision. "To anticipate: a substitution by Rome of Jupiter Capitolinus in the place of the Jewish god is to be explicit again some sixty or so years later in the establishment of Aelia Capitolina. I shall suggest this was not accidental."[33] According to Goodman, once the Jerusalem temple was destroyed, whether by accident or design, it became impossible to apologize for it and rebuild it under Roman jurisdiction. "Apology would suggest error and the possibility that the powerful god of the Jews would spurn the new emperor who had destroyed his sanctuary."[34] Goodman thinks that it would have been possible for Vespasian to incorporate the Jewish God in the Roman pantheon if he had so desired, but he did not because of his fury at the betrayal of the Judean ruling class in the revolt.[35] From a Roman perspective, "the gods delighted in the extinction of the sanctuary where Jewish atheism, directed to an invisible entity, was a reproach to genuine religion ... [with] the victory of Jupiter proclaimed symbolically through the immediate institution of the *fiscus iudaicus*."[36]

However, it is possible that Vespasian and Titus shared in Josephus's idea of divine relocation. Goodman has not considered the effect of a belief in the relocation of the "powerful god of the Jews" on Vespasian and Titus. Josephus implies this belief when he places a speech in Titus's mouth in which the general acknowledges that the deity who dwelled in the Jerusalem temple has relocated.[37] Titus's arch of triumph, erected in the Circus Maximus in 81 and no longer extant, maintained the focus on the city of Jerusalem and not the temple as it proclaimed with untrue flattery that Titus, with the help of his father, "subdued the race of the Jews and destroyed the city of Jerusalem which by all generals, kings or races previous to himself had either attacked in vain or not even attempted at all."[38] The Romans seem to have understood that the God of Israel was unique in that he had only *one sanctuary at a time* where he would manifest his presence.[39] Later sources summarizing Tacitus's lost account of Titus's deliberations before the destruction of the temple, indicate that the general decided to destroy the temple despite suggestions to retain it as a trophy of victory.[40] A belief in divine relocation could be one of the reasons Titus deliberately burns the temple (if Tacitus is correct). The account of Tacitus shows that the divine relocation of the God of Israel is not just an idea of Josephus. This possibility gains more credence because it also explains the destruction of the temple at Leontopolis. The God of Israel needed to be shown to have relocated to Rome by choice; any other sanctuary that might falsely claim residency would have to be eliminated because it might provide an alternative home for the divine occupant.

33. Goodman, "Trajan," 25.

34. Ibid., 24.

35. Goodman, *Ruling Class*, 238.

36. Goodman, "Judaca," 664.

37. Josephus, *B.J.* 5.127. Rives suggests Titus believed the temple to be abandoned, but does not speculate on where Titus believed the deity went! "Flavian Religious Policy," 149.

38. Fergus Millar, "Last Year in Jerusalem: Monuments of the Jewish War in Rome," in Edmondson, *Flavius Josephus and Flavian Rome*, 120.

39. Rives, "Flavian Religious Policy," 159–64.

40. Barnes, "Josephus and Tacitus," 135.

The triumph shared by Vespasian and Titus could be interpreted as expressing the idea of divine relocation (Josephus, *B.J.* 7.149–54). The parade floats show the conquest of Judean cities, but closes with the golden table, the candlesticks and last of all, "the law of the Jews." For Vespasian, Titus, and even Josephus, perhaps the parade of the Torah scrolls embodies the divine transfer of the God of Israel to his new home when the triumph ends in its traditional location, at the temple of Jupiter Capitolinus.[41] The Arch of Titus in the Forum famously depicts the spoils from the temple being carried in the Flavian triumph. Vespasian placed the golden treasures from Jerusalem among many other works of art originally gathered by Nero, in the new Flavian Temple of Peace, treating them as artistic works from the empire. The purple curtain and the scrolls are treated differently and are kept in Vespasian's palace (Josephus, *B.J.* 7.158–62); this implies an imputation of special sanctity to these objects. This distinction only makes sense if the emperor believed that he had not offended the Jewish God and that he would actually benefit from the proximity of the sacred objects. Vespasian has no qualms about redirecting the tax from the Jerusalem temple to the temple in Rome, perhaps because in his eyes, both "Jupiter" and "Yahweh" may be different faces of the same being. Therefore, there was no risk of divine retribution for either the destruction of the temple in Jerusalem or for the redirected tax, because this is actually what the God of Israel wanted to occur. Thus, the imposition of the *fiscus judaicus* would not be punitive for the Jewish diaspora, but actually beneficial for all concerned, both Jews and Romans. From a Roman perspective, the redirected tax functioned as both an outward sign of proper respect for Yahweh from the Romans, and a (required) expression of continued worship of their God by the Jews. In Vespasian's eyes, the rebuilding of the temple in Jerusalem would remain divinely unnecessary as long as the God of Israel received proper care in his new home in Rome.

Domitian

Domitian's rule brings changes. He openly credited Jupiter Best and Greatest with saving his own life during the coup in Rome. In gratitude, Domitian dedicated a temple to Jupiter the Guardian with his own effigy in the lap of the god to thank him for his protection during the sack of the Capitol.[42] Eager to maintain the justification for Flavian rule established by his father and brother, Domitian completed the arch to mark the apotheosis of Titus, which depicts the spoils from the temple carried in the parade of Vespasian and Titus. Domitian maintains the *fiscus judaicus* initially unchanged, but the switch in the name of the tax during his reign, documented at Edfu (see above), suggests a conscious policy change of severing of the established link between the current tax and the old Jerusalem temple tax. This is in keeping with Domitian's active pagan piety (Suetonius, *Dom.*). By this change he may be signaling a rejection of the idea of the God of Israel dwelling in the temple in Rome and by extension, any extraordinary accommodation with his Jewish subject's beliefs.

41. I wonder if Josephus may have hoped to become the "high priest" of the newly located Yahweh in Rome!

42. Goodman, *Rome and Jerusalem*, 465.

Near the end of Domitian's tenure, Suetonius records a change in the implementation of the *fiscus judaicus*. Domitian drastically expands the pool of eligible taxpayers, and introduces draconian collection methods. "Besides other taxes, that on Jews
was levied with the utmost vigor, and those were persecuted who without publically
acknowledging that faith yet lived as Jews, as well as those who concealed their origin
and did not pay the tribute levied upon their people" (*Dom.* 12.2).[43] This is a change
from Vespasian's original tax, which fell upon all Jews who openly maintained their
faith; that left the initiative with the individual.[44] Under Domitian's implementation,
it doesn't matter how you live or what you profess; if you are of the *gens*, then you pay.
It is now the Roman government who determines who is a Jew and not the individual.
An apostate or anyone who left the faith is still responsible for paying the tax. The
definition of Jewishness is based on the tax.[45]

The newly expanded tax pool would include Jews who had become Christians,
whether they maintained links to the synagogue or had become totally gentile in the
way they lived out their new faith. This could become a "pitfall" for Christians.[46]
It would not have included gentile Christians unless they were perceived to have
adopted a Jewish lifestyle when they accepted Christianity. Domitian's reforms may
have placed these Christians into a sort of "no-man's land" under pressure to be either
Jewish or pagan.[47] The aggressive enforcement under Domitian may have created
a cruel dilemma with eternal consequences for Christians: either deny Christ and
sacrifice to the Roman gods; deny Christ and become Jewish; or, embrace Christ and
accept the probably fatal consequences of being labeled an atheist.[48] What is clear is
that Jewish Christians and Jewish apostates would be considered Jews by the Roman
government in order that they might be taxed.[49]

Nerva and Trajan

Nerva changes all this when he succeeds the assassinated Domitian in 96 CE. Early
in his rule, Nerva issues a coin that has the legend FISCI IUDAICI CALUMINA
SUBLATA, which Goodman translates as "the malicious accusation the treasury for
Jewish affairs has been removed."[50] The generally accepted interpretation of this

43. I quote from the Loeb translation as the Latin is challenging.
44. Williams sees no change in policy, only in the execution of the policy. Margaret H. Williams,
"Domitian, the Jews and the 'Judaizers': A Simple Matter of Cupiditas and Maiestas?," *Historia: Zeitschrift
für Alte Geschichte* 39 (1990): 196–211.
45. Goodman, "Diaspora Reactions," 32.
46. Peter Hirschberg, "Jewish Believers in Asia Minor According to the Book of Revelation and the
Gospel of John," in *Jewish Believers in Jesus: The Early Centuries*, ed. Oskar Skarsaune and Reidar
Hvalvik; (Peabody, MA: Hendrickson 2007), 222. Hirschberg believes the threat would have arisen because
the tax was collected by Jewish authorities. I disagree because of the evidence of the Edfu ostraca suggests
the *fiscus judaicus* was collected with other taxes.
47. Magnus Zetterholm, *The Formation of Christianity in Antioch: A Social-Scientific Approach to the
Separation Between Judaism and Christianity* (London: Routledge, 2003), 198–206.
48. Colin J. Hemer, *The Letters to the Seven Churches of Asia in Their Local Setting*, JSNTSup 11
(Sheffield: JSOT Press, 1986), 10.
49. Foster, "Jesus and the *Fiscus Judaicus*," 314.
50. Goodman, *Rome and Jerusalem*, 469.

phrase is that Domitian stopped the "witchhunt" aspect of the enforcement of the tax and it reverted to the more limited pool of taxpayers first enforced by Vespasian.[51] Goodman thinks the coin issue indicates Nerva stopped the tax altogether as part of his campaign to totally divorce himself from the Flavian dynasty.[52] "Such an appeal makes best sense if the reform advertised by Nerva was an end to the collection of the tax."[53] Foster believes this to be an erroneous conclusion by Goodman since the tax continued under Trajan, and cites the Edfu tax receipts as evidence.[54] Goodman agrees the tax again was collected by Trajan, but believes that Trajan *reinstated* the tax.[55] A careful review of the tax receipts at Edfu actually provides some support for Goodman's position. The receipts are for payments made under Vespasian, Titus, Domitian, and Trajan; they do not indicate any payment of the tax under Nerva; as the collection does include receipts from payments under his successor Trajan, the absence of receipts may not be just a by-product of the arbitrariness of archaeological recovery.[56]

Scholars have postulated a much more positive atmosphere toward Judaism under Nerva because of his repudiation of Domitian's tax gathering methods.[57] This has led to the hypothesis that Nerva planned to permit the rebuilding of the temple or at least considered the possibility in a more favorable light. "With the demise of the Flavians," says Goodman, "Jews might reasonably hope to be permitted to rebuild their Temple after it had lain in ruins for 26 years."[58] Nerva's accession occurred when hope for the rebuilding of the temple did seem to be renewed in the Jewish community. "It is likely that all Jews hoped, in vain, for the rapid rebuilding of the sanctuary in Jerusalem. Josephus in the 90s A.D. still assumed that the Temple and its priesthood were central elements of Jewish worship, as did the Christian author of 1 Clement, and priests retained their prestige and still received tithes although their influence gradually declined as their religious functions faded into memory."[59]

The reforms of Nerva have been seen as the context for the Epistle of Barnabas. According to Michele Murray, this noncanonical text was "written because the modification of the *fiscus judaicus* and the expectation of the rebuilding of the Jewish temple in Jerusalem would have generated a heightened sense of purpose and optimism among Jews living in Palestine and in the Diaspora. No doubt it would also have had a profound impact on Christians." [60] Following Peter Richardson and Martin Shuster, Stephen Wilson places the writing of the extracanonical Epistle of Barnabas during

51. Garland, "Matthew's Understanding," 199; Miriam Griffin, "Nerva to Hadrian," in Bowman, *High Empire* 92.

52. Goodman, "Gentile Attitudes," 176. Nerva looks back to Augustus as his model.

53. Goodman, *Rome and Jerusalem*, 469.

54. Foster, "Jesus and the *Fiscus Judaicus*," 315–16.

55. Goodman, *Rome and Jerusalem*, 475. This is only the latest restatement of his understanding of Trajan that carries throughout Goodman's writings.

56. Tcherikover and Fuchs, *Corpus*. No receipts exist for any tax under Nerva, so the absence of Jewish tax receipts should be used with caution.

57. Goodman, *Rome and Jerusalem*, 448; Peter Richardson and Martin B. Shukster, "Barnabas, Nerva and the Yavnean Rabbis," *JTS* 34 (1983): 43. Stephen G. Wilson, *Related Strangers: Jews and Christians 70–170 CE* (Minneapolis: Fortress, 1995).

58. Goodman, "Trajan," 26.

59. Goodman, "Judaea," 667.

60. Michele Murray, *Playing a Jewish Game: Gentile Christian Judaizing in the First and Second Centuries CE*, Studies in Christianity and Judaism 13 (Waterloo: Wilfrid Laurier University, 2004), 47.

Nerva's reign using the present tense mention of the rebuilding of the temple in Barn-abas 16:3–4 as a significant piece of evidence.[61] However, although Wilson acknowl-edges that there is "not a single piece of evidence to connect Nerva to [a] rebuilding of the temple," he nevertheless thinks Nerva is the emperor who is "perhaps the most likely to have approved this."[62] This logic is somewhat circular, as Wilson uses the present tense of the epistle to suggest the hope of a rebuilding effort by Nerva, which in turn he uses to support the proposed date of the epistle! Daniel Schwartz considers that the epistle dates to the time of Hadrian and in total contradiction with Wilson, suggests that the temple being discussed is a temple to Jupiter, not the God of Israel.[63]

If the rule of Nerva did generate a renewed hope in the Jewish community for the rebuilding of the temple, then these hopes would have been dashed in late 97 CE when Nerva adopted Trajan as his heir. I agree with Goodman's reasoning that because Trajan's father was a legionary commander under Vespasian in the Judean campaign, the younger Trajan would have sought to repolish the military credentials of the tri-umph over the Jews, which could have been tarnished by Nerva's policy of giving the Flavian dynasty's achievements less prominence.[64] A heightened reappraisal of the senior Trajan's military reputation would enhance the new heir's military heritage and consequentially increased his appeal to the legions.

Biblical Speculation

Religious identity was a fluid concept in antiquity, just as it is today. The lines between Christian and Jew were the "flowing together of a permeable border; not fixed, but fluid."[65] For Paget, "'flux, fluidity, convergence, blur, negotiation, porousness', these have, to some at least, become the buzz words in the study of the subject."[66] Identity flux is strongest when rethinking is forced on people who would not otherwise take the time from "real life" to consider their identity deeply.

Domitian's rigorous implementation of the *fiscus judaicus* forced individuals to confront their own identity. For example, the tax status of gentile proselytes is unclear; it is probable that they would have paid the tax in its original iteration since this was based on observable behavior.[67] Many would have been openly paying the temple tax before the destruction of the Jerusalem temple since it would have been a mark of their faith. Wilson suggests that these "Judaizers," gentile proselytes to a Jewish-oriented Christianity, are the people "who say they are Jews and are not" of Rev 2:9.[68] They say

---

61. Wilson, *Related Strangers*; Richardson and Shukster "Barnabas."

62. Wilson, *Related Strangers*, 135.

63. Daniel R. Schwartz, *Studies in the Jewish Background of Christianity*, WUNT 60 (Tubingen: Mohr Siebeck, 1992), 151.

64. Goodman, *Rome and Jerusalem*, 475.

65. Daniel Boyarin, *Border Lines: The Partition of Judaeo-Christianity* (Philadelphia: University of Pennsylvania Press, 2004), 15.

66. Paget, *Jews, Christians*, 22.

67. Murray, *Jewish Game*, 20. Murray equates pagan proselytes or "judaizers" in her term, following Wilson, as the targets of the second stricture in Domitian's campaign.

68. Wilson, *Related Strangers*, 73. Wilson suggests they were attracted to Judaism as a safety net under pressure from Domitian, which is echoed in the rigorous enforcement of the *fiscus judaicus*. Wilson's stu-dent, Murray agrees in *Jewish Game*, 59.

they are Jews by paying the tax. Domitian's tax collectors would have expected them to continue to pay the new tax, even if they were not circumcised and not of the *gens*.

For Wilson, the repeated comparisons between the old covenant and the new covenant in the canonical book of Hebrews "give the impression that Judaism (Christian or non-Christian) was an immediate threat" and that the best context for this immediacy is the reign of Nerva.[69] It seems to me that the context of the flux of religious identity that so concerns the author of Hebrews is best found in the impact of the changes introduced to the *fiscus judaicus* by Domitian.[70] As has been widely noted, "the epistle to the Hebrews seems to be addressed to Jewish Christians feeling (and sometimes succumbing to) the pull of Judaism."[71] The Roman government's expanded definition of Jewishness may have caused some Christians to rethink their faith identity, what Philip Church calls a "modified relapse."[72] "If I am going to be treated as a Jew by having to pay the tax, then maybe I still am a Jew and I should explore what that means" they might have said.[73] The economic argument should not be discounted. Historically, overt religious identity change can often be a product of economic pressure. [74] An overt Jewish identity also provided protection against the charge of atheism that Christians were vulnerable to. These combined factors could have led some former believers to turn their backs on overt Christian connections.

The rule of Domitian is a better fit for Hebrews, rather than later in the reign of Nerva, because of the impact of Nerva's reforms. Domitian's death was sudden and violent; the author of Hebrews would have expected to live for decades more under the ruler's policies. He would have anticipated continuing pressure on Jewish Christians to deny the Christian interpretation of Jesus, hence the necessity of writing. Apparently, Nerva's reform of the *fiscus* had the effect of making plain who was a Christian and who was a Jew since scholars have noted that there is a clear distinction in Roman pagan texts between Jews and Christians after 96 CE.[75] Paget notes "the absence of external evidence for Christians paying the *fiscus* may be further proof of social separation and indeed the cause of the phenomenon."[76] Under Nerva, self-identified Christians of Jewish background should have been able to escape paying the tax if they disavowed connections to the synagogue. This economic motive could

---

69. Wilson, *Related Strangers*, 126.

70. I have no intention to rehash the voluminous arguments over the intertwined questions of authorship and date of Hebrews. Suffice it to say that I think Clement of Rome wrote Hebrews and he wrote it just before Nerva's accession. The debate on the issues of date and authorship are summarized in the recent works of my former dean, David L. Allen [even though he is wrong!]; see Allen, *Hebrews*, NAC 35 (Nashville: Broadman & Holman, 2010); and his published dissertation Allen, *Lukan Authorship of Hebrews* (Nashville: Broadman & Holman, 2010).

71. Stephen G. Wilson, *Leaving the Fold: Apostates and Defectors in Antiquity* (Minneapolis: Fortress, 2004), 127–28.

72. Philip Church, *Hebrews and the Temple: Attitudes to the Temple in Second Temple Judaism and in Hebrews*, NovTSup 171 (Leiden: Brill, 2017), 18. Although Church places Hebrews before the destruction of the temple his model of modified relapse is helpful.

73. This reaction occurs in modern societies when identity is dictated by oppressive governments; I have observed this in my own contacts with Syrians whom the government has labeled "Christians."

74. E.g., on Cyprus in the sixteenth century after the Ottoman conquest of the island; Thomas W. Davis, "Archaeology, Identity and the Media in Cyprus," in *Archaeology, Bible, Politics and the Media*, ed. Eric Meyers and Carol Meyers (Winona Lake, IN: Eisenbrauns, 2012), 189–96.

75. Goodman, "Diaspora Reactions," 33. Foster, "Jesus and the *Fiscus Judaicus*," 315.

76. Paget, *Jews, Christians*, 11.

have encouraged many to remain on the Christian side of the identity continuum. They were no longer in danger of being "outed," denounced by an informer who discovered their hidden ethnicity or former religious identity. The easing of the tax enforcement may have even encouraged movement toward a Christian identity among some in the Jewish community.

Under Nerva, the renewed hope for rebuilding the temple would cause a hardening of identity rather than a more open door. At the same time, for Christians, the delay in the parousia would force a deemphasis on the physical land and the temple in favor of a more spiritualized conception of the kingdom of God.[77] For Jews, the fundamental relationship between deity and people was expressed through the sacrifice, mediated by the priests. A rebuilt temple, would once again be a dwelling place for God as the Second Temple became after its completion. Judean identity is "unimaginable" without a temple.[78] This "Third Temple" would provide another conundrum for Christians: How could this be God's dwelling place if his presence on earth is now to be found through his Spirit indwelling the church? With a possible return of the sacrificial rite on the horizon, there would be less room for those in the Roman-defined "Jewish community" who believed the sacrifice was no longer necessary because of Christ. The continuum of identity, loosened under the pressure of Domitian would be severely tightened by the loosening of Nerva.

The *fiscus judaicus* in its original iteration under Vespasian may have caused a blurring of the identity boundary line delineating God and Jupiter, which would be annually interrogated when the tax was collected. This could be an underlying reason for the rather abrupt ending of the first letter of John. John closes his epistle with the warning: "Children, guard yourselves from idols" (1 John 5:21). This is an afterthought with no real connection to what John says before this verse except in the mode of address. Commentators are diverse and contradictory in their opinions regarding this command from John.[79] It is possible that new diaspora converts, raised in a pluralistic and syncretistic world, might be led astray into outward idolatry because they see Jews annually paying a tax founded to maintain the worship of God, which now supports a pagan temple. In the process of inquiring about their new faith, they might encounter the belief that the "Jewish tax" is paid to Jupiter Capitolinus because that temple is the new home of the God of Israel, whom the new believers now worship in Christ. By extension then, could it be acceptable to worship God through Jupiter? John's answer is clear: "Children, stay away!"

77. Philip Alexander, "The Parting of the Ways from the Perspective of Rabbinic Judaism," in Dunn, *Jews and Christians*, 23.

78. John Barclay, "Constructing Judean Identity After 70 CE: A Study of Josephus' Against Apion," in *Identity and Interaction in the Ancient Mediterranean: Jews Christians and Others; Essays in Honor of Stephen G Wilson*, ed. Zeba A. Crook and Philip A. Harland, New Testament Monographs 18 (Sheffield: Sheffield Phoenix, 2007), 107.

79. Raymond Brown ably summarizes the positions in his Anchor Bible volume: Brown, *The Epistle of John: A New Translation with Introduction and Commentary*, AB 30 (New York: Doubleday, 1980).

CHAPTER 6

Gifts of the Nile: Materials That Shaped the Early Egyptian Burial Tradition

Joanna Dębowska-Ludwin and Karolina Rosińska-Balik

Introduction

We are used to thinking about ancient Egypt as "the gift of the Nile." However, in the light of recent field research the famous sentence by Herodotus finds a more profound explanation. The idea of the "gift" may be easily extended from abundance of water in the land surrounded by desert and fertile river mud turning Egypt into the granary of the ancient world to a variety of materials, which were used with the typical ancient Egyptian creativity to build monuments of their civilization, houses but also tombs. The cemetery of Tell el-Farkha serves as an example since it preserved numerous graves of the Proto- and Early Dynastic date, each of them constructed of locally available sources. The abundant materials such as mud, straw, and reed were the base for construction of all typical burial elements of differentiated value, varying according to the amount of work engaged and the level of technological innovation applied. In fact, the materials became the basic factor that shaped Egyptian burial tradition, influencing the form of canonical graves. A closer analysis of all materials used for an early Egyptian burial shows that the idea of value was much more complex than was previously accepted. Foreign resources were highly valued, but technology was also important for the Egyptians and the final effect mattered at least equally, if not even more than the price and rarity of applied materials. Our excavation project was supported by experimental archaeological undertakings, as well as ethnographic studies, which gave us more data to better interpret the economic and social meaning of the ancient materials used as structural elements and furnishing for early Egyptian tombs.

The Background

The site of Tell el-Farkha is located in the eastern Nile Delta, approximately 120 km northeast from Cairo in the Daqahliya province. From north and west it is surrounded by cultivated land, while from south and east it borders on the modern village of Ghazala, quickly growing and constantly endangering the site. Remains of the ancient settlement, along with the cemetery belonging to it, date back from the times of the Lower Egyptian culture activity to the Old Kingdom, having witnessed a millennium of human presence. The site, which is presently composed of three mounds, was first discovered in the 1980s and then for two years excavated by an Italian expedition directed by Rodolfo Fattovich (Chłodnicki et al. 1991; 1992). In 1998, the works were

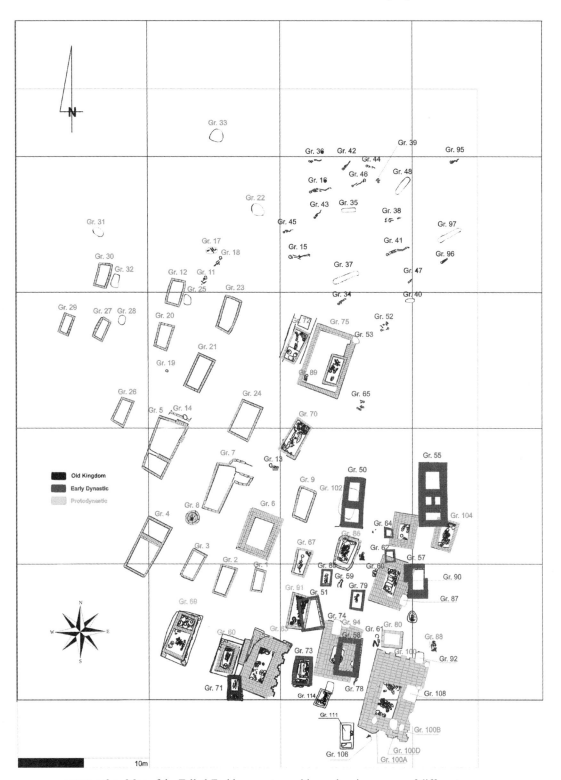

FIGURE 6.1. Map of the Tell el-Farkha cemetery with overlapping graves of different age. Drawing by Marcin Czarnowicz and Karolina Rosińska-Balik.

resumed by a new team, the Polish Archaeological Mission to the Nile Delta, directed by Marek Chłodnicki of the Poznan Archaeological Museum and Krzysztof M. Ciałowicz of Jagiellonian University in Krakow. The site is one of the rather small ones, merely four hectares, therefore at the beginning it seemed a great opportunity to excavate it completely with a focus on observation of life and death in all their aspects at the ancient settlement. However, after twenty years of archaeological activity it became clear that the site hides much more than was supposed—an influential local center of the fourth millennium BCE, with monumental mud-brick architecture, mass beer production, impressive tombs, and examples of the highest quality early Egyptian art, such as gold and ivory figurines, to mention only the most significant discoveries (for more details see Chłodnicki, Ciałowicz, and Mączyńska 2012).

The long history was divided into seven occupational phases. The first two connected with the Lower Egyptian culture, the third one is transitional, the fourth represents a Naqadan character, the fifth Protodynastic, the sixth Early Dynastic, and the final seventh belongs to the Third and Fourth Dynasties of the Old Kingdom. According to our present knowledge, the settlement evolved from a simple Lower Egyptian village, through a local deltaic center of trade and power in the late Predynastic to Early Dynastic times, to be finally abandoned in the Old Kingdom (for more details see, e.g., Ciałowicz 2017). From our point of view, the most interesting are phases 4–6 because it is to them that we can assign the carefully constructed mud-brick tombs found at the site.

2.1. The Cemetery

The first graves were excavated at the site at the Eastern Kom in 2000, and soon it became obvious they are arranged in four separate sepulchral episodes (fig. 6.1). The oldest known example is the so-called Mastaba no. 10, a monumental building approximately eighteen meters by sixteen meters large, composed of the main chamber with a shaft enclosed by three rectangular rooms. The edifice was preserved to the height of about three meters, with its eastern facade covered with a kind of a stucco, probably decorated with niches or waves modeled in mud-brick. The structure dates back to a very distant period of Naqada IIIA2/B1, being among the earliest monumental brick buildings in Egypt (for more details see Ciałowicz and Dębowska-Ludwin 2013). The first regular cemetery discovered so far at the site is dated to the period of Naqada IIIB–C1, that is, the times of Dynasty 0 and the beginning of Dynasty 1, and, as a simplification of the complicated political history of the delta and the site itself, it is called Protodynastic. In fact, graves of the group belong to the most interesting funerary structures ever found in Tell el-Farkha, as they are beautifully constructed and furnished, picturing the highest point of the settlement's prosperity. Many of these tombs are in the characteristic form of a small mastaba, each of them unique and in an almost experimental shape with mud-brick niched facades, clearly traceable remains of cultic activity and carefully composed sets of offerings. Then, after an unexplained occupation break and an episode of housing activity, another cemetery returned to the same location. This time it dates back to the period of Naqada IIIC2–D, and represents a fully stratified community that lived in Tell el-Farkha in the Early Dynastic period, under the reign of early Egyptian pharaohs. The majority of graves in the group represent simple pit inhumations, some of them in reed coffins, usually equipped with very few or no objects. The previously predominating brick structures turned into small constructions of repeatable shapes and offerings types, moreover, the striking attention to detail was replaced by large amounts of badly fired pottery beer jars. The only monumental funerary enclosure of the time makes the impression of a settled social stratification only stronger. Finally, the last scene of sepulchral activity at the site illustrates a group of graves dated to the Third and Fourth Dynasties, which were no longer bricked structures, but only simple pit burials, mostly devoid of any objects. These poor burials also emphasize the falling prosperity of the settlement in Tell el-Farkha, which was soon abandoned (for more detailed discussion on the cemeteries see Dębowska-Ludwin 2018). As the youngest graves at the site were also the simplest and did not implement mud-bricks, in our further discussion we will focus on the three older manifestations of burial tradition practiced in Tell el-Farkha.

Materials

When discussing materials used for graves we need to remember the complexity of an early Egyptian burial. The deceased was the essence, of course, but people of the time believed he or she needed furnishings to cross into the afterlife. The objects required a shelter to fully serve their owner, hence, every grave element was important because only their properly balanced composition opened up perspectives for the future of the deceased. We tend to distinguish architecture from equipment but for the ancient builders both manifestations were equally important, as both served the same goal. That is why we will focus now on three kinds of materials used in a grave: structural, supplementary, and decorative.

Structural materials were used for the sheer tomb construction and are dominated by mud-brick and mud applied as mortar for bounding and coating bricks. Traces of some organic materials are also recovered in brick structures but they seem to play a supplementary role. Thus, thin and often twisted timber planks of low quality and local origin were used as supporting elements in roof constructions, while simple mats or even bunches of reed were implemented to make roof covers. More elaborate woven mats were used as burial chamber inlays and burial covers, whereas reed baskets played the role of low quality coffins. Finally, decorative materials were used for the production of burial equipment. Furthermore, within the category we find pottery (in a way mud, too), organic food products, but also materials interpreted as luxurious—bone and ivory, carnelian, agate, serpentine, basalt, travertine, greywacke, copper, or even gold in the form of various personal objects, such as adornments, stone vessels, or tools.

3.1. Mud-brick

Considering mud-brick as a building material, we should start with its ingredients. The basic component for brick production at that very ancient time was mud, which came from the Nile alluvium and consisted of clay, sand, and some organic remains. All of these elements occurred in different proportions, depending most probably on

FIGURE 6.2. Mastaba no. 10 with its thick walls built with a combination of two brick types. Photograph by Robert Słaboński.

the place of their origin, that is, where by the river the mud was transported from and where it was acquired by people. Also the particular season was of crucial importance, as mud composition was deeply dependent on the Nile floods. Since particular components of bricks are not without significance, in case of deficiency or—the opposite— excess of some ingredients, admixtures must have been provided.

In order to successfully produce bricks, the raw material they were made of must have been plastic but durable. Therefore, in case of shortages of clay in the mud, some straw or chaff was added. Straw, or other organic materials, is responsible for cohesion and the plasticity of the mixture. On the other hand, mud that was too rich in clay required much more time for drying, so a perfect balance was needed. Moreover, to prevent shrinkage and cracking, and to increase the strength of a brick, an admixture

FIGURE 6.3. Forming bricks in a rectangular mold. Photograph by Karolina Rosińska-Balik.

of sand was made. Small fractures of sand filled empty spaces in the mixture and stabilized larger ones, making sand responsible for durability.

When examining large edifices with solid walls at the site of Tell el-Farkha, we noticed they were constructed of two types of bricks (fig. 6.2). The oldest buildings were made of dark bricks with a dominance of mud, but soon another kind of material started to be used widely in the more elaborate structures—light brick containing a lot of sand. There are clear differences in their physical properties, as sandy bricks are much stronger but vulnerable to erosion from rain, while muddy bricks are weaker but more resistant to moisture, which proved especially important in the case of occasional but heavy winter rains. Despite being different in composition, they shared the same shapes.

A typical brick shape observable in all burial structures at Tell el-Farkha is surprisingly similar to modern bricks used in present building—an elongated box, rectangular in section with all edges sharp and straight sides, twice as long as wide. Thus, repeatable form resulted from shaping bricks in a mold—a wooden frame with a handle, as proved by later discoveries and the experiment below (fig. 6.3). Within a single structure bricks shared the same standard size (most often 24 cm × 12 cm × 10 cm), and if in some parts bricks do not match the standard size, it must be the result of later repairs or alterations. The standardization was so deep that the size remained the same, regardless of the type of a particular brick, which could sometimes be used together, side by side, in a single wall. Also, the way of arranging bricks in a wall was the same (for a discussion on particular patterns in brick arrangement see Ździebłowski 2008, and for evidence from nearby sites see, e.g., Midant-Reynes

FIGURE 6.4. Rounded corner inside Mastaba no. 10. Photograph by Robert Słaboński.

et al. 2015), the only difference being the mortar—dark and muddy for walls with a predominance of sandy bricks, and light and sandy for those predominated by the dark ones. Such long-term existence of the brick size standard also proves its practical importance as a handy and versatile building material. Shapes of the structures seem to follow the brick standard, too, since the most typical constructions were rectangular with straight corners and sides. However, we can observe a kind of evolution or improvement in their form, illustrated by rounded corners (fig. 6.4), possible wavy lines or elaborated niches—another hint that suggests bricks were a borrowed invention but their application was local and fully innovative. The fact that all the rounded and uneven building shapes belong only to the most sophisticated structures of the older phases and vanish completely in more typical constructions of the later period strongly supports the assumption. It seems possible that the simplification of architectural forms, characteristic of the sixth occupational phase at Tell el-Farkha, was somehow forced by the simplicity and handiness of a standard brick. This leads us to an experiment.

3.1.1. Brick-Making Experiment

Excavations at the site of Tell el-Farkha resulted in many conclusions concerning the character of bricks and brick buildings, but also raised numerous practical questions. In order to better understand the complex issue, we decided on an experimental production of mud-bricks at the site, which indeed provided several insights concerning

FIGURE 6.5. Experimental drying of bricks. Photograph by Karolina Rosińska-Balik.

the manufacturing process. Connecting our archaeological knowledge with the know-how of a local craftsman, who is still familiar with the largely forgotten ancient technique, we were able to estimate the required ingredients and time needed for the work, as well as the area necessary for drying bricks. Thus, in short, as the experiment itself is the subject of another paper (Rosińska-Balik and Dębowska-Ludwin, forthcoming), to obtain 100 bricks we used 1.2 m³ of mud with natural sand admixture, about 7 kg of straw and 60 L of water. The components created a mixture after around thirty minutes of work, then the mixture aged for about a day to be ready for forming bricks. The forming process took around ninety minutes and finally, the longest stage, drying, which consumed about a week and needed the area of 4.2 m² to properly arrange the bricks so as to facilitate their turning—a procedure essential for drying evenly on all sides to eliminate cracking (fig. 6.5).

With the basic numbers we were ready to simulate the monumental Mastaba no. 10 construction process. It was calculated that, on average, it was possible to manufacture about 75 bricks per hour. With the assumption of a ten-hour workday, a two-worker team could easily make 750 bricks in a day. It is clear that to make the work more efficient, many teams were employed. Such a strategy is confirmed by numerous models showing everyday activities of ancient Egyptians found in noble tombs of the pharaonic age. Even though the models are much younger than the epoch discussed, they obviously refer to the same practices. In the monumental Mastaba no. 10 at the Eastern Kom at Tell el-Farkha one layer consists of about 3000 bricks. Thus, it required 4 days of work, 36 m³ of mud and 210 kg of straw. The bricks left to dry covered an area of

130 m². To erect 3 m high walls, to which height the structure has been preserved, the numbers grow significantly: 135,000 bricks, 1620 m³ of mud, 9300 kg of straw, and the area for drying bricks covers 5850 m². On the basis of our calculation again, a pair of workers was able to lay 2000 bricks per day. Thus, it would take them 83 days to build the structure, plus about 202 days for the brick preparation process, and 7 days for drying. Including off-work days, that is, at least one per Egyptian week of 10 days, it gives us around ten months for the construction and finishing of the building. Of course, the time could be shortened by multiplying working teams, but there were serious limitations, such as the capacity of the settlement. Taking into consideration its size, assigning more than ten teams to the task seems highly improbable, but if it were viable, the time would be reduced to about 10 days of sheer bricklaying. However, such a short time is not the final estimation, as we need to remember brick production and drying, their transport from the manufacturing plant to the construction site, brick seasoning and the time consumed for the preparation of other, perishable elements of the structure, such as, for example, mats, not to mention offerings, which are a separate issue. To sum up, it seems reasonable to estimate the mastaba construction time at about two months, with the assumption of favorable weather conditions and a season free of agricultural work, but not during the annual flood, which in the Nile Delta region severely limited the area that could be used for drying bricks. It becomes clear then that the construction process of such a monumental building was a major organizational challenge.

FIGURE 6.6. Impression of a wooden beam over a roof mat in grave no. 130. Photograph by Joanna Dębowska-Ludwin.

FIGURE 6.7. Modern roof
with wooden beams and mats.
Photograph by Joanna
Dębowska-Ludwin.

3.2. Organic Materials

As was already said, bricks were supplemented with various organic materials of plant
origin. Low quality wood was used for roof constructions. Timber itself has not been
preserved in the local deltaic conditions, but sometimes its impressions or negatives
can be found. As a result, we cannot say anything more detailed about particular plants,
but quite a lot about their application. In the case of graves 67 and 130, a negative of a
wooden, rather thin plank was found. In both graves a single beam was placed perpen-
dicularly in about the middle of the structure length to hold a mat of local reeds that
played the role of the roof. More details were preserved in grave 130 (fig. 6.6), where two
mats were uncovered: one of them placed on the top of burial chamber brick walls and
the second one located over the first one with a beam in between them. It is worth mentioning that the mats were made of long reeds tied together and placed parallel (the lower
mat) or perpendicular (the upper mat) to the grave length. Soon, it became clear that the
practice is another example of long-lasting permanence, when in an old and abandoned,
but modern house built in the mud-brick technique close to the site, we observed the
same type of roof construction with poor quality wooden beams supporting a roof made
of two mats of long reeds placed perpendicular and parallel to the beams (fig. 6.7).

A more elegant form of a roof construction was probably also a kind of screen made
of thin wooden slats arranged crosswise (fig. 6.8), which was found by the entrance of
a vertical shaft leading to the burial chamber in Mastaba no. 10. Unfortunately, it has

FIGURE 6.8. Wooden screen in Mastaba no. 10. Photograph by Robert Słaboński.

been preserved only partially over the brick walls of the shaft, so the interpretation is mainly based on the place of discovery and analogies to other, better preserved roof constructions of similar age. Regardless of its actual function, the unique screen was a structural element of the monumental building.

Apart from simple reed mats used for roofing, also more elaborate examples were commonly used in burials, such as inlays in chambers, or a kind of blanket covering the deceased and their offerings from above. Such an application was probably meant to separate or even protect bodies deposited in graves from direct contact with the ground. In this case the mats were woven from local grasses, most often in a checked design. Once again, the preservation state did not make it possible to identify particular plant species, as all the mats were found in the form of white, mineralized fibers, which are merely a depiction of the objects originally placed in tombs, but clear enough to provide some details of their woven design (fig. 6.9).

Finally, at this point it is worth mentioning the baskets used in some graves as coffins. The story of their preservation is the same as of other organic materials at the site, so the only details we can discuss are their shape and function. They were found in a series of burials of the Early Dynastic cemetery at the site of Tell el-Farkha, always in simple pit graves without bricks, where the pit was completely filled with a coffin (fig. 6.10). Very often the deceased buried inside were devoid of equipment, and even if they were offered something, it was a humble set of few jars. The baskets themselves were rectangular in shape, with slightly rounded corners, which was the result of the plaiting technique, and just as big as a highly contracted human body placed inside. Some of them could have had similarly made lids, others were covered with mats.

FIGURE 6.9. Detail of a mat inlay in grave no. 9. Photograph by Robert Słaboński.

FIGURE 6.10. Negative of a reed coffin in grave no. 135. Photograph by Robert Słaboński.

3.3. Materials for Burial Offerings

Early Egyptian graves would not be complete without offerings. The main category of objects was food (rarely preserved and, as it seems, always of local origin) and pottery, which as a separate subject will not be included in the discussion. It should be added that pottery from graves at Tell el-Farkha forms a large and diversified corpus, which was changing over time to become the basic dating factor for particular burials (for more details see, e.g., Jucha 2012). However, vessels from the graves represent typical forms characteristic of the adjacent settlement (popularity of various forms differs but the collection remains the same), all being locally produced from local sources. We observe a certain pattern of pottery vessel selection in favor of cylindrical jars, plates, bowls, and large wine and beer jars, but here the key seems to be the function of vessels, namely serving and storing food, with no special attention paid to their extra value or imported origin. So, as a rule, the pottery in the Tell el-Farkha graves seems to be only the packaging, rather than an offering in itself.

Leaving aside food and pottery, we come across other materials used for the production of objects deposited in graves. Some of them are seen today as luxurious, but often, this interpretation is based only on the rarity of the material they were made of, with no special attention being paid to the actual value for their ancient owners. In the case of Tell el-Farkha these were stones, metals, and bone, used for the production of personal adornments, cosmetic items, vessels, tools, and some other exceptional and rarely represented types of objects.

3.3.1. Stones

The most common material for nonpottery offerings was various types of stones. The eye-catching kinds, such as carnelian, agate, amethyst, steatite, serpentine, or hematite, accompanied by more frequently used limestone, quartz, and greywacke, were chosen for beads (Rosińska-Balik 2013), which originally created long strings arranged in necklaces or bracelets (fig. 6.11). This kind of offerings was found in merely 20 percent of graves, three-quarters of which belong to the Protodynastic cemetery, and are usually associated with carefully built and equipped small mastabas. The most typical bead shape was squat barrel-like made of carnelian, most probably of local origin and locally produced, which is indicated by little bead workshops, discovered in another area of the site, that is, at the Central Kom (Chłodnicki 2017). Other stones might have been imported, but taking into consideration the relative rarity of noncarnelian beads in the Tell el-Farkha graves, once again, it can be inferred that people collecting offerings relied on local resources.

Another category of stone objects offered to the deceased are vessels, most often in the form of bowls, plates, cylindrical jars, squat barrel jars, or miniature items (Pryc 2012, 299–304), that is, types practical for serving food and used as small containers. They were made of travertine and basalt, supplemented by occasionally used limestone, sandstone, and agate. In general, less than 20 percent of graves at the site were supplied with this kind of offerings. About a half of the discoveries come from the Protodynastic tombs, mostly in the form of a small mastaba. In that period, the most popular were deep basalt bowls and miniature vessels of various stones, composed in

FIGURE 6.11. Colorful set of stone beads from grave no. 130. Photograph by Robert Słaboński.

colorful sets of diversified types, while at the Early Dynastic cemetery typical were deposits of small or miniature jars of travertine in very repeatable shapes, registered in small brick tombs, or as single items in simple pit graves with reed coffins.

The production of stone vessels most probably took place in specialized workshops, as it was obviously much more challenging than making beads of carnelian, because of accessibility of sources and the minimal size and quality of a block useful for further processing. The vessels registered in graves of Tell el-Farkha represent typical objects known from many other sites throughout Egypt, so they might have been imported from such specialized factories, especially when we think about the closest available resources, which are rather remote from the site: Wadi Gerravi at the Eastern Desert for travertine (Klemm and Klemm 2008, 148), Abu Zabal at the outskirts of modern Cairo for basalt (Mallory-Greenough, Greenough, and Owen 1999), Gebel Ahmar near Heliopolis, a modern part of Cairo, for sandstone (Aston et al. 2000: 53), the Nile Valley between Cairo and Esna for limestone (Aston, Harrell, and Shaw 2000, 28–29), or Wadi Abu Gerida at the Western Desert for agate (Aston, Harrell, and Shaw 2000, 26). On the other hand, the picture was not so homogenous, since a sort of local manufacturing or at least repairing was executed at the site, too, which is suggested by the presence of a workshop found at the Western Kom of Tell el-Farkha (Jórdeczka and Mrozek-Wysocka 2012, 291–94).

Finally, a specific type of stone items registered in graves is cosmetic palettes made of greywacke, quite often found with matching grinders (Buszek 2012). At the site they represent shield, zoomorphic, and—most often—geometric shapes with an engraved frame decoration of two or three parallel lines (fig. 6.12). Their forms are typical of the period they represent, the closest possible source of material for their production is Wadi Hammamat (Klemm and Klemm 2008, 297), so it seems likely they were

FIGURE 6.12. Cosmetic palette with a grinder from grave no. 94. Photograph by
Robert Słaboński.

imported objects, used for cosmetic purposes, as they are often visibly worn out in
the center and sometimes preserve remains of some colorants. Numerous discoveries of parts of these objects in settlement layers suggest they were typical personal
items, which is why they were also deposited in the most well-furnished graves of the
Protodynastic cemetery, being absent in younger burials.

3.3.2. Metals

Metals are rarely found in the early history of Egyptian civilization, probably because
they were imported, traded, valuable, and almost always reworked. That is why discoveries of metal object are exceptional, but still present in the graves of Tell el-Farkha.
The most often found material at the site is copper in the form of personal adornments,
such as bracelets or real tools/weapons of various types: adzes, awls, knives, and
harpoons (Czarnowicz 2012). All of them were real and heavy items with clear traces
of use, deposited close to the deceased bodies, in most cases in older, Protodynastic
graves, again those of massive mud-brick structure and carefully collected offerings.
So far, no signs of copper processing have been found at the site, and while every copper item represents a unique discovery, it is highly probable that this kind of objects
was imported as ready-to-use or partially formed tools/weapons/ornaments. Unfortunately, we do not have a clue to the question why some deceased were honored with
such an exceptional offering, when the richest tombs at the site were devoid of such
items. Was it dependent on the profession of a particular grave owner, or their involvement in copper trade? Regrettably, these are the questions we cannot answer now.

Another example of metals in the graves of Tell el-Farkha is a unique discovery of a
stone pendant covered with a golden leaf, which was found in grave 6, a representative
of the Protodynastic cemetery. This triangular pendant decorated with a plaited plant
design was the central part of a completely preserved necklace (fig. 6.13), composed of

FIGURE 6.13. Stone pendant covered with golden foil from grave no. 6. Photograph by Robert Słaboński.

red carnelian and white limestone barrel-shaped beads deposited on a neck of an approximately twelve-year-old child buried in a small beautifully constructed mud-brick mastaba. Although other examples of golden beads were attested at the site (see Dębowska-Ludwin, Rosińska-Balik, and Czarnowicz 2015), this is the only case—so far—connected with burials. The uniqueness of the find proves it was an imported object, not just material, offered to a member of a wealthy family, who died prematurely—a hint that the society was already stratified, or at least, at the beginning of the way.

3.3.3. Bone

Bone implements (Kurzyk 2012, 366–69) registered in graves were made of mammal skeletons, as far as it can be determined, mostly of goat/sheep, sometimes of hippopotamus, and although the accessibility of materials differed significantly, they were all of local origin. Hence, it seems that in this case the material itself was rarely valuable, the feature that made the objects luxurious was the way in which they were produced—often miniature objects with detailed decoration, and what they were meant to be used for—many cosmetic items, such as miniature containers in the form of cylindrical vessels (fig. 6.14) or little fish boxes representing *Tilapia Nilotica* for some, most probably, precious beauty products found in grave 24. Other types of bone objects had more practical function (awls and spoons), or were used for entertainment as game pieces of hippopotamus tooth found in grave 108, but here again they share the same detailed workmanship, which makes each of the items a separate little work of art. Interestingly, the vast majority of bone discoveries comes from the older, Protodynastic tombs of brick construction, with only two graves, numbers 51 and 108, of the Early Dynastic period that contained few bone objects, which suggests once more that at Tell el-Farkha the prospering society of the Protodynastic period was deeply absorbed by the form of a burial, contrary to later times. Moreover, the particular value of a tomb

FIGURE 6.14. Bone miniature
cylindrical vessel in grave
no. 24. Photograph by
Robert Słaboński.

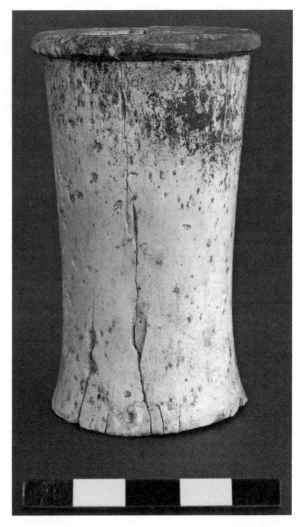

FIGURE 6.14. Bone miniature cylindrical vessel in grave no. 24. Photograph by Robert Słaboński.

was seen rather as the workload connected with the production of every little element of the whole, rather than a simple distinction between local and imported material.

Conclusion

The site of Tell el-Farkha shows that an early Egyptian grave was built of many materials, but the vast majority of them were of local origin. All structural elements and commonly represented types of offerings were made of local mud and plants—gifts of the Nile. Our overview shows that various imported materials were also included in grave goods, but their presence was obviously considered as additional and rather decorative, as if it was nice to have such a beautiful item, but even the richest did not feel obliged to include them in their offerings. On the other hand, the most important factor that influenced the choice of objects and structure types, was their value, seen more as time expenditure and labor investment.

The most elaborate tombs were beautifully equipped and constructed of mud-bricks. The regular and standardized shape of the building material influenced typical shapes of structures, including graves, which after a short period of experimentation were dominated by rectangular elongated forms with straight sides and angles. Mud-brick proved to be a very efficient material, which, with its multistep and time-consuming production process, induced a complicated organization of work, the basis of social structure of the Egyptian civilization. The material proved to be stable, durable, and humidity resistant but was not flexible enough for roof constructions, which is why the basic mud material was supplemented by plants. Various regionally abundant trees, reeds, and grasses were added to the structures to form roofs, however, they were also limited by their length and strength. Short and low quality wooden beams made it possible to build only simple roofing structures over narrow rooms, mats added to the beams had to be large and numerous, and still needed extra support in the form of thick walls. All these elements contributed to a successful building project, which was based on locally accessible sources and was only possible thanks to an appropriate organization and manpower. Luxurious materials, as they are interpreted on the basis of their rarity or imported origin, played nothing but a decorative role, being only an addition, while the most valued and impressive achievement was coordination of work. Was it part of the local Lower Egyptian legacy that even the largest structures were equipped with so few objects, compared to the size of the burial chamber? This is another question we cannot answer; however, we should not underestimate the importance of large and well-coordinated projects, as they became the foundation of the pharaonic state on the Nile.

Many of the preferred building materials introduced in antiquity proved handy and efficient, so practical that they lasted almost till the present time. If it weren't for the breakthrough in modern construction technologies of the last twenty years, so evident in Egypt, which has made it possible to build fast, cheap, and high, the mud structures which are traditional but better adapted to the local climate, would still be popular, and wouldn't have become merely relics of the past.

BIBLIOGRAPHY

Aston, Barbara G., James A. Harrell, and Ian Shaw. 2000. "Stone." Pages 5–77 in *Ancient Egyptian Materials and Technology*. Edited by Paul T. Nicholson, and Ian Shaw. Cambridge: Cambridge University Press.

Buszek, Artur. 2012. "Cosmetic Palettes." Pages 315–22 in *Tell el-Farkha I: Excavations 1998–2011*. Edited by Marek Chłodnicki, Krzysztof M. Ciałowicz, and Agnieszka Mączyńska. Poznan: Poznan Archaeological Museum; Krakow: Krakow Institute of Archaeology, Jagiellonian University.

Chłodnicki, Marek. 2017."Early Dynastic Bead Workshops at the Central Kom of Tell el-Farkha." *Études et Travaux* 30:211–19.

Chłodnicki, Marek, Krzysztof M. Ciałowicz, and Agnieszka Mączyńska, eds. 2012. *Tell el-Farkha I: Excavations 1998–2011*. Poznan: Poznan Archaeological Museum; Krakow: Krakow Institute of Archaeology, Jagiellonian University.

Chłodnicki, Marek, Rodolfo Fattovich, and Sandro Salvatori. 1991. "Italian Excavations in the Nile Delta: Fresh Data and New Hypotheses on the Fourth Millennium Cultural Development of Egyptian Prehistory." *Rivista di Archeologia* 15:5–33.

———. 1992. "The Italian Archaeological Mission of the C.S.R.L.-Venice to the Eastern Nile Delta: A Preliminary Report of the 1987–1988 Field Season." *CRIPEL* 14:45–62.

Ciałowicz, Krzysztof M. 2017. "New Discoveries at Tell el-Farkha and the Beginnings of the Egyptian State." *Études et Travaux* 30:231–50.

Ciałowicz, Krzysztof M., and Joanna Dębowska-Ludwin. 2013. "The Origin of Egyptian Mastabas in the Light of Research at Tell el-Farkha." *Études et Travaux* 26:153–62.

Czarnowicz, Marcin. 2012. "Copper Tools." Pages 345–56 in *Tell el-Farkha I: Excavations 1998–2011*. Edited by Marek Chłodnicki, Krzysztof M. Ciałowicz, and Agnieszka Mączyńska. Poznan: Poznan Archaeological Museum; Krakow: Krakow Institute of Archaeology, Jagiellonian University.

Dębowska-Ludwin, Joanna. 2018. "Socio-Economic Changes in the Early Egyptian Society as Reflected by Graves of the Tell el-Farkha Cemetery." Pages 21–30 in *The Eastern Nile Delta in the Fourth Millennium BC*. Edited by Krzysztof M. Ciałowicz, Marcin Czarnowicz, and Marek Chłodnicki. Krakow: Institute of Archaeology, Jagiellonian University in Krakow.

Dębowska-Ludwin, Joanna, Karolina Rosińska-Balik, and Marcin Czarnowicz. 2015. "Golden Beads in the Context of the Lower Egyptian Culture." *Archéo-Nil* 25:45–56.

Jórdeczka, Maciej, and Małgorzata Mrozek-Wysocka. 2012. "Stone Working Tools and Workshops." Pages 279–96 in *Tell el-Farkha I: Excavations 1998–2011*. Edited by Marek Chłodnicki, Krzysztof M. Ciałowicz, and Agnieszka Mączyńska. Poznan: Poznan Archaeological Museum; Krakow: Krakow Institute of Archaeology, Jagiellonian University.

Jucha, Mariusz A. 2012. "Pottery from the Cemetery." Pages 77–86 in *Tell el-Farkha I: Excavations 1998–2011*. Edited by Marek Chłodnicki, Krzysztof M. Ciałowicz, and Agnieszka Mączyńska. Poznan: Poznan Archaeological Museum; Krakow: Krakow Institute of Archaeology, Jagiellonian University.

Klemm, Rosemarie, and Dietrich D. Klemm. 2008. *Stone and Quarries in Ancient Egypt*. London: British Museum.

Kurzyk, Michał. 2012. "Bone Implements." Pages 357–74 in *Tell el-Farkha I: Excavations 1998–2011*. Edited by Marek Chłodnicki, Krzysztof M. Ciałowicz, and Agnieszka Mączyńska. Poznan: Poznan Archaeological Museum; Krakow: Krakow Institute of Archaeology, Jagiellonian University.

Mallory-Greenough, Leanne M., John D. Greenough, and J. Victor Owen. 1999. "The Stone Source of Predynastic Stone Vessels: Mineralogical Evidence for Quarries in Northern Egypt." *Journal of Archaeological Science* 26:1261–72.

Midant-Reynes, Béatrix, Nathalie Buchez, Gaëlle Bréand, François Briois, Julien Cavero, Anne-Sophie Coupey, Morgan De Dapper, Nathalie Delhopital, Aline Emery-Barbier, Rachid el-Hajaoui, Samuel Guérin, Frédéric Guyot, Christiane Hochstrasser-Petit, Joséphine Lesur, Mathilde Minotti, Ilona Regulski, Jérôme Robitaille, Loic Torchy, and Yann Tristant. 2015. "Tell el-Iswid 2006–2010: The Archaeology of the Eastern Nile Delta in the Fourth Millennium BC." Pages 37–56 in *Aegyptus Est Imago Caeli: Studies Presented to Krzysztof M. Cialowicz on His 60th Birthday*. Edited by Mariusz A. Jucha, Joanna Dębowska-Ludwin, and Piotr Kołodziejczyk. Krakow: Institute of Archaeology.

Pryc, Grzegorz. 2012. "Stone Vessels." Pages 297–314 in *Tell el-Farkha I: Excavations 1998–2011*. Edited by Marek Chłodnicki, Krzysztof M. Ciałowicz, and Agnieszka Mączyńska. Poznan: Poznan Archaeological Museum; Krakow: Krakow Institute of Archaeology, Jagiellonian University.

Rosińska-Balik, Karolina. 2013. "Polish Excavations at Tell el-Farkha (Ghazala) in the Nile Delta: Preliminary Report 2011–2013; Beads from the Eastern and Western Koms 1998–2013; General Remarks." *Archeologia* 64:134–38.

Rosińska-Balik, Karolina, and Joanna Dębowska-Ludwin. Forthcoming. *Mud-brick Building in Ancient Egypt: An Experimental Approach*.

Ździebłowski, Szymon. 2008. "Some Remarks on the Earliest Settlement Mud-brick Structures in Egypt." *GM* 217:111–22.

CHAPTER 7

Computer Analytics in Chronology Testing and Its Implications for the Date of the Exodus

David A. Falk

I AM GRATEFUL to have the opportunity to contribute to this Festschrift in Jim's honor. I first met Jim at Trinity Evangelical Divinity School as a student, and he encouraged me to pursue research in Egyptology. He provided sound advice and direction for me as a student while giving me the freedom to follow the evidence wherever it might lead. Even though I am no longer his student, I hope that this contribution serves to honor my friend Jim.

Approximately midway through my doctoral research, I had begun to take an interest in chronology and began to notice that not all chronologies were created equal. Specifically, I noticed that when a proposed chronology failed to gain scholarly traction it was often because it conflicted with an objective fact that linked one ruler with another ruler elsewhere, putting dates of the two rulers out of synch. With that understanding, I began work in 2014 on a computer analytics project with the objective of being able to test chronologies for internal consistency based upon the synchronisms found in the ancient Near East. That project, *Groundhog: Chronology Test Laboratory*, was completed in early 2017 and ultimately became a test bed to create and validate chronological hypotheses.[1]

Then in November 2017, I was asked to participate in a debate on the date of the exodus at the meeting of the Evangelical Theological Society. During that debate I advocated the position that one should follow the evidence instead of advancing a dogmatic position concerning the date, a position that I still hold. However, in preparing for that debate, I noticed that one's view regarding the date of the exodus was often strongly tied to specific perspectives on ancient Egyptian chronology. Since the tie between chronology and the date of the exodus was so strong, it also seemed natural to test hypotheses on the date of exodus by computer analytics where such a hypothesis proposed a distinct chronology.

Many views exist today as to the identity of the king of Egypt during the exodus and the exodus's corresponding date. Insofar as these dates are based upon historical, archaeological, or exegetical arguments, this paper will critically assess five hypotheses on the date of the exodus and will test each hypothesis for internal consistency using (where applicable) computer analytics as a means of assessment.[2]

---

1. A detailed technical overview and live view of *Groundhog: Chronology Test Laboratory* can be located at http://www.groundhogchronology.com. *Groundhog* was first presented in David A. Falk, "Groundhog: Preliminary Results of a Computational Method for Validating Chronologies" (paper presented at the Sixty-eighth Annual Meeting of the American Research Center in Egypt, Kansas City, MO, 21–23 April 2017).

2. This paper will only consider positions that hold to the exodus as a historic event. Biblical minimalism and other skeptical views will not be engaged as those views persist as philosophical positions, that is, universal negations, which by definition can be subjected to neither computer analytics nor validity testing.

A Traditional Date of the Exodus?

An inevitable issue that emerges with the date of the exodus concerns the role that an absolute date plays in tradition. The reasoning follows along the lines that a suggested date of the exodus runs afoul of the traditions of the church and must be the product of secularism. While an appeal to tradition is dubious on logical grounds, tradition is nonetheless persuasive among those who hold the Bible in high esteem. And without addressing this question adequately, computer analytics, despite being based upon pure mathematics, would probably have little traction.

Hence, the question of the exodus date as a tradition is perhaps as important as the debate on the date itself. Prima facie, those that hold to an early date as "tradition" imply that this is a belief that has been passed down from generation to generation. But even if such a belief were traditional, what kind of tradition would this be? Would it be the unwavering tradition of the apostolic faith once for all given to the saints passed down from the apostolic sees, or would this be a recent dogma that has become recognized as a tradition? And even so, is there a sound reason for the faithful to adopt a tradition without reflection? Therefore, this question does then demand an answer as to whether any commonly cited traditional date of the exodus can live up to being a tradition.

Perhaps, the first suggested absolute date for the exodus descends from Hebrew traditions that were formalized in the medieval period and were first introduced in late antiquity by Rabbi Hillel Hanassi (344).[3] Jewish tradition dated the exodus to AM (*Anno Mundi*) 2448, which is 1312 BCE in the Gregorian calendar.[4] At first blush, this date is closer to the commonly recognized late date (ca. 1250 BCE) than it is to the commonly recognized early date (ca. 1440 BCE), and much of the trajectory for the late date is initially based upon the Hebrew date.

Joseph Scaliger was probably the first Western scholar to attempt to establish a chronology using a mixture of archaeoastronomy, biblical texts, and Byzantine Greek manuscripts that flooded into Europe after the fall of Constaninople in 1453. Scaliger dated the exodus by beginning with the date of the flood AM 1656, adding the birth of Abram (+292 years), then added 75 years until the birth of his son followed by the 430 years for the Egyptian sojourn to derive the date AM 2453, fixing the date of the exodus to 1495 BCE.[5]

Bishop Ussher published his chronology in 1654.[6] Ussher relied upon the belief that four thousand years had passed between the creation of Adam and the birth of Christ, and adjusted the date for Dionysius Exiguus's error in dating the birth of Christ; thus, appealing to the Hebrew *Anno Mundi* calendar to obtain a 4004 BCE date of creation.[7]

---

3. Ludwig Ideler, *Handbuch der mathematischen und technischen Chronologie* (Berlin: Rücker, 1825), 1:569–80.

4. *Anno Mundi* (AM) is a calendar system that starts with a presumed year of creation and counts forward. Several AM calendar systems existed each with different dates of creation. The Byzantine AM calendar began its epoch in 5509 BCE Julian, and the Hebrew calendar began in 3761 BCE Julian, with other luminaries offering other dates for the epoch. For the date, see Jewish Chronicle, "The Date of the Exodus," *Littell's Living Age* 195.2518 (1892): 64.

5. Joseph Scaliger, *Opus novum de emendatione temporum* (Geneva: Typis Roverianis, 1629), 780.

6. Rob Iliffe, "Biblical Chronology," in *Encyclopedia of the Scientific Revolution from Copernicus to Newton*, ed. Wilbur Applebaum (New York: Garland, 2000), 134.

7. For Dionysius's error, see Anne O'Connor, *Finding Time for the Old Stone Age: A History of Palaeolithic Archaeology and Quaternary Geology in Britain, 1860–1960* (Oxford: Oxford University Press,

Ussher calculated his chronology by taking the only fixed date he thought that he could rely upon, the creation epoch, and counting forward through the generations of Genesis. Thus, contrary to what is commonly assumed, Ussher did not date the exodus according to Solomon's foundation of the temple of the Lord (1 Kgs 6:1) but calculated the date of the exodus (1491 BCE) from the moment of creation and only then added 480 years to get the date for Solomon's declaration. Both Scaliger and Ussher used lunar dating as their primary corroborative evidence for their dates but the uncertainty involved with those observations precipitated nearly a century of debate that resolved little.

The advent of the middle class in Europe and museums as public institutions during the eighteenth century saw the influx of artifacts from the ancient Near East into Europe. The deciphering of hieroglyphic and cuneiform scripts in the nineteenth century added considerable amounts of extra-biblical data that were able to shed light upon the biblical texts to the extent that in the late nineteenth century people once again started to suggest new dates for the exodus.

With the advent of Egyptology, C. Richard Lepsius suggested that the pharaoh of the exodus was Merenptah and that the exodus occurred in about 1314 BCE, which he determined based upon the traditional Hebrew date correlated with Manetho.[8] J. Swartz made the suggestion in *The Theological Monthly* that the exodus took place in 1438 BCE during the reign of Thutmose III.[9] An anonymous opinion piece published in *Littell's Living Age* in 1892 mentioned a correction to the date of the Jewish tradition (1312 BCE) using archaeoastronomy coming up with a 1335 BCE date.[10] A. L. Lewis wrote a small piece suggesting that the Israelites could not have entered Canaan prior to 1388 BCE, after the wars of Ramesses II, and dated the exodus between 1430 BCE and 1300 BCE depending upon whether a high or low chronology was ultimately adopted.[11] It can then be observed that much of this debate has been ultimately tied to the issue of Egyptian chronology since as early as 1894 CE. However, only a couple of years later, in 1896, William M. Flinders Petrie discovered the Merenptah Victory Stela that contained the earliest discovered mention of Israel, cementing the veracity of the prevailing view in the minds of mainstream scholarship.

James Orr was perhaps the first person to suggest the modern conception of an early date for the exodus (ca. 1449 BCE), based upon the foundation of the Solomonic Temple and it was his "new hypothesis" that first suggested that the exodus occurred in the first years of Amenhotep II.[12] Orr did this by assuming that the 480 years of 1 Kgs 6:1 had hermeneutical precedence over other texts and connected the Israelites

2007), 1–2. For Ussher's date, see Paul Bahn, "The Antiquity of Man," in *Archaeology: The Key Concepts*, ed. Colin Renfrew and Paul Bahn (New York: Routledge, 2005), 7–8. Year 1 of the Julian calendar is 4713 BCE. So, year 710 of the Julian calendar is 4713–710 which equals 4004 BCE.

8. C. Richard Lepsius, *Letters from Egypt, Ethiopia, and the Peninsula of Sinai: with Extracts from the Chronology of the Egyptians, with Reference to the Exodus of the Israelites*, trans. L. Horner and J. B. Horner (London: Bohn, 1853), 449 (Merenptah); 451, 456 (exodus); 450–51 (Manetho).

9. Old Testament Notes and Notices, "The Pharaoh and Date of the Exodus," *The Old Testament Student* 8 (1889): 302.

10. Jewish Chronicle, "Date of the Exodus," 64.

11. A. L. Lewis, "The Date of the Exodus," *Friends' Intelligencer* 51 (1894): 26.

12. James Orr, *The Problem of the Old Testament: Considered with Reference to Recent History* (New York: Scribner's Sons, 1906), 422–23.

with the Habiru.[13] T. E. Peet figured 1446 BCE for the exodus but was open to the possibility that 1 Kgs 6:1 is not a literal number.[14] Peet seems to have been aware of both
Orr's hypothesis and the Merenptah hypothesis but ultimately refused to pick a side.[15]
It is clear by the time of Peet that the Orr hypothesis had gathered enough steam to
become synonymous with a traditional position. It is remarkable to observe just how
rapidly a forcefully presented view can become recognized as tradition.

Since Orr's publication, his hypothesis has been republished many times by several
authors with only minor variations. Perhaps, the most successful of these republica-
tions was the book by James W. Jack, which popularized Orr's views in 1925.[16] Jack
maintained all the features of Orr's hypotheses but expanded it to a book length,
ascribing the exodus to about 1445 BCE and identifying Amenhotep II as king of the
exodus. Jack connected the Israelites with the Hapiru but as a proponent of the Document Hypothesis he dealt with the problem of the appearance of Rameses in the biblical text by saying that it was a later change by redactors. But Jack also recognized the
late date as the "traditional school" and his own theory as the nontraditional position.[17]

But Jack would be by no means the final copy of the Orr hypothesis, which was
recapitulated by Theodore Robinson, A. Lucas, Bryant Wood, and Douglas Petrovich.[18] And despite being fodder for the unimaginative expository mind, the position
was not by any means universally accepted. Even early on, the position faced criticism. H. H. Rowley critiqued Lucas's rendition of the hypothesis for "concentrating
on one biblical text to the exclusion of all others, and on one archaeological theory,
to the exclusion of all others, so he concentrates on one site to the neglect of all
others."[19] That "one site" was Jericho, the destruction of which John Garstang dated
to the fifteenth century BCE. Already in 1941, cracks were appearing in Garstang's
conclusion, which William F. Albright noted was "devoid of concrete archaeological
foundation."[20] This was before Kathleen Kenyon put the final nail in the coffin of the
fifteenth century destruction theory.[21]

Albright's critique of Garstang's conclusions created a visceral reaction among
conservative scholarship in the latter half of the twentieth century; for example,
John J. Bimson in the 1970s made strides to paint Albright and other proponents of
the late exodus view as the opponents to conservative scholarship while advocating
strongly for an early dating tradition suggesting that the exodus took place around

13. Ibid., 424.

14. T. Eric Peet, *Egypt and the Old Testament* (Liverpool: University of Liverpool Press, 1922), 112.

15. Ibid., 120–21.

16. James W. Jack, *The Date of the Exodus in the Light of External Evidence* (Edinburgh: T&T Clark, 1925).

17. L. E. Binns, review of *The Date of the Exodus*, by J. W. Jack, *Theology* 13 (1926): 175.

18. Theodore H. Robinson, "The Date of the Exodus," *ExpTim* 47 (1935): 53–55. A. Lucas, "The Date of the Exodus," *PEQ* 73 (1941): 110–21. Bryant G. Wood, "The Rise and Fall of the Thirteenth-Century Exodus-Conquest Theory," *JETS* 48 (2005): 475. Douglas Petrovich, "Amenhotep II and the Historicity of the Exodus-Pharaoh," *MSJ* 17 (2006): 81–110.

19. H. H. Rowley, "The Date of the Exodus," *PEQ* 73 (1941): 155.

20. For the cracks appearing, see Rowley, "Date of Exodus," 154. William F. Albright, "The Israelite Conquest of Canaan in Light of Archaeology," *BASOR* 74 (1939): 23; Albright, "The Kyle Memorial Exca-vation at Bethel," *BASOR* 56 (1934): 10.

21. John Garstang and J. B. E. Gartstang, *The Story of Jericho*, 2nd ed. (London: Marshall, Morgan & Scott, 1948), 177–78.

1446 BCE.[22] Most of these negative critiques ultimately failed to establish whether an early dating tradition ever existed. Nevertheless, some later conservative scholars who held to an early date remained unafraid to recognize that the late date had been the dominant view for over a century.[23]

Despite the historical background, Wood promoted Bimson's idea that "the 13th-century exodus-conquest theory was formulated by William F. Albright in the 1930s."[24] While Albright actually moved toward a thirteenth century date view of the exodus earlier in 1921, the significance of Albright's view is not his acceptance of a late date (ca. 1260 BCE) but that he based his view upon a modern Egyptian chronology correlated with what the Bible suggested was the *terminus post quem* of Rameses/Piramesses and Pithom.[25] Albright thought that Tanis was Rameses based upon the Ramesside blocks that were used as the foundation of the Tanite buildings; however, Qantir (not Tanis) was later confirmed to be the site of Piramesses.[26] About seventy-five years later, archaeological teams at Qantir finally confirmed using caesium-magnetometry surveys the *terminus post quem* date of Piramesses to no earlier than the reign of Seti I.[27]

In sum, the early date appears to originate with Scaliger (1629) and takes its modern form with Orr (1906). The late date appears to originate with Rabbi Hillel Hanassi (344) and takes its modern form with Albright (1921). When taken in its historical context, all views have pedigrees that were transformed in the light of modernity, and thus no position on the date of the exodus can claim the weight of tradition. Because all dating hypotheses have a relatively recent origin, each hypothesis must be assessed on the basis of its merits and preferably with the help of objective tests such as that done by computer analytics.

Chronology Testing by Computer Analytics

One tool that can be used for computer analytics is *Groundhog: Chronology Test Laboratory*.[28] *Groundhog* can take a chronology and test it against known synchronisms for internal consistency. This software is based upon a five-hundred-year old mathematical method that was espoused by Luca Pacioli.[29] The algorithm used is similar to the double-entry method used in financial accounting. Since many hypotheses for the date of the exodus also depend upon unique chronologies, this makes each

22. John J. Bimson, *Redating the Exodus and Conquest*, 2nd ed., JSOTSup 5 (Sheffield: Almond, 1981), 15, 74.

23. John Rea, "New Light on the Wilderness Journey and the Conquest," *Grace Theological Journal* 2 (1961): 5.

24. Wood, "Rise and Fall," 475.

25. W. F. Albright, "A Revision of Early Hebrew Chronology," *JPOS* 1 (1921): 60, 79; 66; 63.

26. Labib Habichi, *Tell el-Dabʻa I, the Site in Connection with Qantir: The Previous Discoveries, Its Identification and History*, Denkschriften der Gesamtakademie 23 (Vienna: Österreichische Akademie der Wissenschaften, 2001), 120.

27. Irene Forstner-Müller et al., "Preliminary Report on the Geophysical Survey at Tell el-Dabʻa/Qantir in Spring 2008," *AeL* 18 (2008): 97–99.

28. Further information about *Groundhog: Chronology Test Laboratory* can be found at http://www.lagomorph-rampant.com/chronology/index.html.

29. Alan Sangster and Giovanna Scataglinibelghitar, "Luca Pacioli: The Father of Accounting Education," *Accounting Education* 19 (2010): 424.

hypothesis potentially testable by the validity of its contingent chronology. This makes computer analytics an effective new tool for biblical scholars along with the standard literary and exegetical tools.

Since synchronisms are generally objective data and extended inconsistency effect is a possibility, each chronology is tested against all the known synchronisms from the ancient Near East.[30] Each hypothesis is given the presumption of consistency until testing shows otherwise. So, if a chronology is silent or omits certain details, for example, an Egyptian chronology being silent on the chronology of Babylon, omissions will be supplemented with chronological information that is known to be internally consistent that gives the greatest benefit of the doubt to the hypothesis.

Pertaining to the date of the exodus, most hypotheses will either use a conventional Egyptian chronology or a custom chronological framework. Methodologically, *Groundhog* can be done for any unique chronological hypothesis. Where frameworks are nearly identical, for example, the Albright/Kitchen and Rendsburg hypotheses, *Groundhog* testing needs to be done only once. In general, *Groundhog* has shown that the conventional low or low-middle LB Egyptian chronology is internally consistent.[31] The data available for *Groundhog* testing is currently not granular enough to differentiate between variants of the low chronology, that is, Kitchen/Shaw, Hornung/Krauss/Warburton, and Baines/Málek have all been shown to be internally consistent with the synchronisms of the ancient Near East.[32] Other conventional chronologies, like high Egyptian chronologies, have so far resisted attempts to be harmonized without resorting to large gaps between dynasties. Similarly, custom chronological frameworks

---

30. Synchronisms are metadata that are derived from ancient documents such as letters or treaties. In most cases the agents (sender and recipient) from these documents are either explicitly stated or, less often, one of the agents is implied from its contextual propinquity. The determination of these agents is usually not subject to the interpretation of the modern reader. This makes synchronisms a more reliable source for objective data than what is found in the king lists; e.g., the treaty between Ramesses II and Hattusili III mentions the names of both kings and it is thus difficult to take this as anything but two kings ruling contemporaneously. Extended inconsistency effect occurs when a king list shows an inconsistency against lists that are not directly connected by a synchronism; e.g., a change to the Egyptian chronology can change the dates for the Hittite New Kingdom which in turn becomes inconsistent with the Kassite Dynasty of Babylon. These inconsistencies can show up in lists two or three degrees of separation beyond the original change.

31. The following dates typically define Egyptian New Kingdom chronological frameworks:

	Ahmose I	Amenhotep II	Ramesses II
low chronology	ca. 1540–1515 BCE	ca. 1425–1400 BCE	ca. 1279–1213 BCE
low-middle chronology	ca. 1540–1515 BCE	ca. 1425–1400 BCE	ca. 1290–1224 BCE
high chronology	ca. 1565–1539 BCE	ca. 1439–1413 BCE	ca. 1305–1239 BCE

It should be noted that there is currently no middle chronological position for the Eighteenth Dynasty of Egypt. The low-middle chronology is a composite of the middle dates for the Nineteenth Dynasty with the low dates for the Eighteenth Dynasty.

32. Kenneth A. Kitchen, "Regnal and Genealogical Data of Ancient Egypt (Absolute Chronology I), The Historical Chronology of Ancient Egypt, a Current Assessment," in *The Sychronisation of Civilisations in the Eastern Mediterranean in the Second Millennium B.C.*, ed. Manfred Bietak, 2 vols., Contributions to the Chronology of the Eastern Mediterranean 1 (Vienna: Österreichischen Akademie der Wissenschaften, 2000), 1:39–52. Ian Shaw, "Chronology," in *The Oxford History of Ancient Egypt*, ed. Ian Shaw, new ed. (New York: Oxford University Press, 2003), 480–89. Erik Hornung, Rolf Krauss, and David A. Warburton, "Chronological Table for the Dynastic Period," in *Ancient Egyptian Chronology*, ed. Erik Hornung, Rolf Krauss and David A. Warburton, HdO 83 (Boston: Brill, 2006), 490–95. John Baines and Jaromír Málek, *Atlas of Ancient Egypt*, rev. ed. (Oxford: Andromeda, 2002), 36–37.

that implement an alternative understanding of Egyptian chronology will need to be individually tested. As long as the chronological imperatives are sufficiently fleshed out, these views are in most cases suitable for *Groundhog* testing.

Albright/Kitchen, Ramesses II, About 1250 BCE

The Albright/Kitchen hypothesis is probably the most widely accepted hypothesis today among ancient Near East specialists that still profess a historical exodus. Unlike other views on the dating of the exodus, it did not originate from within the field of Old Testament studies but out of Egyptology and is driven by archaeological imperatives.

Albright was the first to suggest a date for the exodus in the mid-thirteenth century BCE based upon a correlation between Tanite and Israelite culture; however, many of these destruction layers were later discovered to be off by a century or two, putting the entire hypothesis in disrepute. However, the hypothesis was reinvigorated by Kenneth Kitchen who noticed that the archaeology of Qantir/Piramesses/Rameses coincided with a thirteenth century *terminus post quem*.[33] This implied that if the biblical text was to be taken at face value then the exodus could happen no earlier than the accession of Ramesses II. James Hoffmeier contributed greatly to this hypothesis by adding to the archaeological evidence.[34] The view has several advantages such as a strong archaeological basis that conformed to the toponymic associations (for example, *terminus post quem* of the toponyms for Piramesses and Tell el-Retaba/Pithom to no earlier than Ramesses II) as well as being a good fit with sound readings of the biblical text and thirteenth century destruction layers at Tel el-Hezbet/Hazor and Tel el-Sultan/Jericho. Despite objections that have been made to the Albright/Kitchen hypothesis, it is unlikely to be supplanted any time in the foreseeable future.

Rendsburg, Ramesses III, About 1175 BCE

The Rendsburg hypothesis dates the exodus to the reign of Ramesses III and is coordinated with the collapse of the Egyptian New Kingdom following the reign of Ramesses IV.[35] Like the Albright/Kitchen hypothesis, the Rendsburg hypothesis generally agrees with a conventional chronology; however, he sets the date of Ramesses III about seven years earlier (1195–1164 BCE). An important feature of the Rendsburg hypothesis is that it purposes a different understanding of the Merenptah Victory Stela, which is that the text is referring to "the Israelites while still in Egypt," a somewhat problematic reading given that "Israel" in the stela is written with the foreign place or foreign people determinative (Gardiner sign T14) and is included in a list of foreign nations. [36]

33. Kenneth A. Kitchen, *Ancient Orient and the Old Testament* (Chicago: InterVarsity, 1966), 57–75.

34. James K. Hoffmeier, *Israel in Egypt: The Evidence for the Authenticity of the Exodus Tradition* (New York: Oxford University Press, 1996).

35. Gary A. Rendsburg, "The Date of the Exodus and the Conquest/Settlement: The Case for the 1100s," *VT* 42 (1992): 516.

36. Ibid., 517. For the Egyptian determinative, see *KRI* 4:19.7.

The theory is skeptical of a long Egyptian sojourn and proposes that Joseph entered Egypt under Seti I (ca. 1294–1279 BCE), Israel was enslaved under Ramesses II, and Moses led the children of Israel out of Egypt around 1175 BCE, "during the Sea Peoples invasion."[37] Rendsburg gives the genealogical records in Numbers priority but is highly skeptical of a "typically exaggerated passage of time."[38] He figures that the entire biblical narrative from beginning of the Egyptian sojourn until entry into the promised land was four to six generations, and Nashshon (Exod 6:23) lived five generations or "150 years before David."[39] If it is assumed that there was one generation from wandering in the wilderness, this implies that the time in the Egyptian sojourn would have been only four to five generations.

The biblical text states that 70 sons of Jacob entered into Egypt (Gen 46:27; Exod 1:5) and that no less than 603,550 persons left Egypt based upon the *beqaʿ* (half-shekel) head tax (Exod 38:24) and that the half-shekel applied to all adults over the age of twenty regardless of gender (Exod 30:14). Rendsburg suggests that this head-tax figure is the result of a later copyist bringing the figure for the number of persons in line with the 600,000 men of Exod 12:37.[40] However, Exod 38:24 is dealing with matters of silver weight not head count.

The fact is that the country with the highest fertility recorded is Niger with 6.76 children/woman.[41] Assuming maximum fertility, the time from eisodos to exodus that it would take to achieve close to the numbers cited above would be no less than six to seven generations with an additional generation taking place in the wilderness, making it is more likely that more than eight generations were involved in the entire narrative.[42] This outcome would also be consistent with readings of Exod 12:40 found in the Samaritan Pentateuch and Septuagint.

---

37. Gary A. Rendsburg, "The Pharaoh of the Exodus—Rameses III." https://thetorah.com/the-pharaoh-of-the-exodus-rameses-iii.

38. Ibid.

39. Rendsburg, "Date of the Exodus and the Conquest/Settlement," 524.

40. Gary A. Rendsburg, "An Additional Note to Two Recent Articles on the Number of People in the Exodus from Egypt and the Large Numbers in Numbers I and XXVI," *VT* 51 (2001): 395.

41. Central Intelligence Agency, *The CIA World Factbook 2016–17* (Washington, DC: U.S. Government Printing Office, 2016), 545.

42. The population calculations are quite straightforward and assume neither extensive polygamy (which was generally *verboten* in Egypt) nor attrition through mortality. If it is assumed that a generation is twenty-five years as Rendsburg does and if the fertility rate is the same as Niger, the following population growth table is obtained:

Generation	Population	Years
0	140	0
1	473	25
2	1599	50
3	5405	75
4	18269	100
5	61749	125
6	208715	150
7	705447	175

It should be noted that the population for generation 0 is based upon the tradition of the 70 sons of Jacob arriving in Egypt (Gen 46:27; Exod 1:5). While recognizing that not all these sons survived to arrive in

The Rendsburg hypothesis leads to some provocative consequences. If we are to accept this version of events, we must also accept that the population that fled Egypt was on the order of about fifty thousand and that this relatively small group of people managed to conquer Canaan. He further calls into question both time frames and demographics. But if either the time frames or the demographics as represented by the biblical texts are to be believed, this would make Rendsburg's four to five generation sojourn and his identification of Ramesses III as king of the exodus difficult to accept.

Bimson, Thutmose III, About 1470 BCE

The Bimson hypothesis follows along the trajectory introduced with Orr's hypothesis of an early date of the exodus with some very notable distinctions. Instead of dating from the foundation of the Solomonic temple, he pegs his date from the 300 years of Jephthah (Jdg 11:26) whom he dates to about 1130 BCE and, contrary to Orr, suggests that the 480 years of 1 Kgs 6:1 was longer than 480 years.[43]

Bimson does not produce a fully fleshed Egyptian chronology to back up his view, although he does deviate from conventional chronology in some important ways. He states that Thutmose III assumed rule from Hatshepsut between 1483 and 1470 BCE.[44] Since Bimson holds that the exodus took place during the first year of Thutmose III's independent rule in 1470 BCE, this sets Thutmose III's reign to about 1492–1438 BCE, just inside the limits proposed by Rita Gautschy's high chronology.[45] While Gautschy's chronology was shown to be internally consistent with *Groundhog* testing, her chronology is implausible because it proposes gaps between contiguous dynasties; for example, a gap between Kassite and Second Isin Dynasties, and extends the Egyptian Third Intermediate period by thirty years without sufficient warrant.

Bimson's evidential approach does not weigh the preponderance of evidence but instead doubles-down upon ambiguity when possible; for example, he claims no relation between the name of the storage city of Rameses (Exod 1:11) and the tying of that name to Ramesses II, a counterintuitive claim given that Piramesses in ancient Egyptian texts uses the throne name of Ramesses II (P. Anastasi 3.1, 12).[46] However, it is arguable if an ancient Egyptian toponymy could sustain this dubious distinction; for example, Alexandria versus Alexander the Great. Furthermore, I wonder how his claim of a paucity of twelfth and thirteenth century settlements helps his claim of a fourteenth century exodus, since arguing for the former also precludes the latter— a problem that he later recognizes after forcefully making his argument.[47]

Overall, Bimson does not deal with the problems associated with the identification of Thutmose III as king of the exodus; for example, that the royal court during

---

Egypt, e.g., Er and Onan (Gen 46:12), for the sake of basic growth calculations a number of 70 is assumed and with each man having a wife to make 140 persons.

43. Bimson, *Redating the Exodus and Conquest* 94.

44. Ibid., 231.

45. Ibid., 230. Rita Gautschy, "A Reassessment of the Absolute Chronology of the Egyptian New Kingdom and Its 'Brotherly' Countries," *AeL* 24 (2014): 141–58.

46. Bimson, *Redating the Exodus and Conquest*, 35.

47. Ibid., 60, 74, 219.

the Eighteenth Dynasty was seated in Thebes and that Thutmose III campaigned for sixteen seasons in the Levant, the first of which occurred in the twenty-third regnal year when Thutmose III chronicled his military victory over Megiddo, a year after Bimson's supposed year of the exodus. This seems contrary to Deut 11:4, which implies that the Egyptian army had not recovered forty years after being destroyed at the Sea of Reeds. Furthermore, Bimson has to resort to unorthodox interpretations; for example, Thutmose III did not conquer the Levantine cities but simply paraded around them.[48] However, given the extensive records of Thutmose III's campaigns and given that during his independent rule Thutmose III established an empire that dominated the region until the Ramesside period and given his influence in Syria, the Bimson hypothesis is hard to view as credible.

Orr/Wood, Amenhotep II, About 1447 BCE

This hypothesis as it exists today is practically a carbon-copy of the hypothesis fleshed out by Jack who plagiarized the ideas of Orr. Jack believed in the Documentary Hypothesis and held that occurrences of Rameses in the biblical texts were redactions by a later editor. This view is popularized today by Bryant Wood and his protégé, Douglas Petrovich.[49] The view forces a strong hermeneutical imperative upon the 480th year in 1 Kgs 6:1 as a numeric 480 solar years, which compels the interpreter to arrive at an early date of the exodus (ca. 1446 BCE). The hypothesis appeals to the use of chronology in the support of its ideological position; however, its proponents must also reject conventional chronology because, as discussed for the Bimson hypothesis (see above), Thutmose III as the Egyptian king of Egypt plays poorly with the exodus account.

Supporters of this view interpret that Moses being eighty when he spoke to Pharaoh (Exod 7:4) and being forced into exile for forty years (Acts 7:30) must mean that Pharaoh's predecessor must have also reigned at least forty years.[50] The sole king of New Kingdom Egypt then that comes close to fulfilling this interpretation is Amenhotep II because his predecessor, Thutmose III was the only king of the Eighteenth Dynasty who reigned for more than forty years. However, their key interpretation has a problem, which is Exod 4:19 when the Lord tells Moses, "Go back to Egypt, for *all the men* who were seeking your life are dead." The text is clear that multiple men wanted to kill Moses, not just pharaoh's predecessor. This means that the predecessor did not have to live the entire forty years of Moses's exile, only the last surviving person who wanted Moses dead.

The Orr/Wood hypothesis hinges upon Amenhotep II being the pharaoh of the exodus. Orr ascribes the accession of Amenhotep II to about 1449 BCE, with the exodus taking place shortly thereafter.[51] Wood's view of the exodus depends upon

48. Ibid., 218–19.

49. Wood, "Rise and Fall," 479, 482. Douglas Petrovich, *The World's Oldest Alphabet* (Jerusalem: Carta Jerusalem, 2016), 11.

50. Petrovich, "Amenhotep II and the Historicity of the Exodus-Pharaoh," 85.

51. Orr, *Problem of the Old Testament*, 422 n. 6.

Amenhotep II being king, dating him to 1453–1419 BCE.[52] Petrovich likewise dates Amenhotep II's reign to 1455–1418 BCE.[53] Modern proponents of the Orr/Wood theory typically defer to Petrovich's dating for Amenhotep II. While all the proponents of this hypothesis must resort to a nonconventional chronology to support this view, Petrovich is the only author to flesh out a chronology supporting this claim.[54]

In order to achieve Amenhotep II reigning during the 1440s, Petrovich expands Egyptian dates to a high chronology stretching out the Eighteenth and Twentieth Dynasties so that the reign of Amenhotep II noses over the 1446 date. The difference between the conventional date and the Wood/Petrovich dates for Amenhotep II is about thirty years. While the Orr/Wood hypothesis tweaks the Egyptian New Kingdom, it generally leaves the remainder of the conventional low chronology intact.

When this chronology was tested with *Groundhog*, the hypothesis was shown to be inconsistent and therefore must be false. Most significantly the expanded Egyptian dynasties are inconsistent with the Kassite dynasty of Babylon (Amenhotep III ↔ Burna-Buriash II [*EA* 6]).[55] His reconstruction of the chronology of the kings of Israel was also found to be inconsistent with accession of King Omri with the thirty-second regnal year of Asa (Omri Б 0 ↔ Asa Б 31 [1 Kgs 16:23]). *Groundhog* testing has shown that the accession of Amenhotep II could not have taken place prior to 1443 BCE.

Rohl, Dudimose, 1447 BCE

David Rohl uses a set of critiques that he calls the "four pillars" of conventional chronology that he uses to cut a "New Chronology" out of whole cloth.[56] Even though he is an agnostic, Rohl has made inroads into the evangelical community with his raconteur style and being featured in the movie *Patterns of Evidence*. Like Orr/Wood, Rohl gives an early date to the exodus (1447 BCE) but rearranges the dynasties into an ultralow chronology lowering the dates by over three hundred years so that the exodus falls on the short reign of Dudimose, an extremely minor king at the rump end of a crumbling Middle Kingdom.[57]

Rohl gives short shrift to most of the 150 synchronisms that define ancient Near Eastern chronology, and as a result he has had to edit his chronology several times

---

52. Wood, "Rise and Fall," 484.

53. Petrovich, "Amenhotep II and the Historicity of the Exodus-Pharaoh," 81–110.

54. Petrovich, *World's Oldest Alphabet*, 234.

55. Synchronisms are abbreviated using specialized notation. Contemporaneous synchronisms use the notation <king 1> ↔ <king 2>. If a synchronism is anchored to the accession of a king, the symbol Б is used with the regnal year. If anchored to the end of a reign, the symbol ә is used with the regnal year. Regnal years are counted from year 0, so if a reign is anchored against the first year of a king's reign, the notation is "Б 0". Sequential synchronisms use the notation <king 2> → <king 1>; these synchronisms derive the dates for <king 1> from <king 2> but not necessarily the reverse; this is because more often than not later kings are used to derive the dates of earlier kings. The application of synchronisms and their classification is a complex subject beyond the scope of this paper.

It should be noted that this paper only reports inconsistencies that have a variance of greater than ±2 years. Inconsistencies of this magnitude exceed the error that could be caused by variations between calendar systems and thus always represent true defects in a chronology.

56. David Rohl, *A Test of Time: The Bible—From Myth to History* (London: Century, 1995) 153.

57. Ibid., 340–41.

over the last thirty years to salvage it. Every book that he has published offers new dates (sometimes with dates differing even within the same book), propping up the hypothesis with ad hoc reasoning.[58] *Groundhog* has tested several variations of Rohl's chronology (the 1995, 2003, and 2007 revisions) and all revisions of the New Chronology fail to show internal consistency.[59]

Conclusion

The computer analytics supplied by *Groundhog* testing successfully contributed to an assessment of all five hypotheses examined in this paper, even in cases where specific chronologies were not supplied. The tests showed two hypotheses to be internally inconsistent (Orr/Wood and Rohl hypotheses). These two hypotheses disqualify themselves from further consideration because of their failure to maintain a consistent position.

Of the three remaining positions that computer analytics showed to be consistent, *Groundhog* testing of the Bimson hypothesis showed that an internally consistent chronology was only possible by resorting to implausible chronological gaps. In addition, the Rendsburg and Bimson hypotheses have problems with the archaeological evidence making them difficult to accept. This leaves only the Albright/Kitchen hypothesis as the most plausible hypothesis. Despite being the most plausible hypothesis, the Albright/Kitchen hypothesis could still have problems with boundary conditions; for example, the LB destruction of Hazor in the late thirteenth century coinciding too

58. Compare dates for Amenemhat III. Rohl (*Test of Time*, 406) suggests an accession date of 1682 BCE; in 2002 (*The Lost Testament: From Eden To Exile; the Five-Thousand Year History of the People of the Bible* [London: Century, 2002], 137), he dates Amenemhat III to 1678–1635 B.C.; and in 2007 (*Lords of Avaris: Uncovering the Legendary Origins of Western Civilization* [London: Century, 2007], 129), he dates Amenemhat III to 1682–1636, but on p. 132 dates him to 1678–1634 BCE.

59. Inconsistencies in Rohl's 2007 chronology were revealed in Azaraiah Б 15 ↔ Menahem Б 0 (2 Kgs 15:17), Azariah Б 15 ↔ Shallum Б 0 (2 Kgs 15:13), Azariah Б 14 ↔ Zachariah Б 0 (2 Kgs 15:8), Joram Б 0 ↔ Jehoshaphat Б 17 (2 Kgs 3:1), Ahaziah Б 0 ↔ Jehoshaphat Б 16 (1 Kgs 22:51), Asa Б 37 ↔ Omri Б 0 (1 Kgs 16:23), Humban-Nikash I Б 0 ↔ Nabonassar Б 4 (Glassner, 195), Ammurapi ↔ Suppiluliuma II (*HDT*, no. 38), Niqmaddu III ↔ Suppiluliuma II (*TLC*, no. 77), Ammistamru II ↔ Tudhaliya IV (*HDT*, no. 36A), Ammistamru II ↔ Tudhaliya IV (*HDT*, no. 37), Niqmaddu II ↔ Mursili II (RS 17.334, 1–19 [Bryce, 200–201]), Shalmaneser II ↔ Mursili II (RS 17.334, 1–19 [Bryce, 200–201]), *Shalmaneser III ↔ Mursili II (*CTH* 172.2, KUB 23.99)—Rohl (*Test of Time*, 502) claims that the "Shalmaneser" in these texts refers to Shalmaneser III not Shalmaneser I and despite the special pleading, this synchronism is inconsistent with his thesis, Tiglath-Pileser III ↔ Nabonassar (Glassner, 195), Shamshi-Adad V ↔ Marduk-balatsu-iqbi (Glassner, 183), Shalmaneser III ↔ Nabu-apla-iddina ə 0 (Glassner, 183), Adad-nerari II ↔ Shamash-mudammiq (Grayson, 148), Adad-nerari II ↔ Shamash-mudammiq (Glassner, 181), Akhenaten ↔ Niqmaddu II (*EA* 49), Amenhotep III ↔ Ammistamru I (*EA* 45), Tudhaliya IV ↔ Tukulti-Ninurta I (RS 34.265 [Dietrich, 103–139]) , Asher-bel-kala ↔ Marduk-shapik-zeri ə 0 (Glassner, 181), Tiglath-Pileser I ↔ Marduk-nadin-ahhe (Glassner, 181; Grayson, 43–44), Ashur-resha-ishi I ↔ Nebuchadnesser I (Glassner, 181), Ashur-dan I ↔ Zababa-shuma-iddin (Glassner, 179), Ninurta-spil-Ekur ↔ Meli-Shipak II (Frahm, n.p.), Enlil-kuduri-usur ↔ Adad-shuma-usur (Glassner, 179), Ashur-nereri III ↔ Adad-shuma-usur (Tablet K. 3045, *ABL* 924), Tukulti-Ninurta I ↔ Kashtiliash IV (Glassner, 179), Adad-narari I ↔ Nazi-Maruttash (Glassner, 179), Enlil-narari I ↔ Kurgalzu II (Glassner, 179), Ashur-uballit I ↔ Kurgalzu II (Glassner, 179), Ashur-uballit I ↔ Kara-hardash (Glassner, 179), Ashur-uballit I ↔ Burna-Buriash II (*EA* 15), Samsi-Addu I ↔ Yasmah-Adad (ARM 1.113 + LAPO 16.36 [Sasson, 23]), Yahdun-Lim ə 0 ↔ Samsi-Addu I, Samsi-Addu I ↔ Hammurabi (WAB 5, 284 , 11f [Thureau-Dangin, 135–139]), Ishbi-Erra Б 0 ↔ Ibbi-Sin ə 0 (Glassner, 125), and Sarlagab ə 0 ↔ Shar-kali-sharri (*RTC*, 118).

close to the beginning of the Israelite conquest. Yet, this view holds up better to the archaeological and chronological evidence than the other proposed hypotheses.

I would, however, suggest one minor clarification to the Albright/Kitchen hypothesis that would bring it in line with the Levantine archaeological evidence and which necessitates only a minor refinement. By acknowledging the reign of Horemheb to fifteen years instead of twenty-eight years and pushing back the accession date of Ramesses II to a middle chronological position (ca. 1289–1223 BCE), this sets the Battle of Kadesh to about 1284 BCE which may set the date of the exodus to about seventeen years earlier than is typically characterized of the Albright/Kitchen hypothesis. This proposed date (ca. 1267 BCE ±15) is within the error tolerances set out by the hypothesis.[60] *Groundhog* testing done for this revision in chronology showed that this minor adjustment is consistent; thus, it is a viable alternative within the pale of the Albright/Kitchen hypothesis.

---

60. Kitchen (*Ancient Orient and the Old Testament*, 61) suggested a possible range of ca. 1260 BCE ±20 when he held that the accession of Ramesses II was in 1290 BCE and suggested that the mean date could move by a decade or more depending upon the accession date. He would later revise the accession to 1279 B.C. (*Pharaoh Triumphant: The Life and Times of Ramesses II* [Mississauga: Benben, 1982], 239) moving the date to a decade later.

CHAPTER 8

Uniting the World: Achaemenid Empire Lists and the Construction of Royal Ideology

Deirdre N. Fulton and Kaz Hayashi

Introduction

Among the monumental inscriptions dating to the Persian period, there are several royal texts that list the subjugated people under the control of the Achaemenid kings. These inscriptions, oftentimes referred to as empire lists provide a register of the peoples who constituted the sizeable Persian Empire.[1] Enumerating one's territorial holdings may be seen in early antecedents from Elam, Mesopotamia, and Egypt, yet their use in Persian-era propaganda reflects the unique ways in which the Achaemenid monarchy perceived, organized, and portrayed their vast empire. The lists are written in the first-person from the voice of the Persian monarch and catalog the nations within the empire.

Empire lists are most numerous in the time of Darius, appearing in foundation charters, monumental empire lists, and also tribute-bearing lists. Following Darius, subsequent Achaemenid rulers also utilized empire lists as well. While the order in which they place the countries is not completely standardized, the empire lists draw some clearly defined boundaries of the geographical realm of the empire. Past studies of these lists have focused on the order of the names as well as the overall statement of control that the Persian monarchy was attempting to convey.[2] Most studies, however, have focused primarily on Darius's Bisitun monument, which is the earliest known Persian example. A more thorough analysis of all of the monumental empire lists reveals that these inscriptions make important imperial claims and their organization is not arbitrary, but rather built on earlier traditions of laying claim to a vast territory, both by naming the place and by alluding to control over the region. Shorter versions of these texts, called boundary lists, are also important to examine since both help establish the ways in which Achaemenid kings organized their empire and asserted dominion over both the center and the periphery. The organization and rhetorical intent offers a glimpse into understanding how the Persian monarchy conceived of its vast territory. An an analysis of the grouping and sequence of both boundary and empire lists and their organization offers us a glimpse into the royal ideology of empire enumeration.

We are both indebted to James Hoffmeier for his guidance in directing formative periods of our education (Fulton, Wheaton College, and Hayashi, Trinity International University). A version of this paper, titled "Organizing the World" was given by Deirdre Fulton at the Annual Meeting of the Society of Biblical Literature, Boston, November 2018.

1. E.g., see Pierre Briant, *From Cyrus to Alexander: A History of the Persian Empire,* trans. Peter T. Daniels (Winona Lake, IN: Eisenbrauns, 2002), 172.

2. Pierre Lecoq, *Les inscriptions de la Perse achéménide* (Paris: Gallimard, 1997).

Earlier Examples of Empire List

Amélie Kuhrt notes, "Elam, Mesopotamia, and Egypt in particular contributed to the emerging formulation of the Persian imagery of power. This can be particularly clearly seen in the Achaemenid royal monuments and iconography, although these traditions were fundamentally and deliberately reshaped in the process of adoption and adaptation."[3] Kuhrt's statement highlights that other empires and regions contributed to Persian royal ideology, specifically the ways in which the Persian Empire lists speak of land and kingship, and also how they envisioned their subjugated nations.[4] Earlier examples are found in Assyrian images of kingship controlling the "four corners of the universe" (*šar kibrāt erbetti*) and "king of the universe" (*šar kiššati*) as well as topographical lists.[5] These royal titularies are found in earlier examples: "king of the universe" is found in third through first millennium royal inscriptions, and "king of the universe" is common in Neo-Assyrian inscriptions but traces back to Sargon of Akkad.[6] Egypt also used royal titularies to enumerate the power of the king, which is most notably seen in the Pharaonic titulary that includes reference to the king as the unifier of Upper and Lower Egypt. Indeed, the unification of these two territories is embodied in the *sekhemti* crown, combining the Hedjet crown of Upper Egypt with the Deshnet crown of Lower Egypt.

Some of the most notable examples of ancient Near Eastern topographical lists come from New Kingdom Egypt. In the example of Egypt, topographical lists can either be classified according to their physical contexts (e.g., triumph-scenes, stelae, temple walls, columns, statue bases, and battle reliefs), or their textual types, which Kenneth Kitchen further divides into (1) encyclopedic lists, (2) regional lists, and (3) lesser lists.[7] Kitchen identifies several "foundation documents" including three copies of Thutmose III's inscription enumerating 116 names, as well as a supplementary list that contains 152 additional names from Karnak, which contain names from the seven regions either under the Egyptian Empire's control or regions they sought to control.[8] Subsequent pharaohs such as Amenophis II and Haremhab appear to extract from earlier lists to form their "lesser lists," and even Sethos I's major list at Karnak

3. Amélie Kuhrt, "State Communication in the Persian Empire," in *State Correspondence in the Ancient World: From New Kingdom Egypt to the Roman Empire*, ed. Karen Radner (New York: Oxford University Press, 2014), 113.

4. See Briant, *From Cyrus to Alexander*, 177.

5. See Paul Garelli, "La conception de la royauté en Assyrie," in *Assyrian Royal Inscriptions: New Horizons in Literary, Ideological, and Historical Anaylsis*, ed. F. M. Fales, OAC 17 (Rome: Instituto per l'Oriente, 1981), 1–5. David S. Vanderhooft, *The Neo-Babylonian Empire and Babylon in the Latter Prophets*, HSM 59 (Atlanta: Scholars Press, 1999), 21.

6. Vanderhooft, *Neo-Babylonian Empire*, 21; William W. Hallo, *Early Mesopotamian Royal Titles: A Philologic and Historical Analysis*, AOS 43 (New Haven: American Oriental Society, 1957).

7. Kenneth A. Kitchen, "Egyptian New-Kingdom Topographical Lists: An Historical Resource with 'Literary' Histories," in *Causing His Name to Live: Studies in Egyptian Epigraphy and History in Memory of William J. Murnane*, ed. Peter J. Brand and Louise Cooper, CHANE 37 (Leiden: Brill, 2009), 129–36. See also Joannes Simons, *Handbook for the Study of Egyptian Topographical Lists Relating to Western Asia* (Leiden: Brill, 1937).

8. Kitchen, "Egyptian New-Kingdom Topographical Lists," 129–36. See earlier works on Thutmose III's toponym lists by Donald B. Redford, "A Bronze Age Itinerary in Transjordan (Nos. 89–101) of Thutmose III's List of Asiatic Toponyms," *JSSEA* 12 (1982): 55–74; Redford, *The Wars in Syria and Palestine in Thutmose III: The Foundations of the Egyptian Empire in Asia*, CHANE 16 (Leiden, Brill, 2003), 43–56;

and Ramesses III's list at Medinet Habu both directly borrow from Thutmose III's foundation document, but also edit their respective list through omitting and adding names.[9] While there may have been a historical reality to these lists, Kitchen observes that they also functioned heraldically "to proclaim the universal dominion of the pharaoh over all lands."[10] Additionally, certain shorter lists referred to as heraldic, function to "symbolize the might of Pharaoh."[11] The concept of land and kingship, therefore, were intricately connected, and the vastness of the king's empire reflected the strength of the king.

The Land in Persian Imperial Ideology

Similar to the Egyptian antecedents, Persian territorial lists had both practical and ideological uses. This connection between land and kingship was also central to royal ideological propaganda. The Persian Empire controlled an immense imperial territory that was divided into provinces known as satrapies.[12] While scholars depend on multiple sources to reconstruct the Achaemenid administration, these empire lists provide the most valuable source of primary evidence.[13] The empire lists include: Darius's Bisitun inscription (DB), two inscription from Darius's tomb at Naqsh-i Rustam (DNa, DNe), Darius's inscription from Persepolis's south terrace wall (DPe), a Babylonian inscription of Darius on a stone slab from Susa (DSaa), an inscription preserved on numerous fragmentary clay tablets from Susa (DSe), a partial inscription on glazed bricks (DSm), a fragmentary text on a marble slab (DSv), the Daiva inscription (XPh), Darius's statue found at Susa (DSab), and the Suez Canal Stela—and the labels accompanying the portrayal of subject peoples on the tomb at Persepolis (A?P/A³Pb) should also be added, totaling twelve "empire lists."[14]

The Land in Praise of Ahura Mazda

Most empire lists either begin with a praise for Ahura Mazda followed by an identification of the king (DNa, DSe, XPh, DZc), or vice versa (DB, DSm).[15] In these introductory lines praising Ahura Mazda, the king acknowledges Ahura Mazda as the creator of the earth and heavens, as well as the giver of kingship (DNa, DZc, DSab,

---

James K. Hoffmeier, *Israel in Egypt: The Evidence for the Authenticity of the Exodus Tradition* (New York: Oxford University Press, 1997), 176–98.

9. Kitchen, "Egyptian New-Kingdom Topographical Lists," 131–32.

10. Ibid.

11. Ibid., 134.

12. For a discussion of the unique characteristics of the Persian Empire, see Richard Stoneman, *Xerxes: A Persian Life* (New Haven: Yale University Press, 2015).

13. Bruno Jacobs and Josef Wiesehöfer identify three groups of primary sources: Herodotus's writings, Alexander historians, and *dahyāva* lists. See Bruno Jacobs, "Achaemenid Satrapies," *Encyclopædia Iranica*, http://www.iranicaonline.org/articles/achaemenid-satrapies; Josef Wiesehöfer, "Provinz (persich)," *Das wissenschaftliche Bibelllexikon im Internet*, http://www.bibelwissenschaft.de/stichwort/31492.

14. Jacobs, "Achaemenid Satrapies," lists eleven of the lists. A twelfth, the tomb at Persepolis, should be included in this list as well.

15. Exceptions include A?P/A³Pb and DNe where no royal titular appears, and in DSab, a royal titular appears on the statue, but not immediately preceding the list of names.

DSe, XPh) and a "large kingdom containing good horses and good men" (DZc).[16] In a few of the empire lists, immediately preceding the catalog of subject peoples, the king credits Ahura Mazda with placing numerous subject nations under the king's rule, as exemplified by the statement "By the favour of Ahura Mazda, these are the countries of which I was king outside Persia" (XPh).[17] Darius's famous tomb inscription at Naqsh-i-Rustam (DNa) offers an explanation as to why Ahura Mazda is said to grant the various nations to Darius: Ahura Mazda sees "this earth in commotion," Darius battles and seizes countries outside of Persia, fulfilling Ahura Mazda's desire to put the world "in its proper place." The introductory praise for Ahura Mazda portrays the king's reign over multiple nations as divinely sanctioned.

The Land and King in Royal Titular Formulae

A royal titular formula either appears following the introductory praise for Ahura Mazda or independently from the divine praise, and communicates two principle Achaemenid imperial ideologies: the supremacy of the Persian king, and the Persian Empire's control over various peoples. While the length and content of a royal titular formula differs depending on the specific empire list, DNa provides an example of one of the most extensive royal titular formula: "I (am) Darius the great king, king of kings, king of countries containing all kinds of men, king on this great earth far and wide, son of Hystaspes, an Achaemenid, a Persian, an Aryan, having Aryan lineage."[18] The titular formula consist of six parts, albeit with minor differences depending on the inscription: (1) The king's name, (2) "the great king," (3) "king of kings," (4) "king of countries (containing all kinds of men)," (5) "king of this great earth (far and wide)," and (6) the king's lineage.

Every royal titular accompanying an empire list contains the first four elements.[19] The royal titles "great king" and "king of kings" elevate the Persian king's superior position, whereas titles four and five emphasize the king's control over his empire.[20] The Old Persian designation *xshâyathiya dahyûnâm* is difficult to translate with certainty since *dahyûnâm* (sing. *dahyu-*) can mean both country and people. Yet several inscriptions extend this formula to *xšayathiya dahyunam paruzananam* "king of all kinds of people" to specify that the king reigns over all the inhabitants within the various countries under his realm. Several inscriptions further add the royal designation *xšayathiyam ahyaya bumiya* "king of the earth," emphasizing the extent of the earth as "far and wide."[21] The royal titular "king on this great earth far and wide" (DNa, DSe, DZc, XPh), Pierre Briant argues, "expresses the immensity of the space conquered

16. Amélie Kuhrt, *The Persian Empire: A Corpus of Sources from the Achaemenid Period* (London: Routledge, 2010), 485. All translations of inscriptions are from Kuhrt, except for DNe, DSm, and DSv, which are English translations from Lecoq, *Les inscriptions de la Perse*.

17. See also DSm, DSv.

18. Kuhrt, *Persian Empire*, 502. An equally lengthy formula appears in two other empire lists of Darius (DSe and DZc) and adopted by Xerxes (XPh).

19. See, e.g., XPh, DB, DNa, DPe, DSab, DSe.

20. Kuhrt, *Persian Empire*, 151–52 n. 2. The title "king of kings" rarely appears in Mesopotamian royal formulae. Instead, the formula appears more commonly in Urartian inscriptions.

21. The formula appears in A²Sd, A²Sa, A²Ha, D²Sb, A³Pa. See DSe, DZc, XPa, XPb, XPc, XPd, XPf, XPh, XE, XV, A¹Pa.

and controlled by the Great King and the Persians."[22] Both the introductory section praising Ahura Mazda and the royal titular formulae highlight two Achaemenid imperial ideologies: the Persian king's superior royal status granted by Ahura Mazda and Ahura Mazda's gracious act in giving the king far-reaching control over the various subject nations.

Two Types of Land Description: Boundary Lists and Empire Lists

Following these introductory formulae, the empire lists also contain catalogs of toponyms. These lists have received substantial scholarly attention due to the insights they offer on the Persian political structure and administration, however, the purpose of the empire lists remains contested.[23] There are two major interpretations concerning the purpose of the empire lists, both based on how one translates the Old Persian word *dahyu-* (pl. *dahyāva*). The first position claims the empire lists represent the Persian Empire's administrative districts, and thus the phrase should be translated as "land" or "country." According to Ronald G. Kent, the *dahyāva* lists provide a record of the different lands under the control of the Achaemenid rulers Darius and Xerxes, and satraps such as Dādaršīš in Bactria and Vivāna in Arachosia were ruling districts that appear as *countries*.[24] Bruno Jacobs further asserts that the *dahyāva* lists were organized based on administrative hierarchy, arguing that the names missing in the lists belong to lower levels of the hierarchy.[25]

The administrative model, however, has been met with opposition. Hilmar Klinkott identifies certain characteristics that betray the likelihood of the lists reflecting an administrative document: the lists vary in length and lack important commercial and military sites such as Syria, Cilicia, and Karmania, certain administrative units are duplicated, there is inconsistency in the use of administrative names, and the term *dahyu-* appears outside of administrative contexts and can either mean "land" or "ethnic group."[26]

Klinkott's final point articulates the second interpretation that identifies the items enumerated in the *dahyāva* lists as "people."[27] Indeed, J. M. Cook notes that Darius's

22. Briant, *From Cyrus to Alexander*, 177–79.

23. For a discussion, see Wiesehöfer, "Provinz (persich)."

24. Roland G. Kent, "Old Persian Texts IV: The Lists of Provinces," *JNES* 2 (1943): 302. See also Rüdiger Schmitt, "Der Titel 'Satrap,'" in *Studies in Greek, Italic and Indo-European Linguistics: Offered to Leonard R. Palmer on the Occasion of His Seventieth Birthday, June 5, 1976*, ed. Anna Morpurgo Davies and Wolfgang Meid, IBS 16 (Innsbruck: Institut für Sprachwissenschaft der Universität Innsbruck, 1976), 373.

25. Jacobs, "Achaemenid Satrapies."

26. Hilmar Klinkott, *Der Satrap: Ein achaimenidischer Amtsträger und seine Handlungsspielräume*, Oikumene 1 (Frankfurt: Antike, 2005), 79–85. See also Josef Wiesehöfer, *Ancient Persia: From 550 BC to 650 AD*, trans. Azizeh Axodi, new ed. (London: Tauris, 2001), 60. Klinkott argues that Hasta belonged to Arachosia; the Drangians were part of the satrap of Arachosia; Sattagidia was part of Arachosia, and the names were used synonymously; Sagartia appears to be part of Media. Certain inconsistencies are present; specifically, the names Maka, Ethiopia, and Elam are written in various ways.

27. Jack M. Balcer, "Persian Occupied Thrace (Skudra)," *Historia: Zeitschrift für Alte Geschichte* 37 (1988): 1–21; P. J. Junge, "Satrapie und Natio: Reichsverwaltung und Reichspolitik im Staate Dareios' I," *Klio* 34 (1942): 28–31; T. Cuyler Young Jr., "The Consolidation of the Empire and Its Limits of Growth Under Darius and Xerxes," in *Persia, Greece and the Western Mediterranean c. 525–579 B.C.*, ed. John Boardman et al., 2nd ed., CAH 4 (Cambridge: Cambridge University Press, 1988), 53–111; Pierre Lecoq, "Observations sur le sens du mot *dahyu* dans les inscriptions achéménides," *Transeu* 3 (1990): 131–40.

tomb facade at Naqsh-i Rustam records the names as ethnicities corresponding to the figures represented on the relief, which suggests that the entities represent people.[28] George Cameron's linguistic study argues this position as well based on the Elamite version of the *dahyāva* lists. The Elamite inscriptions attach personal markers (sg.: *-r*, pl.: *-p*) to indicate personal human beings, and eighteen of the twenty-three land names in DB, as well as the Elamite construction of "King of *da-a-ia-ú-iš* (loan word of Old Persian *dahyu-*)," bear this personal marker.[29] Additionally, Cameron points out that the Elamite determinative for people (a vertical wedge) appears most commonly before the cognate term for the Old Persian word *dahyu-*.[30]

Overall, the variation of the lists' lengths, the apparent duplication of the same geographical area, as well as the inconsistency in term counter the impression that the empire lists represent an administrative document enumerating the empire's districts. The lexical flexibility of *dahyu-* as either meaning "land" or "people," as well as Cameron's argument of the use of Elamite personal markers, suggests that the *dahyāva* lists at least included both geographical areas and ethnic peoples, or as Christopher Tuplin suggests, "they simply express the empire's extent in terms of ethnic groupings."[31] This suggestion leads to the question: If the "empire lists" did not function as an administrative document, what is its intended purpose? The empire lists likely contain a rhetorical function communicating the Achaemenid royal ideology.[32] The ideology communicated by the empire list may be understood in light of several inscriptions identified here as "boundary lists" that outline the extent of the Persian Empire.

Boundary Lists

The boundary lists are a series of texts that briefly outline the extent of the Persian Empire. One example is Darius's Akkadian inscription found on the south wall of the Persepolis terrace (DPg), which states:

> A great god is Ahuramazda, who is the greatest among all the gods, who created heaven and earth, created mankind, who gave all well-being to mankind who dwell therein, who made Darius king, and bestowed on Darius the king kingship over this wide earth, in which there are many lands: Persia, Media, and the other lands of other tongues, of mountains and plains, from this side of the sea to that side of the sea, from this side of the desert to that side of the desert.[33]

The introductory divine praise acknowledges Ahura Mazda as the creator of heaven and earth, and further describes the deity as granting Darius kingship over the "wide earth, in which there are many lands." The following section then describes the extent

---

28. J. M. Cook, "The Rise of the Achaemenids and Establishment of Their Empire," in *The Median and Achaemenian Periods*, ed. Ilya Gershevitch, CHI 2 (Cambridge: Cambridge University Press, 1985), 244.

29. George G. Cameron, "The Persian Satrapies and Related Matters," *JNES* 32 (1973): 48.

30. Ibid., 49.

31. Christopher Tuplin, "The Administration of the Achaemenid Empire," in *Coinage and Administration in the Athenian and Persian Empires: The Ninth Oxford Symposium on Coinage and Monetary History*, ed. Ian Carradice, BARIS 343 (Oxford: British Archaeological Reports, 1987), 113.

32. Klinkott, *Der Satrap*, 67.

33. Kuhrt, *Persian Empire*, 483.

of Darius's kingdom, first by referring to Persia and Media, which represents the center of the Persian Empire, and then by listing the periphery in terms of their topographical features with the formula "from X to Y." The inscription makes Persia and Media the focal point by exclusive use of their toponyms. The coupling of topographical features (mountains and plains, this sea to that sea, this desert to that desert) forms a merism that includes everything within these boundaries. Briant notes that the imagery used in DPg stresses "the immensity of the imperial space and also the ethnic, cultural, and linguistic diversity of the peoples subject to the 'king of the countries.'"[34] Darius's inscription, therefore, delineates the far-reaching extent of the Persian Empire without mentioning any specific peoples by name.

A trilingual inscription from the apadana at Persepolis and Hamadan (DPh and DH), however, records a different version to delimit the kingdom's extent.[35] The text reads, "King Darius proclaims: This (is) the kingdom which I hold, from the Saca who are beyond the Sogdiana, from there as far as Kush, from the Indus as far as Sardis, which Ahuramazda, the greatest of gods, bestowed upon me."[36] Three of the locations (Kush, Indus, and Sardis) are clearly identifiable. The location of Saca poses more difficulty since the term is neither a toponym nor a Persian satrap. Instead, Saca refers to the various nomadic tribes that lived in the central Asian steppe. Although three primary Saca are known from inscriptions—*Sakâ haumavargâ* "Haoma-drinking Saca," *Sakâ tigrakhaudâ* "Saca with pointed hats," and *Sakâ paradrayâ* "Saca across the sea"—the descriptions "who are beyond the Sogdiana" clarifies which tribe is identified. Sogdia was a northeastern satrap within the Persian Empire, hence, the Saca identified in the inscription must be the *Sakâ haumavargâ* "Haoma-drinking Saca" dwelling in the northeastern region of the Persian Empire.[37] The extent from Saca to Kush (ancient Sudan) draws a northeast to southwest extension. The Indus represents the southeastern extent of the Persian Empire and Sardis, located within the satrap of Lydia, represents the empire's northwestern region.[38] The description "The Indus as far as Sardis," therefore stretches from the southeastern to the northwestern extent of the kingdom.

Darius's trilingual inscription also outlines the boundaries of the Persian Empire, but it does so by referring only to the four locations that represent the northwest, southwest, northeast, and southeast. The formula connecting these extremities (from Saca to Sogdiana and from Kush to Sardis), precludes the need for a more detailed list, for the formula implies the inclusion of all the nations within these borders.

Thus, two features characterize the boundary lists: an inscription that emphasizes (explicitly or implicitly) the Persian Empire's center and a boundary list that inserts geographical and ethnic names into the formula "from X as far as Y" to express the kingdom's extent as well as everything it contained.[39] When the more detailed empire lists are read in light of these boundary lists, it becomes apparent that the empire lists

34. Briant, *From Cyrus to Alexander*, 179.
35. There are six known copies of this inscription, all written on precious metals.
36. Kuhrt, *Persian Empire*, 576
37. Ibid., 482 n. 2. Kuhrt explains, "*Hauma* was an intoxicating drink ritually drunk in Iranian cult" as well as a Persian designation for a people group located in central Asia.
38. While there is the satrap of Thrace further east, as well as Scythia further north, the reference of Sardis seems to encompass this northwestern region.
39. Kuhrt, *Persian Empire*, 18.

also communicate a similar ideology by listing more countries with their own sequential patterns.

Empire Lists

Most of the empire lists mention that the king controlled and collected tribute from each group referenced in the catalog, yet these lists were created not for administrative purposes but rather for different political and ideological purposes.[40] Apart from the question of whether these lists enumerate countries or peoples, scholars have questioned whether these lists were created as a means of enumerating the contents of the empire or the dimensions of the empire. That is, are the names meant to be a realistic picture of the peoples under the control of the empire or to outline the extent of the empire?

As we have argued, these lists are not intended to be a catalog of the different administrative districts. Briant argues that the Persian monarchs were intentionally choosing specific groups, and hence that the lists are "nothing but a selection of subject countries."[41] If choice were taking place, the empire lists were meant to show Persian dominance over specific groups of people, or a selection of representative nations. In order for this content-based interpretation to be true, one must ask why each name is included in each catalog and conversely why certain names are not included. Certain omissions are difficult to explain, especially the aforementioned Phrygia, Cilicia, and Syria, to name a few.

Another model that could be applied to these lists in order to understand how the Persian monarchy conceived of an ideological empire is a dimensional interpretation. In other words, while these lists illustrate a clear sense of territorial space controlled by Persian kings, they focus on the boundaries of the empire. The lists begin with the core of the empire, but quickly draw one out to the peripheries in all directions. For this model to be tenable, it is necessary to delineate the periphery, because this creates the boundaries of the empire. The orientation, however, is also essential to understand.

Briant indeed notes a geographical orientation reflected in the Bisitun inscription. He divides the list into five geographical groupings: (1) center (Persia, Elam), (2) south-southeast axis (Babylonia, Assyria, Arabia, Egypt), (3) west-east axis (those of the Sea, Sardis, Ionia, Media, Armenia, Cappadocia), (4) center-east axis (Parthia, Drangiana, Aria, Chorasmia, Bactria, Sogdiana), and (5) southeast-west axis (Gandhara, Scythia, Sattagydia, Arachosia, Makran).[42]

Similarly, Bruce Lincoln argues for a concentric geographical orientation as the chief structuring device of the empire lists. Persia represents the absolute center, since Persia always appears first on the list, except for inscriptions that explicitly refer to either a conquest or payment of tribute.[43] The Medes, Elamites, and Babylonians represent the second sphere and appear along with the Persians. Media, Elam, and Babylonia not only share close geographic and cultural proximity with Persia but

---

40. Briant, *From Cyrus to Alexander*, 177.

41. Ibid.

42. Ibid., 180.

43. Bruce Lincoln, *Religion, Empire, and Torture: The Case of Achaemenid Persia, with a Postscript on Abu Ghraib* (Chicago: University of Chicago Press, 2007), 23. In conquest or payment of tribute examples, Persia is not listed.

also contain Persian capital cities (Ecbatana, Susa, and Babylon).[44] The third sphere constitutes all other peoples that stretch in the four cardinal directions.[45] According to Lincoln, the sequence of the third sphere begins with one cardinal point (the north-south axis is regularly treated first, then east-west axis) and moves from the center to the outer periphery, then rotates ninety degree and repeats the sequence until all four cardinal directions are covered.[46]

While both Briant and Lincoln suggest the geographical dimension plays a role in organizing the empire lists, neither scholar takes the entire available corpus into consideration, relying primarily on Darius's Bisitun inscription to demonstrate their theoretical models.[47] The following section builds upon these two scholars work by incorporating all the available empire lists, and argues that all the empire lists can be grouped into two designations: center-east-west and center-west-east empire lists.

Center-East-West Empire Lists

Seven inscriptions (DNa, DNe, DSe, XPh, A?P/A^{3}Pb, DSab, Suez Canal) list subject names in a center-east-west sequence. While the individual inscriptions contain minor variations in number of names and its sequence, one can detect an overall organizational sequence (especially between DNa, DNe, DSe, and A?P/A^{3}Pb).

The current study identifies a three-part geographical division to the empire lists (see appendix 8.1). The first group constitutes the center. Briant and Lincoln both agree that the empire lists begin with the center of the Persian Empire, but Briant only includes two names (Persia and Elam) whereas Lincoln argues that the first and second central sphere consist of four names (Persia, Media, Elam, and Babylonia). Except for the few inscriptions lacking the name Persia (DNa and DSe), every center-east-west empire list mentions Persia-Media-Elam (always in this sequence). Lincoln includes Babylon within his second sphere along with Media and Elam, but this is likely due to his dependence on the DB inscription that follows the center-west-east orientation, in which Babylon often marks the beginning of the western group of names (see discussion below). In the center-east-west empire lists, however, Elam concludes the central group, and names representing the eastern group (most often Parthia) follow.

Lincoln observes that the empire lists begin with central locations and then the names move out toward the periphery, thereby following a centrifugal pattern.[48] In contrast to Lincoln's division of the third concentric sphere into the four cardinal directions (i.e., north, west, south, and east), the current study suggests certain lists are organized in center, east, then west groups that can further be subdivided into

44. Ibid.

45. Ibid., 24.

46. Lincoln also comments that certain peoples (Nubians, Carians, and Makans) tend to appear at the end, even though this means breaking the sequence; ibid.

47. While Lincoln consults seven lists (DB, DNa, DPe, DSe, DSm, XPh, A^{3}Pb), his conclusions are based on DB rather than the entire corpus, *Religion, Empire, and Torture,* 23 table 4. Briant follows suit and only refers to six lists (DB, DNa, DPe, DSe, DSaa, XPh) with passing references to the Suez Canal stelae and Darius's statue, *From Cyrus to Alexander,* 173.

48. Lincoln, *Religion, Empire, and Torture,* 24. Also, Wiesehöfer notes that this centrifugal organization follow Assyrian and Babylonian models. Wiesehöfer, *Ancient Persia,* 60.

northeastern, southeastern, northwestern, and southwestern groups. The eastern group usually begins with the sequence of Parthia-Areia-Bactria-Sogdiana and concludes by referring to Caria (see appendix 8.1). The eastern group is further subdivided into a northeastern group (Parthia-Areia-Bactria-Sogdiana-Chorasmia) and southeastern group (Drangiana-Arachosia-Sattagydia-Gandara-India) that both stretch outward from the center.[49] Briant essentially sees this division in his proposal of center-east axis and southeast-west axis, and this subdivision into a northeastern group and southeastern group.[50]

The reference to Babylon marks the shift to the western group of names. Almost every name that appears in this section lies west of the center, except Maka, which generally appears near the end of the inscription.[51] Like its eastern counterpart, the western group can be further subdivided into a southwestern group (Babylonia-Assyria-Arabia-Egypt)—but with certain outliers (namely Assyria)—and northwestern group (Armenia-Cappadocia-Sardis-Ionia-Scythia-Thrace-Petasos Wearing Ionian) that emanates from the center toward the periphery.[52] The final names on the list are in the west but are found in both the northwest (Caria) and southwest (Libya-Nubia).[53]

Center-West-East Empire Lists

Five inscriptions all attributed to Darius constitute the center-west-east empire list model: DB, DSaa, DPe, DSm and DSv.[54] In contrast to the center-east-west empire lists that often contained about thirty names (A?P/A³Pb, DNe, DNa, XPh) the center-west-east group only contain around twenty-three names, and indeed the DB names the subject people and then states "all twenty-three peoples/countries."[55] Despite their relative consistency, the center-west-east empire lists exhibit greater variety in sequence. The lists clearly group names in a center-west-east geographical sequence, yet it is unclear whether a further north and south subdivision is intended (see appendix 8.2). The western group begins with four southwestern names, then moves from the center

49. Lincoln seems to group these two eastern groups into one. *Religion, Empire, and Torture*, 23–24.

50. Based on the Bisitun inscription, Briant (*From Cyrus to Alexander*, 180) lists five names that constitute the southeast-west axis (Gandhara, Scythia, Sattagydia, Arachosia, Makran). In light of the seven inscriptions belonging to the center-east-west inscriptions, however, Maka should be omitted, and the names constituting this group, should be Drangianian-Arachosian-Sattagydian-Gandaran-India-hauma-drinking Saca, and pointed-hat Saca. XPh places Drangianian and Arachosian at the beginning of the eastern group, and retains the sequence of Sattagydia-Gandara-India-hauma-drinking and pointed-hat Sacas, but separates these names, then places these within the western group.

51. Ibid.

52. Assyria is problematic since it is north of Persia. This pattern of listing Babylon and Assyria together, however, appears to be a scribal convention.

53. The subdivision, therefore largely agree with Briant's proposal for a south-southeast axis and west-east axis, albeit the current study places Media with the center group. Briant, *From Cyrus to Alexander*, 180. In contrast to Lincoln's proposal that divides between a western group (those of the sea, Lydia, Ionia) and northern group (Media, Armenia, Cappadocia), these two groups should be treated as representing the northwestern arena. Lincoln, *Religion, Empire, and Torture*, 24.

54. Even though Darius's Akkadian inscription on a marble slab is very fragmentary with only five names confidently restored.

55. Kuhrt, *Persian Empire*, 141 col. 1. DSaa and DSm list twenty-four names, and DSm could have very likely originally have contained a few more names, but due to the break on the glazed brick, it is unclear.

toward the outside (Babylonia-Assyria-Arabia-Egypt). The four names that follow lie in the northwestern region (Countries of the sea-Lydia-Ionia-Armenia-Cappadocia); however, they lack a clear inner to outer movement.[56] Similarly, the eastern group begins with northeastern names and moves from the center to the periphery (Parthia-Drangiana-Areia-Chorasmia-Bactria-Sogdiana), but the following group of eastern names seems to reflect the periphery, hence they lack a clear centrifugal orientation.

The comparison between the center-east-west empire lists with the center-west-east empire lists reveals the following differences. First, the sequence of names is different in the center group. While the center-east-west empire list follows the sequence of Persia, Media, and Elam, the center-west-east empire list always mentions Elam before Media. Second, the eastern group varies in sequence. While the center-east-west group mostly follows the sequence of Parthian-Areian-Bactrian-Sogdian-Chorasmian, the center-west-east group instead prefers the order of Parthia-Drangiana-Areia-Chorasmia-Bactria-Sogdiana.[57] Third, several western toponyms (i.e., Thrace, Libya, Nubia, and Caria) appear in the center-east-west empire lists, but are omitted in the center-west-east empire lists. The omission of subjects begs the question: Why omit certain names?

Examining these lists with a dimension-driven model in mind accounts for what Briant interprets as a selection of peoples, and one does not have to justify the presence or absence of certain groups. Specific areas around the periphery are not necessary to enumerate because they are included within other names that are registered on the empire lists. Certain place-names are metonymic, and thus include the people groups that appear to be missing. In other words, when Ionia is mentioned, there is no need to catalog every group along the coast of Anatolia. These places are included without listing them. This dimension-driven model focuses on more of a geographically oriented message than the contents-driven model does. The empire lists illustrate the vastness of Persian dominance, which strengthens the center and thus bolsters the position of the king.

To summarize, two types of inscriptions sketch the extent of the vast Persian Empire: boundary lists and empire lists. Both lists have two primary aims: first, to stress the centrality of Persia, and second, to outline the vastness of the Persian Empire that the king controlled. The two types of lists fulfill this goal in different ways. The boundary list either explicitly or implicitly affirms the centrality of Persia and depicts the extent of the Persian Empire by connecting the borders of the empire, either figuratively by referring to geographical features or in a more concrete way by picking subjects that represent the northeast, southeast, northwest, and southwest corners of the empire. The empire lists either follow the center-east-west or center-west-east geographical organization, but both groups begin with the central sites (Persia, Elam, Media) and then list names from the center toward the empire's periphery. Their organization elevates Persia's place among the nations and further expresses the far-reaching control and dominance over

56. The individual sequence of Lydia-Ionia and Armenia-Cappadocia shows a movement from the inside to the outside. The placement of Armenia-Cappadocia after Lydia-Ionia on a macro level, however, reflects a movement from periphery to the center.

57. The two hieroglyphic inscriptions (DSab and Suez Canal stele) do not follow the standard center-east-west sequence, and the only center-west-east list that does not follow the conventional sequence is DPe. These inscriptions, nonetheless, only exhibit minor modification to the sequence.

every direction of the wide empire, possibly reflecting an essential element of Persian royal ideology for "the aspiration to global dominance over space."[58] The extent of this Persian imperial ideology stretches far beyond the capital or central region of the Persian Empire and is most clearly seen from an empire list placed in the land of Egypt.

A Final Empire List: The Statue of Darius at Susa

In 1972, a statue of Darius was discovered during excavation of the southwestern facade of a monumental gate at Susa.[59] Based on the statue's iconography, quadrilingual inscription, and material, scholars agree that the statue originated from Egypt— perhaps originally placed at the Atum Temple at Heliopolis—then the statue was transported to Susa, possibly during Xerxes's reign when Egypt revolted against Persia.[60] The statue's iconography and inscriptions combine Persian and Egyptian features.[61] Even though the statue was apparently constructed at an Egyptian workshop, the sculptor applied a Persian measurement and anatomical proportion, rather than a Twenty-Sixth Dynasty Saite proportion.[62]

The statue's iconography clearly portrays the king in Persian vesture: the king garbed in a colored Persian robe, girded in a belt with a sheathed Elamite-style dagger, adorned with an Iranian bracelet, and wearing strapless royal Persian shoes.[63] The sculpture, however, depicts the king in an Egyptian posture. The bent left arm goes across the abdomen with the left hand clenching a stem of a plant (likely a lotus), the right arm stretches down the side of the body, and the hand holds a stone cylinder.[64]

---

58. Reinhold Bichler, "Persian Geography and the Ionians: Herodotus," in *Brill's Companion to Ancient Geography: The Inhabited World in Greek and Roman Tradition*, ed. Serena Bianchetti, Michele Cataudella, and Hans-Joachim Gehrke (Leiden: Brill, 2016), 19.

59. Now housed in the National Museum in Tehran, inventory number 4112. Several scholars assume Darius's statue is the only extant human sculpture in the round from the Achaemenid period. See, e.g., Jean Perrot, "Le palais de Darius : Nouvelles données archéologiques," *CRAIBL* 154 (2010): 424. Oscar Muscarella points to a fragment of a royal head and four other fragments of a sculpture of a human (one possibly a hero) in the round from Apadana. Oscar W. Muscarella, "Fragment of a Royal Head," in *The Royal City of Susa: Ancient Near Eastern Treasures in the Louvre*, ed. Prudence O. Harper, Joan Aruz, and Françoise Tallon (New York: Metropolitan Museum of Art, 1992), 219–21. Scholars further postulate that the Darius statue likely formed a pair with another statue that possibly stood either at the northern or eastern end of the passage, see, e.g., Jean Perrot, and Daniel Ladiray, "La porte de Darius a Suse," *Cahiers de la Délégation archéologique française en Iran* 4 (1974): 44; Heinz Luschey, "Die Darius-Statuen aus Susa und ihre Rekonstruktion," in *Kunst, Kultur und Geschichte der Achämenidenzeit und ihr Fortleben*, ed. Heidemarie Koch and D. N. Mackenzie, AMI 10 (Berlin: Reimer, 1983), 191–206. See also Shahrokh Razmjou, "Assessing the Damage: Notes on the Life and Demise of the Statue of Darius from Susa," *Ars Orientalis* 32 (2002): 81–104.

60. Razmjou, "Assessing the Damage," 86. For the discussion on the different theories regarding the statue's date and origin, see Margaret Cool Root, *The King and Kingship in Achaemenid Art: Essays on the Creation of an Iconography of Empire*, Acta Iranica 19 (Leiden: Brill, 1979), 72; John Curtis and Shahrokh Razmjou, "The Palace," in *Forgotten Empire: The World of Ancient Persia*, ed. John Curtis and Nigel Tallis (London: British Museum, 2005), 99.

61. Margaret Cool Root, "Circles of Artistic Programming: Strategies for Studying Creative Process at Persepolis," in *Investigating Artistic Environments in the Ancient Near East*, ed. Ann C. Gunter (Washington, DC: Smithsonian Institute, 1990), 115–39, esp. 129. See also Guitty Azarpay, "Proportional Guidelines in Ancient Near Eastern Art," *JNES* 46 (1987): 183–203.

62. Azarpay, "Proportional Guidelines," 190. See also Root, "Circles of Artistic Programming," 130.

63. Razmjou, "Assessing the Damage," 81.

64. For a list of examples of reliefs at Persepolis that portray the king holding a lotus see Razmjou, "Assessing the Damage," 102 n. 6. For the stone cylinder, see ibid, 83. For hypotheses concerning what the

The vertical pillar on the back of the statue also indicates a clear Egyptian sculptural tradition, symbolizing the divine protective presence.

Multiple inscriptions are engraved upon the statue. Each tip of the belt tassels contains Egyptian hieroglyphic inscriptions that extol Darius as the king of Upper and Lower Egypt and a perfect god who reigns over the two lands, with Darius's name in a royal cartouche.[65] Additionally, a trilingual cuneiform inscription (Old Persian, Elamite, and Babylonian) adorns the robe's right-side pleat, and a different Egyptian hieroglyphic text runs down the left-side pleat.[66]

The cuneiform inscription largely follows a standard Old Persian inscriptional sequence, beginning with praise for Ahura Mazda and followed by an extended titular formula describing Darius as "the king of kings, king of countries, king of this great earth," and then a blessing asking Ahura Mazda to protect Darius.[67] In between the praise of Ahura Mazda and the royal titular formula, the inscription inserts certain details, identifying Darius as the one responsible for the statue's commission, so that people may know that Persia rules over Egypt. The cuneiform inscription therefore reflects a strong Achaemenid ideology praising the Persian deity and Persian supremacy. The cuneiform text, however, also contains peculiar features uncommon to typical Old Persian inscriptions, such as adopting foreign rhetorical features and changing the orientation of the cuneiform signs to force the readers to turn their heads sideways.[68] These factors lead Razmjou to conclude that "although the monument was meant to invoke Achaemenid visions of kingship and identity, it was intended to do this in an Egyptian context."[69]

The hieroglyphic inscription shows a clear contextualized message aimed at its Egyptian audiences.[70] There is no mention of Ahura Mazda, only the Egyptian deities Atum, Re, Neith, Montu, and Horus. The inscription also associates Darius with Atum of Heliopolis to justify his reign as divinely sanctioned and to eulogize Darius as the conqueror and king of Upper and Lower Egypt who crushes the "nine bows" (a traditional expression used to refer to Egypt's enemies).[71] Thus the hieroglyphic text

stone cylinder may represent, see Henry P. Colburn, "Art of the Achaemenid Empire, and Art in the Achaemenid Empire," in *Critical Approaches to Ancient Near Eastern Art*, ed. Brian A. Brown and Marian H. Feldman (Berlin: de Gruyter, 2014), 786; and Henry G. Fischer, "An Elusive Shape Within the Fisted Hands of Egyptian Statues," *Metropolitan Museum Journal* (1975): 9–21.

65. Translation in Kuhrt, *Persian Empire*, 478.

66. Razmjou, "Assessing the Damage," 85.

67. For the transliterated text and French translation, see François Vallat, "La triple inscription cunéiforme de la statue de Darius 1er (DSab)," *RA* 68 (1974): 157–66. Vallat also notes that the opening praise for Ahura Mazda differs from all other initial evocation except the stele of the Suez Canal (158). For an English translation, see Kuhrt, *Persian Empire*, 478.

68. Razmjou, "Assessing the Damage," 87, referring to Clarisse Herrenschmidt, "Les creations d'Ahuramazda," *Studia Iranica* 6 (1977): 37 ; and Perrot and Ladiray, "Porte de Darius," 43–56.

69. Razmjou, "Assessing the Damage," 87. See also Jennifer Finn, "Gods, Kings, Men: Trilingual Inscriptions and Symbolic Visualizations in the Achaemenid Empire," *Ars Orientalis* 41 (2011): 242 for a discussion of royal ideology.

70. Christopher Tuplin, "Darius' Suez Canal and Persian Imperialism," in *Asia Minor and Egypt: Old Cultures in a New Empire; Proceedings of the Groningen 1988 Achaemenid History Workshop*, ed. Heleen Sancisi-Weerdenburg and Amélie T. Kuhrt, Achaemenid History 6 (Leiden: Nederlands Instituut voor Het Nabije Oosten, 1991), 244.

71. Kuhrt, *Persian Empire*, 479 n. 8.

adopts traditional Egyptian motifs to depict Darius in line with past Egyptian pharaohs and to justify his reign as sanctioned by the Egyptian gods.

The iconography of the statue base is also of note. An Egyptian motif known as *sma-tawy* adorns the front and back of the base, depicting the god Hapi binding the lotus and papyrus to symbolize the union between Upper and Lower Egypt.[72] This symbol often appears in association with a king, inscribed below a cartouche containing the king's name. The lotus and papyrus symbol is usually found on a throne or a statue base.[73] The accompanying inscription reads, "I give you all life and strength, stability, health and joy. I give you all countries of the plain and all countries of the mountains, united under your sandals. I give you Upper Egypt and Lower Egypt, who adore your beautiful face, like that of Re, eternally."[74] Both the iconography and inscription therefore communicate Darius's position as the ruler and unifier of Upper and Lower Egypt.

Darius's dominion, however, goes beyond Egypt. The reference to all the countries of the plain and mountains finds commonalities with Darius's Babylonian inscription at Persepolis (DPg) that also uses topographical features as a merism to convey all the earth. Moreover, the imagery of countries united under the king's sandals is also iconographically depicted with Darius's statue. The king is standing upon a base with twenty-four fortification rings containing names of subjugated peoples in Egyptian hieroglyphs, and atop each ring is a kneeling figure with palms raised upward that personifies each ethnonym.[75] In traditional Egyptian iconography, a fortification ring usually encloses ethnic or geographic names of prisoners of Egypt and above the ring portrays a prisoner with hands tied behind his back.[76]

The left and right side of the base each feature twelve subject peoples. The left side lists nations generally from the west side of the empire (front to back: Babylonia, Armenia, Sardis, Cappadocia, Skudra [Thrace], Eshur [Syria], Hagor [northwest Arabia], Kemi [Egypt], the land of Tjemhou [Libya], the land of Nehsy [Nubia], Maka, India), and the right-side lists people from the center and east of the empire (Back to front: Persia, Media, Elam, Aria, Parthia, Bactria, Sogdia, Arachosia, Sattagydia, Chorasmia, Saka marshlands and plains).[77] Compared to other center-east-west empire lists, DSab reflects two primary differences: reversing the sequence of names and omitting and adding toponyms.[78] The changes were probably made to suit an Egyptian audience: it includes Syria, historically significant to the Egyptians, and moves Arabia-Egypt between Syria and Libya due to their geographical proximity.

---

72. Ibid., 479 n. 13.

73. Colburn, "Art of the Achaemenid Empire," 786.

74. Kuhrt, *Persian Empire*, 478–79.

75. The same list of nations appears on the Tell el-Maskhouta canal stelae of Darius.

76. Michael Roaf, "The Subject Peoples on the Base of the Statue of Darius," *Cahiers de la Délégation archéologique française en Iran* 4 (1974): 73–159; Root, *King and Kingship*, 69–70.

77. According to Root, placing the eastern lands at the king's left side and the western land at the right may reflect Egyptian influence, since the left is considered the east due to the orientation of the Nile. Root, *King and Kingship,* 70 n. 73.

78. For the eastern group, DSab reverses the standard sequence of Parthia-Areia, Drangia-Arachosia, Sardis-Cappadocia. For the western group, DSab reverses the sequence of Sardis-Cappadocia. DSab omits standard names that appear in every other center-east-west empire lists, including: Sattagydia, Gandara, Assyria, Ionia, Scythians, and Caria.

When read right-to-left, both sides emanate from the center of the Persian Empire (right: Persia, Media, Elam; Left: Babylonia, Armenia) and stretch outward to the fringes of the empire (right: Arachosia, Sattagdia, Chorasmia, and Saka marshlands and plains; left: land of Tjemhou [Libya], land of Nehsy [Nubia], Maka, India). The centrality of Persia, however, does not communicate the superiority of Persia. In fact, Henry Colburn rightfully notes that the inclusion of Persia among the empire's subjects "visually at least, puts the Persians on par with everyone."[79]

The preceding analysis of the iconography and inscription of Darius's statue and its base demonstrates that while the statue heavily adopts Egyptian artistic conventions, it also reflects clear Persian features with intentional modifications to convey its Achaemenid ideology in an Egyptian context. First, the statue's posture, the podium's *sma-tawy* symbol, and the inscription's text convey Darius as king of Egypt. Second, the statue's position over the twenty-four ethnonyms, Darius's extended titular formula in the cuneiform text, and the hieroglyphic text on the base that depicts all countries of both the plains and the mountains under Darius's feet point to the Achaemenid dominion over the world. Third, the personified depiction of subject nations as supporters, rather than bound prisoners, and the incorporation of Persia among the twenty-four place names communicate that the various nations as a collective entity (including Egypt) support the Persian king's political and religious authority over the nations.

Conclusion

This study offers a model for understanding the organizing principle and rhetorical intent of the empire lists. First, the introductory praise for Ahura Mazda and the royal titular formula both elevate the king as the rightful, divinely sanctioned ruler over the wide kingdom containing many nations. Second, the extent of this empire is delineated in two types of inscriptions: boundary lists and empire lists. In contrast to scholars who identify the empire lists as administrative documents, the current study aligns with scholars who view the empire lists as primarily reflecting royal ideology and suggests that both the boundary lists and empire lists bolster the centrality of Persia and describe the vastness of the empire subsumed under the king, albeit in unique ways. The boundary lists employ the formula "fro°m° X to Y" and either refer to geographical features (mountains and plains, this sea to that sea, this desert to that desert) or to four sites that represent the northeastern, southeastern, northwestern, and southwestern corners of the empire. In contrast to the boundary lists that connect the empire's outer boundaries (and in extension include everything in between), the empire lists constitute twelve inscriptions organized geographically either in a center-east-east or center-west-east sequence. All empire lists emphasize the centrality of Persia by first listing the names that represent the empire's central region (Persia, Media, Elam). Then, the empire lists continue to enumerate subjects extending westward and eastward. Their organizing principle therefore both highlights the centrality of Persia

79. Colburn, "Art of the Achaemenid Empire," 787.

and reflects the royal Achaemenid ideology of the king's control over the empire's outer periphery. Finally, this paper concludes with a detailed discussion of Darius's statue from Susa that likely originated in Egypt. Both the statue's iconography and its inscription reflect a merging of Achaemenid and Egyptian artistic conventions, all the while retaining the prominence of Persian culture. The inclusion of Persia among the list of subjects, as well as depictions of subject peoples with raised hands and palms facing upward, however, indicates that the Persian king's aim was not simply to subjugate the various people. Instead, the ideology envisioned was for all the nations to support the Persian king who unites the world.

Appendix 8.1: Center-West-East Empire List[80]

	DNe	A?P/A³Pb	DNa	DSe	DSab & Suez Canal	XPh
Center	Persian	Persian			Persia	
	Mede	Mede	Media	Media	Media	Media
	Elamite	Elamite	Elam	Elam	Elam	Elam
East						**Arachosia**
						Armenia
						Drangiana
	Parthian	**Parthian**	**Parthia**	**Parthia**	**Areia**	**Parthia**
	Arian	**Areian**	**Areia**	**Areia**	**Parthia**	**Areia**
	Bactrian	**Bactrian**	**Bactria**	**Bactria**	**Bactria**	**Bactria**
	Sogdian	**Sogdian**	**Sogdiana**	**Sogdiana**	**Sogdiana**	**Sogdiana**
	Chorasmian	**Chorasmian**	**Chorasmia**	**Chorasmia**	**Arachosia**	**Chorasmia**
	Drangian	**Drangianian**	**Drangiana**	**Drangiana**	**Drangiana**	
	Arachosian	**Arachosian**	**Arachosia**	**Arachosia**	**Sattagydia**	
	Sattagydian	**Sattagydian**	**Sattagydia**	**Sattagydia**	**Chorasmia**	
				Maka		
	Gandaran	**Gandaran**	**Gandara**	**Gandara**		
	Man of Sind	**Indian**	**India**	**India**		
	Hauma drinking Saka	**Hauma drinking Saca**	**Saca who drink Hauma**	**Saca who drink Hauma**	**Saca of Marsh**	
	Saca with pointed hats	**Pointed-hat Saca**	**Saca with pointed hats**	**Saca with pointed hats**	**Saca of the Plain**	

80. From Kuhrt, *Persian Empire,* except for DNe, DSm, and DSv.

	DNe	A?P/A³Pb	DNa	DSe	DSab & Suez Canal	XPh
West	Babylonian	Babylonian	Babylonia	Babylonia	Babylon	Babylonia
	Syrian	Assyrian	Assyria	Assyria		Assyria
	Arab	Arab	Arabia	Arabia		**Sattagydia**
	Egyptian	Egyptian	Egypt	Egypt		Lydia
	Armenian	Armenian	Armenia	Armenia	Armenia	Egypt
	Cappadocian	Cappadocian	Cappadocia	Cappadocia		Ionians
	Lydian	Sardian	Sardis	Sardis	Sardis	Dwellers beyond the Sea
	Greek	Ionian	Ionia	Ionians	Cappadocia	Maka
	Scythian	Scythian	Scythians	Scythians		Arabia
	Thracian	Thracian	Thrace	Thrace	Thrace	**Gandara**
	Macedonian	Petasos-wearing Ionian	Petasos-wearing Ionians	Ionians beyond the sea	Syria	**Indus**
					northwest Arabia	
					Egypt	Cappadocia
	Libyan	Libyan	Libya		Libya	Dahae
						Scythains who drink haoma
	Kushite	Nubian	Nubia		Nubia	**Scythians who wear pointed hats**
	Maka	Maka	Maka		Maka	Thrace
					India	Akaufaka
						Libyans
	Carian	Carian	Caria	Caria		Carians
						Nubians

Appendix 8.2: Center-West-East Empire Lists

	DB	DSaa	DPe	DSm	DSv
Center	<u>Persia</u>	<u>Persia</u>		<u>Persia</u>	
	<u>Elam</u>	<u>Elam</u>	<u>Elam</u>	<u>Elam</u>	
		<u>Media</u>	<u>Media</u>		<u>Media</u>
West	*Babylonia*	*Babylon*	*Babylonia*	*Babylonia*	*. . .*
	Assyria	*Assyria*	*Arabia*	*Syria*	
	Arabia	*Arabia*	*Assyria*	*Arabia*	
	Egypt	*Egypt*	*Egypt*	*Egypt*	
	Those of the sea	*The Sealands*	*Armenia*		
			Cappadocia		*Cappadocia*
	Lydia	*Saris (Lydia)*	*Lydia (Sardis)*	*Lydia*	*. . .*
	Ionia	*Ionia*	*Ionians*		*Assyria*
				Greece	
	<u>Media</u>			<u>Media</u>	
	Armenia	*Urana (Armenia)*		*Armenia*	
	Cappadocia	*Cappadocia*		*Cappadocia*	
East			**Sagartia**		**India**
	Parthia	**Parthia**	**Parthia**	**Parthia**	**. . .**
	Drangiana	**Drangiana**	**Drangiana**	**Drangiana**	
	Areia	**Areia**	**Areia**	**Areia**	
	Chorasmia	**Chorasmia**		**Chorasmia**	**Chorasmia**
	Bactria	**Bactria**	**Bactria**	**Bactria**	**. . .**
	Sogdiana	**Sogdiana**	**Sogdiana**	**Sogdiana**	
			Chorasmia		
			Sattagydia		
			Arachosia		
			India		
	Gandara	**Gandara**	**Gandara**	**Gandara**	
	Scythia	*Cimmeria (Scythians)*	*Scythians*		
	Sattagydia	**Sattagydia**		**Sattagydia**	
	Arachosia	**Arachosia**		**Arachosia**	
	Maka	**Qadie (Maka)**	**Maka**	**Sind**	
				Thrace	
				Macedonia	
				. . .	

Geophysical Research in Pelusium: On the Benefits of Using the Resistivity Profiling Method

Tomasz Herbich

Introduction

Professor James K. Hoffmeier, to whom this article is dedicated, spent many years in northern Sinai. There are many references in this volume to his work in the area. Studies in the field of earth sciences, that is, with the prefix "geo": geology and geomorphology, were very important in his research. They allowed the tracking of changes in the landscape that took place in the ancient period. This knowledge was essential for studying settlements and communication routes in the area (e.g., Hoffmeier and Moshier 2006, 2013). In Tell el-Borg, another research method came into play—geophysics. The author of this article had the pleasure and honor of carrying out geophysical research there (Herbich 2014).

In the last two decades, at least a decade later than in Europe, the use of geophysical methods has become an important part of research for archaeologists operating in the Nile Valley both in Egypt and Sudan, as well as in the delta (Herbich et al. 2005; Herbich 2003, 2012, 2013). Of the three geophysical methods commonly used in archaeology: the magnetic, georadar, and resistivity methods, the studies have been dominated by the magnetic method. There are various reasons for this; the two most important ones are the climatic conditions of the Nile Valley and the properties of building materials used there.

The most commonly used construction material in the Nile Valley was the sun-dried mud-brick, characterized by high magnetic susceptibility (usually between ca. 2×10^{-3}SI–4×10^{-3}SI). The magnetic properties of Nile mud were discovered in the 1960s during research in Mirgissa (Hesse 1967, 1970). The method gave good results in the registration of mud buildings covered by sand, which is devoid of magnetic properties, that is, in conditions of strong contrast between the magnetic values of archaeological structures and their surroundings. Remarkable progress has been made since the end of the 1990s, when—thanks to the use of high resolution instruments—it became possible to register structures built of mud-brick erected on the alluvium (where the contrast between the buildings and their surroundings is much smaller; Pusch 1999; Pusch, Becker, and Fassbinder 2000). The short time required for measurement allowed one to condense the measuring grid, as well as to investigate large areas in a short period of time (Herbich 2015).

The low efficiency of the resistivity method, compared to the magnetic method, is caused by the fact that measurements taken on sand are extremely difficult due to its very high resistivity. Additionally, in alluvial areas the resistivity method is mainly effective when searching for stone and burnt brick structures. Moreover, it requires good contact between the electrodes and the ground. The very low humidity of surface layers in Egypt and Sudan makes the measurement procedure (requiring watering the places where the electrodes are inserted) time-consuming. The third of the aforementioned methods, the georadar method, has so far proven to be useful mainly in tracing voids in rock beddings, as well as stone structures in sandy environments (e.g., Herbich, von der Osten-Woldenburg and Zych 2011). The effectiveness of the method in alluvial Nile areas is limited by high groundwater levels; the method seems to be mainly useful when searching for stone structures, although recent research results successfully showed mud architecture (Ullrich and Wolf 2015; Herbich and Ryndziewicz 2019).

The purpose of this article is to show that under certain conditions, using the undervalued resistivity method can give good results, especially when the same area is also tested using a different geophysical method. The research was carried out in an area very well known to Professor Hoffmeier—in North Sinai, in the Hellenistic-Roman city of Pelusium. It will serve as a case study to prove this point. Magnetic and resistivity methods were used in the research of the site (fig. 9.1).[1]

The Site

At the time when Pelusium was established, it was located at the mouth of the most eastward branch of the Nile (named Pelusian after the city). The exact founding date of the city is unknown, but most likely it took place mid-first millennium BCE. At the time of its heyday, during the Graeco-Roman period, it occupied an area about five to six kilometers long, and was one of the most important cities in Egypt. Written sources confirm the city's importance in international trade, while there is little information about its topography. The texts mention ports, custom offices, temples, a hippodrome, and a fortress. Without a doubt, there were many public utility buildings (Carrez-Maratray 1999). The city declined with the end of the first millennium CE, and was abandoned in the times of the Crusaders. The fall of the city, apart from political reasons, was caused by the silting of the Pelusian branch of the Nile, which inhibited water transport into the Nile Delta and further south, as well as geological processes that caused the sea coastline to move away from the city (Bietak 1975; Coutellier and Stanley 1987). Presently, the northern border of the city is more than three kilometers away from the sea. In the early twentieth century, when archeologists became interested in Pelusium, the only structure with a clear plan was the Byzantine fortress erected at the end of sixth century CE, covering an area of approximately 80,000 m². At that time, the temple (dedicated to Zeus) and the theater were identified (Clédat 1914). Considerable information about the city's buildings was gained when research was carried out there at the end of the twentieth century, following the return of Sinai to Egypt, and during a rescue operation undertaken when the canal that irrigates

---

1. The research, led by Tomasz Herbich, was carried out in 2005–2009. Artur Buszek, Szymon Maślak, Robert Ryndziewicz and Dawid Święch assisted in the fieldwork. The change in the political situation in Egypt prevented the completion of the research. The measurements were carried out as part of a research project of the Polish Center of Mediterranean Archaeology of the University of Warsaw, in cooperation with the Institute of Archaeology and Ethnology of the Polish Academy of Sciences.

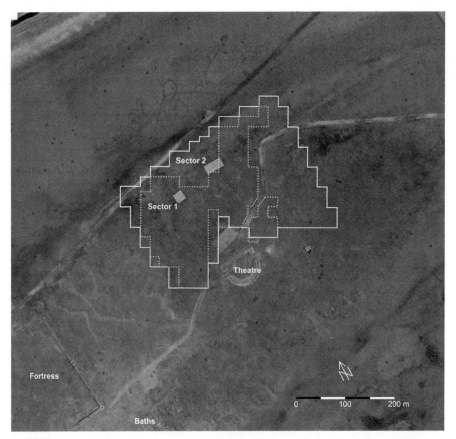

FIGURE 9.1. The area of the geophysical survey shown on a satellite image (Google Earth).
The area of the magnetic survey has been marked with a solid line, and the area of the resistivity survey with a dotted line. Sectors 1 and 2: excavation by the Polish Centre of Mediterranean Archaeology, University of Warsaw.

northwest Sinai with Nile water was being constructed. As a result, foundations of a
theater and baths from the Roman period, and a Byzantine church, were uncovered.
A second theater and cemeteries were identified in the eastern part of the city (bibliography in Jakubiak 2009). The research undertaken by the mission of the Polish
Centre of Mediterranean Archaeology of the University of Warsaw, on the northern
edge of the city, on the eastern side of the fortress, led to the discovery of foundations
of a residence richly decorated with mosaics (Jakubiak 2007, 2008).

However, there were no studies that would give more accurate data on the plan
of Pelusium—the layout of the streets, the sizes of insulae, identification of areas in
terms of their function in the city (public, residential, industrial). The state of preservation of the city does not allow such data to be obtained solely based on the analysis
of the surface. The site is now a broad plain with slight height differences, covered
by considerably moist saline silt, with no architectural remains visible on the surface,
other than single columns, stone blocks, and brick fragments (fig. 9.2). A geophysical
survey, as part of the Polish Centre of Mediterranean Archaeology research program,
made it possible to obtain such data.

FIGURE 9.2. The northern part of the survey area. The walls of the Byzantine fortress seen in the background. Photograph by Tomasz Herbich.

The Method

Initially, the author only intended to use the magnetic method in Pelusium, its effectiveness previously verified on dozens of other sites in Egypt. The results are widely known thanks to numerous publications. In some Egyptological periodicals, the principles of the method have also been presented in the introductions to presentations of results (Mathieson, et al. 1999).

The results of magnetic tests obtained during the first test season only allowed the exact borders of the built-up area, the general orientation of the buildings, and the layout of streets to be determined (more on this below in the description of results) (Jakubiak 2008). Despite the small size of the area covered by research (28,000 m²), it could already be concluded that the magnetic maps did not provide enough information to reconstruct plans of individual buildings. The reason for this was the building material: burnt brick. Burned clay, due to the phenomenon of thermoremanent magnetization, becomes a material with high magnetic susceptibility (Aspinall, Gaffney, and Schmidt 2008). Walls built using this material come out on magnetic maps only when the spaces between the walls are devoid of any materials with equally high magnetic susceptibility (e.g., rubble from burnt bricks from destroyed upper parts of the walls, Bevan 1994). In this situation, it was decided to test the resistivity profiling method—and in the case of positive test results—research would be continued using both methods.

The resistivity profiling method was sporadically used in Egypt. The method registers the horizontal range of structures, based on their ability to conduct electric current.

FIGURE 9.3. Magnetic survey with the use of a fluxgate gradiometer. Photograph Tomasz Herbich.

During the survey, changes in resistance are observed in the layer, determined by the layout of four electrodes: two potential and two current (Schmidt 2013). By maintaining constant spacing between the electrodes, changes are registered to a constant depth. In Egypt, this method had already been used in the 1980s by Ian Mathiesson in Amarna (Mathieson 1984), as well as the author in Tell Atrib (Myśliwiec and Herbich 1988). The analysis of results at the time, based on hand-drawn maps or graphs, only allowed to separate zones of various resistances; such analysis essentially made the reconstruction of building plans impossible.

The results of the tests in Pelusium showed that the walls made from burnt bricks cause anomalies that allow the reconstruction of building plans. The positive result was achieved thanks to a high contrast between the resistivity of alluvium soil (below 0.5 ohm-m), and of burnt brick walls (above 1 ohm-m). Such low resistivity (all values are below 2 ohm-m) was the result of high soil moisture, as well as very high salinity.

To carry out the magnetic survey, Geoscan Research FM256 fluxgate gradiometers were used, measuring the gradient of the vertical vector of the Earth's magnetic field intensity (fig. 9.3). Measurements were taken along lines half a meter apart, and twenty-five centimeters apart on the line (eight measurements per square meter). The resistivity survey was carried out using the Geoscan Research RM15 resistance meter, applying the twin-probe array (with a half meter distance between the traversing electrodes, fig. 9.4), along lines one meter apart, with measurements taken every half meter (two measurements per square meter).

FIGURE 9.4. Resistivity survey with the use of a resistivity meter with a twin-probe array. Photograph by M. Kurzyk.

The Result

The magnetic survey covered an area of 88,000 m², and was sufficient to determine the effectiveness of the method in reconstructing the plan of the city of Pelusium. On the magnetic map, the northern range of the buildings (and also the edge of the riverbed) is clearly visible (fig. 9.5). Linear anomalies in a perpendicular arrangement, consistent with cardinal directions, 100 to 400 m long, were interpreted as streets. The arrangement of the anomalies clearly corresponds to the orientations of buildings, consistent with the orientation of the streets. However, after a closer analysis of the magnetic image, it turns out that it is only possible to clearly define the outer walls of only four structures: a round structure in the southern part of the research area, 45 m in diameter (fig. 9.5), another round structure 15 m in diameter at the western border of the research area (square H2 in fig. 9.6A), a rectangular structure measuring 40 m × 14 m located in the northeast corner of the area (between squares C4 and B6 [eastern corner] in fig. 9.7A), and finally, a rectangular structure measuring 17 × 8 m, located in the center of the area shown in figure 9.6A. The latter structure, characterized by uniform magnetic field values, corresponds to either a nonbuilt-up area or a type of a mud-brick platform. The only building with a visible internal plan is the already mentioned rectangular structure in the northeast corner of the research area. In most cases, it is extremely difficult to determine the width of the streets, because it is impossible to determine which lines correspond to their edges (e.g., the anomaly between the north corner of H3 and western part of

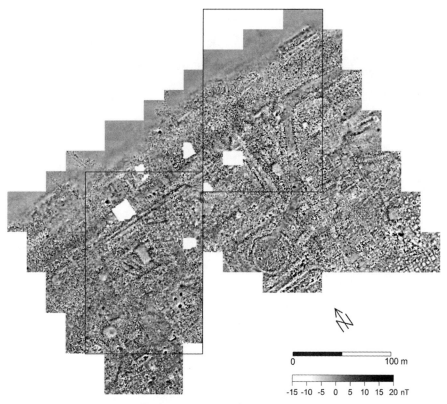

FIGURE 9.5. Magnetic map. The left rectangle marks the area presented in figure 9.6, the right rectangle marks the area presented in figure 9.7.

I4 in fig. 9.7A). An exception is the anomaly corresponding to the main street of the northern part of the city, running along the east-west line, where two very clear, almost 120 m long, linear anomalies form the edges the street (between D2 and A6 in fig. 9.6A).

A comparison of the magnetic map and the resistivity map shows that in a few cases we can more clearly define what the magnetic map presents, or confirm that the assumptions formed on the basis of the magnetic map were correct. And so, on the magnetic map, in the area where the linear anomalies cross at right angles, indicating that the area has been built over (squares C3, C4, D3, and D4, fig. 9.6A), the resistivity map shows a complex of anomalies with high resistivity values, corresponding to a building with a square plan (with a side of twenty-five meters), with a clearly visible northern and eastern edge (fig. 9.6B). The resistivity map also shows the interior plan of the building, with rows of different sized rooms, especially visible in its eastern part. A linear magnetic anomaly running parallel to the northern edge of the building, at a distance of four meters, clearly marks the northern edge of the street. This anomaly corresponds to the southern edge of the building, excavated in sector I (fig. 9.1). The resistivity image confirms the width of the street (fig. 9.6B).

We can observe an analogous situation in an area located forty meters toward the east from the one described above. On the magnetic map, we can see a complex of linear anomalies in a perpendicular arrangement, with most anomalies oriented north-south (in B5, C5, B6, and C6 squares, fig. 9.6A), adjoining from the south with an anomaly corresponding to the street running east-west. On the resistivity map, in the corresponding area, we can observe a corner of a building of considerable size, with clearly outlined western and northern edges, and rows of rectangular rooms located along the western edge (fig. 9.6B). At the same time, the western line precisely defines the edge of the street, which we could suspect exists based on the results the magnetic map, but we could not precisely locate it. The resistivity map also indicates the exact point where the streets intersect (in the northwestern part of B5, fig. 9.6B).

Another area where the resistivity map gave a much more detailed image of the buildings than the magnetic map is visible a bit further to the east, on the south side of the street on the east-west line mentioned above. The arrangement of linear anomalies on the magnetic map, visible between the northern corner of H3, and the eastern part of I4 (fig. 9.7A), does not answer the question whether the street is five meters or ten meters wide. However, the resistivity image clearly shows that the width of the street is greater than presumed (fig. 9.7B). The magnetic map suggests a presence of a building in this area, but it is impossible to say anything about its plan. The resistivity image, however, shows the northern and western edge of the building, and two rows of rectangular and square rooms located along its western edge.

The comparison of the magnetic map and the resistivity map also made it possible to assess the condition of building foundations, and to determine what material they were made of. Linear anomalies corresponding to a rectangular building, registered as a result of magnetic measurements on the northern edge of the site (with its center in B5, fig. 9.7), are in most cases negative (i.e., the values of their magnetic field are lower than their surroundings). Such anomalies may suggest that the foundations were made of stone (limestone lacks magnetic properties, and Egyptian sandstones have low magnetic susceptibility). The use of the most durable construction material, which is stone, seems logical, considering that the building is located on the riverbank, and therefore in a place more exposed to the destructive effects of water. Stone surrounded by muddy alluvium would have a much higher resistivity value than the environment. However, the anomalies that correspond to that building on the resistivity map, have lower resistivity values compared to their surroundings. This can only mean one thing: the anomalies in fact correspond to the so-called "ghost walls," that is, foundation ditches, created when the building material that forms the walls has been completely removed. Ghost walls were discovered in a number of places in Pelusium (Jakubiak 2007). The construction of the fortress created a great demand for bricks at the end of the sixth century. The fact that the building was made of bricks is confirmed by a number of disturbances visible on the map in the spaces between the ghost walls. These anomalies correspond to fragments of bricks, probably left during the disassembly of the building.

The comparison of the magnetic and resistivity maps at the western edge of the research area (figs. 9.5 and 9.6), where the round structure with a diameter of fifteen meters is located, also could indicate the type of material that was used for its construction. A negative anomaly corresponds to the building on the magnetic map (in the western corner of H2, fig. 9.6A). On the resistivity map (fig. 9.6B) an anomaly with a significantly higher resistivity value than its surroundings is visible. This allows us to suppose that the structure causing these anomalies is made of stone—limestone or sandstone.

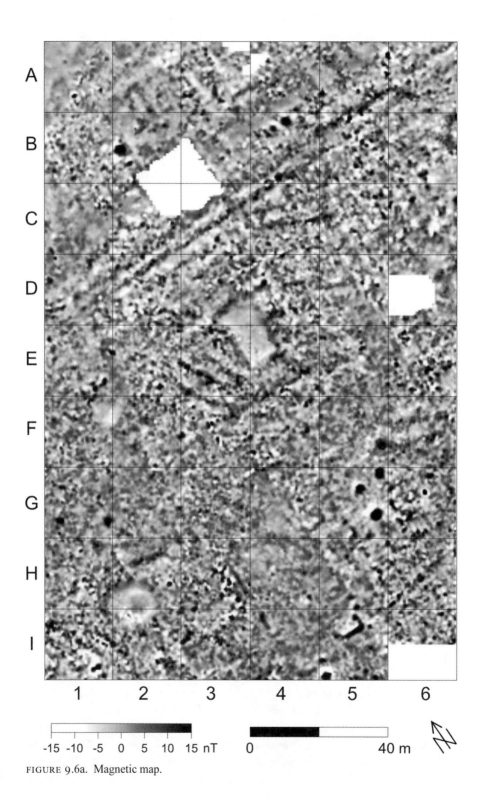

FIGURE 9.6a. Magnetic map.

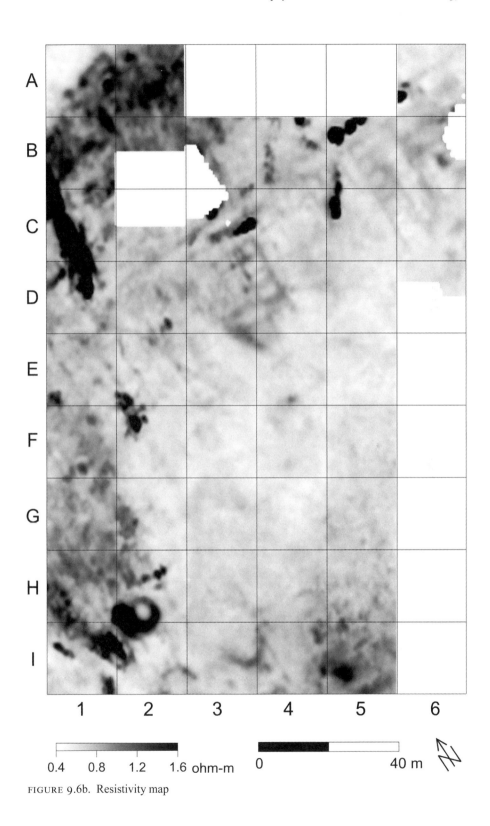

FIGURE 9.6b. Resistivity map

140   Tomasz Herbich

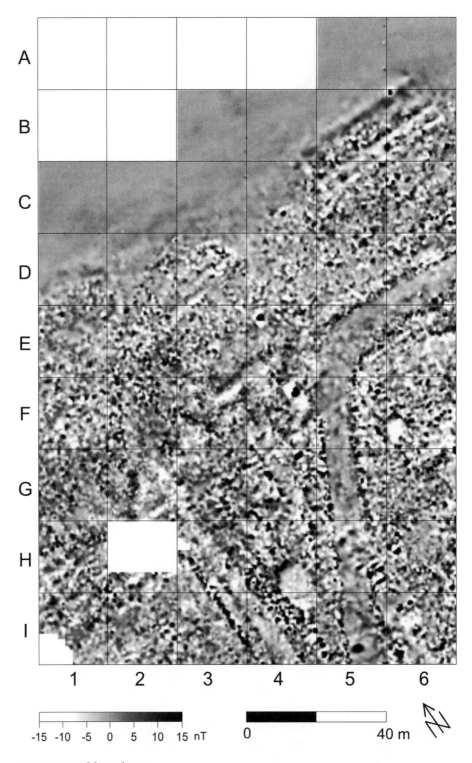

FIGURE 9.7a. Magnetic map.

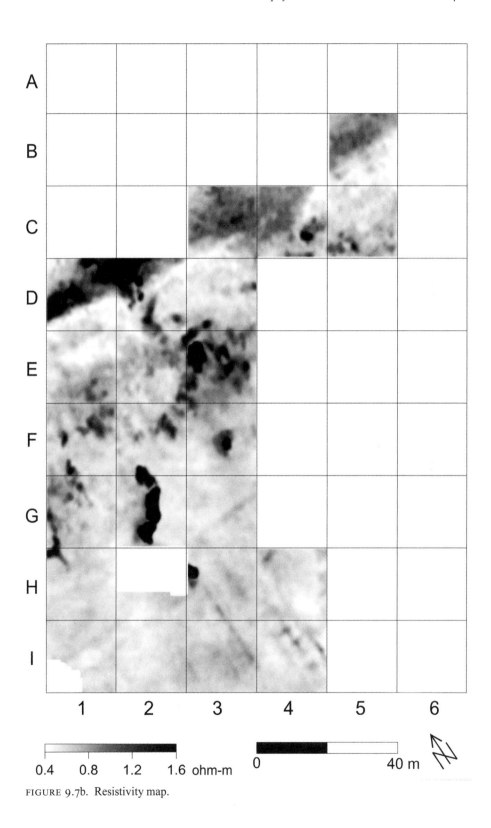

Final Remarks

The presented material clearly shows that in geological conditions conducive to carrying out resistivity surveys (low resistivity of soil and good contact between the soil and electrodes), it is worthwhile to use this method—despite it requiring more effort than the magnetic one. The benefits of using two or more geophysical methods on one site have been known to archaeological geophysicists for a long time, and this methodology of measurements has been used many times, however, mainly in European archaeology. In Egyptian archaeology, surveys using several geophysical methods have been carried out, but these were mostly studies of small areas (e.g., Ibrahim, Sherief and Al-Metwally 1998; Kamei et al. 2002). Resistivity measurements in Pelusium covered an area of 45,000 m², and it seems that it still is the largest area covered by resistivity profiling at an archaeological site in Egypt (at least among the published research).

The political situation in north Sinai prevented the continuation of archeological research in Pelusium. Despite already having consent from the Egyptian authorities, it was impossible to complete the magnetic measurements. As the project had to be abandoned, it was also unfortunately impossible to carry out the resistivity survey in the areas that had earlier been covered by magnetic research.

Professor Hoffmeier and the author represent completely different specialties in the field of archaeology. But one thing, of course apart from an interest in Egyptian archaeology, now connects them: the impossibility to continue research in Sinai. However, it is doubtful whether this unfortunate connection makes them happy.

BIBLIOGRAPHY

Aspinall, Arnold, Christopher Gaffney, and Armin Schmidt. 2008. *Magnetometry for Archaeologists*. Lanham, MD: Altamira.

Bevan, Bruce W. 1994. "The Magnetic Anomaly of a Brick Foundation." *Archaeological Prospection* 1:93–104.

Bietak, Manfred, ed. 1975. *Tell el-Dabʿa II: Der Fundort im Rahmen einer archäologisch-geograpchischen Untersuchung über das ägyptische Ostdelta*. Denkschriften der Gesamtakademie 4. Vienna: Österreichischen Akademie der Wissenschaften.

Carrez-Maratray, Jean-Yves. 1999. *Péluse et l'angle oriental du delta Égyptien aux époques grecque, romaine et byzantine*. Cairo: Institut français d'archéologie orientale.

Clédat, Jean. 1914. "La temple de Zeus Cassios à Péluse." *ASAE* 13:79–85.

Coutellier, Vincent, and Daniel J. Stanley. 1987. "Late Quaternary Stratigraphy and Paleography of the Eastern Nile Delta, Egypt." *Marine Geology* 77:257–75.

Herbich, Tomasz. 2003. "Archaeological Geophysics in Egypt: The Polish Contribution." *Archaeologia Polona* 41:13–55.

———. 2012. "Geophysical Methods and Landscape Archaeology." *Egyptian Archaeology* 41:11–14.

———.2013. "Geophysical Surveying in Egypt: Periodic Report for 2011–2012." Pages 241–45 in *Proceedings of the Tenth International Conference on Archaeological Prospection, Vienna May 29–June 2 2013*. Edited by Wolfgang Neubauer, Immo Trinks, Roderick B. Salisbury, and Christina Einwögerer. Vienna: Österreichischen Akademie der Wissenschaften.

———. 2014. "Results of the Magnetic Survey at Tell el-Borg, North Sinai, March 2006 and 2007." Pages 346–63 in *Tell el Borg I: The "Dwelling of the Lion" on the Ways of Horus*. Edited by James K. Hoffmeier. Winona Lake, IN: Eisenbrauns.

———. 2015. "Magnetic Prospecting in Archaeological Research: A Historical Outline." *Archaeolgia Polona* 53:21–68.

Herbich, Tomasz, Matt Adams, Pascale Ballet, David O'Connor, and Ulricht Hartung. 2005. "Geophysics in Egyptian Archaeology." *Dossiers d'Archeologie* 308:62–70.

Herbich, Tomasz, Harald von der Osten-Woldenburg, and Iwona Zych. 2011. "Geophysics Applied to the Investigation of Graeco-Roman Coastal Towns West of Alexandria: the Case of Marina el-Alamein." Pages 209–31 in *Classica Orientalia: Essays Presented to Wiktor Andrzej Daszewski on His 75th birthday*. Edited by Henryk Meyza and Iwona Zych. Warsaw: University of Warsaw, DiG.

Herbich, Tomasz, and Robert Ryndziewicz. 2019. "Geophysical Surveying in Egypt and Sudan: Periodical Report for 2017–2018." Pages 169–72 in *New Global Perspectives on Archaeological Prospection: Thirteenth International Conference on Archaeological Prospection, 28 August–1 September 2019, Sligo, Ireland*. Edited by James Bonsall. Oxford: Archaeopress.

Hesse, A. 1967. "Mesures et interprétation en prospection géophysique des sites archéologiques du Nil." *Prospezioni Archeologiche* 1:43–48.

———. 1970. "Introduction géophysiques et notes techniques." Pages 51–121 in *Mirgissa I*. Edited by Jean Vercouter. Paris: Geuthner.

Hoffmeier, James K., and Stephen O. Moshier. 2006. "New Paleo-Environmental Evidence from North Sinai to Complement Manfred Bietak's Map of the Eastern Delta and Some Historical Implications." Pages 165–74 in vol. 2 of *Timelines: Studies in Honour of Manfred Bietak*. Edited by Ernst Czerny, Irmgard Hein, Hermann Hunger, Dagman Melman, and Angela Schwab. OLA 149. 3 vols. Leuven: Peeters.

———. 2013. "'A Highway out of Egypt': The Main Road from Egypt to Canaan." Pages 485–510 in *Desert Road Archaeology*. Edited by Frank Förster and Heiko Reimer. Africa Prehistorica 27. Köln: Barth Institut.

Ibrahim, E. H., M. R. Sherief, and A. A. Al-Metwally. 1998. "Shallow Geophysical Investigations on Tell el Farama, Northwest Sinai, Egypt." *Archaeological Prospection* 5:91–100.

Jakubiak, Krzysztof. 2007. "Tell Farama (Pelusium), Report on the Third and Fourth Seasons." *Polish Archaeology in the Mediterranean* 17:125–35.

———. 2008. "Pelusium: Still Egyptian or Maybe Oriental Town in the Western Sinai; Results of the Last Excavations on the Roman City." Pages 221–35 in vol. 2 of *Proceedings of the Fifth International Congress on the Archaeology of the Ancient Near East, Madrid, April 3–8 2006*. Edited by Joaquín Córdoba, Miquel Molist, Carmen Pérez, Isabel Rubio, Sergio Martínez. 2 vols. Madrid: Universidad Autónoma de Madrid.

———. 2009. "Tell Farama, Pelusium: City Urban Planning Reconstruction in the Light of the Last Researches." Pages 67–74 in *Proceedings of the Fifth Central European Conference of Egyptologists: Egypt 2009; Perspectives of Research, Pułtusk 22–24 June 2009*. Edited by Joanna Popielska-Grzybowska and Jadwiga Iwaszczuk. Acta Archaeologica Pultuskiensia 2. Pułtusk: Pułtusk Academy of Humanities.

Kamei, Hiroyuki, Magdy Ahmed Atya, Tareq Fahmy Abadallatif, Masato Mori, and Pasomphone Hemthavy, P. 2002. "Ground-Penetrating Radar and Magnetic Survey to the West of al-Zayyan Temple, Kharga Oasis, al-Wadi al-Jadeed (New Valley), Egypt." *Archaeological Prospecting* 9:93–104.

Mathieson, Ian J. 1984. "A Resistivity Survey at el-Amarna." Pages 99–123 in *Amarna Reports I*. Edited by Barry J. Kemp. Occasional Papers 1. London: Egypt Exploration Society.

Mathieson, Ian, Elizabeth Bettles, Jon Dittmer, and Colin Reader. 1999. "The National Museums of Scotland Saqqara Survey Project, Earth Sciences 1990–1998." *JEA* 85:21–43.

Myśliwiec, Karol, and Tomasz Herbich. 1988. "Polish Archaeological Activity at Tell Atrib in 1985." Pages 177–89 in *Archaeology of the Nile Delta, Egypt: Problems and Priorities*. Edited by Edwin van den Brink. Amsterdam: Netherlands Foundation for Archaeological Research in Egypt.

Pusch, Edgar. 1999. "Towards a Map of Piramesse." *Egyptian Archaeology* 14:13–15.

Push, E., Helmut Becker, and Jörg W. Fassbinder. 2000. "Palast—Tempel—Auswärtiges Amt? Oder: sind Nilschlammauern magnetisch zu erfassen?" *AeL* 11:135–53.

Schmidt Armin. 2013. *Earth Resistance for Archaeologists*. Lanham, MD: Altamira.

Ullrich, Burkart, and Pawel Wolf. 2015. "Hamadab near Meroe (Sudan): Results of Multitechnique Geophysical Surveys." *Archaeologia Polona* 53:392–95.

CHAPTER 10

The Genealogies of Genesis 5 and 11 and Comparative Studies: Evidence for a Seam

Richard S. Hess

THE STUDY OF THE BIBLICAL GENEALOGIES at the beginning of Genesis has been enhanced by the use of the ancient Near Eastern comparative material. The purpose of this paper will be to review some key aspects of that study, with special attention to comparative material relevant to the genealogies of Gen 5 and 11, and to suggest how this comparative material may shed light on questions surrounding the interpretation of the genealogies. In order to do this a review will be made of some of the most important texts and analyses that have been ascribed relevance for the genealogies (Hebrew *tôlĕdôt*) of Gen 5 and 11. The study will consider recent work on the ancient Near Eastern context of the personal names as found in these genealogies. This will lead to an examination of discussions of the literary, text critical, and onomastic contexts for the texts of Gen 5 and 11. It will be noted how all three of these areas point toward a specific seam or break at the same point in the text of the genealogies. Study of the origins, distinctions, and comparative materials make contributions to understanding these ancient texts.

Ancient Near Eastern King Lists and Genesis 5 and 11

We begin with a review of the ancient Near Eastern comparisons to the genealogies as a whole. In so doing we consider the special role of ancient Near Eastern king lists and related materials. In the Schweich Lectures of 1916 Leonard W. King argued similarities between the Sumerian King List and the genealogies and other details of Gen 4–6.[1] He and others, such as George A. Barton, argued for the origins of the names in these lists as coming from the Sumerian King List.[2] A thorough study of the Sumerian King List appeared in the 1939 monograph of Thorkild Jacobsen.[3] He concluded that the antediluvian section of the list was a separate piece added later, and that the composition of the work about the time of the Ur III period served to promote national feeling. These views were generally confirmed by scholars with the development by William

---

1. Leonard W. King, *Legends of Babylon and Egypt in Relation to Hebrew Tradition* (London: Oxford University Press, 1918), 37–38.
2. George A. Barton, *Archaeology and the Bible*, 7th ed. (Philadelphia: American Sunday School Union, 1937), 324.
3. Thorkild Jacobsen, *The Sumerian King List*, AS 11 (Chicago: University of Chicago Press, 1939).

Hallo from a national feeling to an ideal of unity under one king as the purpose of the Sumerian King List.[4]

In 1957 Wilfred Lambert noted that the Old Babylonian style of the early second millennium BCE consistently used the expression, "X *mâr* Y" to identify a biological son or one who was adopted into that relationship.[5] However, after 1600 BCE the Kassite period of Babylon changed their usage of this expression to include reference to descendants who might be separated by some generations. This conclusion could be used as evidence for the presence of gaps in the genealogies of Gen 1–11, if they or the traditions behind them were produced after 1600 BCE. The opposite would be true if the ultimate origin of these works dates from before 1600, and especially if they had cultural connections with the Old Babylonian world. However, the form, "son of," does not occur in the genealogies of the first part of Genesis.

Using four texts, including LKA 76, Ki 1904-10-9, and Kouyunjik 5119 and 7987, Erica Reiner, with the acknowledged assistance of Benno Landsberger, reconstructed an important textual tradition dealing with the antediluvian sages, the *apkallu*.[6] The list describes seven *apkallu*, whom it designates as the *purādu*-fish of the sea. Reiner observes connections with the records of the later account of the Greek historian Berossus about Oannes and monsters in the form of fish who taught humanity the crafts of civilization. The *apkallu* are not kings, but are associated with them as sages. Each *apkallu* corresponds to a successive king. In their role as inventors and builders of civilization, they invite comparison with the line of Cain in Gen 4:17–24. J. J. Finkelstein supplemented this association of the *apkallu* with the antediluvian king list.[7] He discussed the lengthy reigns of these kings, something long noted as an important comparison with the long-lived line of Gen 5. However, the Sumerian King List includes kings who reigned as briefly as 6,000 years and as long as 72,000 years. These numbers are impossibly higher than Gen 5, where the oldest figure, Methuselah, lives 969 years. Nevertheless, they provide comparative evidence of common traditions that recognized a flood where those who lived before the flood survived much longer than their descendants.

Four comparisons may be made concerning the *apkallu* and their antediluvian kings, and the line of Cain and that of Seth. Along with (1) the dual lines of *apkallu* and kings compared with the lines of Cain and of Seth, as well as (2) the long lives of the "second line" (kings and line of Seth) in each case, we may add that (3) the "first line" (*apkallu* and the line of Cain) did not continue after the flood (there is one *apkallu*, but not a line) while the "second line" did continue. A fourth point of comparison is made by Finkelstein, concerning the similar names in the two lines of Genesis (e.g., Enoch, Lamech, and Methushael/Methuselah) and those of the *apkallu* and their associated antediluvian kings, "Enmedugga in the time of Anmeluanna (i.e., Enmeluanna); Enmegalamma in the time of Anmegalanna (i.e., Enmegalanna); Enmebulugga in the

4. William W. Hallo, "Royal Hymns and Mesopotamian Unity," *JCS* 17 (1963): 112–13; Hallo, "Beginning and End of the Sumerian King List in the Nippur Recension," *JCS* 17 (1963): 52–57. For a list of other scholars in agreement with Jacobsen, see Thomas C. Hartman, "Some Thoughts on the Sumerian King List and Genesis 5 and 11B," *JBL* 91 (1972): 26–27 nn. 5, 7.

5. Wilfred G. Lambert, "Ancestors, Authors, and Canonicity," *JCS* 11 (1957): 1.

6. Erica Reiner, "The Etiological Myth of the 'Seven Sages,'" *Or* 30 (1961): 1–11.

7. J. J. Finkelstein, "The Antediluvian Kings: A University of California Tablet," *JCS* 17 (1963): 39–51.

time of Enmeušumgalanna."[8] The comparisons of the biblical names with Sumerian names, however, did not hold up as well. Already in 1964, E. A. Speiser concluded that direct borrowing from Sumerian was unlikely and preferred intermediate routes, perhaps via Hurrian.[9] Since then there has been no convincing evidence for a linguistic relationship between these groups of names.[10] Further, the ideology of the Sumerian King List and the attempts to compare the groupings of name lists in terms of ten generations are now seen as not unique to the Sumerian King List and Genesis, but as common West Semitic forms.[11]

In 1965 Lambert published an important essay on the book of Genesis and the Old Babylonian account known as the Atrahasis Epic.[12] As in Gen 1–11, this places the stories of creation and of a flood in the context of a larger literary narrative. Looking at the antediluvian king lists as well, Lambert suggests a common inheritance in all these examples in which the flood story does not occur by itself but in a larger context that can and often does include lists of kings who precede and follow it.[13] Therefore, there may be grounds for comparing these king lists with the genealogies in terms of the similar literary contexts in which they occur.

A year later, in 1966, Finkelstein brought to scholars' attention one of the most important cuneiform texts related to the early genealogies of Genesis.[14] This was BM 80328, which contained a list of the names of the rulers of the first dynasty of Babylon, ending with the third ruler after Hammurabi, Ammiditana. Some of the initial names on the list correspond with known Amorite tribes and with the names of the first part of the Assyrian King List. The first three names in the list may be double names, similar to those separate names in the Assyrian King List. Thus, in line 2 of the Hammurabi list there is *Tu-ub-ti-ya-mu-ta,* likely a linkage of the first two names on the Assyrian King List, *Tu-di-ya* and *A-da-mu.*[15] Both genealogies are thus related and attest to a conscious awareness of tribal origins. Further, this text is not strictly a king list. It is a prayer to the shades of the dead, a *kispu* ritual, the first twenty-eight lines of which form an added list of names from earliest to latest.[16] In the present document this list of names is part of a larger context whose purpose is religious. This may be compared with the genealogies of Gen 5 and 11, which form part of a larger context.

Hallo ascribed the "genealogical orientation" to the coming of the Amorites (ca. 2000 BCE), groups of people who arguably have connections with the emergence of the Old Babylonian dynasty, the early Assyrian rulers, and the Israelite traditions of Genesis.[17] Abraham Malamat compared the Hammurabi list of names with the

---

8. Finkelstein, "Antediluvian Kings," 50.

9. E. A. Speiser, *Genesis,* AB 1 (Garden City, NY: Doubleday, 1964).

10. Gerhard F. Hasel, "The Genealogies of Gen 5 and 11 and Their Alleged Babylonian Background," *AUSS* 16 (1978): 364–65. Hasel adds other objections to this comparison including the long-noted facts that the king lists deal with royal lineage and length of reigns while the biblical genealogies deal with nonroyal lifespans.

11. Abraham Malamat, "King Lists of the Old Babylonian Period and Biblical Genealogies," *JAOS* 88 (1968): 163–73; Hartman, "Some Thoughts on the Sumerian King List," 28–32.

12. W. G. Lambert, "A New Look at the Babylonian Background of Genesis," *JTS* 16 (1965): 287–300.

13. Ibid., 292.

14. J. J. Finkelstein, "The Genealogy of the Hammurapi Dynasty," *JCS* 20 (1966): 95–118.

15. Ibid., 99. Finkelstein credits this observation to Benno Landsberger.

16. W. G. Lambert, "Another Look at Hammurabi's Ancestors," *JCS* 22 (1968): 1–2.

17. William W. Hallo, "Antediluvian Cities," *JCS* 23 (1971): 62–63.

Assyrian King List and the biblical genealogies in greater detail.[18] In form and function he found similarities with Gen 5 and 11. For example, there are eleven names in lines 1–8 of the Hammurabi dynasty, twelve kings in lines 1–7 of the first column of the Assyrian King List, and perhaps ten names in both Gen 5 and 11. Thomas Hartman also supported this connection between Gen 5 and 11 and the other Amorite genealogies.[19]

In 1975 Robert Wilson published an initial paper on the subject of biblical genealogies.[20] In it he summarized earlier work and then argued that Malamat had incorrectly assumed the historiographic value of biblical genealogies and that the assertion of the characteristic Amorite genealogy of about ten generations has not been proven. He suggested that the similarities between the opening names of the Assyrian King List and the earlier names of the Hammurabi dynasty presume that these societies found a common Amorite origin. However, the chronological order of the names could not be assumed. The genealogies may originally have included segmented parts, where some of the names that now appear were in fact contemporaries rather than in a parent-child relationship.

Wilson criticized the earlier literary study of the Old and New Testament genealogies by Marshall Johnson as inadequate due its lack of form critical and tradition critical analysis, as well as a lack of awareness of the more detailed ancient Near Eastern and anthropological parallels.[21] Wilson undertook this task in a monograph that appeared in 1977.[22] His study of ancient Near Eastern king lists attempted to read into them a good deal of the fluidity that he had identified in the tribal genealogies obtained from anthropological research. He saw this fluidity operating in the biblical genealogies, including those of Genesis. Wilson argued that Gen 4 and 5, the lines of Cain and of Seth, were drawn from the same source but served different functions. The editors changed the order and names to reflect that purpose.

While interesting in itself, is too much imported from oral and tribal genealogies and superimposed on written genealogies of the ancient world? In his review of Wilson's work, Lambert noted some important points.[23] He observed that the Sumerians of the third millennium BCE did not betray any interest in descent from a particular line in order to establish legitimacy for a royal office. On the other hand, the Old Babylonian period king list and that of the first dynasty did reflect the Amorite practice of extending legitimacy through a king's line of descent.[24] Thus differing functions defined different king lists. They were not uniform in the ancient world. Lambert also made the important point that, by the second millennium BCE, king lists were drawn from Babylonian year-name lists and from Assyrian *limmu* lists, and were used to establish systems for reckoning time. To fulfill this purpose, parentage was

---

18. Malamat, "King Lists of the Old Babylonian Dynasty."

19. Hartman, "Some Thoughts on the Sumerian King List."

20. Robert R. Wilson, "The Old Testament Genealogies in Recent Research," *JBL* 94 (1975): 169–89.

21. Ibid., 172–73. See Marshall D. Johnson, *The Purpose of the Biblical Genealogy: With Special Reference to the Setting of the Genealogies of Jesus*, SNTSMS 8 (Cambridge: Cambridge University Press, 1969).

22. Robert R. Wilson, *Genealogy and History in the Biblical World*, YNER 7 (New Haven: Yale University Press, 1977).

23. W. G. Lambert, review of *Genealogy and History in the Biblical World*, by Robert R. Wilson, *JNES* 39 (1980): 75–77.

24. W. G. Lambert, "The Seed of Kingship," in *Le palais et la royauté (archeology et civilization): XIXe R.A.I. Paris, 21 juin–2 juillet 1971*, ed. Paul Garelli (Paris: Geuthner, 1974), 427–40.

not important, but the sequence of rulers was essential. This practical application was not recognized by Wilson, but provides evidence for the stability of dates and times, rather than the fluidity to which Wilson refers.

David T. Bryan observed that attempts to make broad generalizations about genealogies and their common origins are overstated.[25] The *apkallu* list and the Sumerian King List did not originate together. Therefore, any similarities in names should not be assumed as indications of a common origin for the two. Further, the names in the Hammurabi king list and those in the Assyrian King List, while similar, are not identical. This, along with a list of differences in literary structure and content between Gen 4 and 5, suggest that these two lists should not be assumed to have drawn their names from the same origins.

I pursued the differences between ancient Near Eastern king lists and the genealogies of Gen 1–11 in a study published in 1989.[26] It remains my contention that the contextual data must have priority over the comparative, especially when different purposes are involved in creating the name lists. In terms of the ancient Near Eastern lists, formal differences are found between the Genesis genealogies and the Sumerian King List. The latter contain no regular genealogical notices. They use the term "son of" (DUMU) to identify relationships. The same is true of the list of rulers of Lagash and of the Assyrian and Babylonian King Lists. The Hammurabi King List simply lists the names, with no kinship description. All of this is unlike the genealogies of Gen 5 and 11 where kinship references include "son," but also notes about begetting.

This point further needs to be made with reference to the direction of the king list. The ancient Near Eastern king lists, especially the West Semitic ones, tend to begin with the latest generation and work backward in time. This is the opposite of the genealogies in Genesis. They begin with the earliest figure and move forward in time.[27]

The *apkallu* list and their corresponding kings are two different lists. The same is true of Gen 4 and 5, as already noted. Finally, there is a contrast between the lists of kings, as well as scribes and priests, in the ancient Near East, and the lists of Gen 1–11 which are exclusively concerned with kinship. Combined with the forward movement in time, this feature provides a distinctive function for the genealogies of Gen 5 and 11. They push the reader forward in history. The ideal in the genealogies is not backward looking to some glorious past or a noble figure with whom the list connects. Instead, it moves forward with the expectation of better things to come in the future.

Two lists of kings have also appeared among the Ugaritic texts, discovered at Ras Shamra near the Mediterranean coast of Syria and generally dated to the thirteenth century BCE. There is a king list from Ugarit (*KTU* 1.113) that was published in 1968.[28]

---

25. David T. Bryan, "A Reevaluation of Gen 4 and 5 in Light of Recent Studies in Genealogical Fluidity," *ZAW* 99 (1987): 180–88.

26. Richard S. Hess, "The Genealogies of Genesis 1–11 and Comparative Literature," *Bib* 70 (1989): 241–54.

27. This is true even for the Assyrian King List. Although it begins with the seventeen earliest kings, the second group of ten kings names first the latest ruler and the end of the list indicates the earliest ruler.

28. *COS* 1.104. For the publication, see Charles Viroulleaud, "Les nouveaux textes mythologiques et liturgiques de Ras Shamra (XXIVe Campagne, 1961)," in *Ugaritica 5: Nouveaux Textes Accadiens, Hourrites et Ugaritiques des Archives et Bibliothèques Privées d'Ugarit: Commentaires des Textes Historiques*, ed. Jean Nougayrol et al., Mission de Ras Shamra 16, Bibliothèque Archéologique et Historique 80 (Paris: Geuthner, 1968), 545–95, esp. 561–62; and Dennis Pardee, RSOu 4, 165–78.

On its recto, the tablet (RS 24.257) contains a partially preserved poetic (repetitive) text in which tambourines (Ugaritic *tp*) and flutes are raised in honor of the "Pleasant One." The reverse contains two columns where only the second column is preserved in a readable form.[29] Although partially broken, the first readable line contains the name Ammistamru. There follow thirteen lines, apparently going back to the first known king, Yaqaru. Each royal name is preceded by the Ugaritic word *'l,* "god." This may indicate that the kings have died, that they are somehow divine, that a deity associated with each king is referenced, or a combination of these points. Like Gen 5 and 11, the context is a religious one, but unlike the biblical genealogies, there is no family or chronological relationship identified between these rulers. There seems to be a sequence from later to earlier kings.

The second list of kings also occurs in a religious context. It is a list of patrons of the Ugaritic dynasty, described as commemorating the accession to kingship of Ammurapi who was the last king of Ugarit (*KTU* 1.161).[30] The legendary Rephaim, here kings of old, are summoned to this feast or *marzēaḥ.* The names of four kings listed as Didanites are otherwise unknown. Two other leaders, Ammistamru and Niqmadu, are known as rulers at Ugarit. The text is disputed in terms of its interpretation. The unclear nature of the king list does not allow for specific comparison with the biblical texts. More generally, all West Semitic lists of kings that we have reviewed share with the genealogies of Gen 5 and 11 a religious context.

When Lambert wrote some sixty years ago, he argued that king lists using "son of" before 1600 BCE intended the understanding to be one of biological father and son with no gaps in descendants. For those after 1600 this was not always the case. Nevertheless, there was a historical importance to king lists because of their use in reckoning chronology.

However, the 1966 publication of the Hammurabi list changed some perspectives. As a list of Amorite (and therefore West Semitic) ancestors of the current king in the Old Babylonian period, it was both a list closest to the genealogies of Gen 5 and 11 in terms of cultural origins and in terms of serving a religious purpose different from what would be described as exclusively a king list. As noted, this list seems to have conflated its earliest names when compared with those names in the Assyrian King List. Further a comparison between this Hammurabi dynasty list and the Assyrian King List supports the claim that the many similar names in the same order occur in the first eight slots of the Hammurabi genealogy (*COS* 1.134) as do the first twelve names of the Assyrian King List (*COS* 1.135).[31] Both lists include additional names that do not occur in the other list. Comparisons between these early lists, reaching back well before 2000 BCE, suggest the presence of gaps and of conflations of names. The same may be true of the Ugaritic king list but there is nothing to compare it with. Nevertheless, the conclusion regarding early West Semitic or Amorite king lists is that gaps are possible in the genealogical sequence.

29. The first column preserves three and four letters at the end of two lines that can be reconstructed as the names of Ugaritic kings Niqmepa and Ammistamru.

30. *COS* 1.105. For a translation and the publication history, see Richard Hess, *Israelite Religions: An Archaeological and Biblical Survey* (Grand Rapids: Baker Academic, 2007), 110–11.

31. Alan R. Millard, "2. Historiography," in *COS* 1.134–138:461–70, esp. pp. 461–63.

Genealogies of Genesis 5 and 11 and Biblical Chronology

The areas of research in these genealogies have gone forward in other directions. Work has addressed the question of the intention of the genealogies as sources for chronological information.

The term "sons" appears with "daughters" in the Genesis lists but the emphasis on the "son" who succeeds his father in the line includes the *hiphil* form of the *yld* root and the name of that son. This raises questions about the meaning of this form of begetting the son and whether or not evidence can be brought to bear in terms of dating these family lines.

The traditional understanding dates at least from the earliest Hellenistic Jewish historian for whom records exist. Clement of Alexandria records how the second century BCE historian Eupolemus used the genealogies to calculate 5,149 years from Adam until his own time (*Strom.* 1.141, 4). From that time until the nineteenth century it was common to assume that the genealogies of Genesis were guides to determining the age of the human race. In 1890 William Henry Green challenged the dominant view by arguing that Gen 5 and 11 contained gaps that rendered them useless as indicators of absolute chronology.[32] Green contends that the third-person masculine singular *hiphil* form of *yld*, "he begot, has caused to be born," can refer both to biological sons and daughters as well as to later descendants, grandchildren, and their offspring, for example. As evidence he cites Deut 4:25, where children and grandchildren are explicitly mentioned, and 2 Kgs 20:18 (= Isa 39:7) where the "children" are those offspring of Hezekiah who will go into captivity a century later. Thus, Green argues that these phenomena, where the number of generations in between cannot be determined, must allow for lengthy gaps between the figures named in the genealogies of Gen 5 and 11.

In an important essay, Jeremy Sexton concedes that these examples allow for a genealogical gap.[33] That is, he agrees that Enosh in Gen 5:9–11, may be the father, grandfather, or great-grandfather of Kenan. However, Sexton asserts that the text states Kenan was born when Enosh was ninety years of age. For Sexton, there may be genealogical gaps but not chronological ones. Thus, the *hiphil* of *yld* followed by a direct object marker and a name requires that the stated name-bearer was born in the conditions pertaining to the verb and its modifiers. In this case, those conditions include the age at which the birth took place. Thus, there are no chronological gaps in the manner in which the text presents its data. As for the Septuagint and New Testament plus of Cainan as the son of Arpachshad (see Luke 3:36 and Jub. 8:1–5), Sexton concludes that the Septuagint preserves the original text with its longer chronology.[34]

Taking a different approach has been the work of the chronogenealogists, a term invented and championed by Gerhard Hasel.[35] Like others already mentioned, Hasel

---

32. William Henry Green, "Primeval Chronology," *BSac* 47 (1890): 285–303.

33. Jeremy Sexton, "Who Was Born When Enosh Was 90? A Semantic Reevaluation of William Henry Green's Chronological Gaps," *WTJ* 77 (2015): 193–218. Sexton credits the first publication of the key points of this argument to Smith Bartlett Goodenow, *Bible Chronology Carefully Unfolded* (New York: Revell, 1896), 317–27.

34. Sexton, "Who Was Born When Enosh Was 90," 212–18.

35. Gerhard. F. Hasel, "Genesis 5 and 11: Chronogenealogies in the Biblical History of Beginnings," *Origins* 7 (1980): 23–37; Hasel, "The Meaning of the Chronogenealogies of Genesis 5 and 11," *Origins* 7 (1980): 53–70.

argued for historical and chronological intent in the genealogies of Gen 5 and 11.[36] Unlike others, however, Hasel did not prefer the Septuagint or any other tradition over the Masoretic Text. He found the greater irregularity in numbers of years in the Hebrew text to witness to the likelihood that they had not been retouched by a later editorial hand. Bolstered by additional arguments from others such as Travis Freeman and Bernard White, it seems that the genealogies of Gen 5 and 11 are intended to be used chronologically. With their detailed summary of years lived before and after begetting the representative of the next generation, they are unlike any other genealogy in or outside the Bible.[37]

White follows earlier work in noting the uniquely chronological nature of the genealogies of chapters 5 and 11, unlike any other in the Bible or the ancient Near East.[38] White concludes that the appearance of the numbers of years for each of the members of the genealogies of Gen 5 and 11 demonstrates that they must have been designed to provide numerical totals. Further, several notes, especially at the beginning and end of the genealogies, indicate that the relationship is one of fathers and their biological sons. This intentional chronology establishes a "paragenealogy" from Adam to Joshua, that provides broad and overarching chronological information intended to allow for the calculation of human history from the first human until the entrance of Israel into the promised land.

The arguments presented above are important. However, a careful study reveals that the conclusions may not always be supported by the evidence. On a surface level of comparison there are differences between the presentation of the lines of Seth and of Shem. For example, the line of Shem nowhere totals the ages each figure lived while that of Seth provides a total for each person. If it matters that these two genealogies are different from other genealogies, then it matters that each one has a structure different from the other.

Further, if these genealogies are different from the other biblical genealogies, then assumptions about the function of the *hiphil* form of *yld* followed by the direct object marker do not necessarily hold here as they do many other places. Even in the non-genealogical usage of this form in Lev 25:45, the text describes the "begetting" of a *mišpāḥâ*, an extended family or clan. Could something different also be envisioned in Gen 5 and 11? Genesis 1–11 is generally recognized as a separate piece of literature in comparison with the rest of Genesis. In these eleven chapters the use of the *hiphil* form of *yld* is restricted to the lines of Seth and Shem in chapters 5 and 11, with the single exception of Gen 6:10 which continues the genealogy of chapter 5 and completes the line of Shem with Noah begetting three sons. Therefore, there is no other usage of this verb form embedded in these opening chapters of Genesis. Given only these attestations and the apparently more flexible usage of the *hiphil* form of *yld* in one (Lev 24:45) of only eight other occurrences outside of Gen 1–11 in the Pentateuch,

36. Jonathan Sarfati, "Biblical Chronologies," *TJ* 17 (2003): 14–18; Travis R. Freeman, "The Genesis 5 and 11 Fluidity Questions," *TJ* 19 (2005): 83–90; Bernard White, "Revisiting Genesis 5 and 11: A Closer Look at the Chronogenealogies," *AUSS* 53 (2015): 253–77.

37. Travis R. Freeman, "A New Look at the Genesis 5 and 11 Fluidity Problem," *AUSS* 42 (2004): 259–86; White, "Revisiting Genesis 5 and 11," 255–61.

38. White, "Revisiting Genesis 5 and 11," 256–77.

we should be hesitant to draw the conclusion that the verb must have the sense of begetting a biological son in the next generation.

This of course is not the only literary argument for a strictly "ungapped" linear and chronological sequence in the genealogies. However, it does open the issue to reconsidering what may be the possible meanings and purposes of the numbers and names listed in these texts.

Genealogies of Genesis 5 and 11 and Textual Criticism

In general, the text of Genesis in the Masoretic tradition is considered reliable and old. However, there are variants in the numbers of years found in the genealogies of Gen 5 and 11 among the Masoretic, Septuagint, and Samaritan text traditions.[39] While the Samaritan text tradition appears to be derivative, Emanuel Tov notes that scholars have disagreed as to whether the Masoretic or the Septuagint preserves the earliest numbers, or whether both are derivative.[40] He believes that the differences are the product of recensions rather than individual scribal errors or corrections.[41] The total number of years lived for the figures of Gen 5 are the same in both the Masoretic and Septuagint textual traditions. However, in general the Septuagint expands the total number of years covered by each genealogy. One theory proposes that it may serve to project the biblical chronology earlier than the Egyptian chronology known at the time of the Septuagint's translation, as noted by Sexton.[42] However, this suggestion is conjectural.

A larger question has to do with the appearance of Cainan in the Septuagint list of Gen 11, as a successor to Arphaxad and a predecessor of Shelah. The Masoretic text preserves no knowledge of this figure while the Septuagint attests the name in Gen 10:24; 1 Chr 1:18; and in the recurrence of this list in Luke 3:36 and Jub. 8:1–5. If the name was not originally in the list then how does it appear in the Septuagint, in the later New Testament, and in other texts that use the Septuagint? If the name was originally in the list, then is not this evidence for a gap in the genealogy of the Masoretic Text?

Regardless of the answer one chooses, there seems to be something unusual going on in the text here at the beginning of the line of Shem in Gen 11. Even in the Masoretic Text there is an interruption in the regularity of the reporting. In the genealogies of chapters 5 and 11 the normal manner of indicating that figure A lived X number of years and then begat B is introduced by the customary *waw*-consecutive form, *wayᵉhî* "he lived." This verb form is the normal signal that the text has moved forward to the next generation. In terms of a temporal sequence this verbal form is exactly what one would expect. It occurs as each new generation is introduced from Adam in Gen 5

---

39. See Gordon J. Wenham, *Genesis 1–15*, WBC 1 (Waco, TX: Word, 1987) 131, 250 for summaries of the different numbers. The chronology of the flood in Gen 8 reflects similar variations in these textual traditions.

40. Emanuel Tov, *Textual Criticism of the Hebrew Bible*, 3rd ed. (Minneapolis: Fortress, 2012), 305–6.

41. Emanuel Tov, "The Genealogical Lists in Genesis 5 and 11 in Three Different Versions," in *Textual Criticism of the Hebrew Bible, Qumran, Septuagint: Collected Essays, Volume 3*, ed. Emanuel Tov, VTSup 167 (Leiden: Brill, 2015) 221–38.

42. Sexton, "Who Was Born Before Enosh Was 90?"

until Terah in Gen 11. There are two exceptions in the Masoretic Text. They occur at
the beginning of the genealogy of Shem. While Shem's generation is introduced by
wayᵉhî (11:11), this is true neither for Shem's successor Arphaxad nor for his successor,
Shelah. The form reemerges as the introductory verb in 11:16 with Eber, the successor of Shelah. For Arphaxad and Shelah, however, there is a significant difference.
In place of *wayᵉhî*, these two generations begin with a *waw* followed by the name of
the relevant person, Arphaxad in 11:12 and Shelah in 11:14. There then appears the odd
verbal form, *hay*. This is analyzed as a shortened form of a third-person masculine
singular *qal* perfect of the same root as *wayᵉhî*. However, it is an unusual form.[43]

The reason for *hay* is not clear. Here it serves our purpose to note that it is one
more interruption in these otherwise remarkably regular genealogies. Note that it also
occurs for both the predecessor and the successor of the already noted Cainan, who
appears in the genealogy of the Septuagint (and New Testament) but not in the genealogy of the Masoretic Text.

Genealogies of Genesis 5 and 11 and Personal Names

The remaining area to investigate has to do with the personal names associated with the
name-bearers in each generation. Such a study would not only examine any Hebrew or
other etymology of the name, but would also reflect on whether the elements and form
of the name occur at any specific time or at multiple times in the well-attested history
of the use of personal names in the ancient Near East. We refer to this as the onomastic
profile of a name. We know, for example, that the personal names in the genealogies
of Gen 5 and 11 are not attested in later Israelite or Jewish names before a period well
into the Roman era. Even Jewish and Christian names from the early centuries CE
attest a few examples of Adam and Sarah but nothing else from the early chapters of
Genesis.[44] It seems clear that the personal names of Gen 5 and 11 date from a period
before or outside of Israelite and Jewish naming customs of the first millennium BCE.

In order to examine the onomastic profile of the names and their elements we will
review the work done in my *Studies in the Personal Names of Genesis 1–11*.[45] That
work can be consulted for details of the meaning of specific names. The greater interest here is whether these names have an identifiable etymology and where these names
and their elements occur in the ancient Near East. The following names appear in the
genealogy of Seth in Gen 5: Adam, Seth, Enosh, Kenan, Mahalalel, Jared, Enoch,
Methuselah, Lamech, and Noah. All these names have relatively clear West Semitic
etymologies except Kenan and Lamech. Kenan possesses the first three consonants
of Cain, *qyn,* followed by a hypocoristic name ending. The name carries the sense
of a metal smith in South Arabian. It is not attested earlier than the eighth century
because no South Arabian inscriptions are known from any earlier period. Lamech

43. This change in verb form does not appear in the Septuagint.

44. Richard S. Hess, "Names," in *Dictionary of Daily Life in Biblical and Post-Biblical Antiquity: Volume III, I–N*, ed. Edwin M. Yamauchi and Marvin R. Wilson (Peabody, MA: Hendrickson, 2016), 429–58,
esp. 451–55.

45. Richard S. Hess, *Studies in the Personal Names of Genesis 1–11*, AOAT 234 (Kevelaer: Butzon &
Bercker; Neukirchen-Vluyn: Nerkirchener, 1993; repr. Winona Lake, IN: Eisenbrauns, 2009).

is an otherwise unknown name and etymology. The "selah" element of Methuselah as well as Enosh, Enoch, and Noah do not occur in other personal names from any known period. The other names are commonly attested in West Semitic names of early and late periods. There are two exceptions to this: Adam and the "methu" element of Methuselah. These two occur only in the second millennium BCE and earlier. They do not occur in the first millennium BCE.

When we come to the genealogy of Shem we have the following names: Shem, Arphaxad, Cainan, Shelah, Eber, Peleg, Reu, Serug, Nahor, Terah, and Abram. Of these we have already discussed Cainan. We have also noted Shelah, which is the same as the "selah" element of Methuselah. The elements of Shem, Eber, Reu, and Abram occur in Amorite names of the early second millennium BCE and West Semitic personal names of later periods. Peleg, Serug, Nahor, and Terah appear primarily as place names in the region of northern Syria and the border area of southern Turkey. Arphaxad has no known etymology and no onomastic profile. If it is a two-element name it is not clear as to what the two elements refer. Further, its repetitive consonant plus *patakh* vowel plus consonant closing the syllable is most unusual. It may be that by the time Gen 11 was compiled the pronunciation had been forgotten and in its place a three-syllable repetition was used. As noted, Shelah is the only other name here that does not occur in personal or place names of any period.

There are the unusual circumstances of the name Cainan (see above) and the names that are best related to places, such as Peleg, Serug, Nahor, and Terah. Among the names in these genealogies whose elements appear in other personal names, none of these are limited to the first millennium BCE. All these names have elements that occur in the second millennium BCE and some occur earlier. A few, such as Adam and the first element in Methuselah, only appear in the second millennium BCE or earlier.

Returning to Arphaxad, it is important to note that its occurrence in Gen 10:22 places the name in the context of four other names that all occur as place names or as names of people groups: Elam, Ashur, Lud, and Aram. Genesis 10:24 mentions Arphaxad as the father of Shelah (Cainan in the Septuagint) in a manner not unlike 10:13–14: "Egypt was the father of the Ludites, Anamites. . . ." Again, the same is true in 10:15–18 "Canaan was the father of Sidon his firstborn, and of the Hittites, Jebusites. . . ." In all of these the description is that of people groups rather than individuals. As with several of the other names in the line of Shem, the picture is less one of a specific individual and more one of place names or one in the context of people groups.

I am not able to identify more about the name Arphaxad. However, the evidence suggests that the nature of this word does not require that it be interpreted as a single personal name.

Summary Conclusion

In conclusion, there are multiple pieces of evidence that question whether one can assert without doubt that there are no gaps anywhere in the genealogies of Gen 5 and 11. Gaps do occur in early West Semitic king lists outside the Bible. Although different from the biblical genealogies, these king lists remain closer in form and context to the biblical genealogies than any other sequence of persons moving chronologically through time.

Further, it has not been demonstrated that the grammatical forms employed in the genealogies must define a biological father to son relationship in every instance. The large chronological periods of time, those that the biblical text does describe in its later chronological overview of the whole history of humanity, do not exhibit the precision of specific dates.

Text critical study of the genealogies of Gen 5 and 11 results in some differences of chronology between major textual traditions, such as the Masoretic Text and the Septuagint. For the most part the names are consistent and in order. However, the appearance of Cainan between Arphaxad and Shelah in the Septuagint and other traditions, as well as in the New Testament genealogy of Jesus in Luke 3:6, raises significant questions about whether there may be a seam in the genealogy at this point.

Finally, the study of the personal names in terms of etymology and onomastic profile raises questions for names such as Lamech and Arphaxad. Lamech may itself be a name that signifies a turning point in the generation in both the lines of Cain and of Seth.[46] In the case of Arphaxad the vocalization of the name invites speculation that something is going on that was lost early in the tradition, just as the Gen 10 context allows for more than a personal name at this point.

In all this, we cannot prove that there are gaps in the genealogies. Rather, we can ask questions that have not been answered to date by the models provided.

---

46. See Richard S. Hess, "Lamech in the Genealogies of Genesis," *BBR* 1 (1991): 21–25.

Sety I's Military Relief at Karnak and the Eastern Gate of Egypt: A Brief Reassessment

Hesham M. Hussein

Introduction

The military relief of Sety I (1290–1279 BCE) at Karnak is an important pictorial document for the history of ancient Egypt's eastern frontier.[1] Inscribed on the north exterior wall of the great hypostyle hall, the relief comprises a series of scenes commemorating the king's first military campaign, which took place through the Way(s) of Horus and beyond, in what is today northern Sinai and Palestine.[2] The relief also commemorates Sety's establishment along the Way(s) of Horus of a chain of military fortresses (see fig. 11.1).[3] Representations of the campaign are divided into three registers. A doorway in the center separates the registers into a series of six war scenes, distributed on the east/northeast and west/northwest exterior walls of the great hypostyle hall.[4] Unique hieroglyphic texts accompany the relief and are distributed in vertical and horizontal lines. These texts are describing and narrating the actions that were taking place in

For English editing, I am indebted to Gina du Bois, copyeditor UEE, for reviewing and editing my article.

1. James Henry Breasted, "Ramses II and the Princes in the Karnak Reliefs of Seti I," *ZÄS* 37 (1899): 132–41; J. G. Wilkinson, "Letters to Sir William Gell from Henry Salt, J. G. Wilkinson, and Baron von Bunsen," *JEA* 2 (1915): 141–42; Alan H. Gardiner, "The Ancient Military Road Between Egypt and Palestine," *JEA* 6 (1920): 99–116; R. O. Faulkner, "The Wars of Sethos I," *JEA* 33 (1947): 35–38; Raphael Giveon, *Les Bédouins Shosou des documents égyptiens*, Documenta et monumenta Orientis antique 18 (Leiden: Brill, 1971), 41–43; Anthony J. Spalinger, "The Northern Wars of Seti I: An Integrative Study," *JARCE* 16 (1979): 29–47; Epigraphic Survey, *Reliefs and Inscriptions at Karnak, Volume 4: The Battle Reliefs of King Sety I*, OIP 107 (Chicago: Oriental Institute of the University of Chicago, 1986), 16–26, pls. 6, 8; Clive Broadhurst, "An Artistic Interpretation of Sety I's War Reliefs," *JEA* 75 (1989): 229–34; *KRI* 1:12–17; Dominique Valbelle, "La (Les) route(s) d'Horus," in *Hommages à Jean Leclant*, ed. Catherine Berger-El-Naggar et al., 4 vols. (Cairo: Institut français d'archéologie orientale, 1994), 379–86. Peter J. Brand, *The Monuments of Seti I: Epigraphic, Historical and Art Historical Analysis*, PAe16 (Leiden: Brill, 2000), 122, 197–206; Giacomo Cavillier, "The Ancient Military Road Between Egypt and Palestine Reconsidered: A Reassessment," *GM* 185 (2001): 23–31, fig.1; Agnèse Degrève, "La campagne asiatique de l'an 1 de Séthy Ier représentée sur le mur extérieur Nord de la Salle Hypostyle du Temple d'Amon à Karnak," *RdÉ* 57 (2006): 47–76, pls. 8–13; James K. Hoffmeier, ed., *Tell el-Borg 1: Excavations in North Sinai* (Winona Lake, IN: Eisenbrauns, 2014), 1–61; Franck Monnier, "Une iconographie égyptienne de l'architecture defensive," *ENiM* 7 (2014): 180–86, fig. 6. This chronology for Sety I is proposed by Erik Hornung, Rolf Krauss, and David A. Warburton, eds., *Ancient Egyptian Chronology*, HdO 83 (Leiden: Brill, 2006), 493.

2. Gardiner, "Ancient Military Road," 99–116; Eliezer D. Oren, "The Ways of Horus in North Sinai," in *Egypt, Israel, Sinai: Archaeological and Historical Relationships in the Biblical Period*, ed. Anson F. Rainey (Tel Aviv: Tel Aviv University, 1987), 71; Valbelle, "La (Les) route(s) d'Horus," 379–86.

3. Eliezer D. Oren and J. Shershevsky, "Military Architecture Along the 'Ways of Horus': Egyptian Reliefs and Archaeological Evidence," *ErIsr* 20 (1989):9, pl. 1.

4. Epigraphic Survey, *Battle Reliefs of King Sety I,* 3–26, pl. 1.

FIGURE 11.1. Scene of Sety I's triumphal return from campaigning in the East. North exterior wall, great hypostyle hall, Karnak. Photograph by Mostafa Al Saghir, head of Karnak Temple.

every scene. Almost all the fortresses and structures were labeled and were given a name.

The lower register's east-side reliefs narrate geographically Sety's campaign, from its starting-point at Tjarou to its conclusion at Pa-Cannan, in five relative scenes.[5] Two battles took place along the Way(s) of Horus, the first combat occurring at the halfway point, near the fortresses and water reservoirs. The second (final) conflict took place just outside the city of Pa-Cannan, where the king defeated the rebels and brought an end to the chaos caused by the Shasu peoples.[6]

Sety's Triumphal Return to Egypt

The current study focuses specifically on the sixth scene—that of Sety's triumphal return to Egypt from his eastern campaign. The scene will be divided, for the purpose of elucidation, into three related units that provide a geographical and environmental pictorial description of the eastern gate of ancient Egypt. The epigraphic survey plates used in this study are numbers 6 and 8.

In the center of the first unit (see fig. 11.2), Sety stands in his chariot, driving before him three rows of bound captives. The second unit (see fig. 11.2) shows the campaign as it is about to enter Egypt's eastern gate, across a crocodile-infested freshwater canal labeled "the dividing water."[7] This canal runs directly into the salt water of the Mediterranean, abundant with fish.[8] On the opposite (western) side of the canal an audience awaits the king. The third unit (see fig. 11.3) shows the king at the end of the triumphal procession, presenting prisoners and booty to Amun-Re.

5. Ibid., 3–26, pls. 1, 2.
6. Ibid., pls. 3, 5.
7. Oren, "Ways of Horus," 71.
8. See James K. Hoffmeier and Stephen O. Moshier, "New Paleo-Environmental Evidence from North Sinai to Complement Manfred Bietak's Map of the North Eastern Delta and Some Historical Implications," in *Timelines: Studies in Honour of Manfred Bietak*, ed. Ernst Czerny et al., 3 vols., OLA 149 (Leuven: Peeters, 2006), 2:165–74.

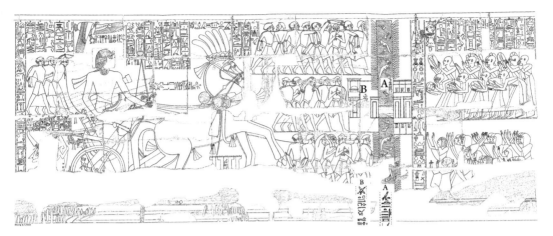

FIGURE 11.2.   Scene of Sety I's triumphal return from campaigning in the East and a formal triumphal audience waiting for the victorious king on the canal's west bank. North exterior wall, great hypostyle hall, Karnak. Source: Epigraphic Survey, *Reliefs and Inscriptions at Karnak, Volume 4: The Battle Reliefs of King Sety I*, OIP 107 (Chicago: Oriental Institute of the University of Chicago, 1986), pl. 6; courtesy of the Oriental Institute of the University of Chicago.

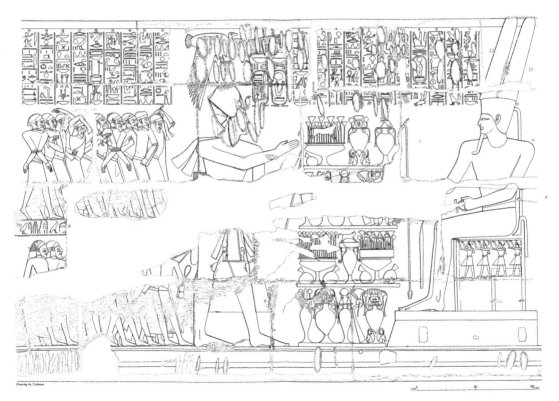

FIGURE 11.3.   Sety I presents prisoners and booty to Amun-re. North exterior wall, great hypostyle hall, Karnak. Source: Epigraphic Survey, *Reliefs and Inscriptions at Karnak, Volume 4: The Battle Reliefs of King Sety I*, OIP 107 (Chicago: Oriental Institute of the University of Chicago, 1986), pl. 8. Courtesy of the Oriental Institute of the University of Chicago.

FIGURE 11.4. Schematic representation of the structures depicted on both sides of the canal in Sety I's military relief at Karnak. Illustrated by Hesham M. Hussein.

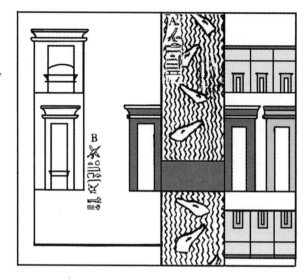

In 1920, Alan Gardiner provided a description and interpretation of the relief.[9] What is notable is his interpretation of the structures separated by the canal (see figs. 11.4, 11.5). He considered the structures collectively, as a single fortress consisting of three buildings with doors, all represented as a rectangular space. Gardiner interpreted the entrance to the fortress from the east side of the canal to be through a large portal, after which one passed through a second portal onto a bridge, and then through a third portal on the other side of the waterway [A] "Ta dnit."[10] Gardiner did not conjecture the purpose of the two gates situated adjacent to each other on the west side of the canal.

Significantly, recent investigations and discoveries in north Sinai are enabling archaeologists to merge archaeological, textual, and geological data with the epigraphic and pictorial sources to widen our understanding of Sety's relief and shed new light on its interpretation. It is now proposed that the frontier city of Tjarou be identified with Tell Heboua I and Tell Heboua II in north Sinai.[11] These two sites are located less than one kilometer apart and are separated by traces of a freshwater canal.[12]

9. Gardiner, "Ancient Military Road," 104.

10. In 2011, Nicholas Wernick introduced a slightly different interpretation of the canal complex. He considered the buildings as a single structure with the canal running between them, with two gates located on the king's (i.e., east) side, and another two gates located on the west side, making four gates in all. See Nick Wernick, "The Images of Fortifications in the Sety I Battle Reliefs: Comparing Art and Archaeology," in *Current Research in Egyptology: Proceedings of the Tenth Annual Symposium, University of Liverpool 2009*, ed. Judith Corbelli, Daniel Boatright, and Claire Malleson (Oxford; Oxbow, 2011), 159.

11. Mohamed Abd el-Maksoud, *Tell Heboua (1981–1991): Enquête archéologique sur la deuxième période intermédiaire et le nouvel empire à l'extémite orientale du delta* (Paris: Éditions Recherché sur les Civilisations, 1998); Mohamed Abd el-Maksoud and Dominique Valbelle, "Tell Heboua-Tjarou. L'apport de l'épigraphie," *RdÉ* 56 (2005): 1–43; Abd el-Maksoud and Valbelle, "Tell Heboua II: Rapport préliminaire sur la décor et l'épigraphie des éléments architectoniques découverts au cours des campagnes 2008-2009 dans la zone central du Khetem de Tjarou," *RdÉ* 62 (2011): 1–39.

12. Bruno Marcolongo, "Evolution du paléo-environement dans la partie orientale du delta du Nile depuis la transgression flandrienne (8000 B.P.) par rapport aux modèles de peuplement anciens," *CRIPEL* 14 (1992): 23–31.

FIGURE 11.5. Scene of the structures separated by the canal [A]. North exterior wall, great hypostyle hall, Karnak. Reprinted by permission of CNRS-CFEETK: © CNRS-CFEETK 58330/A. Chéné.

Egyptologists suggest that Heboua II can be identified with structure [B], "Khetm Fortress of Tjarou" as it is labeled in the Karnak relief, which was controlling Egypt's eastern gate (I will not analyzing the role of Khetem or its structure in this article), and that Heboua I refers to the buildings on the other side of the canal.[13] The canal [A] is interpreted as the body of freshwater, formed by the Pelusiac branch of the Nile, traces of which today separate Heboua I and II. A number of scholars heretofore assumed that Sety's triumphal-return scene represented "Tjarou," the starting-point, as an extensive complex of buildings composed of two massive fortified structures separated by a canal and connected by a bridge.[14] I offer, based on excavation I have recently participated in during my work at Tell Heboua I and II, that there are no architectural similarities between the typology (shape and plan) of the massive fortified walls of Tell Heboua I or Tell Heboua II and the building complex depicted on both sides of the canal, which is not named or labeled in the accompanying hieroglyphic text. Additionally, a monumental gateway at Tell Heboua I has been discovered in the middle of the western wall, on the Egyptian side of the fortified walls. Also a monumental gateway at Tell Heboua II has been discovered in the middle of the northern fortified wall.[15]

The Canal Scene

According to Gardiner's interpretation, the building complex depicted on both sides of the canal consists of multiple elements and a total of three doors.[16] Unfortunately, the complex is not named in the accompanying inscription.[17] However, if we look closer to this specific part of the returning scene, I believe that we can see more than just structures and portals.

The objective of the current study is to illuminate the premises adjacent to the canal (with the exception of structure [B] "Khetm of Tjarou"), in order to understand their typology and function. These unique structures are not represented elsewhere on the north exterior wall of the hypostyle hall.[18] The canal complex (see figs. 11.4, 11.5)

13. James K. Hoffmeier, "Reconstructing Egypt's Eastern Frontier Defense Network in the New Kingdom (Late Bronze Age)," in *The Power of Walls—Fortifications in Ancient Northeastern Africa: Proceedings of the International Workshop Held at the University of Cologne 4th–7th August 2011*, ed. Friederike Jesse and Carola Vogel (Cologne: Barth Institut, 2013), 168; James K. Hoffmeier and Mohamed Abd el-Maksoud, "A New Military Site on 'The Ways of Horus,'" *JEA* 89 (2003): 196; James K. Hoffmeier and Stephen O. Moshier, "A Highway Out of Egypt: The Main Road From Egypt to Canaan," in *Desert Road Archaeology in Ancient Egypt and Beyond*, ed. Frank Forster and Heiko Riemer, Africa Praehistoria 27 (Cologne: Barth Institut, 2013), 499.

14. Mohamed Abd el-Maksoud, "Tjarou porte de l'Orient," in *Le Sinaï durant l'antiquité et le Moyen-Age: 4000 ans d'histoire pour un désert*, ed. Dominique Valbelle and Charles Bonnet (Paris: Errance, 1998), 61–65; Cavillier, "Ancient Military Road," 24; Hoffmeier and Abd el-Maksoud, "New Military Site," 171–73; Hoffmeier, "Reconstructing Egypt's Eastern Frontier," 168; Hoffmeier, *Excavations in North Sinai*, 56.

15. Morris suggested that the location of the Heboua I monumental gateway on the Egyptian side of the fort should have been located along the "Canaanite" wall of the fortress (eastern enclosure), based upon the Karnak relief and also upon practical requirements. See Ellen Morris, *Architecture of Imperialism: Military Bases and Evolution of Foreign Policy in Egypt's New Kingdom*, PAe 22 (Leiden: Brill, 2005), 409.

16. Gardiner, "Ancient Military Road," 104.

17. *Battle Reliefs of King Sety I*, pl. 6.

18. There are similarities between Sety I triumphal returning scene and other returning scenes during the New Kingdom, except the other scenes have neither a canal nor its adjacent complex. See Epigraphic

too has no parallel, except in Amarna period scenes, where we can detect similarities between Sety's canal gates and the Amarna period doors.[19]

To better understand the unique elements of the canal scene it is conducive to deconstruct its constituents as follows (from left to right; see figs. 11.4, 11.5): structure B; a large gate on the canal's eastern side; a bridge over the canal; a large gate on the canal's western side and another large gate adjacent to it; and six doors organized into two groups of three each, one group depicted above the two adjacent gates and the other shown beneath.

According to the sequence of scenes, Sety I headed west past Khetm of Tjarou [B], then proceeded through the canal's eastern gate, and from there crossed the bridge leading to the western side of the canal, where he was welcomed by the priests, officials, and commanders of Upper and Lower Egypt.

A New Interpretation of the Canal Scene

The triumphal returning scene of King Sety I is believed to be an important visual documentation and a mine of information, also it is counted to be part of the propaganda of the triumphal procession that follow the military campaign of King Sety. Indeed, the triumphal scene provides a pictorial documentation of how the ancient Egyptian celebrated the return of their victorious king and his army. The king led the Egyptian forces to victory, and put an end to the chaos caused by the Shasu. Likewise, the scene gives clues to how the eastern gate and entry point of ancient Egypt were planned.

In my reinterpretation of the canal scene (see figs. 11.4, 11.5), I first consider the large gate east of the bridge, the bridge itself, and the first large gate west of the bridge as possible components of an entry-control system for monitoring and controlling the movements of people and materials into and out of Egypt.[20] Therefore, I hypothesize that these two gates and the bridge may have been part of the fortress structure [B], the "Khetm Fortress of Tjarw," which is situated on the east side of the canal as an official entry point at Egypt's eastern border.[21]

I next consider the second large western gate and the six doors, whose location and function do not make immediate sense.[22] I propose that the gate and six doors function

---

Survey, *Medinet Habu—Later Historical Records of Ramses III*, OIP 9 (Chicago: University of Chicago, 1932), 2: pls. 77, 98.

19. Norman de Garis Davies and Geoffrey Thorndike Martin, *The Rock Tombs of el Amarna: Vol. 6: Tomb of Parennefer, Tutu, and Aÿ* (London: Egypt Exploration Fund, 1908), pls. 17–18. A new limestone block has been discovered inside the tomb of Iwrkhy, south of King Unas causeway. A canal scene similar to the King Sety I relief is depicted on the block. Iwrakhy's scene depicted a waterway filled with crocodiles, the upper part of a gate on the canal's eastern side, a bridge over the canal, and chariots and soldiers. It is clear that Iwrakhy's scene was an informal copy of King Sety I's relief, but unfortunately, the rest of the scene is missing. For more information, see Ola El Auguizy, "The *Khetem* of Tjaru: New Evidence," in *NeHeT* 6 (2018): 1–7, pl.1a.

20. The two gates (eastern and western) are depicted as a rectangular structure, consisting of two doorposts, a single stone architrave (lintel), and a cavetto cornice. It is noteworthy that neither gate is depicted with a threshold.

21. For more information about the role of Khetem fortresses, see Morris, *Architecture of Imperialism*, 804–9.

22. Furthermore, the location of the two adjacent large portals to the west side of the canal has an important meaning if we reorganize and relocate the canal scene components.

FIGURE 11.6. Author's schematic interpretation of Sety I's triumphal gate depicted in Karnak relief. Illustrated by Hesham M. Hussein.

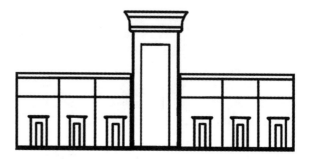

together as one architectural unit (see fig. 11.6). That the doors are depicted as a solid block is perhaps due to a lack of space available to the artist and the artist's desire to render the maximum amount of information, or for other artistic reasons, the unusual nature of perspective in Egyptian art. These doors are organized into two groups of three each, they appear to flank both sides of the second western gate, possibly rendering this gate the "triumphal gate" in Sety's procession of triumphal return. It is fitting that the gate would have been facing the king, with his campaign, as he reentered Egypt upon his return.

Also, I assume that the triumphal gate of Sety I is part of a triumphal gateway, which consists of two components, the main one represented by a triumphal gate. The second consists of two controlling gates and a bridge (see fig. 11.7). I think that the canal scene complex is supposed to present the first depiction of a triumphal gate.

Monumental gates and portals were well known in ancient Egypt. Temple gates of the Ramesside and Ptolemaic periods were huge structures carved with scenes. Monumental entrances and doors clearly had their own decorative programs and were often at least two stories tall.[23]

In the ancient world, the monumental triumphal gate was a ceremonial structure in the shape of a rectangular gate, with one or more passageways. Textual resources from later periods assumed that triumphal gateways were built for celebrating the victories of kings, generals, and their armies, and also to commemorate important events.[24]

We know that monumental gateways were features of civilizations such as the Egyptian, Hittite, Assyrian, Babylonian, and Mycenaean. Surviving examples include the Ishtar Gate of Babylon (605–562 BCE) and the Gate of All Nations at Persepolis (486–465 BCE).[25]

During the Roman period, triumphal gates and arches were well known and played an important role in triumphal celebrations.[26] The Romans constructed triumphal gates

23. Dieter Arnold, *The Encyclopedia of Ancient Egyptian Architecture* (Princeton: Princeton University Press, 2003), 75.

24. Sarah Midford, "Roman Imperial Triumphal Arches," *JCAV* 27 (2014): 11–15; James C. Anderson, *Roman Architecture and Society*, Ancient Society and History (Baltimore: Johns Hopkins University Press, 1997), 265.

25. For the Ishtar Gate, see Piotr Bienkowski and Alan R. Millard, eds., *Dictionary of the Ancient Near East* (London: British Museum, 2000), 43. For the Gate of All Nations, see Vesta S. Curtis and Sarah Stewart, eds., *Birth of the Persian Empire* (London: Tauris, 2005), 127; Gwendolyn Leick, *Dictionary of the Ancient Near East Architecture* (London: Routledge, 1988), 161.

26. S. Midford, "Roman Imperial Triumphal Arches," 11–15.

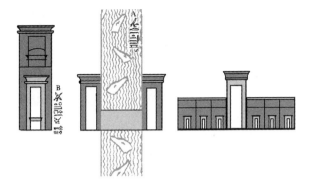

FIGURE 11.7. Schematic interpretation of Sety I's triumphal gateway complex depicted in Karnak Relief. Illustrated by Hesham M. Hussein.

as statements of power, highlighting the military accomplishments of the emperors.[27] From Roman Egypt there are known examples of triumphal gates: the gate of Diocletian (284–305 CE) at the northeast corner of Philae Island, the gate from "Antinoupolise-Sheikh 'bda" near Minya, as well as a gate at al-Qasr in the Bahria Oasis.[28] It is thought that Alexandria was adorned with triumphal gates and arches.[29]

The Triumphal Procession of Sety I

The triumphal procession has been around for a long time. Ancient civilizations considered the triumphal procession as a projection of power and glory. The earliest depiction of a triumphal procession from ancient Egypt dates to the early Dynastic period and can be recognized on the verso of the famous Narmer Palette (3150–3125 BCE).[30] Several New Kingdom examples have also survived.[31]

According to Sety I's relief, the Shasu battle was followed by a triumphal procession that consisted of the victorious king and his army, the king's chariot and horses, the Shasu captives and their (captive) leaders, the triumphal gateway, the magistrates, priests, and flower-bouquet holders, and, finally, the offerings scene to the deity Amun-Re.

27. Anderson, *Roman Architecture and Society*, 265.

28. (Leiden: Brill, 2013), 362; Philip Parker, *The Empire Stops Here: A Journey Along the Frontier of the Roman World* (London: Vintage, 2009), 408. For the one near Minya, see Edme François Jomard, *Description de l'Égypte, Antiquités* (Paris: De l'imprimerie impériale, 1809), 4: pls. 57–58. For the gate at al-Qasr, see Patrizio Pensabene, *Elementi architettonici di Alessandria e di altri siti egiziani*, Repertorio d'arte dell'Egitto greco-romano 3 (Rome: Bretschneider, 1993), 33–34, fig. 41; Alan B. Lloyd, ed., *A Companion to Ancient Egypt*, 2 vols. (Chichester: Wiley-Blackwell, 2010), 1:365.

29. Kenneth A. Sheedy, "Scenes from Alexandria in the Time of Domitian," in *Egyptian Culture and Society: Studies in Honour of Naguib Kanawati*, ed. Alexandra Woods, Ann McFarlane, and Susanne Binder, 2 vols., Supplement aux annales du service des antiquités de l'égypte cahier 38 (Cairo: Conseil suprême des antiquitiés, 2010), 2:212–13; Guiseppe Botti, *Plan de la ville d'Alexandrie à l'époque ptolémaique* (Alexandria: Carrière, 1898), 62.

30. David O'Connor, "Context, Function and Program: Understanding Ceremonial Slate Palettes," *JARCE* 39 (2002): fig. 3; Alan B. Lloyd, *Ancient Egypt State and Society* (Oxford: Oxford University Press, 2014), 60.

31. Epigraphic Survey, *Medinet Habu—Later Historical Records of Ramses III* 3: pls. 77, 98.

The Karnak relief depicted every stop of Sety's triumphal procession, shown running from left to right in one extended row. The first scene (figs. 11.1, 11.2) illustrated the victorious king standing erect in his triumphal chariot, proceeding in glory toward Egypt's eastern gate.[32] His quiver contains no arrows: a sign that the war is over. The chariot is pulled by two horses named, in the accompanying inscription, "the first horse of his majesty L.P.H., Amun Gives Him Power."[33] The king is driving three rows of bound captives before his chariot while dragging another row behind him. Three prisoners' heads project from the back of the chariot "making 27 prisoners in all," referred to as Shasu.[34] The king, his army, and captive are moving through the triumphal gate.

The second scene (fig. 11.2) depicts priests, officials, and commanders of Upper and Lower Egypt in two rows to the west of the triumphal gateway, awaiting the victorious king.[35] The top row of the audience presents flower bouquets to the king and his army.[36] The last scene of the triumphal procession (fig. 11.3) depicts the final destination, the temple of Amun-Re, where the king stands before the god, leading two rows of Shasu captives and "making 19 captives in all," presenting four rows of spoils to Amun-Re.[37]

If we consider the canal scene structures as a triumphal gate, this will be the first known triumphal gate from the ancient world and indeed possibly the origin of the Roman triumphal arches. Moreover, the triumphal procession scenes of Sety I at Karnak will be the first completely documented triumphal procession from the ancient world.

32. Ibid., pl. 6.

33. Aiman Eshmawy, "Names of Horses in Ancient Egypt," in *Proceedings of the Ninth International Congress of Egyptologists: Actes du neuvieme congres international des Egyptologues; Grenoble, 6–12 Septembre 2004*, ed. Jean-Claude Goyon and Christine Cardin, 2 vols. OLA 150 (Leuven: Peeters, 2007), 2:667.

34. A. Gaballa, "Narrative in Egyptian Art" (Ph.D. diss., University of Liverpool, 1967), 321.

35. Epigraphic Survey, *Battle Reliefs of King Sety I*, pl. 6.

36. The flowers are considered a symbol of triumph and victory.

37. Epigraphic Survey, *Battle Reliefs of King Sety I*, 23–26, pl. 8.

CHAPTER 12

Ma'at in the Amarna Period: Historiography, Egyptology, and the Reforms of Akhenaten

Mark D. Janzen

Introduction

Any study of Ma'at in the Amarna period finds itself in the middle of a fascinating Egyptological paradox. On the one hand, there is Ma'at—long recognized by Egyptologists as representative of Egyptian conceptions of truth and order. Juxtaposed to this is the figurehead of the Amarna period—the iconoclastic, controversial, and "heretical" king, Akhenaten. Thus, one hand holds orthodoxy, while the other contains revolution and controversy. Additionally, in spite of a seemingly limitless amount of research, "Egyptologists know that the notoriety of the Amarna Period is matched only by its obscurity."[1] This obscurity affects the interpretations of wide range of topics: Amarna religion, foreign policy, chronology, and so on.[2] This creates a frustrating yet fascinating dynamic, as it becomes all too easy to characterize the period and its actors in extreme terms, often leaving little room for middle ground.[3] Notwithstanding these inherent problems, the following discussion examines the use of Ma'at in iconographic and textual sources from the Amarna period in order to shed more light on both the conceptual understanding of Ma'at in the Amarna period and to present a more nuanced approach to Akhenaten's reforms. It is hoped that an understanding will emerge that avoids the often-polarizing approaches some scholars have taken toward this time period and its ruler.

Ma'at: A Brief Overview

As the Egyptian goddess of cosmic order, truth, and justice, Ma'at has long been recognized as not only a goddess but also as one of the foundational elements of ancient

It is an honor and my great pleasure to dedicate this article to James Hoffmeier, who has had an enormous impact on my own career. My interest in both archaeology and Egyptian history stems from my time with Professor Hoffmeier at Trinity. In fact, I took his archaeology course on a whim during my first semester of graduate work and within a few weeks changed my major. His exacting scholarship has inspired many of us, whether in regard to Egyptology or biblical studies, or his particular niche—the intersection of the two. I wish him all the best in his future endeavors and eagerly await his next book!

1. William J. Murnane, "The End of the Amarna Period Once Again," *OLZ* 96 (2001): 9.

2. For thorough discussion of the plethora of chronological issues during the end of the Amarna period see Marc Gabolde, *D'Akhenaton à Toutânkhamon*, Collection de l'Institut d'Archeologie et d'Historie de l'Antiquite 3 (Lyon: Université Lumière-Lyon 2, 1998); reviewed also in Murnane, "End of the Amarna Period." For more on the foreign policy of Akhenaten, see Raymond Cohen and Raymond Westbrook, eds., *Amarna Diplomacy: The Beginnings of International Relations* (Baltimore: Johns Hopkins University Press, 2000).

3. Murnane, "End of the Amarna Period," 9.

Egyptian society.[4] The goddess represented "divine harmony and balance of the universe, including the unending cycles of rising and setting of the sun," speaking perhaps to one of her many aspects that would find significance in the reforms of Akhenaten.[5] As a concept, Ma'at is the personification of truth, order, and unity, while as a specific goddess Ma'at is usually identified visually as a woman with a single ostrich feather in her hair.[6] Egypt's remarkable longevity and continuity can largely be explained by the sense of tradition and the unchanging values emphasized in Ma'at.[7]

As the goddess of truth, Ma'at is connected to daily conduct and righteousness.[8] Personal ethics were rooted in the concept of Ma'at. Of equal, if not greater, significance is the connection of Ma'at to kingship and royal legitimacy.[9] An Old Kingdom text, The Teaching for Kagemni, connects notions of keeping Ma'at with royal favor:

> Do Ma'at for the king (for) Ma'at is what the king loves . . .
>   speak Ma'at to the king, (for) Ma'at is what the king loves.[10]

In short, kingship is the "effective power of the order of Ma'at."[11] Thus, for Akhenaten to effectively reform Egyptian society and religion, he must take Ma'at into account either by outright rejection or by integrating the concept into his religious reforms. Ma'at was simply too central to Egyptian society—for king and commoner alike— to be ignored by an individual seeking to enact such sweeping changes.

Akhenaten: "Sophisticated" Monotheist or Radical Tyrant?

For his part, Akhenaten remains one of the most thoroughly researched figures in ancient history.[12] No doubt, his successors would be displeased to find their efforts at

---

4. Among the more important studies are Jan Assmann, *Ma'at: Gerechtigkeit und Unsterblichkeit im Alten Ägypten* (Munich: Beck, 1990) as well as Erik Hornung, *Conceptions of God in Ancient Egypt: The One and the Many*, trans. John Baines (Ithaca: Cornell University Press, 1982).

5. Quotation from Donald B. Redford, ed., *The Ancient Gods Speak: A Guide to Egyptian Religion* (Oxford: Oxford University Press, 2002), 189.

6. Emily Teeter, "Multiple Feathers and Maat," *Bulletin of the Egyptological Seminar* 7 (1985–1986): 43. Though the single feather is attested most often, there are examples where Ma'at is depicted wearing multiple feathers (43–47). Furthermore, the use of the feather may hearken back to Ma'at's association with Shu. See Irene Shirun-Grumach, "Remarks on the Goddess Maat" in *Pharaonic Egypt: The Bible and Christianity*, ed. Sarah Israelit-Groll (Jerusalem: Magnes, 1985), 173–201. Shirun-Grumach connects this understanding of Ma'at to her role as a "personal air goddess" (174). While the term "personal" is unclear here, her connection of Ma'at and Shu (air deity) is an interesting one that may in fact be alluded to in Amarna iconography (see below).

7. Emily Teeter, *The Presentation of Maat: Ritual and Legitimacy in Ancient Egypt*, SAOC 57 (Chicago: Oriental Institute of the University of Chicago, 1997), 1.

8. Emily Teeter, "A Preliminary Report on the Presentation of Maat," *ARCE Newsletter* 134 (1985–1986): 3.

9. Teeter, *Presentation of Maat*, 2.

10. *Urk* 1:195.6–8; Miriam Lichtheim, *Maat in Egyptian Autobiographies and Related Studies*, OBO 120 (Göttingen: Vandenhoeck & Ruprecht; Fribourg: Universitätsverlag, 1992), 61.

11. Vincent A. Tobin, "Ma'at and ΔIKH: Some Comparative Considerations of Egyptian and Greek Thought," *JARCE* 24 (1987): 115.

12. The same could be said of the Amarna period as well. There is perhaps no time period in all of ancient history that was been written about with greater frequency. As Martin puts it, "Scarcely a month

erasing his memory and name have failed in such grand fashion. In the past approximately 150 years, Akhenaten has had an extraordinary "cultural afterlife."[13] It is no
stretch to say that he has been subjected to more interpretations using radically differing methods than any figure in Egyptian history. These interpretations have changed
over time, being based largely on whatever was fashionable when they were written.[14]
For James Breasted, Akhenaten was the "first individual" in history, pioneering a religion with a "gospel of beauty and beneficence of the natural order."[15] On the opposite
extreme, Donald Redford calls the controversial king a "misshapen individual."[16]

Akhenaten is popular even among more mainstream intellectualists. Akhenaten the
idealist inspired Sigmund Freud's final work—*Moses and Monotheism*.[17] One look
at Freud's title sums up another vein of Akhenaten mania—the search for monotheism and the perceived influence Akhenaten had on the authors of the Bible and other
monotheistic faiths. As Redford states, "For some he is a forerunner of Christ, to others a great mystic whose teaching is still relevant."[18] Akhenaten maintains a strange,
amorphous relevance down to the present with diverse individuals or groups, who
have little in common, championing him on racial, religious, or even sexual grounds.[19]

In many respects then, Egyptologists have been fighting a losing battle to recover
the factual Akhenaten. In some cases their frustration is obvious and understandable;
to ignore the facts "in favor of flights of fantasy is utter folly."[20] Yet, prominent Egyptologists are not immune from making speculative judgment-calls about Akhenaten.
At one point, Redford refers to him as "an iconoclastic freak."[21] Speculating to an
alarming degree, he presents Akhenaten as "a recluse with a single fixation" who
was "apt to grow tired of extended periods of concentration necessary to pursue a
consistent foreign policy."[22] One wonders how Redford was able to so effortlessly
enter into the head of the king, and his statements might be more indicative of his
own leanings than Akhenaten's. Redford even claims to know why Aziru, a rebellious
former vassal, defected: "His defection was as much due to his loathing of the person
of the pharaoh."[23] It seems that Redford's own loathing of Akhenaten has led to him
assuming the Aziru must have shared that feeling. To his credit, Redford does not

passes without a publication appearing on the Amarna period." See Geoffrey T. Martin, *A Bibliography
of the Amarna Period and Its Aftermath: The Reigns of Akhenaten, Smenkhkare, Tutankhamun and Ay
(c. 1350–1321 B.C.)* (London: Kegan Paul, 1991), 1.

13. Dominic Montserrat. *Akhenaten: History, Fantasy, and Ancient Egypt* (London: Routledge, 2003), 1.
14. Donald B. Redford, *Akhenaten: The Heretic King* (Princeton: Princeton University Press, 1984), 4.
15. James H. Breasted, *Dawn of Conscience* (New York: Scribners, 1933), 294.
16. Redford, *Akhenaten*, 4.
17. Monserrat, *Akhenaten*, 6; 95–107.
18. Redford, *Akhenaten*, 4.
19. The quickest way to demonstrate this point is to simply look at Monserrat's table of contents
(*Akhenaten*). Monserrat's book is a brilliant summary of the various interpretations these groups have placed
upon Akhenaten and, to my knowledge, is the finest summary of why Akhenaten remains so profoundly
influential to this day.
20. Redford, *Akhenaten*, 5. This is an interesting quote because Redford himself is guilty of such flights
of fantasy!
21. Ibid., 158. Redford's comment here is referring to the clash between traditional religion and
Akhenaten's reforms. However, to call Akhenaten a "freak" is hardly the hallmark of empirical, data-based
scholarship.
22. Ibid., 202–3.
23. Ibid., 203.

hide his biases, concluding his book with the following: "I cannot conceive of a more tiresome regime under which to be fated to live."[24] One must question whether such vehement views about the person of Akhenaten have colored Redford's understanding of Akhenaten's religious reforms.

Breasted's comment, noted above, is indicative of the other extreme. Cyril Aldred also stands opposite Redford and is quite fond of Akhenaten and the Amarna period. Akhenaten's presentation of himself as a family man strikes a "humane and sympathetic" chord.[25] Aldred claims that Akhenaten is more "rational" and "advanced" than other pharaohs due to a "more rational belief in a universal sole god."[26] The obvious implication here is that Akhenaten is superior simply because his religious views align better with modern monotheistic faiths than Egyptian orthodoxy.[27] Even more transparent are claims from the previous generation of scholars that Akhenaten has founded a "religion so pure that one must compare it to Christianity in order to find its faults."[28]

Can scholars who so clearly wish to champion Akhenaten and his reforms as "advanced" be trusted when interpreting their complexities? Is Aldred, for example, looking for monotheism in the same way that Redford looked for evidence of Akhenaten the tyrant? What is truly amazing is that both Redford and Aldred are first-rate Egyptologists looking at primarily the same corpus of data. This is the Akhenaten phenomenon at its most pronounced: even professional Egyptologists are at times unable to lay their biases aside.[29]

If the man Akhenaten is elusive, then what claims can one reasonably make about his reforms? This is compounded not just by the fact that the Amarna period remains a hotbed for controversy but also because other than the Great Hymn to the Aten, no texts from the period explicitly state Amarna theology.[30] For a New Kingdom pharaoh, Akhenaten left shockingly few texts of his own, let alone anything approaching a systematic theology of Atenism.[31] Redford is only slightly more even-tempered when speaking of Akhenaten's reforms than when writing of the pharaoh's character: "Thus, the ever-growing symbolism in art, cult, and magic can no longer be realized . . . every growing creative thought of an intelligent polytheism is repressed. . . . No truth can

24. Ibid., 234–35. See also Montserrat, *Akhenaten*, 12–14.

25. Cyril Aldred, *Akhenaten: King of Egypt* (London: Thames & Hudson, 1988), 305; more generally see pp. 303–6.

26. Cyril Aldred, *Akhenaten and Nefertiti* (New York: Brooklyn Museum, 1973), 79.

27. Montserrat, *Akhenaten*, 14.

28. Arthur E. P. B. Weigall, *The Life and Times of Akhnaton, Pharaoh of Egypt* (Edinburgh: Blackwood, 1910), 62. Such claims are, of course, a reflection of the times when Weigall lived, yet Weigall's work, despite a century of further research remains popular with nonspecialists. See Aiden Dodson, *Amarna Sunset: Nefertiti, Tutankhamun, Ay, Horemheb, and the Egyptian Counter-Reformation* (Cairo: American University in Cairo, 2009), xxi–xxiii.

29. There are numerous excellent, recent treatments of Akhenaten and his reforms that do avoid such extremes. Among others see, Dodson, *Amarna Sunset*; James K. Hoffmeier, *Akhenaten and the Origins of Monotheism* (Oxford: Oxford University Press, 2015); Barry J. Kemp, *The City of Akhenaten and Nefertiti: Amarna and Its People* (London: Thames & Hudson, 2012); David P. Silverman, Josef W. Wegner, and Jennifer Houser Wegner, *Akhenaten and Tutankhamun: Revolution and Restoration* (Philadelphia: University of Pennsylvania Museum of Archaeology and Anthropology, 2006).

30. Robert Hari, *New Kingdom Amarna Period*, Iconography of Religions, Egypt 6 (Leiden: Brill, 1985), 4.

31. Erik Hornung, "The Rediscovery of Akhenaten and His Place in Religion," *JARCE* 29 (1992): 48.

come from anyone but the king."[32] Akhenaten's monotheism comes at the expense of Egyptian polytheism, a tragedy to Redford.

For no less a doyen than William M. Flinders Petrie, Akhenaten's reforms reflect a logical and scientific rationality:

> If this were a new religion invented to satisfy our modern scientific concep-
> tions, we could not find a flaw in the correctness of this view of the energy of
> the solar system ... a position which we cannot logically improve upon at the
> present day.[33]

Here Petrie brings a whole new discipline into the equation—*science.* Akhenaten is not merely a reformer; he's scientifically accurate to the point that, at least in Petrie's own day, Petrie could claim that science could not logically improve upon Akhenaten's reforms.

Others find a vein of natural philosophy in Akhenaten's reforms. Jan Assmann writes:

> Amarna theology concentrates on the one aspect of god as life, and occupies itself
> with a uniquely explicit and forceful description of visible reality, so as to lead
> everything back to one source of life in the sun. We stand here at the origin less
> of the monotheistic world religions than of natural philosophy. If this religion had
> succeeded, we should have expected it to produce a Thales rather than a Moses.[34]

James Allen builds on the foundation provided by Assmann, speaking of Akhenaten's teaching about nature he opines: "Its fundamental principle, that of light, is a natural concept—in fact, superior to those which the early Greek philosophers came up with—and not a god in the traditional sense of Egyptian religion."[35] Both Assmann and Allen make an interesting contribution in revealing a tendency toward natural philosophy in Akhenaten's reforms. However, in claiming that Akhenaten founded natural philosophy more so than an Egyptian religion, Assmann and Allen seem to proceed on the basis of a false analogy. Worshiping an element of nature or the cosmos does not equate to a philosophical system. If Akhenaten were truly a precursor to Thales, then Akhenaten would have treated the Aten as Thales treated water. But, Akhenaten clearly worshiped the Aten; Thales did not worship water. Moreover, if, as Allen states, Akhenaten's conception of light shared little in common with traditional Egyptian religion, one must wonder why Akhenaten built temples for the Aten, made offerings to it, and generally venerated it as a deity.

---

32. Donald B. Redford, "The Sun-disc in Akhenaten's Program: Its Worship and Antecedents, I," *JARCE* 13 (1976): 47.

33. William M. Flinders Petrie, *A History of Egypt*, 2nd ed., 6 vols. (London: Methuen, 1895), 2:214.

34. Jan Assmann, *Ägypten: Theologie und Frömmigkeit einer frühen Hochkultur*, Urban-Tashenbücher 366 (Stuttgart: Kohlhammer, 1984), 248–49; quoted in James P. Allen, "The Natural Philosophy of Akhenaten," in *Religion and Philosophy in Ancient Egypt*, ed. William Kelly Simpson, YES 3 (New Haven: Yale University Press, 1989), 89–102.

35. Allen, "Natural Philosophy of Akhenaten," 99–100.

Debates about the timing and extent of Akhenaten's monotheism or henotheism muddy the waters as well. At present, the consensus among Egyptologists is that Akhenaten was a monotheist, but this remains a contentious topic.[36] Aiden Dodson puts a poignant emphasis on the problem: "Egyptologists who produce new interpretations can run the risk of being accused of such things as slandering the Founder of Monotheism (note capitalization)."[37] Emblematic of Dodson's point are statements like Robert Hari's: "there can be no doubt we have, for the first in the history of humanity, the establishment of a monotheistic religion."[38]

To understand the extent of Akhenaten's monotheism, several key events from his reign must be noted. First, major changes took place following the young king's Sed-festival (jubilee) in year four or five, when Akhenaten sacrificed solely to the Aten, and not to other deities, as tradition demanded, revealing the already elevated status of the Aten.[39] Redford rightly observes,

> All the evidence militates in favor of the kaleidoscope of revolutionary changes associated with Akhenaten's program having taken places at his jubilee, or in anticipation thereof. This includes the new style of art, the new, outlandish representation of the king, the first steps in overt iconoclasm, and the introduction of the disk (Aten) as an icon, and the enclosing of the didactic name in cartouches.[40]

Second, shortly after Akhenaten changed his name in year five or six of his reign, he began to persecute other deities. Jacobus van Dijk writes, "probably at that same time as this name change took place, the traditional gods were banned completely and a campaign was begun to remove their names and effigies (particularly those of Amun) from monuments."[41] Unfortunately, no royal decree survives to disclose the king's intent, yet iconoclasm is obvious.[42] Akhenaten replaced his previous name, Amenhotep IV, with his new name on temples in Thebes devoted to the Aten.[43] Iconoclasm in his fifth year targeted the Theban triad in particular (Amun, Mut, and Khonsu), and, on blocks from Karnak, Akhenaten made clear his intention, claiming all the gods beside the Aten had "died."[44] Third, this was likely done in connection to the

---

36. For two of the more important works arguing against Akhenaten's monotheism, see Siegfried Morenz, *Egyptian Religion*, trans. Ann E. Keep (Ithaca: Cornell University Press, 1973), 147; Nicholas Reeves, *Akhenaten: Egypt's False Prophet* (London: Thames & Hudson, 2001), 118. For a useful recent summary of scholarship on each side of the debate see Edwin Yamauchi, "Akhenaten, Moses, and Monotheism," *Near East Archaeological Society Bulletin* 55 (2010): 1–15. Summaries can also be found in Hoffmeier, *Akhenaten and the Origins of Monotheism*, 206–10; and Mark D. Janzen, "Akhenaten and the Amarna Period," in *Behind the Scenes of the Old Testament: Cultural, Social, and Historical Contexts of Ancient Israel*, ed. Jonathan S. Greer, John W. Hilber, and John H. Walton (Grand Rapids: Baker Academic, 2018), 253–59.

37. Dodson, *Amarna Sunset*, xxii.

38. Hari, *New Kingdom Amarna Period*, 3.

39. Janzen, "Akhenaten and the Amarna Period," 255–56.

40. Donald B. Redford, "Akhenaten: New Theories and Old Facts," *BASOR* 369 (2013): 19.

41. Jacobus van Dijk, "The Amarna Period and Later New Kingdom," in *The Oxford History of Ancient Egypt*, ed. Ian Shaw (Oxford: Oxford University Press, 2000), 270.

42. Hoffmeier, *Akhenaten and the Origins of Monotheism*, 195.

43. Redford, *Akhenaten*, 140–41.

44. William J. Murnane, *Texts from the Amarna Period in Egypt*, ed. Edmund Melzer, SBLWAW 5 (Atlanta: Scholars Press, 1995), 31; Redford, "Akhenaten: New Theories and Old Facts," 14–15. On the

move to Akhetaten—a final attack before the next phase of reforms.[45] Overall, clear connections exist between the Sed-festival, name change, iconoclasm, and move to Akhetaten.[46]

By the time Akhenaten moved the capital to Amarna, his religion of light had undergone several phases: (1) Aten and the traditional gods coexisted until (2) the king abandoned them and allowed them to be neglected, before (3) he ultimately subjected them to iconoclasm.[47] These phases help explain the extent of Akhenaten's monotheism. Initially, the Aten was worshiped while other gods were at least tolerated—an essentially henotheistic religion. The final years at Thebes hinted at changes to come, and the iconoclasm there is demonstrative of monotheism.[48] A final change to the didactic name of the Aten, "Living Re, Ruler of the Horizon, Rejoicing in the Horizon in His Name of Re, the Father, who has come as the Sun-disc" took place after the move to Akhetaten.[49] The removal of, "Horakhty" and "Shu" from the earlier names "was meant to remove any doubt that Aten is connected to these gods."[50] Iconography echoes this change as important visual elements of solar theology are lacking—the Re-Horakhty falcon, the scarab beetle, the winged sun-disc, and the solar boat.[51] Thus, only the Aten was considered a god, despite the previously strong connections to earlier solar theology. By this time, Akhenaten seems to have settled his theology, culminating in a form of monotheism that is more explicit than earlier in his reign.

Akhenaten and Ma'at: Did the King Reform "Truth and Order"?

If Akhenaten can reasonably be established as a monotheist (especially during that latter portion of his reign) what does that mean for his understanding of Ma'at? Much like with the treatment of other solar deities, some scholars have claimed that Ma'at underwent significant changes during Akhenaten's reign. Hari contends that Ma'at became such "an abstract principle that her name came to be written only in phonetic hieroglyphs, without the image of a seated goddess wearing on her head the characteristic feather."[52] Aldred also notes the phonetic spelling of Ma'at as a shift based on "doctrinal reform."[53] A few obvious problems jump to mind with these comments, not the least of which is the fact that there are examples of the feather-goddess

---

desecration of other gods, see the useful summary in Hoffmeier, *Akhenaten and the Origins of Monotheism*, 202–3.

45. Redford, "Akhenaten: New Theories and Old Facts," 23–26.

46. Janzen, "Akhenaten and the Amarna Period," 255–56; Hoffmeier, *Akhenaten and the Origins of Monotheism*, 194.

47. William J. Murnane, "Observations on Pre-Amarna Theology During the Earliest Reign of Amenhotep IV," in *Gold of Praise: Studies on Ancient Egypt in Honor of Edward F. Wente*, ed. Emily Teeter and John A. Larson, SAOC 28 (Chicago: Oriental Institute of the University of Chicago, 1999), 303–12.

48. Jan Assmann, *Of God and Gods: Egypt, Israel, and the Rise of Monotheism* (Madison: University of Wisconsin Press, 2008), 29.

49. Redford, *Akhenaten*, 186.

50. Hoffmeier, *Akhenaten and the Origins of Monotheism*, 206.

51. Redford, "Akhenaten: New Theories and Old Facts," 27.

52. Hari, *New Kingdom Amarna Period*, 5.

53. Aldred, *Akhenaten: King of Egypt*, 278.

determinative (Gardiner sign list, C10) used in the writing of the term stemming from Amarna itself.[54] If Ma'at became an overly abstract principle, one should not find scenes of the king keeping Ma'at in traditional fashion; an aspect examined below concerning iconography.

Additionally, Hari admits that explicitly theological texts are lacking, but his generalization of Akhenaten's specific treatment of the all-important concept of Ma'at is based only on the *absence* of Ma'at in the Great Hymn to the Aten.[55] Leaving aside the obvious issue of basing an argument on the absence of evidence, this is problematic because Ma'at is in fact present in other hymns to the Aten with both types of spelling attested (goddess determinative used and not used—see table 12.1).[56] Also, it is far too simplistic to say that changing the writing of the term Ma'at to no longer include the goddess determinative proves that Akhenaten "eliminated" Ma'at. In fact, it seems the precise opposite is true. That a pharaoh so determined to avoid depicting deities other than the Aten felt the need to still reference Ma'at, even if in frequently modified spellings, is a commentary itself on the importance of Ma'at. Again, the writing "Ma'at" without the determinative is not exclusive, merely preferred.

Akhenaten also needed to address other deities who were associated with more mundane terms or concepts. For example, Aldred noted that the word Mut, meaning mother, received a similar treatment as Ma'at, with the vulture of the goddess replaced by a full spelling in glyphs, rather than the vulture ideogram ( ), which could represent the goddess.[57] A critique of the validity of this statement would move beyond the bounds of the discussion, but one parallel must be noted here. Mut as "mother" would have been as impossible for Akhenaten to replace conceptually as Ma'at, meaning essentially "truth/order." The fact that he generally eliminated the vulture ideogram has not been used to claim that he attempted to do radically alter the Egyptian conception of motherhood, so why should the spelling of Ma'at be any different? Modification of the spelling of a particular term does not equate to changing the meaning. For that matter, it is fair to question whether the Egyptians themselves would have made any distinction between the concepts (motherhood; truth) and the deities (Mut; Ma'at). Caution is required in order to avoid introducing a potentially false dichotomy. But this point is also a critique of scholars like Redford who claim that the multiplicity of divine names and forms was "foreign to Akhenaten."[58] How can a scholar such as Redford, who clearly knows that Akhenaten wrote the names of at least Ma'at, the Aten, and Re-Horakhty in different forms, make such a statement?[59]

54. For the sign list, see Alan H. Gardiner, *Egyptian Grammar*, 3rd rev. ed. (Oxford: Oxford University Press, 1957), 449. More on the feather-goddess determinative below, but see Norman de Garis Davies, *The Rock Tombs of el Amarna: Part III and IV—The Tombs of Panehesy and Meryra II*, Egypt Exploration Fund 37 (London: Gilbert & Rivington, 1905), part 4: pls. 32–33.

55. Hari, *New Kingdom Amarna Period*, 2–5; See also Erik Hornung, *Akhenaten and the Religion of Light* (Ithaca: Cornell University Press, 1999), 52–53.

56. Davies, *Rock Tombs of el Amarna*, part 4: pls. 32–33.

57. Aldred, *Akhenaten: King of Egypt*, 278, 222, fig. 20.

58. Redford, "Sun-disc," 47.

59. Redford, "Sun-disc," 53; Redford, *Akhenaten*, 172–74. One solution is that Akhenaten was changing things as he went along, and while this is certainly true, scholars rarely mention this phenomenon when generalizing about Akhenaten's reforms. If true, this counters claims like Redford's (above) about the king making sweeping, sudden, and dramatic changes.

TABLE 12.1. Attestations of the spelling of Ma'at from Amarna.

Tomb owner and location	Spelling with the goddess determinative (𓂝𓁦, or only 𓁦)	Spelling without the goddess determinative (variations of 𓐰)	Spelling without the goddess determinative but with the feather (variations of 𓐠𓏏𓆄)
Apy, right doorjamb	Line 1	Lines 2, 3	
Apy, short hymn to Aten	×2		
Ay, ceiling			A, C
Ay, left doorjamb	Line 1	Line 2 (×2)	
Ay, east thickness	Line 5	Lines 7, 12, 5, 16	
Ay, west thickness		Lines 1 (×2), 13	
Ay, right outer jamb	Line 1	Line 2	
Ay, left outer jamb		Line 2 (×2)	
Huya, east wall	Caption text ×1		
Huya, north wall	Door lintel ×1		
Mahu, short hymn to Aten	Line 1 ×2		
May, north wall	Line 11	Lines, 1, 2, 4 8	
May, south wall		Line 1	
May, left doorjamb		Line 1	
May, right doorjamb		Line 1	
Meryre, south. wall		West side ×1	
Meryre, east wall		Lower half ×1	
Meryre, south door		×2	
Meryre, inner wall, west side		Line 4	
Meryre, antechamber, south wall, east side			×1
Meryre, antechamber, south wall, west side			×1
Meryre, antechamber, doorjamb		×6	
Meryre, panel A		×2	
Meryre, entrance, left doorjamb		×4	
Rames, exterior left doorjamb	Line 1	Line 3	
Tutu, short hymn to Aten	Line 11		
Tutu, right outer jamb	Line 1		
Tutu, architrave A	×2		
Tutu, entrance ceiling	×1		
Tutu, left doorjamb	Lines 1, 2		
Tutu, south thickness	Lines 1, 6-9	Line 7	
Tutu, north thickness	Lines 1 (×2), 9		
Tutu, west wall	Line 5	Line 16	

The degree to which one views the extensiveness of Akhenaten's monotheistic reforms has the potential to impact one's views of his conception of Ma'at. Additionally, the degree to which one believes he was a tyrant forcing his views on the populace potentially affects how one understands the concept of Ma'at as it pertains to nonroyal persons. It has been claimed that Akhenaten alone was the "fount and dispenser of Maat."[60] If this statement is true then there should be evidence from both the textual and iconographic record, to which the discussion now turns.

60. Lichtheim, *Maat in Egyptian Autobiographies*, 61.

Iconography

For the purposes of discussion, the iconography of Akhenaten's reign is divided between two distinct time periods—pre-Amarna (Thebes) and Amarna (Akhetaten), after the king had moved the capital.[61] This is in keeping with the structure employed by Emily Teeter, whose work on the monuments at Thebes has proven useful to this discussion.[62]

Changes in the relationship between the king and the gods were already taking place during the reign of Akhenaten's father, Amenhotep III.[63] After Akhenaten's reign, his predecessors were quick to dismantle his monuments, especially at Thebes.[64] These factors combine to create a complex situation in analyzing the earliest portions of Akhenaten's reforms. The *talatat*, as they are now known, are all that remains of Akhenaten's temples at Thebes, and in most cases the blocks were reused by his successors in other structures.[65] Approximately forty-seven thousand *talatat* have been cataloged and photographed, very few have been published, further complicating matters.[66]

There remains, however, important evidence from the *talatat* regarding Akhenaten's understanding of Ma'at. Teeter found approximately thirty examples of scenes depicting the presentation of Ma'at, demonstrating that this scene was more common in the early portion of Akhenaten's reign than in the periods immediately after.[67] For all the influence he wielded on his son, Amenhotep III presented Ma'at in only four surviving scenes; more examples stem from earlier in the Eighteenth Dynasty as well the latter half of the New Kingdom.[68] Although this is partially explained by Akhenaten's removal of cult statues with which to interact, leaving Akhenaten with fewer types of ritual actions to conduct than his father, that the king continued to present Ma'at is significant. It symbolized the king's legitimacy by portraying him as upholding the principles inherent in Ma'at.[69] The main difference between the Amarna and later periods in this type of scene is that the Amarna period examples contain no dedicatory inscriptions and no recitations "from the normally mute Aten."[70]

61. Some scholars opt for an intermediate phase, or they attempt to divide the phases by regnal years. This is problematic because of the lack of chronologically explicit texts. Clearly, Akhenaten's reforms did not take place all at once, but using the capitals as parameters allows the discussion to be structured around something concrete. See Redford, "Sun-disc," 53–56.

62. Teeter, "Preliminary Report," 5.

63. Harry Smith, "Ma'et and Isfet," *BACE* 5 (1994): 80. For more on Amenhotep III see Arielle P. Kozloff and Betsy M. Bryan, *Egypt's Dazzling Sun: Amenhotep III and His World* (Cleveland: Cleveland Museum of Art, 1992).

64. Teeter, "Preliminary Report," 5.

65. Ibid., 5. For more on the problems of working with *talatat* see Ray Smith and Donald B. Redford, eds., *The Akhenaten Temple Project: Vol 1, Initial Discoveries* (Warminster: Aris & Phillips, 1976); and Redford, ed., *The Akhenaten Temple Project: Vol. 2, Rwd–Mnw, Foreigners and Inscriptions* (Warminster: Aris & Phillips,1988).

66. Teeter, "Preliminary Report," 6. A similar problem relates to the *talatat* and Akhenaten's *Sed* festival. See Jocelyn Gohary, *Akhenaten's Sed-festival at Karnak*, Studies in Egyptology (London: Kegan Paul, 1992). Akhenaten's potential celebration of a *Sed* festival at Karnak would be another important link between the so-called heretic and standard Eighteenth Dynasty pharaonic ideology, at least during the early portion of his reign. It is possible that by later in his reign he abandoned the practice (ibid., 63).

67. Teeter, "Preliminary Report," 8.

68. Teeter, *Presentation of Maat*, 14.

69. Ibid., 1.

70. Ibid., 49. For a general discussion of the inscriptions that otherwise accompany presentation scenes, see the general discussion in Jan Bergman, "Zum, 'Mythos vom Staat' im alten Ägypten," in *The Myth of*

Additionally, Akhenaten did not need to depict Ma'at in anthropomorphic form to convey all that Ma'at represented, as the ostrich feather (or feathers) has been shown to represent Ma'at.[71] Thus, we may speak of the attestation of Ma'at in iconography as either the seated goddess or the specific feather(s) associated with her. Another possible iconographic element of Ma'at is the connection between Ma'at and the spouts on *nemset*-vessels in the Amarna period, a case convincingly made by Sayed Tawfik.[72] In a scene on a block from an Aten temple in Thebes, Nefertiti is twice seen offering Ma'at as a form of worship to the Aten, exactly as Akhenaten might have.[73] On the left she presents the typical Ma'at figure seated on the *neb* basket, while to the right she offers the *nemset*-vessel which clearly has a feather spout as well as a hawk head and sun-disc.[74] The connection of the hawk head and disc with Ma'at is reminiscent of Heliopolitan ideals, as discussed above. Akhenaten never completely rejected anthropomorphic representations of the sun god either; such depictions were never targets of his iconoclasm. Nefertiti was also presented as upholding Ma'at in typical pharaonic fashion by smiting a captured enemy.[75]

Talatat from the IXth Pylon at Karnak depict Akhenaten in the classic smiting pose and both the king and queen presenting to the Aten.[76] In this latter scene, Akhenaten is clearly presenting Ma'at with the goddess seated on a *neb* basket. The text reads, "the King of Upper and Lower Egypt Neferkheperure Wa-en-re [institutes the offerings] for his father Re, as an offering menu for every day in Memphis."[77] This scene is obviously from early in Akhenaten's reign as he still refers to the sun-disc as Re. This is in keeping with the "early" name of the Aten.[78] What is most significant from the *talatat* at Thebes is that, other than the presence of Nefertiti in some examples, there is nothing whatsoever to suggest that Ma'at, or the king's understanding of it early in his reign, has undergone any changes in Ma'at role as truth and cosmic order in relation to solar deities and royal legitimation.[79]

---

the State: Based on Papers Read at the Symposium on the Myth of the State Held at Åbo on the 6th–8th September 1971, ed. Haralds Biezais, Scripta Instituti Donneriani Aboensis 6 (Uppsala: Almqvist & Wiksell, 1972), 85–86.

71. Teeter, "Multiple Feathers." The names of the Aten could also be offered for Ma'at (see notes 90, 94, and 96).

72. Sayed Tawfik, "Aton Studies 5: Cult Objects on Blocks from the Aton Temple(s) at Thebes," *MDAIK* 35 (1979): 335–41.

73. Tawfik, "Aton Studies," 85. Nefertiti's role as upholder of Ma'at is intriguing. Commenting on what it means for kingship in the Amarna period is beyond the scope of this discussion. Suffice to say that scenes of either Nefertiti or Akhenaten presenting Ma'at both reveal Akhenaten's understanding of Ma'at. That Nefertiti is depicted in this fashion is significant, but she is not acting due to a different conceptual understanding of Ma'at itself. In fact, there is good evidence to suggest that Nefertiti was seen on equal footing with Akhenaten; see J. R. Harris, "Nefertiti Rediviva," *Acta Orientalia* 35 (1973): 5–13.

74. Tawfik, "Aton Studies," 338, fig. 4; see also Teeter, "Multiple Feathers," 45, fig. 6.

75. Harris, "Nefertiti Rediviva," 9; John D. Cooney, *Amarna Reliefs from Hermopolis* (New York: Brooklyn Museum, 1965), 82–85 (no. 51a).

76. See also Hari, *New Kingdom Amarna Period*, pl. 8.

77. Redford, "Sun-disc," 53–54.

78. Redford, "Sun-disc," 54. Redford also points out that deities like Atum, Hathor, Osiris, and Anubis are still attested from tombs in this period (53). Again, this is to be expected as the king's reforms would have taken some time and may not have spread too far from Amarna.

79. Ma'at is also depicted in full anthropomorphic form in the tomb of Khereuf: Epigraphic Survey, *The Tomb of Khereuf*, OIP 102 (Chicago: Oriental Institute of the University of Chicago, 1980), pl. 9.

Thus far, all examples hail from Thebes and from early in the king's reign; it is now time to examine iconography at Akhenaten's famous capital at Amarna, Akhetaten. Here Ray Smith and Donald Redford claim that they have been "unable to find at Amarna the ... offering object ... of the goddess Ma'at ... seated in a bowl."[80] This is a significant comment if true, as it would mark a noteworthy shift from the scenes that survive on the Karnak/Theban *talatat*.

Perhaps the most interesting scene from Amarna is a fragment of a parapet containing two sides (fig. 12.1).[81] Carved in sunken relief on both sides, the parapet shows parts of the figures of both the king and the queen making offerings to the Aten.[82] Stylistically, the art is conventional, even stereotypical of the Amarna period.[83] The young king is now following his own artistic conventions, rather than Eighteenth Dynasty ones. On both sides, the larger, deeper-cut figure is badly damaged and the queen is far more visible.[84]

On the verso side, the queen "elevates a very complicated offering in the form of a woman who wears four ostrich feathers, seated on a *neb* basket."[85] This figure is clearly intended to be Ma'at, who sits in a *neb* basket in the scenes mentioned earlier, and who, of course, is depicted with multiple ostrich feathers.[86] The total number of feathers, four, is familiar from depictions of Shu, but the feather is clearly not the straight Shu feather. It is worth questioning if there might be some connection between Ma'at, Shu or Tefnut, and the queen intended here, however, Baudouin van de Walle's identification of the figure as solely Shu or the abstract concept of air is unconvincing.[87] Teeter's argument that the posture of the figure is unmistakably patterned after Ma'at is more persuasive, and it is far more likely given the conceptions of Ma'at discussed above and the fact that the figure is seated on a *neb* basket.[88] Though connections to Shu may be in kept in mind, there is little reason to suppose that this particular figure is Shu, absent any relationship to Ma'at. A more emphatic correlation between Shu and Ma'at, particularly the Ma'at feather, can be seen in object 26.7.767 from the New York Metropolitan Museum of Art. Here the figures are symbolic representations of Akhenaten and Nefertitii as Shu (left) and Tefnut (right), with Shu holding a Ma'at feather.[89]

80. Smith and Redford, *Akhenaten Temple Project*, 1:24.

81. Brooklyn Museum object 41.82. Aldred, *Akhenaten and Nefertiti*, 104–5, fig. 18. See also T. G. H. James, *Corpus of Hieroglyphic Inscriptions in the Brooklyn Museum I: From Dynasty I to the End of Dynasty XVIII* (Brooklyn: Brooklyn Museum, 1974), 134–35, pl. LXXVI. James's plate contains the texts but not the scenes. See also J. D. Cooney and William Kelly Simpson, "An Architectural Fragment from Amarna," *Brooklyn Museum Bulletin* 12.4 (1951): 1–12; figs. 2–3.

82. Aldred, *Akhenaten and Nefertiti*, 104.

83. Cooney and Simpson, "Architectural Fragment," 10–12.

84. Aldred, *Akhenaten and Nefertiti*, 104.

85. Teeter, "Multiple Feathers," 45.

86. Is it possibly intended to be Nefertiti herself as Ma'at? See also Aldred, *Akhenaten and Nefertiti*, 104.

87. Baudouin van de Walle, "Survivances mythologiques dans les coiffures royals de l'époque atonienne," *CdÉ* 55 (1980): 23–36, esp. 29–30.

88. Teeter, "Multiple Feathers," 45–46.

89. There is good reason to suppose that Shu is meant to represent Akhenaten. When Amenhotep III died he assumed the mythical role of Atum-Re. Shu is the son of Atum-Re. Thus, Akhenaten is presenting himself as Shu and making claims about the divinity of both him and his father. For more, see W. Raymond Johnson, "The Revolutionary Role of the Sun in the Reliefs and Statuary of Amenhotep III," *Oriental*

Returning to the parapet, Ma'at is holding the life-giving names of the Aten, rather than holding the usual *'nḫ* sign.[90] This provides a wonderful example of the type of changes Akhenaten felt necessary to emphasize in his reforms. Ma'at is still depicted with life-giving connotations, but Akhenaten has tweaked the symbolism to include the Aten. Ma'at is then in turn raising a pair of cartouches with the earlier names of the Aten, all of which are also seated on a *neb* basket.[91] Above the scene is an inscription, which reads "son of Re, living in Ma'at" (*s3 R' anḫ m M3at*). Enough of the king's figure survives to allow one to read the earlier names of Aten inscribed on his arms and chest.[92] Ma'at here is written with the seated goddess determinative (Gardiner sign list, C10), demonstrating that at Amarna while the earlier form of the name of Aten was in use, the goddess determinative could be employed.[93]

On the recto side (fig. 12.4b) the queen also upholds the names of the Aten upon a *neb* basket. The connection between Ma'at, the royal figures, and the Aten is emphatic. The king and queen uphold Ma'at by raising not the stereotypical seated goddess, but the names of the Aten and a form of the goddess Ma'at represented by Nefertiti herself.[94] This shift in depiction is perhaps a prelude to Akhenaten's later determination not to directly portray deities except the Aten. This fact, however, is countered by the presence of the Ma'at goddess determinative in the hieroglyphs. This twist on the usual iconography of Ma'at is indicative of Akhenaten's artistic policies, yet he makes reference to Ma'at, and the scene as a whole is clearly reminiscent of a presentation scene. That he went to such unusual lengths to portray and uphold Ma'at demonstrates once more that the concept was simply too central to kingship and Egyptian society for Akhenaten to move entirely away from it. Finally, if it is true that Nefertiti is to be identified as the goddess Ma'at, it is possible that scenes depicting Akhenaten embracing Nefertiti are another means by which the king upholds or is "living on Ma'at."[95]

Institute News and Notes, 151 (1996); http://oi.uchicago.edu/research/pubs/nn/fal96_epi.html. Also see Kozloff and Bryan, *Egypt's Dazzling Sun*.

90. Teeter, *Presentation of Maat*, 92. For examples of the life-giving rays of the Aten, see Norman de Garis Davies, *The Rock Tombs of el Amarna: Parts I and II—The Tomb of Meryra*, Egypt Exploration Fund 37 (London: Gilbert & Rivington, 1903), part 1 pls. 22 and 25; part 2 pls. 5, 8, 10, 12, 13, 15, 33, and 34; Davies, *Rock Tombs of el Amarna*, part 4 pl. 5.

91. Teeter, "Multiple Feathers," 45.

92. Aldred, *Akhenaten and Nefertiti*, 104.

93. James, *Corpus of Hieroglyphic Inscriptions*, pl. 76, no. 306.

94. Nefertiti's association with other deities is well known as well. She could be associated with Tefnut and Hathor, for instance. For Tefnut see J. R. Harris, "A Fine Piece of Egyptian Faience," *Burlington Magazine* 119 (1977): 340–43; for Hathor see Geoffrey T. Martin, *The Royal Tomb at el-Amarna I: Objects* (London: Egypt Exploration Society, 1974), 15.

95. Smith, "Ma'et and Isfet," 80. The phrase "living on Ma'at" will be discussed more below. For examples of scenes of embracing, see Norman de Garis Davies, *The Rock Tombs of el Amarna: Part V and VI—The Tombs of Huya and Ahmes*, Egypt Exploration Fund 37 (London: Gilbert & Rivington, 1908), part 6, pl. 3; Davies, *Rock Tombs of el Amarna*, part 3, pls. 8–9; part 4, pl. 22.

Evidence of a less obvious sort is available if one accepts the widely held notion that food offerings are synonymous with Ma'at offerings (see Ragnhild Bjerre Finnestad, *Image of the World and Symbol of the Creator: On the Cosmological and Iconological Values of the Temple of Edfu*, Studies in Oriental Religion 10 [Wiesbaden: Otto Harrassowitz, 1985], 154; Jan Assmann, *Der König als Sonnenpriester: Ein kosmographischer Begleittext zur kultischen Sonnenhymnik in thebanischen Tempeln und Gräbern*, Abhandlungen des Deutschen Archäologischen Instituts Kairo 7 [Glückstadt: Augustin, 1970], 63–65). Additionally, there is textual evidence from tombs in the Amarna period to support this understanding. See Davies, *Rock Tombs of el Amarna*, part 4, pl. 31.

Regardless of whether the location was Thebes or Amarna, Akhenaten made several concessions to incorporate the concept of Ma'at into his reforms, if not in traditional fashion. Caution is still required here as these are admittedly unique scenes; far more common are scenes where Akhenaten offers the names of the Aten absent any explicit connection to Ma'at.[96]

Textual Data

As mentioned above, Hari claimed that Akhenaten refused to allude to "anything that recalls the traditional pantheon. . . . The image of the goddess (Ma'at) had to be replaced . . . by phonetic readings."[97] This claim is puzzling. Most explicit is the simple fact that Ma'at was included in the epithets of Akhenaten, who lives in Ma'at / truth (*anḫ m Mȝat*) in both his own monuments and from the tombs of his officials.[98] Beginning with the earliest portion of his reign, before he had changed his name, one finds in a simple taxation decree the epithet "who lives in Maat."[99] The same epithet occurs on a graffito from Aswan, as well as a scarab from Luxor, using the goddess determinative.[100] The epithet occurs in later texts such as the Later Proclamation from the boundary stelae at Amarna.[101] Not surprisingly, the phrase also appears on small objects, like shabtis.[102] Previously, this important phrase was the sole prerogative of the gods who had their own family groups—father, mother, offspring. Akhenaten's understanding of the Aten involved no family of deities, so those who "live on Ma'at" were now the king and his family, clear evidence that the king's understanding of Ma'at contains both traditional roots and innovations suitable to Amarna religion.[103]

From middle Egypt, the statue of the mayor of the town of Nefrusy, Yuni, says that Yuni is "the true follower" and that he may "live true."[104] As far as the mention of deities is concerned, Yuni is the "beloved of Re," and he also speaks of the "Ka of Khnum." His wife's statue also mentions Re and Khnum, as well as Osiris, echoing a more orthodox understanding of Egyptian deities.[105] A letter from Apy, the steward of Memphis, contains the phrase "who lives in Ma'at," dating to year 5 of Akhenaten's reign.[106] The Aten itself is said to live on Ma'at in a funerary stela (J.E. 34182), which may provide an interesting example from the period of transition to Akhetaten.[107]

96. To cite but a few examples, see Aldred, *Akhenaten and Nefertiti*, figs. 35, 47; Ali Radwan, "Einige Aspekte des Vergöttlichung des ägyptischen Königs," in *Ägypten: Dauer und Wandel*, DAIK Sonderschaft 18 (Mainz: von Zabern, 1985), 61, fig. 12. See also Teeter, *Presentation of Maat*, 91.

97. Hari, *New Kingdom Amarna Period*, 13.

98. See, e.g., Murnane, *Texts from the Amarna Period*, 41.

99. Ibid., 30.

100. For the graffito from Aswan, see ibid., 41; Labib Habachi, "The Graffito of Bak and Men at Aswan and a Second Graffito Close by Showing Akhenaten Before the Hawk-headed Aten," *MDAIK* 20 (1965): 85–92. For the taxation decree, consult Maj Sandman, *Texts from the Time of Akhenaten*, Bibliotheca Aegyptiaca 8 (Brussels: Fondation Egyptologique Reine Elisabeth, 1938), 149.

101. Sandman, *Texts from the Time of Akhenaten*, 119–30; Murnane, *Texts from the Amarna Period*, 81–89.

102. Martin, *Royal Tomb at el-Amarna*, 57, pl. 16 no. 152.

103. Silverman, Wegner, and Houser Wegner, *Akhenaten and Tutankhamun*, 32–33.

104. Murnane, *Texts from the Amarna Period*, 47–48.

105. Ibid. 49.

106. Ibid., 50–51.

107. Sandman, *Texts from the Time of Akhenaten*, 178–79; Murnane, *Texts from the Amarna Period*, 51.

There are several attestations from the Tomb of Kheruef (Theban Tomb 192) pre-dating the move to Akhetaten. In one scene, Queen Tiye is portrayed facing the gods; among them is Ma'at.[108] The Hymn to the Rising Sun from this tomb provides a hint of the changes to come, and also claims that Ma'at embraces the sun, while the Hymn to the Setting Sun says that Re feeds on Ma'at, connecting Ma'at to sustenance.[109] Here one can readily agree with Assmann's assertion that Ma'at was viewed as a life-giving substance.[110] Those who contend that Ma'at cannot be understood in such a fashion because of its mythic symbolism are, frankly, missing the point.[111] One of Ma'at's mythical roles is sustenance; the texts make that clear. Assuming that a mythic concept cannot pertain to a more concrete aspect like nutrition is to erroneously adopt modern understandings of myth that have little to do with ancient Egyptian conceptions.

Concerning the inscriptions from the tombs of Amarna (table 12.1), one finds numerous attestations of Ma'at in the unfinished tomb of Ay.[112] Here the earlier name of the Aten is used, meaning that work in the tomb began before the change to the final form of the didactic name of the Aten (Year 9). Akhenaten continues to be the one "who lives on Ma'at" on the East Thickness (3×), the West Thickness (3×), the outer jambs (3×) and the inner door jambs (2×).[113] On the East Thickness, Ma'at is explic-itly connected to the Aten itself, as Akhenaten is in the "image like Aten, the ruler of Ma'at who issued from continuity."[114] This epithet refers to Akhenaten, as usual, but the connection to the Aten is significant; this is also in keeping with the king's role in upholding Ma'at, in this case as the "ruler of Ma'at." Ay says of Akhenaten while speaking to the Aten, "Your son (Akhenaten) *presents* Maat to your benign counte-nance" (emphasis added).[115] Ma'at as an offering seems to be the intent, providing a link to the scenes discussed above. Furthermore, Ma'at is written both with (𓐙𓂝𓁐 line 5) and without (𓂝 ; line 5 second occurrence and line 7) the 𓁐 determinative.[116] Within two short lines, *both* spelling types are attested, making it difficult to claim that the spelling of Ma'at proves anything whatsoever about the understanding of Ma'at in the Amarna period, at least prior to the final form of the didactic name. Since dating the tombs is difficult due to their incomplete condition, caution is required. Regardless,

---

108. Epigraphic Survey, *Tomb of Kheruef*, 32–33, pl. 9.

109. For the Hymn to the Rising Sun, see ibid., 38 pl. 20; Murnane, *Texts from the Amarna Period*, 59. For the Hymn to the Setting Sun, see Epigraphic Survey, *Tomb of Kheruef*, 30–32, pl. 7; Murnane, *Texts from the Amarna Period*, 60.

110. Assmann, *Ma'at*.

111. For an example of this argument, see Vincent A. Tobin, *Theological Principles of Egyptian Religion* (New York: Lang, 1989), 84–85.

112. It should be noted that tombs for Akhenaten's officials are difficult to date and most are unfinished. Their order of construction is not clear. Based on the name of the Aten used, many of them must have been started immediately after the move to Amarna. Two exceptions to this are the tombs of Huya (TA1) and Meryre (TA2). For more, see Dodson, *Amarna Sunset*, 27–99. For the tomb of Ay, see Davies, *Rock Tombs of el Amarna: Parts V and VI*.

113. For the East Thickness, see Davies, *Rock Tombs of el Amarna*, part 6, pls. 25, 38, 39. For the West Thickness, see ibid., plate 27; Sandman, *Texts from the Time of Akhenaten*, 93–96. For the jambs, see Davies, *Rock Tombs of el Amarna*, part 6, plates 32 and 34; Sandman, *Texts from the Time of Akhenaten*, 98–100.

114. Murnane, *Texts from the Amarna Period*, 111.

115. Ibid., 111; Davies, *Rock Tombs of el Amarna*, part 6, 28.

116. Ibid., pl. 25.

Akhenaten did not change the spelling of Maʿat in uniform fashion immediately following the move to his new capital.

Still on the East Thickness of his tomb, Ay also claims that the king "placed Maʿat in my innermost being."[117] He also says that "Waenre (Akhenaten) rejoices in Maʿat" due to his being knowledgeable like the Aten.[118] Maʿat might therefore be considered one effective outcome of knowledge of the Aten.

On the West Thickness of Ay's tomb Maʿat is written without the goddess determinative all three times, and each example is simply the epithet.[119] The left jamb of the inner door says, "Long live the Good God, who is pleased with Maʿat."[120] Here the goddess determinative is used in the spelling of Maʿat, while just a line later, in the standard "who lives on Maʿat" epithets, the determinative is not used (twice).[121] The exact same situation repeats itself on the right doorjamb with the first spelling using the goddess determinative while the other two do not.[122] It is possible, though far from certain, that when used in repetitious epithets, the shorter form of Maʿat (no determinative) was preferred.

The word Maʿat occurs twice on the ceiling of Ay's tomb. The first use is adjectival, not in reference to the goddess herself: "the righteous one who has done what his lord says."[123] The second reference juxtaposes Maʿat with falsehood: "who abandoned falsehood in order to do Maʿat."[124] In both cases, a full phonetic spelling is given with the feather used instead of the goddess determinative: [hieroglyphs].[125] Thus, a third spelling is attested; taken as whole, there was no standard spelling of Maʿat from Ay's tomb.[126]

The standard epithet containing Maʿat was also found in the tomb of Apy/Ipy the steward, with Maʿat written both with and without the goddess on the right doorjamb.[127] Just as with the doorjambs from Ay's tomb, the first reference is spelled with the goddess determinative, while the other two omit it. The two references to Maʿat from the tomb of Rames follow the same pattern with the first using the goddess determinative (line 1) and the second omitting it (line 3).[128] Another spelling with the goddess determinative is found on the left doorjamb of the tomb of Suti (line 1).[129] Overall, the doorjambs from the tombs of various officials at Amarna consistently spell Maʿat with the goddess determinative in the first line.

117. Murnane, *Texts from the Amarna Period*, 111, 118; Davies, *Rock Tombs of el Amarna*, part 6, 28 pl. 25 line 12, p. 33 pl. 32. See also the influential study by Rudolf Anthes, *Die Maat des Echnaton von Amarna*, Journal of the American Oriental Society Supplement 14 (Baltimore: American Oriental Society, 1952), 10.

118. Murnane, *Texts from the Amarna Period*, 111.

119. Davies, *Rock Tombs of el Amarna*, part 6, pl. 27; Sandman, *Texts from the Time of Akhenaten*, 93–96.

120. Murnane, *Texts from the Amarna Period*, 117. Davies, *Rock Tombs of el Amarna*, part 6, 34, pl. 32.

121. Davies, *Rock Tombs of el Amarna*, part 6, pl. 32, line 2.

122. Ibid., pl. 32.

123. Murnane, *Texts from the Amarna Period*, 119.

124. Ibid., 119.

125. Davies, *Rock Tombs of el Amarna*, part 6, pl. 33.

126. See also the texts on the west architrave and the ceiling of Ay's tomb Davies, *Rock Tombs of el Amarna*, part 6, pls. 32, 34; Murnane, *Texts from the Amarna Period*, 119.

127. Davies, *Rock Tombs of el Amarna*, part 4, pl. 39. The goddess determinative is used in line 1, but not in lines 2 and 3.

128. Ibid., pl. 37.

129. Ibid., pl., 39.

Of the nine references to Ma'at in the tomb of May, only one is spelled using the goddess determinative (North Thickness, line 11).[130] Here Akhenaten is said to be "knowledgeable like the Aten, content with Ma'at."[131] On the other hand, Tutu's tomb contains several references to Ma'at spelled with the goddess determinative. The king is said to "live on Ma'at" on the right outer doorjamb (𓇋𓈖𓐪𓏏) and on Architrave A (𓐪 [2×]).[132] This second example is significant as even at Amarna Egyptian artisans could use the goddess determinative as a substitute for a full spelling; the same spelling is used on the south thickness, (lines 1, 6 and 7) and north thickness (line 1).[133] Traces of the goddess determinative also survive on a damaged portion of the ceiling.[134] This is the exact opposite of claims that the goddess determinative was replaced by a purely phonetic spelling! These examples demonstrate that even at Amarna the determinative alone could suffice as a spelling of Ma'at.

The shorter hymn to the Aten is attested from various officials' tombs, usually heavily damaged. Still, attestations of the word Ma'at survive. Artisans spelled Ma'at with the goddess determinative in shorter hymn to the Aten in Apy's tomb, line 1 (2×) and Tutu's tomb, line 11.[135] The determinative is absent from the spelling of Ma'at in the shorter hymn to the Aten in the tombs of Mahu, line 2 (2×) and Apy, line 6.[136]

From the tomb of the Chief Steward of the King's Wife Tiye, Huya, we find the phrase "Arisen in the beauty of Ma'at," with Ma'at written using the goddess determinative.[137] This is interesting for several reasons. First, this writing uses *only* the goddess determinative 𓐪, just as the example from Tutu's tomb on Architrave A. Second, the connection between Ma'at and the rising of the Aten is emphatic. Third, the connection of Ma'at with beauty may have required writing the determinative in a more physical sense. Others have pointed out the connection of Ma'at with beauty; suffice to say, it is yet another nuance of Ma'at that finds expression in the Amarna period.[138] Finally, and most significantly for this study, this tomb dates to Year 12 based on a caption text, when the final form of didactic name of Aten was used.[139] Thus, Ma'at could be spelled with the goddess determinative even during the final phase of Akhenaten's reforms.[140]

130. Davies, *Rock Tombs of el Amarna*, part 5, pls. 2, 4. For the spelling with the determinative, see ibid., pl. 2, line 11.

131. Murnane, *Texts from the Amarna Period*, 144.

132. Davies, *Rock Tombs of el Amarna*, part 6, pls. 13, 14.

133. Ibid., pls. 15,16. See table 12.1 for the few references to Ma'at from Tutu's tomb that do not use the goddess determinative.

134. Ibid., pl. 14.

135. Davies, *Rock Tombs of el Amarna*, part 4, pl. 32.

136. Ibid., pl. 32.

137. Murnane, *Texts from the Amarna Period*, 134; Davies, *Rock Tombs of el Amarna*, part 3, pl. 8. Ma'at receives its full spelling in another place from this tomb—the north wall, lintel door (see Davies, *Rock Tombs of el Amarna*, part 3, pl. 16)—in a full spelling of Amenhotep III's name, Nebmaatre.

138. See Maulana Karenga, *Maat: The Moral Ideal in Ancient Egypt* (Los Angeles: University of Sankore Press, 2006), 88–89.

139. Dodson, *Amarna Sunset*, 11–12, fig. 10.

140. Caution is required, however, as the only other tomb that certainly dates to after year 12 is Meryre's, where Ma'at is not spelled with the goddess determinative. See Davies, *Rock Tombs of el Amarna*, part 1, pls. 7, 30, 34, 35, 36, 38–41.

In many of the examples above the officials purposefully linked their keeping Ma'at with their service to their king; indeed, it is the basis for their lofty status. Ay specifically referred to Akhenaten's teaching (above), and says it is the king who placed Ma'at in his body, making explicit connections between Akhenaten, Ma'at, and notions of sustenance. Tutu called Akhenaten "the ruler who lives by Ma'at" in keeping with the king's epithets. Huya connected Ma'at to beauty. In short, the tombs of officials at Amarna demonstrate several of the standard aspects of the concept of Ma'at in connection to the king.

However, as vital as the king's role was in his subjects' keeping of Ma'at, it was not an exclusive royal prerogative, despite Assmann's claim that during the Amarna period Ma'at was eliminated as ethical standard and absorbed into the idea of the Aten and the king himself.[141] Thus, in Assmann's view, the people no longer used the traditional understanding of Ma'at to govern their behavior, but rather justified their actions based on the king. Assmann seems to have overlooked texts of officials that document both their direct worship of the Aten and their upholding the ethics of Ma'at. These texts connect the god and king as noted by Assmann, but not as exclusively as he suggests.[142] For example, Tutu directly praises the Aten himself and then brags that he has committed no wrongdoings because "Ma'at has made her place in me" and that *he* has "executed Ma'at for the king."[143] Louis Žabkar notes that the importance of such statements lies in the removal of Osirian judgment from Amarna religion; the deceased confesses directly to the Aten.[144] As Teeter summarizes:

> Although the relationship of the king and sun god is very prominent in these texts, the non-royal devotee's direct appeal to the god and the numerous references to Maat suggest that Assmann's conclusions are subject to question.[145]

Overall, though Akhenaten's role in keeping Ma'at was a vital component of his reforms, his officials upheld Ma'at as well.

Concluding this tour of Amarna tombs, there is good reason to dispute the contention of scholars that the image of the seated goddess Ma'at was replaced by purely phonetic spellings. Though it is true that the deity herself is not pictured in full anthropomorphic form in Amarna art, the determinative is used several times (see table 12.1), and the spellings vary enough that neither can be said to be the standard form. Additionally, ethical conceptions of Ma'at and her role in the confessions of the deceased were not eliminated during the Amarna period. The king's role as a conduit to the Aten and the teacher of Ma'at to his subjects is clear in the textual record, but this does not mean that only he had access to the Aten or that Ma'at lost all ethical connections during the Amarna period.

---

141. Assmann, *Ägypten: Theologie*, 11–14, 232–81. Teeter, *Presentation of Maat*, 85.

142. Teeter, *Presentation of Maat*, 85.

143. Ibid., 85. See also Louis V. Žabkar, "The Theocracy of Amarna and the Doctrine of the Ba," *JNES* 13 (1954): 94–95. In other cases, the official addresses the *ka* of the king, the *ka* of the queen, the Aten and the *ka* of the king, or the Aten and the *ka* of the queen (see ibid., 95).

144. Ibid., 94–95.

145. Teeter, *Presentation of Maat*, 85.

Conclusion

The concept of Maʿat is alive and well in the Amarna period even if the goddess herself is not depicted in her fullest anthropomorphic form. This has led to the speculation that while the concept of Maʿat endured, "the deity was perhaps being phased out."[146] While such a view is possible, it may not be valid to assume that the Egyptians viewed the goddess Maʿat and the concept of Maʿat as separate. For a deity so ubiquitous in iconography and texts, it is telling that throughout Egyptian history Maʿat was not venerated independent of other deities, meaning she was not worshiped so much as incorporated into the worship of other deities.[147] This also partially explains why Akhenaten was able to retain Maʿat even as he sought to change Egyptian religion.

Regardless, the concept of Maʿat was clearly too central to Egyptian society in general and kingship specifically for Akhenaten to replace it or simply ignore it. A pharaoh attempting religious reform to Akhenaten's degree would need to be especially direct in claiming that he "lives on Maʿat." Likewise, there is very little within the conceptualizations of Maʿat that points toward a fundamental epistemological shift; rather, Maʿat was simply placed in a different context—that of Akhenaten's religion reforms.[148] Debates that center on whether Maʿat was "truth" or "moral order" have been avoided because of uncertainty as to whether the Egyptians would have made such distinctions.[149] Maʿat represented truth and unity; it was ever the means by which pharaohs asserted their right to rule precisely because they kept the cosmos ordered. Nonroyals continued to emphasis their righteous deeds based on ethical conceptions of Maʿat.

In the midst of all the changes he was initiating, Akhenaten desperately needed to connect himself to Maʿat. The message that he "lived on" and upheld Maʿat gained increased significance as a unifying element. His views on Maʿat are, therefore, no more "sophisticated" than those of any other pharaoh, nor does Akhenaten come across as a tyrant forcing his views on a helpless populace. Surely, part of his motivation in upholding Maʿat was to appease an uncertain populace. For that matter, archaeological evidence increasingly reveals the skepticism of the populace. Even at Amarna they clearly did not fully embrace his radical ideology. Amarna households and cemeteries attest to the retention of elements of traditional Egyptian religion—small figures of traditional gods like Thoth, depictions on coffins of gods like Anubis, and above all molds for protective amulets, whose importance for health and home no doubt trumped any concern for pharaoh's edicts.[150]

In seeking to "purify the cult of the sun and to create a new and special place for it,"[151] Akhenaten was attempting enough as it was; there was no need to revolutionize

146. Silverman, Wegner, and Houser Wegner, *Akhenaten and Tutnakhamen*, 40.
147. The only surviving structure devoted to her is a small temple inside the precinct of Montu at Karnak.
148. Karenga, *Maat*, 92. See also Roland G. Bonnel, "The Ethics of El-Amarna," in *Studies in Egyptology Presented to Miriam Lichtheim*, ed. Sarah Israelit-Groll, 2 vols. Jerusalem: Magnes, 1990), 1:71–97.
149. E.g., see the opposing views of Anthes and Breasted. Anthes, *Die Maat des Echnaton*, 1–36; Breasted, *Dawn of Conscience*, 369.
150. Kemp, *City of Akhenaten*, 230–63; see also Silverman, Wegner, and Houser Wegner, *Akhenaten and Tutankhamen*, 37.
151. Kemp, *City of Akhenaten*, 263.

the meaning of Maʿat or, even more radically, to remove Maʿat. In an era of upheaval, Maʿat played prominent roles in both the reign of Akhenaten and those of his successors who were so determined to undo his reforms. It is fitting to conclude by agreeing with the The Maxims of Ptahhotep:

Great is Maʿat, and its foundation is firmly established;
... in the long run it is Maʿat which endures.

CHAPTER 13

"I Have Made Every Person Like His Fellow"

Jens Bruun Kofoed

Introduction

When, in 1983, I moved to Copenhagen to commence my theological studies at the University of Copenhagen, I was utterly unaware that *Journal of the Ancient Near Eastern Society* had just published the article, "Some Thoughts on Genesis 1 and 2 and Egyptian Cosmology," and I had no idea whatsoever that, later in my career, the author, Jim Hoffmeier (1983), would become a dear friend and mentor. After all these years it is a privilege, therefore, to offer a few additions to the important observations made in the above-mentioned article in honor of his scholarship.

Since the *JANES* publication quite a few articles on the potential Egyptian background to Gen 1 and 2 have been published (J. P. Allen 1988; Currid 1991; Redford 1992; Atwell 2000; Hasenfratz 2002; Strange 2004; Johnston 2008; see also the earlier Kilian 1966; Schmidt 1967; Gordon 1982), and though many still consider a Babylonian background the most likely, it has now been demonstrated that Gen 1 and 2 makes just as much sense as an appropriation of and polemic against *Egyptian* traditions.

The purpose of this paper is not to duplicate what has already been suggested but to add some observations on a relatively neglected point for comparison between the Egyptian and biblical texts, namely the reason for and purpose of the creation of humanity, and thus to make a modest contribution to the understanding of the Egyptians' conception of their createdness and its implications for biblical studies.

The Sources

There are no treatises on theological anthropology from ancient Egypt. Insights have to be gleaned from relatively sparse clues in texts composed in different genres (funerary texts, myths, hymns, prayers, instructions, narratives, prophecies) written or inscribed on various materials (walls, coffins, monuments, papyri) over a very long period of time (third to first millennia BCE).[1]

---

1. Pyramid texts are cited from James P. Allen's *The Ancient Egyptian Pyramid Texts* referring to the (new) spell numbers utilized there with Kurt Sethe's older numbering in parenthesis (J. P. Allen 2015; Sethe 1962). Coffin texts not included in *COS* are quoted from Raymond O. Faulkner's *The Ancient Egyptian Coffin Texts* (1973). Texts from The Book of the Dead are quoted from Thomas George Allen's *The Book of the Dead or Going Forth by Day: Ideas of the Ancient Egyptians Concerning the Hereafter as Expressed in Their Own Terms* (1974). A few texts not included in the abovementioned corpora are quoted from

Creation Order

Erik Iversen, in his book on *Egyptian and Hermetic Doctrine* (1984, 16), argues that humanity's special position in the cosmic hierarchy is evidenced by their position in lists enumerating the various species of beings, since they occasionally were placed before the gods. Though Iversen only refers explicitly to the Memphite Theology of the Shabaka Stela, other texts seem to support his assertion.

From the Old Kingdom a pyramid text from the tomb of Pepi I (ca. 2289–2255 BCE) places people before gods in the creation order: "Pepi was given birth by his father Atum . . . when people had not yet come into being, when the gods had not yet come into being" (J. P. Allen 2015, 179; P 511 [PT 571]).

In The Great Cairo Hymn of Praise to Amun-Re from the Second Intermediate period, we find the same sequence in the praise of Amun-Re as the one "from whose two eyes mankind came forth, on whose mouth the gods came into being" (*COS* 1.25:39).

The same sequence is evidenced in a New Kingdom mortuary text inscribed on the back wall in the tomb of Paheri, scribe of the treasury and mayor of the towns of Nekheb and Iunyt (El-Kab and Esna) during the reigns of Thutmose I (1503–1493 BCE) and Queen Hatshepsut (1479–1458 BCE). In his prayer for offerings, Amun is addressed as "Sole one, primordial, eldest, Primeval, without [equal], [Creator] of men and gods, Living flame that came from Nun, [Maker] of light for mankind" (*AEL* 2:15).

Papyrus Harris I, in a list of temple endowments from the reign of Ramesses IV (1155–1149 BCE), describes Ptah in his manifestation as Tatenen, the primordial mound, as "Ta-Ténen, père des dieux, Grand dieu de la première fois, Qui a façonné les humains, qui a créé les dieux" (Grandet 1994, 284, introduction, 2–4), and the same order is found on a Ramesside stela, where Ptah is described as "[n]oble god of the first occasion, who built people and gave birth to the gods, original one who made it possible for all to live" (*COS* 1.13:20, cols. 1–4).

Also from the New Kingdom we have a hymn introducing the Book of the Dead describing Ptah/Tatenen as "thou Creator of mankind and Maker of the substance of the gods" (Budge 1969, 5). Also relevant are a great number of Book of the Dead spells. Spell 15A5 reads: "When thou [Re-Harakhte] hast warded off the Disease Demons as (thou dost) men and gods." The same sequence is found in spells 15A2, 15B3, 42, 114, 116, 124, 125, 130, 134 (2×), 148, 152, 175 (2×), 177, 181 (3×), and 185B (T. G. Allen 1974, 18, 20, 22, 48–49, 92, 93, 96, 99, 107, 109–10, 140, 151, 184–86, 193, 195, 205). In the same funerary genre, The Book of Dead of Nesi-Khonsu from the late New Kingdom or early Third Intermediate period describes Amun-Re as the one "from whose divine eyes come forth men and women; at whose utterance the gods come into being" (Budge 1969, 652).

From the Late period, the Great Hymn to Khnum states that the creator god "made mankind, created gods," "brought forth all that is . . . to feed men and gods," and "fashioned men, engendered gods" (*AEL* 3:113–14).

E. A. Wallis Budge's *The Book of the Dead* (1969), James Henry Breasted's *Ancient Records of Egypt* (1906), Miriam Lichtheim's volumes on *AEL* (vols. 1–3) and Pierre Grandet's *Le papyrus Harris* (1994).

A number of texts, however, give the opposite sequence. From the Book of the Dead, spell 15 announces that "Gods and men come to thee [Atum] bowing down," whereas spell 185E states that "[t]hey that exist, behold, they are with [thee], both Gods and men" (T. G. Allen 1974, 15, 206). In the Memphite Theology, in the section describing Ptah's creation by thought and expression, it is stated that Ptah "is preeminent in every body and in every mouth—of all the gods, all people, all animals, and all crawling things that live—planning and governing everything he wishes" (*COS* 1.15:22, col. 54).[2] In a New Kingdom hymn to the Sun God inscribed on the Stela of the Brothers Suti and Hor from the reign of Amenhotep III (1388–1350 BCE), Aten is titulated "Beneficent mother of gods and men" (*COS* 1.27:44; second hymn line 11). The slightly earlier Coffin Text 1130 also places the gods before humanity (see below). In the Legend of Isis and the Name of Re, from the Ramesside Papyrus Turin 1993, the creator god is said to have made "gods, men, flocks, herds, reptiles, birds, and fish, the kingship of gods and men altogether" (*COS* 1.22:33).

The Third Intermediate period Banishment Stela addresses Amun as the one "who supplies the necessities of gods and men" (Breasted 1906, 319, §655).

From the Late period the same order is found in the Great Hymn to Khnum, a Morning Hymn to Khnum (2×), and Nesuhor's Prayer (*AEL* 3:110; Breasted 1906, 507, §991).

Though the evidence seems to back Iversen's (1984) assertion *quantatively*, caution must be exercised, since we may be dealing with stock phrases or perspectival order that carry little *qualitative* weight. Such a conclusion may be supported by the Great Cairo Hymn of Praise to Amun-Re from the Second Intermediate period, where Amun-Re, in the beginning of the hymn, is praised in his manifestations as Khepri and Atum: "Khepri in the midst of His bark, Who issued command that the *gods* might be, Atum, who made the *common man*." A few lines later in the same hymn, however, we find the opposite sequence in the description of Amun-Re as the one "From whose two eyes *mankind* came forth, On whose mouth the *gods* came into being" (*COS* 1.25:38–39; emphasis added). The same variation is found in the Great Hymn to Khnum and in the variations of spell 15 from the Book of the Dead.

How Was Humanity Created?

Also relevant for our discussion are descriptions of the how of humanity's creation. As a precursor to the New Kingdom books of the underworld, the Book of Two Ways (Coffin Texts 1029–1130) has the creator announcing that "I made the gods evolve from my sweat, while people are from the tears of my Eye" (CT 1130; *COS* 117:27; see also Lesko 1977, 130).[3] The same manner of creation is described in quite a number of texts.

---

2. As for the date of composition, Allen argues that "for a long time the original was thought to derive from the Old Kingdom or even earlier, but advances in our understanding of Egyptian grammar and theology have now made a date in the Nineteenth Dynasty more likely" (J. P. Allen 2002, 21 and the literature listed in n. 1).

3. That the gods' "sweat" was considered aromatic is evidenced by the parallelism between "sweat" and "perfume" in Third Intermediate period Papyrus Berlin 3055: "You have your sweat, O gods. You have your perfumes, O goddesses. You have the perfume of your bodies" (*COS* 1.34:56).

In a spell from the Middle Kingdom Coffin Texts, the creator god Atum states that "people ... emerged from my eye" (CT 80; *COS* 1.8:12), and in the abovementioned Hymn of Praise to Amun-Re from the Second Intermediate period, the creator is described as the "One, alone, who made that which is, From whose two eyes mankind came forth" (*COS* 1.25:39). From the Ptolemaic period, Papyrus Bremner-Rhind describes how "the evolution of people" happened "from the tears that came from my [i.e., Atum's] Eye" (*COS* 1.9:15).

J. P. Allen (*COS* 1.8:12 n. 14), in a note to Coffin Text 80, acknowledges that the explanation of humanity as emerging from the creator's eye is "a reference to the 'etymological' etiology of human beings (*rmṯ*) from the 'tears' (*rmyt*) of the sun (the creator's 'eye')," but, in a comment on the juxtaposition of gods evolving from sweat and people from tears in Coffin Text 1130, Allen (*COS* 1.17:27 n. 10) nevertheless argues that "[a]lthough both people and the gods derive from the creator, the latter evolved directly from the creator's substance, whereas people are a secondary creation." Garry Shaw (2014, 35), in a similar vein, describes the creation of humanity as "an accidental consequence of the Eye's despair, anger and sadness." Philippe Derchain (1992, 219) states, however, that "the tradition that has him [humanity] born from the tears of a god depends merely on a play on words between *rmj*, 'cry,' and *rmt*, 'man,'" and no attempt seems to have been made to draw any moral or metaphysical conclusions from this assonance. Geraldine Pinch (2002, 66) concurs by stating that "most such mythical wordplay was ephemeral or relatively insignificant." A First Intermediate period text, the Instruction for Merikare, seems to support the latter understanding by its description of humankind as the creator god Re's images, "who came from his body" (*COS* 1.35:64). The concept should probably be understood as a "democratic" version of the royal appeal to the creator god Atum in the earlier Pyramid Text 155 to "elevate him [king Una] to you, encircle him inside your arms: he is your son of your body, forever" (J. P. Allen 2015, 39; W 155 [PT 222]). Since "body," is perhaps even more substantial than "sweat," there seems to be no ontological or substantial difference between the creation of humankind and the gods. As for the *cause* of the eye's weeping, the various versions of the tears myth explain the weeping both as a sign of joy (e.g., the Bremner-Rhind Papyrus) and sorrow (e.g., Coffin Text 714), and though Pinch (2002, 67) notes that "most versions of the tears myth provide an explanation for the perpetually sorrowful and imperfect state of humanity," such a conclusion may stretch the argument further than the evidence can support.

In the tradition of humanity being created by Khnum, no difference is made between the creation of humanity and other creatures. According to the Late period Great Hymn to Khnum from the temple of Esna, Khnum is said to have "fashioned men, engendered gods" and to have formed "all men and beasts" on his potter's wheel (*AEL* 3:114). When the New Kingdom Instruction of Amenemope states that "man is clay and straw, the god is his builder" (*COS* 1.47:121) the juxtaposition is between the creator god (presumably Khnum) and humanity, not between the engendered gods and humanity, and the point in the instruction has more to do with humanity's responsibility in the upholding of cosmic order than with the metaphysical character of humanity.

What the texts do show, however, is that, just as the first pair of sexually differentiated gods, Shu and Tefnut, were created—not born—by the suprasexual demiurge Atum, humankind was also created (sexually differentiated) by the creator god himself, whereas subsequent generations of *both* gods and men were "born." Humanity, in other words, shares in the same divine essence as the created gods and occupies the highest rank in the created order. The fact that mankind, in these traditions, is created *before the sun*, only adds to the picture that humanity is the apex of creation.

Humanity and the Created Order

That humans had such a position in the created order is confirmed by the Instruction of Merikare, where the creator god is described as a shepherd caring "well" for his flock by his initial creation (past tense) and by continually upholding creation (present tense):

> Well tended is mankind—god's cattle,
> He made sky and earth for their sake . . .
> He shines in the sky for their sake;
> He made for them plants and cattle,
> Fowl and fish to feed them . . .
> He makes daylight for their sake,
> He sails by to see them (*COS* 1.35:64).

In Coffin Text 1130 the creator god Atum claims as one of his "deeds" that "I have made the four winds, so that every person might breathe in his area" (*COS* 1.17:26), and the Great Hymn to Aten describes how the creator god ordered the world so that, wherever humanity was placed, creation was meant to supply their needs:

> You set every man in his place,
> You supply their needs;
> Everyone has his food,
> His lifetime is counted . . .
> You supply their needs;
> You made Hapy in duat,
> You bring him when you will,
> To nourish the people,
> For you made them for yourself (*COS* 1.28:46).

It is clear from the texts that the creator god not only cared for humankind but for all his creatures. In the Great Cairo Hymn of Praise to Amun-Re, Amun is the one "Who made that on which the gnat lives, The worm and the flea likewise, Who made the sustenance of the mice in [their] holes, Who vivifies the winged creatures in every tree" (*COS* 1.25:39), and the same hymn makes clear that not only humanity but all creatures were given the breath of life, since Amun is the one "Who gave breath to the one in the egg, Who vivifies the son of the slug" (Averbeck 1994, 39). The same idea is found in Coffin Text 80, where Atum states about creatures of the air (falcons), land (jackals, pigs), and water (hippopotami, crocodiles, fish) that "I will lead them and enliven them, through my mouth, which is Life in their nostrils. I will lead my breath into their throats" (*COS* 1.8:13). Humanity, as implied by this text, was just one "animal in the jungle," but other texts do make clear that, despite this biotic sameness, humanity was singled out as ontologically unique. It is nowhere stated, for example, that the creator god "hears" the cry or "soothes" the suffering of animals. Humanity, on the other hand, is the unique recipient of precisely such an attention and intervention on behalf of the creator god. A few examples: Atum, in Coffin Text 80, is the one "Who hears the prayer of the one who is in distress" (*COS* 1.25:38), and in the Instruction for Merikare, humanity is also singled out as a special object of the creator god's care:

> He has built his shrine around them,
> When they weep he hears.
> He made for them rulers in the egg,
> Leaders to raise the back of the weak.
> He made for them magic as weapons
> To ward off the blow of events,
> Guarding them by day and by night (*COS* 1.35:66).

In the New Kingdom Prayer to Re-Harakhti, Atum is described as "protector of millions, who delivers hundreds of thousands, the helper of the one who cries to him (*COS* 1.29:47), and in the Late period Great Hymn to Khnum, the creator god is the one who "soothes suffering by his will," when "he makes women give birth" (*AEL* 3:112). Moreoover, the creator god is also known to show compassion when the supplicant confesses their sin and asks for mercy. In an ostracon from the New Kingdom, Amun is described as "grand de courroux" but, nevertheless, "seigneur de miséricorde" (Ostracon Caire 12224; Posener 1975, 201), and in the inscription on the Votive Stela of Nebre, the supplicant, "who lay sick unto death, [in] the power of Amun, through his sin" appeals to Amun as the one who "rescues him who is in *dat*; For you are he who is [merciful], When one appeals to you, You are he who comes from afar" (*AEL* 2:106; see also the following Votive Stela of Neferabu on p.107). The stela, in Ashraf Iskander Sadek's (1987, 227) words, demonstrates "confidence in the might and mercy." The strongest expression of the creator god's mercy and humanity's intrinsic value over against other creatures, however, is found in the First Intermediate period Admonition of Ipuwer, where the sun god Re is described as the one who, despite the "fire in [humanity's] heart," nevertheless "spends a day collecting them":

> He is the herdsman of all, and there is no evil in his heart."
> His herds are few (but) he spends a day collecting them,
> (Because) fire is in their heart.
> Would that he had perceived their nature in the first generation,
> Then he would have smitten the evil,
> He would have stretched out his arm against it,
> He would have destroyed their seed and their heirs,
> While the people still desired to give birth (*COS* 1.42:97).

It is not that Re is unaware of humanity's evil nature, and the evil is, importantly, located not in the creator god but in humanity's nature, but humanity's intrinsic value is nevertheless so high that the creator god goes to great length to save him. Or as

R. T. Rundle Clark (1959, 70) has it: "When [Re] punishes the wicked they remain his kinsfolk; he does not withhold himself completely from them but treats them as errant members of his family."

Another text with implications for the understanding of humanity's uniqueness and special value in the created order, is the tale of Djedi in Papyrus Westcar from the Second Intermediate period (*AEL* 1:215). In the tale King Khufu summons the magician Djedi to his court because he has heard that he can join a severed head: "His majesty said: 'Is it true, what they say, that you can join a severed head?' Said Djedi: 'Yes, I can, O king, my lord.' Said his majesty: 'Have brought to me a prisoner from the prison, that he be executed.' Said Djedi: 'But not to a human being, O king, my lord! Surely, it is not permitted to do such a thing to the noble cattle!'" (*AEL* 1:219). Though Khufu's interest in Djedi's skills may have been triggered by the well-documented fear of losing one's head in the afterlife (Pinch 2004, 162), the tale nonetheless implies that some things ought not to be done to human being because of their intrinsic worth and value. Furthermore, as Verena M. Lepper (2008, 176) has argued, the tale also betrays an equalitarian ideal where Djedi, a peasant, interacts on equal footing with the king:

> Weil es sich bei allen Dreien um hochgestellte Persönlichkeiten handelt, wird hier der sozioökonomishce Hintergrund nicht als Unterschied deutlich, sondern als Gemeinsamkeit der Redeweisen. Die Protagonisten Heben sich gegenüber den Sprechenden der vergangenen wie auch der zukünftigen Geschichte dadurch ab. Djedi, der in rechtlicher Hinsicht ein blosser *nds* ist, bewegt sich damit durch seine Weishet (die sich in seiner Sprache widerspiegelt) auf einer Ebene mit dem König. Dies wird schon allein durch den Inhalt seiner Reden deutlich. Er is ein dem König ebenbürtiger Gesprächespartner, der diesen sogar kritisiert.

What Is the Purpose of the Creation of Humanity?

The reason *why* humanity was created is not very explicit in the texts, but the Great Cairo Hymn of Praise to Amun-Re implies that humanity was created to honor and worship their creator:

> Jubilation to you, because you have wearied yourself with us.
> Let the earth be kissed for you, because you have created us . . .
> Let us adore your might in as much as you have made us,
> Let {us} act for you because you have borne us (*COS* 1.25:39).

Numerous texts from the Old Kingdom and throughout the Late period describe the *king* as the image of god (Ockinga 1984), but the Instruction of Merikare states, significantly, that not only the king but *humankind* was fashioned in the image of the creator god, thereby implying that the *imago dei* was accredited to the king only representatively or *par excellence*: "[Humans] are his images, who came from his body" (*COS* 1.35:64). New Kingdom hymns to Amun also refer to the creator god making people "in his own image" (Pinch 2002, 67; see also Hornung 1982, 134; Karenga 2004, 218–19). All men and women, in other words, were created to be rulers.

The purpose of creating humanity, however, was first and foremost connected to procreation and the sustaining of world order. As for procreation, Amun, in Papyrus Leiden I 350, is described not only as self-creator and creator of the first gods and humans, but also as involved in humanity's procreation: "You are come in fathers, maker of their sons, in order to make functional heirs for your children" (*COS* 1.16:24; 80th ch., lines 10–11). J. P. Allen (1988, 50–51), in a comment to his translation of the quoted lines, explains that "the process of development that began with the creator extends into the generational process of continuing life." In the Great Hymn to Aten, the creator god is described in a similar manner as the one "Who makes seed grow in women, Who creates people from sperm" (*COS* 1.28:45), and the same idea is present in the Great Hymn to Khnum, where Khnum is praised for forming "the loins to support the phallus in the act of begetting . . . the male member to beget, the womb to conceive." Thus all creatures are called to give thanks, because Khnum is a manifestation of "Ptah-Tatenen, creator of creators" (*COS* 1.46:113). Though Ewa Wasilewska (2000, 141) has recently criticized Siegfried Morenz's (1973, 184–85) suggestion that people were created "in order to carry his [the creator god's] procreative purpose," the selection of texts quoted above seems to disprove her conclusion that "there is no evidence for this hypothesis" (Wasilewska 2000, 141). Procreation was indeed understood to be one of humanity's divinely ordained responsibilities.

Unlike procreation, the upholding of *ma'at*, world order, defined by John Baines (1995, 12) as "both the harmonious cooperation which was projected as a social ideal and the constant struggle to maintain the cosmos against the forces which threatened it," was initially the responsibility of the king and only gradually became the concern of important state officials, judges, and—of course—the temple clergy. In an Old Kingdom spell designated for "emerging from the Duat," king Uni (2375–2345 BCE) is said to "having put Maat in it in place of disorder" (J. P. Allen 2015, 42), and in spell 424 from the pyramid of Pepi (2332–2283 BCE), the king is described as the one who "sets up [*ma'at*] like the sun" (J. P. Allen 2015, 344). We find the same expectations in the First Intermediate period Admonition of Ipuwer, where the king in office is blamed for the social and political upheavals, and a future king is expected to put an end to contemporary adversities: "Behold, it has befallen that the land is deprived of kingship by a few people who ignore the custom." And because the king is unable or unwilling to maintain justice and order, "sadness overwhelms, misery is everywhere" (*COS* 1.42:96–97).

In the Middle Kingdom a commoner—The Eloquent Peasant—expressed his complaint about being unjustly beaten, robbed and threatened to silence by one of the high steward Rensi's officials with reference to *ma'at*. Putting his case before Rensi, he describes the crime committed against him as a violation of *ma'at* for which Rensi—and ultimately the king—is responsible: "Behold, justice flees from you, Banished from its seat! When the magistrates do wrong" (*COS* 1.43:101). When Rensi presents the case to his superior, King Nebkaure, "it pleased the heart of his majesty more than anything in this whole land" (*COS* 1.43:104), because he acknowledged *ma'at* as a democratic concept, and that a person's character was more important than their social status.

Also, from the Middle Kingdom, Coffin Text 1130 provides us with the perhaps most explicit idea of human equality:

I have done four good deeds inside the portal of the Akhet.
I have made the four winds,
so that every person might breathe in his area.
That is one of the deeds.
I have made the great inundation,
so that the poor might have control like the rich.
That is one of the deeds.
I have made every person like his fellow.
I did not decree that they do disorder:
it is their hearts that break what I said.
That is one of the deeds.
I have made their hearts not forget the West,
for the sake of making offerings to the nome gods.
That is one of the deeds (*COS* 1.17:26–27).

All the necessities of life—air, water, food, justice, afterlife—the text states, should be equally available to all men of all social classes. J. P. Allen (*COS* 1.17:27 n. 8) remarks that, "since creation involved the establishment of order, subsequent disorder in the world derives not from the creator but from human failings," and that the sentence "I have made every person like his fellow" means that "the natural order must necessarily involve no such distinctions." This vision of an ideal, fully equalitarian society was never realized, of course, but, as it is phrased by Henri Frankfort et al. (1949, 107), "it was still a valid sublimation of the highest aspirations of the time. Wistfully it says: All men should be equal; the creator-god did not make them different."

Since the texts that most explicitly betray a democratic understanding of the image of god and an equalitarian society date to the turbulent First Intermediate period and the Middle Kingdom, many scholars have argued that it is evidence of a process of democratization that took place after the collapse of the Old Kingdom. The "idea," as Mark Smith (2017, 4.7.1) dubs it, was that "privileges formerly restricted to royalty were now usurped by non-royal individuals who had gained access to copies of spells and rituals that were believed to confer them." Though Leonard H. Lesko (1977, 5–6) argued that "this is still a good characterization," such an idea, Smith (2017, 4.7.1) asserts, "is not supported by the evidence at our disposal. Instead, already in the Old Kingdom, Egyptian rulers and their subjects shared the same aspirations for the afterlife and hoped to fulfill these by the same means" (see also Silverman 1991, 72 n. 86).

From the New Kingdom period onward a more profound democratization took place, however, and the elite's concern over their postmortem judgment—the weighing of their heart against a feather as the symbol of *ma'at*—by way of prayers, spells and passwords seems to have spread to other classes in society. The chapterization of the spells in the extremely popular Book of the Dead demonstrates that, by the time of the New Kingdom, scribes could be consulted by those who could afford it to produce custom-made books for an individual or a family. By the time of the Late period, R. James Ferguson (2016, 17) notes, the judgment against the feather of *ma'at* "takes on strongly moral tones and goes beyond merely prescriptive concerns with ritual conduct or mortuary customs. Likewise, judgment also ceases to be absolute and involves the notion of a person doing well in terms of the situation that life had provided them" (see also Silverman 1991, 73).

Summary

Summing up the analysis, the texts describe the intrinsic value of humanity by deriving it from the fact that humankind shares in the same divine essence as the created gods, occupies the highest rank in the created order, and is the special object of the creator god's provision and compassion. The purpose of creating humanity was to honor and worship the creator god by procreation and sustainment of world order, and though there arguably is a hierarchical focus on the king in the early texts, other texts suggest that a process of democratization or diffusion of the king's privileges took place from the First Intermediate period and onward. A few Middle Kingdom texts are very explicit in stressing the democratic and equalitarian implications for Egyptian society, and though the standards of conduct implied by such an understanding of humanity's intrinsic worth was rarely acknowledged, let alone met, such a standard nevertheless stands as a powerful ideal that, given the texts' popularity, informed the community's social structures and beliefs thereby—at least in principle—safeguarding the value of the individual from government overreach.

Implications for Biblical Studies

Despite the significant differences between the Egyptian texts and biblical creation texts (outlined in the literature mentioned in the introduction), the anthropological (and harmatological) observations from our analysis demonstrate that there are perhaps more parallels than dissimilarities. Though humans, in the biblical account, are not an emanation of the creator god as is the case in at least some Egyptian texts, a person's intrinsic worth and the individual and societal implications thereof stand in remarkable parallel to Egyptian thinking: Humanity is created in the image of g/God as the apex of the created order and as g/God's vice-regents with the purpose of honoring the c/Creator by procreation and sustainment/expansion of world order. Humanity's failure to follow the way of ma'at/the instructions of God/Yahweh is not derived from the c/Creator but from a defect in humanity's nature, and though humans deserves punishment for their failure and/or are subject to natural evil, g/God nevertheless shows compassion and provides for them.

The substantial parallels between the texts do not prove, of course, that, for example, Gen 1 is dependent on Egyptian texts, but they do invite us to be cautious in using Mesopotamian creation texts as a pretext for determining the date of composition of the biblical account. It is a commonplace that Gen 1 makes perfect sense as a postexilic appropriation of and polemic against *Babylonian* traditions, but since the *anthropological* parallels makes even more sense vís-a-vís the Egyptian texts, the author(s) may have had the Egyptian rather than the Mesopotamian beliefs in mind. Again, this does not in itself invalidate a postexilic date of composition for the creation account in its present form. John Strange (2004, 353), for example, has suggested that "as Gen 1:1–2:4

is considered to be postexilic, i.e., after ca. 450, perhaps even as late as the early
Hellenistic period, in classical source criticism belonging to the late priestly source
(P), when there was a considerable Jewish element in the Egyptian population with
connections to Jerusalem, it is quite feasible that there should be a direct connection
between the two documents or at least the theology behind both." Strange, however,
also points to other periods with direct Egyptian influence on "Cana'anite, Israelite
and Jewish religion," and though Strange sticks to the historical-critical dating of the
text, his documentation of Egyptian influence in earlier periods clearly permits that the
account could have been composed in or had an oral or written prehistory stretching
back to the Late Bronze or Early Iron Age, when both Trans- and Cisjordan were part of
the Egyptian Empire. That is precisely what Hoffmeier (1980, 48), two decades earlier,
suggested in his *JANES* article: "In the years following their occupation of Canaan
there was ongoing contact with Egypt. There is no reason to doubt that there could have
been literary influence on Hebrew cosmology as there was in other areas of Hebrew
literature." If that is the case, and the parallels discussed in this essay clearly allow
for it, maybe the author(s) and tradents of the creation traditions of Genesis should be
found among people who were native to Egypt but for some reason settled in Canaan.

BIBLIOGRAPHY

Allen, James P. 1988. *Genesis in Egypt: The Philosophy of Ancient Egyptian Creation
     Accounts*. YES 2. New Haven: Yale Egyptological Seminar.
———. 2002. "From the 'Memphite Theology.'" *COS* 1.15:21–23.
———. 2015. *The Ancient Egyptian Pyramid Texts*. 2nd ed. WAW 38. Atlanta: SBL Press.
Allen, Thomas George. 1974. *The Book of the Dead or Going Forth by Day: Ideas of the
     Ancient Egyptians Concerning the Hereafter as Expressed in Their Own Terms*. SAOC 37.
     Chicago: University of Chicago Press.
Atwell, James E. 2000. "An Egyptian Source for Genesis 1." *JTS* 51:441–77.
Averbeck, Richard E. 1994. "The Sumerian Historiographic Tradition and Its Implications for
     Genesis 1–11." Pages 79–102 in *Faith, Tradition, and History: Old Testament Historiogra-
     phy in Its Near Eastern Context*. Edited by A. R. Millard, James K. Hoffmeier, and
     David W. Baker. Winona Lake, IN: Eisenbrauns.
Baines, John. 1995. "Kingship, Definition of Culture, and Legitimation." Pages 3–47 in
     Ancient Egyptian Kingship. Edited by David B. O'Connor and David P. Silverman. PAe 9.
     Leiden: Brill.
Breasted, James Henry. 1906. *Ancient Records of Egypt, Volume IV: The Twentieth to the
     Twenty-Sixth Dynasties*. Ancient Records 4. Chicago: University of Chicago Press. http://
     archive.org/details/BreastedJ.H.AncientRecordsEgyptAll5Vols1906.
Budge, E. A. Wallis. 1969. *The Book of the Dead*. 2nd ed. rev. and enlarged. London: Rout-
     ledge; Kegan Paul.
Clark, R. T. Rundle. 1959. *Myth and Symbol in Ancient Egypt*. London: Thames & Hudson.
Currid, John D. 1991. "An Examination of the Egyptian Background of the Genesis."
     BZ 35:18–40.
Derchain, Philippe. 1992. "Egyptian Anthropology." Pages 219–23 in *Greek and Egyptian
     Mythologies*. Edited by Yves Bonnefoy. Translated by Wendy Doniger. Chicago: Univer-
     sity of Chicago Press.
Faulkner, Raymond O. 1973. *The Ancient Egyptian Coffin Texts: Spells 1–354*. Warminster:
     Aris & Phillips. http://archive.org/details/TheAncientEgyptianCoffin1.
Ferguson, R. James. 2016. "The Ancient Egyptian Concept of Maat: Reflections on Social
     Justice and Natural Order." Centre for East-West Cultural & Economic Studies Research

Papers 15. Robina: Bond University. https://research.bond.edu.au/en/publications
/the-ancient-egyptian-concept-of-maat-reflections-on-social-justic.

Frankfort, Henri, H. A. Groenewegen-Frankfort, John A. Wilson, and Thorkild Jacobsen. 1949. *Before Philosophy: The Intellectual Adventure of Ancient Man, An Essay on Speculative Thought in the Ancient Near East*. Pelican Books A198. Harmondsworth: Penguin.

Gordon, Cyrus H. 1982. "Khnum and El." Pages 203–14 in *Egyptological Studies*. Edited by Sarah Israelit-Groll. Scripta Hierosolymitana 28. Jerusalem: Magnes.

Grandet, Pierre. 1994. *Le papyrus Harris I (BM 9999), tomes 1 et 2*. Biblioteque d'Etude 109. Cairo: Institut français d'archéologie orientale.

Hasenfratz, Hans-Peter. 2002. "Patterns of Creation in Ancient Egypt." Pages 174–78 in *Creation in Jewish and Christian Tradition*. Edited by Henning Graf Reventlow and Yair Hoffman. JSOTSup 319. Sheffield: Sheffield Academic.

Hoffmeier, James K. 1983. "Some Thoughts on Genesis 1 and 2 and Egyptian Cosmology." *JANES* 15:39–49.

Hornung, Erik. 1982. *Conceptions of God in Ancient Egypt: The One and the Many*. Ithaca: Cornell University Press.

Iversen, Erik. 1984. *Egyptian and Hermetic Doctrine*. Opuscula Graecolatina 27. Copenhagen: Museum Tusculanum.

Johnston, Gordon H. 2008. "Genesis 1 and Ancient Egyptian Creation Myths." *BSac* 165:178–94.

Karenga, Maulana. 2004. *Maat: The Moral Ideal in Ancient Egypt; A Study in Classical African Ethics*. New York: Routledge.

Kilian, Rudolf. 1966. "Gen 1:2 und die Urgötter von Hermopolis." *VT* 16:420–38.

Lepper, Verena M. 2008. *Untersuchungen zu PWestcar: Eine philologische und literaturwissenschaftliche (Neu-)Analyse*. ÄA 70. Wiesbaden: Harrassowitz.

Lesko, Leonard H. 1977. *The Ancient Egyptian Book of Two Ways*. Berkeley: University of California Press.

Morenz, Siegfried. 1973. *Egyptian Religion*. Ithaca: Cornell University Press.

Ockinga, Boyo. 1984. *Die Gottebenbildlichkeit im alten Ägypten und im Alten Testament*. ÄAT 7. Wiesbaden: Harrassowitz.

Pinch, Geraldine. 2002. *Handbook of Egyptian Mythology*. Santa Barbara: ABC-CLIO.

———. 2004. *Egyptian Mythology: A Guide to the Gods, Goddesses, and Traditions of Ancient Egypt*. Oxford: Oxford University Press.

Posener, Georges. 1975. "La piété personelle avant l'âge Amarnien." *RdÉ* 27:195–210.

Redford, Donald B. 1992. *Egypt, Canaan, and Israel in Ancient Times*. Princeton: Princeton University Press.

Sadek, Ashraf Iksander. 1987. *Popular Religion in Egypt During the New Kingdom*. HÄB 27. Hildesheim: Gerstenberg.

Schmidt, Werner H. 1967. *Die Schöpfungsgeschichte Der Priesterschrift*. Wissenschaftliche Monographien zum Alten und Neuen Testament 17. Neukirchen-Vluyn: Neukirchener Verlag.

Sethe, Kurt. 1962. *Übersetzung und Kommentar zu den altägyptischen Pyramidentexten*. 2nd ed. 6 vols. Hamburg: Augustin.

Shaw, Garry J. 2014. *The Egyptian Myths: A Guide to the Ancient Gods and Legends*. New York: Thames & Hudson.

Silverman, David P. 1991. "Divinities and Deities in Ancient Egypt." Pages 7–87 in *Religion in Ancient Egypt: Gods Myths, And Personal Practice*. Edited by Byron E. Shafer. London: Routledge.

Smith, Mark. 2017. *Following Osiris: Perspectives on the Osirian Afterlife from Four Millennia*. Oxford: Oxford University Press.

Strange, John. 2004. "Some Notes on Biblical and Egyptian Theology." Pages 345–58 in *Egypt, Israel, and the Ancient Mediterranean World: Studies in Honor of Donald B. Redford*. Edited by Gary N. Knoppers and Antoine Hirsch. PAe 20. Leiden: Brill.

Wasilewska, Ewa. 2000. *Creation Stories of the Middle East*. London: Kingsley.

CHAPTER 14

The Founding of the Temple in Ancient Egypt: Ritual and Symbolism

Ash Melika

AMONG THE ACADEMIC TOPICS that have captured the attention of James Hoffmeier throughout his lustrous career is ancient Egyptian religion. As a token of appreciation, I dedicate these observations to him.

The founding of the temple rituals are well attested in the textual, representational, and archaeological evidence of ancient Egypt, Mesopotamia, Anatolia, Persia, and Syria-Palestine.[1] In this paper, I will investigate the rituals that comprise the founding of the temple in ancient Egypt. Specifically, I will focus on the temple of Edfu from the Ptolemaic period for representational and textual sources. I will also investigate the material culture of different periods that shed light on the subject, but particularly, the Texte de la Jeunesse, the Berlin Leather Roll, and the Poetical Stela from the New Kingdom period.[2] This paper does not examine all the evidence, textual or otherwise, of temple building in ancient Egypt, yet of the examined data an illustration of the overall structure of this phenomenon is brought to light mostly from the New Kingdom and beyond.

Any investigation of the subject of temple building in the ancient world must take into account the multileveled symbolic signification or representation of this cultural

---

1. The most complete study to date of Egyptian temple foundation ritual accounts has been done by James M. Weinstein, "Foundation Deposits in Ancient Egypt" (PhD diss., University of Pennsylvania, 1973); Weinstein, "Foundation Deposits," *OEAE* 1:559–61; see also Alexandre Moret, *Du Caractère Religieux de la Royauté Pharaonique* (Paris, Leroux, 1902), 130–42; Friedrich Wilhelm von Bissing and Hermann Kees, *Das Re-Heiligtum des Königs Ne-Woser-Re (Rathures) II: Die Kleine Festdarstellungen* (Leipzig: Duncker, 1923), 3–13; Pierre Montet, "Le Rituel de Fondation des Temples Égyptiens," *Kêmi* 17 (1964): 74–100; Ann R. David, *Religious Ritual at Abydos (c. 1300 B.C.)*, (Warminster: Aris & Phillips, 1973), 69–74; Sanaa Abd El-Azim el-Adly, "Das Gründungs und Weiheritual des Ägyptischen Tempels von der Frühgeschichtlichen zeit bis zum Ende des Neuen Reiches" (PhD diss., Eberhard-Karls-Universität, 1981); K. Zibelius-Chen, "Tempelgründung," *LÄ* 6 (1986): 385–86; and more recently, Richard H. Wilkinson, *The Complete Temples of Ancient* Egypt, (London: Thames & Hudson, 2000), 38–39; Sylvie Cauville, *Offerings to the Gods in Egyptian Temples*, trans. Bram Calcoen (Leuven: Peeters, 2012), 263–68; Janusz Karkowski, "'A Temple Comes to Being': A Few Comments on the Temple Foundation Ritual," *Études et Travaux* 29 (2016): 111–23. Studies investigating the founding of a temple in the ancient Near Eastern world are explored by: Victor Hurowitz, *I Have Built You an Exalted House: Temple Building in the Bible in the Light of Mesopotamian and Northwest Semitic Writings*, JSOTSup 115 (Sheffield: JSOT Press, 1992); Richard S. Ellis, *Foundation Deposits in Ancient Mesopotamia*, YNER, 2 (New Haven: Yale University Press, 1968). Also, the recent edited volume by Mark J. Boda and Jamie Novotny, eds., *From the Foundations to the Crenellations*: *Essays on Temple Building in the Ancient Near East and Hebrew Bible*, AOAT 366 (Münster, Ugarit-Verlag, 2010), is an in-depth study of temple-building from different periods and regions of the ancient Near East and Israel. Unfortunately, Egypt is not included in the first section of the book, which covers the ancient Near East.

2. See notes 6, 12, and 15 below.

pattern. Particularly, the founding of the temple is embedded in a more complex ritual paradigm that conveys a plethora of meaning encapsulated in symbols. One cannot just give a descriptive analysis of the founding of the temple rituals without investigating where it fits within the scheme of the whole of culture. Symbols exhibited in rituals do not have inherent meaning; they must be interpreted. Hence the founding of the temple ritual in ancient Egypt reflects religious symbols whereby its meaning is integrated within the whole cultural system.

Temple Building Ritual Paradigm

Temple-building accounts in ancient Egypt are often based on fragmentary textual, representational, and archaeological evidence; there is no complete account that comprehensively describes the procedure. The temple building genre combines mythical accounts and ritualistic performances that complement each other, but they do not necessarily always appear in the same episode. Based on the textual, representational, and archaeological data examined, which is not conclusive, the general features of temple building in ancient Egypt proceed in the following sequence:[3]

I.   Divine Command and Plan[4]
  1. Divine commission.
  2. Divine selection of a sacred site.
  3. The king announces his plan to build a temple.
  4. The temple pattern is revealed.
II. The King Officiates the Foundation Ritual and Initiates Construction[5]
  1. The king accompanied by the gods departs from his palace (Ptolemaic period).
  2. The king arrives at the sacred site (Ptolemaic period).
  3. The king lays the measurement of the building: "Stretching of the cord."
  4. The king digs the foundation trench: "Hoeing the earth."
  5. The king shapes and deposits the first brick: "Molding of the brick."

3. Arvid S. Kapelrud, "Temple Building: A Task for Gods and Kings," *Or* 32 (1963): 62, has compared the temple building accounts of Gudea of Lagash, Moses, and Solomon and reaches similar conclusion: "In the cases where a king is the actual temple builder the following elements are most often found: 1. Some indication that a temple has to be built; 2. The king visits a temple overnight; 3. A god tells him what to do, indicates plans; 4. The king announces his intention to build a temple; 5. Master builder is engaged, cedars from Lebanon, building-stones, gold silver etc. procured for the task; 6. The temple finished according to plan; 7. Offerings and dedication, fixing of norms; 8. Assembly of the people; 9. The god comes to his/her new house; 10. The king is blessed and promised everlasting domination." Hurowitz, *I Have Built You*, 109–10, lists six features or stages comprising this genre in the Solomonic temple account: 1. King decides to build a temple and divine approval; 2. Preparations, which includes material and workmen; 3. Construction and description—namely structures, furnishings, inspection, assembling, and installation of furnishing; 4. Dedication festivities and prayers; 5. Divine promises and revelation; and 6. Blessing and curses.

4. This section is after the Berlin Leather Role, see note 00 below.

5. Sections II–III are mainly based on the decorative program and texts of the temple of Horus at Edfu (see table 14.1), and follow the work of Weinstein, "Foundation Deposits in Ancient Egypt," 6; Montet, "Rituel de foundation," 74–100; Karkowski, "A Temple Comes to Being," 113–14; Wilkinson, *Complete Temples*, 38; Cauville, *Offerings to the Gods*, 263–68; and Faiza Mahmoud Sakr, "New Foundation Deposits of Kom el-Hisn," *SÄK* 33 (2005): 349–55, respectively.

TABLE 14.1. Foundation rituals decorative program in the Second Hypostyle Hall. Numbers refer to the temple plan of figure 14.1.

Wall	Scene 1	Scene 2	Scene 3	Scene 4	Scene 5
Southwest wall (108–109)	King departs from his palace.	King arrives at the sacred site.	"Stretching of the cord"		
West wall (110–114)	King pours sand into the foundation trench.	King places the plaques of gold and precious stones at the four corners of the temple.	King purifies the temple.	King consecrates the temple.	King presents the temple to the gods.
Southeast wall (117–118)	King departs from his palace.	King molds the first brick.	King hacks the earth.		
East wall (119–120)	King lays the foundation stone.	King purifies the temple.	King consecrates the temple.	King presents the temple to the gods.	

      6. The king pours sand into the foundation trench: "Pouring of the sand."

     7a. The king places the plaques of gold and precious stones at the four corners of the temple.

     7b. The placement of foundation deposit.

     8. The king transports the first stone block and situates it into place with a lever.

  III. The King Instigates the Final Initiation Rites

     1. king scatters *bsn* (natron or gypsum) around the temple to purify it.

     2. The king consecrates and presents the temple to its respective god(s).

     3. The king offers worship

Important points:

- The events pertaining to the founding of a temple did not follow the same sequence and are not all present in the same temple.
- The decorative program exhibited different episodes that are not ordered in the same chronological manner (table 14.1).
- The most complete episodes of the founding of the temple are found in the New Kingdom and especially, in the Ptolemaic period.
- The most important foundation ritual was the "Stretching of the cord."
- Rituals in theory were conducted by pharaoh and did not always mirror the real timing of construction.
- The founding of the temple merges the material world and the unseen divine realm.

Again, my analysis of this topic is greatly hampered by scarce data, which makes this examination inconclusive concerning details of the rituals and the sequence thereof. Given the evidence at hand, however, a preliminary survey can be established.

Divine Command and Plan

The first step in the founding of a temple in ancient Egypt is the king is divinely com-missioned to construct a temple for the deity. This desire on behalf of the king is a response to divine instructions—hence, the origination of the project is from the deity. Religiously, the king embodied the divine office of kingship through his union with the royal *Ka*—divine life force. At his coronation there were certain duties spoken to him by the gods that he was mandated to carry out in order to maintain this divine force. Thus embodying divine and human attributes, he became the mediator between the gods and humans; his role first and foremost was to maintain *ma'at*—order, harmony, first state of creation. To establish *ma'at*, he, among other things, had to build, renew, and restore temples of the gods.

At the Karnak temple, on the southern exterior wall of Hatshepsut's offering cham-bers is an inscription that relays the story of Thutmose III 's divine nomination to kingship as youth, commonly known as Texte de la Jeunesse.[6] Its style is biographi-cal, encompassing kernels of historical descriptions of Thutmose III's early career and theological reflections.[7] The scenery features the king sitting within a pavilion; beneath his throne, two lions are facing opposite directions and in between is the *smȝ-tȝwy* symbol exemplifying the unity of Upper and Lower Egypt. The damaged relief displays the king facing forty-nine columns of fragmented inscriptions. The pha-raoh is portrayed addressing some of his court officials. This representation parallels a scene of Senwosret I on the same wall positioned further east, but only the begin-ning of his inscriptions are preserved.[8] The configuration of the decorative program established by Thutmose III heightens the connection between himself and the royal ancestral line to affirm the identity politics of the past (Middle Kingdom), and more importantly, establish ritual efficacy of the eternal existence of the deified king so as to secure order and stability in Egypt.[9]

---

6. For the text, see Kurt Sethe, *Urkunden der 18. Dynastie: Übersetzung* (Leipzig: Hinrichs, 1961), 155–75. A convincing and detailed examination of the date of the text is presented by Peter F. Dorman, *The Monuments of Senenmut: Problems in Historical Methodology* (London: Kegan Paul, 1988), 15–16, 47–50, 56–58, 64–65; and Anthony Spalinger, "Drama in History: Exemplars from Mid Dynasty XVIII," *SÄK* 24 (1997): 269–78. Both scholars agree that the composition is dated to the early years of the king's sole rule. For literary and historical reviews, see Dimitri Laboury, *La statuaire de Thoutmosis III: Essai d'interprétation d'un portrait royal dans son contexte historique*, Aegyptiaca Leodiensia 5 (Liège: Centre informatique de philosophie et lettres, 1998), 547–60; Peter Laskowski, "Monumental Architecture and the Royal Building Program of Thutmose III," in *Thutmose III: A New Biography*, ed. Eric Cline and David O'Connor (Ann Arbor: University of Michigan Press, 2006), 184–92; and Elizabeth Blyth, *Karnak: Evolu-tion of a Temple* (London: Routledge, 2006).

7. Laskowski "Monumental Architecture," 184, distinguishes between two dates for this text: the time of the occurrences depicted in the text, and the date that the actual inscription was inscribed on the temple wall. Spalinger, "Drama in History," 277, convincingly argues that the narrative is nonfictional, recount-ing the early events of Thutmose III. For comments concerning the use of the term "biography" instead of "autobiography" in describing first-person accounts in Egyptian literary texts, see Elizabeth Frood, *Bio-graphical Texts from Ramessid Egypt*, WAW 26 (Atlanta: Society of Biblical Literature, 2007), 3–6.

8. Habachi has pointed out that both scenes have been reproduced by Thutmose III from an older scene from the temple of Senwosret I. See Labib Habachi, "Devotion of Thutmose III to His Predecessors: Apro-pos of a Meeting of Sesostris I with His Courtiers," in *Mélanges Gamal Eddin Mokhtar*, ed. Paule Posener-Kriéger, 2 vols., Bibliothèque d'étude 97 (Cairo: Institut Français d'Archéologie Orientale), 1:349–59.

9. On the importance of the veneration of Senwosret I by Hatshepsut and Thutmose III, see Jadwiga Iwaszczuk, "The Legacy of Senwosret I During the Reign of Hatshepsut and Thutmose III", *Études et Travaux*, 27 (2014): 161–78.

The inscriptions are a form of literature known as *Königsnovelle* ("king's novel"). According to Antonio Loprieno, this category of literature refers "to a form of Egyptian narrative which focuses on the role of the king as recipient of divine inspiration or as protagonist of the ensuing decision-making process."[10] The king in this type of literature assumes the divine plan and by extension aligns himself with the counsel of the gods, he then communicates his plans to court officials.

Texte de la Jeunesse begins with a trance-like experience of Thutmose III in the temple, namely while serving in the temple the prince encounters the god Amun, he is taken to the heavens and given a series of oracles that pronounced him king. After he is crowned by the creator god Re and given different royal titles, he is handed the royal position to lead Upper and Lower Egypt and defeat its enemies; the king addresses his father Amun in return and describes how he has engaged in projects required of him as pharaoh:

ḳd=j pr=f m kȝt nḥḥ [jt]=j rd nṯr.t=j
d=j wsḫ swt jr wj sḏß=ḥȝwt=f tp ȝ

I have built his house as a work of eternity ... my [father] the one who created my divine essence; I made sure that for the one who created me, I allocate his altars on earth. (cols. 17–18).[11]

In the text the divine selection of Thutmose III has come about through direct divine revelation, and in response the king initiates the building and maintenance of Amun's temple so as to enact the divine will and reciprocate divine favor. Another text that has the features of a *Königsnovelle* and sheds light on the subject matter is the building inscription of Senwosret I—known as Berlin Leather Roll (P. Berlin 3029).[12] The Berlin Leather Roll is a New Kingdom text copied in hieratic of presumably a hieroglyphic inscription on the wall of the temple of Atum at Heliopolis or a stela made by Senwosret I.[13] The king is addressing his court officials in the following

10. Antonio Loprieno, "The 'King's Novel,'" in *Ancient Egyptian Literature: History and Forms*, ed. Antonio Loprieno, PAe 10 (Leiden: Brill, 1996), 277. Also see Irene Shirun-Grumach, "Kadesh Inscriptions and Königsnovelle," in *Proceedings of the Seventh International Congress of Egyptologists*, ed. Christopher J. Eyre, OLA 82 (Leuven: Peeters, 1998), 1067–73; Beate Hofmann, *Die Königsnovelle: "Strukturanalyse am Einzelwerk,"* ÄAT 62 (Wiesbaden: Harrassowitz, 2004); and Anthony Spalinger, "Königsnovelle and Performance," in *Times, Signs and Pyramids: Studies in Honour of Miroslav Verner on the Occasion of His Seventieth Birthday*, ed. Vivienne Gae Callender et al. (Prague: Charles University Press, 2011), 351–74.

11. Unless otherwise noted, all translations are by the author.

12. For a translation, see *AEL* 1:115–18; R. B. Parkinson, *Voices from Ancient Egypt: An Anthology of Middle Kingdom Writings* (London: British Museum Press, 1991), 40–43. For the text, see Adrian de Buck, *The Building Inscription of the Berlin Leather Roll*, AnOr 17 (Rome: Pontifical Biblical Institute, 1938), 48–57. For textual analysis, see Hans Goedicke, "The Berlin Leather Roll (P Berlin 3029)," in *Festschrift zum 150 Jährigen Bestehen des Berliner Ägyptischen Museums* (Berlin: Akademie, 1974), 87–104; and Matthias Müller, "Die Administrativen Texte der Berliner Lederhandschrift," in *From Illahun to Djeme: Papers Presented in Honour of Ulrich Luft*, ed. Eszter Bechtold, András Gulyás, and Andrea Hasznos, BARIS 2311 (Oxford: Archaeopress, 2011), 173–81; Rolf Gundlach, "The Berlin Leather Roll (pBerlin 3029)," in *Palace and Temple: Architecture—Decoration—Ritual; Fifth Symposium on Egyptian Royal Ideology*, ed, Rolf Gundlach and Kate Spence (Wiesbaden: Harrassowitz, 2011), 103–14.

13. Whether this is a New Kingdom text that is reproduced from a Middle Kingdom copy, or it is a New Kingdom original despite its Middle Kingdom setting is still a subject of much debate, yet the former

manner: (1) he expresses his divinely sanctioned plan to build a temple; (2) the officials support and praise his plan; (3) the king commissions his chief administrator to carry out the plan; and (4) the king officiates the founding ceremony ritual. Jan Assmann contends that this type of royal literature in the New Kingdom stresses divine purpose and intention in the initial installation of the king.[14] He points out that the case is quite clear in the Berlin Leather Roll where one finds linguistic features in the text that highlight divine volition. The text states:

> He begat me to do what should be done for him, to accomplish
> what he commands to do.
> He appointed me shepherd of this land, knowing him who would herd it for him.
> He gave to me what he protects, what the eye in him illuminates.
> He who does all as he desires conveys to me what he wants known . . .
> He advanced me to Lord of the Two Parts . . .
> He destined me to rule the people, made me to be before mankind.
> He fashioned me as palace-dweller, an offspring not yet issued from the
>   thighs . . .
> I excel by acting for my maker, pleasing the god with what he gave.
> [I am] his son and his protector, he gave me to conquer what he conquered.
>   (*AEL* 1:116–17)

The divinely created king is predestined to follow in the will of the deity, he is therefore given a specific plan to build a temple, to which he responds immediately. The context of the above texts portrays the king as a son of the gods and divinely appointed to the office of kingship, and based on this divine status, he reenacts the will/deed of the gods, one of which is to build temples. The speeches given by both kings (Senwosret I and Thutmose III) confirm that the king's pursuit of building a temple is reinforced by divine providence, which in effect legitimizes their rule as well as their undertaking of such a costly project. Along the same line, in the so-called Poetical Stela of Thutmose III, the god Amun addresses the king saying:[15]

> I give you protection my son, my beloved. . . . Whom I begot in my divine body, Thutmose, everliving, Who does for me all that my *ka* desires. You have built my temple as work of eternity. . . . Your monuments surpass those of all former kings. I command you to make them, I am satisfied with them; I have placed you on the Horus-throne of millions of years, that you may lead the living forever.

argument seems more plausible. See Philippe Derchain, "Les Débuts de L'Histoire [Rouleau de Cuir Berlin 3029]," *RdÉ* 43 (1992): 35–47; Aldo Piccato, "The Berlin Leather Roll and the Egyptian Sense of History," *Lingua Aegyptia* 5 (1997): 137–59; and Andréas Stauder, *Linguistic Dating of Middle Egyptian Literary Texts*, Lingua Aegyptia Studia Monographica 12 (Hamburg: Widmaier, 2013), 249–57.

14. Jan Assmann, "State and Religion in the New Kingdom," in *Religion and Philosophy in Ancient Egypt*, ed. William Kelly Simpson, YES 3 (New Haven: Yale University Press, 1989), 70.

15. For a translation, see *AEL* 2:38; Jürgen Osing, "Zur 'Poetischen Stele' Thutmosis' III," in *Literatur und Politik im pharaonischen und ptolemäischen Ägypten: Vorträge der Tagung zum Gedenken an Georges Posener, 5.–10. September 1996 in Leipzig*, ed. Jan Assmann, and Elke Blumenthal, Bibliothèque d'étude 127 (Cairo: Institut français d'archéologie orientale, 1999), 75–86. On the relationship between this text and that of Texte de la Jeunesse, see Laskowski "*Monumental Architecture*," 187–88.

The king again is seen as divinely created (*wtt*) and erects (*s'ḥ'*) a temple and monuments according to the command (*wḏ*) of Amun. It is worth noting that the divine command of the gods is always supplemented with wisdom and power that is bestowed upon the king to construct the temple at the divinely appointed time and space, and with the precise building designs. In the Leather Roll the officials applaud the king by saying: "*Hu* is <in> your mouth, *Sia* is behind you, O King! What you plan comes about" (*AEL* 1:117). The king possesses *Hu*, the personification of divine utterance and *Sia*, the personification of divine understanding. This characterization of the king emphasizes the fact that he has the same creative force that appeared in the beginning of creation, and therefore is imbued with the accurate knowledge and plan of the temple's architectural pattern. Namely, he chooses at the right time the appointed landscape, dimensions, material to be used for construction, and appoints the right personnel, interior design, and furniture of the temple.

Foundation Rituals

The foundation ritual sequences evolved from the earliest times of Egyptian history and were performed at the construction locations of new or renewed temples. The separate foundation rites were collectively known as *pḏ sš* "stretching of the cord," which was the central ritual performed all throughout ancient Egyptian history.[16] New Kingdom kings valued this antiquated ritual and recorded it on their temple walls in its archaic form, as is attested in Thutmose III's small temple at Medinet Habu and Amenhotep III's temple at Luxor, to name a few. The ritual performance took several days and the king was the central figure. As founder and builder of the temple, the king received provision and support from the deities. It should be highlighted that there is no complete arrangement of the scenes at any given temple, a selection is always made from the entire decorative program.[17]

The foundation rituals represented on the walls (reliefs and texts) of the temple of Horus at Edfu dating to the Ptolemaic period are the most comprehensive to date.[18] Namely, they preserve the most sequentially complete foundation ritual episodes.

16. Alexander Badawy, *Philological Evidence About Methods of Construction in Ancient Egypt* (Cairo: Institut français d'archéologie orientale, 1956), 51–74. The Stretching of the cord foundation ritual is attested in the Palermo Stone: First Dynasty, probably King Den, *pḏ sšnw ḥm-sšȝt 'ȝ wr ḥwt-nṯr swt-nṯrw*, Stretching the cord (in foundation ceremony) by the Seshat-priest for the great door of the temple Thrones of the Gods. King Nynetjer (Second Dynasty): *ḫ'(t) (n)swt pḏ sšnw ḥwt ḥrw-rn*, Appearance of the King of Upper Egypt, Stretching the cord for the temple Horus-Ren. And King Djoser (Third Dynasty): *ḫ'wwi nswt-biti pḏ sšnw ḥwt- nṯr qbḥ-nṯrw*, Dual Appearance of the King of Upper and Lower Egypt, Stretching the cord for the temple Refreshment of the Gods. See Toby A. H. Wilkinson, *Royal Annals of Ancient Egypt: The Palermo Stone and Its Associated Fragments*, Studies in Egyptology (London: Kegan Paul, 2000).

17. Karkowski, "A Temple Comes to Being," 112.

18. See Sylvie Cauville, *Edfou*, Bibliothèque générale 6 (Cairo: Institut français d'archéologie orientale, 1984); Sylvie Cauville and Didier Devauchelle, "Le temple d'Edfou: Étapes de la construction, nouvelles données historiques," *RdE* 35 (1984): 31–55; Maxence de Rochemonteix and Emile Chassinat, eds. *Le temple d'Edfou I*, 2nd ed., 4 vols. (Cairo: Institut français d'archéologie orientale, 1984–1987); Emile Chassinat, ed., *Le temple d'Edfou II*, 2nd ed., 2 vols. (Cairo: Institut français d'archéologie orientale, 1987–1990); and Emile Chassinat. ed., *Le temple d'Edfou III–XIV* (Cairo: Institut français d'archéologie orientale, 1928–1934). For other inscriptions or reliefs referencing the foundations ceremony, see Weinstein, "Foundation Deposits in Ancient Egypt," 21 n. 3.

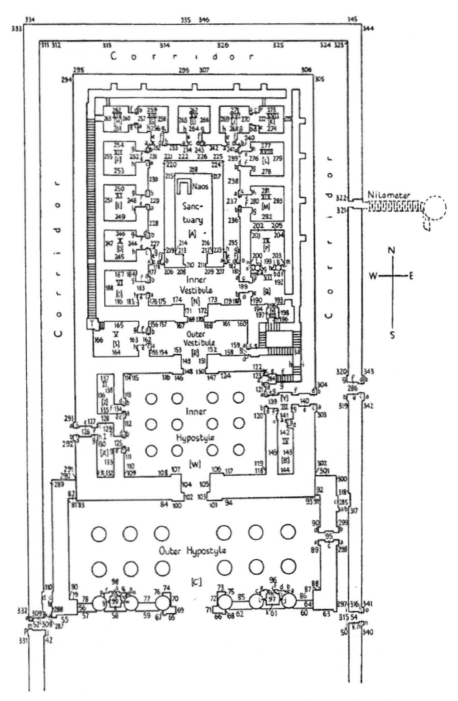

FIGURE 14.1. Temple of Edfu plan (North part). Source: Bertha Porter and Rosalind L. B. Moss, *Topographical Bibliography of Ancient Egyptian Hieroglyphic Texts, Reliefs, and Painting 6: Upper Egypt; Chief Temples (Excluding Thebes), Abydos, Dendera, Esna, Edfu, Kôm Ombo, and Philae* (Oxford: Oxford University Press, 1939), 130. Reproduced with permission of the Griffith Institute, University of Oxford.

The scenes also most likely mirror an accurate record of the long foundational ritual from early Egyptian history, as the Ptolemaic kings were keen on representing themselves fully in line with Egyptian traditions to legitimize their rule. Many of the foundational reliefs are located in the second hypostyle hall built by Ptolemy IV, and in the outer hypostyle hall added by Ptolemy VII (fig. 14.1, table 14.1). The scenes are not represented in sequential totality in any of the decorative programs, and some are repeated throughout the temple. Further, there are foundation ceremony texts that are scattered throughout the temple as well. The decorative scenes in the second hypostyle hall represent most of the ritual sequences on three separate walls: the south, west, and east walls (table 14.1). In principle, the texts and reliefs display a thematic discourse of the ritual. Hence it seems plausible that such scenes constituted a script of ritual acts that the king himself essentially performed—at least in the main temple projects—despite the inconvenience of such rituals.[19] An important event, such as this, carried significant political and religious meaning, and did not happen often in a monarch's lifetime. Perhaps in the insignificant projects the king's deputy would perform the rite.

3.1 The King Leaves His Palace to Found a Temple

The first two scenes in the Horus temple at Edfu were not included in the earlier decorative program or textual sources of earlier foundation rituals (figs. 14.2–3).[20] On the south wall of the second hypostyle hall, Pharaoh Ptolemy IV leaves his palace accompanied by two standard-bearers and the god Iunmutef. He then arrives at the designated site where the temple was going to be constructed. The inscription indicates that the king leaves his palace "to make monument to his father," and that "he guides the delightful procession to the great place to do the rites to his father Horus of Behdet, Ihy, bull of the sky."[21] Before the king stands the god Iunmutef "Pillar of his mother," a manifestation of the god Horus acting as the ritual performer. His name has been interpreted to mean different things, but it's more likely that it refers to the pillar that holds the sky goddess.[22] The god is depicted as a young *sem*-priest, wearing a wig, a side lock, leopard skin robe, and a broad collar. His apparel represents divine kingship as it embodies the young Horus. The god Iunmutef is walking in the same direction as the king, yet his upper torso and head are turned toward the king to offer him incense—the text in front of him reads: *jrt sntr* "offering incense." The god takes on the priestly role in the divine (*ntrw*) realm to ritualistically revive, transform, and preserve the divine force of the king and his initiatives of founding the temple, which of course is an essential element of upholding the ideal cosmic state of preservation

---

19. A. Rosalie David, *A Guide to Religious Ritual at Abydos* (Warminster, Wilts.: Aris & Phillips, 1981), 51.

20. Weinstein, "Foundation Deposits in Ancient Egypt," 8.

21. Chassinat, *Edfou III*, 112.

22. For the different interpretations, see Hermann te Velde, "Iunmutef," *LÄ* 3:212; Also see Steven R. W. Gregory, "The Role of the *'Iwn-mwt.f* in the New Kingdom Monuments of Thebes," *British Museum Studies in Ancient Egypt and Sudan*, 20 (2013): 31, who interprets the name as a manifestation of the king: "the pillar supporting creation, or rather the embodiment of that pillar, the 'Pillar of his Mother,' i.e., the Horus aspect of kingship itself which passed from king to king." For an in-depth study of the god Iunmutef, see Ute Rummel, *Iunmutef: Konzeption und Wirkungsbereich eines altägyptischen Gottes*, DAIK Sonderschrift 33 (Berlin: de Gruyter, 2010).

FIGURE 14.2. The king departs from his palace (Edfu Temple). Photograph by Ash Melika.

FIGURE 14.3. The king arrives at the sacred site (Edfu Temple). Photograph by Ash Melika.

FIGURE 14.4. Stretching of the cord (Edfu Temple). Photograph by Ash Melika.

manifested in the first act of creation.[23] Examining the scenes and texts of Iunmutef in the Mansion of Millions of Years at Thebes, Ute Rummel states, "His actions all focus on the vivification, regeneration, and deification of the ruler."[24] Steven Gregory goes further and argues that the god personifies the ideal state of creation, which is passed down from one king to another.[25] The king proceeds and holds the ankh sign (life and revitalization) in his left hand and with his right he holds the hands of Hathor, who is introducing him to the god Horus. The emphasis on the kingly divine association and collaboration highlights the god's approval of the project.

3.2 The Stretching of the Cord Ritual

At the sacred site the king begins the most frequent ritual act represented in Egyptian sources, the Stretching of the cord (*pd sš*).[26] The ritual included three distinct phases: selecting the four corners of the temple, "Stretching the cord," and "Loosening the

---

23. Gregory, "Role of the *'Iwn-mwt.f* , 28.

24. Ute Rummel, "Generating 'Millions of Years': Iunmutef and the Ritual Aspect of Divine Kingship," in *Les temples de millions d'années et le pouvoir royal à Thèbes au Nouvel Empire*, ed. Christian Leblanc and Gihane Zaki, Memnonia, Cahier supplémentaire 2 (Cairo: Dar el-Kutub, 2010), 206–7.

25. Gregory, "Role of the *'Iwn-mwt.f*," 37–38.

26. See note 16 above.

cord."[27] The second scene at the Edfu temple displays the king standing facing the goddess Seshat, known at Edfu as the "Mistress of the Foundation Plans and the Writings, First of the House of Life," a title that accurately personifies the goddess (fig. 14.4). She also has well-established connections with providing animation to the concept of "lifetime."[28] The king marks the four corners of the temple at night by using a surveying instrument called the *merkhet*, a notched wooden ruler with two plumblines.[29] The tool is utilized to align the temple's plan according to the location of the stars of a northern circumpolar consolation (Great Bear, i.e., Ursa Major).[30] It is probable that the actual survey happened by specialists before the ceremony, and the king symbolically performed the ritual; or, a priest specialist could have impersonated Seshat and guided the king in the technicalities of the ritual.[31] Once the temple's four corners were accurately determined in accord with astronomical orientations, the king and the goddess Seshat used a club to drive long poles (that are tightly wrapped with a cord) in the ground at the appropriate angles of the temple. The cord might have been tied to the stakes at the four corners of the structure to link the parameters of the temple.[32] Ropes generally played an important role in measurement in ancient

27. Weinstein, "Foundation Deposits in Ancient Egypt," 9.

28. For a detailed discussion on the goddess Seshat see, Dagmar Budde, *Die Göttin Seschat*, Kanobos 2 (Leipzig: Wodtke & Stegbauer, 2000); Thomas Schneider, "Das Schriftzeichen 'Rosette' und die Göttin Seschat," *SÄK* 24 (1997): 241–67; Gerald A. Wainwright, "Seshat and the Pharaoh," *JEA* 26 (1941): 30–40. On the connection of the goddess with kingship ideology, see Anthony Spalinger, *The Great Dedicatory Inscription of Ramesses II: A Solar-Osirian Tractate at Abydos*, CHANE 33 (Leiden: Brill, 2009), 7 n. 24. On her representation in the book of Thoth, see Richard Jasnow and Karl-Theodor Zauzich, *The Ancient Egyptian Book of Thoth: A Demotic Discourse on Knowledge and Pendant to the Classical Hermetica* (Wiesbaden: Harrassowitz, 2005), 19–22. On the iconography of Seshat and its astronomical relevance in temple construction, see Juan Antonio Belmonte, Miquel Ángel Molinero, and Noemi Miranda, "Unveiling Seshat: New Insights into the Stretching of the Cord Ceremony," in *In Search of Cosmic Order: Selected Essays on Egyptian Archaeoastronomy*, ed. Juan Antonio Belmonte and Mosalam Shaltout (Cairo: Supreme Council of Antiquities Press, 2009), 193–210. Seshat is always portrayed with kings in the Stretching of the cord rite, an exception to this principle is attested in two cases: Queen/Pharaoh Hatshepsut and the God's wife of Amun, Amenirdis I. For the former, see Karkowski, "A Temple Comes to Being," 113, pl. 1a; for the latter, see Mariam F. Ayad, *God's Wife, God's Servant: The God's Wife of Amun (c. 740–525 BC)* (London: Routledge, 2009), 118.

29. Martin Isler, "The Merkhet," *Varia Aegyptiaca* 7 (1991): 53–67.

30. For a general discussion see, Zbyněk Žába, *L'Orientation Astronomique dans L'Ancienne Egypt, et la Precession de L'Axe du Monde* (Prague: Editions de l'académie Tchécoslovaque des Sciences, 1953); and Christian Leitz, *Studien zur ägyptischen Astronomie*, ÄA 49 (Wiesbaden: Harrassowitz, 1991).

31. The Berlin Leather Roll (II, 13–15) indicates that the king delegated the rite of the Stretching of the cord to the chief lector priest: "the chief lector priest, scribe of the divine book, stretching the cord and loosening the rope" (ḫri-ḥˀb.t ḥry-tp zš-mḏˀ.t-nṯr pḏ šs wḥ' wˀwˀ.yt). The text reveals, however, that the king is personally overseeing the ritual, so it is possible that the chief lector priest, who might have been a specialist in astronomical particularities, impersonated the goddess Seshat and guided the king, as well as recited the proper ritual prescriptions. I'm not aware, however, of a similar text, whereby the chief lector priest performs the foundation rite instead of the king. For a detailed discussion on this office, see Roger Forshaw, *The Role of the Lector in Ancient Egyptian Society*, Archaeopress Egyptology 5 (Oxford: Archaeopress, 2014), 51–64.

32. For previous and somewhat different explanations concerning the actual methods of the usage of the poles and the cord in this ritual, see Žába, *Orientation Astronomique*, 61–62; Alexander Badawy, *A History of Egyptian Architecture* (Berkeley: University of California Press, 1968), 63; Martin Isler "An Ancient Method of Finding and Extending Direction" *JARCE* 26 (1989): 191–206; more recently, Connie Rossi, *Architecture and Mathematics in Ancient Egypt* (Cambridge: Cambridge University Press, 2007), 154–59; and Rosalind Park, "Stretching the Cord," in *Proceedings of the Seventh International Congress of Egyptologists: Cambridge, 3–9 September 1995*, ed. C. J. Eyre, OLA 82 (Leuven: Peeters, 1998), 839–48, who, in my opinion, does not make a strong case arguing that the cord in the foundation ritual refers figuratively to the nautical cord. I find the arguments of Isler and Rossi to be the most detailed and convincing; namely,

Egyptian society; this is attested in the linguistic and artistic evidences. The word *snṯ* means to "plan, measure out, found," and has a looped cord determinative, reflecting the relationship between the measuring ropes and constructing a building.[33] In the Eighteenth Dynasty several nonroyal tombs display reliefs of land surveyors measuring the field using a long cord (*nwḥ*). Also, from the same period there are three kneeling votive statues—Amenemhat-Serer, Penanhor, and Senenmut—inscribed with the title "Overseer of the Fields," holding a measuring cord as it rests on their laps on top of which surmounts a sacred measuring device bearing the ram's head of Amun (in the case of Senenmut it was substituted for a human's head).[34] Finally, the episode ends with the *wḥꜥ wꜣwꜣt*, "Loosening of the cord," a perplexing act, since its purpose is not described in the relief or texts. It might be that after the extents were marked on the ground, the cord was loosen and slipped from the stakes to the ground to mark the extension of the whole perimeter. At any event, although the complete details of the ritual are not well-defined, what is suggestive is that the temple is positioned according to divine orientation and sacred alignment within the cosmic order.

The King Initiates Construction

The fourth episode, known as *bꜣ tꜣ* "Hoeing the earth," features pharaoh holding a large hoe (*ḥnn*) with both hands, digging the first foundation trench of the temple before Horus and Hathor (fig. 14.5). The king says to Horus: "I dug the foundation of the temple. I broke down for you the earth to the limit of Nun, to complete your work for eternity."[35] "The limit of Nun" most likely reflects the water table, since a title in a different relief of the same scene states: "Dig a hole to the water level so that your house is firm." Hence, Nun is associated with the foundation layers of temples. According to Egyptian myths, the first temple was built on the primeval mound which Nun, the primeval waters, gave rise to.[36]

   After the trenches were dug, the king returns and performs a ritual generally inscribed as *bꜣ tꜣ*, "Molding of the brick," yet at Edfu, a more prescriptive title is added: "Molding the brick at the four corners of the temple" (fig. 14.6).[37] The king stands

the stakes and cord were primarily used to accurately mark out and extend the direction of the structure. Rossi does not believe, however, that they were used to measure the perimeter of the temple.

   33. See Badawy, *Philological Evidence*, 57. For the usage of the word in the founding of Akhetaten by Akhenaten, see James Hoffmeier, *Akhenaten and the Origins of Monotheism* (Oxford: Oxford University Press), 148.

   34. See Rossi, *Architecture and Mathematics*,154 nn. 30–31. In addition, for Senenmut's statute, see Catherine H. Roechrig, Renée Dreyfus, and Cathleen Keller, eds., *Hatshepsut: From Queen to Pharaoh* (New York: Metropolitan Museum of Art, 2005), 122–24. The image of a land surveyor using a long cord are exhibited in the following Theban tombs: Menna (TT 69), Khaemhet (TT 57), Amenhotpsesi (TT 75), Djeserkareseneb (TT 38), and Nebamun (location unknown—the relief is in the British Museum). For the use of ropes in building material, see Dieter Arnold, *Building in Egypt, Pharaonic Stone Masonry* (New York: Oxford University Press, 1991), 63, 268–69, 282–83.

   35. Montet, "Rituel de Fondation," 85.

   36. H. Rotsch, "The Primeval Ocean Nun and the Terminology of Water in Ancient Egypt," in *L'acqua nell'antico Egitto: Vita, rigenerazione, incantesimo, medicamento*; *Proceeding of the First International Conference for Young Egyptologists: Italy, Chianciano Terme, October 15–18, 2003*, ed. Alessia Amenta, Maria Michela Luiselli, and Maria Novella Sordi, Egitto Antico 3 (Rome: Bretschneider, 2005), 229–40.

   37. Montet, "Rituel de Fondation," 87.

FIGURE 14.5. Hoeing the earth (Edfu Temple). Photograph by Ash Melika.

FIGURE 14.6. Molding of the brick (Edfu Temple). Photograph by Ash Melika.

before Horus holding a mold that rests on a table.[38] The accompanying inscription describes the king as mixing the mud-brick material, and ascribes to him the title "Heir of Khnum, Strength of Arm, who administers the land, and raises temples for the gods."[39] Khnum is the potter creator god who fashions gods, humans, and animals.[40] The king is symbolically initiating the building process through his preparation of mud-brick for the four corners of the foundation of the temple. On the whole, temples in New Kingdom and beyond were built with stone material, except for the outer massive enclosure walls in which mud-brick laid in wavy lines was utilized to mimic the primeval waters of Nun.[41] The Molding of the brick ritual possibly reflects the

38. Mud-brick was only used in temples for building enclosure walls, the rest of the structure was built with hard stones. On the use of mud-brick in building material, see Barry Kemp, "Soil (including Mud-brick Architecture)," in *Ancient Egyptian Materials and Technology*, ed. Paul T. Nicholson and Ian Shaw (Cambridge: Cambridge University Press, 2000), 78–103.

39. Montet, "Rituel de Fondation," 87.

40. Paul F. O'Rourke, "Khnum," *OEAE* 2:231–32; D. Abou-Ghazi, "Favours to the King from Khnum in the Pyramid-Texts," *The Intellectual Heritage of Egypt: Studies Presented to László Kákosy by Friends and Colleagues on the Occasion of His 60th Birthday*, ed. Ulrich Luft (Budapest: Chaire d'Égyptologie, 1992), 27–32.

41. Byron E. Shafer, ed., *Temples of Ancient Egypt* (Cornell University Press, 1997), 5 n. 34.

FIGURE 14.7. Pouring of the sand (Edfu Temple). Photograph by Ash Melika.

symbolic purpose of the outer enclosure walls in which the king, an heir of Khnum, is inaugurating a sacred landscape demarcating between chaos and order, the sacred and profane.

The sixth foundation ritual is labeled as *wšꜣ-šʿ*, "Pouring of the sand," the king is portrayed pouring sand from a large bucket into the foundation trenches before the deity (fig. 14.7).[42] A layer of sand was generally used with mud-brick to fill and level foundation trenches in temple constructions, as evident in various archeological sites, for example, the Karnak temple complex.[43] Further, sand in Egyptian mythology is symbolically significant, representing the primeval mound in the first act of creation, as well as operating as a purifying element.[44] More importantly, it prescriptively acts as a defensive component protecting from enemies by rendering them as an ineffective

42. Penelope Wilson, *A Ptolemaic Lexicon: A Lexicographical Study of the Ptolemaic Texts in the Temple of Edfu*, OLA 78 (Leuven: Peeters, 1997), 264–65.

43. Donald Redford et al., "East Karnak Excavations, 1987–1989," *JARCE* 28 (1991): 79. Moreover, King Seti I at his temple in Abydos is portrayed pouring sand before the gods Re-Harakhti, Amun-Re, and Isis; see Bertha Porter and Rosalind L. B. Moss, *Topographical Bibliography of Ancient Egyptian Hieroglyphic Texts, Reliefs, and Painting VI: Upper Egypt; Chief Temples (Excluding Thebes), Abydos, Dendera, Esna, Edfu, Kôm Ombo, and Philae* (Oxford: Oxford University Press, 1939), 13, 14, 17.

44. See Robert Ritner, *The Mechanics of Ancient Egyptian Magical Practice*, SAOC 54 (Chicago: Oriental Institute of the University of Chicago, 1993), 155–57, and references therein.

FIGURE 14.8. King places the sacred plaques in the foundation (Edfu Temple). Photograph by Ash Melika.

grit, and as an offensive substance that fragments the enemies.[45] This ceremonial performance might be pointing to a defense ritual, whereby the temple is purified and its landscape set apart as a sacred domain.

The seventh rite, not seen in temple reliefs before the Ptolemaic period, portrays the king presenting Horus with a tray on which seventeen (twenty-four at the Dendra temple) small plaques and precious stones are stacked (fig. 14.8). The accompanying inscription reads: "Placing the plaques of gold and costly stones at the four corners of the temple. . . . I did this for the corners of your temple in order to complete your work for eternity."[46] The king placed small plaques made out of gold, copper, silver, lapis lazuli, turquoise, and other precious material in the foundation deposit at the four corners of the temple. These plaques are found in numerous archeological material cultures from the Eleventh Dynasty onward—and they have evolved in size, shape, and material. According to James Weinstein, during the Ramesside period a smaller size plaque made from different materials and distributed more widely began to appear.[47] He adds that the plaques represented at the wall reliefs in the Edfu and Dendra temples were these smaller precious stones.[48]

Perhaps this rite included or is an extension of the foundation deposit ceremony, in which votive offerings were placed beneath the foundations of important buildings (temples, tombs, forts, etc.) before their construction.[49] The votive offerings were

45. See *AEL* 3:130.
46. Montet, "Rituel de Fondation," 92–95.
47. Weinstein, "Foundation Deposits in Ancient Egypt," 421–22.
48. Ibid., 422.
49. On the foundation ceremony, see Weinstein, "Foundation Deposits in Ancient Egypt," 559–61; Pierre Montet. "Le Rituel de Fondation des Temples," *CRAIBL* 104 (1960): 172–80; Michel Azim,

placed in a pit or trench at crucial intersections, such as entrances or corners of the structure. Evidence of foundation deposits from the archaeological records is numerous and they date from the Old Kingdom to the Greco-Roman era. Various votive offerings, inscribed and uninscribed, are found in these pits, which included: plaques, tools and vessels, mud-brick models, and food offerings.[50] The only direct hint of the foundation deposit ceremony in connection with the Stretching of the cord episode is found in a Fifth Dynasty fragmented relief from the sun temple of Niuserre at Abu Ghurob.[51] The scene portrays the king in a kneeling position holding two jars in each hand, in front of him is a U-shaped trench containing the heads of a bull and a goose and an outstretched hand of an unrecognizable figure holding a vessel. Behind the king there are two Stretching of the cord scenes. However due the loss of the upper part of the relief and lack of inscriptions it is difficult to identify some of the figures and why the Stretching of the cord scene is represented twice. The significance of this relief is that it links the foundation deposits with the foundation ceremony and it portrays evidence of a sacrificial rite.

At any rate, the offering of the plaques at the four corners of the temple ceremonially emphasized the precious material and valuables that were to be used in the building and its furniture. Pierre Montet also proposed that the material supernaturally safeguarded the temple, and the number seventeen might have an astrological connection.[52] As for the deposit ceremony, it was a purposeful ritual utilizing objects that figuratively implied the perpetual establishment of the temple, highlighting the role of the king as its founder and builder.[53] Possibly, the sacrificial act consecrated the temple and its landscape ushering in the new phase of actually building the temple. After the votives were laid in the deposit, sand was poured again to fill the pits, an act related to the Pouring of the sand ritual.[54]

In the eighth and last ceremony in the foundation ritual, the king initiates the beginning of the construction project by moving the first stone block into its place (fig. 14.9). In the accompanying inscriptions the king states: "I grabbed a lever with my own hands, working to build your temple."[55] The king is identifying with the builders—in essence, he is the main constructor of the temple. By this act, he signaled that the

"Découverte de Dépôts de fondation d'Horemheb au IXe pylône de Karnak," *Karnak* 7 (1982): 93–120. François Schmitt, "Les Dépôts de Fondation à Karnak, Actes Rituels de Piété et de Pouvoir," *Karnak* 16 (2017): 351–71; Sakr, "New Foundation Deposits of Kom El-Hisn," 349–55. Karkowski, "A Temple Comes to Being," 114, suggests that the foundation deposit ceremony should be included as part of the foundation ritual and might have followed the Stretching of the cord ceremony. I agree with this observation but would add that its sequence best fits within this rite during the Ptolemaic period, or immediately following the Pouring of the sand rite in earlier times.

50. The inscriptions usually include the name of the king who commissioned the building and, at times, the name of the deity to whom the temple is dedicated. Inscribed foundation deposits began in the Middle Kingdom and continued to the Ptolemaic period; Sylvie Marchand, "Histoire Parallèle: La Céramique et Les Dépôts De Fondation De L'Égypte Ancienne," *Égypte Afrique and Orient* 36 (2004): 8.

51. Ludwig Borchardt and Heinrich Schäfer, "Vorläufiger Bericht über die Ausgrabungen bei Abusir im Winter 1899/1900," *ZÄS* 38 (1900): pl. 4.

52. Montet, "Rituel de Fondation," *CRAIBL*, 177.

53. By the Ptolemaic period foundation deposits included dedicatory formulae, hence functioned more as commemorative objects, see Weinstein, "Foundation Deposits in Ancient Egypt," 437; Marchand, "Histoire Parallèle," 17.

54. Weinstein, "Foundation Deposits in Ancient Egypt," 422.

55. Montet "Rituel de Fondation," 95.

FIGURE 14.9. King transports the first block into place (Edfu). Photograph by Ash Melika.

temple area has been consecrated and therefore the beginning of the construction will resume under his supervision. The king alongside the gods, ceremonially, are providing the stone material to build the temple for "eternity."

Consecration of the Temple

Once the temple was completed, the place of worship was to be sanctified through consecration rituals to ensure the accommodation of the deity; again, the king played the central role in these rituals. After all, building or renewing temples was a royal prerogative that only the king was responsible for, since he was infused with the numinous nature of the deities.

The consecration rituals prepared the way for the deity to physically descend and inhabit his/her house on earth.[56] In the Edfu temple, there are several scenes that relay the final initiation rites before the temple became fully operational. The first scene in this sequence is entitled *wpš bsn*, "spinkling *bsn*" (fig. 14.10). The scene portrays the

56. Montet, "Rituel de Fondation," *CRAIBL*, 178.

FIGURE 14.10. Sprinkling natron (Edfu Temple). Photograph by Ash Melika.

king scattering, in an oval shape, balls of *bsn*, "natron"[57] around the temple structure (represented by a miniature *naos*), and with his left hand holding a mace. The accompanying inscriptions elucidate the function of this ritual: "I scatter for you the beautiful natron of El-Kab. . . . I sanctify and I chase evil around Behdet."[58] In another scene the king in this rite is said to purify the temple also with resin (incense), four vases, four red pots, southern grains, and northern grains.[59] Clearly, this is a purification ritual whereby the king is warding off all the enemies and sanctifying all parts of the

57. The word refers to some crystalline element, such as natron or gypsum, see John R. Harris, *Lexicographical Studies of Ancient Egyptian Minerals* (Berlin: Akademie, 1961), 190–91; *Wb* 1:475. *Bsn* is used by Ramsesses in the Great Hypostyle hall, see Peter J. Brand, Rosa E. Feleg, and William J. Murnane, *The Great Hypostyle Hall in the Temple of Amun at Karnak: Volume I, Part 2: Translation and Commentary*, SAOC 142 (Chicago: Oriental Institute of the University of Chicago, 2019), 50. In this ritual, natron was most likely the substance used, see Weinstein, "Foundation Deposits in Ancient Egypt," 15–16.

58. Chassinat, *Edfou II*, 32–33. Joachim F. Quack explains that "purification scenes are usually placed at the beginning of a ritual, in order to define the place, persons, and objects involved as being pure" ("Conceptions of Purity in Egyptian Religion," in *Purity and the Forming of Religious Traditions in the Ancient Mediterranean World and Ancient Judaism*, ed. Christian Frevel, Christophe Nihan, Dynamics in the History of Religion 3 [Leiden: Brill, 2013], 117).

59. Chassinat, *Edfou VII*, 52–56.

FIGURE 14.11. Consecration
and presentation of the
temple (Edfu Temple). Photograph by Ash Melika.

temple—walls, sanctuary, and the rest.[60] Hence, the temple landscape and building
have been sanctified for the deities to inhabit.

Following the sprinkling of *bsn* scene the king consecrates and offers the temple
to the deity (fig. 14.11). The king holds in one hand a scepter and staff, and gestures
with his other hand a sign of offering the completed temple to the god. The short title
of this rite is "Giving the temple to his lord" (*rdỉt pr n nb.f*).[61] The text formula states:
"I consecrate your house for you, Give your palace to divine places."[62] This scene is
very important in the founding ritual process because it is the culmination of all the
ceremonial events.[63] The rite is a process in which the temple is brought to life as
the divine presence animates it, preparing it for the daily divine services and festival
ceremonies. Namely, the profane space enters the divine timeless process of revivification of the cosmos as it was demonstrated in the first act of creation. The consecration
ritual is further associated by two texts at the Edfu temple designated as the Ritual of
the opening of the mouth.[64] The content and structure of the ritual has been published

60. Concerning purification rituals, see Quack, "Conceptions of Purity in Egyptian Religion," 115–58.
61. Chassinat, *Edfou VII*, 58. At other instances the titles *swḏ kȝt n nb.s or swḏ pr n nb.f* is utilized, see
Aylward M. Blackman and Herbert W. Fairman, "The Consecration of an Egyptian Temple According to
the Use of Edfu," *JARCE* 32 (1946): 82 n. 32.
62. Chassinat, *Edfou III*, pl. LXI.
63. Cauville, "*Offerings to the Gods*," 267.
64. Blackman and Fairman, "Consecration of an Egyptian Temple."

FIGURE 14.12. The king offers worship and adoration (Edfu Temple). Photograph by Ash Melika.

by Aylward Blackman and Herbert Fairman who explain the function of the ritual in these words: "The idea evidently was not that only the cultus-statues were enabled to come alive and active through the due performance of this rite, but the figures in the wall-reliefs also and the entire edifice with all its appurtenances."[65] Eugene Cruz-Uribe adds that the ritual also invoked the protective forces of the deities that maintained the sustainability of life in the cosmos.[66] Finally, after the revivification of the temple through the immanent presence of the deities, the pharaoh stands before the presented temple raising both his hands in an adoration ritual worshiping the gods (fig. 14.12). This scene concluded the ritual, and the structure is now transformed from a mere temple building to an operational temple of worship.

Conclusion

In sum, the founding of the temple in ancient Egypt includes primarily four common stages: (1) divine command; (2) divine plan/foundation rituals; (3) construction ceremonies; and (4) dedication rituals. The first stage of building a temple involves a divine

65. Ibid, 85.
66. Eugene Cruz-Uribe, "Opening of the Mouth as Temple Ritual," in *Gold of Praise: Studies on Ancient Egypt in Honor of Edward F. Wente*, ed. Emily Teeter and John A. Wilson, SAOC 58 (Chicago: Oriental Institute of the University of Chicago, 1999), 71–72.

commission from the deity to the king, then the king is given the plan of construction that he is to follow. Subsequently, the foundation rituals are carried out, which include rites that comprise the phases before and during the building stages. Once the temple has been built and is fully operational, the consecration ritual is enacted to dedicate the building to the deity; the deity, in turn, responds with divine recognition and the temple is transformed from the realm of the profane (common) to sacred space. Thus, the founding of the temple comprises all ritual activities performed before and during the building stages and the postbuilding rites and ceremonies.

Symbolically, the temple was built on a sacred foundational site, and it was oriented according to east-west axis (more common), an astronomical significance, or paralleling the Nile River.[67] Even the measurements and dimensions of the temple were impregnated with mythical meaning.[68] In the New Kingdom and beyond, the temples built for the gods reached their archetypical model: enclosure walls, pylon, open courtyard, hypostyle hall, offering chamber, bark chamber, and the holy of holies or inner chamber.[69] The selection of the landscape to build a temple symbolized the primordial mound coming forth from the waters of Nun. According to Egyptian creation myths, out of Nun rose the primeval mound on which the first temple was built. Hence, in ancient Egypt, the temple built by the pharaoh, under the supervision of the deity, was at the heart of the cosmogonic myth, in which temple rituals reenacted this first act of creation to create order and stability in the cosmos.

67. E.g., the Luxor temple (*Ipet-resyt*, "Southern Ipet") is known to be the birth of the god Amun, see W. Raymond Johnson, "Monuments and Monumental Art under Amenhotep III: Evolution and Meaning," in *Amenhotep III; Perspectives on His Reign*, ed. David O'Connor and Eric Cline (Ann Arbor: University of Michigan Press, 2004), 66–67. On sacred space and the selection of foundation sites, see Peter F. Dorman and Betsy M. Bryan, eds., *Sacred Space and Sacred Function in Ancient Thebes: Occasional Proceedings of the Theban Workshop*, SAOC 61 (Chicago: Oriental Institute of the University of Chicago, 2006); G. Vittmann, "Orientierung," *LÄ* 4: 607–9; and Badawy, *History of Egyptian Architecture*, 183.

68. Erik Hornung, *Idea into Image: Essays on Ancient Egyptian Thought*, trans. Elizabeth Bredeck (New York, Timken, 1992), 118–19.

69. Badawy argues that the temple of Khonsu is an archetypical New Kingdom temple, see Steven Snape, *Egyptian Temples*, (Princes Risborough: Shire, 1996), 29. It must be noted, however, that this model was not completely replicated in every situation, New Kingdom temples and beyond were similar but not exact in structure and decoration program. Many temples in Thebes remain more or less intact, however, they are located in a concentrated site and are not reflective of all Egyptian temples, see Stephen Quirke, *Ancient Egyptian Religion* (London: British Museum, 1992), 76.

CHAPTER 15

Goliath's Head Wound and the Edwin Smith Papyrus

Edmund S. Meltzer

WHEN I TAUGHT JIM HOFFMEIER introductory Middle Egyptian at the University of Toronto—as I recall, it was in the 1973–1974 academic year—both of us were graduate students. In the ensuing years, which have grown into decades, we have been friends, colleagues and coworkers. We have studied with several of the same teachers, Professors Redford, Williams, Millet, and Mills; we have both worked on the Akhenaten Temple Project; and about ten years after that first encounter in Middle Egyptian, we coedited a Festschrift for Ron Williams, in which Jim wrote one of what has grown into an increasingly long list of impressive studies fruitfully comparing ancient Egyptian texts, art and archaeological finds with the Hebrew Bible.[1] I always look forward to seeing Jim at the American Research Center in Egypt and other meetings, and he is one of the most dedicated and decent people I know. It is thus a pleasure to dedicate to him a reflection on a perhaps off-the-beaten-track comparison between a biblical passage and an ancient Egyptian text.

The episode of David and Goliath has typically been compared with the combat between Sinuhe and the Champion of Retjenu in the Middle Egyptian story of Sinuhe.[2] However, after having immersed myself for several years in the trauma cases of the Edwin Smith Papyrus, in collaboration and constant dialogue with Dr. Gonzalo M. Sanchez MD, a neurosurgeon, a different perspective has occurred to me.[3] A number of the most important and striking (no pun intended, maybe) cases in the Edwin Smith Papyrus are skull fractures, and I began to wonder how the brief and apparently terse account of the David-Goliath duel (1 Sam 17:48–51) compares with the head trauma cases of the ancient Egyptian manual.

I would like to thank Dr. Gonzalo M. Sanchez MD for reading and discussing a draft of this paper and for making very helpful suggestions and sending additional references and materials.

1. For the Akhenaten Temple Project, see Donald B. Redford, et al., *The Akhenaten Temple Project, Vol. 2: Rwd–Mnw, Foreigners and Inscriptions*, Aegypti Texta Propositaque 1 (Toronto: Akhenaten Temple Project; University of Toronto Press, 1988). For the Festschrift, see James K. Hoffmeier and Edmund S. Meltzer, eds., *Egyptological Miscellanies: A Tribute to Professor Ronald J. Williams*, Ancient World 6 (Chicago: Ares, 1983). James K. Hoffmeier, "Some Egyptian Motifs Related to Enemies and Warfare and Their Old Testament Counterparts," in Hoffmeier and Meltzer, *Egyptological Miscellanies*, 53–70.

2. E.g., Günter Lanczkowski, "Die Geschichte vom Riesen Goliath und der Kampf Sinuhes mit dem Starken von Retenu," *MDAIK* 16 (1958): 214–18; see also Hans Goedicke, "Sinuhe's Duel," *JARCE* 21 (1984): 197–201.

3. Gonzalo M. Sanchez and Edmund S. Meltzer, *The Edwin Smith Papyrus: Updated Translation of the Trauma Treatise and Modern Medical Commentaries* (Atlanta: Lockwood, 2012); also Sanchez and Meltzer, "Edwin Smith Speaks and His Papyrus Lives," paper presented at the Annual Meeting of the American Research Center in Egypt, Providence, RI, April 2012.

The Biblical account reads as follows:

David put his hand into the bag; he took out a stone and slung it. It struck the
Philistine in the forehead; the stone sank into his forehead, and he fell face down
on the ground. Thus David bested the Philistine with sling and stone; he struck
him down and killed him. David had no sword; so David ran up and stood over
the Philistine, grasped his sword and pulled it from its sheath; and with it he
dispatched him and cut off his head. (1Sam 17:49–51 NJPS)

One point about the sequence of events has to be clarified; when Goliath fell face
down, he was incapacitated but not yet dead.[4] The "killed him" of the above translation
is anticipatory or summarizing, because it was not until David took Goliath's sword
that he "dispatched," that is, killed or slew him (Hebrew *wayəmōtətēhû*).

There are several cases in the Edwin Smith Papyrus that invite comparison with
Goliath's wound: cases #7 ("Frontal Cutting Wound with Compound Skull Fracture
Penetrating the Frontal Air Sinus"), #8 ("Closed Head Injuries with Comminuted
Skull Fracture," comprising what we have labeled as 8A and 8B), and #9 ("Wound in
the Forehead, Fracturing the Outer Table of the Frontal Bone").[5] While the location
of the Case #7 and Case #9 injuries in the forehead area seems to provide an obvious
though perhaps superficial parallel with Goliath's head trauma, the situation is considerably more complicated. The description in Case #9 of "a wound in his forehead,
smashing in/burst fracturing the bony plate of his braincase" seems on the face of it to
be a description applicable to Goliath's injury, but the course of treatment prescribed
in Case #9 strongly suggests that the injury is less catastrophic than those described
in Case #8, although it is obviously also severe.[6] It is very interesting that Case #9 is
the only one in the Edwin Smith Papyrus "trauma treatise" in which a ritual power
procedure (a translation and concept that Dr. Sanchez and I prefer to the commonly-
used "magic") is prescribed.[7] That, perhaps paradoxically, along with the treatment by
means of "ground ostrich eggshell with oil," followed by "powdered ostrich eggshell,"
essentially a graft employing "biomimetic" material, suggests that this was actually
a case in which healing was considered somewhat likely.[8] It is also significant that
the most negative verdict, "a medical condition that cannot be handled/dealt with,"
is not stated for Case #9 while it is for both Case #8A and #8B.[9] Looking again at the
latter, the descriptions "a crushed fracture in his braincase" and "a smashed in/burst
fracture of his skull" seem more similar to the biblical statement that "the stone sank

4. The observation that, according to the text, Goliath was killed by David after falling to the ground,
has been made in print by Vladimir M. Berginer, "Neurological Aspects of the David-Goliath Battle:
Restriction in the Giant's Visual Field," *Israel Medical Association Journal* 2 (2000): 725–27; and Deirdre E. Donnelly and Patrick J. Morrison, "Hereditary Gigantism: The Biblical Giant Goliath and His Brothers," *Ulster Medical Journal* 83 (2014): 86–88. I thank Dr. Sanchez for sending me these articles. Dr. Sanchez and I agree that Dr. Berginer's suggestion that Goliath's shield-bearer was a guide necessitated by the
giant's impaired eyesight is far-fetched.
5. For #8, see Sanchez and Meltzer, *Edwin Smith Papyrus*, 86–94. For #9, see ibid., 71–103.
6. Ibid., 96.
7. Ibid., 96–97, 101–3.
8. Ibid., 99–101.
9. Ibid., 88, 303.

into his forehead."[10] It is clear from the descriptions in the Edwin Smith Papyrus that the Case #8 traumas are closed injuries, that is, the skin is unbroken, while #8B evidences "greater damage," sufficient "to allow palpation of tissues and brain pulsations through the unbroken scalp," along with bleeding from the patient's nostrils and ears, which also occurs in the uncomplicated course of Case #7.[11] Some idea of the physical impact of a Case #8 injury can perhaps be gotten from the head of Soldier #14 of the slain soldiers of Nebhepetre Mentuhotpe excavated by Herbert Winlock.[12] We think that an example of a Case #9 injury can be identified on the skull of Soldier #25.[13] The description of Goliath's injury does not definitely clarify whether or not the skin was broken, and does not mention any nasal or aural bleeding.

Case #7 of the Edwin Smith Papyrus immediately shows a significant difference from the two subsequent cases, because it is a slash wound, inflicted by a blade, not a crushing impact, and it is described as "penetrating to the bone, and perforating the membranous lined sinus cavities of his braincase."[14] Two examples of what seem to be Case #7 type traumas can be seen on Soldiers #14 and #23 of the group published by Winlock.[15] The account of Case #7 comprises an uncomplicated injury and what Dr. Sanchez and I have designated as two alternative courses. In the first alternative course, the complication is tetanus (Egyptian *ti3*), which receives its first known designation and clinical description in this document.[16] Tellingly, the simple or uncomplicated course receives the second verdict, "a medical condition I will fight with."[17] The condition of the patient who has contracted tetanus is given the third verdict, "a medical condition that cannot be handled/dealt with."[18] In the second alternative course, the patient is described as pallid and weak, but no separate verdict is stated, though his weakness and pallor are described as showing that "he is entering into an incurable condition"[19]

It is envisioned by the Egyptian Master Physician (as Dr. Sanchez and I have dubbed the unknown author of the Edwin Smith Papyrus) that a patient inflicted with a Case #8A trauma could be ambulatory though impaired.[20] As Dr. Sanchez says in his medical commentary to Case #8, regarding the verdict of "cannot be handled," "This verdict does not necessarily reflect a lethal situation," but "points to the reality of a fixed neurological deficit . . . the patient was cared for by those measures for head injuries applied in treating other cases of severe head injuries in the Edwin Smith Papyrus with a sitting position and supportive measures, continued until the crisis passed."[21] The "fixed neurological deficit" seems also to be a good description of the "incurable condition" envisioned by Explanation J, which elaborates on the second

10. Ibid., 87.
11. For #8B, see ibid., 88, 92–93. For #7, see ibid., 74.
12. Ibid., 94, fig. 8 d.
13. Ibid., 101, fig. 9 a.
14. Ibid., 73.
15. Ibid., 80, fig. 7.
16. Ibid., 79–85.
17. Ibid., 74.
18. Ibid., 74, 303.
19. Ibid., 75, 76.
20. Ibid., 87–88.
21. Ibid., 92.

alternative course of Case #7. In the medical commentary to the catastrophic fracture
of Case #8B, Dr. Sanchez states that "The patient's outlook is poor."[22] The question of
whether Goliath could have survived his wound, and what his condition would have
been, was preempted by the subsequent actions of David.

As I have looked at the Egyptian and Hebrew texts, a somewhat tantalizing lexical
question has also occurred to me. The account in 1 Sam 17:49 says that "the stone sank
[*tiṭĕbaʿ*] into his forehead." Another case in the Edwin Smith Papyrus, #32 ("Cervi-
cal Vertebral Compression Fracture"), uses a word *ḏfyt* "compressing/penetration."[23]
The Hebrew root *ṭbʿ* is often equated with Egyptian *ḏbʿwt* and variants, "signet, seal,"
though phonetic difficulties have been noted.[24] If not for the absence of the *ʿayin*, one
might be tempted to speculate whether a comparison of the Hebrew with the root of
Egyptian *ḏfyt* might be suggested; perhaps this proposal could be suggested as an
instance of a biliteral base as a possible explanation of the Egyptian term's missing
an *ʿayin*.[25] Another example of the correspondence Egyptian *f* : Hebrew *b* is suggested by Jim's and my teacher Donald Redford: Egyptian *drf* "writing, script" (taking the determinative, Gardiner sign list Aa 10, as a stylus or writing implement) and
Hebrew *dārbān* "goad"; and Murtonen lists the Semitic (including Hebrew) root *bšl*
"ripen, boil, cook," and so on and Egyptian *fsi/psi* "cook," while noting that "Eg. /y/
= Semitic /l/ is unusual."[26]

Finally, the use of the sling as a weapon prompts me to recall that Jim and I both
have had the archaeological experience of uncovering sling stones at East Karnak,
a testimony of conflicts that took place in Upper Egypt during the later phases of the
site.[27]

I am very gratified to dedicate these meanderings, reflections and reminiscences to Jim,
who is a jolly good fellow, and who is also both an Egyptologist and an archaeologist.

22. Ibid., 93.

23. Ibid., 208–9; Raymond O. Faulkner, *A Concise Dictionary of Middle Egyptian* (Oxford: Griffith
Institute, 1962), 322.

24. A. Murtonen, *Hebrew in Its West Semitic Setting: A Comparative Survey of Non-Masoretic Hebrew
Dialects and Traditions, Part One: A Comparative Lexicon*, Studies in Semitic Languages and Linguistics
13 (Leiden: Brill, 1989), 203. For the Egyptian writings, see Faulkner, *Concise Dictionary*, 322.

25. On biliteral roots and their expansion in Egyptian and Semitic as well as elsewhere in Afro-Asiatic,
see the literature cited in Sanchez and Meltzer, *Edwin Smith Papyrus*, 129, n. 156, as well as Sabatino
Moscati, ed., *An Introduction to the Comparative Grammar of the Semitic Languages: Phonology and
Morphology*, Porta Linguarum Orientalium 6 (Wiesbaden: Harrassowitz, 1969), 72–75.

26. Donald B. Redford, "Some Observations on the Northern and North-Eastern Delta in the Late
Predynastic Period," in *Essays in Egyptology in Honor of Hans Goedicke*, ed. Betsy M. Bryan and David
Lorton (San Antonio: Van Siclen, 1994), 209; Faulkner, *Concise Dictionary*, 315. Murtonen, *Comparative
Lexicon*, 122–23; Faulkner, *Concise Dictionary*, 94, 98. For initial *i* : *l*, see Edmund S. Meltzer, "'Heart':
ib or **inb* in Egyptian?" *JNES* 36 (1977): 149. Also, since *fsi* and its *Nebenform psi* are third-weak (3ae
inf.) roots of which *-i* is the most typical ending, the possibility of a biliteral base or kernel again needs to
be considered.

27. I have presented a popular account in "Akhenaten's Lost Temples," *Fate* 32.1 (January 1979): 49.

CHAPTER 16

Did the Patriarchs Meet Philistines?

Alan Millard

AN ANCIENT BOOK TELLS of two groups of people meeting at certain times and in a certain area. No other source provides that information or indicates that either group was in the region at that time. Later documents do show that one group was there centuries after and the other group could have been. Since the book in its present form was created later still, it is easy to label its reports anachronistic, assuming that a writer at the later time, or afterward, supposed the situation of his own day applied in previous centuries. However, there are many examples of ancient books preserving unique pieces of information that historians have discounted in recent times, then shown to be correct. The book in question is Genesis, the two groups the Philistines and Israel. Abimelech, king of Gerar (Gen 20:2) is presented as "king of the Philistines" when he meets Isaac (Gen 26:1, 8) and living in "the land of the Philistines" in episodes concerning both patriarchs (Gen 21:32, 34; 26:1, 8, 14–18). Have historians discounted the evidence of these passages too hastily?

The appearance of the Philistines in the biographies of Abraham and Isaac has long been treated as an anachronism because the first mention of the Philistines in ancient inscriptions comes in the reign of Ramesses III, where they are among the Peoples of the Sea whose threatening hosts his forces repelled on land and sea about 1175 BCE.[1] Apart from an Egyptian list of about 1100 BCE., the Philistines do not recur in any contemporary record until the Assyrian king Adad-nerari III (810–783 BCE) boasts of tribute from Philistia (*palastu*) as well as Samaria and Edom. The situation for Israel is similar: the famous Israel Stele of Merenptah is the oldest report to name her.[2] No other inscriptions do that until Shalmaneser III tells how his army faced Ahab the Israelite's force at the Battle of Qarqar in 853 BCE and a few years later Mesha of Moab celebrated his triumph over Israelites east of the Dead Sea on the Moabite Stone. Edom and Moab, too, are first named in Egyptian texts of the thirteenth and twelfth centuries BCE, then not again until the Assyrian and Moabite inscriptions of the ninth century. In fact, there are many such gaps in past records and so in present

---

1. For a recent summary, see Aren M. Maeir and Louise A. Hitchcock, "The Appearance, Formation and Transformation of Philistine Culture: New Perspectives and New Finds," in *"Sea Peoples" Up-to-Date: New Research on Transformations in the Eastern Mediterranean in the Thirteenth–Eleventh Centuries BCE*, ed. Peter M. Fischer and Teresa Bürge, Contributions to the Chronology of the Eastern Mediterranean 35 (Vienna: Österreichschen Akademie der Wissenschaft, 2014), 149–62. See now Shirly Ben-Dor Evian, "Ramesses III and the 'Sea-Peoples': Towards a New Philistine Paradigm," *Oxford Journal of Archaeology* 36 (2017): 267–85.

2. Translated by James K. Hoffmeier, "The (Israel) Stele of Merneptah (2.6)," *COS* 2.6:40–42.

knowledge of ancient history, however much historians try to fill them.[3] Could there be such a gap in the earlier history of the Philistines?

The "Sea Peoples" were known to the Egyptians a century before Ramesses III's reign, when some of them fought with Ramesses II and Merenptah. Altogether, there are eight names in Egyptian texts, but the pharaohs' lists vary and no one of them need be considered complete, like the biblical lists of the inhabitants of the promised land. In Canaan, and especially in the area of the five cities of the Philistines (Ashdod, Ashkelon, Ekron, Gaza, and Gath), clear signs of occupation by people with strong connections to the cultures of Cyprus and the Aegean are found in strata of the twelfth and eleventh centuries. Notable among them is the painted pottery often called Philistine ware plentiful at sites of the twelfth century BCE. May some predecessors of the Philistines have reached the shores of the Eastern Mediterranean earlier still? One name the Egyptians record among allies of the Libyans whom Merenptah defeated is the Lukka. That is not the earliest occurrence of the name, which is to be identified with the region of Lycia. At Byblos in the Obelisk Temple, early in the second millennium BCE, stood a stele inscribed in Egyptian hieroglyphs for a man with an Anatolian name, Kukun, who came from Lukka, a place later appearing in Hittite texts slightly older than Merenptah's.[4]

At several sites in the Levant, whole pots or fragments from the Minoan era of Crete, or derivatives of them, (ca. 1750–1550 BCE) have been found, from Ugarit, Beirut and Hazor to Tel Haror (possibly ancient Gerar).[5] At Tel Nami, north of Dor, seeds of a bean-like vegetable were excavated. They had been imported from the Minoan world and, because they required special knowledge to prepare to avoid giving diners a form of paralysis, they imply one or more persons from the Minoan area visiting Canaan, or a Canaanite traveling there to learn the skill.[6] Wall paintings in the style well known from the palace at Knossos in Crete were fashionable in the eastern Mediterranean about 1750–1550 BCE, indicating the presence of craftsmen able to design and create them. Fragmentary examples have been discovered at several sites: the famous figures of men leaping over bulls occur at Tell el-Dabʿa in the Eighteenth Dynasty, Cretan designs at Alalakh and parts of animals, birds, and buildings at Tell Kabri. A bull-leaping motif is part of relief decoration on a vase from the Old Hittite period, about the seventeenth century BCE from central Anatolia and was also engraved on cylinder seals that may be a little older, so it could be conjectured that the sport passed from the Near East to Crete. At Tel Haror in the ruins of a late Middle

---

3. See Alan R. Millard, "Ramesses Was Here . . . and Others, Too!," in *Ramesside Studies in Honour of K. A. Kitchen*, ed. Mark Collier and Steven R. Snape (Bolton: Rutherford, 2011), 305–12.

4. William F. Albright, "Dunand's New Byblos Volume: A Lycian at the Byblian Court," *BASOR* 155 (1959): 31–34.

5. Robert S. Merrillees, "The First Appearances of Kamares Ware in the Levant," *AeL* 13 (2003): 127–42; J. Alexander MacGillivray, "Lebanon and Protopalatial Crete: Pottery, Chronology and People," in *Interconnections in the Eastern Mediterranean: Lebanon in the Bronze and Iron Ages; Proceedings of the International Symposium, Beirut, 2008*, ed. Anne-Mari Maila Afeiche, Baal Hors série 6 (Beirut: Ministère de la Culture, Direction Générale des Antiquités, 2009), 187–93. Eliezer D. Oren mentioned "an elegant carinated chalice on a high foot with Minoan-type tall handles" beside Cypriot wares in a shrine, "Haror, Tel" in *The New Encyclopedia of Archaeological Excavations in the Holy Land*, ed. Ephraim Stern, Ayelet Lewinson-Gilboa, and Joseph Aviram, 4 vols. (Jerusalem: Israel Exploration Society, 1993), 2:581.

6. Mordecai E. Kislev, Michal Artzy, Marcus Ezra, "Import of an Aegean Food Plant to a Middle Bronze IIA Coastal Site in Israel," *Levant* 25 (1993): 145–54.

Bronze Age temple, a potsherd of Cretan origin was unearthed which was incised with three signs of the Minoan Linear A script. Although its purport is unclear—the script is not properly understood—for some reason, someone took the jar, or perhaps only the sherd, to southern Canaan where it was left.[7] These elements make it clear that there were contacts between Crete and the Levant long before the appearance of Philistines in Egyptian documents.[8] The ancient name for Crete was Kaphtor, which appears as an adjective, "Kaphtorite" in descriptions of clothing, shoes, and weapons in Babylonian tablets from Mari, shoes being sent from Mari to king Hammurabi of Babylon, and returned.[9] While biblical writers knew that name (Amos 9:7; Jer 47:4; Deut 2:23; Gen 10:14; 1 Chr 1:12), the Philistines might have been a related group, or their name may have replaced an older name, no longer current when the book of Genesis reached its final form, although place names in Gen 14 were given their later equivalents and Kiriath-Arba is identified as Hebron in Gen 23:2. If later writers imagined these episodes, either they deliberately distanced the patriarchal circumstances from the Philistines of later centuries by titling Abimelech "king" of Gath, avoiding the apparently Philistine word *seren* used later, and placing him in Gerar, which was not a main Philistine city later on. The king bore a West Semitic name, as did his counselor Ahuzzath (Gen 26:26), while Phicol, his commander, had a name that may be Anatolian (Gen 21:22; 26:26).[10]

Excluding the Genesis passages as anachronistic for the early second millennium BCE results from the widespread assumption that ancient writers imagined earlier times as reflections of their own. This was clearly expressed by Julius Wellhausen, "we attain to no historical knowledge of the patriarchs, but only of the time when the stories about them arose in the Israelite people; this latter age is here unconsciously projected, in its inner and outward features, into hoar antiquity, and is reflected there like a glorified mirage."[11] That has been repeated by others, among them, in 1999, Thomas L. Thompson who stated, "A biblical narrative reflects the historical context of its writing rather than the more distant past of its referent."[12] More recently the archaeologist Israel Finkelstein restated the position with regard to the Hebrew books as a whole, "biblical . . . authors lived centuries after many of the text-described events

---

7. Eliezer D. Oren et al., "A Minoan Graffito from Tel Haror (Negev, Israel)," *Cretan Studies* 5 (1996): 91–117; Gary A. Rendsburg, "On the Potential Significance of the Linear A Inscriptions Recently Excavated in Israel," *AuOr* 16 (1998): 289–91; Peter M. Day et al., "Petrographic Analysis of the Tel Haror Inscribed Sherd: Seeking Provenance Within Crete," *Aegaeum* 20 (1999): 191–96.

8. Constance von Rüden, "Minoanizing Paintings in the Eastern Mediterranean," in *The Encyclopedia of Ancient History*, ed. Roger S. Bagnall et al. (New York: Wiley & Sons, 2018); Tunç Sipahi, "New Evidence from Anatolia Regarding Bull-Leaping Scenes in the Art of the Aegean and the Near East," *Anatolica* 27 (2001): 107–25.

9. For a comprehensive survey, see Karen Polinger Foster, "Mari and the Minoans," *Groniek* 217 (2018) 343–62.

10. These observations have long been made. I am indebted to the essays by T. C. Mitchell "Philistia," in *Archaeology and Old Testament Study: Jubilee Volume of the Society for Old Testament Study, 1917–1967*, ed. D. Winton Thomas (Oxford: Clarendon, 1967), 404–27; and Kenneth A. Kitchen "The Philistines" in *Peoples of Old Testament Times*, ed. Donald J. Wiseman (Oxford: Clarendon, 1973), 53–78, for initial stimulus.

11. Julius Wellhausen, *Prolegomena to the History of Israel*, trans. J. Sutherland Black and Allan Menzies (Edinburgh: Black, 1885), 318–19.

12. Thomas L. Thompson, *The Mythic Past: Biblical Archaeology and the Myth of Israel* (London: Basic Books, 1999), 66, 67.

ostensibly took place and self-evidently promote the ideology and theology of their own time and place."[13] Yet the same attitude when taken to some Babylonian narratives has proved to be misleading.

One ancient literary text relates the victory of a king over rebel subjects. The text has no clear archaeological context, so the handwriting is the best clue to the time when the surviving copy was written. That proves to be several centuries after the king reigned, so the questions arise: Is the text, and others like it, legend, or folk-lore, or fiction created to glorify a king of the writer's time, or is it based on reality, on events that took place in the past? Making an analysis of the text in 1995, an eminent historian argued that it was a creation of the period when the copy was made, although incorporating elements from an earlier one. The king of the scribe's time, or his supporters, had it created to serve a political purpose. Reasons for his argument lay in various differences from the ancient king's own inscriptions. He found, for example, royal titles present that the king did not use and a predecessor's freeing of the eventual rebels to be unsubstantiated. That analysis followed a wider-ranging study that treated this and other narratives as propaganda for current rulers and their policies, offering past kings as models, while inventing their exploits to suit the situations of the day. Accordingly, this and related literary, poetic texts should not be used for reconstructing the history of the ancient king, rather, they can be used sources for the period in which they were written.[14]

Hardly had those views been published when a renewed examination of one of the actual inscriptions of the ancient king revealed that it contained the very titles that had been held to be wrong and a report of the episode of freeing the eventual rebels that had been rejected. The literary account is now seen to contain reliable information from the earlier time.

The king in question is Naram-Sin of Akkad, who ruled approximately 2213–2176 BCE. The text is The Great Revolt Against Naram-Sin, for which there are two copies made in the Old Babylonian period, around 1800–1600 BCE. One objection to the proposal that this was propaganda for a king in that era is the failure to fit its narratives clearly to an apt situation. The suggestions made have some plausibility, yet they are purely hypothetical; they have no factual basis. When the text is placed beside documents contemporary with the events it describes, it is obvious that they have much in common. In fact, a small fragment from the period of Naram-Sin's dynasty bears a few lines of the same story.[15]

One Assyriologist who argued that the text about Naram-Sin was created long after his death, claimed historians should "examine texts with a view to learning not

---

13. Address to a joint session of the American Schools of Oriental Research and the Society of Biblical Literature, Boston, November 2017; http://www.asor.org/anetoday/2018/01/reflections-archaeology-biblical-historiography.

14. Mario Liverani, "Model and Actualization: The Kings of Akkad in the Historical Tradition," in *Akkad The First World Empire: Structure, Ideology, Tradition*, ed. Mario Liverani (Padua: Sargon, 1993), 41–67.

15. See Timothy Potts, "Reading the Sargonic 'Historical-Literary' Tradition: Is There a Middle Course? (Thoughts on The Great Revolt against Naram-Sin)," in *Historiography in the Cuneiform World, Proceedings of the XLVe Rencontre Assyriologique Internationale*, ed. Tvi Abusch, et al. (Bethesda, MD: CDL, 2001), 391–408; William W. Hallo, "New Directions in Historiography (Mesopotamia and Israel)," and "Polymnia and Clio," in *The World's Oldest Literature: Studies in Sumerian Belles-Lettres*, CHANE 35 (Leiden: Brill, 2010), 431–51, 453–69.

what they tell us about the events they purport to describe, but what they tell us about themselves and the reasons for describing these events in a given way."[16] While he is surely right that texts should be examined to find out what they reveal about their composition, that should not preclude examining them to learn what they tell about the events they purport to describe. If that attitude were adopted across ancient history, very little ancient history could be written, for the context of composition need not determine the context of the content. This does not assume a credulous approach to ancient texts. Rather, they have to be analyzed carefully in the light of all available knowledge. Such analysis has to avoid imposing modern concepts on them, expecting chronological order, or dismissing assertions of supernatural intervention, starting with a "hermeneutic of suspicion" attempting to seek only what interests of the writers the text served, attempting, on the other hand, to understand the mentality of their authors. The examples given demonstrate the dangers of treating the texts in too negatively a critical way.

The duty of the historian to assess information received is at least as old as Herodotus. The "Father of History" compiled his work about the Persian War against the Greeks in the fifth century BCE, and included many anecdotes that have little relevance to the war. Mingling with the battles and political intrigues are details of impressive sights he had seen, of strange customs and wonders others had told him. Herodotus frequently states that he relied on what he was told, sometimes commenting that he does not believe the report, for example, the conveyance of water through a leather pipe in western Arabia (book 3.9). He may give more than one account of something, with a note of which he prefers, such as differing explanations of the oracle of Dodona (book 2.54-57). Not surprisingly, writers ancient and modern have impugned *The Histories* of Herodotus as containing little more than gossip. Today Herodotus is heard with more respect. His accounts of Scythian kings buried with retainers and numerous horses, or his description of Babylon are accepted as valuable sources of information because archaeological discoveries have largely substantiated them.[17] Even his more extraordinary tales have become credible in the light of research and discovery. In book 3.102–104, he tells of large ants in India that, as they burrow, throw out sand containing gold dust. A classical scholar called that "a remarkable tall story" in 1970, despite it having been clearly established as reflecting fact long before. The "ants" are marmots and the region is the Karakorum mountains of Baltistan.[18] Numerous other examples could be presented where authors in the distant or more recent past offered reports that were to be discounted in modern times and then shown to be credible.

If there were Philistines at Gerar in the Middle Bronze Age, they could only be identifiable through written records, in the same way as the Philistines at the end of the Late Bronze Age are only identifiable because of written texts. Pottery and other artifacts at certain sites can show connections with Cyprus and the Aegean but cannot reveal the

---

16. Steve Tinney, "A New Look at Naram-Sin and the 'Great Rebellion,'" *JCS* 47 (1995): 2.

17. For a recent discovery of the tomb of a chieftain with a woman, thirty-three other people, and fourteen horses, see *Ancient-Origins.net* 16 February 2016, https://www.ancient-origins.net/news-history -archaeology/examining-stunning-treasures-and-macabre-slaughter-siberian-valley-kings-020745; for Babylon, see O. E. Ravn, *Herodotus' Description of Babylon* (Copenhagen: Nordisk, 1942).

18. See A. W. Lawrence, *Herodotus: Rawlinson's Translation Revised and Annotated* (London: Nonesuch Press, 1935), 308–10; and *The Times*, 4th December, 1996, 12.

names of their makers or owners, or the identity of any group they belonged to. The Minoan-style pottery scattered across Middle Bronze Age Levantine sites may indicate no more than trading links, but the beans at Tel Nami and the Linear A graffito at Tel Haror could point to a foreign presence in those places. At Gerar king Abimelech, with his Semitic name, might employ foreign, Philistine, mercenaries, or rule a few migrant families; the narratives do not expect their readers to envisage hordes like those the forces of Ramesses III faced. If there were a few Philistines in Gerar in the Middle Bronze Age, their names would not be expected in the Execration Texts that place rulers with West Semitic names in Ashkelon later known as Philistine (*ḥâl-yaqim*, *mura(n)*).[19] Were it not for the El Amarna letters the presence of a few Indo-European rulers in Canaanite towns would be untraceable (e.g., Shuwardata, Intaruta).[20]

Beside the questions of ancient writers' ability to report long-past events and gaps in surviving written documents, gaps in material remains should also be reckoned with. A few decades ago the journal *Levant* published a detailed study of "The Small Cuboid Incense-Burner of the Ancient Near East."[21] The objects are found across the Near East at sites of the first millennium BCE and continuing into the Roman period. The author observed three examples from Ur that the excavator, (Sir) Leonard Woolley, had placed in the second millennium and suggested that their date be lowered to agree with others from the Neo-Babylonian or Persian periods. Whether Woolley's dating is right, or not, while the study was in preparation, numerous specimens of such incense burners from the second millennium, even as early as its opening centuries, were being found at sites on the middle Euphrates.[22] Knowing that almost all of these small cuboid incense-burners belonged to the first millennium led to the wrong assumption that every one was made in that era.

Every crumb of information from the past deserves critical scrutiny and that should be equally as positive as negative. Biblical commentators have long approached the texts from a negatively critical standpoint, producing negative results, claiming that without independent support the statements of the texts cannot be accepted. Nevertheless, discovery after discovery points to the accuracy of biblical narrators and the reality of the circumstances they portray. Jim Hoffmeier has illustrated this effectively in his books *Israel in Egypt* and *Ancient Israel in Sinai*, dealing with situations for which there are next to no written records apart from the Hebrew Bible.[23] These paragraphs attempt to add a little weight in favor of the patriarchal biographies as a tribute to a long-standing and valued scholar and friend.

---

19. Anson F. Rainey in *The Sacred Bridge: Carta's Atlas of the Biblical World*, ed. Anson F. Rainey and R. Steven Notley (Jerusalem: Carta, 2006), 52, 58.

20. Richard S. Hess, *Amarna Personal Names*, ASOR Dissertation Series 9 (Winona Lake; IN: Eisenbrauns, 1993), 87, 88, 151.

21. Michael O'Dwyer Shea, "The Small Cuboid Incense-Burner of the Ancient Near East," *Levant* 15 (1983): 76–109.

22. See Alan R. Millard, "The Small Cuboid Incense Burners: A Note on Their Age," *Levant* 16 (1984): 172–73; Wolfgang Zwickel gave an extensive survey in *Räucherkult und Räuchergeräte: Exegetische und archäologische Studien zum Räucheropfer im Alten Testament*, OBO 97 (Fribourg: Universitätsverlag; Göttingen: Vandenhoeck & Ruprecht, 1990), 62–69.

23. James Hoffmeier, *Israel in Egypt: The Evidence for the Authenticity of the Exodus Tradition* (Oxford: Oxford University Press, 1997); Hoffmeier, *Ancient Israel in Sinai : The Evidence for the Authenticity of the Wilderness Tradition* (Oxford: Oxford University Press, 2005).

CHAPTER 17

Writing Trauma: Ipuwer and the Curation of Cultural Memory

Ellen Morris

IT IS MY PLEASURE to dedicate this essay to Jim Hoffmeier, a cherished friend and a scholar whose work on Egypt's eastern border fortresses continues to be fundamental to my own understanding of pharaonic imperialism. For this contribution, I've chosen to write on another subject close to his heart, namely the potential of narratives that are often dismissed as "literary" or "folkloric" to yield valuable information about Egypt's society and its history. In particular, this essay—which focuses on the embedding of cultural trauma in social memory—is intended to compliment his own consideration, in his book *Israel in Egypt* (Hoffmeier 1997), of the role of famine in intensifying intercultural contact.

The literary work known as the The Admonitions of an Egyptian Sage survived in only a single manuscript, dated to the Nineteenth Dynasty, the verso of which bore a hymn to the god Amun. Since its original decipherment, the text has frustrated scholars on almost every level. Its date, purpose, and historical worth are much contested. Minority opinions place it as early as the immediate aftermath of the Old Kingdom or as late as the Eighteenth Dynasty, while current consensus dates it linguistically to the late Twelfth or the Thirteenth Dynasty (Parkinson 2002, 50; Enmarch 2008, 4–25; Stauder 2013, 509). Whether this date would be coeval with its original composition, however, is not at all certain. Ipuwer, the text's narrator—who will here, for simplicity's sake, be referred to also as its author—was remembered as an overseer of singers (*jmj-r ḥsjw*).[1] If the original composer was indeed, first and foremost, a singer, it is likely that the work survived in oral form long before it was transcribed.

The text's date and genre, of course, have bearing on whether Egypt's frightening descent into chaos—about which Ipuwer admonishes the Lord of All—should be seen as relevant to the First Intermediate Period, the Second Intermediate Period, or to neither. Indeed, many scholars suggest that the work is essentially ahistorical and represents a theodic "reproach to god." Even the identity of Ipuwer's interlocutor is enigmatic, as the Lord of All might be the creator god, the king, or an intentionally obfuscating conflation of the two. A thorough discussion of all these debates may be found in Roland Enmarch's (2008) foundational study of the text, *A World Upturned: Commentary on and Analysis of The Dialogue of Ipuwer and the Lord of All*.

As if these points of confusion weren't enough, the text's evocation of chaos and misery seems to serve no discernable purpose. Unlike references to fear, hunger, and

---

1. The Egyptians often indulged in pseudepigraphy. Thus, even if Ipuwer was in fact a composer of note, there is still no guarantee that he would have been responsible for the work attributed to him.

strife in the tombs and steles of individuals who lived through the First Intermediate Period (Vandier 1936; Moreno García 1997, 3–92), the text does not paint a picture of chaos in order that its author might be seen as an effective force for good. Throughout, Ipuwer remains but a passive spectator. Nor does the narrative advertise the coming of a future king, who would bring order to chaos (as was the case for the Prophecies of Neferty), or else offer a royal apologetic and road for recovery (as in The Teaching for King Merikare). Finally, unlike The Lamentations of Khakheperre-sonbe and The Man Who Was Weary of Life, the text does not serve as an exploration of the troubled psyche of its narrator. Rather, for the entirety of the text, Ipuwer gazes outward onto a present that he depicts as unremittingly bleak and essentially unrecognizable.

Given the absence of any redemptive message, it is extremely difficult to understand the text's purpose or the nature of its reception. For a work whose purported author was enumerated among the canonical literary greats, as the Egyptians remembered them (Enmarch 2008, 26), Ipuwer's admonitions seem never to have found a home in scribal schools. At a loss for how to view the text, most scholars in recent years have denied it any historical relevance whatsoever. Richard Parkinson (2002, 207), for example, states that "the contradictions that express chaos . . . signal the fictional nature of the text, while the elaborate use of wordplay foregrounds its character as a rhetorical tour de force." For his part, Enmarch (2008, 39) concludes similarly that

> this sort of lament does not portray real contemporary chaos, or even describe a specific dramatic situation. . . . Instead these laments form a schematic anti-ideal "inverted world" (verkehrte Welt) that elaborates the topos of order versus chaos. The setting of Ipuwer is vague, with no clear references to specific historical events, emphasizing the lament descriptions' timeless relevance.

There is, however, another way of interpreting the text, and that is that the chaos described by Ipuwer is timeless only inasmuch as the societal suffering occasioned by the most ecologically devastating famines virtually always conforms to a broadly recognizable set of symptoms.

In this essay, I seek to bolster a hypothesis formulated by Fekri Hassan (2007) in "Droughts, Famine and the Collapse of the Old Kingdom: Re-reading Ipuwer," namely that the terrifying transformation of Ipuwer's world was wrought by famine. To support his claim, he presented ecological evidence for a pronounced environmental downturn at the end of the Old Kingdom, which has since been substantiated by a wide variety of other studies (cf. Arz, Lamy, Pätzold 2006, 432, 439–40; Marshall et al. 2011, 147, 159; Manning et al. 2014, 401, 414; Welc and Marks 2014, 124). In addition to arguments concerning the dating and composition of the text, Hassan also briefly alluded to catastrophic Nilotic famines that took place in 963 CE and 1200–1202 CE in order to make his case that The Admonitions of an Egyptian Sage faithfully represented the breakdown of social order typical in times of famine.

The effects of severe famines have been well documented throughout the world, and although each bears its own culture-historical peculiarities, societal responses to famines tend to follow quite similar trajectories. Unlike food crises, which may be managed via careful rationing and the distribution of grain from central stores, famines are—due to natural and cultural causes—intractable. Short in duration and mercifully infrequent, they are nonetheless singularly traumatic events set off in stark relief from the comfortingly familiar life that precedes and postdates them. Indeed, according to historian David Arnold (1988), the bewilderment and terror occasioned by famines must be counted among their most defining characteristics.

> Famine signifies an exceptional (if periodically recurring) event, a collective catastrophe of such magnitude as to cause social and economic dislocation.... It was a multiple crisis of subsistence, survival and order. The more protracted and intense the crisis the more the normal order of things collapsed and gave way to all that was abnormal and horrific. (Arnold 1988, 6, 19)

It is the aim of this essay, then, to take Ipuwer's words seriously and to place the chaos described by him in conversation with records of famines from other periods in Egypt's history, from other countries, and with the work of scholars who focus on trauma and social memory.

Writing Trauma

The memories of survivors of trauma are notoriously unreliable. In his book *Writing History, Writing Trauma*, Dominick LaCapra (2001) discusses the difficulties historians face in evaluating truth claims embedded in narratives of survivors that are often supercharged with emotion. By way of example, he asks: If an Auschwitz survivor speaks vividly of witnessing four chimneys go up in flames, when historians know that only a single chimney met this fate in an uprising of inmates, should this invalidate her entire narrative? Or, should one conclude, as does LaCapra, that the survivor's retelling

> may, to a greater or lesser extent, be (or not be) an accurate enactment, reconstruction, or representation of what actually occurred in the past. It may involve distortion, disguise, and other permutations relating to processes of imaginative transformation and narrative shaping, as well as perhaps repression, denial, dissociation, and foreclosure. But these issues have a bearing only on certain aspects of her account and could not invalidate it in its entirety. (LaCapra 2001, 88–89)

This problem of discerning the effect of emotion and distortion on truthful narratives was further complicated for LaCapra by the book *Fragments: Memories of a Wartime Childhood* (Wilkomirski 1997), written by a man who claimed to have spent his childhood in a Nazi death camp. For many survivors and Holocaust experts who read it, the narrative rang true, and the points of confusion were attributed to the author's age at internment and to the long-term effects of trauma. Other particularly disturbing details, such as the tiny babies that he reported had chewed their fingers to the bone, gave pause. Yet, as LaCapra noted, events that were in equal measure surreal and horrific abounded in the camps and "what is plausible or implausible in events of the Holocaust is notoriously difficult to determine" (LaCapra 2001, 33).

So, too, it is with first-hand famine narratives, which are also often inextricably entangled in emotion and suffused with the macabre (Arnold 1988, 17). Accounts of cannibalism, for instance, have been associated with many of the most desperate famines. In some cases, these claims—especially with regard to necrophage—have been found credible. More often, it seems, rumor transmogrified into truth, and such reports served to emphasize that in this new hellish version of reality there was nothing humane left in humanity (Tuchman 1978, 24; Edgerton-Tarpley 2008, 211–33; Ó Gráda 2009, 63–68; Herrmann 2011, 57–58). Claims of cannibalism made by Ankhtifi and Hekanakht—two men who lived through separate periods of low Niles that bookended the First Intermediate Period—are often rightly viewed with suspicion, as in both cases the practice supposedly occurred in a region that did not have the benefit of the narrator's patronage. Yet, perhaps this abrupt dismissal misses the point, for references to cannibalism, true or not, may serve as an effective barometer for the severity of a crisis. Despite the fact that a great many instances of food insecurity are known from Medieval Egypt, for instance, chroniclers make reference to cannibalism sparingly. Such charges generally occur only with regard to famines known from other lines of evidence to have been extraordinarily devastating, for example, those of 1064–1065, 1199–1201, 1294–1296, 1402–1404; 1694–1695, 1790–1792 (al-Baghdādi 1965, 56r–59l; al-Maqrīzī 1994, 38, 41; Raphael 2013, 71–72, 85, 91; Sabra 2000, 153; Hassan 1997, 11; Mikhail 2011, 217).

Ipuwer—who, like the author of *Fragments: Memories of a Wartime Childhood*, may or may not have witnessed tragedy and who, like him, has been accused of a certain amount of "overwriting"—is uncharacteristically silent on the subject of cannibalism. There is no question, however, that much of his narrative is at once both hyperbolic and vague, as Enmarch observes. Does this, however, invalidate its claim to truth, especially as these two traits also characterize the narratives of survivors of famines as well as those of their direct descendants?

When Cormac Ó Gráda, a historian of the Great Irish Famine of 1847, for instance, compared contemporaneous accounts of this famine with the compilations of individual and societal memories collected in the 1930s and 1940s, he was impressed with the extent to which these memories were selective. Accounts nearly always lacked specifics and were tales of hardships that had fallen upon others. In assessing these materials Ó Gráda (2001, 130–31) concluded,

> Asking folklore or oral tradition to bridge a gap of a century or more and generate reliable evidence on the famine was asking a lot. The long gap between the event and the collection of the evidence allowed ample time for confusion, forgetting and obfuscation.... And yet the folklore record at its best is vivid, harrowing, telling and, sometimes, intriguing and puzzling. Rejecting what it has on offer would be going too far.

As will be discussed toward the end of this essay, first-hand narratives and folk accounts of famines both tend to be composed after a significant amount of time has elapsed; thus, the two share many of the same stylistic traits.

In the analysis that follows, those elements of Ipuwer's narrative that bear a strong resemblance to eyewitness accounts of famine are highlighted. In many cases, it will be seen that Ipuwer's descriptions of the harbingers and horrors of starvation do not, in fact, appear overblown. It will also be argued that some details in Ipuwer's narrative suggest an origin in observation rather than extrapolation. By the same token, however, this analysis also endeavors to make note of those aspects of Ipuwer's text that either omit well-attested aspects of famines or else place a seemingly idiosyncratic emphasis on particular elements of them. Finally, the essay ends by revisiting the subject of why trauma is written and how it tends to be received.

The Onset of Crisis

It is here asserted that the litany of social ills Ipuwer describes ultimately arose as a result of famine. In his narrative, not only were customary dietary staples like barley, bread loaves, and sycamore figs nowhere in evidence, but people suffered from a hunger so overwhelming that it drove adults to steal food from children and to seek out other nourishment formerly deemed fit only for birds or swine (Ipuwer 5.1–5.2; 6.1–6.3; 16.1–16.3). In famines, as attested cross-culturally, the exploitation of starvation foods plays a central role (Arnold 1988, 79–80; Azeze 1998, 63–64; Ó Gráda 2009, 73–78). During analogous crises in Egypt, such as those that occurred in 1064–1065, 1199–1201, and 1294–1296 CE, for instance, people resorted to the consumption of dogs, cats, carrion, the excrement of animals, garbage, and even, purportedly, human corpses (al-Baghdādī 1965, 55*l*; al-Maqrīzī 1994, 38; Sabra 2000, 143, 167; Hassan 1997, 11; Mikhail 2011, 217; Raphael 2013, 85, 91; Davis 2017, 113). It is likewise characteristic of the most advanced states of famine that food-sharing networks—even among close family members—finally break down. Indeed, relief workers operating in places as diverse as Austria and Uganda have reported the necessity of enacting measures to prevent mothers from consuming rations intended for their own children (Dirks 1980, 30).[2]

In Ipuwer's narrative there is no mention of the failure of the Nile. Mentuhotep son of Hepi, by contrast, made reference to the "little inundation" that caused his province hardship during the First Intermediate Period (Bell 1971, 16). Likewise, in the Prophecies of Neferty, set in the same era, it was stated that "the river of Egypt is empty, and the waters may be crossed on foot. Men search for water that the ships may sail, but the watercourse has become a river bank" (Simpson 2003, 216). Ipuwer's omission, however, is not unusual. In her study of pharaonic famine texts, Barbara Bell observed that low Niles are most often referred to elliptically in Egyptian texts, through references to sandbanks, hunger, and dry conditions. This reticence, she suggests, was perhaps due to "some religious taboo, or at least a superstitious disinclination about speaking critically of the Nile" (Bell 1971, 13). Ipuwer evidently felt no compunction, however, about describing the effects of drought on land that the inundation had not reached. The desert, he said, was throughout the land, and all that grew had been transformed into brushwood (Ipuwer 3.1, 13.2).

Droughts that struck North Africa and the Eastern Mediterranean often happened independently of low Niles, but when the two cooccurred the scale of suffering in

2. A couplet from an Ethiopian famine song laments, "Ah, Year Seventy-Seven, I wish I was not born! My own mother snatching away, the scraps of food in my hand" (Azeze 1998, 59–60).

Egypt was particularly intense. In 1181, for instance, the historian Aḥmad ibn ʿAlī Taqī al-Dīn al-Maqrīzī wrote that "the Nile dried up so that it became but a ford. . . . Numerous islands of sands formed" (Raphael 2013, 81), while again in 1201 it was said that the riverbed of the Nile had dried up entirely (al-Maqrīzī 1994, 41). John Russell Young, who visited Egypt during the notoriously devastating drought of 1877–1879, likewise described the effects of this deadly combination on the land, stating, "Today the fields are parched and brown, and cracked. The irrigating ditches are dry. You see stumps of the last season's crop. But with the exception of a few clusters of the castor bean and some weary, drooping date palms, the earth gives forth no fruit. A gust of sand blows over the plain and adds to the somberness of the scene" (Davis 2017, 3–4).

Droughts and Displacements

Although the author of The Admonitions of an Egyptian Sage paid far less attention to the infiltration of Easterners into the Nile Delta due to drought than did, for instance, the authors of The Prophecies of Neferty or The Teaching for King Merikare, such incursions were nonetheless a subject of concern. Tribes of the desert, Ipuwer states, had become Egyptians everywhere. Bowmen had settled, and foreign people now not only lived in the delta, but they had also begun to take up its trades (Ipuwer 1.9; 2.2; 4.5–8). Such large-scale incursions of climate refugees were, in fact, typical of situations in which region-wide droughts occurred prior to (or in the absence of) Nile failure, as the honoree of this volume has discussed at length with respect to pharaonic Egypt (Hoffmeier 1997, 52–69).

There exist ample parallels in medieval records as well. In the severe drought of 1294–1296, for instance, it is estimated that thirty to fifty thousand Libyans from Cyrenaica migrated to the Nile Valley just in advance of a catastrophic failure of the inundation (al-Maqrīzī 1994, 43; Sabra 2000, 141–42). Dramatic rises in immigration during hard times, whether occurring in the First Intermediate Period, the end of the Late Bronze Age, or today, tend to result in a xenophobic backlash as well as in promises by leaders to combat such infiltrations and put preventative measures in place. It is thus significant that one of the few preserved statements of the Lord of All involves a pledge to do better in this respect (Ipuwer 14.12–15.3). So too, Neferty prophesies, will Amenemhet I stop such infiltrations, while Merikare's father enumerates his successes in this regard with pride (Simpson 2003, 161–62, 220; Morris 2017).

If the immigration of foreigners to Egypt is entirely typical of times of drought, the most severe Nile failure tended to prompt movement in the opposite direction, as occurred in 1199–1201, 1402–1404, and 1449–1452 (al-Baghdādi 1965, 55l, 61r-l; Sabra 2000, 153, 160). The author of Ipuwer is silent on this subject, perhaps because this option would have been far more difficult during the pharaonic period than during medieval times, when an investment in infrastructure greatly facilitated travel out of Egypt by land and sea. Internal movement within the country, however, should have been a phenomenon worthy of note, as it was for ancient observers such as Ity of Gebelein and Ankhtify of Moʿalla. Indeed the latter remarked that the entire country had been transformed into locusts, journeying northward and southward in search of food (Bell 1971, 8–10)!

When famines were localized, people moved from dearth to plenty (Sabra 2000, 167). As a bedouin man explained it to former US president Ulysses S. Grant in 1877, during the latter's poorly timed pleasure trip, "The Nile has been bad, and when the Nile is bad, calamity comes and the people go away to other villages" (Davis 2017, 3). In times of severe famine, however, it became common for villagers to move toward the cities, where centralized stores of grain might be found in greater density (al-Baghdādi 1965, 55*l*, 60*l*; al-Maqrīzī 1994, 41; Sabra 2000, 160; Mikhail 2011, 217; Raphael 2013, 57, 66). Such "unusual wandering"—especially toward cities—is, in fact, characteristic of famines wherever they occur (Dirks 1980, 27; Ó Gráda 2009, 81–89). While Ipuwer's statement that fine linen was now used by Egyptians to make bedouin-style tents (Ipuwer 10.1–2) may hint at such internal displacement, the phenomenon received less attention from him than it likely deserved.

Property Theft and Banditry

Yet another of the notable silences in The Admonitions of an Egyptian Sage is the unrest caused by the rising price of food. In one of the few oblique references to this phenomenon, Ipuwer laments, "Riches are throughout the land, (but) ladies of the house say, 'Would that we had something we might eat!'" (Ipuwer 3.2–3.3; Enmarch 2008, 224). As hunger worsens in a famine, the acquisition of food increasingly becomes a life or death matter. Given that prices tended to rise directly upon even the forecast of an insufficient flood, such inflation in the cost of food served both as a harbinger and as a concomitant cause of famine (Sabra 2000, 137).

No records of prices have survived from the First Intermediate Period, but inflation may be indirectly signaled via an epidemic of tomb robbery, as also cooccurred with spikes in the price of grain in Egypt's Twentieth Dynasty. At that time, as the ecological crisis that marked the end of the Late Bronze Age worsened, authorities cracked down on a rash of tomb robbery in Thebes, generating a tremendous paper trail. According to Papyrus B.M. 10052, one woman told authorities that she had utilized one deben (ca. 91 g) of silver from her husband's share of the ill-gotten gains to buy grain. Another woman, caught with loot in her possession, explained it away stating, "I got it in exchange for barley in the year of the hyenas, when there was a famine" (Kemp 1991, 243). While such exchanges sound improbable and could be conceived of as attempts on the part of the thieves to garner sympathy from their judges, a tale survived of a woman who was unable to sell a thousand dinar necklace for flour during the famine that lasted from 1064–1072 (al-Maqrīzī 1994, 38). Certainly, there is no doubt that relative worth in times of famine is radically reassessed.

If inflation presages famine, so too does crime. Thus, Indian Famine Codes considered an uptick in crime as one of the early warning signs of famine, and statistics kept in Ireland during the Great Famine demonstrate that rates of burglary and robbery quintupled (Ó Gráda 2009, 52–53). Perhaps because Ipuwer claimed allegiance with the erstwhile elite, he expands at great length on what he viewed as an epidemic of crime. Both Ipuwer and the Lord of All, for instance, decry the practice of tomb robbery (Ipuwer 7.2; 16.13–14), a subject also discussed as emblematic of the First Intermediate Period in The Teaching for King Merikare (Simpson 2003, 159). Crimes against the living, however, were of even greater concern to Ipuwer. Robbers, he said, did not hesitate to steal cattle and other valuables from the rich, and the owners of property were even on occasion forced to defend it from rooftops and guardhouses (Ipuwer 1.1; 2.2–3; 2.9; 7.5; 8.3–4; 8.9; 13.3). Indeed, this last observation is reminiscent of 'Abd al-Baghdādi's (1965, 65r) eyewitness report that in the great famine of 1199–1201 "it was necessary to fortify entrances, and salaried guardians were employed to guard property." Perhaps not surprisingly, even gardens, in times of famine, required guarding (Dirks 1980, 29).

It was not solely the rich, however, who were preyed upon as unrest grew in pace with the worsening crisis. Farmers could be set upon in their fields (Ipuwer 1.4; 2.1), and travel too was dangerous. Bandits lay in wait for passersby, stealing their belongings and not infrequently murdering them in the process (Ipuwer 5.11–12; 13.4–5). "Look, the land has knotted together in gangs," Ipuwer laments (Ipuwer 7.7). "If three men go on the road, (only) two are found! The many slay the few" (Ipuwer 12.13–14). Everyone, it seemed, was afraid (Ipuwer 2.9; 5.7; 9.14–10.1; 15.14–16.1). Such a deteriorated state of security is common to famine narratives in Medieval Egypt as well. Writing again of the famine that he witnessed in 1199–1201, al-Baghdādi stated that no single route was safe from murders. Indeed, captains would even offer discounted passage "and then butcher their passengers and divide their effects" (al-Baghdādi 1965, 60r). So too, al-Maqrīzī (1994, 37) stated of the famine that occurred from 1064–1072, "The lands remained uncultivated and fear prevailed. Land and sea routes became unsafe, and travel became impossible without a large escort; otherwise one would be exposed to danger."

Social Banditry, Strikes, Riots, and Revolution

Bandits are rarely, if ever, a homogenous group. Many were no doubt driven to crime out of desperation. Other bands of thugs, the Lord of All implies, may have consisted of former troops gone rogue, as indeed is frequently attested in weak and failed states alike (Ipuwer 14.14–15.1; White 2013, 151–52, 168). There is, however, yet another class of bandits that would certainly have been of concern to a member of the old guard elite, like Ipuwer, and that is social bandits. Such men, as Eric Hobsbawm (1959, 13–29) has famously explicated, saw their actions as righting social wrongs perpetrated by the rich against the poor—a situation that may well have felt more urgent and justified as access to food increasingly became a life and death matter.

Social bandits, for instance, were especially active between Sohag and Girga during the 1877–1879 famine that killed more than ten thousand people in Upper Egypt. At this time the government, despite being fully aware of the suffering of the peasantry, had continued to overtax farmers, often beating them and confiscating their property when the deteriorating ecological situation meant that they were unable to meet their obligations. Peasant protest at such treatment led the government to send two thousand troops into the region, at which point fifty or sixty individuals headed for the hills. Those that fled their villages raised the call of social revolt, employing "a rhetoric of social justice, vowing to unite those peasants oppressed by the state's overtaxation and brutal treatment of its subjects" (Cole 1999, 89). While relatively few peasants found the resolve to join this band, local sympathies were with them, and their activities rendered travel in the region unsafe for government officials and their sympathizers (Cole 1999, 87–89).

Studies of famine narratives reveal that in addition to the ubiquitous victims, tales are frequent of both heroes and villains. The former acted to alleviate suffering while the latter caused it (Edgerton-Tarpley 2008, 79–89).[3] Social inequality among the haves and have-nots is never more starkly visible than during a famine, and it is notable that in virtually all of the eyewitness accounts of famine from ancient Egypt, presented on tomb walls and commemorative stele, members of the elite were at great pains to emphasize their status as heroes. These men claimed to have utilized grain stores to nourish those in their district first and those in neighboring districts second. They forgave tax debt, and when they could not prevent deaths they subsidized funerals.[4] They ensured peace by rationing water for the fields and invested in agricultural improvements so as to maximize what harvests there were to be had in those "years of misery" and "painful years of distress." When forced by necessity, they imported grain and facilitated its equitable distribution. As important as what these self-proclaimed heroes did do, however, was what they didn't. They didn't utilize their positions of strength to dispossess others of their houses, fields, or property. Nor did they seize a man's daughter—which was perhaps a reference to the radically increased prevalence of slavery and prostitution in times of famine (Vandier 1936; Bell 1971, 8–17; Moreno García 1997, 3–92).[5]

What is fascinating and absolutely unexpected, then, considering Ipuwer's presumed status as a member of the elite, is that nowhere in his exceedingly long descriptive text do heroes make an appearance. Neither Ipuwer, nor the remaining owners of wealth, nor the Lord of All step in to alleviate the sufferings of those less fortunate than themselves. Indeed, as even Ipuwer himself admitted, "Officials do not associate with their people, who cry out(?)" (Ipuwer. 2.5; Enmarch 2008, 222).

In the narratives of historic food crises that never escalated to the status of famines and in other tales of heroic but doomed efforts at combatting ecological calamities, the quick and efficient role of the governing elites in remitting taxes and in redistributing grain to the poor was absolutely essential (Shoshan 1980, 463–66; Ó Gráda 2009, 195–202). Indeed, in *Poverty and Charity in Medieval Islam: Mamuk Egypt, 1250–1517*, Adam Sabra (2000, 141) asserts that the "message [of famine narratives] is clear: the Mamluk ruler enjoys legitimacy by virtue of his care for his subjects." Thus, almost certainly, the extravagant quantities of grain stockpiled by the king, temple officials, and the elite in ancient Egypt were only tolerated because of a governing moral economy that mandated the sharing of such stores in times of need. If pharaonic society was by and large built on a nested system of patron-client relationships, as Mark Lehner (2000)

3. Along these lines, the sociologist Pitrim Sorokin (1942, 14) in his "Law of Diversification and Polarization" postulated that disaster has the power both to bring out the very best of people or, conversely, the very worst.

4. In cases when the death toll was not yet unmanageable, elites in later famines also occasionally subsidized funerals (Sabra 2000, 147).

5. The author of Ipuwer barely touches upon two of the most common strategies of survival in famines: prostitution and the selling of oneself or one's family members into slavery (see Edgerton-Tarpley 2008, 192–97; Ó Gráda 2009, 56–60). The single exception is perhaps his observation "[Lo]ok, rich ladies and great ladies, owners of riches, are giving away their children (in return) for beds" (Ipuwer 8.7–8.8).

and Barry Kemp (2012, 163) have recently argued, then the most seemingly stale of all elite boasts—that of regularly giving bread to the hungry—must have been treated by workers and dependents in times of real hunger not as a platitude but as an obligation.

In an ideal world, then, patrons and people in positions of power would step up to their duty to provide for the needy in times of famine. Cross-culturally, however, famines often brought out the worst in elites, many of whom took to hoarding rather than sharing both to ensure their own well-being and also to potentially turn a profit, as prices for the commodity they commanded had now skyrocketed (al-Maqrīzī 1994, 39–40, 43; Sabra 2000, 136–37, 145, 159; Raphael 2013, 60, 63, 66). In such cases, laborers were let go or else were woefully stinted in their wages (Arnold 1988, 82–83). Thus, it came to pass in Ipuwer's narrative—as in many famines no doubt both before and since—that the poor were forced to take matters into their own hands.

When wages were cut, ceased, or were simply rendered insufficient to purchase basic foodstuffs, the response on the part of laborers was often to refuse to work altogether. The first-known labor strike occurred in the Twentieth Dynasty, during the period of inflation and rampant tomb robbery discussed above. Ipuwer's observations that "washermen have not agreed(?) to carry <their(?)> loads" and that "all craftsmen . . . have (ceased) to work" (Ipuwer 1.2, 9.6; Enmarch 2008, 221, 232), however, suggest that such tactics were not, in fact, unprecedented. Craftworkers and wage laborers have historically numbered among the most vulnerable in times of crisis (Sabra 2000, 146–47, 161–62). In the famine that occurred between 1199 and 1201, for instance, the making of crafts ceased altogether (al-Maqrīzī 1994, 42). Moreover, out of the nine hundred makers of rush mats in Cairo, al-Baghdādi (1965, 64r) reported that no more than fifteen made it out of that particular ecological disaster alive!

The worst famines have two stages: anger and despondency.[6] The former, which requires more strength, occurs when hunger pains are acute enough to provoke panic, but not so acute as to be physically debilitating. Historic accounts of famine in Egypt are filled with references to food riots, which frequently targeted granaries and bakeries; these occurred, for instance, during the crises of 1294–1296, 1336–1337, 1415–1416, 1694–1695, 1784–1787 (al-Maqrīzī 1994, 45; Sabra 2000, 144, 155; Mikhail 2011, 217–18). Indeed, drawing on his own studies of Mamluk grain riots as well as the work of George Rudé on French and English equivalents in the Eighteenth and Nineteenth centuries, Boaz Shoshan (1980, 460) concludes that

> the moral economy gave crowds what might be called legitimacy to riot whenever their expectations concerning grain supplies were not met. . . . Seen in this light, grain riots cannot be regarded merely as an impulsive reaction to dearths and famines, but rather they appear as a coherent form of political action—a critique of rulers.

Ipuwer, too, reports on a food riot that had turned violent: "the storehouse is razed, its guard stretched out on the ground" (Ipuwer 6.4). While a description such as this could

---

6. Robert Dirks adopts Hans Selye's three-stage response system of the human body to stress—alarm, resistance, and exhaustion—to subdivide progressive reactions to famine (Dirks 1980, 26–31). Culturally speaking, however, the first two stages are easily conflated.

be interpreted prosaically as a smash-and-grab raid on food supplies, other portions of his narrative make it clear that attacks such as this were in some instances directed expressly at the extractive organs of the government.

Ipuwer laments the targeting of offices and deliberate destruction of records. According to him,

> office<s> have been opened and th<eir> inventories removed; dependent people have become the owner<s> of dependents. O, yet scribes are slain, and their writings removed. . . . O, yet scribes of the field-register, their writings have been obliterated; the life-grain of Egypt is a free-for-all (Ipuwer 6.7–6.9; Enmarch 2008, 228).

Documents targeted for destruction, then, seem to have stipulated which people belonged to the category of serf or dependent laborer, who had rights to specific fields, and what taxes were in arrears. If, once all such records were obliterated, the life-grain of Egypt was indeed a free-for-all the masses must have been elated. Indeed, Ipuwer's admonitions provide an otherwise rare glimpse into the hatred harbored by many toward the disciplinary arm of the state. His distress at attacks on pharaonic rules, regulations, and labor prisons, for example, makes for a stark contrast with the evident exhilaration felt by commoners at storming their own version of the Bastille. As Ipuwer recounts it, nobles did indeed lament while the poor rejoiced:

> O, yet the rulings of the labor enclosure are cast (lit. put) out, and one walks on th in the alleys; wretches tear them up in the streets. . . ; (the) ordinance <of> the House of Thirty has been stripped bare. O, yet the great labor enclosure is in commotion; wretches come and go in the great domains (Ipuwer 6.9–6.12; Enmarch 2008, 228).

The burning of public records and the storming of prisons are, of course, two classic revolutionary goals. It is thus of interest that, according to Ipuwer, an antiauthoritarian sentiment had swept over much of the population.

Regarding this insurgency, he writes, "Every town says, 'Let's drive out the strong among us!" (Ipuwer 2.7–2.8; Enmarch 2008, 223). Adding, "porches, pillars, and partition walls(?) are burnt . . . the ship of the south is in an uproar, towns are hacked up" (Ipuwer 2.10–2.11; Enmarch 2008, 223). Evidently deprived of its revenues through popular resistance to taxation (Ipuwer 3.10–3.12; 10.3–10.5), and both fearful and impoverished through want, the crown found itself unable to reassert order or even to protect itself from the wrath of those it had once ruled. The palace fell in an hour, and "wretches" removed the king (Ipuwer 7.1–7.6).

As stated at the outset of this essay, the proper milieu into which Ipuwer's account should be placed and how much credence to give it are much debated. There is little doubt, however, that during famines populist anger and weak governments felt to be venial and corrupt made for a combustible mix (Dirks 1980, 27–30). If more governments didn't fall during Egypt's later history, it seems often to have been due to the fact that the country was at that point part of an empire, and the king resided elsewhere. Antiauthoritarian actions, infighting, and serious strife, however, were

certainly witnessed in a series of famines that took place in the tenth century, as well as
in 1055–1056, 1294–1296, and 1790–1796 (al-Maqrīzī 1994, 29–30, 36–37, 47; Mikhail
2011, 229–30; Raphael 2013, 189–90).

Debilitation, Disease, Despondency, and Death

Outbursts of anger are to some degree a luxury typical only of the early stages of famine. What follows, in the worst-case scenario, is far more disheartening: namely, mute
suffering in the face of an enormous death toll. A combination of migration, starvation,
and pestilence (brought on by the increasingly compromised immune systems of the
malnourished) has been known to account for the loss of up to half of a total population. Indeed, in Egypt at a local level, it was not uncommon for entire villages to be
depopulated in the course of a famine (al-Baghdādi 1965, 641; Arnold 1988, 20–21;
al-Maqrīzī 1994, 45; Mikhail 2011, 217). Ipuwer seems to describe just such a scenario,
when he laments: "pestilence is throughout the land, blood is everywhere; there is no
lack(?) of death.... [H]e who places his brother in the earth is everywhere" (Ipuwer
2.5–2.6; 2.13–2.14; Enmarch 2008, 222–23). "O, yet the many dead," he notes, "are
buried in the river" (Ipuwer 2.6–2.7; Enmarch 2008, 222).

A rendition of the various dates when disease and pestilence—two of the four
horsemen of the apocalypse—rode roughshod together across Egypt is unnecessary,
for the two were always inseparable, and their combined death toll was by all accounts
stunning (Sabra 2000, 137; Raphael 2013, 56). One line in The Admonitions of an
Egyptian Sage, open to differing interpretations, may well be relevant: "O, yet the
river is blood and one drinks from it; one pushes people aside, thirsting for water"
(Ipuwer 2.10; Enmarch 2008, 223). While it is possible that Ipuwer is here specifically
referencing the prevalence of selfishness and the dearth of empathy that often characterize famines, his imagery may, in fact, be far grimmer. What might be described
is the increasing need to push aside dead bodies in order to reach the water (Bell
1971, 12).

While seemingly hyperbolic, the picture Ipuwer would be painting is not without
parallel. In his eyewitness account of the famine that occurred in Egypt between 1199
and 1201, al-Baghdādi stated that the death toll was so extraordinary that corpses were
commonly thrown in the Nile. He himself paid people to clear bodies in this manner,
and, on other occasions, he witnessed numerous corpses "swollen and inflated like
water skins filled with air" float by. Indeed, he wrote of observing body parts scattered
at the water's edge during a boat trip as well as of having talked to a fisherman who
claimed "that he had seen pass close to him, in a single day, four hundred corpses that
the waters of the river carried with them" (al-Baghdādi 1965, 61r). Certainly, in at least
three other epidemics (e.g., 963–971, 1294–1296, 1790–1796) deaths were stated to
have been so numerous that recourse was taken to pitching bodies in the Nile, tossing
them in wells, or interring them in hastily excavated mass graves (al-Maqrīzī 1994, 31,
45–46; Mikhail 2008, 256). Likewise, in 1791, when an estimated one to two thousand
people died each day, it was stated by a chronicler that "there was not any work left for
people except death and its attendant matters" (Mikhail 2011, 222). The official count
of the dead from this epidemic amounted to three hundred thousand.

Bringing new life into this world of death was understandably fraught. Demographic losses during famines tend to be exacerbated due to the fact that female fertility plummets in such situations. Ipuwer observed this for himself, stating, "women are barren(?) and can't conceive; Khnum cannot create because of the state of the land" (Ipuwer 2.4; Enmarch 2008, 222). Such a decline in fertility—well documented in places as diverse as India, China, Leningrad, and Athens—not surprisingly, is thought to be both situational and physiological (Stein and Susser 1975; Ó Gráda 2009, 103–7; Raphael 2013, 73). Even when babies are born, however, many don't survive long, dying because they were delivered prematurely or due to the malnourishment of their mothers. Still others are victims of infanticide (Ó Gráda 2009, 61). Classical authors agree that this was a practice Egyptians abhorred in times of plenty (Strabo, *Geography* 17.2, 5; Diodorus Siculus, *Library of History* 1.77, 7), yet Ipuwer reports that the crisis in his day was so dire that even the children of the wealthy and "children of prayer are placed on high ground" (Ipuwer 5.6; Enmarch 2008, 226; also Ipuwer 4.3; 5.6).

It is almost impossible to contemplate how it must have felt to live through a time when one's familiar world devolved into a state of chaos, misery, and death. According to Ipuwer, one common consequence was a debilitating depression (Ipuwer 1.8; 3.13–3.14), which resulted in suicidal thoughts that plagued all, even the very young and those that occupied the uppermost stratum in society (Ipuwer 4.2–4.3). Indeed, for many sufferers, according to Ipuwer, such thoughts manifested in action. Concerning this he states simply, "the crocodiles gorge, but do not seize (for) men go to them themselves" (Ipuwer 2.12; Enmarch 2008, 223). Data on suicides during famines, as Ó Gráda points out, is rarely available in more than an anecdotal form, but he notes spikes that occurred in both India and Finland during 1867–1868, when records were indeed kept. Deaths by drowning during famines are reported by Livy in Rome during the fifth century BCE and for India in 1291 CE. Moreover, it was apparently common to see the poor "everywhere . . . hopelessly, apathetically killing themselves" in the course of a famine that struck China in 1931 (Ó Gráda 2009, 62–63).

With regard to pharaonic Egypt, it is notable that the only known cultural meditation on suicide—The Man Who Was Weary of Life—seems to have been quoted by the author of The Admonitions of an Egyptian Sage and to have been put to papyrus perhaps as early as the reign of Senwosret II. Given its heavy subject matter and the similarity of its narrator's critiques to those of Ipuwer, it is perhaps not surprising that it, too, is known from only a single manuscript (Parkinson 2002, 50; Simpson 2003, 184–85; Enmarch 2008, 24). Clearly, while the effects of trauma might linger, the ability of such dispiriting subject matter to attract widespread interest did not.

Why Write Trauma?

If Ipuwer has been accused of hyperbole, it is not by scholars who have delved indepth into the effects of famine on society. While any long-lived Egyptian was likely to have experienced worrisome food crises, famines that raged out of control and caused widespread suffering and death occurred far more infrequently. Indeed, the famines discussed in this essay, which qualify for such a dubious distinction, were limited to those that occurred in 963–971, 1064–1072, 1199–1201, 1294–1296, 1372–1373,

1402–1404, 1415–1416, 1459–1452, 1694–1695; 1784–1787; 1790–1796, and 1877–1879. Thus, only in the fifteenth and in the eighteenth century would it have occurred that an individual might have been unfortunate enough to witness more than one of these catastrophic events.

The only positive aspect one can point to regarding famine in Egypt is that it occurred infrequently and for a duration that rarely exceeded a few years of concentrated misery, save for periods of extended ecological downturns. Demographically, societies tend to recover from even the worst famines within a decade or so (Ó Gráda 2009, 123), and so it comes to pass that societal memory inevitably fades in the face of normality. The fragility of memory even among survivors, however, has often been noted. For instance, one of the challenges Fekade Azeze (1998, 28–29) faced in compiling material for his book *Unheard Voices: Drought, Famine and God in Ethiopian Oral Poetry* is that within a decade of the Ethiopian famine, which lasted from 1984–1985, most peasants had forgotten (or perhaps repressed) the poems that they themselves or others had composed during their time of suffering.

The curation of social memory is made even more difficult by the fact that survivors suffering from posttraumatic stress are often famously reticent to speak of their experiences to their descendants or to contemporaries who have only experienced situations of peace and plenty. It is worth noting, however, that the reluctance of survivors to communicate often lessens as they age. Facing the recognition that their memories might well die with them and also that history that is forgotten runs the risk of repetition, survivors often begin to speak of the unspeakable only after many years have passed. It is notable that the stories that emerge, then, well seasoned with time and steeped in the personal preoccupations of the narrator, on occasion, bear a marked resemblance to The Admonitions of an Egyptian Sage.

In *Tears From Iron, Cultural Responses to Famine in Nineteenth-Century China*, Kathryn Edgerton-Tarpley (2008) discusses a vivid account of the "Incredible Famine" that ravaged north China from 1876–1879. Known in Chinese as the "Song of the Famine Years" (*Huangnian ge*), it was composed by an ordinary man by the name of Liu Xing, who concluded the song with an exhortation:

> I fear taking these disaster years as past and not thinking [of them]. Thus I wrote this song to hand down to the generations. Upon obtaining this song, hide it in your home and read it often to your sons and younger brothers. People of the whole household, remember it in your hearts (Edgerton-Tarpley 2008, 227).

It is both affirming and disheartening, then, that Edgerton-Tarpley first became aware of this particular song from a yellowed handwritten manuscript that a collector—whose grandfather and mother had told him of the famine in his youth—had bought from the grandfather of a fellow villager. He did so because he wanted to preserve these memories and to pass them on. To his dismay, however, he found children to be uninterested in them. "Those who have full bellies," he explained, "don't want to hear about such circumstances" (Edgerton-Tarpley 2008, 43).

The Song of the Famine Years tells of a drought that parched the fields and forced people to resort to famine foods. Prices rose, crops again failed, and then the corpses began to pile up, exposed to the open air. According to Edgerton-Tarpley (2008, 48),

Liu describes how hungry people gathered in crowds that refused to disperse. During the day, they begged, but at night they plotted rebellion. In the countryside, some "evil people" formed gangs armed with guns and rope whips. Entering villages in the dark of night, they stole valuables and grain and tore the clothing off women.

People swiped food from one another, ate cats and dogs, and finally resorted to cannibalism, eating first the dead and then their own family members. All businesses, he said, closed for trade. Everyone attempted to sell their belongings. Women sold themselves, and a pestilence swept through the population. Although corpses were interred in mass graves, they piled up like mountains (Edgerton-Tarpley 2008, 47–50).

The points of comparison with Ipuwer's narrative should be obvious, but the tales converge in other respects as well. It is fascinating that both texts reference the destruction of ornate wooden furniture for firewood (Ipuwer 3.5; Edgerton-Tarpley 2008, 49), a necessity driven home by al-Baghdādi's description of Egyptians resorting to the destruction of architectural elements within their own houses to maintain fires in their hearths and ovens (al-Baghdādi 1965, 62*l*, 64*l*). Moreover, two years into the famine Liu laments that no offerings were placed in ancestral halls, nor did people sing traditional songs or perform the rites and celebrations that always accompanied the New Year's holiday. Affection for and trust in the emperor had also ceased. For Ipuwer, too, faith in god and king had all but vanished along with the performance of religious cult (Ipuwer 5.7–5.9; 11.1–12.13). Rituals, like riots, studies have shown, tend to decrease in prevalence the longer a famine wears on with no relief in sight (Dirks 1980, 27–28, 31; Arnold 1988, 75–78). "If I could perceive, and know where god is, then I would act for him!" Such sentiments, Ipuwer asserts, had became increasingly and understandably common (Ipuwer 5.3; Enmarch 2008, 226).[7]

In Trauma, Emphasis Is Personal

If famines have a way of resembling one another, what differs most about the stories they inspire is emphasis. In Ipuwer's case, his narrative is most strongly colored by his concern for the plight of the rich. Here his pity appears misplaced, for famines are not—at their start, at least—equal opportunity killers. The Great Famine in Ireland, for example, is in this respect typical. As Ó Gráda writes, "A disaster that struck the poor more than the rich . . . the famine's impact was very uneven; poverty and death were closely correlated, both at a local level and in cross-section. . . . It produced a hierarchy of suffering" (Ó Gráda 2001, 121, 123). The plight of the poor was nearly always precarious. Thus, what is shocking in the Song of the Famine Years is not that many of the poorest families perished. It is rather that among the scions of the great families over half starved to death (Edgerton-Tarpley 2008, 50).

---

7. Ipuwer's reproaches to god are closely echoed in some Ethiopian famine songs. One asks, for example, "When I shout 'My God! . . . Oh my dear God!' Why are You silent? Why pretend You are not there? When I know You *are*! (Why pretend You have nothing? When I know You *have*!)" (Azeze 1998, 98).

Like cannibalism, the suffering of the rich served as an exclamation mark in famine narratives—a way to emphasize that the particular famine being described was truly exceptional. For instance, concerning the famine of 1064–1072 in Egypt, al-Maqrīzī (1994, 38) writes that even the Fatamid Caliph

> was compelled to sell everything in his palace, including precious objects, clothes, furniture, weapons, and the like. He was reduced to sitting on a mat, his administrative apparatus collapsed, and his dignity was lost. The women of the palaces came out—their hair undone and screaming: "Hunger! Hunger!"

Or, as Ipuwer had put it long ago "Look, rich ladies have come to (the point of) hunger!" (Ipuwer 9.1; Enmarch 2008, 231). Likewise, the chronicler Ibn al-Dawādārī indulged in black humor with reference to the scourge of 1294–1296, quipping, "Many died, those who were lucky and those who were poor" (Raphael 2013, 92–93). The sufferings of the nobility were also noted, somewhat more soberly, with respect to the famines of 1199–1201, 1372–1373, 1449–1452, 1469–1470, and 1790–1796 (al-Baghdādī 1965, 64*l*, Shoshan 1980, 467; Sabra 2000, 147, 159, 162).

Famine and Opportunity

Ipuwer's concern for the sufferings of his own social class is not particularly surprising, especially as plotlines that feature a Dickensian fall from riches to rags exert a lurid fascination and have provided plotlines for pulp fiction ever since the genre was invented. What is strange, however, is Ipuwer's insistence that the fall of the rich was counterbalanced by an enrichment of the poor (Ipuwer 2.4–2.5; 3.2–3.4; 3.14–4.1; 4.8–4.14; 5.2; 7.8–8.5; 8.11; 9.1–9.2; 9.4–9.5). It is this aspect of the text, more than any other, that has caused scholars to dismiss it as essentially ahistorical (*AEL* 1:150; Enmarch 2008, 63–64).

Ipuwer's insistence that riches were redistributed on a large scale is without a doubt overplayed and flies in the face of cross-cultural observations about societal dynamics during famines. It may not, however, be entirely baseless. The unusual opportunities for social advancement that occurred during the famine of 1199–1201 were remarked upon by al-Baghdādī (1965, 62*l*), who wrote:

> Meanwhile it is a thing worthy of admiration that a group of people who until now have always been of limited means, are become happy this year. Some have amassed wealth by trade in wheat; others in receiving rich inheritances. Some others have been enriched, and no-one knows the origin and cause of their fortune.

By way of redeeming Ipuwer's credibility, then, it is important to briefly consider three broad mechanisms that tend to facilitate income redistribution and the mixing of social classes both during and after particularly devastating famines: crime and social banditry, revolt and the destabilization of the erstwhile nobility, and the readjustment of resources in the wake of demographic changes.

Ipuwer himself ties social inversion in part to the enrichment of robbers (Ipuwer 2.9). The prevalence of social banditry during famines has already been discussed, and there is little doubt that anger toward wealthy families and institutions that hoarded grain must have run high. As Ó Gráda (2001, 129) observes,

> Not only are famines uneven [in terms of their effects on social classes] but they are also, always and everywhere, deeply divisive tragedies. The charity and solidarity that bind communities together are strengthened for a while, but break as the crisis worsens: hospitality declines, crime and cruelty increase."[8]

Lessened security, increased resentment, and desperation no doubt led to the frequent targeting of the wealthy—not only with respect to the property found in their homes but so too that interred in their "houses of eternity," as tombs were known in Egypt. Providing that robbers survived the famine and were not forced by necessity to sell their goods for grain, the breakdown in order did indeed provide an opportunity for wealth to be redistributed at knifepoint.

Famines radically reduce the ability of a state both to inspire allegiance and to enforce it. Likewise, as discussed above, the righteous anger of a mob can lead to the downfall of a ruler whose legitimacy has been lost together with those that had most directly profited from his regime. Thus the centers that grew to greatest prominence in Egypt's Intermediate Periods were often new to power, as were the elites that erected monumental architecture and tombs therein. The hereditary nobles who had been ousted with an old regime did not necessarily constitute the cornerstone upon which the new order was founded. Nor were they the primary beneficiaries. In the wake of the famine's political consequences, then, it may well have seemed to Ipuwer as if the poor had become rich and the rich poor.

If famine has two stages—anger and despondency—the third cross-culturally attested avenue of social advancement is occasioned simply by survival. The worst famines typically resulted in a great deal of unclaimed property. As al-Baghdādī (1965, 64l) observed after the famine of 1199–1201, Egypt's richest estates were for the most part totally deserted due to the death or flight of their inhabitants. The seizure of the possessions of those that fled or died during the famine that raged from 1790–1796 likewise constituted a unique opportunity for enrichment (Mikhail 2011, 224). Indeed, the virulence of the plague that accompanied this particular famine had been such that not only did it kill Egypt's leader, but "successors immediately rose to power only to die themselves three days later. Those who replaced them also died in the course of a few days. . . . Leaders came to power in the morning and died by late afternoon. . . . Many large Cairene families were decimated by the plague" (Mikhail 2008, 256). New families, however, undoubtedly rose to take their place.

The effects of plague on societies that emerged from it are perhaps best known from records of the Black Plague, which hit Europe in waves during the fourteenth century. Reports suggest that for some survivors, the plague's aftermath proved a boon.

---

8. Although not discussed here, instances of cruelty, selfishness, and the fraying of even familial bonds are noted in Ipuwer's narrative (Ipuwer 1.1; 5.10; and 9.3) as well as in later historical and anthropological accounts of famine (Tucker 1981, 222; Dirks 1980, 28, 30).

With a glut of merchandise on the shelves for too few customers, prices at first plunged and survivors indulged in a wild orgy of spending. The poor moved into empty houses, slept on beds, and ate off silver. Peasants acquired unclaimed tools and livestock, even a wine press, forge, or mill left without owners, and other possessions they never had before (Tuchman 1978, 117).

Thus in the aftermath of a massive loss of life, the plight of many survivors may well have improved due to the demand for their labor and to their ability to lay claim to the property of people who had perished.[9]

What is fascinating, however, is that such social advancement did not come uncontested. Instead, the medieval equivalents to Ipuwer did their best to stem such tides. Thus, governments throughout Europe issued ordinances to regulate wages and to restrict the bargaining power of laborers and artisans (Cohn 2007, 479). Such ordinances were not at all dispassionate. Rather, as Samuel Cohn (2007, 480) explains,

> these new laws reflect elites' further anxieties about class. . . . The laws alleged that labourers now "demanded quality wines and meats beyond their station." For these elites the world had suddenly been turned upside down: to quote a Florentine decree of 9 October 1348, "while many citizens had suddenly become the poor, the poor had become rich," The Florentine chronicler Stefani said much the same.

This jealous desire to safeguard their own status prompted governing elites in Florence and England to enact sumptuary laws, legislating that servants and workers were no longer permitted access to clothing, jewelry, or luxury goods deemed inappropriate to their social class. As recent revisionist historical work has shown, however, those that benefited most from the plague in its immediate aftermath were not the poor, but rather those survivors that had maintained a grip on their riches and could use them to invest in other sources of wealth (Cohn 2007, 481). Thus, the laws, while indeed prompted by some degree of true social advancement on the part of the lower classes, are perhaps better understood as symptomatic of exactly the type of elite anxiety and fear of falling that permeates The Admonitions of an Egyptian Sage.

The Reception of Trauma Literature

Widespread trauma creates societal scars that often endure in art. Some creative meditations, such as the famine songs of Ethiopia, are composed in the thick of tragedy, though the words are not always preserved. Ipuwer, who was remembered as an overseer of singers (Parkinson 2002, 308), makes mention of the fate of artists during his time: "[Music]ians are at the loom(?) within the weaving rooms, their weavers' songs being dirges; the tellers [of words(?) are at] quernstones" (Ipuwer 4.12–4.13; Enmarch

---

9. Ipuwer may indirectly reference the growing demand for laborers when he states that Upper Egypt had become empty fields and that even when the inundation met a mark of plentitude no one plowed (Ipuwer 2.3; 2.11). His observation anticipates al-Maqrīzī's (1994, 42) statement, with respect to the famine of 1199–1201, that "When God succored His creatures through the flooding of the Nile, no one was left to plow or sow."

2008, 226). This observation—that new songs were indeed being composed and sung, but in an era without official patronage—is reminiscent of much artistic production in times of societal chaos.

Mohommed Othman, for instance, wrote an article in *Al-Monitor* in 2015 on the sad irony that right at the point when the most urgent stories remain to be told of life in the Gaza Strip, its literary scene is almost extinct. He states,

> Writer-novelist Yousra al-Ghul said that culture has become a luxury for Gazans, indicating that publishing is in crisis.... "Funding is weak and so no one is sponsoring these writers, so [the writers] isolate themselves. The Gaza Strip is packed with a lot of young novelists from both sexes. They participate in Arab competitions, but [these efforts will remain meaningless] until publishing houses start printing them."

In the famines and food crises of the First Intermediate Period, for instance, the literary genre of the dirge may well have been invented and sung, as uniquely appropriate to its time. But the second step in the artistic process—namely, the commitment of an oral composition to writing—may well have been delayed until the reassertion of political stability, when artists were once again provided with the funds, leisure, equipment, and encouragement to pursue their craft exclusively.

As touched upon in the beginning of this essay, there are a variety of times that "bearing witness"—undertaking to retell a traumatic event in unsparing detail—becomes a priority. The first appears to be in the face of impending death. This might be the death of the individual holding the memory, as was often the case for Holocaust survivors. So too Liu Xing, whose Song of Famine memorialized China's Incredible Famine of 1876–1879, waited twenty years before committing his narrative to writing in order to cause others to remember. For those who listen to such stories, the tenacity of memory is remarkable. Thus, in researching her book on the Incredible Famine, published in 2008, Edgerton-Tarpley (2008, xiv) was able to interview elderly inhabitants of Shanxi who had heard first-hand reports of the famine directly from their own grandparents. So, too, roughly a century later, the Irish Folklore Commission succeeded in assembling a wide variety of tales that were still in circulation about life during the Great Irish Famine of 1847.

If a recognition of the transience of living memory is one impetus for the writing of trauma, so too is its repetition. The target demographic for memoires penned by those battling cancer is not the young and healthy. Analogously, stories of societal traumas may be all but forgotten until the lessons learned from those experiences prove once again valuable. Thus, in China, there was little widespread interest in curating memories of the Incredible Famine until roughly eighty years later, when the country again faced a critical shortage of food due to Mao's failed Great Leap Forward. At that time the government sent out local historians to gather and publish famine songs, poems, stele inscriptions, and other sources. These, interestingly enough, were often employed by Mao's government so as to downplay the difficulties of its current crisis (Edgerton-Tarpey 2008, 5, 228–30).

If recent linguistic analysis is correct in its tendency to date much of the pessimistic literature, including The Admonitions of an Egyptian Sage, to the Thirteenth Dynasty, a parallel with the resuscitation of interest in the Incredible Famine during Mao's time may well be apt. During the Thirteenth Dynasty rulers cycled in and out of power at a dizzying rate, perhaps even due to a plague—the likes of which may be witnessed in the roughly contemporary levels of Tell el-Dabʻa (Bietak 1996, 35–36). Nile floods may well have been erratic, foreigners had taken up residence in the delta, and toward the end of the period the central government failed altogether. Thus, it is perhaps only natural that writers of this time should have expressed an interest in the last era during which disorder had threatened the natural and political world, prompting them to copy down older famine songs and perhaps even to compose new works modeled after the old.

What is fascinating about The Admonitions of an Egyptian Sage, which is the longest and most relentless of its genre, is that the composition seems to have existed outside the literary canon, at least insomuch as it survived in only a single manuscript, which is dated to the Nineteenth Dynasty. Unlike the Prophecies of Neferty, plausibly a dirge of similar antiquity that was tied up in a neatly propagandistic bow at its end and served up to school children as part of a scribal curriculum, Ipuwer's song was curated and respected, but seemingly stayed on its shelf. Indeed, it has been suggested that when it was recopied parts of its original text were no longer decipherable (Gardiner 1969, 2).

Just when the narrative was copied down on Papyrus Leiden I 344 is uncertain, but the hand of the scribe that penned the hymn to Amun, which shared its papyrus, was dated paleographically to the late Nineteenth or Twentieth Dynasty (Gardiner 1969, 1). If The Admonitions of an Egyptian Sage had been copied at some point between Merenptah's time and the end of the dynasty, it may well, once again, have seemed particularly relevant. A drought had struck the ancient Mediterranean world at that time and inspired revolts among Egypt's subject territories as well as invasions from Libyan tribes and Aegean climate refugees, who were fleeing famine and upheaval in their own homelands. Moreover, after Merenptah's death the country suffered from a succession of short-lived rulers of little legitimacy and civil strife. Perhaps, it was at that point that a particularly learned scribe felt it was time to take Ipuwer's lamentation down from the shelf and to dust it off for a new audience.

Writing trauma, either *in* or *in response to* a period of societal turmoil, preserves painful memories in hopes of preventing future occurrences. Historical and climatological evidence indicates that periods that saw the natural world wreak havoc on the social world were few and far between, typically sparing multiple generations at a time from their universal misery. When they did occur, the events of such periods caused tremendous anxiety and suffering, and spawned narratives populated both with heroes and villains—though who exactly was cast in what role no doubt differed according to the teller and the intention. Regarded with indifference in times of order and plenty, works like Ipuwer's may well, like Homer's shades, have drawn new life from fresh blood.

BIBLIOGRAPHY

Arnold, David. 1988. *Famine: Social Crisis and Historical Change*. Oxford: Basil Blackwell.
Arz, Helge W., Frank Lamy, and Jürgen Pätzold. 2006. "A Pronounced Dry Event Recorded Around 4.2 ka in Brine Sediments from the Northern Red Sea." *Quarternary Research* 66:432–41.

Azeze, Faqada. 1998. *Unheard Voices: Drought, Famine and God in Ethiopian Oral Poetry*. Addis Ababa: Addis Ababa University Press.

Baghdādī, 'Abd al-. 1965 [1204]. *The Eastern Key*. Translated by K. H. Zand et al. London: Allen & Unwin.

Bell, Barbara. 1971. "The Dark Ages in Ancient History I: The First Dark Age in Egypt." *AJA* 75:1–26.

Bietak, Manfred. 1996. *Avaris: The Capital of the Hyksos; Recent Excavations at Tell el-Dab'a*. London: British Museum Press.

Cohn, Samuel. 2007. "After the Black Death: Labour Legislation and Attitudes Towards Labour in Late-Medieval Western Europe." *The Economic History Review*. NS 60:457–85.

Cole, Juan Ricardo I. 1999. *Colonialism and Revolution in the Middle East: Social and Cultural Origins of Egypt's 'Urabi Movement*. Cairo: American University in Cairo Press.

Davis, Mike. 2017. *Late Victorian Holocausts: El Niño Famines and the Making of the Third World*. New York: Verso.

Dirks, Robert. 1980. "Social Responses During Severe Food Shortages and Famine." *Current Anthropology* 21:21–32.

Edgerton-Tarpley, Kathryn. 2008. *Tears from Iron : Cultural Responses to Famine in Nineteenth-Century China*. Berkeley: University of California Press.

Enmarch, Roland. 2008. *A World Upturned: Commentary on and Analysis of The Dialogue of Ipuwer and the Lord of All*. Oxford: Oxford University Press.

Gardiner, Alan H. 1969. *The Admonitions of an Egyptian Sage from a Hieratic Papyrus in Leiden (Pap. Leiden 344 recto)*. Hildescheim: Olms.

Hassan, Fekri A. 1997. "Nile Floods and Political Disorder in Early Egypt." Pages 1–23 in *Third Millennium BC Climate Change and Old World Collapse,* Edited by H. Niizhet Dalfes, George Kukla, and Harvey Weiss. NATO ASI 49. Berlin: Springer.

———. 2007. "Droughts, Famine and the Collapse of the Old Kingdom: Re-reading Ipuwer." Pages 357–77 in *The Archaeology and Art of Ancient Egypt: Essays in Honor of David B. O'Connor, Volume I*. Edited by Zahi A. Hawass and Janet Richards. Cairo: Supreme Council of Antiquities.

Herrmann, Rachel B. 2011. "The 'Tragicall Historie': Cannibalism and Abundance in Colonial Jamestown." *William and Mary Quarterly* 68:47–74.

Hobsbawm, Eric J. 1959. *Primitive Rebels*. Manchester: University of Manchester.

Hoffmeier, James K. 1997. *Israel in Egypt: The Evidence for the Authenticity of the Exodus Tradition*. Oxford: Oxford University Press.

Kemp, Barry. 1991. *Ancient Egypt: Anatomy of a Civilization*. New York: Routledge.

———. 2012. *The City of Akhenaten and Nefertiti: Amarna and Its People*. London: Thames and Hudson.

LaCapra, Dominick. 2001. *Writing History, Writing Trauma*. Baltimore: Johns Hopkins University Press.

Lehner, Mark. 2000. "Fractal House of Pharaoh: Ancient Egypt as a Complex Adaptive System, a Trial Formulation." Pages 275–353 in *Dynamics in Human and Primate Societies: Agent-Based Modeling of Social and Spatial Processes*. Edited by Timothy A. Kohler and George J. Gummerman. New York: Oxford University Press.

Manning, Sturt W., Michael W. Dee, Eva M. Wild, Christopher Bronk Ramsey, Kathryn Bandy, Pearce Paul Creasman, Carol B. Griggs, Charlott L. Pearson, Andrew J. Shortland, and Peter Steier. 2014. "High-precision Dendro-[14]C Dating of Two Cedar Wood Sequences from First Intermediate Period and Middle Kingdom Egypt and a Small Regional Climate-related [14]C Divergence." *Journal of Archaeological Science* 46:401–16.

Maqrīzī, Aḥmad ibn 'Alī Taqī al-Dīn al-. 1994 [1405]. *Mamluk Economics: A Study and Translation of al-Maqrīzī's Ighāthah*. Translated by Adel Allouche. Salt Lake City: University of Utah Press.

Marshall, Michael H., Henry F. Lamb, Dei Huws, Sarah J. Davies, Richard Bates, Jan Bloemendal, John Boyle, Melanie J. Leng, Mohammed Umer, and Charlotte Bryant. 2011.

"Late Pleistocene and Holocene Drought Events at Lake Tana, the Source of the Blue Nile." *Global and Planetary Change* 78:147–61.

Mikhail, Alan. 2008. "The Nature of Plague in Late Eighteenth-Century Egypt." *Bulletin of the History of Medicine* 82:249–75.

———. 2011. *Nature and Empire in Ottoman Egypt: An Environmental History.* Cambridge: Cambridge University Press.

Moreno García, Juan Carlos. 1997 *Études sur l'administration, le pouvoir et l'idéologie en Égypte, de l'Ancien au Moyen Empire.* Ægyptica Leodiensia 4. Liège: C.I.P.L.

Morris, Ellen F. 2017. "Prevention Through Deterrence Along Egypt's Northeastern Border: Or the Politics of a Weaponized Desert." *Journal of Eastern Mediterranean Archaeology and Heritage Studies* 5:133–47.

Ó Gráda, Cormac. 2001. "Famine, Trauma and Memory." *Béaloideas* 69:121–43.

———. 2009. *Famine: A Short History.* Princeton: Princeton University Press.

Othman, Mohommed. 2015. "Gaza Writers Lose Out as Culture Becomes Afterthought." *Al-Monitor: the Pulse of the Middle East.* May 15. https://www.al-monitor.com/pulse/ru/originals/2015/05/palestine-gaza-writing-books-authors-social-media-publishing.html.

Parkinson, R. B. 2002. *Poetry and Culture in Middle Kingdom Egypt: A Dark Side to Perfection.* New York: Continuum.

Raphael, Sarah Kate. 2013. *Climate and Political Climate: Environmental Disasters in the Medieval Levant.* Brill's Series in the History of the Environment 3. Leiden: Brill.

Sabra, Adam. 2000. *Poverty and Charity in Medieval Islam: Mamluk Egypt, 1250–1517.* Cambridge: Cambridge University Press.

Shoshan, Boaz. 1980. "Grain Riots and the 'Moral Economy': Cairo 1350–1517." *Journal of Interdisciplinary History* 10:459–78.

Simpson, William Kelly, ed. 2003. *The Literature of Ancient Egypt: An Anthology of Stories, Instructions, Stelae, Autobiographies, and Poetry.* 3rd ed. New Haven: Yale University Press.

Sorokin, Pitirim A. 1942. *Man and Society in Calamity.* New York: Dutton.

Stauder, Andréas. 2013. *Linguistic Dating of Middle Egyptian Literary Texts.* Lingua Aegyptia Studia Monographica 12. Hamburg: Widmaier.

Stein, Zena, and Mervyn Susser. 1975. "Fertility, Fecundity, Famine: Food Rations in the Dutch Famine 1944/5 Have a Causal Relation to Fertility, and Probably to Fecundity." *Human Biology* 47:131–54.

Tuchman, Barbara W. 1978. *A Distant Mirror: The Calamitous Fourteenth Century.* New York: Ballantine.

Tucker, William F. 1981. "Natural Disasters and the Peasantry in Mamlūk Egypt." *JESHO* 24:215–24.

Vandier, Jacques. 1936. *La famine dans l'Egypte Ancienne.* Cairo: Institut français d'archeologie orientale.

Welc, Fabian, and Leszek Marks. 2014. "Climate Change at the End of the Old Kingdom in Egypt Around 4200 BP: New Geoarchaeological Evidence." *Quaternary International* 324:124–33.

White, Sam. 2013. *The Climate of Rebellion in the Early Modern Ottoman Empire.* Studies in Environment and History. Cambridge: Cambridge University Press.

Wilkomirski, Binjamin. 1997. *Fragments: Memories of a Wartime Childhood.* New York: Schocken.

CHAPTER 18

Old Kingdom Exotica at Pharaoh's Court and Beyond: Dwarfs, Pygmies, Primates, Dogs, and Leopards

Gregory Mumford

IT IS A DISTINCT PLEASURE to write an article in honor of James ("Jim") Hoffmeier, a friend and project director with whom I have worked at Tell el-Borg (north Sinai) in recent years, plus a well-respected and prolific colleague whose many and wide-ranging works I have consulted since the advent of my studies in the 1980s regarding both Egyptology and the ancient Near East. Selecting a pertinent topic for his Festschrift was initially tricky, since Jim's interests are equally broad and varied, but this final selection has been drawn and expanded from a portion of a manuscript I am currently completing.[1] In researching the broader relations between Egypt, sub-Saharan Africa and other regions, I became intrigued by three or four imports that often appear together in different groupings with dwarfs, especially during the Old Kingdom, namely sub-Saharan African dogs, felines (usually leopards), and primates (i.e., baboons; monkeys); while Egyptian dwarfs appear frequently alongside these exotic imports, they are overshadowed somewhat by the novelty and rarity of imported sub-Saharan "pygmies" who are distinguished by a different nomenclature in Egyptian texts.[2] This paper supplements the Old Kingdom portion of Veronique Dasen's 1993 seminal study on *Dwarfs in Ancient Egypt and Greece*, by adding some less well-known and new examples (e.g., Worcestor Art Museum 1931.99; see figures 18.1–2); it applies some quantification and statistical analyses to the apparent Old Kingdom preference for using indigenous dwarfs as handlers of imported dogs, primates, and sometimes felines (e.g., from Nubia, sub-Saharan Africa, Punt, and occasionally the adjacent deserts and oases); and it reviews the presence of Egyptian dwarfs and foreign pygmies in other professions and activities in the Old Kingdom (and later periods).[3]

1. This in-progress book delves into much greater depth concerning questions on the location of Punt, the many different Nubian and sub-Saharan African interrelations with Egypt, plus Egyptian interactions with other places, including Arabia, the Near East, East Mediterranean, and elsewhere from late Prehistory through the Persian period.

2. The term "dwarf" is retained here owing to its widespread usage in past-current literature, while avoiding other nonacceptable terms in conjunction with the emerging preference for utilizing the expression "little people" by the Little People of America (LPA) and the Little People of Canada (LPC). For further details on the LPA association's changing name and preferences, see https://en.wikipedia.org/wiki/Little_People_of_America.

3. See Filer (2001) for additional commentary on Dasen's study.

FIGURE 18.1. Line drawing, by Greg Mumford, of a dwarf called Widj (*W-[i]-ḏ*), with a *tjesem*-dog and long-tailed monkey, initially extracted from a low resolution, online photograph of a Sixth Dynasty mastaba tomb marsh scene, no. 1931.99, currently displayed in the Worcester Art Museum (https://worcester.emuseum.com/search/1931.99).

Distinguishing Indigenous Dwarfs from Foreign Types

Determining the ethnicity, and in a few instances the occurrence of actual dwarfism, can be problematic at times regarding the transmission of dwarfs and pygmies in ancient Egyptian scenes and figural arts (see table 18.1, nos. 1, 32, 34, 37, 44, 54, 59, and 67).[4] However, most ancient Egyptian depictions and sculptures adopted some typical features to indicate indigenous Egyptian (and foreign) dwarfs, in contrast to other conventions and stereotypes for portraying and distinguishing between regular Egyptians and foreigners (in this study mainly Nubians, Puntites, and other peoples from sub-Saharan Africa).[5]

Aside from nonillustrated references or allusions to pygmies, the Old Kingdom lacks clear depictions of either sub-Saharan African dwarfs or pygmies, be they

4. Buszek (2008, 41) discusses this problem regarding the ambiguous identity of two figurines at Tarkhan and Tell Ibrahim Awad as either dwarfs or children, but adds that better publication of the objects might have enabled a more precise determination.

5. Verma 2014, 94. See also an earlier study on dwarfs in ancient Egypt by el-Aguizy 1987. "Regular" is being used here to designate both people lacking clear dwarfism in art and the (late) Old Kingdom guidelines, conventions, and styles applied to portraying primary figures and, to a lesser extent, secondary figures in art (see Robins 1994, 64–72, figs. 4.1–5). Verma (2014, 94) and others have already noted some of the stylistic conventions discernable in Old Kingdom portrayals of dwarfs.

FIGURE 18.2. An ex situ marsh scene (no. 1931.99) from an initially unidentified but recently rediscovered tomb at Saqqara, containing a depiction of a dwarf, Widj, currently displayed in the Worcester Art Museum and republished here courtesy of the Worcester Art Museum; Bridgeman Images license 1037891.

Nubian, Puntite, or from elsewhere in sub-Saharan Africa (e.g., Yam).[6] Owing to the excitement caused by the apparent rarity in obtaining a pygmy (*dng*) during both Djedkare Isesi and Pepy II's reigns, one might predict that any such portrayal in an Old Kingdom setting would have been emphasized via additional features or emphasized components, including perhaps a caption. In contrast, regular-sized Nubians tend to be fairly distinct in Egyptian art, including hairstyle, darker skin tones (i.e., in painted compositions), facial features, and sometimes clothing and jewelry (e.g., S. Smith 2003; Booth 2005).

6. See Silverman (1969, 53–55, 59) for a discussion on the precise usage of "pygmy" (*dꜣng*; *dꜣg*) in relatively few Old Kingdom and later contexts, plus an absence of archaeological portrayals of the *dꜣng*/*dꜣg* mentioned in Harkhuf and the Pyramid Texts.

TABLE 18.1. Dwarfs, leopards/cheetahs, primates, *tjesem*-dogs, and other occurrences in Old Kingdom pyramid complexes and elite tombs.

Date/Period	Tomb, etc.	Tomb Owner's Titles	Dwarfs	Associated Scene	References
1. (Dasen no. 14, henceforth D14) Early Dynasty 4; Swinton 2014, 46, 96, IV.1; 2–4 no. 55	**Neferma'at** Mastaba (Petrie no. 16), Meidum	Prophet of goddess Bubastis and Shesmetet; Priest of Min; etc. (son of Sneferu)	Attendant "Little boy" (dwarf?) 2 young men/dwarfs?	**Neferma'at facade** Man with leopard **Itet (wife):** Boy with "apes" (a monkey and baboon) and an ibis **Elsewhere:** Two "young men" with monkey and baboon	Porter and Moss 1934, 92–93; Neferma'at facade, 93 Itet facade; Osborn and Osbornová 1998, 32 fig. 4-4, 33 fig. 4-5; Dasen 1993, 254 no. 14 dwarf(?)
2. (D11) Dynasty 4 (Khufu to Shepseskaf); Swinton 2014, 46, 96, IV.4–6 no. 40	**Meres'ankh III** Rock-cut chapel G7530+7540 east field, Giza	King's daughter of his body; etc.	Dwarf (female) Dwarf (female)	**G7530:** With a monkey (in a scene of offering-bearers) **G7540:** Alongside four female attendants	Porter and Moss 1974, 197, Room I scene (3) in G7530, and 199, chapel north wall in G7540; Thompson 1991, 95 n. 17; Dasen 1993, 111, fig. 9.3, 253 no. 11
3. (D 12) Late Dynasty 4 (Khephren Menkaure); Swinton 2014, 46, 96, IV.5–6 no. 49	**Nebemakhet** Mastaba LG86 central field, Giza	King's son of his body; Chief Justice; Vizier; etc.	Three dwarfs	Jewelry production scene (alongside other industries, plus tomb owners with two baboons)	Porter and Moss 1974, 231, room II (6), register III, 356 section 9d (crafts appendix); Dasen 1993, 253 no. 12
4. (D 13) Dynasty 4 (temp. Menkaure); Swinton 2014, 47, 96, IV.5 no. 113	**Debheni** Rock tomb LG 90 ("Tomb of Hammed es Samaan"), Giza	Overlord of Nekheb; Secretary of the Toilet-house; Master of the largesse in the Mansion of Life; etc.	2 attendants 2 attendants Dwarf (female) with female dancers	**Room I scene (1)** I dog behind them **Room I scene (1)** I monkey behind **Room I scene (3)** in a scene with female dancers and clappers, plus a monkey under the nearby chair of the male tomb owner; Attendants with dog and monkey.	Porter and Moss 1974, 235–36, room I, scene (1) with regular attendants, scene (3), register V, plus scene (1) at entry doorway; Dasen 1993, fig. 9.16, 253–54 no. 13, pl. 18.1

TABLE 18.1. (*cont'd*) Dwarfs, leopards/cheetahs, primates, *tjesem*-dogs, and other occurrences in Old Kingdom pyramid complexes and elite tombs.

Date/Period	Tomb, etc.	Tomb Owner's Titles	Dwarfs	Associated Scene	References
5. (D =no) Dynasty 4 (Old Kingdom); not in Swinton	**Petety** Tomb/burial complex of Petety (Tomb GSE 1923), upper tombs, the artisan's cemetery, Giza	**Titles:** The King's acquaintance; the eldest inspector of the small ones (or commoners) of good reputation, i.e., *smsw nds shd nfrw.* **Burial shaft** Achondroplastic dwarf(?) with large head versus body, or a disability.	Burial shaft no. 5: dwarf? (in one of nine burial shafts)	**Skeleton** of 40–45 year old, female dwarf(?) (in wooden coffin)	Hawass 2003, 116–17, Dynasty 4; pottery in shaft; Hawass 2004, 27, 35, figs. 1–2, pl. 1; Hawass and Senussi 2008, 18 date; Lehner and Hawass 2017, 349–50.
6. (D =no) Dynasty 4 or 5; not in Swinton	**Per-en-ankh (Perniankhu)** Mastaba tomb G1700, west field (near tomb of Seneb), Giza	King's acquaintance; *nmiw?* (dwarf?) of the Great Palace; the one who pleases his majesty every day; the king's dwarf (*nmiw*)*, and the administrator of the treasury. Interpreted as a dancing dwarf. *(See Fischer 2002, 35–39 for this part of his titles and name)	Dwarf (male; tomb owner) Dwarf statue	**Skeleton:** The tomb contained a skeleton of a 40 year old male with achondroplasia (or possibly hypochondroplasia); Hawass 2011, 80, photo of skeleton **Statue:** 48 cm high basalt statue of an achondroplastic dwarf	Thompson 1991, 97 n. 20; Hawass 1991, 157–59; Filer 1995, 55–57, 60; Sampsell 2001, 67–69, 68, photo; Hawass 2003, 66–69; Hawass 2006, 136; Kozma 2006, 305, 307; Kozma 2008, 3106, 3107 fig. 4; Kozma 2010, 2558; Hawass 2011, 77–85

TABLE 18.1. (cont'd) Dwarfs, leopards/cheetahs, primates, tjesem-dogs, and other occurrences in Old Kingdom pyramid complexes and elite tombs.

Date/Period	Tomb, etc.	Tomb Owner's Titles	Dwarfs	Associated Scene	References
7. (D = no) Dynasty 4–5 (Old Kingdom); not in Swinton	**Female dwarf** burial in the workmen's cemetery, lower tombs, Giza	**Achondroplastic female dwarf and child** (mother died during pregnancy); about three feet tall	Dwarf and child	**Skeleton** of female dwarf and unborn child	Hawass 2003, 118; Filer 1995, 56–57; Hawass 2006, 173; Hawass and Senussi 2008, 16 date; Lehner and Hawass 2017, 350
8. (D = no) Dynasty 4–5 (Old Kingdom); not in Swinton	**Female dwarf** burial in the workmen's cemetery, lower tombs, Giza	**Female dwarf** about three feet tall	Dwarf	**Skeleton** of female dwarf	Hawass 2003, 118; Hawass and Senussi 2008, 16 date; Lehner and Hawass 2017, 350
9. (D25) Late Dynasty 4 to early Dynasty 5; not in Swinton	**Queen Khentkaus I** rock-cut step pyramid tomb (mastaba) LG 100, center field, Giza	Various titles	Dwarf (frag.)	In a scene holding a staff or sandals	Porter and Moss 1974, 288–89; Dasen 1993, 256; no. 25 dwarf not noted in PM III
10.a (D41) Redated to Dynasty 4–5 (vs. Dynasty 6); Swinton 2014, 138–39, dates it to Sahure (Dynasty 5)	**Seneb (Sonb)** Mastaba West Field Giza	**Titles:** See below, but including "Director of dwarves in charge of dressing" (Hawass 2011, 83)	Dwarf	Town owner shown in scenes and statues (either achondroplasia, or possibly hypochondroplasia);	Porter and Moss 1974, 101–3; Thompson 1991, 92 n. 7, dated to Dynasty 4–5; Hawass 1991, 161; Dasen 1993, fig. 9.19a–d, 259–60 no. 41; Sampsell 2001, 65, 69; Hawass 2011, 83

TABLE 18.1. (*cont'd*) Dwarfs, leopards/cheetahs, primates, *tjesem*-dogs, and other occurrences in Old Kingdom pyramid complexes and elite tombs.

Date/Period	Tomb, etc.	Tomb Owner's Titles	Dwarfs	Associated Scene	References
10b. (D113) Redated to Dynasty 4–5 (vs. Dynasty 6); Swinton 2014, 138–39, places his tomb in the period of King Sahure, vs. dates by Cherpion (see Sampsell 2001, 72) (early-mid Dynasty 4) or later dates (Dynasty 6)	Seneb (Sonb) Mastaba west field, Giza	Titles: Great one of the litter; Overseer of the dwarfs in charge of linen; Overseer of the *iwhw* (= animal tenders?); Priest of Wadjet, Khufu, Radjedef, the great bull which is at the head of *Spt*, and the bull *Mrhw*; Companion of the house; controller of the palace; Overseer of weaving in the Palace, the administration of the crown of Lower Egypt, the administration of the *mw*, and the crew of the *kz*-ships; Keeper of the God's seal of the *Wn-hr-bw* boat; etc.	(a). Wooden dwarf statue (b). Dwarf statue base in granite (c). Limestone statue group with dwarf	30 cm high; disintegrated (in Hildesheim, Pelizaeus Museum) Missing/unknown Cairo Museum JdE 51.280	Porter and Moss 1974, 102, statue a, 102 chapel III, statue base; el-Aguizy 187, 55–56; Thompson 1991, pl. 16, dated to Dynasty 4–5; Hawass 1991, 161; Dasen 1993, 276–77, no. 113 a, b, and c, pl. 28.2 frontispiece; Filer 1995, 57; Filer 1995, 53, 54, fig. 24; Sampsell 2001, 65–67, 66 photo, 72 for Cherpion redating Seneb's tomb to Dynasty 4; Kozma 2006, 306–7, fig. 4.
11. (D15) Early Dynasty 5; Swinton 2014, 47, 96, IV.6–V.2, no. 106	Kanufer Mastaba G2150 west field, Giza	Overseer of commissions; Herdsman of the White Bull; Director of the Palace	Dwarf	Carrying a monkey upon his head, in scene with people bringing items	Porter and Moss 1974, 77, offering room scene (1), doorway; Dasen 1993, 254 no. 15, pl. 18.2
12. (D20) Early(?) Dynasty 5; not in Swinton	'Ankhma're Rock tomb G7837+7843 east field, Giza	Titles?	Room I (6): Dwarf Room II (7): Dwarf	G7837: Leading a dog (under palanquin) G7843: With a dog and a monkey	Porter and Moss 1974, 206, room I scene (6) in G7837 and room II scene (7) in G7843; Dasen 1993, 255 no. 20

TABLE 18.1. (cont'd) Dwarfs, leopards/cheetahs, primates, *tjesem*-dogs, and other occurrences in Old Kingdom pyramid complexes and elite tombs.

Date/Period	Tomb, etc.	Tomb Owner's Titles	Dwarfs	Associated Scene	References
13. (D17) Early Dynasty 5; Swinton 2014, 45, 98, V.2–3 no. 21	**Wehemka** Mastaba D.117 west field, Giza	Scribe of the archives and of recruits; Steward; etc.	Dwarf (male attendant); name: Neferhuu	Bringing various articles (basket; sandals) alongside female bearers	Porter and Moss 1974, 115, chapel doorway (3); Dasen 1993, 111, fig. 9.3, 254 no. 17
14. (D32) Early Dynasty 5; Swinton 2014, 40, 47, VI.1L–2E no. 99	**Ka'aper (Kai-aperu)** Tomb loc. unknown; north of Step Pyramid, Saqqara	Judge; Boundary official; Scribe of the king's expedition in Wenet, Serer, Tepa and Ida; etc.	Dwarf Regular harpist	In a scene before a flutist, with arms raised, while a monkey is beside a harpist: probably a paired dwarf and monkey, albeit in adjacent scenes; a rare or unique? scene of a solo dance by a dwarf.	Porter and Moss 1978, 501, chapel scene (4); Thompson 1991, 93 n. 10; Dasen 1993, fig. 9.18, 257–58 no. 32; Kinney 2012, 62, 63, fig. 13
15. (D26) Dynasty 5 context; not in Swinton	**Unknown** From Sahure Pyramid complex, Abusir	Fragmentary relief originating from Ty	Dwarf	In a scene with a man and his dog	Dasen 1993, 256, no. 26, citing Porter and Moss 1974, 332.
16. (D27) Dynasty 5 context; not in Swinton	**Unknown** From Neuserre Pyramid complex, Abusir	Fragmentary relief originating from elsewhere	Dwarf (zwerges)	In an unpublished scene	Dasen 1993, 256, no. 27, unpublished citing Porter and Moss 1974, "33" (for 337–39?).
17. (D19) Early–mid Dynasty 5 (redated to Dynasty 4; temp. Khafre); Swinton 2014, 46, 96, IV.5– V.1 no. 60	**Nesutnufer** Mastaba G4970 west field, Giza	Overseer of strongholds of the Heliopolitan-East nome; Leader of the land of the Thinite and Aphroditopolite nomes; etc. (perhaps Seneb's son?)	Two dwarfs Title+names: *Iswu*, Re djed-ef-ankh; *Iswu*, Ankh; *iwdj-sw*; attendants and two Nubians	In a scene holding a fly whisk and headrest, accompanied by offering-bearers, plus two Nubians bringing animals	Porter and Moss 1974, 144, chapel scenes (5)–(7); Dasen 1993, 112, fig. 9.4, 255, no.19; Sampsell 2001, 72 redating; perhaps Seneb's son.

TABLE 18.1. (*cont'd*) Dwarfs, leopards/cheetahs, primates, *tjesem*-dogs, and other occurrences in Old Kingdom pyramid complexes and elite tombs.

Date/Period	Tomb, etc.	Tomb Owner's Titles	Dwarfs	Associated Scene	References
18. (D33) Dynasty 5 (temp. Neferirkare or later); not in Swinton	**Neferirtenef** Mastaba D55 east of Step Pyramid, Saqqara	Judge; Overseer of scribes; Prophet of Sahure; Prophet of Re in the Sun temples of Userkaf and Neferirkare; etc.	Dwarf (title: retainer)	Leading a dog and monkey (below the tomb owner and his wife)	Porter and Moss 1979, 583, 584, chapel, scene (8); Harpur 1987, 503, fig. 133 top, left side; Thompson 1991, 94, fig. 3; Dasen 1993, fig. 9.10, 258, no. 33
19. (D29) Dynasty 5 (temp. Neuserre+); Swinton 2014, 141, redates it to Djedkare (Dynasty 5)	**Ty (Mariette)** Tomb no. 60 (D22), north of Step Pyramid, Saqqara	Overseer of the Pyramids of Neferirkare and Neuserre, and of the Sun-temples of Sahure, Neferirkare, Ra'neferef, and Neuserre; etc.	Dwarf (title: *iwḥw* = tender?; name: Pepi) Dwarf	**Pillared hall scene:** Leading a dog and monkey (below palanquin) **Inner hall scene:** Dwarf holding a baton, leading a monkey alongside man with a dog.	Porter and Moss 1978, 470, room II, pillared hall, scene (6)–(7), and 475 room VI, inner hall, scene (44), register VII; Dasen 1993, 257, no. 29, pl. 20.1–2; Jones 2000, 7–8, no. 29
20. (D37) Dynasty 5 (temp. Neuserre or Menkauhor); Swinton 2014, 46, 100, V.6L–8E no. 44	**Ni'ankh khnum** and **Khnemhotep** Mastaba (no number, plan lxvi), near Unas Pyramid, Saqqara	(a). Prophet of Re in the Sun-temple of Neuserre; Overseer of manicurists of the Great House; etc. (b). Prophet of Re in the Sun-temple of Neuserre; Overseer of manicurists of the Great House; etc.	Craftsmen Dwarf	No apparent dwarfs in the scene of industries, including jewelry production In a scene carrying a box and placed beneath palanquin	Porter and Moss 1978, 641, 643, outer hall, scene (19), register III; Dasen 1993, 258–59, no. 37 dwarf not noted in PM III., pl. 22.2
21. (D22) Mid-Dynasty 5 or later; not in Swinton	**Itisen** Mastaba and rock tomb (no number, plan xxxii), central field, Giza	Greatest of the Ten of Upper Egypt; Director of scribes in the Great Broad Hall; Prophet of Ma'at; etc.	Attendants and dwarf (at end of line)	In a scene leading two dogs, a monkey, and a baboon (in register IV); below scenes of a palanquin and attendants (I–II), and bearers (III)	Porter and Moss 1974, 252, pillared offering room, scene (2), register IV; Dasen 1993, 255; no. 22 dwarf not noted in PM III.

TABLE 18.1. (cont'd) Dwarfs, leopards/cheetahs, primates, tjesem-dogs, and other occurrences in Old Kingdom pyramid complexes and elite tombs.

Date/Period	Tomb, etc.	Tomb Owner's Titles	Dwarfs	Associated Scene	References
22: (D24) Mid-late Dynasty 5; Swinton 2014, 45, 96, IV.2 no. 19	**Wepemnefert** (called Wep) Rock tomb (no number, plan xxiii, E 9), central field, Giza	Secretary of the Toilet-house; Boundary official of Dep; Master of the largesse in the Mansion of Life; etc.	Two groups of two dwarfs (n = 4)	Manufacturing jewelry (alongside baking scene, and other industries)	Porter and Moss 1974, 282, offering-room (6), register III; Thompson 1991, 93, 94, fig. 7; Dasen 1993, fig. 9.14, 256, no. 24, pl. 19.2a–b
23: (D36) Mid-late Dynasty 5; Swinton 2014, 46, V.6 no. 53	**Nufer / Nefer (and K3-ḥ3)** Mastaba near Teti Pyramid, Saqqara	Inspector of the wa'bt; Director of singers; etc.	Two groups of two dwarfs (n = 4) Attendant \ \ Dwarf	**Offering room (1):** In a scene near the tomb owner's family and dog; **Offering room (3):** A scene of boat-building with a monkey and baboon, plus an official with a sunshade bearer **Offering room (4):** In a scene with two scribes, holding a scribal palette (also described as holding a box)	Porter and Moss 1979, 639, 640, offering-room, scene (1)–(2), (3), register II, and 640, offering-room scene (4), register I; Thompson 1991, 93 n. 12; Dasen 1993, 112, fig. 9.5, 258, no. 36; Filer 1995, 58–59.
24: (D30) Late Dynasty 5; not in Swinton	**Kaemrehu** Mastaba 79 (D2; S905), north of the Step Pyramid, Saqqara	Secretary of the Toilet-house; Prophet of the Pyramid of Neuserre; etc.	Two dwarfs	In a scene making jewelry, alongside other industries.	Porter and Moss 1978, 485, 486, chapel, scene (2), register IV; Dasen 1993, 257, no. 30
25: (D*) Citing the reign of Djedkare Isesi (i.e., Dynasty 5); not in Swinton	**Harkhuf** Rock tomb Qubbet el Hawa, Elephantine		A dancing pygmy from Punt	**Text:** "a pygmy who dances for the god from the land of the Horizon dwellers, just like the pygmy which the seal-bearer of the god Wer-djed ed-ba brought back from the land of Punt in the time of Izezi."	Thompson 1991, 95, 97 using dng; Strudwick 2005, 332.

TABLE 18.1. (*cont'd*) Dwarfs, leopards/cheetahs, primates, *tjesem*-dogs, and other occurrences in Old Kingdom pyramid complexes and elite tombs.

Date/Period	Tomb, etc.	Tomb Owner's Titles	Dwarfs	Associated Scene	References
26. (D34) Late Dynasty 5 (temp. Isesi to Unas); Swinton 2014, 45, 132, V.9 no. 27	Ptahhotep II (Tjefi) Mastaba complex D64 west of Step Pyramid, Saqqara	Chief Justice, Vizier; Inspector of prophets of the Pyramids of Menkauhor and Isesi; Inspector of *wa'b*-priests of the Pyramid of Neuserre; etc.	Two groups of two dwarfs (n = 4) Attendants	**Offering-room:** In a scene making jewelry, near the tomb owner and other attendants, including one attendant with a dog and monkeys, harpist and singer. **Offering-room:** Bringing leopard and lion in cages, hyenas and dogs on leashes, small animals in boxes	Porter and Moss 1979, 600, offering-room, scene (16), register (b), 602, offering-room, scene (18), register II; Dasen 1993, 258, no. 34, pl. 21
27. (D16) Late Dynasty 5 (Unas); Swinton 2014, 47, 120, V.9M no. 85	Senedjemib, good name Mehi Mastaba LG26, G2378 west field, Giza	Chief Justice; Vizier; King's architect and builder in the Two Houses; etc.	Two groups of two dwarfs (n = 4)	Manufacturing jewelry (alongside people making vases)	Porter and Moss 1974, 88, register III chapel hall (6); Dasen 1993, fig. 9.3, 254, no. 16
28. (D18) Dynasty 5; Swinton 2014, 47, 128, V.2–3 no. 90	Seshemnufer I Mastaba G4940 west field, Giza	Royal chamberlain; One belonging to the estate "Mansion of Har-kheper"; Prophet of Heket; Judge; Boundary official; etc.	Dwarf (female) Female offering-bearer	In a scene holding a box on her head, with another female bearer	Porter and Moss 1974, 142–43 (not noting a dwarf); Dasen 1993, 254–55, no. 18, pl. 19.1a–b
29. (D21) Dynasty 5; not in Swinton	Tjenti Mastaba east of Tomb LG 68, Giza	Director of the dining hall of the Great House; Overseer of the *ka* servants; etc.	Dwarf	In a scene leading a bull, alongside other animals	Porter and Moss 1974, 210 (not noting a dwarf); Dasen 1993, 255, no. 21

TABLE 18.1. (cont'd) Dwarfs, leopards/cheetahs, primates, *tjesem*-dogs, and other occurrences in Old Kingdom pyramid complexes and elite tombs.

Date/Period	Tomb, etc.	Tomb Owner's Titles	Dwarfs	Associated Scene	References
30. (D28) Dynasty 5 (temp. Neuserre or later); not in Swinton	**Kaemnefert** Mastaba no. 57 (D23) north of the Step Pyramid, Saqqara	Prophet of Re in the Sun-temples of Userkaf, Neferir ka-re and Neuserre; Prophet of Khephren and Sahure wa'b-priest of the the pyramids of Sahure and Neuserre	Dwarf	In a scene with a staff, leading a monkey, following a palanquin.	Porter and Moss 1978, 467–68; Dasen 1993, 256–57, no. 28
31. (D31) (late) Dynasty 5; not in Swinton	**Nikauhor** Mastaba S915, Saqqara	Prophet of Re in the Sun-temple of Userkaf; Prophet of Userkaf; etc.	Dwarf Attendants	In a scene carrying sandals, in a line of attendants	Porter and Moss 1978, 498; Dasen 1993, 257, no. 31
32. (D38) Dynasty 5; not in Swinton	**Kai-khent** Lower Tomb/"Tomb of Afa" rock tomb, Hammamiya	Chief of the Tens of Upper Egypt; Overseer of works in the central nomes of Upper Egypt; etc.	Dwarf Dwarf(?) title/name: scribe Keresi	In a scene leading an ox; in a scene at the prow of a boat	Porter and Moss 1937, 8; Thompson 1991, 93, 95, 96, fig. 5; Dasen 1993, 259, no. 38
33. (D39) Dynasty 5; not in Swinton	**Kaemnefert** Rock tomb, El-Hagarsa	King's priest; Overseer of *nswtyu*;	Dwarf (female) Female attendants	In a scene bringing furnishings (a tall shrine-type box), with other female bearers	Porter and Moss 1937, 35 Dynasty 4; Thompson 1991, 94, fig. 10, 95; Dasen 1993, 112, fig. 9.6, 259, no. 39
34. (D35) Late Dynasty 5 (Unas); Swinton 2014, 46, V.9 no. 50	**Queen Nebet** Twin mastaba by Unas Pyramid, Saqqara	King's wife (of Unas); Companion of Horus; etc.	Dwarf (female) Other female attendants	Carrying sandals and a box, in a register behind the queen, with other female attendants (bringing wine)	Porter and Moss 1978, 623, 624, room II, scene (8), register IV; Thompson 1991, 95 n. 17; Dasen 1993, 258, no. 35
35. (D23) Late Dynasty 5 or early Dynasty 6; not in Swinton	**Ireru** Mastaba (no number, plan xxiii, E 8), central field, Giza	Overseer of the storeroom of the King's repast; King's wa'b-priest; etc.	Dwarf Others	Leading a bull/ox (in a scene with a scribe and butchers)	Porter and Moss 1974, 280, west chapel, between false doors; Dasen 1993, fig. 9.12, 255–56, no. 23

TABLE 18.1. (*cont'd*) Dwarfs, leopards/cheetahs, primates, *tjesem*-dogs, and other occurrences in Old Kingdom pyramid complexes and elite tombs.

Date/Period	Tomb, etc.	Tomb Owner's Titles	Dwarfs	Associated Scene	References
36. (D55) Late Dynasty 5 (Unas) or Dynasty 6; not in Swinton	**Kairer** Mastaba (no number, plan lxv), near Unas Pyramid, Saqqara	Titles?	Two groups of two dwarfs (n = 4) Other workers	Four dwarfs making jewelry (in scene with people making statues, plus industrial scenes in registers beside tomb owner and wife)	Porter and Moss 1979, 631, room II, scene (9), registers I–II; Dasen 1993, 263, no. 55
37. (D112) Dynasty 5–6; not in Swinton	**Petpennesut** Limestone statue from mud-brick mastaba tomb G1105, Giza	**Tomb owner:** No titles for this dwarf (name only)	One limestone dwarf (?) statue 48 cm high	**Statue** of standing dwarf with a kilt; base inscribed with his name.	Porter and Moss 1974, 55, plan X; Dasen 1993, 275, 276, no. 112.
38. (D114) Dynasty 5–6; not in Swinton	**Unknown** Mastaba tomb G7715 east field, Giza	**Servant statuette** Cairo Museum, JdE 72.144	One limestone dwarf statue 4.7 cm high	**Statue** of standing, naked dwarf carrying four pottery vessels	Porter and Moss 1974, 203, Dynasty 6; Dasen 1993, 277, no. 114.
39. (D115) Dynasty 5–6; not in Swinton	**Nikauinpu** Mastaba tomb number (?) west field?, Giza	**Servant statuette** Chicago, Oriental Institute, 10627	One limestone dwarf statue 21.4 cm high	**Statue** of standing, naked dwarf carrying a bag over left shoulder	Porter and Moss 1974, 300, Dynasty 5–6; Dasen 1993, 277, no. 115, pl. 29.1.
40. (D116) Dynasty 5–6; not in Swinton	**Nikauinpu** Mastaba tomb number (?) west field?, Giza	**Servant statuette** Chicago, Oriental Institute, 10641	One limestone dwarf statue 12.5 cm high	**Statue** of a seated, naked dwarf with a harp; the dwarf displays classic achondroplasia.	Porter and Moss 1974, 301, Dynasty 5–6; Thompson 1991, 93 n. 11; Dasen 1993, 277, no. 116, pl. 29.3a–b; Kozma 2006, 310, fig. 10

TABLE 18.1. (cont'd) Dwarfs, leopards/cheetahs, primates, tjesem-dogs, and other occurrences in Old Kingdom pyramid complexes and elite tombs.

Date/Period	Tomb, etc.	Tomb Owner's Titles	Dwarfs	Associated Scene	References
41. (D117) Dynasty 5–6; (tomb unknown)	**Khnumhotep** (ex situ statue, most probably from a tomb for him at Saqqara)	**Prob. tomb owner** Cairo Museum, CG 144; Chief of the perfumers(?); Overseer of linen (or clothing); ka servant.	One limestone dwarf statue 46 cm high Titles/name: Overseer of linen, and ka servant; Khnumhotep	**Statue** of standing dwarf with a kilt on a base; his statue has a large cranium and an elongated skull, but normal facial features.	Porter and Moss 1979, 722–23, late Dynasty 5 or Dynasty 6; el-Aguizy 1987, 56; Thompson 1991, 92 n. 6; Dasen 1993, 277–78, no. 117, pl. 29.2; Filer 1995, 57, 58. fig. 30, 60; Sampsell 2001, 64–65; Kozma 2006, 308; Hawass 2011, 83
42. (D118) Dynasty 5–6; (tomb unknown)	**Unknown provenance**	**Servant statuette** Baltimore, Walters Art Gallery (WAG) 71.504	One ivory dwarf statue 8.9 cm high	**Statue** of standing, naked dwarf with hands on chest, a peg-hole in the head (for carrying something on his head?)	Dasen 1993, 278, no. 118, pl. 30.1; Kozma 2010, 2558, fig. 5 cat. no. 71.504
43. (D46) Dynasty 5–6; Swinton 2014, 100, V.8(?)	**Seshemnufer Tjeti** (called Theti) Mastaba (no number, plan xxxii); cemetery GIS, Giza	Chief of bat; Sole companion; Director of the Two Seats; etc.	Dwarf (frag.) Title+name: Overseer of linen, Nefer wedenet.	In a scene with a dog and monkey on a leash; below a palanquin with the tomb owner.	Porter and Moss 1974, 227, room I, fragment probably from south wall; Dasen 1993, 261, no. 46
44. (D47) Dynasty 5–6; Swinton 2014, 100, V.6L–8E	**Ni'ankh Khnum** (no number, plan xxiii, B-6) central field, Giza	Overseer of commissions of the Great House; Inspector of Nubians; King's adorner and Keeper of gold; etc.	Dwarf(?) Other attendants	In a scene leading an ox (along with offering-bearers and butchers); shown smaller, but proportionate (may not be a dwarf).	Porter and Moss 1974, 248, chapel scene between false doors; Dasen 1993, 261, no. 47 questioned identity as dwarf

TABLE 18.1. (cont'd) Dwarfs, leopards/cheetahs, primates, *tjesem*-dogs, and other occurrences in Old Kingdom pyramid complexes and elite tombs.

Date/Period	Tomb, etc.	Tomb Owner's Titles	Dwarfs	Associated Scene	References
45. (D56) Dynasty 5–6; Swinton 2014, 100, V.8L–9E	**Akhtihotep** Mastaba tomb by King Unas Pyramid, Saqqara	Secretary of the toilet-house; Prophet of Khnum in all his places; Prophet of Heka; etc.	Dwarf	In a marsh scene, standing behind people catching birds.	Porter and Moss 1979, 635–36, Dynasty 5 or Dynasty 6, chapel scene (3); Dasen 1993, 263, no. 56
46. (D =no) Dynasty 6 (temp. Pepi I); not in Swinton	**Ni-ankh-pepi** The Black Rock tomb chapel A (n.1), Meir	Governor; Overseer of Upper Egypt; Treasurer of the king of Lower Egypt; Overseer of prophets; etc.	Dwarf ("pygmy")	Fragmentary scene: Dwarf holding an oblong item (a stick?; a leash?) to a dog's mouth; both are under the tomb owner's chair.	Blackman and Apted 1953, 27, pl. 19; Thompson 1991, 95 n. 14.
47. (D49) Early Dynasty 6; Swinton 2014, 45, 102, VI.1M–E no. 15	**'Ankhma'hor** Sesi Mastaba near Teti Pyramid, Saqqara	Chief Justice; Vizier; Inspector of prophets and Tenant of the Pyramid of Teti; etc.	Three groups of two dwarfs (n = 6) Dwarf	**Room II scene 7:** Making jewelry (alongside other industries) **Room II scene 8:** Holding a fruit basket, with a monkey on his shoulder (near tomb owner, son, and other attendants)	Porter and Moss 1978, 512, 513, room II, scene (7) register III, and scene (8); Thompson 1991, 94, fig. 4; Dasen 1993, 261, no. 49; Osborn and Osbornová 1998, 40, fig. 4-35, 120.
48. (D51) Early Dynasty 6 (temp. Teti); Swinton 2014, 47, 100, no. 111 VI.1E–M	**Kagemni (Gemnikai)** (Memi) Mastaba near Teti Pyramid, Saqqara	Chief Justice, Vizier; Overseer of the Pyramid-town of Teti; etc.	Dwarf Other attendants	In a scene leading a monkey and dogs (under a palanquin, near attendants and sunshade bearers)	Porter and Moss 1978, 523, room IV, scene (22); Dasen 1993, 262, no. 51; Osborn and Osbornová 1998, 40, fig. 4-34, 120

TABLE 18.1. (cont'd) Dwarfs, leopards/cheetahs, primates, *tjesem*-dogs, and other occurrences in Old Kingdom pyramid complexes and elite tombs.

Date/Period	Tomb, etc.	Tomb Owner's Titles	Dwarfs	Associated Scene	References
49. (D52) Early Dynasty 6 (temp. Teti); Swinton 2014, 45, 46, VI.1L–2E no. 38	**Mereruka** (Meri) Mastaba near Teti Pyramid, Saqqara	Chief Justice; Vizier; Inspector of prophets and tenants of the Pyramid of Teti; etc.	Two groups of dwarfs (n = 4) Dwarf and attendants Two dwarfs Twelve female dwarfs Title: Supervisor of the treasury	**(A). Room III:** in a scene making jewelry with other jewelers, etc. **(A). Room IV:** in a scene with a monkey and two dogs, plus other attendants, **(A). Room XIII:** in a scene leading a monkey and three dogs (under nearby palanquin and other attendants) **(B). Room V:** a scene with a monkey and two dogs beneath a palanquin and twelve associated female dwarf attendants, men, women, etc.; box of "myrrh"	Porter and Moss 1978, 525, 528, room III, scene (20), 529, room IV, scene (27), and 532 room XIII, scene (74) in Mereruka's chapel; Osborn and Osbornová 1998, 40, fig. 4–33; Sampsell 2001, 62 photo; Porter and Moss 1978, 534, 535, room V, scene (108); Thompson 1991, 91 n. 5, 95; Dasen 1993, fig. 9.9, fig. 9.11, 262 no. 52, pl. 22.1a–b, 23a–b
	Waʿtetkhet Hor (wife of Mereruka)				
	Meryteti chapel		Dwarf	**(C). Room III:** dwarf with offering-bearers	
50. (D48) Early Dynasty 6 (Pepy I); Swinton 2014, 46, VI.1L–2, no. 79	**Khentika Ikhekhi** Mastaba near Teti Pyramid, Saqqara	Real Chief Justice; Vizier; Inspector of prophets of the Pyramids of Teti and Pepy I; etc.	Dwarf Title+name: Overseer of the household (Steward) ʿAnkhef	Egyptian dwarf holding a cloth(?) and giving a box to the seated tomb owner	Porter and Moss 1978, 508, 510, room IX, scene (38), doorway; Thompson 1991, 92, 94, fig. 2; Dasen 1993, fig. 9.8, 261 no. 48
51. (D =no) Dynasty 6 (Tomb of King Pepy I)	**Pepy I** Pyramid burial complex, Saqqara	Pyramid Text spell 517 of King Pepy I (P465)	Pygmy (vs. dwarf)	Pepy spell 465 to the ferryman about Pepy I: "He is a dwarf/pygmy of the god's dances, an entertainer before his [great] seat" (Allen 2005, 159)	Faulkner 1969, 191, utterance 517, no. 1189; Thompson 1991, 95, 97 using *ting*; Allen 2005, 159 (Pepi I corridor), 383 (P 465 = PT517), 407, 451

TABLE 18.1. (*cont'd*) Dwarfs, leopards/cheetahs, primates, *tjesem*-dogs, and other occurrences in Old Kingdom pyramid complexes and elite tombs.

Date/Period	Tomb, etc.	Tomb Owner's Titles	Dwarfs	Associated Scene	References
52. (D =no) Dynasty 6 (Tomb of King Merenre)	**Merenre** Pyramid burial complex, Saqqara	Pyramid Text spell 517 of Merenre (M357)	Pygmy (vs. dwarf)	Pepy spell 465 to the ferryman about Merenre (see Allen 2005, 159)	Faulkner 1969, 191 utterance 517, no. 1189; Thompson 1991, 95, 97 using *dng*; Allen 2005, 229 (Merenre corridor), 387 (M 357 = PT517), 407, 451
53. (D =no) Dynasty 6 (Tomb of Queen Neith)	**Queen Neith** Pyramid burial complex, Saqqara	Pyramid Text spell 517 of Queen Neith (N545)	Pygmy (vs. dwarf)	Pepy spell 465 to the ferryman about Queen Neith (see Allen 2005, 159)	Faulkner 1969, 191 utterance 517, no. 1189; Thompson 1991, 95, 97 using *dng*; Allen 2005, 392 (N 545 = PT517), 407, 451
54. (D40) Early Dynasty 6; not in Swinton	**Hetepniptah** Mastaba G2430 west field, Giza	Overseer of tenants of the Great House; Director of the Palace; Secretary of his Lord; etc.	Dwarf(?)	Leading a dog(s) and monkey, placed below palanquin.	Porter and Moss 1974, 94, chapel doorway (2); Dasen 1993, 259, no. 40, questioned identity as dwarf
55. (D44) Early Dynasty 6; not in Swinton	**Nefer/Nufer** (good name Idu [I]) Mastaba G5550, west field, Giza	Chief Justice; Vizier; etc.	Dwarf Titles+name: Overseer of linen, *ka* servant, Merri	Carrying monkey above head (appears under chair of tomb owner)	Porter and Moss 1974, 165, chapel south wall; Dasen 1993, 260, no. 44
56. (D50) Mid-Dynasty 6; Swinton 2014, 45, 102, VI.1L–2, no. 36	**Mereri** Mastaba near Teti Pyramid, Saqqara	Count; Overseer of the department of tenants of the Great House; etc.	Dwarf Title+name: Overseer of linen, *ka* servant Redi	In a scene carrying a box, situated behind the family of the tomb owner; in a marsh scene	Porter and Moss 1978, 518, outer hall, scene (3); Thompson 1991, 92, 92, fig. 1; Dasen 1993, 262, no. 50
57. (D45) Late Dynasty 5 to early Dynasty 6; not in Swinton	**Nunetjer** Mastaba (no number, plan xix [1]) cemetery GIS, Giza	No titles (wife: Henutsen)	Dwarf (female or male?) Female dancers, etc.	Dancing in a scene holding sistrum (and directing dancers), with some female dancers and clappers (near wife and daughter); a monkey under tomb owner's chair	Porter and Moss 1974, 217, chapel, west wall registers I–II (female dwarf imitating female dancer); Thompson 1991, 93, 96 fig. 6; Dasen 1993, fig. 9.17, 260–61, no. 45; Kinney 2012, 62–64, fig. 14

TABLE 18.1. (cont'd) Dwarfs, leopards/cheetahs, primates, *tjesem*-dogs, and other occurrences in Old Kingdom pyramid complexes and elite tombs.

Date/Period	Tomb, etc.	Tomb Owner's Titles	Dwarfs	Associated Scene	References
58. (D43) Dynasty 6; not in Swinton	**Khentkawes** Mastaba (no number, plan xxxiv) west field, Giza	Prophetess of Hathor; Mistress of Dendera; etc.	Dwarf (may not be female) Attendants	Placed before seated couple (parents?), holding a fly-whisk(?) near attendants and men bringing animals	Porter and Moss 1974, 149, room II (2), doorway; Dasen 1993, fig. 9.7, 260, no. 43 described with kilt
59. (D42) Dynasty 6; not in Swinton	**Inpuhotep** Mastaba (no number, plan xxxiv) west field, Giza	Prophet of the shrine of Anubis in Aphroditopolis; Prophet of Sahure and Neuserre; Prophet of Re in the Sun-temple of Neuserre; etc.	Two dwarfs(?)	Shown smaller, but proportionate, and bringing cattle	Porter and Moss 1974, 107, chapel doorway; Dasen 1993. 260, no. 42, questioned regarding identity as dwarfs
60. (D =no) Late Dynasty 6; not in Swinton	**Shepsipumin/ Kheni** Rock tomb H24. Akhmim El-Hawawish	Count; Treasurer of the king of Lower Egypt; *sem*-priest; director of every kilt; keeper of the headdress; etc.	Dwarf Title-name: Keeper of the monkeys (*iri?-gf*), Hebeb	A fragmentary scene with a dwarf holding a leash for a probable monkey and holding sandals; under a palanquin	Kanawati 1981, 26, fig. 21; Thompson 1991, 93 n. 13.
61. (D*) Late Dynasty 6 (temp. Pepy II); not in Swinton	**Harkhuf** Rock tomb, Qubbet el Hawa, Elephantine	Governor; etc.	Pygmy (vs. dwarf): A dancing pygmy from Iam (Yam)	**Text:** "you have brought back a pygmy who dances for the god from the land of the Horizon dwellers"	Thompson 1991, 95, 97 using *dng*; Sampsell 2001, 69; Strudwick 2005, 332
62. (D59) mid-Dynasty 5 to early Dynasty 6 vs. late Dynasty 6; Swinton 2014, 143–44 redating to early to mid-Dynasty 6	**Inti** Rock tomb, Deshasheh	Overseer of commissions; Overseer of royal monuments; Ruler of the Residence.	Three dwarfs Dwarf	Following a row of offering-bearers: one carrying box on his head and a collar; two in fragmentary metalworking scene; at the stern of a boat holding unidentified item	Porter and Moss 1934, 121–22, chapel scene (3) and (6); Thompson 1991, 95 n. 15; Dasen 1993, fig. 9.13b, 264, no. 59; Filer 1995, 58–59, fig. 33.

TABLE 18.1 (*cont'd*) Dwarfs, leopards/cheetahs, primates, *tjesem*-dogs, and other occurrences in Old Kingdom pyramid complexes and elite tombs.

Date/Period	Tomb, etc.	Tomb Owner's Titles	Dwarfs	Associated Scene	References
63. (D60) Dynasty 6	**Ipi or Heribi** Rock tomb (no. 481), Beni Hasan	Ruler of the Residence; Intimate **Subsidiary burial** of dwarf in Pit S14: Coffin (no body?)	Dwarf Pit S14 had a coffin for this dwarf.	A scene showing a dwarf holding a baton with a hand, and a dog nearby, below a chair.	Porter and Moss 1934, 161; Dasen 1993, 264–65, no. 60
64. (D61) Dynasty 6	**Serfka** Rock tomb, el-Sheikh Sa'd	Seshemta of the Hare-nome; Prophet of Khufu and Userkaf; Overseer of the New Towns; Overseer of the central nomes of Upper Egypt; etc.	Dwarf / Four dwarfs / Dwarf	With a monkey on a leash, below tomb owner's chair; Jewelry production; Leading a dog and holding a baton(?)	Porter and Moss 1934, 187–88, outer hall scenes and (6); Thompson 1991, 93, 95, 96, fig. 8; Dasen 1993, fig. 9.15a–b, 265, no. 61; Filer 1995, 57, 59, fig. 32.
65. (D62) Dynasty 6; not in Swinton	**Ibi** Rock tomb, Deir el Gabrawi	Nomarch of the Anteopolite nome; Assistant prophet of the pyramid of Neferkare; etc.	Two pairs of dwarfs (n = 4)	Jewelry production scene, standing beside box, holding a mirror, below chair of tomb owner	Porter and Moss 1934: 243–44, hall scene (12)–(13); Thompson 1991, 92 fig. 9, 95; Dasen 1993, 265, no. 62
66. (D63) Dynasty 6; not in Swinton	**Nenankhpepy** Rock tomb, Hierakonpolis (Kom el-Ahmar)	Seal-bearer; etc.	Dwarf	Unpublished scene of a "rachitic achondroplast" dwarf standing on a palanquin of Men-pepi	Porter and Moss 1937, 197, Dynasty 6; omitting mention of a dwarf; Dasen 1993, 266, no. 63
67. (D58) Dynasty 6 (tomb unknown)	**Unknown** Ex situ mastaba tomb block from Saqqara(?)	No details	Female dwarf(?) Name: Sankhwt hwt-hrw	**Door jamb frag.:** A standing female, holding a box, with a smaller female behind her	Dasen 1993, 264, no. 58, private collection: G. Michailidis Collection
68. (D53) Dynasty 6; Swinton 2014, 33, 46, 122, VI.1L, no. 69(?)	**Hesy, Hapi** Mastaba, Saqqara	Various titles (may be Swinton 2014, 33, no. 69)	Dwarf / Dwarf	**Portico west wall:** Standing behind man catching birds **Western facade:** Leading a monkey and dog; near a line of attendants	Dasen 1993, 263, no. 53 unpublished; now published by Kanawati and Abd er-Razeq 1999; see Swinton 2014: 33. no. 69(?), 182

TABLE 18.1. (cont'd) Dwarfs, leopards/cheetahs, primates, *tjesem*-dogs, and other occurrences in Old Kingdom pyramid complexes and elite tombs.

Date/Period	Tomb, etc.	Tomb Owner's Titles	Dwarfs	Associated Scene	References
69. (D54) Dynasty 6; Swinton 2014, 27, 46, 102, VI.1M no. 47	**Nikauisesi** Mastaba, Saqqara	Various titles (see Swinton 2014, 27, no.47: Count; Sole companion; Overseer of priests; Lector priest; etc.)	Dwarf Title+name: Overseer Iri n-ptah(?) Dwarf Name: Iri? Dwarf(?) Title+name: Treasurer Iti	In a scene standing behind tomb owner Accompanying a monkey and 3 dogs, below a palanquin, carrying a box and leading a dog	Dasen 1993: 263 no. 54 unpublished; now published by Kanawati and Abd er-Razeq 2000; see Swinton 2014, 27, no. 47, 182
70. (D64) Dynasty 6 (tomb unknown)	**Unknown** Ex situ block without provenance	Hanover, Kestner Museum, 1935.200.201	Dwarf	Standing on a boat cabin and holding something in his left hand	Dasen 1993, 266, no. 64
71. (D57) Early Dynasty (tomb recently rediscovered)	**Ni'ankhnesut** Ex situ mastaba tomb block from Saqqara	Kofler-Truniger Collection A.90	Left dwarf Title+name: Treasurer, Hetep Right dwarf	Fragmentary scene; dwarf holding bag and leading a monkey and leopard (cheetah/panther). Dwarf carrying sandals and leading two dogs	Porter and Moss 1979, 696, private collection: Kofler Truniger collection; Dasen 1993, 263, 264, no. 57
72. (D =no) Early Dynasty (probably post Teti) (tomb recently rediscovered)	**Ni'ankhnesut** Ex situ mastaba tomb blocks, from Saqqara	Worcester (Mass.), Art Museum, No. 1931.99; Lector priest of (king) Teti; etc.	Dwarf Name: Widj (*Wiḏ*)	In a scene leading a long-tailed monkey and dog on a leash; near other officials and a marsh scene	Porter and Moss 1979, 696; Worcester Art Museum: Image online (https://worcester.emuseum.com/search/1931.99).
73. (D =no) Late Dynasty 5 to early Dynasty 6; not in Swinton; assigned V.8–9?	**Khunes(?)** Rock tomb 2, Zawyet el Maiytin (also called Zawyet Sultan and Z. el-Amwat)	Overseer of commissions; Ruler of the residence; etc.	Dwarfs Attendants Attendant	Thompson (1991, 95) notes dwarf(s) in a scene of jewelry making from Zawyet el Maiytin, which may fit Khunes Attendants with dogs and a baboon Man with dog	Porter and Moss 1934, 134–35; see also 135, hall scenes (8)?, (10); Harpur 1987, 118, 195; Thompson 1991, 95; Gillam, York University, Dec. 2014 season at Khunes and Kheteti (ARCE archives)

Puntites are usually portrayed differently from Nubians: In the better-represented (later) New Kingdom depictions of Puntites, one sees a different people in their appearance and dress.[7] The adult males and females, and children, are shown with a regular physique and reddish skin, excepting the queen of Punt who is portrayed as quite overweight. Many males have shoulder-length hair with a goatee curled at the end, while other males are clean-shaven, perhaps representing youths (e.g., the sons of the ruler of Punt); the chief of Punt appears to have a closely shaved head without a fillet. Otherwise, men frequently sport a plain headband with a back knot and short hanging ends, while other males are shown bare-headed. The male adults often have a bead necklace and wear short, wrap-around kilts, with a single or double fold hanging in front, and a belt with a short strip of material hanging from its back. The kilts vary a little: some have a longer front fold ending in tassels; one fragmentary scene displays a more typical short Nubian kilt; a few kilts may display horizontal banding. A few high-ranking male Puntites, such as the chief, place a dagger through their belts, while others may carry throw-sticks, clubs, or another type of implement. The Puntite women seem to wear an ankle-length skirt, but no upper garment. The queen of Punt and her daughter sport a semitransparent skirt (fine linen?) through which their legs are shown, while another woman has a solid, ankle-length skirt, perhaps reflecting leather, wool, or a coarser grade of linen. Like the males, the queen and princess have a bead necklace, bracelets, and anklets; the Puntite queen also has a headband. The young Puntite children are shown naked. Other ethnic groups, such as the Medjay, southern Libyan tribes, later Kushites, and others, also display distinguishing features, some of which change over time.[8]

It is exceedingly problematic to confirm the presence and appearance of pygmies (*dng*) in ancient depictions, let alone via their more sporadic and less common occurrence in textual sources. In contrast, the various sculptures and other evidence for dwarfs are usually much easier to identify and more common, and appear well before the Old Kingdom: A dwarf burial occurs in the Badarian period at Mostagedda, while dwarf figures appear in mortuary contexts during the Naqada period at el-Ballas and Naqada; dwarf figures, images, and other data appear in mortuary and cultic settings from the Early Dynastic period at Elephantine, Hierakonpolis, Abydos, Saqqara, Tell Ibrahim Awad, and Tell el-Farkha.[9] In addition, the

7. See Panagiotopoulos (2006, 395, fig. 11.8), who includes an illustration from TT.100 (Rekhmire's tomb).

8. See Leahy 1999, 445–47; (Libyans); 2001, 291 (Libyans); Williams 1999, 485–87 (Medjay); Leclant 1999, 423–28 (Kushites); Kendall 2001, 250–52 (Kushites); 2007, 401–6; and Naunton 2010, 120–39 (Libyans and Nubians). For more in-depth studies on Egypt and Nubia, see S. Smith 2003; Redford 2004; Török 2009.

9. A dwarf skeleton occurs in Badarian Grave 3510 at Mostagedda (Brunton 1937, 42, pl. 10; Buszek 2008, 35, 36 n. 3). Some Predynastic figures of dwarfs include two females and/or "odd little dwarf-like figures" that Buszek (2008, 37 n. 12) suggests might originate from el-Ballas (see W. Smith 1949, 4–5, fig. 6 right and lower row); Naqada has yielded figures of a male dwarf, two dwarf females, and a child with a dwarf. For discussion, see Buszek 2008, 37 nn. 13–15.The Early Dynastic to early Old Kingdom shrine at Elephantine produced one potential dwarf figurine in faience (Buszek 2008, 39 nn. 22–23). The Main Deposit at Hierakonpolis contained several dwarf figures in ivory (Quibell and Petrie 1898, 7, pls. 11, 18 no. 7, 19; Quibell and Green 1899, 13–14, 34, 37–38; discussion in Buszek 2008, 38 nn. 19–20). Abydos has yielded several figures and pieces from dwarfs from cultic contexts (Buszek 2008, 38 n. 21), while the subsidiary burial complex associated with Kings Djer, Den, and Semerkhet at Abydos produced nine tomb stelae (Dasen 1993, 251–53 nos. 1–9, pl. 17.2–3, dwarfs Shedj, Djedj, Hep, Seti-inpu, Wedj-wesekh,

skeletons of a few Early Dynastic dwarfs are also attested in royal and elite mortuary settings at Abydos and Saqqara.[10]

Although the Old Kingdom has many depictions of dwarfs, several dwarf skeletons, and a variety of textual references to different types of dwarfs (see further below), there is also much ambiguity regarding the nature of some late Old Kingdom rough amulets that might form a precursor to later dwarf-type, *pataikos*-figures, namely "Ptah the dwarf."[11] It is not until the Middle Kingdom, however, that dwarfs and perhaps pygmies become more popular in different settings, as amulets and household deities, and exported abroad: for example, beginning in the Middle Kingdom, hybrid dwarf-and-leonine Bes-figures appear on "magic wands" and in later amulets and other media.[12] Although these dwarf-type figures had been equated initially with having originated from either the Near East or sub-Saharan Africa (i.e., as either pygmies or dwarfs), they are now believed to have developed out of a rearing lion-figure motif (Wilkinson 2003, 102). The increasing popularity of Nubians and dwarf figures and motifs in Egypt and the East Mediterranean parallels both the Middle through New Kingdom periods of intensifying relations between Egypt and Nubia, plus Egypt's expanding connections abroad.[13] In contrast, regarding the more elusive portrayal of and references to pygmies, only a few Hellenistic period examples have

Sima-netjer, and two Nofrets; Buszek 2008, 36 n. 7), plus a quartzite bowl bearing an image of a dwarf wearing a kilt (Dasen 1993, 251 no. 3, pl. 17.1). A cultic deposit at Tell Ibrahim Awad contained a number of dwarf figures and images (Buszek 2008, 39 n. 24, 45–55); Tell Farkha in the eastern delta has produced thirteen ivory dwarf figures from the Protodynastic to the First Dynasty (Buszek 2008, 54–55, catalogue nos. 1–13, pls. I–V; Ciałowicz 2011, 57–60, 59 fig. 6.8). In addition, an Early Dynastic limestone cylinder without provenance bore a depiction of four dwarfs (Dasen 1993, 253, no. 10, fig. 9.1).

10. In addition to nine stelae from dwarf burials at Abydos, the First Dynasty burial complexes of Djer and Semerkhet have yielded three subsidiary burials with dwarf skeletons (Dasen 1993, 251–52 nos. 1, 3–8; Petrie 1900, 13 section 15, chambers L–M; Petrie 1901, 24, pl. 6A:14 dwarf humerus), while one "dwarf" skeleton (contra the identification by the excavators as having rickets) is known from a subsidiary burial (no. 58) near elite tomb 3504 at Saqqara (Emery 1954, 36, no. 58, fig. 14, pl. 25; Buszek 2008, 36 n. 4).

11. Andrews (1994, 39) notes that these crude *pataikos* amulets, which were initially interpreted as "Ptah-Sokar" amulets, are not sufficiently detailed and identifiable until the New Kingdom, and, are best done in the Third Intermediate period through Late period (Andrews 1994, 39, fig. 36; Wilkinson 2003, 123, upper right figure). Andrews (1990, 68–69) discusses the linkage between Ptah, a patron deity of craftsmen, his ability to take on the form of dwarfish *pataikoi* (i.e., relayed by Herodotus ca. 450 BCE), and the substantial role and presence of dwarfs in Old Kingdom jewelry manufacture. Györy (2002, 491 n. 1) places the origin of *pataikos* amulets with late Old Kingdom type amulets of "men with arms akimbo", See some late Old Kingdom examples published by Brunton, who includes a "dwarfs(?)" subtype from Qau and Badari, and a parallel dwarf-figure from Mahasnah (Brunton 1928, 8, class 3 "children," 14, pl. 93 class/type L3–15, Sixth through Eighth Dynasties), and other examples from the Sixth through Eighth Dynasties at Mostagedda (Brunton 1937, pl. 46 tomb register with amulet types, pl. 56, class/type L nos. 5–14).

12. Bes figures are typically male, naked with a bow-legged, dwarf body, feature a lion's mane and tail, have a long protruding tongue and fangs, a plumed headdress, and, in later periods, often carry musical instruments (e.g., a tambourine) and weaponry such as knives, a sword and shield, snakes, or other things (Andrews 1994, 39–40, 40 fig. 37; Wilkinson 2003, 123). Despite having indirect roots in the Old Kingdom, Bes figures mainly appear in the Middle Kingdom, and especially from the New Kingdom period and later (Wilkinson 2003, 102–4, illustrations; see also Romano 1989).

13. E.g., the popularity of Nubians, or Africans in general, outside Egypt is first attested via an African face modeled on a faience bead/pendant that was exported to Cyprus during Middle Bronze Age I, ca. 1900–1800 BCE (see Karageorghis 1988, 8–9 fig. 1, MB I tomb at Lapithos), while many more examples appear in seals, amulets, weights, and a gold diadem in Late Bronze Age contexts (Karageorghis 1988, 10–15, figs. 2–6). See Herrmann (1994, 316–91 Bes figures, and 404–92 Patake amulets) for the widespread occurrence of dwarf figures of Bes and Pataikos in Syria-Palestine during the Late Bronze Age through Iron Age.

sufficient details to warrant an equation with pygmies: for instance, one Kabeiric skyphos jar shows a postulated "pygmy with a fat stomach," which has been equated with the protuberant abdomen characterizing many modern African pygmies.[14]

Regarding the potential Old Kingdom import of sub-Saharan African pygmies into Egypt, we are left to rely mainly on assessing more explicit, albeit fairly rare, inscriptional references. The evidence for the possible export of Puntite pygmies, or sub-Saharan African pygmies obtained by Puntites, is restricted largely to a few Old Kingdom and later references (see table 18.1 nos. 25, 51–53, 61; Silverman 1969, 55; Török 2009, 56). The best-known and most explicit example represents Harkhuf's trading mission to Yam (later Irem?), near the advent of Pepy II's reign (late Sixth Dynasty), during which he obtained a *dng* ("pygmy"). This pygmy is described as originating from Punt via Yam, the latter of which may have been situated in Upper Nubia (Kerma?), or possibly even further south (perhaps beyond Khartoum?); the same account refers to another Puntite pygmy being obtained in the earlier reign of Djedkare-Isesi (Fifth Dynasty).[15] Otherwise, the Pyramid Texts link several rulers with "... a *deneg* ["pygmy"] of the god's dances, an entertainer before his [great] seat" (table 18.1 nos. 51–3).[16] Hence, one might expect a potential ancient depiction of sub-Saharan pygmies to display such things as a smaller stature in comparison to adjacent figures (excepting echelon perspective), a body with more proportional features (versus dwarfs with achondroplasia), an exaggerated or protrubent abdomen, some similarities to other Egyptian portrayals of Nubians in skin tones, facial features and hair, and perhaps an emphasis upon music and ritual dancing (with which pygmies are linked particularly in the Pyramid Texts).[17] A literature review to-date shows that the Old Kingdom has yet to yield any clear physical portrayals of sub-Saharan African pygmies versus the less ambiguous and usually indigenous Egyptian dwarf figures.

The ancient Egyptians perceived and specified a difference between *nm(w)*, usually translated as "dwarfs," who were not uncommon in ancient Egypt (see table 18.1), and the aforementioned much rarer and distinct "little people," namely *dng*, *dꜣng*, or *dꜣg*, interpreted and translated frequently as "pygmies," who might represent either *actual* pygmies or possibly another variety of dwarfism from sub-Saharan Africa.[18] Since

14. Snowden (1970, 23, 37 fig. 6, 273 n. 6) cites modern anthropologists observing this feature. In contrast, see Turnbull (1983) for a further discussion and illustrations of the Mbuti pygmies and their broad range of physical features, including slighter to more rounded abdomens.

15. Regarding Yam's location in Upper Nubia, or perhaps even south of Khartoum, see O'Connor (1986, 155–57; 2003). See also Kendall (1997, 2007) for discussion on Yam and Kerma's role in late Old Kingdom trade. Concerning Old Kingdom Egypt's long-distance contact with sub-Saharan Africa, a survey in the Laqiya region of northern Sudan, in Wadi Shaw (which lies to the west of the third cataract), has yielded a sherd from a Fourth Dynasty "Meidum bowl," which may suggest an earlier usage of the Abu Ballas Trail from Dakhleh Oasis. See Kuper 2002, 9, pl. 23; Kröpelin and Kuper 2007, 222 n. 14; Mumford 2017.

16. See Faulkner 1969, 191, spell 517, section 1189; and Allen 2005, 159, 383, 407, 451.

17. Some Middle Kingdom and later models of Bes and/or dwarf-figures display dancing (e.g., the ivory dancing dwarfs from Lisht), while the more typical composite Bes figures contain various additional links with dancing, music (e.g., tambourines), and sub-Saharan Africa features (e.g., lion's mane; lion's tail; sometimes a leopard garment) (see Tyldesley 2007, 27–28, fig. 22).

18. For dwarfs, see Shennum 1977, 46 dwarf *nm*[w]; Faulkner 1962, 133 *nm(w)* "dwarf"; *DLE*, 2, s.v. *nmw* "dwarf"; *DLE*, 5, 29 dwarf, *nmw*; Hannig 1995, 413 *nmw* "Zwerg" (dwarf; "midget"), "Verwachsener" (deformed); see also Dawson 1938, 186–87 n. 2; he cites an Egyptian bronze figurine of an African pygmy in the Cairo Museum. Of note, the term *nmw/nmi*, however, tends to be used for achondroplastic dwarfs from the Middle Kingdom through Late period. See Thompson 1991, 95, 97; and el-Aguizy 1987, 53. For

Egyptian dwarfs were fairly common in pharaonic Egypt, especially in Old Kingdom
tomb scenes, young King Pepy II's excitement about the pending delivery and novelty
of a *dng* from Punt, including his reference to a past, well-remembered and celebrated
duplicate occasion (Kitchen 2004, 26), imply that a sub-Saharan *dng* reflected a sufficiently rare and different physique than the dwarfs found in Egypt that this term
may very well indicate a true pygmy.[19] In the past few centuries and until today pygmies have resided in the forests of Uganda, Rwanda, Burundi, the Congo, and further
south in sub-Saharan Africa.[20] Of note, the discovery at Tell Asmar (Mesopotamia)
of a sealed, securely dated (ca. 2500 BCE), and well-analyzed sample of copal attests
to the occurrence of some long-distance trade, albeit down-the-line, five thousand
miles from Zanzibar (East Africa) to southern Mesopotamia during the same period as
Egypt's Old Kingdom.[21] Hence, taking into consideration such contemporary, down-
the-line, long-distance "trickle trade," it is not implausible that pygmies might have
been in contact with or sent to Punt (Eritrea and northeast Ethiopia) and/or Yam (upper
Nubia?) in the third millennium BCE via regional, commercial relations along the
White Nile from Uganda.[22] Presumably pygmies would have represented enough of a
rarity for the entrepreneurial Puntites and/or others to recognize and send northward
to their pharaonic customers who seemed eager to obtain all sorts of diverse exotica
from sub-Saharan Africa.[23] On the other hand, pygmies also appear to have played an
important ideal, albeit rare, role in a ritual dance (*jbꜣ nṯr*) affiliated with the Egyptian
ruler in the Pyramid Texts (see Silverman 1969, 54), but perhaps often required an
indigenous Egyptian dwarf substitute.

In order to elicit such delight in young King Pepy II, and to retain the fame and
memorability of a similar occasion at the court of Djedkare-Isesi many decades before,
the African and/or Puntite pygmies (*dng*) must have displayed substantive differences
from the indigenous and quite well-known Egyptian dwarfs (*nmw*), and presumably
also any northern Nubian dwarfs. Sub-Saharan African pygmies and/or dwarfs may
also have formed such an appealing exotic import to the royal court during the Old

---

pygmies, see Shennum 1977, 120 (pygmy, *dng*); Faulkner 1962, 314 (*dng*, "pygmy"); Hannig 1995, 983 (*dng*,
dng, *dg*, "Zwerg" [dwarf; midget], or Pygmäe [Pygmy]); see also Dawson 1938, 185; Seyfried 1986, 1432,
1433–34 n. 4 (*dlg* and *dng*/*dng*), 1434 n. 5 (Urk. I, 128, 5.17; 129.17; and 130, 14 [Harkhuf]), Jones 2000, 1008
(*dng* "pygmy"); Lesko's *DLE* lacks references to either *dng* or its variants. See also Fischer 2002, 38, who
discusses the application of *dng* to achondroplastic dwarfs when utilizing the ear determinative, plus "the
tendency of such dwarfs to be prone to deafness." For sub-Saharan Africa, see Sowada 2009, 201; el-Aguizy
1987, 54; Dawson (1938, 185–89) also discusses pygmies versus dwarfs.

19. Sampsell (2001, 71) estimates that at any one time during the Old Kingdom, Egypt may have had
around fifty to seventy dwarfs of various types within a population of approximately a million if one incor-
porates the current rates of occurrence of dwarfism identified in recent populations.

20. See Turnbull 1983. The postulated past links between the modern Mbuti pygmies and the ancient
Egyptians are intriguing, but remain unproven. See Hallet and Pelle 1973.

21. Moorey 1994, 79. See also Chami 2004, 100; 2006, 137, who asserts that copal-bearing trees (*Trachy-
lobium*) originally grew along the East Africa coast until the demand for gum copal deforested this region
in the nineteenth century CE; he adds that copal is commonly found in substantial quantities in Neolithic
contexts at East African sites.

22. The location(s) of Punt is debated variously, ranging from northeast Sudan to Eritrea, northeast
Ethiopia, Somalia, and southwest Arabia (see Herzog 1968; Manzo 1999; Kitchen 2004; Breyer 2016).

23. See also Herzog (1968, 56–58). The distance between Uganda and the confluence of the Nile with
the Atbara river is one thousand miles, which is a fair distance, but not impossible, especially if pygmy
populations extended much further north than today. On the other hand, an African dwarf might have suf-
ficed as a "novelty," regarding the Ancient Egyptians' wishes/needs, in place of a pygmy.

Kingdom (e.g., Djedkare-Isesi and Pepy II), that it became fashionable for the elite, including courtiers, to employ Egyptian dwarfs frequently as caretakers for their imported African animals: green monkeys, baboons, *tjesem*-hounds, and leopards/cheetahs (see table 18.1).[24] This appeal for exotic sub-Saharan African pygmies and little people may continue somewhat in successive periods, such as via an Eighteenth Dynasty captioned image of a potential Puntite dwarf or pygmy at Soleb Temple in Lower Nubia, and a pygmy on a Late period tambourine from Akhmim.[25] However, by the New Kingdom the elite tend to hire either regular Egyptians or Nubians as tenders for imported sub-Saharan African animals. Regarding the popularity of dwarfs throughout the pharaonic era, from the Middle Kingdom and later the household deity Bes displays features that have been debated to represent either a pygmy or dwarf, albeit with greater favor being placed on his dwarfen features.[26] The continuing popularity of such figures is exhibited in an unprovenanced, Persian period, or later, bronze figurine of a pygmy.[27]

Associations Between Dwarfs and Imported Animals

Various past studies have already noted the frequent juxtaposition of Egyptian dwarfs with imported African primates, dogs, and occasionally spotted felines (usually leopards). This study illustrates a less well-known, Old Kingdom depiction of a dwarf leading a *tjesem* hound and a monkey from an ex situ marsh scene from a recently rediscovered late Old Kingdom tomb of Ni-ʿankh-nisut at Saqqara (see figs. 18.1–2; Daoud 2007).[28] Although Egypt did contain some indigenous primates and dogs, including the offspring of imported species and their breeding within Egypt (especially by Late period animal cults; see Germond 2001; Ikram 2004, 2005), the continuity and frequency of expeditions to sub-Saharan Africa, which usually retrieved some primates, dogs, and leopards, argue that Egypt's need may have exceeded both the indigenous supply and required supplemental replenishment (i.e., new breeding stock).

24. For scenes of dwarfs accompanying leopards, cheetahs, green monkeys, baboons, and *tjesem*-hounds, see Dawson 1938, 185–89; Dasen 1993; many illustrations throughout the relevant sections in Osborn and Osbornová 1998, 40, and following; and consult Sampsell 2001, 60–73.

25. A *sed*-festival relief from Amenhotep III's temple at Soleb contains a depiction of a small male with a caption identifying him as originating from Punt. See Dasen 1993, 43; Breyer 2016, 188 n. 7. Dasen (1993, 43 n. 51) viewed a sketch drawing of this "danseur de Pount," provided by Jean Lecant, but was unable to confirm whether the Soleb relief portrayed a pygmy versus a miniature male figure. It remains unpublished, while Soleb also has a series of toponyms with a regular-sized, Asiatic-style, bearded figure beside the name "Punt" (Giorgini, Robichon and Leclant 1998, pl. 230, second-to-the- last figure on lower right). Dasen 1993, 43, 154 fig. 9.28a–b interpreted the Late period figure as possibly representing either a pygmy or a black dwarf, being a counter-balance to a depiction of the dwarf-deity Bes who appears on the other side of the tambourine.

26. See Baines 1985, 128, 129, fig. 84; el-Aguizy 1987, 58; and Verma 2014, 94.

27. This figurine occurs in the Cairo Museum, entry no. 27708 (Daressy 1900, 124–25, plate); it dated epigraphically to the Persian period, or the Twenty-ninth through Thirtieth Dynasties, while it may date stylistically as late as the Ptolemaic-Roman period.

28. This scene does not appear to have been included in Dasen's study of Egyptian dwarfs and is included here as one of several additions to the study of Old Kingdom dwarfs. This writer (Mumford) has submitted a fuller study (August 2019) focusing on assessing this ex situ marsh scene from the Worcester Art Museum in a forthcoming Festschrift for Ronald J. Leprohon.

Importing Primates

Ancient Egypt applied several terms to identify different types of monkeys, including *htw*, or sometimes *h̠tw* ("ape"), *iʿn/iʿnj* (Hamadryas "baboon" [*Papio hamadryas*]), *ʿnr* (Anubis "baboon" [*Papio anubis*]), *ky* ("monkey"; sometimes translated as "short-tailed monkey"), and *gf*, sometimes *gif* (a "long-tailed [green] monkey" [*Ceropithecus aethiops*]).[29] Of interest, the terms *iʿn*, *ʿnr*, and *ky* normally adopt the hieroglyphic determinative for a short-tailed sacred baboon (*Cynocephalus hamadryas*), while the term *gf/gif* uses a determinative illustrating a long-tailed monkey.[30] Another type of long-tailed monkey (i.e., the Patas/Red monkey [*Erythrocebus patas*]) also appears in ancient Egypt, but it is fairly similar in form to *gf*-monkeys; it also lacks a known ancient Egyptian designation, and it is usually difficult to distinguish from ancient Egyptian depictions of *gf*: green monkeys.

Many primates originally resided in the Nile Valley and adjacent regions during prehistoric times, but their natural habitats and populations shifted southward gradually during the late Predynastic through Early Dynastic periods. However, their emerging popularity as pets (i.e., mainly monkeys) and sacred cult animals (i.e., baboons) meant that the ancient Egyptians maintained domestic primate populations artificially within Egypt and through replenishment with and/or the supplementation of additional primates and breeding stock via periodic importation from sub-Saharan Africa and elsewhere.[31] Regarding the Hamadryas baboon (*Papio hamadryas* [Egyptian *iʿn*]), it is believed to have disappeared from Egypt in the late First Dynasty, while its overall geographic distribution apparently became increasingly restricted until today, occurring primarily in eastern Sudan, Ethiopia, Somalia, and the Red Sea hill country of

29. For ape, see Shennum 1977, 5 ("ape") and Faulkner 1962, 160 (masc. *htw*, fem. *htt*). *Wb.* 2:503, s.vv. "ht.w" and "ht.t" "ein tier" (animal). For Hamadryas baboon, see Shennum 1977, 9 ("baboon") and Faulkner 1962, 11 (masc. *iʿn*, fem. *iʿnt*, masc. pl. *iʿnw*). *Wb.* 1:41, s.vv. "iʿnj" "Pavian" (male baboon), "iʿnt" "weibliche *Pavian*" (female baboon). *ʿnr* is an Old Kingdom term for baboon, like *iʿn*. See Wb. 1:192, s.v. "ʿnr" "Pavian" (baboon]). For "short-tailed monkey," see *Wb.* 5:110, s.vv. "kjw" and "kj.t" "affin" (female monkey). For "long-tailed monkey," see Shennum 1977, 97 ("monkey") and Faulkner 1962, 285 (masc. *ky*, fem. *kyt*, masc. pl. *kyw*). This term is used in the Tale of the Shipwrecked Sailor in designating one type of monkey from Punt. For *gf*, see Shennum 1977, 97 ("monkey [long-tailed]") and Faulkner 1962, 289 (masc. *gf*, fem. *gft*, masc. pl. *gfw*). This is also found in the Tale of the Shipwrecked Sailor to distinguish another type of monkey from Punt. See also Gardiner 1957, 461, E33. See *Wb.* 5:110 (*gif*, *gwf*, and *gif.t* "kleiner affe, meerkatze" and "affin, weibliche meerkatze" [a small monkey, female monkey]).

30. For the short-tailed determinative, see Gardiner 1957, 461, sign list E32 and notes. The popularity and common appearance of the short-tailed monkey, namely baboon, in Egypt is suggested by the many variants of this type of monkey (Grimal, Hallof, and Van der Plas 2000, 1 A-6 sign list A431 [a man facing a standing baboon], 1 E-1 sign list E32, E35–36, E36A, E37, E37A, E38–46, E46A, E47–51, E51A, E52–58, E58A, E59–63, E63A, E64–68, E68A, E69–71, 1 E-3 sign list E190, E194, E196, E213, E233, E245–49, and 1 E-4 sign list E269–72). Gardiner (1957, 461, sign list E33) indicates a distinct long-tailed monkey associated with the term *gf* or *gif*. The relative scarcity of this imported, sub-Saharan long-tailed monkey is emphasized by the single obvious type of ideogram illustrating it (Grimal, Hallof, and Van der Plas 2000, 1 E-1 sign list E33).

31. Janssen and Janssen (1989, 21) assert that monkey populations had definitely become extinct in Egypt by the New Kingdom, and had been imported from Nubia as early as the Old Kingdom. A distribution map is published in Manzo 1999, 133 pl. 8, "diffusion du babouin." Regarding other factors and sources for primates imported into Egypt, Goudsmit and Brandon-Jones (2000, 111–19) have suggested that the presence of more macaques in the Lower Galleries at Saqqara (ca. 200–30 BCE), versus the earlier Upper Galleries (ca. 400–200 BCE), reveals a shift in importing baboons from the traditional Nile-Red Sea sources and trade networks to obtaining barbary macaques from northwest Africa. They suggest this shift might tie into the 202 BCE Roman defeat of Hannibal (Carthage) and west Phoenician trade.

southwestern Arabia.[32] The Anubis baboon is quite similar, but it is less frequently portrayed, and its exact distribution is uncertain during the pharaonic period. It favors savannah land and is currently found south of the Sahara, across central Africa.[33] Like baboons, green monkeys are found in both savannah and wooded regions throughout sub-Saharan Africa. Their earliest known depiction dates to the Fourth Dynasty, with further illustrations throughout the Old, Middle, and New Kingdoms, with sculpted figures appearing on various New Kingdom items, and many mummified remains from Late period animal cemeteries at Heliopolis, Medinet Gurob, Tuna el-Gebel, Dendera, and Thebes.[34] Red (Patas) monkeys have a slightly less extensive range, but are found in the southern Sahara and central Africa, including in the southern Nile river basin (Osborn and Osbornová 1998, 41). They are depicted in Predynastic rock art, but are tricky to distinguish from green monkeys in pharaonic art.[35] The Late period animal cemetery at Dendera yielded the mummy of a patas monkey.

Of interest, Salima Ikram, Nathaniel Dominy, and Gillian Leigh Moritz, recently carried out oxygen isotope analysis of the hair from two New Kingdom baboon mummies in the British Museum: The specimen from the Valley of the Kings yielded a close match with all of the modern baboon specimens from Eritrea and some specimens from eastern Ethiopia (i.e., comparing the similarities in specific environments, including plants eaten over long periods). In contrast, the tested Egyptian specimens did not correspond with modern baboons from Somalia and Mozambique.[36]

Importing and Replenishing Dog Breeds

A few ancient Egyptian terms are known to specify domesticated "dogs" (*iw*; *iwiw*) and "hounds" (*ṯsm*), the latter Egyptian term for which has broad applications to

32. The Hamadryas baboon likely began to be imported into Egypt in the early Old Kingdom: depictions of it reappear in the Fourth and Fifth Dynasties (e.g., Tombs of Nefermaat, Nebemchut, and Uarna) and Eleventh and Twelfth Dynasties (e.g., Tombs of Khety, Baqt III, Nehera, and Khnumhotep), and New Kingdom (e.g., Qurnah tomb; Tomb of Rekhmire; Tutankhamun's tomb; Eighteenth Dynasty papyri; Hatshepsut's mortuary temple; Ramesses II obelisk; Ramesses III's mortuary temple). See Osborn and Osbornová 1998, 32–37, figs. 4-4 to 4-22. Some of these scenes show the baboons being brought either from Nubia or from Punt. Osborn and Osbornová (1998, 33) admit that actually relatively little is known about their ancient distribution.

33. The Anubis baboon is depicted sporadically from the Old Kingdom to early Ptolemaic period, and is mummified frequently in Late period cults (Osborn and Osbornová 1998, 38–39). They are shown being exported from Punt.

34. Green monkeys are portrayed in Old Kingdom tombs (e.g., Nefermaat; Debehen; Ptahhotep; Mereruka; Gemnikai; ʿAnkhmʿAhor), Middle Kingdom tombs (e.g., Ukhotep; Baqt III; Nehera; Uarna), New Kingdom tombs (e.g., Anen; Rekhmire; Kenamun; Huy), temples (Nubian tribute scene in Beit el-Wali temple of Ramesses II; monkeys in scene of Punt from Hatshepsut's mortuary temple), and decorated artifacts (e.g., cosmetic spoon) (Osborn and Osbornová 1998, 39–41, figs. 4-6, 4-7, 4-12, 4-18, 4-29 to 4-38, and 13-44; Ricke, Hughes, and Wente 1967, pls. 7–9).

35. Osborn and Osbornová (1998, 42, figs. 4-39 to 4-41) reproduce some Predynastic rock art with patas monkeys.

36. See https://www.independent.co.uk/life-style/history/baboon-mummy-analysis-reveals-eritrea-and-ethiopia-as-location-of-land-of-punt-1954547.html. The similarities between modern baboons in Somalia and Yemen suggest that Yemen would lack a positive match for the baboon sample from Egypt; strontium isotope testing is planned for additional confirmation. The generic baboon mummy illustrated in *The Independent*, however, represents a Late period baboon (see Quirke and Spencer 1992, 93, fig. 71).

various breeds, and is sometimes translated as "greyhounds."[37] Hence, the somewhat generic hieroglyphic dog-ideogram, namely sign list E14, is frequently applied to the two to three known different terms for dogs in ancient Egypt, namely *iw*, *iwiw*, and *tsm*.[38] However, the diverse breeds of dogs attested via skeletal remains, mummified canines, and pictorial renditions of varying quality and accuracy, reveal that Egypt actually had more breeds of dogs (*Canis familiaris*) than the surviving limited designations and generic ideogram might otherwise imply.[39]

The domestication of wolves (*Canis lupus pallipes*) in Southwest Asia, ca. 10,000–8000 BCE, forms the earliest known ancestors of Near Eastern, Egyptian, and African domestic dogs.[40] However, the first documented appearance of domesticated dogs in Egypt occurs at Merimde Beni-Salame in northern Egypt during the Badarian period.[41] Douglas Brewer notes that Prehistoric to Predynastic depictions reveal three basic variants: a short, stocky dog which is variously called a "pariah," Pomeranian, or later a mastiff; a larger robust dog with a straight tail and labeled a "pariah," or "mongrel"; and a thin greyhound-like dog with a curled tail, which is often called a "greyhound," a "hunting dog," a "hound," or a *tjesem*.[42]

During the Dynastic period, there is an increase in the depiction of different types of dogs in Egypt, including the *tjesem* (with an emphasized curl in its tail), the saluki (having a slightly curved tail), the greyhound (with a slightly curved tail), the pariah, the mastiff, and some smaller types (e.g., Pomeranian; Osborn and Osbornová 1998, 60–67, figs. 7-25 to 7-53). The breed of dogs of prime concern here are the popular hunting dogs, also called sight-dogs with curved tails, who can be subdivided into two types: the *tjesem*-dogs, which are similar to the African *Basenji*, and the salukis, which are shown as the most frequent export to Egypt as tribute from Nubia and Punt during the New Kingdom.[43] Although Rosalind Janssen and Jack Janssen have noted

37. For "dog," see Shennum 1977, 43 "dog" (*iw*, *iwiw*) and Faulkner 1962, 12 (*iw* "dog," and *iwiw* "dog"); *Wb*. 1:48, s.v. "iw" ("Hund" [dog]) in Middle and New Kingdoms; 50, s.v. "iwiw" ("Hund" [dog]). For "hound," see Shennum 1977, 75 ("hound" *tsm*) and Faulkner 1962, 308 *tsm* ("hound"); *Wb*. 5:409, s.v. "tsm" ("Windhund, Hund" [greyhound, dog]); this term appears in The Tale of the Shipwrecked Sailor in regard to gifts of hounds from Punt. For "greyhound," see Gardiner 1957, 459, sign list E14 "greyhound"; the term *tjesem* (or "tesem") itself is not breed-specific, but the dog type portrayed by the ideogram is one form of "sight dog." See Brewer, Clark and Phillips 2001, 32–33.

38. E.g., *iw* and *tsm* cited in Gardiner (1957, 459 sign list E14 "greyhound" [*slughi*]). Several variants are known for this ideogram (Grimal, Hallof, and Van der Plas 2000, 1 A-4 A248 [a man walking a dog], A248A [a man holding a dog], and A248B [a sitting man holding a dog by the leash], 1 E-1 sign list E14, E14A, E14B, and E14C). Of note, the latter variants, E14B and E14C appear to have heavier torsos, while E14A and E14C have longer tails. See also Grimal, Hallof, and Van der Plas 2000, 2 E-3 sign list E14C, E14, A248, A248A, A248B.

39. Brewer, Clark and Phillips 2001, 34; Rice 2006, 72–73 fig. 22, who discusses the mummy of a possible *tjesem*-dog.

40. Osborn and Osbornová 1998, 57. It is debated whether jackals contributed to the genetic background of dogs.

41. These dogs display more wolf-like traits than later domesticated examples (Osborn and Osbornová 1998, 57); other Predynastic dog burials occur at Mostagedda, Badari, Mahasna, Abadiyeh, Nag ed-Der, Heliopolis, Maadi, and Wadi Digla (Brewer, Clark and Phillips 2001, 28).

42. Brewer, Redford, and Redford 1995, 116; Osborn and Osbornová 1998, 57–59, figs. 7-7 to 7-18. Brewer suggests that mastiffs may have originated from Mesopotamia (Brewer, Clark and Phillips 2001, 32–39).

43. Osborn and Osbornová 1998, 41, fig. 4-37 [Eighteenth Dynasty tomb of Rekhmire], 41, fig. 4-38 [Ramesses II's Beit el-Wali temple], and 66, fig. 7-47 [Eighteenth Dynasty tomb of Amenmose]; salukis are often termed "Egyptian greyhounds."

that some of almost eighty known examples of dog names may be Nubian, they assert that most of these names seem to derive from Libya, which is also known to have sent dogs to Egypt (perhaps via the Abu Ballas Trail and Dakhleh Oasis during the Old Kingdom; see Janssen and Janssen 1989, 11–12; Mumford 2017).

Both types of nonindigenous dogs were definitely bred in Egypt throughout the pharaonic period, according to Brewer and others: The saluki-type dog population most likely flourished in Nubia and Punt (Brewer, Clark and Phillips 2001, 34), and could be used to replenish or strengthen Egypt's local stock of salukis. The *tjesem*-dogs are also noted as being imported from Punt, such as in the Middle Kingdom Tale of the Shipwrecked Sailor (see Simpson 2003). On the other hand, Brewer has noted that the origin of the *tjesem* breed of sight-dogs (*tesem*) is still debated regarding whether it originated from East Africa or Southwest Asia.[44] He notes the presence of bones from a similar sight dog found in the Ubaid period in Mesopotamia and suggests a Southwest Asian origin in late Prehistory (see Brewer, Clark and Phillips 2001, 33). However, he also admits that pharaonic period Egypt is well-documented as having imported both *tjesem*-dogs and the second type of sight-dogs, namely salukis, from Nubia (Brewer, Clark and Phillips 2001, 33–34, figs. 3.8–10). Brewer compared skeletal data with pictorial evidence for the various types of ancient Egyptian dogs and concluded that pharaonic Egypt followed a general breeding program to maintain at least a few basic dog breeds with particular traits to aid in specific tasks, such as obtaining sight hounds for hunting, namely the *tjesem* and salukis.[45] Other usages for dogs included pets, guard dogs, police dogs, patrol dogs, and cult animals (Janssen and Janssen 1989, 9–13; Brewer, Clark and Phillips 2001, 43–47).

Importing Leopards, Cheetahs, and/or Ambiguous Spotted Felines ("Panthers")

Although leopards (*Panthera pardus* [formerly *Felis pardus*]) and cheetahs (*Acinonyx jubatus* [formerly *Felis jubata*]) are quite distinct animals, not only in body form, spotting, habits, and preferred habitats, their identification is sometimes problematic in ancient Egyptian art and terminology. Dale Osborn and Jana Osbornová cite two Egyptian terms for "leopard": the first term *ꜣby* is also more broadly translated as "panther," while an older variant term, *bꜣ-šmꜥ* (see *ꜣbj-šmꜥ*), may also be translated specifically as "leopard," or more generally as "panther."[46] Regarding cheetahs, both authors indicate an older ancient Egyptian designation, *bꜣ* (see *ꜣbj*), and an older variant term, *bꜣ-mḥ* (see *ꜣbj-mḥ*), both of which have been translated as either "cheetah,"

---

44. Rice 2006, 33 favors the *tjesem*-dog's origin from Punt, which he argues is most likely located in East Africa.

45. Brewer, Clark and Phillips 2001, 40–43, fig. 3.18; Rice (2006, 89–90) discusses the *tjesem*-hound's superiority in maintaining speed over a distance in chasing game.

46. For *ꜣby*, see Shennum 1977, 108 ("panther" *ꜣby*) and Faulkner 1962, 2 (*ꜣby* "panther"); Osborn and Osbornová 1998, 119; *Wb.* 1:7, s.vv. "*ꜣbj*" ("panther" [panther]), "*ꜣbj.t*" ("das weibliche tier" [i.e., female panther]). For *bꜣ-šmꜥ*, see *Wb.* 1:7, s.v. "*ꜣbj šm*'" ("leopard"), 415, s.v. "*bꜣ-šm*'" ("leopard"); Osborn and Osbornová 1998, 119.

or "panther."[47] Of note, Raymond Faulkner translates *bỉ* as "leopard," which actually reveals a periodic ancient Egyptian (and modern) confusion, or ambiguity, over what species are meant exactly by this and other labels.[48] These ancient Egyptian words also use slightly different determinatives to indicate either a live "leopard," "cheetah," "panther," or a hide from one of these animals. The former circumstance may be specified by using a hieroglyph showing the full profile of a "panther," while the latter situation often has a "panther" head in profile alongside the symbol for animal hide.[49] The alternate words for "leopard" and "cheetah" also often omit a specific panther ideogram, and instead display more ambiguous determinatives: a sedge plant associated with "Upper Egypt" is used for leopards (*bỉ-šmˁ*) versus a papyrus clump affiliated with "Lower Egypt (*bỉ-mḥ*)" appearing with cheetahs.[50] Leopards are portrayed clearly in First Dynasty and later pharaonic art, while depictions of cheetahs are not confirmed until the Middle Kingdom and later (Osborn and Osbornová 1998, 120, 122).

Leopards and cheetahs do reside in similar habitats, but while leopards may dwell in forested regions and hunt a broader range of game, cheetahs are found mainly in savannah to semidesert environments and subsist on a narrower range of prey, especially gazelles.[51] Osborn and Osbornová suggest that leopards resided throughout most of Egypt during the pharaonic period, but this would probably mean habitats along the fringe of the Nile floodplain, or vegetation areas away from human habitation (it is uncertain to what extent leopards inhabited the pharaonic through Ptolemaic–Roman landscape in Egypt).[52] Two subspecies of leopards (*Panthera pardus*) are attested in Egypt, namely *Panthera pardus jarvisi* and *Panthera pardus pardus*. These animals are extremely rare in Egypt today, with one confirmed sighting of a *Panthera pardus pardus* in 1913 in the Qattara Depression in the Western Desert, other occurrences in 1994 at Gebel Elba, some verified sightings in the South Sinai mountains during the

47. Osborn and Osbornová 1998, 119, including hieroglyphic forms. For both variants, see *Wb.* 1:7, s.vv. "ỉbj mḥ" ("der Gepard" [cheetah]), 415, s.vv. "bỉ" ("panther"), "bỉ-šmˁ" ("leopard"), "bỉ mḥ" ("der Gepard" [cheetah]).

48. Shennum 1977, 77 ("leopard" *bỉ*) and Faulkner 1962, 16 *bỉ* ("leopard"). See Osborn and Osbornová 1998, 120 fig. 7-222 for an image of a "leopard" below the term *bỉ* for "cheetah." It is also possible that the illustration was simply not quite as clearly executed and had meant to portray a cheetah.

49. Gardiner's sign list E24 illustrates a long-tailed feline in profile, which represents the ideogram commonly used for *ỉby*, which is translated either as "panther" or "leopard" (Gardiner 1957, 460 E24). A variant ideogram occurs for this feline, showing it running in a "flying gallop" motif (Grimal, Hallof, and Van der Plas 2000, 1 E-5 sign list E24 and E24A, and 2 E-5 sign list E24 and E24A). Gardiner sign list F9 displays the head of a "leopard" (*bỉ*) (Gardiner 1957, 462 F9). This ideogram has a few variants (Grimal, Hallof, and Van der Plas 2000, 1 F-1 sign list F9, 1 F-2 sign list F90). For the hide, see *Wb.* 1:415, s.v. "bỉ" ("leopardenfell" [leopard fur/hide]).

50. Gardiner sign list F28 is the most common determinative used to indicate a leopard or panther "hide," but does have variants F27 and F29 (see Gardiner 1957, 464 F28). Of interest, the symbol (i.e., Gardiner sign list F28) used to indicate a leopard/panther hide sometimes has the value *ỉb*, which appears in place names such as *ỉbw* (Elephantine) and *ỉbḏw* (Abydos), and might imply that this typical southern product, namely exotic animal hides, played a secondary role in the adoption of the name *ỉbw* for Elephantine. See Gardiner 1957, 483, sign list M26 sedge plant for *Šmˁw* "Upper Egypt," or a southern connotation (*rswt*). See Gardiner 1957, 481, sign list M16 papyrus clump for *Tỉ-mḥw* "Lower Egypt," or a marsh connotation M15.

51. Leopards adapt to a broad range of environments versus cheetahs. See Osborn and Osbornová 1998, 119, 122.

52. Osborn and Osbornová 1998, 119. They also note that leopards resided in the Western Desert oases, along the coastal desert strip, in the Eastern Desert, and in the Sinai until recent times. A map of their distribution appears in Manzo 1999, 132, pl. 6 ("diffusion du léopard").

1950s, and more recent bedouin claims for leopard sightings at Gebel Serbal and Feiran in south Sinai (Hoath 2003, 106–7). Presumably leopard populations originally spanned much of prehistoric North Africa, prior to the desertification of this region that left isolated pockets of African wildlife within and near oases and other clusters of vegetation and game. Although the ancient Egyptians are well-attested obtaining leopard and cheetah hides from sub-Saharan Africa, textual-pictorial evidence does indicate their being hunted in Egypt's adjacent deserts. For example, the Middle Kingdom literary piece, The Eloquent Peasant, mentions leopard skins as one of the products supplied from the Wadi Natrun ("Salt Field").[53] In addition, very small populations of leopards still survive in isolated areas in Algeria and Morocco, the western and southern parts of Arabia, various areas in the Middle East, including Anatolia (Turkey), and further away in parts of Asia (Hoath 2003, 106–7; see also Osborn and Osbornová 1998, 119).

Like leopards, cheetahs initially had a fairly broad range across prehistoric North Africa, the northern Sinai, and beyond, especially in savannah habitats. A few cheetahs survive in Egypt's northwestern coastal desert (e.g., the Qattara Depression and its environs), and northern Libya, but are virtually extinct in these regions.[54] Cheetahs also used to have a much broader range, residing in many areas within the Middle East, including the Arabian Peninsula, Levant, Anatolia, Iran, Pakistan, and India.[55] Hence, both cheetahs and leopards were obtainable from various non-sub-Saharan sources, ranging from Egypt's adjacent deserts to more distant habitats, but still represented exotic wildlife found *outside* the Nile floodplain.

In general, spotted felines, whether representing leopards, cheetahs, or other felines, are utilized as pets, trophies (i.e., tribute scenes), hide fittings, and garments in ancient Egypt.[56] In their application as garments, spotted feline hides, which may come from leopards, are used mainly as a form of cloak covering the torso of *sem*-priests, but also appear sometimes as full-length, leopard/feline-style clothing worn by a few elite males and females.[57] Regarding some statements asserting that the pharaonic Egyptians trained and used cheetahs for hunting, a closer scrutiny of the evidence by Osborn and Osbornová has shown there is no firm evidence for this supposition.[58] Otherwise, leopards, cheetahs, and other spotted felines served as a rarer form of exotic pet, being tended either by regular-sized people or dwarfs.

53. This Middle Kingdom tale survives in Papyri Berlin 3023, Berlin 3025, Berlin 10400, and British Museum 10274 (also designated as P. Butler 527) (*AEL* 2:169, 170 line 14, 182 n. 1).

54. Hoath (2003, 104–5) notes that two cheetahs were reportedly killed in Libya in 1980, and in Egypt in 1993 and 1994; a few cheetahs may still reside in the Qattara Depression (i.e., traces of tracks and hides) and north Sinai (1946 report), and are almost entirely reliant on hunting Dorcus gazelles.

55. Cheetahs have disappeared from most of the Middle East, but may possibly exist in small numbers in isolated parts of Arabia, and survive in the region to the south of the Caspian Sea. See Hoath 2003, 104.

56. See Driel-Murray 2000, 302, who also notes that some exotic feline hides were utilized for shields and quivers in the Middle and New Kingdoms—in addition to the more common application of cow hides.

57. Most leopard hides, also called panther skins, which include some imitation leopard hides (e.g., Tutankhamun), are worn by *Sem*-priests as a cloak-like overgarment. See Watson 1987, 9, 39–40, 55, illustrated on 34 pl. 3 left (fig. 65) and 39 figs. 66–67; Harpur 1987, 126, 129, 236; Sauneron 2000, 41. A few Early Dynastic through Old Kingdom affluent males and females wear probable imitation leopard garments. See Driel-Murray 2000, 302. In the Fourth Dynasty, Princess Nefertiabt wears a full-length, yellow sheath-dress covered in black spots arranged in petal-style clusters, presumably imitating a leopard skin garment. See Malek 1986, 78–79, photo; Arnold and Ziegler 1999, 242–44, cat. nos. 50–51; Callendar 2006, 120 ("panther skin"); Prince Wep-em-nefret wears a similar body length, "feline pelt" (Arnold and Ziegler 1999, 245–46 cat. no. 52).

58. See Osborn and Osbornová 1998, 122–23, who also note that cheetahs are reputed to be easily tamed.

TABLE 18.2. Selected scenes of leopards, cheetahs, primates, *tjesem*-dogs and other occurrences *lacking* (i.e., excluding) dwarfs in Old Kingdom tombs.

Date/period	Tomb etc.	Tomb owner's titles	Nondwarf attendants	Associated scene	References
1. (D14) Dynasty 4; (more details in table 18.1)	Neferma'at Mastaba (Petrie no. 16), Meidum	Prophet of goddess Bubastis, and Shesmetet; Priest of Min; etc. (son of Sneferu)	Attendant "Little boy" (dwarf?) 2 young men/dwarfs?	Neferma'at facade Man with leopard Itet (wife): Boy with "apes" (a monkey and baboon) and an ibis Elsewhere: Two "young men" with monkey and baboon	Porter and Moss 1934, 92–93, 93 Neferma'at facade, 93 Itet facade; Dasen 1993, 254, no. 14 dwarf(?)
4. (D13) Dynasty 4 (more details in table 18.1)	Debheni Rock tomb LG 90 ("Tomb of Hammed es-Samaan") Giza	Overlord of Nekheb; Secretary of the Toilet-house; Master of the largesse in the Mansion of Life;etc.	2 attendants 2 attendants Attendants	Room I scene (1) 1 dog behind them Room I scene (1) 1 monkey behind Room I scene (3) Attendants with dog and monkey.	Porter and Moss 1974, 235–36, Room I, scene (1) with regular attendants, scene (3), register V, plus scene (1) at entry doorway
14. (D32) Dynasty 5 (more details in table 18.1)	Ka'aper (Kai-aperu) Tomb loc. unknown; Saqqara	Judge, Boundary official; Scribe of the king's expedition in Wenet, Serer, Tepa and Ida; etc.	Regular harpist	a monkey is beside a harpist: (i.e., probably a paired dwarf and monkey, albeit in adjacent scenes)	Porter and Moss 1978, 501, chapel scene (4); Kinney 2012, 62–63, fig. 13
17. (D19) Dynasty 5 (redated to Dynasty 4) (more details in table 18.1)	Nesutnufer Mastaba G4970 west field Giza	Overseer of strongholds of the Heliopolitan-East nome; Leader of the land of the Thinite and Aphroditopolite nomes; etc. (perhaps Seneb's son?)	Accompanied by offering-bearers, plus two Nubians bringing animals	Some offering-bearers plus two Nubians bringing animals	Porter and Moss 1974, 144, chapel scenes (5)–(7); Sampsell 2001, 72 redating; perhaps Seneb's son

TABLE 18.2. (cont'd) Selected scenes of leopards, cheetahs, primates, *tjesem*-dogs and other occurrences *lacking* (i.e., excluding) dwarfs in Old Kingdom tombs.

Date/period	Tomb etc.	Tomb owner's titles	Nondwarf attendants	Associated scene	References
20. (D37) Dynasty 5 (more details in table 18.1)	**Ni'ankh khnum** and **Khnemhotep** Mastaba near Unas Pyramid, Saqqara	(a–b). Prophet of Re in the Sun-temple of Neuserre; Overseer of manicurists of the Great House; etc.	Craftsmen	No apparent dwarfs in the scene of industries, including jewelry production	Porter and Moss 1978, 641, 643, outer hall, scene (19), register III
23. (D36) Dynasty 5; (more details in table 18.1)	**Nufer/Nefer (and K3-h3i)** Mastaba near Teti Pyramid Saqqara	Inspector of the *wa'bt*; Director of singers; etc.	Attendant	**Offering room (3)** A scene of boat building with a monkey and baboon, plus an official with a sunshade bearer	Porter and Moss 1979, 639, 640, offering-room, scene (1)–(2), (3), register II, and 640, offering room, scene (4), register I
26. (D34) Dynasty 5 (more details in table 18.1)	**Ptahhotep II Tjefi** Mastaba complex D64 Saqqara	Chief Justice, Vizier; Inspector of prophets of the Pyramids of Menkauhor and Isesi; Inspector of *wa'b*-priests of the Pyramid of Neuserre; etc.	Attendants	**Offering-room:** Bringing leopard and lion in cages, hyenas and dogs on leashes, small animals in boxes	Porter and Moss 1979, 600, offering-room, scene (16), register (b), 602, offering room, scene (18), register II
28. (D18) Dynasty 5; (more details in table 18.1)	**Seshemnufer I** Mastaba G4940, west field Giza	Royal chamberlain; One belonging to the estate "Mansion of Har-kheper"; Prophet of Heket; Judge; Boundary official; etc.	Attendant	Female offering-bearer	Porter and Moss 1974, 142–43 (not noting a dwarf)
49. (D52) Dynasty 6 (more details in table 18.1)	**Mereruka** Meri mastaba near Teti Pyramid, Saqqara	Chief Justice, Vizier; Inspector of prophets and tenants of the Pyramid of Teti; etc.	Attendant	**(A). Room IV:** In a scene with a monkey and two dogs, plus other attendants	Porter and Moss 1978, 525, 528 529, Room IV, scene (27) in Mereruka's chapel; Osborn and Osbornová 1998, 40, fig. 4-33

TABLE 18.2. (cont'd) Selected scenes of leopards, cheetahs, primates, *tjesem*-dogs and other occurrences *lacking* (i.e., excluding) dwarfs in Old Kingdom tombs.

Date/period	Tomb etc.	Tomb owner's titles	Nondwarf attendants	Associated scene	References
The following tombs continue the sequence from table 1: i.e., key scenes/genres lacking dwarfs.					
74. (other) Early Dynasty 5; Swinton 2014, 47, IV.6–V.2 no. 88	**Seshethotep** Called Heti Mastaba G5150 LG 36 west field, Giza	King's son of his body; Overseer of all works of the king; Greatest of the Ten of Upper Egypt; etc.	Nubian (with other persons)	In a scene of offering-bearers carrying young hyena and bringing other animals	Porter and Moss 1974, 150 chapel, scene (5) and (7) false doors
75. (other) Mid-Dynasty 5; not in Swinton	**Tepem'ankh** Mastaba No. 76 (D.11) north of Step Pyramid, Saqqara	*Wa'b*-priest of the Pyramids of Sneferu, Khephren, Menkaure, Userkaf, and Sahure; Prophet of Khufu and Menkaure, and of the Sun-temple of Userkaf; etc.	Attendants	**Block CG 1556:** A scene with two men and boys accompanying baboons (one baboon is noted as being a male).	Porter and Moss 1978, 483, 484, Room I, passage, scene (5), adjoining block CG 1556 in Cairo Museum
76. (other) Dynasty 5 (temp. Isesi or later); not in Swinton	**Kapuptah** Mastaba ex situ block CG 1711–1567, from Saqqara	Prophet of Re and Hathor in the Sun temple of Neferirkare; Prophet of the Pyramid of Djedkare (Isesi); etc.	Seated tomb owner and some offering-bearers	**Block:** A monkey tied to a chair, plus an adjacent scene with offering-bearers.	Porter and Moss 1979, 693, wall blocks CG 1711 and 1567
77. (other) Dynasty 5–6; not in Swinton	**In-Sneferu Ishtef** Mastaba, east of Sneferu's North/Red Pyramid, Dahshur	Inspector of tenants of the Great House; etc.	Seated tomb owner	**Wall paintings:** A scene with the deceased tomb owner seated in a chair, beneath which a monkey is situated.	Porter and Moss 1981, 891, no. 2 found east of the North/Red Pyramid of Sneferu

TABLE 18.2. (*cont'd*) Selected scenes of leopards, cheetahs, primates, *tjesem*-dogs and other occurrences *lacking* (i.e., excluding) dwarfs in Old Kingdom tombs.

Date/period	Tomb etc.	Tomb owner's titles	Nondwarf attendants	Associated scene	References
78. (other) Dynasty 5–6; not in Swinton	**Sahotpu** good name Tepu Mastaba tomb (LG 53) cemetery GIS Giza	Judge; Overseer of scribes; Director of the Broad Hall; Secretary of judgment; etc.	Male attendant	Leading a dog with a monkey perched on its back; another scene with a dog under chair of tomb owner	Porter and Moss 1974, 222, chapel scenes (2) and (3)
79. (other) Early Dynasty 6 (temp. Teti); Swinton 2014, 47, VI.1 no. 81	**Sabu Ibebi** Mastaba 37 south chapel north of Step Pyramid, Saqqara	Greatest of the Directors of craftsmen in the Two Houses on the day of the festival; Supervisor of prophets of the Pyramids of Unis and Teti; Prophet of Re in the Sun temples of Userkaf, Neferirkare, Neuserre and Menkauhor; etc.	Attendant	A scene with one of the attendants accompanied by a baboon, plus other attendants; near a palanquin carrying the tomb owner	Porter and Moss 1978, 460, south chapel, scene (3), register I
80. (other) Dynasty 6; not in Swinton	**Unknown** Ex situ mastaba tomb block from Saqqara (west of Step Pyramid)	Ex situ block: Tomb owner?	Male attendant	Accompanying a baboon in a scene with other men and wild animals	Porter and Moss 1979, 613, finds from western side of Step Pyramid

The Popularity of Dwarfs in Relation to Exotic Pets, Plus Other Roles in the Old Kingdom

Ancient Egyptian dwarfs and sub-Saharan African pygmies appear in a variety of contexts and roles during the Old Kingdom. Old Kingdom Egyptian dwarfs hold various ranks, ranging from commoners (e.g., Giza workmen's cemetery) to higher-ranking officials (e.g., Khnumhotep; Seneb), being attested by their tombs, depictions, and statuary (table 18.1, nos. 1–80), plus four to five(?) dwarf bodies at Giza and apparently originally in a burial at Beni Hasan (see table 18.1 nos. 5?, 7, 8, and 41?). Aside from only a few known middle-class through higher-ranking dwarfs, most Old Kingdom Egyptian dwarfs appear in jewelry production scenes (table 18.18.3: twelve tombs with forty-one to forty-three dwarfs), where they dominate such scenes versus nondwarfen workers (tables 18.1–18.2).[59] The next most popular scenes consist of dwarfs tending or being associated with primates (monkeys and baboons), *tjesem*-dogs (greyhounds), and sometimes spotted felines (leopards and cheetahs), all of which represent typical imports from Punt and sub-Saharan Africa in general (table 18.1); dwarfs are less frequently associated with leading cattle or even an ibis, a genre otherwise dominated by nondwarfs (table 18.1). Both dwarfs and regular-sized attendants appear carrying a wide range of items, including pots, boxes, bags, baskets, headrests, sandals, cloth, staffs, batons, flywhisks, and mirrors (table 18.1). Many scenes display dwarfs in close proximity to the tomb owner and his family, including banquet scenes, a carrying chair (palanquin), and marsh scenes.[60] Dwarfs also appear in scenes of music and dancing, directing dancers, accompanying dancers, dancing with a monkey, and playing instruments (e.g., sistra; harps; table 18.1).[61] More sporadic depictions illustrate dwarfs in boats, holding a scribal palette for a scribe, and fragmentary scenes of a less clear nature (table 18.1). In contrast, the few known Old Kingdom references to pygmies from sub-Saharan Africa reveal an emphasis upon dancing and an association with the Egyptian king and royal court, a role that apparently could also be filled by indigenous Egyptian dwarfs (table 18.1; see Sampsell 2001, 69; Hawass 2006, 136).

It is this potential linkage between the exotic dancing pygmies from sub-Saharan Africa and the postulated substitution of Egyptian dwarfs for (dancing) pygmies that is intriguing regarding the frequent presence of dwarfs as animal handlers/tenders for imported and derived animal breeds from sub-Saharan Africa, and especially Punt. Although many elite tombs display regular-sized Egyptian and sometimes Nubian animal tenders, a significant number of tomb owners chose to feature Egyptian dwarfs

59. Harpur (1987, 112) tallied about eighteen Old Kingdom jewelry manufacturing scenes from Saqqara, Giza, Meir, Dishasha, el-Sheikh Said, and Deir el-Gabrawi, in which she observed that dwarf-jewelers virtually always occur in contrast to other industries that are dominated by regular-sized laborers. See Swinton (2012, 176) regarding the benefits of dwarfs working with threading beads, including more nimble fingers and noncalloused hands, plus possible associations with the patron deity of craftsmen, Ptah, who is occasionally attested appearing as a dwarf.

60. See Vasiljević (2016, 117–25) for a comparison of Old Kingdom and Middle Kingdom scenes of dwarfs, plus a special status for Seneb in affiliation with his title "the Great one of the carrying chair" in conjunction with other Old Kingdom scenes illustrating dwarfs near carrying chairs.

61. See Gillam (2005, 113–14, 152, the dwarf Djeho) for a discussion on Old Kingdom and later dwarfs' roles in ritual dancing, including specific later dances facilitating resurrection/rebirth (i.e., of the divine child), the latter of which, it is theorized, may be linked to the resemblance of dwarfs to newborns.

TABLE 18.3. Dwarfs and pygmies in various roles, including multiple aspects (i.e., noted in one or more scenes/genres).

Different settings, scenes and roles in which dwarfs appear:	Dynasty 4	Dynasties 4–5	Dynasty 5	Dynasties 5–6	Dynasty 6	Totals for Dynasties 4–6	Catalogue nos. with multiple occurrences of dwarfs (excluding nondwarfs: table 2)
Dwarf tomb owners	—	2	—	1; x?	1?	2–4+x?	6; 10; 37; 41?; 63?
Dwarf bodies in tombs	1?	2	—	x?	—	2–4+x?	5?; <6>; 7; 8; 41?
Dwarf statues and statuettes (in/from tombs)	—	4	—	5; 1?	—	9–10?	6; 10 (3); 37?; 38; 39; 40; 41; 42
Dwarf making jewelry	3	—	14	4	20	41–43?	3 (3); 22 (4); 24 (2); 26 (4); 27 (4); 36 (4); 47 (6); 49 (4);
Nondwarfs making jewelry	—	—	—	—	—	some	62 (2); 64 (4); 65 (4); 73 (2+)
Dwarf with monkey	2?; 2	—	7	1	10;1?	20–23?	1 (2); 2; 4; 11; 12; 18; 19 (2); 21; 30; 43; 47; 48; 49 (1); 54?; 55; 60; 64; 68; 69; 71; 72
Nondwarf with monkey	—	—	—	—	1	1+	
Dwarf with baboon	2?	—	1	—	—	1–3?	1 (2); 21
Nondwarf with baboon	—	—	—	—	—	—	
Dwarfs in tombs showing dogs, primates & leopards elsewhere (indirect)	5	—	9	—	4	18	1; 3 (3); 4; 14; 15; 17; 19; 21; 23 (2+); 26 (1+); 26; 49 (3+); 57
Dwarf with dog	2	—	4	1	11;1?	16–17?	12 (2); 18; 19; 43; 46; 48; 49 (2); 54?; 63; 64; 68; 69 (2);
Nondwarf with dog	—	—	1	—	1	4	71; 72
Dwarf with feline	—	—	—	—	1	1	71
Nondwarf with feline	—	—	—	—	—	some	
Dwarf with cattle/ox	—	—	2	1; 1?	2?	3–6?	29; 32; 35; 44; 59? (2)
Nondwarf with cattle	—	—	—	—	—	many	
Dwarf with ibis	1?	—	—	—	—	1?	1
Alongside/near other animals	—	—	2	—	1	3	17; 29; 58
Accompanying attendants	2	—	8	1	5	16	2 (2); 11; 13; 17; 19; 28; 31; 33; 34; 44; 48; 49; 62; 67; 68

TABLE 18.3. (cont'd) Dwarfs and pygmies in various roles, including multiple aspects (i.e., noted in one or more scenes/genres).

Different settings, scenes and roles in which dwarfs appear:	Dynasty 4	Dynasties 4–5	Dynasty 5	Dynasties 5–6	Dynasty 6	Totals for Dynasties 4–6	Catalogue nos. with multiple occurrences of dwarfs (excluding nondwarfs: table 2)
Dwarf associated with dancers and music	1	—	1	—	1	3	4; 14; 57
Dwarf bringing various items (e.g., boxes; bag; basket; pots; sandals; cloth; staff; baton; stick?; fly-whisk; headrest; mirror; harp; sistrum; lost item)	—	1	8	5	16	30	9; 13; 17; 20; 28; 30; 31; 33; 34; 38; 39; 40; 41; 42; 46; 47; 50; 56; 57; 58; 60; 62; 63; 64; 65; 67; 69; 70; 71 (2)
Dwarf in boat (prow; stern)	—	—	1?	—	2	2–3?	32?; 62; 70
Dwarf holding scribal palette	—	—	1	—	—	1	23
Dwarfs in undefined scene	—	—	2	—	—	2	15; 16
Dwarfs with family (including marsh scenes; chair; palanquin)	1	—	15	—	31	47	4; 12; 18; 19; 20; 21; 23; 26 (4); 34; 43; 45; 46; 47; 48; 49 (2); 49 (12); 50; 55; 56; 57; 58; 60; 63; 64; 65; 66; 68; 69; 72
Pygmy in textual reference	—	—	1	—	1	2	25*; 61
Pygmy in Pyramid Texts	—	—	—	—	3	3	51; 52; 53
TOTAL of dwarf occurrences, including multiple roles:						66–73?	66–73? Individual mortuary contexts
TOTAL of dwarf images, etc., excluding multiple roles:	22	9	76–77?	18–23?	108–113?	232–245?	232–243(?) individual dwarfs occur in 66–73(?) settings
Sub-total: Isolating "pygmies"	—	—	1	—	4	5	Above: 5 = pygmies

as animal handlers in life, perhaps emulating the royal court and others in employing exotic and unusual pets and people.[62] For instance, a Sixth Dynasty relief from the Saqqara tomb of Kaigemni illustrated two dwarfs holding leashes to bring a leopard, a long-tailed monkey, and two dogs (*ṯsm*).[63] From the same period, the tomb of Mer-eruka portrays two dwarfs leading a long-tailed monkey and three *ṯsm*-dogs, while the tomb of ʿAnkhmʿahor depicts a dwarf carrying a monkey and a basket of *dom* palm nuts.[64] Since *ṯsm*-hounds, baboons, monkeys, leopards, and sometimes pygmies, are increasingly associated with products from Punt (including a box of myrrh in one example: table 18.1, no. 49), their increasing juxtaposition alongside Egyptian dwarfs may reflect a growing desire among the elite to showcase their status and ownership of such exotica. This ownership of exotic animals might reflect royal largesse from recent state expeditions to Nubia and Punt, and/or otherwise locally obtained items, perhaps emulating and showing off the wonders brought back to Egypt by periodic royal missions to Punt and more regular trade with Nubia.[65]

After the Old Kingdom, the pairings between Egyptian dwarfs and foreign exotica become less common, while regular-sized Nubian handlers appear alongside African animals more frequently in later New Kingdom mortuary and temple scenes (e.g., tribute).[66] However, Egypt and the Mediterranean area's interest in and the popularity of sub-Saharan Africa, its products, and pygmies continue to grow in the succeeding Iron Age, culminating particularly during the Hellenistic–Roman periods, but also maintaining its appeal until recent times.[67]

Conclusions

Much more work can be done, and needs to be done, regarding elucidating the sources, nature, and extent of the trade in diverse exotic fauna, including strontium analysis of nonindigenous animals and their remains (e.g., mummified animals, preserved hides and items associated with them) from different periods of ancient Egypt.[68] Such sci-

62. E.g., the Fifth Dynasty tomb of Ptahhotep displays an Egyptian servant holding leashes for one long-tailed monkey and three *ṯsm*-dogs. See photograph in Osborn and Osbornová 1998, 39, fig. 4-31.

63. See photograph in Osborn and Osbornová 1998, 40, fig. 4-34, 120.

64. See line drawing details in Osborn and Osbornová 1998, 40, figs. 4-33 and 4-35, 120.

65. E.g., some later ancient Egyptian scenes illustrate long-tailed monkeys giving birth in the wild in Egypt, or near the Nile Valley, thereby suggesting that Egypt began to have an alternate indigenous source of both wild and domestic long-tailed monkeys. See Osborn and Osbornová 1998, 39 fig. 4-30, Twelfth Dynasty tomb of Ukhotep at Meir: hunting scene.

66. See Taylor (1991, 33, fig. 37; 34 fig. 38) for painted scenes showing Nubians delivering tribute from the Eighteenth Dynasty Tomb of Huy and Ramesses II's temple at Beit el-Wali.

67. For Hellenistic–Roman textual references to and frequent depictions of sub-Saharan African pygmies (i.e., sixth century BCE and following), including via Herodotus (ca. 450 BCE), see Snowden 1970, 8, 23, 37 fig. 6, 105, 266 n. 72; and Karageorghis 1988. Dasen (2013, 2239) relates that the Roman period portrayal of pygmies included Nilotic hunting scenes, fighting animals, comical behavior, and exaggerated grotesque appearance. Recent appeal is partly expressed through the rediscovery of ancient Egypt and Egyptomania, the "Age of Exploration," and a present-day fascination with Africa that pervades many cultures and ethnic groups across the globe. See O'Connor and Reid 2003.

68. The recent discovery of blocks from Sahure's causeway (el-Awady 2006) demonstrates how continuing archaeological discovery expands our perception of the nature and extent of Egypt's contact with Punt.

entific analysis could reveal greater precision regarding narrowing down the original habitats—albeit via modern conditions and matches—for the various animals and animal products imported into Egypt, be they dogs, felines, and primates, or certain other animal imports. Chemical analyses might also be applied to key foreign human interments in ancient Egypt to trace an individual's geographic upbringing, migration, and resettlement.[69] Although such analyses and their findings may not *resolve* the geographic location(s) of Punt, which probably shifted and fluctuated over time, such investigations should clarify immensely the broad, complex, and still largely elusive trade networks that appear to have existed between pharaonic Egypt and sub-Saharan Africa.[70]

BIBLIOGRAPHY

Aguizy, Ola el-. 1987. "Dwarfs and Pygmies in Ancient Egypt." *ASAE* 71:53–60.
Allen, James P. 2005. *The Ancient Egyptian Pyramid Texts*. WAW 23. Atlanta: Society of Biblical Literature.
Andrews, Carol. 1990. *Ancient Egyptian Jewelry*. New York: Abrams.
———. 1994. *Amulets of Ancient Egypt*. London: British Museum.
Arnold, Dorothea, and Christiane Ziegler, eds. 1999. *Egyptian Art in the Age of the Pyramids*. New York: Metropolitan Museum of Art.
Awady, Tarek el-. 2006. "King Sahura with the Precious Trees from Punt in a Unique Scene!" Pages 37–44 in *The Old Kingdom Art and Archaeology: Proceedings of the Conference Held in Prague, May 31–June 4, 2004*. Edited by Miroslav Bárta. Prague: Czech Institute of Egyptology, Faculty of Arts.
Baines, John. 1985. *Fecundity Figures: Egyptian Personification and the Iconography of a Genre*. Warminster: Aris & Phillips.
Blackman, Aylward M., and Michael Ross Apted. 1953. *The Rock Tombs of Meir, Part V*. Archaeological Survey of Egypt 28. London: Egypt Exploration Society.
Booth, Charlotte. 2005. *The Role of Foreigners in Ancient Egypt: A Study of Nonstereotypical Artistic Representations*. BARIS 1426. Oxford: Archaeopress.
Brewer, Douglas J., Terence Clark, and Adrian Phillips. 2001. *Dogs in Antiquity: Anubis to Cerberus; The Origins of the Domestic Dog*. Warminster: Aris & Phillips.
Brewer, Douglas J., Donald B. Redford, and Susan Redford. 1995. *Domestic Plants and Animals: The Egyptian Origins*. Warminster: Aris & Phillips.
Breyer, Frances. 2016. *Punt: Die Suche nach dem "Gottesland."* CHANE 80. Leiden: Brill.
Brunton, Guy. 1928. *Qau and Badari II*. British School of Archaeology in Egypt 45. London: Quaritch.
———. 1937. *Mostagedda and the Tasian Culture*. British Museum Expedition to Middle Egypt 1. London: Quaritch.

69. E.g., such chemical analysis on human skeletal material has proved invaluable in tracing some widespread travel by at least one individual (the so-called "Amesbury Archer") from the Alps to Stonehenge, ca. 2500–2300 BCE (by affiliated radiocarbon dating), and thereby has implications for broader travel networks across western Europe (Feder 2018, 229–30, 303; Morgan 2008; Renfrew and Bahn 2019, 120).

70. See Kitchen (2005, 11–12, map 3) for a summary on the most probable location of Punt in eastern Sudan, Eritrea, and their environs during the Old through New Kingdoms, plus other suggestions and possible gradual shifts in its general location from north to south in post New Kingdom times. Suggestions regarding the location of Punt itself have evolved in relation to the discovery of more textual, pictorial, and archaeological data on this land, ranging from improbable and less likely equations to more likely and probable identifications, including Uganda, Southwest Arabia, East Africa, Somalia, Northeast Sudan, Eastern Ethiopia, and Eritrea. See also Manzo 1999. See Mitchell 2005, for a broader geographic and chronological treatment on sub-Saharan African trade.

Buszek, Artur. 2008. "Dwarf Figurines from Tell el-Farkha." Pages 35–55 in *Studies in Ancient Art and Civilization 12*. Edited by Joachim Śilwa. Krakow: Instytut Archeologii Uniwersytetu Jagielloriskiego.

Callender, Vivienne G. 2006. "The Iconography of the Princess in the Old Kingdom." Pages 119–26 in *The Old Kingdom Art and Archaeology: Proceedings of the Conference Held in Prague, May 31–June 4, 2004*. Edited by Miroslav Bárta. Prague: Czech Institute of Egyptology, Faculty of Arts.

Chami, Felix. 2004. "The Egypto-Graeco-Romans and Panchaea/Azania: Sailing in the Erythraean Sea." Pages 93–103 in *Trade and Travel in the Red Sea Region: Proceedings of Red Sea Project I; Held in the British Museum, October 2002*. Edited by Paul Lunde and Alexandra Porter. Society for Arabian Studies Monograph 1. BARIS 1269. Oxford: Archaeopress.

———. 2006. *The Unity of African Ancient History: 3000 BC to AD 500*. Dar es Salaam: E & D.

Ciałowicz, Krzysztof M. 2011. "The Predynastic/Early Dynastic Period at Tell el-Farkha." Pages 55–64 in *Before the Pyramids: The Origins of Egyptian Civilization*. Edited by Emily Teeter. OIMP 33. Chicago: Oriental Institute of the University of Chicago.

Daressy, M. George. 1900. "Statuette grotesque égyptienne." *ASAE* 4:124–25, plate.

Dasen, Véronique. 1993. *Dwarfs in Ancient Egypt and Greece*. Oxford Monographs on Classical Archaeology. Oxford: Clarendon.

———. 2013. "Dwarfs." Pages 2238–40 in vol. 4 of *The Encyclopedia of Ancient History*. Edited by Roger S. Bagnall, Kai Brodersen, Craig B. Champion, Andrew Erskine, and Sabine R. Huebner. 13 vols. Oxford: Blackwell Publishing.

Daoud, Khaled. 2007. "Notes on the Tomb of Niankhnesut, Part I: Reliefs and Inscriptions." *SAK* 36: 23–30.

Dawson, Warren R. 1938. "Pygmies and Dwarfs in Ancient Egypt." *JEA* 24:185–89.

Driel-Murray, Carol van. 2000. "Leatherwork and Skin Products." Pages 299–319 in *Ancient Egyptian Materials and Technology*. Edited by Paul T. Nicholson and Ian Shaw. Cambridge: Cambridge University Press.

Emery, Walter B. 1954. *Excavations at Sakkara: Great Tombs of the First Dynasty II*. Excavation Memoir 46. London: Egypt Exploration Society.

Faulkner, Raymond O. 1962. *A Concise Dictionary of Middle Egyptian*. Oxford: Griffith Institute. Repr. 1981.

———. 1969. *The Ancient Egyptian Pyramid Texts*. Warminster: Aris & Phillips.

Feder, Kenneth L. 2018. *Frauds, Myths, and Mysteries: Science and Pseudoscience in Archaeology*. 9th ed. Oxford: Oxford University Press.

Filer, Joyce M. 1995. *Disease*. Egyptian Bookshelf. Austin: University of Texas Press.

———. 2001. Review of *Dwarfs in Ancient Egypt and Greece*, by Veronique Dasen. *JEA* 87:187–90.

Fischer, Henry G. 2002. "Some Titles Associated with Dwarfs and Midgets." *GM* 187:35–39.

Gardiner, Alan. 1957. *Egyptian Grammar: Being an Introduction to the Study of Hieroglyphs*. 3rd ed. Oxford: Griffith Institute, Ashmolean Museum.

Germond, Philippe. 2001. *An Egyptian Bestiary: Animals in Life and Religion in the Land of the Pharaohs*. London: Thames & Hudson.

Gillam, Robert A. 2005. *Performance and Drama in Ancient Egypt*. Duckworth Egyptology. London: Duckworth.

Giorgini, Michela S., Clément Robichon, and Jean Leclant. 1998. *Soleb V: Le temple bas-reliefs et inscriptions*. Cairo: Institut francais d'archeologie orientale.

Goudsmit, Jaap, and Douglas Brandon-Jones. 2000. "Evidence from the Baboon Catacomb in North Saqqara for a West Mediterranean Monkey Trade Route to Ptolemaic Alexandria." *JEA* 86:111–19.

Grimal, Nicolas-Christophe, Jochen Hallof, and Dirk van der Plas. 2000. *Hieroglyphica Sign List/Liste de Signes/Zeichenliste*. Publications Interuniversitaires de Recherches Égyptologiques Informatisées Volume 1. Utrecht: Centre for Computer-Aided Egyptological Research.

Győry, Hedvig. 2002. "Changes in Styles of Ordinary Pataikos Amulets." Pages 491–502 in *Egyptian Museum Collections Around the World: Studies for the Centennial of the Egyptian Museum, Cairo*. Edited by Mamdouh Eldamaty and Mai Trad. 2 vols. Cairo: American University in Cairo Press.

Hallet, Jean-Pierre, and Alex Pelle. 1973. *Pygmy Kitabu*. New York: Random House.

Hannig, Rainer. 1995. *Grosses Handwörterbuch Ägyptisch–Deutsch: Die Sprache der Pharaonen (2800–950 v. Chr.)*. Kulturgeschicte der Antiken Welt 86. Mainz: von Zabern.

Harpur, Yvonne. 1987. *Decoration in Egyptian Tombs of the Old Kingdom: Studies in Orientation and Scene Content*. Studies in Egyptology. London: Kegan Paul.

Hawass, Zahi. 1991. "The Statue of the Dwarf *Pr-n(j)-ʿnh(w)* Recently Discovered at Giza."*MDAIK* 47:157–62, pls. 12–14.

———. 2003. *Secrets from the Sand: My Search for Egypt's Past*. New York: Abrams.

———. 2004. "The Tombs of the Pyramid Builders: The Tomb of the Artisan Petety and His Curse." Pages 21–39 in *Egypt, Israel, and the Ancient Mediterranean World: Studies in Honor of Donald B. Redford*. Edited by Gary N. Knoppers and Antoine Hirsch. PAe 20. Leiden: Brill.

———. 2006. *Mountains of the Pharaohs: The Untold Story of the Pyramid Builders*. New York: Doubleday.

———. 2011. *Newly Discovered Statues from Giza 1990–2009*. Cairo: Ministry of State for Antiquities.

Hawass, Zahi, and Ashraf Senussi. 2008. *Old Kingdom Pottery from Giza*. Cairo: Publication Department, Supreme Council of Antiquities.

Herrmann, Christian. 1994. *Ägyptische Amulette aus Palästina/Israel mit einem Ausblick auf ihre Rezeption durch das Alte Testament*. OBO 138. Fribourg: Universitätsverlag; Göttingen: Vandenhoeck & Ruprecht.

Herzog, Rolf. 1968. *Punt*. DAIK Ägyptologische Reihe 6. Gluckstadt: Augustin.

Hoath, Richard. 2003. *A Field Guide to the Mammals of Egypt*. Cairo: American University in Cairo Press.

Ikram, Salima. 2004. *Beloved Beasts: Animal Mummies from Ancient Egypt*. Cairo: Supreme Council of Antiquities.

———, ed. 2005. *Divine Creatures: Animal Mummies in Ancient Egypt*. Cairo: American University in Cairo Press.

Janssen, Rosalind, and Jack Janssen. 1989. *Egyptian Household Animals*. Shire Egyptology 12. Aylesbury: Shire.

Jones, Dilwyn. 2000. *An Index of Ancient Egyptian Titles, Epithets and Phrases of the Old Kingdom*. 2 vols. BARIS 866. Oxford: Archaeopress.

Kanawati, Naguib. 1981. *The Rock Tombs of El-Hawawish: The Cemetery of Akhmim, Volume II*. Sydney: Macquarie Ancient History Association.

Kanawati, Naguib, and Mahmud Abd er-Razeq. 2000. *The Teti Cemetery at Saqqara, Volume VI: The Tomb of Nikauisesi*. Australian Centre for Egyptology Reports 14. Warminster: Aris & Phillips.

Karageorghis, Vassos. 1988. *Blacks in Cypriot Art*. Houston: Menil Foundation.

Kendall, Timothy. 1997. *Kerma and the Kingdom of Kush 2500–1500 B.C.: The Archaeological Discovery of an Ancient Nubian Empire*. Washington: National Museum of African Art, Smithsonian Institution.

———. 2001. "Kush." *OEAE* 2:250–52.

———. 2007. "Egypt and Nubia." Pages 401–16 in *The Egyptian World*. Edited by Toby A. H. Wilkinson. Routledge Worlds. Abingdon: Routledge.

Kinney, Lesley J. 2012. "Music and Dance." Pages 53–71 in *Behind the Scenes: Daily Life in Old Kingdom Egypt*. Edited by Ann McFarlane and Anna-Latifa Mourad. The Australian Centre for Egyptology Studies 10. Oxford: Aris & Phillips.

Kitchen, Kenneth A. 2004. "The Elusive Land of Punt Revisited." Pages 25–31 in *Trade and Travel in the Red Sea Region: Proceedings of Red Sea Project I, Held in the British*

Museum, October 2002. Edited by Paul Lunde and Alexandra Porter. Society for Arabian Studies Monograph 1. BARIS 1269. Oxford: Archaeopress.

———. 2005. "Ancient Peoples West of the Red Sea in Pre-Classical Antiquity." Pages 7–14 in *People of the Red Sea: Proceedings of Red Sea Project II, Held in the British Museum, October 2004*. Edited by Janet C. M. Starkey. Society for Arabian Studies Monograph 3. BARIS 1395. Oxford: Archaeopress.

Kozma, Chahira. 2006. "Historical Review: Dwarfs in Ancient Egypt." *American Journal of Medical Genetics* 140A:303–11.

———. 2008. "Historical Review II: Skeletal Dysplasia in Ancient Egypt." *American Journal of Medical Genetics* 146A:3104–12.

———. 2010. "The Ancient Egyptian Dwarfs of the Walters Art Museum." *American Journal of Medical Genetics* 152A:2556–62.

Kröpelin, Stefan, and Rudolph Kuper. 2007. "More Corridors to Africa." *CRIPEL* 26:219–29.

Kuper, Rudolph. 2002. "Routes and Roots in Egypt's Western Desert: The Early Holocene Resettlement of the Eastern Sahara." Pages 1–12 in *Egypt and Nubia: Gifts of the Eastern Desert*. Edited by Renée F. Friedman. London: British Museum.

Leahy, Anthony. 1999. "Libyans." Pages 445–47 in *Encyclopedia of the Archaeology of Ancient Egypt*. Edited by Kathryn Bard. New York: Routledge.

———. 2001. "Libya." *OEAE* 2:290–93.

Leclant, Jean. 1999. "Kushites." Pages 423–28 in *Encyclopedia of the Archaeology of Ancient Egypt*. Edited by Kathryn Bard. New York: Routledge.

Lehner, Mark, and Zahi Hawass. 2017. *Giza and the Pyramids: The Definitive History*. Chicago: University of Chicago Press.

Malek, Jaromir. 1986. *In the Shadow of the Pyramids: Egypt During the Old Kingdom*. Cairo: American University in Cairo Press.

Manzo, Andrea. 1999. *Échanges et contacts le long du Nil et de la Mer Rouge dans l'époque protohistorique (IIIe et IIe millénaires avant J.-C.): Une synthèse préliminaire*. Cambridge Monographs in African Archaeology 48. BARIS 782. Oxford: Archaeopress.

Mitchell, Peter. 2005. *African Connections: Archaeological Perspectives on Africa and the Wider World*. African Archaeology Series 7. Walnut Creek, CA: Alta Mira Press.

Moorey, P. R. S. 1994. *Ancient Mesopotamian Materials and Industries: The Archaeological Evidence*. Oxford: Oxford University Press.

Morgan, James. 2008. "Dig Pinpoints Stonehenge Origins." http://news.bbc.co.uk/2/hi /science/nature/7625145.stm.

Mumford, Gregory. 2017. "Pathways to Distant Kingdoms: Land Connections." Pages 35–57 in *Pharaoh's Land and Beyond: Ancient Egypt and Its Neighbors*. Edited by Pearce Paul Creasman and Richard H. Wilkinson. Oxford: Oxford University Press.

Naunton, Christopher. 2010. "Libyans and Nubians." Pages 120–39 in *A Companion to Ancient Egypt*. Edited by Alan B. Lloyd. Blackwell Companions to the Ancient World. Malden, MA: Wiley-Blackwell.

O'Connor, David. 1986. "The Locations of Yam and Kush and Their Historical Implications." *JARCE* 23:27–50.

———. 2003. "Where Was the Kingdom of Yam?" Pages 155–57 in *The Seventy Great. Mysteries of Ancient Egypt*. Edited by Bill Manley. London: Thames & Hudson.

O'Connor, David, and Andrew Reid, eds. 2003. *Ancient Egypt in Africa*. Encounters with Ancient Egypt. Walnut Creek, CA: Left Coast Press.

Osborn, Dale J., and Jana Osbornová. 1998. *The Mammals of Ancient Egypt*. Natural History of Egypt 4. Warminster: Aris & Phillips.

Panagiotopoulos, Diamantix. 2006. "Foreigners in Egypt in the Time of Hatshepsut and Thutmose III." Pages 370–412 in *Thutmose III: A New Biography*. Edited by Eric H. Cline and David O'Connor. Ann Arbor: University of Michigan Press.

Petrie, William M. Flinders. 1900. *The Royal Tombs of the First Dynasty 1900, Part I*. Egypt Exploration Fund/Society Memoir 18. London: Kegan Paul, Trench, Trubner.

———. 1901. *The Royal Tombs of the Earliest Dynasties 1901, Part II*. Egypt Exploration Fund Memoir 21. London: Kegan Paul, Trench, Trubner.

Porter, Bertha, and Rosalind L. B. Moss. 1934. *Topographical Bibliography of Ancient Egyptian Hieroglyphic Texts, Reliefs, and Paintings: Vol. IV, Lower and Middle Egypt*. Oxford: Griffith Institute, Ashmolean Museum.

———. 1937. *Topographical Bibliography of Ancient Egyptian Hieroglyphic Texts, Reliefs, and Paintings: Vol. V, Upper Egypt; Sites*. Oxford: Griffith Institute, Ashmolean Museum.

———. 1974. *Topographical Bibliography of Ancient Egyptian Hieroglyphic Texts, Reliefs, and Paintings: Vol. III, Memphis, Part 1; Abu Rawash to Abusir*. 2nd ed. Oxford: Griffith Institute, Ashmolean Museum.

———. 1978. *Topographical Bibliography of Ancient Egyptian Hieroglyphic Texts, Reliefs, and Paintings: Vol. III, Memphis, Part 2; Saqqara to Dahshur; Fascicle 1 (III²:393–574)*. 2nd ed. Oxford: Griffith Institute, Ashmolean Museum.

———. 1979. *Topographical Bibliography of Ancient Egyptian Hieroglyphic Texts, Reliefs, and Paintings: Vol. III, Memphis, Part 2; Saqqara to Dahshur; Fascicle 2 (III²:575–776)*. 2nd ed. Oxford: Griffith Institute, Ashmolean Museum.

———. 1981. *Topographical Bibliography of Ancient Egyptian Hieroglyphic Texts, Reliefs, and Paintings: Vol. III, Memphis, Part 2; Saqqara to Dahshur; Fascicle 3 (III²:777–1014)*. 2nd ed. Oxford: Griffith Institute, Ashmolean Museum.

Quibell, James Edward, and Frederick Wastie Green. 1899. *Hierakonpolis Part II*. British School of Archaeology in Egypt 5. London: Quaritch. Repr. London: Histories and Mysteries of Man, 1989.

Quibell, James Edward, and William M. Flinders Petrie. 1898. *Hierakonpolis Part I*. British School of Archaeology in Egypt 4. London: Quaritch. Repr. London: Histories and Mysteries of Man, 1989.

Quirke, Stephen, and A. Jeffrey Spencer, eds. 1992. *The British Museum Book of Ancient Egypt*. London: Thames & Hudson.

Redford, Donald B. 2004. *From Slave to Pharaoh: The Black Experience of Ancient Egypt*. Baltimore: Johns Hopkins University Press.

Renfrew, Colin, and Paul Bahn. 2019. *Archaeology: Theories, Methods, and Practice*. 8th ed. London: Thames & Hudson.

Rice, Michael. 2006. *Swifter than the Arrow: The Golden Hunting Hounds of Ancient Egypt*. London: Tauris.

Ricke, Herbert, George R. Hughes, and Edward F. Wente. 1967. *The Beit el-Wali Temple of Ramesses II*. University of Chicago Oriental Institute Nubian Expedition 1. Chicago: University of Chicago Press.

Robins, Gay. 1994. *Proportion and Style in Ancient Egyptian Art*. Austin: University of Texas Press.

Romano, James F. 1989. "The Bes Image in Pharaonic Egypt." PhD diss., New York University.

Sampsell, Bonnie M. 2001. "Ancient Egyptian Dwarfs." *KMT* 12.3:60–73.

Sauneron, Serge. 2000. *The Priests of Ancient Egypt*. Translated by David Lorton. New ed. Ithaca: Cornell University Press.

Seyfried, Karl-Joachim. 1986. "Zwerg." *LÄ* 6:1432–35.

Shennum, David. 1977. *English-Egyptian Index of Faulkner's Concise Dictionary of Middle Egyptian*. Aids and Research Tools in Ancient Near Eastern Studies 1. Malibu, CA: Undena.

Silverman, David. 1969. "Pygmies and Dwarves in the Old Kingdom." *Serapis* 1:53–62.

Simpson, William Kelly, ed. 2003. *The Literature of Ancient Egypt: An Anthology of Stories, Instructions, Stelae, Autobiographies, and Poetry*. 3rd ed. New Haven: Yale University Press.

Smith, William Stevenson. 1949. *A History of Egyptian Sculpture and Painting in the Old Kingdom*. 2nd ed. Boston: Museum of Fine Arts.

Smith, Stuart Tyson. 2003. *Wretched Kush: Ethnic Identities and Boundaries in Egypt's Nubian Empire*. New York: Routledge.

Snowden, Frank M. 1970. *Blacks in Antiquity: Ethiopians in the Greco-Roman Experience*. Cambridge: Belknap Press of Harvard University Press.

Sowada, Karin N. 2009. *Egypt in the Eastern Mediterranean During the Old Kingdom: An Archaeological Perspective*. OBO 237. Fribourg: Academic Press; Göttingen: Vandenhoeck & Ruprecht.

Strudwick, Nigel. 2005. *Texts from the Pyramid Age*. WAW 16. Atlanta: Society of Biblical Literature.

Swinton, Joyce. 2012. "Workshops." Pages 167–84 in *Behind the Scenes: Daily Life in Old Kingdom Egypt*. Edited by Ann McFarlane and Anna-Latifa Mourad. Australian Centre for Egyptology Studies 10. Oxford: Aris & Phillips.

———. 2014. *Dating Old Kingdom Tombs of the Egyptian Old Kingdom*. Archaeopress Egyptology 2. Oxford: Archaeopress.

Taylor, John H. 1991. *Egypt and Nubia*. Cambridge: Harvard University Press.

Thompson, Elizabeth. 1991. "Dwarfs in the Old Kingdom in Egypt." *BACE* 2:91–98, pl. 16.

Török, László. 2009. *Between Two Worlds: The Frontier Region Between Ancient Nubia and Egypt 3700 BC–AD 500*. PAe 29. Leiden: Brill.

Turnbull, Colin. 1983. *The Mbuti Pygmies: Change and Adaption*. Case Studies in Cultural Anthropology. New York: Harcourt Brace College.

Tyldesley, Joyce. 2007. *Egyptian Games and Sports*. Shire Egyptology 29. Princes Risborough: Shire.

Vasiljević, Vera. 2016. "Dogs, Dwarfs, and Carrying Chairs." Pages 117–32 in *Change and Innovation in Middle Kingdom Art: Proceedings of the Meketre Study Day Held at the Kunsthistorisches Museum, Vienna (3rd May 2013)*. Edited by Lubica Hudáková, Peter Jánosi, and Andrea Kahlbacher. Middle Kingdom Studies 4. London: Golden House Publications.

Verma, Sasha. 2014. *Cultural Expression in the Old Kingdom Elite Tomb*. Archaeopress Egyptology 1. Oxford: Archaeopress.

Watson, Philip J. 1987. *Costume of Ancient Egypt*. Costume Reference. New York: Chelsea House.

Wilkinson, Richard H. 2003. *The Complete Gods and Goddesses of Ancient Egypt*. London: Thames & Hudson.

Williams, Bruce B. 1999. "Medjay." Pages 485–87 in *Encyclopedia of the Archaeology of Ancient Egypt*. Edited by Kathryn Bard. New York: Routledge.

CHAPTER 19

Judges 10:11: A Memory of Merenptah's Campaign in Transjordan

Steven Ortiz and S. Cameron Coyle

JIM HOFFMEIER HAS BEEN one of the leading Egyptologists to research the context of the Egyptian sojourn of the Israelites in their Egyptian context.[1] In addition to his contributions as an ancient historian and biblical scholar, he has also written as a philologist. One of Jim's contributions is the retranslation of Merenptah's victory stela in the three volume *The Context of Scripture*. Hence, we humbly attempt to walk in Jim's footsteps and add a footnote to his work as a historian of Egypt and ancient Israel.

The mention of a people called Israel in the late thirteenth century BCE victory hymn of the Egyptian pharaoh Merenptah has long intrigued scholars seeking to reconstruct Israel's earliest history. Chief among the questions surrounding Merenptah's mention of Israel are the issues of where this people was encountered and whether or not they can be equated with the Israel known from the Hebrew Bible. A consensus of sorts has been forming in recent years, placing Merenptah's Israel in the Cisjordanian highland villages. Nevertheless, those who have focused on the historical geography have noted that one of the cities, Yanoam, is actually better located in Transjordan. Rainey had recently proposed a contrary view that Israel was located in Jordan. We are supporting this view and propose that there is an earlier memory in the book of Judges that perhaps alludes to the encounter with Merenptah's forces. We will review the current proposal to place the Israel of Merenptah's victory poem in the Cisjordan and provide evidence to dismiss this view in favor of a Transjordanian Israel. Our attention will then turn to the biblical text, where an explicit mention of Israel's encounter with Merenptah is, unfortunately, absent.

We will suggest that a Transjordanian skirmish between Merenptah's forces and early Israelite settlers serves as a valid option for the historical referent of the claim made in Judg 10:11 that God had previously saved Israel from the Egyptians.

Merenptah's Canaanite Campaign

> The (foreign) chieftains lie prostrate, saying "Peace."
> Not one lifts his head among the Nine Bows.

---

1. James K. Hoffmeier, *Israel in Egypt: The Evidence for the Authenticity of the Exodus Tradition* (New York: Oxford University, 1997); Hoffmeier, *Ancient Israel in Sinai: The Evidence for the Authenticity of the Wilderness Tradition* (Oxford: Oxford University, 2005).

Libya is captured; while Hatti is pacified;
>   Canaan is plundered, Ashkelon is carried off,
>   And Gezer is captured.
>   Yenoam is made into non-existence;
> Israel is wasted, its seed is not;
>   And Hurru is become a widow because of Egypt.
> All lands united themselves in peace.
>   Those who went about are subdued by the king of Upper and Lower Egypt . . . Merneptah.[2]

Literary Structure of the Victory Poem

The beginning point for our discussion of the geography of Merenptah's campaign is the literary structure of the victory poem itself. In 1985, Gösta Ahlström and Diana Edelman proposed that the poem was arranged in a ring structure.[3] According to their reading, "Canaan" and "Israel" are to be viewed as references to subregions of the Cisjordan, with "Canaan" referring to the coastal areas and "Israel" representing the less populated hill country.[4] Their proposal, however, has not received wide support.[5]

That same year, Lawrence Stager also proposed a literary structure for the victory poem.[6] Contrary to Ahlström and Edelman's view of "Israel" as a geographic locale, Stager argued that "Israel" referred to an ethnic group, and that this group stands parallel in the poem with "Hurru."[7] No doubt Stager is correct in affirming the reference to "Israel" as to an ethnic group, as it alone among the names listed in the poem is accompanied by the Egyptian determinative symbol for a foreign people (a throw-stick with a seated man and woman, above three strokes); the other entities all carry the determinative for a foreign city-state, land, or region (a throw-stick with hill-country).[8] Stager maintained that this people group of "Israel" was located in the Cisjordanian hill country.[9]

Slightly later, Frank Yurco suggested his own structure for the victory poem, arguing "Canaan" and "Hurru" to be synonyms in parallel with one another, and indicating "Ashkelon," "Gezer," "Yanoam," and "Israel" to all be entities within Canaan/ Hurru.[10] Yurco was influenced by his related discovery that a series of wall reliefs

---

2. James K. Hoffmeier, "The (Israel) Stela of Merneptah (2.6)," *COS* 2:40–41.

3. Gösta W. Ahlström and Diana Edelman, "Merneptah's Israel," *JNES* 44 (1985): 59–61.

4. Ibid., 60.

5. See critique and references in Michael G. Hasel, "Israel in the Merneptah Stela," *BASOR* 296 (1994): 45–61. Ahlström later modified their proposal in response to specific criticisms, but his modifications did not alter the association between Israel and the Cisjordanian hill country. See his updated arguments in Gösta W. Ahlström, "The Origin of Israel in Palestine," *SJOT* 2 (1991): 19–34.

6. Lawrence E. Stager, "Merenptah, Israel and Sea Peoples: New Light on an Old Relief," *ErIsr* 18 (1985): 56*–64*.

7. Ibid., 61*.

8. Michael G. Hasel, *Domination and Resistance: Egyptian Military Activity in the Southern Levant, ca. 1300–1185 B.C.*, PÄe 11 (Leiden: Brill, 1998), 198–99.

9. Stager, "Merenptah, Israel and Sea Peoples," 61*.

10. Frank J. Yurco, "Merenptah's Canaanite Campaign," *JARCE* 23 (1986): 189.

at Karnak were originally produced by Merenptah and that they possibly depict the battles described in the victory poem.[11]

Subsequently, Anson Rainey and Michael Hasel independently developed a similar structure for the poem.[12] Like Yurco, they view "Canaan" and "Hurru" as synonymous toponyms in parallel with one another, with the city-states of "Ashkelon," "Gezer," and "Yanoam," and the people group "Israel" to be located within "Canaan"/"Hurru." The poem is structured, according to this view, in a chiastic manner, with the four Canaanite entities at the center. Hasel's outline of the poem's structure is reproduced here in figure 19.1.[13]

From this structure it is clear that Ashkelon, Gezer, Yanoam, and Israel are grouped together as entities within Canaan/Hurru. Having recognized this structural feature of the text, it is generally noted that there appears to be a progressive geographical sequence within this group of toponyms, beginning close to Egypt and moving further away to the northeast.[14] If this is indeed the case, then we can look to find Merenptah's Israel somewhere beyond the territory that precedes it in the poem.[15] The locations of Ashkelon and Gezer are well established and will not be reviewed here, other than to note briefly that these first two sites support the suggestion of a geographical sequence moving away from Egypt. This leaves only the location of Yanoam to be determined, to which we now turn our attention.

The Location of Yanoam

The location of Yanoam is debated. Interestingly, Hasel summarily observes that, "Since [Yanoam] is mentioned in the Merenptah Stela between the toponyms of Gezer and Israel, it was most often assumed that the site was located in Cisjordan."[16] Such an assumption is unwarranted, however, since it must also assume that Merenptah's Israel was located in the Cisjordan. A review of the literature reveals that sites from both sides of the Jordan River have been proposed for Yanoam.

---

11. Yurco, "Merenptah's Canaanite Campaign," 189–215; Yurco, "3,200 Year Old Picture of Israelites Found in Egypt," *BAR* 16.5 (1990): 20–38. See also Stager's comments in "Merenptah, Israel and Sea Peoples," 56*–64*, and Hasel's review in *Domination and Resistance*, 199–201. Bimson suggested that Yurco's view of the reliefs has overly influenced his understanding of the structure of the poem, John J. Bimson, "Merenptah's Israel and Recent Theories of Israelite Origins," *JSOT* 49 (1991): 20.

12. Anson F. Rainey, "Anson Rainey Replies," *BAR* 18.2 (1992): 73–74; Anson F. Rainey and R. Steven Notley, *The Sacred Bridge: Carta's Atlas of the Biblical World* (Jerusalem: Carta, 2006), 99. Hasel, "Israel in the Merneptah Stela," 48 (fig. 1), 50–51. Independently arriving at the same idea is Hasel's claim; ibid., 55 n. 8.

13. Adapted from Hasel, "Israel in the Merneptah Stela," 48.

14. Michael G. Hasel, "Merenptah's Reference to Israel: Critical Issues for the Origin of Israel," in *Critical Issues in Early Israelite History*, ed. Richard S. Hess, Gerald A. Klingbeil, and Paul J. Ray Jr., BBRSup 3 (Winona Lake, IN: Eisenbrauns, 2008), 50.

15. We should note, however, that a geographical progression among the city-states of Ashkelon, Gezer, and Yanoam does not necessarily require that Israel be located along the same trajectory. It is possible that Israel is listed last not because of geographical relationships, but rather because of its nature as a people group, as opposed to the preceding city-states.

16. Hasel, *Domination and Resistance*, 147.

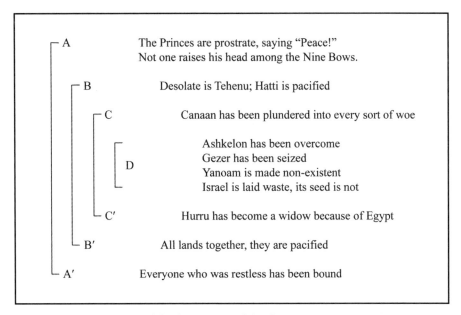

FIGURE 19.1. Hasel's proposal for the structure of the victory poem.

Tell en-Na'ameh

This site in the Huleh Valley was first proposed as Yanoam by H. Clauss in 1907.[17] He was later joined by William F. Albright, who claimed that survey finds indicated occupation at the site throughout the Bronze Age.[18] Few scholars, however, have adopted this suggestion.

Tell el-'Abeidiyeh

John Garstang suggested that Yanoam be identified with Tell el-'Abeidiyeh in 1931.[19] This Jordan Valley site is just south of the Sea of Galilee, on the Cisjordanian side of the river. The proposed identification was adopted by Yohanan Aharoni, whose limited excavations at the site revealed a Late Bronze Age occupation.[20] The site has also been cautiously suggested by William Dever as a possible location for Yanoam, though he offers no justification for the identification.[21]

17. H. Clauss, "Die Städte der El-Amarnabriefe und die Bibel," *ZDPV* 30 (1907): 1–79.

18. William F. Albright, "Bronze Age Mounds of Northern Palestine and Hauran: The Spring Trip of the School in Jerusalem," *BASOR* 19 (1925): 12–13; Albright, "The Jordan Valley in the Bronze Age," *Annual of the American Schools of Oriental Research* 6 (1926): 18–24.

19. John Garstang, *The Foundations of Biblical History: Joshua, Judges* (London: Constable, 1931), 73.

20. Yohanan Aharoni, *The Settlement of the Israelite Tribes in Upper Galilee* (Jerusalem: Magnes, 1957), 125–29 [Hebrew]; Aharoni, *The Land of the Bible: A Historical Geography*, trans. Anson F. Rainey, rev. ed. (Philadelphia: Westminster, 1979), 165.

21. William G. Dever, *Who Were the Early Israelites and Where Did They Come From?* (Grand Rapids: Eerdmans, 2003), 202. Dever's terse discussion of the point, despite his commitment to a Cisjordanian location for Merenptah's Israel, leaves much to be desired and is quoted here in full: "'Yanoam' is usually identified as an important town in northern Canaan, perhaps *el-'Abeidiyeh* in the Jordan Valley."

Tel Yin'am

This site (Tell en-Na'am in Arabic) was originally identified as Yanoam by Aapeli Saarisalo early in the twentieth century.[22] The proposal was widely accepted early on, despite being criticized by Albright.[23] Hasel seems to favor the identification in his work, though he maintains that the evidence is not sufficient for a firm correlation.[24] Excavations at the site were carried out by Harold Liebowitz, beginning in 1975.[25] A large Late Bronze occupation was uncovered in excavation, but this stratum (VIB) was destroyed in a massive conflagration, which, according to Hasel's analysis, is incongruent with Egyptian policy of the period.[26] Thus it is difficult to associate the destruction of this stratum with Merenptah's campaign against Yanoam. Liebowitz has rejected the proposed identification of the site with Yanoam, and instead suggests the site may be biblical Jabneel.

Tell esh-Shihab

The Transjordanian site of Tell esh-Shihab was identified as Yanoam by Nadav Na'aman in 1977.[27] Na'aman's proposal has two lines of argument. He first argues from textual evidence that Yanoam must be located in the Transjordan, in the area of the southern Bashan region. He then suggests Tell esh-Shihab as an acceptable candidate for the location of the ancient city.

Regarding his textual argument, Na'aman first points to Amarna letter EA 197. In this letter, Yanoam appears alongside known cities from the Bashan, suggesting that it too was located in that region. Similarly, Yanoam appears in a topographical list from the period of Amenhotep III where it is listed with a number of Syrian cities. Na'aman suggests that if Yanoam was located in the Cisjordan, it would be out of place on this list. Yanoam again is listed with two known Syrian cities and a third unknown site in a second topographical list, this one from the period of Ramesses II.[28] Na'aman persuasively argues that these three textual witnesses to Yanoam's location all require a Transjordanian site.

On the basis of limited archaeological evidence, Na'aman suggests the Transjordanian site of Tell esh-Shihab, west of Edrei on the Yarmuk River, as the ancient site of Yanoam. Supporting this claim is a depiction of Yanoam on a Karnak relief of Seti I, which shows the city surrounded by a bush-lined river. Na'aman describes Tell

---

22. Aapeli Saarisalo, *The Boundary Between Issachar and Naphtali: An Archaeological and Literary Study of Israel's Settlement in Canaan*, Annales academiae scientiarum Fennicae 21 (Helsinki: Suomalaisen Kirjallisuuden Seuran Kirjapainon, 1927), 112–18.

23. For extensive references, see Hasel, *Domination and Resistance*, 147.

24. Ibid., 188.

25. Harold Liebowitz, "Yin'am, Tel," in *The New Encyclopedia of Archaeological Excavations in the Holy Land*, ed. Ephraim Stern, Ayelet Lewinson-Gilboa, and Joseph Aviram, 5 vols. (Jerusalem: Israel Exploration Society, 1993), 4:1515–16.

26. For the destruction, see ibid. For its incongruence with Egyptian policy, see Hasel, *Domination and Resistance*, 149–50.

27. Nadav Na'aman, "Yeno'am," *TA* 4 (1977): 168–77.

28. Ibid., 168–69.

esh-Shihab as "surrounded almost completely by the Yarmuk gorge."[29] Additionally, a stela of Seti I was discovered at the tell, suggesting the site was indeed involved in the campaign recorded at Karnak. Finally, survey evidence suggests the site was occupied throughout the Bronze Age, but abandoned during the Iron Age. This occupational history would seem to correspond well with the textual witnesses to Yanoam, which are also present only during the Bronze Age.[30]

To summarize, the textual data leads us to believe that Yanoam should be sought in the Transjordan, particularly in the southern Bashan region. This point holds regardless of one's opinion regarding the site of Tell esh-Shihab. However, the limited data available from Tell esh-Shihab do support the possibility that the site could be identified as ancient Yanoam. While further evidence is needed to make a firm identification, it would seem that Tell esh-Shihab is the best option proposed thus far for locating Yanoam.[31]

Further Considerations

Among the more vocal proponents of the Cisjordanian hypothesis in recent years has been Dever. Dever has sought to equate Merenptah's Israel with his proto-Israelites of the Cisjordanian hill country villages.[32] Having mapped Merenptah's campaign from Ashkelon and Gezer to a Cisjordanian Yanoam, Dever states,

> A simple glance at the map here ... will show anyone with an unprejudiced eye *the one place left*, the one where Israel in the late thirteenth century *must have been*: the central hill country. Is it merely a coincidence that most of the thirteenth through twelfth century BCE villages recently brought to light by archaeology are located precisely there?[33]

Dever conveniently leaves the Transjordanian Bashan region off his map, and out of his discussion. It would seem that a truly unprejudiced eye would need to deal with the Transjordanian evidence prior to considering the Cisjordanian hill country to be the only remaining option.

In a 2007 article, Rainey argued strongly in favor of Israelite settlement moving from the Transjordan to the Cisjordan.[34] His argument included a consideration of the location of Yanoam as part of a larger discussion regarding the location of

29. Ibid., 169.
30. Ibid.
31. This conclusion is not widely shared, as most scholars continue to seek Yanoam in the Cisjordan. However, Anson F. Rainey strongly supported the identification, "Whence Came the Israelites and Their Language?" *IEJ* 57 (2007): 56; Rainey, *Sacred Bridge*, 82. Rainey's support was due in large part to the textual aspects of Na'aman's argument. For an overview of the consensus regarding the Cisjordanian position, see references in Ann E. Killebrew, *Biblical Peoples and Ethnicity: An Archaeological Study of Egyptians, Canaanites, Philistines, and Early Israel 1300–1100 B.C.E.*, ABS 9 (Atlanta: Society of Biblical Literature, 2005), 155, 188 nn. 25–26.
32. Dever, *Who Were the Early Israelites*, 201–8.
33. Ibid., 205–6 (emphasis added).
34. Rainey, "Whence Came the Israelites," 41–64.

Merenptah's Israel. Here Rainey briefly overviewed Na'aman's arguments in favor of a Transjordanian context for Yanoam, and affirmed Tell esh-Shihab as a possible candidate.

In a recent response to Rainey's arguments, Dever has attempted to defend his Cisjordan-based indigenous origins theory for early Israel against Rainey's suggestions.[35] He responds specifically to Rainey's argument in favor of locating Merenptah's Israel in the Transjordan, stating:

> This is a truly incredible claim, one for which Rainey obviously cannot cite authorities. The best way to locate Merneptah's Israelites is by way of elimination, i.e., drawing a map based on the text's battle itinerary. The general area—Canaan and the land of the Hurrians—is obvious; and the text specifies the coastal area (Ashkelon and Gezer), extending up to lower Galilee (Yanoam?).
>
> But there is a clear lacuna, precisely in the central hill-country of western Palestine, where the 300 or so Iron IA Proto-Israelite villages that we know are located (as even Rainey agrees). *This* is Merneptah's Israel. There is absolutely no mention, even a veiled reference, to any areas of Transjordan—even though the Egyptians knew the area well in New Kingdom times.[36]

Dever's comments are quoted here in full to demonstrate his failure to deal with the evidence at issue. First, at the end of his initial paragraph, Dever misplaces his question mark. It is not the stela's mention of Yanoam that is questionable, but rather Dever's assumed association of that site with the lower Galilee region. Dever goes on to deny that there is any mention of Transjordanian areas in the stela, "[not] even a veiled reference," without dealing with any of the evidence placing Yanoam in the southern Bashan—evidence which Rainey had reviewed and Na'aman had clearly documented. Thus Dever's claim regarding the "clear lacuna" in the text which points "precisely" to the Cisjordanian central hill-country rings hollow.

If Yanoam is, indeed, to be located in the southern Bashan, as we have argued here, then the reconstructed geographical sequence of Merenptah's campaign places the Egyptian forces in the Transjordan just prior to the encounter with Israel. It would seem that if there is a valid geographical sequencing to the Canaanite entities named in the victory poem, this region, around the southern Bashan, is the most likely candidate for the location of Merenptah's Israel.

Two points should be noted at this juncture. First, a Transjordanian context for early Israel is not out of step with the archaeological evidence available today. Based on his work at Tell el-'Umayri, Larry Herr has argued for some time that the Transjordanian and Cisjordanian hill countries have strong cultural ties with one another.[37] He has also cautiously suggested, following Cross, that the earliest Israelite settlement could have

---

35. William G. Dever, "Earliest Israel: God's Warriors, Revolting Peasants, or Nomadic Hordes?" *ErIsr* 30 (2011): 4*–12*.

36. Ibid., 5* (emphasis original).

37. Larry G. Herr, "Tell el-'Umayri and the Madaba Plains Region During the Late Bronze–Iron Age I Transition," in *Mediterranean Peoples in Transition: Thirteenth to Early Tenth Centuries BCE; in Honor of Professor Trude Dothan*, ed. Seymour Gitin, Amihai Mazar, and Ephraim Stern (Jerusalem: Israel Exploration Society, 1998), 260; Herr, "Tall al-'Umayri and the Reubenite Hypothesis," *ErIsr* 26 (1999): 74*.

been in the Transjordan.[38] Dever has noted the similar settlement patterns for the Late Bronze–Iron I transition in the Cisjordanian and Transjordanian highlands, as well as their material culture similarities.[39] While Dever prefers to differentiate between "proto-Israelites" in the west and "prototribal states" in the east, such a distinction is difficult to make on the basis of the material culture alone.[40]

Second, suggesting that Merenptah's Israel was located in the Transjordan does not require a denial of the Israelite character of the Cisjordanian hill country villages. The question at hand is not really "where was Israel?," but rather, "where was Israel *encountered by Merenptah*?" Given the similarities in settlement patterns and material culture, coupled with the biblical tradition of Israel settling both sides of the Jordan, we lack any compelling reason to restrict the Israelite settlement to either side of the river.

Locating Merenptah's Israel in the Biblical Text?

Having argued in favor of a Transjordanian context for the encounter between Israel and Merenptah's forces, we now turn our attention to the biblical text.

Judges 10:11 and the Egyptians

In Judg 10:6–16 we find the introduction to the Jephthah narrative. The cycle begins with the general notice that Israel had again done "evil in the sight of the LORD" (10:6), before listing the specific foreign gods the people had been worshiping.[41] As a result of their idolatry, the people had been "sold" (10:7) by God to the Philistines and the Ammonites, the latter of whom had oppressed "all the Israelites that were beyond the Jordan in the land of the Amorites, which is in Gilead" (10:8) for eighteen years. The Philistines now disappear from the text, and the narrative focuses almost exclusively on events transpiring in the Transjordanian region of Gilead: Gilead is the place where the Ammonites encamp when they come to fight (10:17); the "commanders of the people of Gilead" search for a leader and proclaim that "he shall be head over all the inhabitants of Gilead" (10:18); most of the action in the narrative takes place at "Mizpah of Gilead" (11:29); and even Jephthah himself is associated with the region, being referred to as "Jephthah the Gileadite" (11:1).

In response to their oppression, the people confess their idolatry to God, whose reply was likely not what the people were hoping for:

> And the LORD said to the Israelites, "Did I not deliver you from the Egyptians and from the Amorites, from the Ammonites and from the Philistines?

---

38. Frank Moore Cross, "Reuben, First-Born of Jacob," *ZAW* 100 (1988): 46–65. Herr, "Tall al-'Umayri and the Reubenite Hypothesis," 74*.

39. Dever, "Earliest Israel," 8*. See also the discussion regarding survey data in Eveline J. van der Steen, *Tribes and Territories in Transition: The Central East Jordan Valley in the Late Bronze Age and Early Iron Ages; a Study of the Sources*, OLA 130 (Leuven: Peeters, 2004), 78–101.

40. Dever, "Earliest Israel," 8*.

41. All biblical quotations are taken from the NRSV.

The Sidonians also, and the Amalekites, and the Maonites, oppressed you; and you cried to me, and I delivered you out of their hand. Yet you have abandoned me and worshiped other gods; therefore I will deliver you no more. Go and cry to the gods whom you have chosen; let them deliver you in the time of your distress." (Judg 10:11–14)

It is this response from God, with its appeal to past examples of divine deliverance, that we will focus on here.

The mention of "the Egyptians" in this pericope has traditionally been understood as a reference to the exodus from Egypt.[42] In support of this view, Robert Boling has argued in favor of an "historical, geographical, and social logic" behind the grouping of the names of previous oppressors, in which the opening references to Egypt and the Amorites are seen to hark "back to the beginning of the story of Israel and its initial successes in Transjordan."[43] Arthur Cundall, who seeks to identify a biblical referent for each of the oppressors in this passage, suggests that the reference here must be to the exodus since there is "no historical evidence of any oppression subsequent to the settlement in Canaan."[44] It would seem, however, that this association depends as much on presumption as it does evidence. The lack of other options, cited by Cundall, seems to be the strongest argument in favor of the association, and it receives only limited support from the relative position of "the Egyptians" in the list.

There are other issues with this interpretation, which, although minor, open the possibility for an alternative view. First, there are a total of nine references in the book of Judges to Egypt or the Egyptians (Judg 2:1, 12; 6:8, 9, 13; 10:11; 11:13, 16; 19:30). Of these nine, our passage is the only occurrence that lacks an explicit reference to the exodus.[45] Judges is generally viewed as a very systematic and cyclical composition, artfully employing repetition and standardized phrases throughout the book. Within our pericope we can see this feature at work; there are seven foreign gods listed in 10:6 as snares to the people, while the divine response of 10:11–12 recounts seven occurrences of past deliverance. Within such a writing style it seems significant that eight out of nine occurrences refer explicitly to the exodus while only 10:11 makes a vague reference to a former deliverance from the Egyptians. While the exodus could be the proper referent of 10:11, the context does not require this interpretation.

A second issue to consider is whether a *biblical* referent is necessary. We do not have any biblical referent for an oppression associated with the Sidonians, nor the

---

42. Robert G. Boling, *Judges*, AB 6A (Garden City, NY: Doubleday, 1975), 192; Arthur E. Cundall, *Judges: An Introduction and Commentary*, Tyndale Old Testament Commentary (London: Tyndale Press, 1968), 139; C. F. Burney, *The Book of Judges with Introduction and Notes* (London: Rivingtons, 1920), 294–97; Carl Friedrich Keil and Franz Delitzsch, *Joshua, Judges, Ruth: Biblical Commentary on the Old Testament*, trans. James Martin (Grand Rapids: Eerdmans, 1950), 376; Victor H. Matthews, *Judges and Ruth*, New Cambridge Bible Commentary (Cambridge: Cambridge University Press, 2004), 115.

43. Boling, *Judges*, 192.

44. Cundall, *Judges*, 139.

45. Six of the references (2:1; 6:8, 13; 11:13, 16; 19:30) speak of Israel coming up (עלה) from Egypt, one (2:12) speaks of going out (יצא) from Egypt, and one (6:9) speaks of being delivered (נצל) from the hand of the Egyptians. This last occurs together with עלה (אָנֹכִי הֶעֱלֵיתִי אֶתְכֶם מִמִּצְרַיִם וָאֹצִיא אֶתְכֶם מִבֵּית עֲבָדִים וָאַצִּל אֶתְכֶם מִיַּד מִצְרַיִם). An anacolouthon occurs in the present passage, with the verb "to save" (ישע) appearing only at the end of 11:12.

Maonites. In the case of the Sidonians, some have suggested this to be a reference to the Deborah narrative, essentially equating the Sidonians with the Canaanites.[46] Nothing in the context, however, suggests any connection between the two, and only a desire to find a biblical referent for the event would lead one to accept the idea. Similarly, some have read "Midianite" for "Maonite," following the LXX, though this variant is not easily explained.[47] It is also unclear why the mention of the Amorites would refer to the initial encounter between these peoples and the Israelites under Moses; these encounters are remembered as Israelite successes, while the context of this passage is deliverance from oppression. With three of the seven former oppressors lacking a clear biblical referent, it seems unnecessary to require that a biblically attested event stand behind the otherwise vague reference to the Egyptians.

A New Proposal

It is noteworthy that this divine response is given within a clear Transjordanian context. The events of the narrative all take place in Gilead, and the people involved are all Gileadites. While the exodus may be the only *biblical* referent available for the mention of the Egyptians in 10:11, our arguments above have provided the potential for a different *historical* referent—Merenptah's campaign. If Merenptah's Israel was located in the Transjordan, it could very well be the case that the memory present in this pericope of a past deliverance from the Egyptians, recounted to a Gileadite audience, recalls Israel's encounter with Egyptian forces in Gilead rather than the events of the exodus.

All we know of Merenptah's battle with the Israelites is the little we learn from the stela. Merenptah claims victory, but clearly exaggerates. An Egyptian victory in the Gilead against the Israelites would have been a hard blow to a people still in the process of settling the land. However, the battle did not result in a lasting Egyptian presence and oppression of the local population. This fact would help to justify the remembrance of the event and its aftermath as an example of deliverance rather than as a defeat. This may also help explain why the book of Judges does not include a more explicit account of the battle; the book is concerned with narratives of deliverance from extended periods of oppression rather than single battles.

Conclusion

In conclusion, our review of the geography of Merenptah's victory poem revealed the importance of the location of Yanoam for determining the possible location of Merenptah's Israel. From the Late Bronze Age textual sources we learned that Yanoam must be sought in the southern Bashan region of the Transjordan, and we agreed with Na'aman that Tell esh-Shihab appears to be the best candidate for identifying the site of the ancient city. We also found justification for a Transjordanian Israel in the close cultural connections evidenced in the archaeological record between the highland

---

46. Cundall, *Judges*, 139.
47. Boling, *Judges*, 192.

sites on both sides of the Jordan River. We then reviewed Judg 10:11 and the vague reference to a past deliverance from the Egyptians. Here we saw that there is no compelling reason to consider the exodus to be the intended referent of this passage, and that an equally valid option is to understand Merenptah's encounter with Israel to be the historical background to this passing reference.

CHAPTER 20

Digging for Data: A Practical Critique of Digital Archaeology

Miller C. Prosser

Introduction

Did you know that there is a field of study known as digital archaeology? Sounds exciting. Armies of silver, shimmering, semiautonomous robots hovering in formation over an ancient site, sifting through dirt, collecting artifacts in their load bays, performing chemical analysis on soil samples, and uploading results to a distant server. Of course, this description is facetious. Even though the term has a bit of a futuristic ring to it, digital archaeology refers simply to the integration of computers and other digital tools in the process of archaeological investigation. Archaeologists have been using digital tools for many decades now; but in the last decade, the speed of uptake has increased, such that scholars are now pausing to ask if these new tools have changed the way archaeology is practiced.[1]

What Is Digital Archaeology

There is little agreement on what constitutes digital archaeology. Even today, we're not convinced that there is any one definition of, or one way to do digital archaeology. It is less important to establish that a thing called digital archaeology exists than it is to define what we mean when we use this term. (Spoiler alert: I am not sure such a thing

It is a great pleasure to honor the academic career of a teacher and mentor. Jim's earnest dedication to his students made studying under his tutelage both inspirational and intellectually challenging. His passion inspired a group of young college students to practically demand a second year of Middle Egyptian hieroglyphs. Jim accepted the challenge, even inviting the three of us to study and read texts around his dining room table for a term. Reflecting on those sessions, I realize only now what patience this must have taken from our long-suffering teacher, enduring hours of halting translation. Now many years later, it has been an unexpected pleasure to reconnect professionally with Jim, supporting his use of the OCHRE database system for the Tell el-Borg excavation. In fact, Jim's history with the database stretches back to previous iterations of the system, before it evolved into what is now OCHRE.

    1. See, e.g., Gordon, Walcek Averett, and Counts (2016, 3). On the slow adoption of digital tools in archaeological practice, Roosevelt (Roosevelt et al. 2015, 326) points out some key differences in digital archaeology versus archaeology prior to digital practices: "In parallel with the commercial digital electronics market, the practice of archaeology has been on a steady, decades-long march towards incorporation of computer-based technologies in every step of the archaeological process. Among the many steps inherent in this process, two recent examples stand out for their importance. The first is the direct digital recording of observations at the time and location of actual excavation; the second is the real-time integration of observations into a database that provides always up-to-date, interconnected views of the overall excavation."

FIGURE 20.1.
A reflective lens on
digital archaeology

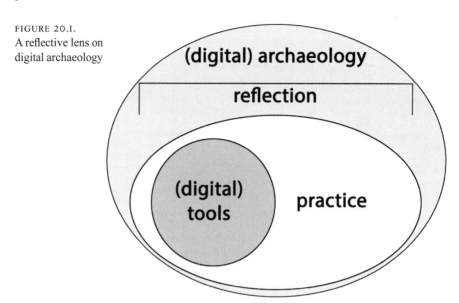

exists.) What is the threshold for defining archaeology as digital archaeology: The use of a digital camera, a registered objects list in a word processing document instead of on a printed form? What minimal threshold must be reached before archaeology becomes "digital?" This line of rhetoric may seem facile, but it is meant to raise a challenging point, what is it that adds the "digital" to digital archaeology?

I want to separate out a few nodes of observation and define how they relate within a broader superstructure that may be called digital archaeology (see fig. 20.1). The first node is the area of digital tools. This refers to hardware and software. The second node envelops the first one but includes more, that is, the node of practice. Practice refers in part to the use of the digital tools, but more broadly also to planning, modeling of data, creating open data sets, and more. These two nodes interact in practical ways. Then at a level above these two is an overarching framework, or lens, through which we view them. Let's call this the reflective lens. By viewing our tools and practice through this lens we hope to understand the role they play and the effect they have on our research. These three elements, if we accept the reductive simplicity, make up a sphere that may be called digital archaeology. Take another look at the figure. Cover up the word digital. What we're left with is a model that could just as easily be one representation of archaeology in general, before the digital advent. So, my point is that while the introduction of digital strategies into the world of archaeology may result in slightly different tools, practice, and reflection, we are not discussing something manifestly different than traditional archaeology.

In each node, digital archaeology may introduce new features. We have new tools (drones, total stations, dSLRs); but we still use most of the old tools (trowels, brushes, strong backs). We have some new practices (creating linked data sets and long-term digital archiving); but we still use most of the old practices (description, classification, interpretation). We may need to reflect slightly differently due to the nature of the digital world, but we still need to contend with many of the issues of archaeological method and theory (Costopoulos 2016, 1).

Reflection

Does the use of digital tools in the practice of archaeology require a deeper reflection on their impact than would the use of trowels and tape measures? Is there something inherent in the use of digital tools that require us to reflect more intentionally than we would when we used paper? No one pauses to question the ethical concerns of creating top plans with pencil and paper, possibly because there were no other options, possibly also because there is no hidden functionality of paper. If there is something unique about digital tools that make this reflection a requirement, it may be the perceived potential of computers for research. Paper had very little potential, other than eventual publication, again on paper. Computers have a great deal more potential, more than what we can probably understand. So, it is an attempt to understand as best we can this potential, and an attempt to understand how to use the tools that drives us to reflect. Once we allow ourselves to be freed from the preprinted excavation record sheet, we may still wonder what an appropriate digital data capture method might be.[2] What are the impacts of such a change? Some intentional reflection is necessary in this process.

Technology is seductive. The new and shiny bevels of the newest Apple device demand to be touched. At this moment, we can converse with the software in our devices, exchanging jokes, finding directions, and generally conducting a digital romance. With very little effort, our device can fool us into thinking that it is sentient. When applied to archaeology, technology can give the mistaken impression that positive outcomes are guaranteed. But anyone who has used a database can tell you that positive or desired outcomes are *absolutely not* guaranteed.[3] Even if we're not talking about experimental new technology, but something that has been well tested, positive outcomes are not guaranteed. There are many factors that could undermine positive outcomes. Perhaps, an example would be instructive. If we lump together various types of information into the same field in a database, we will not be able to extract information based on one aspect of this data. So, a description such as "partially preserved stamped amphora handle" should be atomized into discrete fields: at least (1) level of preservation, (2) presence of seal impression, and (3) vessel part. This level

2. Excavation data are complex. Overly systematized data capture risks oversimplifying our data. As Caraher (2015) observes: "As workflows fragment, however, and narrative notebooks give way to standardized forms, context sheets, digital models, and other regularized expression of trench-side or survey unit knowledge, the significance of this embodied knowledge recedes into the background. Foregrounded, instead, is the systematized regularity of digital data which de-authorizes, overwrites, and 'black boxes' the complexities of excavation and survey."

3. Even if I quibble with his description of relational databases as the most sophisticated method of recording data, I agree with the core of Llobera's (2011, 206) observations, which are worth quoting at length. "With the increasing use of information systems, traditional forms of recording archaeological contexts have given place to databases and other forms of digital media. While their application is not contested by anyone, their use among archaeologists remains less than optimal. The most sophisticated and widely used method of recording context in archaeology is the relational database. However, there has been remarkably little discussion of how easy or efficient it is to store, access, and query data stored in such types of database. Commonly, databases are designed for data entry, moreover, for a particular form of data entry. Emphasis is on recording data and less on how easy it is to retrieve the data or to generate data output in a certain form. The truth is that, even when archaeologists use complex relational entity databases, their queries remain very simple and limited in scope. Our ability to find new links among attributes of archaeological entities stored inside a database is curtailed by its limited interface (traditionally in the form of a table)."

of descriptive atomization then allows the user to find all amphora handles, or any vessel part that has been stamped, with the ability to include or exclude broken items. This level of atomization can be achieved in different ways, but the point remains. Before launching a new project, one must consider carefully the nature of data that will be encountered. Therefore, we reflect on the use of digital tools, the way they may impact our work, and even the way we they should free us from predigital strictures.

This sort of reflection can take many forms. Some have expressed concern about the unintended consequences of efficiency, solutionism, and less traditionally scholarly work.[4] From my experience, the field of archaeology does not currently risk morphing in a manner such that a traditional method of removing dirt is replaced by noninvasive methods aided by not-yet-invented technologies. Until then, archaeologists do what archaeologists have always done, but now with tools that enhance, update, or sharpen previous methods (see Huggett 2013, 16; and bibliography cited there). Some of our new digital tools may frustrate individuals for whom previous predigital methods were sufficient; but we should not stop considering the potential efficiencies and improvements in accuracy that digital tools can provide.

In this vein, we are warned about the potential "deskilling" of researchers, the process by which predigital skills and the attendant affordances are lost when replaced by digital tools that achieve the ends faster (see Caraher 2016, 422–23; Kersel 2016, 478; Walcek Averrett, Gordon, and Counts 2016, vii). Quite rightly, these critics caution that efficiency alone is not sufficient reason to adopt a new tool. In addition to considerations of slow versus fast, I would emphasize the spectrum of accurate versus careless. Data capture can be fast and accurate (machine-generated data), slow and accurate (reliable student workers), fast and careless (scraping the web), or slow and careless (I shall refrain from naming names). In terms of deskilling ourselves and our staff, while this may be a reality, there will always be another skill for us to learn and practice. Does anyone teach a student volunteer how to record points with a tape measure, or how to use grid paper to create a top plan? If these skills are still practiced, they are supplemented by digital skills such as the use of a total station and the creation of shape files and raster images in a GIS program. Again, these digital skills are not necessarily or inherently fast. Using a GIS program to draw a vector shape file that

4. Regarding the broader field of digital humanities, one may offer the warning that universities are seeking to replace traditional, slow academic research with new, fast, methods that produce immediate deliverables. E.g., by replacing manual close readings of texts with the ingestion of many texts and the performance of analysis by computation reading, an English department replaces traditional research with outcomes that are immediately valuable in commercial applications. See Allington, Brouillette, and Golumbia (2016) and Kansa (2016, 454–58). Time will tell if we should have listened to Cassandra or if we are witnessing rather the growing pains of a newly expanding field, not yet sure of its own definition. However one interprets the rise of particular strains of digital humanities in the university—whether it be a neoliberal takeover or not—one hopes that the proper application of digital tools and practices is one that supplements traditional modes of academic research, or even further democratizes that process to allow the ivory tower to invite more participation. It would not be a system in which traditional (read "slow" or "deliberate") research is replaced by preprogrammed analysis. One could perhaps argue that digital archaeology risks losing its traditional mooring if we expect answers from linked data sets, if we assume the digital tool will know something on our behalf. I would argue further that digital archaeology becomes corrupted once we define it as the process of creating the tools: the software, the hardware even. This is not digital archaeology. This is computer science, or more properly development. Leave these tasks to those trained in computer science.

represents a cobblestone pavement containing a thousand polygons is certainly not fast. But it is accurate (if done correctly, of course) and it delivers more potential for integration and use with other project data. Ultimately, apart from speed and accuracy, which are valuable, digital tools when properly applied do not obviate the traditional process of archaeological interpretation.

We are warned that the choice of a new digital tool (some may say toy) should be made with a clear understanding of the potential and limitations of that tool. Beware the "black box," a term that refers to hardware or software whose inner workings are a mystery to all but the computer specialist. Many have noted that, in general, there has been a lack of intentionality in the development and deployment of new digital tools, with little to no consultation with the archaeologists who will be using these tools (see, e.g., Sobotkova et al. 2016; Huggett 2015a, 93). So, on the one hand, an archaeologist is required to be something of an interested party in the creation of their new digital tools. On the other hand, they are warned not to rely too heavily on digital tools they do not fully understand. This is a hard balance to strike. Few archaeologists are trained as computer scientists, which almost guarantees some level of "black box" experience. Is there a place for the traditional archaeologist in digital archaeology? Archaeologists are both reassured and warned about digital tools, that they "can collect data and they can begin to integrate them into the contextual systems that we think of as information, but they cannot perform the leap of informed imagination" (Rabinowitz 2016, 504). One can forgive the archaeologist for being confused as to where to start and how to make the right choices when embarking on or expanding a project's digital strategies.

Practical Critique

What is a practical critique? A practical critique is one that asks questions and suggests solutions. Jeremy Huggett (2015a, 94) discusses the "grand challenge" that digital archaeology should aspire to answer. The argument is passionate and persuasive but provides no tangible advice or practical solutions. It is important to consider the issues of digital archaeology, as Huggett and others do. As the line of reasoning goes, we must reflect on the meaning behind the various tools before simply using them.

From my perspective there is a more primary and practical concern. Do any of these tools work? Do they represent the research accurately, or do they obscure it in ways that confuse or mislead future researchers? The ideal tool should be designed as agnostic, flexible, customizable, extensible; and it should address and respond to the research.

Choosing Digital Tools Intentionally

One major and surprisingly overlooked advantage made possible by digital archaeology is the freedom from restriction: in data capture, data modeling, analysis, and publication. It is remarkable how often both tools and practice in digital archaeology are designed on predigital models. Data capture forms are made to look like paper record sheets familiar to the project. Data is listed and constrained in spreadsheet tables as if to replicate the appendix of a printed volume. As Marcos Llobera (2011, 217) so clearly states, "There is little recognition that the intersection of information systems (computers primarily) and archaeology provides new paradigms and/or research venues."

Instead of focusing on familiarity or speed in the data capture process, an archaeologist's primary demand should be that their data, as recorded in the computer, be modeled in such a way that it reflects more closely the real world.[5] Archaeological data is not business data. It does not lend itself to being stored in spreadsheets. The lack of homogeneity in our data requires a more flexible data model.

Huggett (2015a, 93) observes that "the digital archaeologist has been convinced to use digital tools that were developed for other purposes, typically for the business world," and that "this is the reason why digital tools can be a hinderance to academic research in the Humanities." One may argue that little "convincing" was needed as business tools like Microsoft Access and FileMaker—and even Excel and Word—were perceived as the only tools available for the task. I hope we no longer use heavy machinery to flatten ancient sites, trying to see what is beneath. Construction machinery doesn't work so well in archaeology. It erases exactly what we wish to preserve. Spreadsheets and relational tables do the same thing if applied in the way that most users apply them. These tools typically lump data together into cells in ways that violate a more natural form of the data. It would be hard to overstate the effect these tools have had in shaping and limiting the type of research that is possible in digital archaeology. Quite simply, tools adopted from other fields negatively affect our research in ways we tend not to notice.

The tools we use should reflect the reality of the world we are studying. Spreadsheets reflect the reality of the world they are meant to capture: highly repetitive, predictable, homogeneous financial data. From its early implementation in a digitized form, the spreadsheet model is meant to reproduce an accounting ledger, with rows of line items and columns recording figures.[6] The strategy of organizing data into rows and columns is also employed in the familiar relational database model, which is the underlying organizational strategy for Microsoft Access and FileMaker. In the case of the relational database model, data are stored in tables, where each row represents one entry, and each column represents a category or field of data that describes that entry. For example, row one in a table may represent a coin and the columns may represent the material, date minted, minting authority, decorative motif, and measurements of

5. See Schloen and Schloen (2014) who challenge the traditional paradigm for modeling textual data.

6. In the business world of the early and mid-twentieth century, spreadsheets were just one part of a broader computerized approach to corporate accounting. See,e.g., a chapter titled "On the Evolution of Budgeting and Budget Simulation" in Mattessich (1964), which lays out some of the early uses of data sets in the business world. This chapter, and the volume in general, proposes various processes for working on data sets such as sales budgets. The output of these processes is spreadsheets. It is from this context that programs like Microsoft Excel have evolved. For the business world, the development of these programs was meant to address issues of cost, labor, accuracy, and speed in the handling of accounting data. To achieve these ends, the data needed to be organized in highly regularized formats, so the digital computer could ingest them. As a representative example, take the following passage from an early volume on the use of computers in business: "Punched-card machines can perform work on data and produce reports much faster, more accurately, and more efficiently than can be done manually if the data are standardized in the initial stages.... Thus homogeneous, or like, items can be grouped together very easily" (Awad 1968, 11). As I argue throughout this paper, humanities data are not homogeneous, and we should not allow ourselves to be restricted by a mode of thinking and mode of representing knowledge developed for sales and accounting.

the coin. The typical database will be defined by many of these tables, linked together by common fields such as registration number, find spot, or some other common column in each table. These database tables are easily converted to the spreadsheets that many of us are familiar with. So, both the spreadsheet and the relational database employ the same basic data model. This data model, which was created to record highly regularized and homogeneous data like account numbers, phone numbers, addresses, invoice numbers, inventory, and the like, forces us to conceive of our data in a similar fashion. We are required to think of our data as highly repetitive, as fitting into a limited number of predefined categories, and as something that is not allowed to break these bounds. Archaeologists, and humanists more broadly, should bristle at these limitations if not flat out reject them. With a measure of intentionality, and with at least some involvement in the development process, a researcher should demand tools that are created to address their own research.

To reiterate the point I wish to make in this section, I turn again to Huggett (2012, 205) who observes that "our tools shape the way we organise reality." With this premise as the starting point, I encourage more intentionality in the creation and choice of digital tools for archaeology. In practice, this means beginning by reflecting on the reality of archaeological investigation. What is it that we do? What do we find? How do we describe our activities? This challenging step forces us to think outside the bounds of rows and columns. We should allow ourselves the freedom of describing small finds, for example, using all the terms we want and no more than needed. This sort of process requires thinking of the small find not as a row that must be fitted improperly into a predefined table, but as the item as we see it in our hand. This juglet has a beak spout and a geometric decoration on the body. The next juglet has an unusual base with a reddish tint. Instead of creating a table with a "Decoration" field and a "Spout" checkbox, simply record the observable details that pertain to each item.[7]

Consequently, the digital tool we use to capture these observations must allow for this type of freedom.[8] Further, the tool must allow for the representation of uncertainty and disagreement. If our object is a small corner fragment of some clay object, we may wish to describe it as a "figurine or a spindle whorl." The data model must allow for this sort of ambiguity. Then if in the future a newly hired specialist concludes that the fragmentary item can only be a loom weight, this conclusion should be allowed to stand alongside the previous observations. The idea is that a history of scholarship, including disagreements and uncertainty, is central to our field of research. The data model must support this central tenant of archaeological research. If we can free our minds from conceiving of the data store as parallel to a table or a printed appendix, we stand to completely reform and improve our digital archaeology experience.

---

7. The term "item" is significant in this context. The database model that allows each individual small find to exist on its own terms, outside of the bounds of a table, is called the item-based model. Each item, each thing, each place, each photo is an individual item that can be organized, reorganized, and linked in many ways.

8. In this paper, I do not intend to explicate the virtues of an XML data format versus a JSON format, for example, or even to delve into the technical details that would make these types of observations possible. I wish only to emphasize here that we should not limit our observations to a restrictive and often predefined table.

The Grand Challenge

Huggett (2015b, 83) has wondered why digital archaeology has not risen to the "grand challenge." As he explains, a grand challenge is an achievement that is seen as possible only with great effort. Putting a man on the moon was a grand challenge. Eradicating cancer is a grand challenge not yet achieved as of this writing. Huggett provides an evaluative rubric for identifying what a grand challenge for digital archaeology might look like. It must deal with the fundamental essentials of archaeology. It must be of impressive scope. It must be revolutionary, what some might describe as paradigm-shifting. It should be understandable, even to the public, as being something of a valuable step forward. It should be measurable. Finally, it should be a collaborative effort. He argues that "as digital archaeologists we should be more ambitious, and develop innovative digital tools and methodologies which have the potential not just to transform archaeology but also multiple academic fields and communities beyond" (83).

A Response

While it is valuable to identify the need to strive toward lofty goals like a grand challenge, identifying the challenge is not the challenge. We should *answer* the challenge. What would it mean to answer a grand challenge? Revolutionizing the digital tools and practice of archaeology is not quite like the challenge of reaching the moon or of curing cancer. In obvious ways, these challenges are far more world changing. But even on a more practical level, it is possible to know when those types of challenges are answered: when boots touch the moon or when cancer types begin to be cured. But there is no such clear-cut answer for creating tools for digital archaeology. This sort of challenge can be answered only by an ongoing answer, one that continues to answer. To use terms drawn from grammatical analysis, not an aorist, punctiliar answer, but a progressive or iterative present tense answer. The challenge is never answered. It is always being answered. We could never expect to take stock of our digital work and conclude that it is done.

If we feel we have begun to answer the challenge, are we allowed to say so, or would we be accused of hubris?[9] Would it be possible to maintain the attention of the audience for long enough to convince them that an answer has been achieved? Any real attempt at answering the challenge would be so holistic that it could not be described easily in any short paper or presentation.

---

9. Those who develop and support tools for digital archaeology must be sensitive to the perception that talking about these tools may be perceived as a sales pitch. When does a discussion about best practice become a marketing piece? Kansa (2016, 448) asks, "At what point do marketing and branding imperatives become self-serving goals unto themselves? How does marketing buzz impact the way we understand and evaluate the scholarship encoded in digital archeology?" These are valid considerations and yet it should be possible to talk at conferences, publish papers, print brochures, write books, or even set up booths in exhibition halls without being considered a business venture. There is still an honest desire to work with new people, not as a financially motivated act, but in the pursuit of knowledge through research. It is my hope that the reader will not mistake what follows as either software documentation or a sales technique.

This paper promised a practical critique, one that provides answers and evidence of progress toward a solution. In the concluding portion, I wish to demonstrate how the OCHRE database environment is actively addressing the grand challenge of humanities research.[10] The Online Cultural and Historical Research Environment (OCHRE) was developed through the collaboration of an archaeologist (David Schloen) and a computer scientist (Sandra Schloen). The program has evolved over the course of a decade of use for data capture and analysis. OCHRE was adopted as the project database by various research projects at the Oriental Institute of the University of Chicago, expanding its scope to include projects working on ancient texts, lexicography, history, and other topics. With the creation of the OCHRE Data Service of the Oriental Institute, we began supporting projects at other research institutions around the world. As of this writing, the OCHRE Data Service consists of Sandra Schloen (manager and developer), Miller Prosser (research database consultant), David Schloen (advisor), and Charles Blair (advisor). We have benefited immensely from the contributions of dozens of graduate student workers, postdoctoral scholars, and summer interns, too many to name here. See http://ochre.uchicago.edu for more information about OCHRE and the data service.

The grand challenge asks that we be more ambitious, that we expand beyond archaeology to address other research fields, that we approach something revolutionary or paradigm-shifting. Consider briefly some of the daily activities of projects using OCHRE. The following examples are projects that are using the same highly general OCHRE data model to fit their own research.

OCHRE began as a digital tool for archaeological projects and continues to be used as such. OCHRE was used in the inaugural 2016 field season of the University of Chicago excavation at Tell Keisan for data capture, barcode generation, registration, GIS recording, field and small find photography integration, pottery analysis, supervisor notes, and inventory management. Most of the data was born-digital, meaning that it was recorded directly in the OCHRE application, not transcribed from paper records. No data was stored in data sets outside the project in OCHRE. This tightly integrated approach to data allowed the dig directors and supervisors to perform daily analysis and strategize the weekly direction of digging. At the end of the season, the team returned from the field with only a small stack of paper, as opposed to multiple storage boxes full of dirty papers that would later need transcribing and digitizing.[11] Throughout the summer season, OCHRE supported the fundamental essentials of archaeological practice, as recommended by Huggett's rubric.

---

10. For a more in-depth explanation of OCHRE and the underlying principles, see S. Schloen and Prosser (forthcoming).

11. In addition to the University of Chicago Tell Keisan Excavations, OCHRE is used by other archaeology projects as the primary data capture tool and database including the Chicago-Tübingen Archaeological Project in Sam'al (http://zincirli.uchicago.edu), the Tel Shimron Excavations (http://www.telshimronexcavations.com), the Tell Tayinat Archaeological Project (https://tayinat.artsci.utoronto.ca), the Gadachrili Gora Regional Archaeological Project Expedition (http://www.archaeology.utoronto.ca/g.r.a.p.e.html), the Hippos-Sussita Excavation Project (http://hippos.haifa.ac.il), the Jaffa Cultural Heritage Project (http://jaffa.nelc.ucla.edu), the Leon Levy Expedition to Ashkelon (http://digashkelon.com), and the Zeitah Excavations (https://www.pts.edu/Zeitah_Excavations). Each of these projects has slightly different recording, storage, and analysis procedures, for which they customize their OCHRE projects, defining project terminology and data organization.

The international, multi-institutional collaborative project called Computational Research on the Ancient Near East (CRANE, https://www.crane.utoronto.ca) uses OCHRE as a tool for integrating data across various archaeological research projects working in the Orontes watershed region. Like most research projects, the CRANE project began with years of legacy data in various formats. With a little janitorial work, this data was ingested into OCHRE to be used in a variety of analyses. The various projects retain their own nomenclature. None was forced to adopt the terminology of the other. In other words, CRANE researchers were not forced to agree upon a common terminology, a task that always seems doomed from the start.[12] To highlight just one of the many achievements of CRANE, the project is compiling an extensive record of sites surveyed in Syria and the surrounding region, recording data about the original survey and surveyed site locations. As of this writing, over 6,700 sites have been documented. Where a site has been surveyed multiple times over the course of decades, the observations of each surveyor are recorded, creating a history of scholarship regarding the survey of the region.

The Ras Shamra Tablet Inventory is part archaeological and part philological. The project is working to incorporate data regarding the excavations at Ras Shamra-Ugarit. It also is creating text editions of the alphabetic Ugaritic and logosyllabic Akkadian texts from Ugarit. Each text is broken down into individual signs, words, and phrases. Detailed epigraphic commentary is recorded on a sign-by-sign basis. Where readings are uncertain, various metadata categories are used to capture this information. Editorial disagreements are also being included, to indicate where project editors differ from previous editors. Words are documented in a dynamic glossary and parsed according to project-defined properties. The project has also integrated the world's largest corpus of tablet images of the texts from Ras Shamra-Ugarit (https://ochre.lib .uchicago.edu/RSTI).

The Corinth-East of Theater project is using OCHRE to document its corpus of ceramics. From classifications and measurements of individual ceramic pieces, to automated aggregations of entire lots of ceramics, the project uses OCHRE to keep track of the massive data set. Once the primary work of curating and cataloging is complete, the project will produce a digital publication to make this valuable information available to the public via OCHRE's publication mechanisms.

The Hoard Analysis Research Project, part of the larger CRESCAT project, is analyzing the archaic Greek coin hoards discovered throughout the ancient Near East.[13] The project is interested in studying the distribution of coins in hoards, and the distribution of hoards across the region. The project uses OCHRE to model this data in such a way that the database can pass subsets of data to a University of Chicago server

---

12. A project taxonomy defines the terminology used in that project. Where two projects agree, they can use the same terminology. Where they differ, they can create their own taxonomy of terms. If two projects use different words for the same thing, OCHRE's internal thesaurus provides a mechanism for relating two terms that should be related. These strategies allow the CRANE researchers to query for similar objects across the various CRANE subprojects.

13. CRESCAT (A Computational Research Ecosystem for Scientific Collaboration on Ancient Topics, Spanning the Full Data Life Cycle) is an NSF-funded research project based at the University of Chicago. It is a multi-institutional project that seeks to interconnect existing software tools and apply them to a broad range of research projects.

running the R statistics package and receive results returned to the OCHRE application.[14] Through this process, the project is able to analyze and visualize the data in ways that allow them to discover previously unnoticed patterns of distribution.

The Persepolis Fortification Archive project is creating digital editions of cuneiform Elamite texts and alphabetic Aramaic texts.[15] The Persepolis Fortification Archive is approaching one million cuneiform signs transcribed! They have already exceeded three hundred thousand words identified. The project has produced roughly forty terabytes of digital images, using an integrated photographer's interface in OCHRE to associate an image directly with the tablet in the database. This user interface allows the photographer to add the data to the project and immediately to upload the image to the appropriate directory on the project server. As soon as the photographer produces the image, it becomes available to project members around the world. The project has identified over three thousand unique seals based on the many thousands of seal impressions preserved on tablet surfaces. The Persepolis Fortification Archive leverages OCHRE's highly granular data model to extract a network of data representing which personal names occur in texts sealed by specific seals. This data set helps inform our understanding of administrative practice at Persepolis. The scope and ambition of this project is ongoing, answering the grand challenge.

The Economics in Late Babylonian Archives project is investigating the economic transactions in the Murašû archive. Like the Ras Shamra Tablet Inventory and Persepolis Fortification Archive, the Economics in Late Babylonian Archives begins with highly atomized textual content. Next, they identify the various types of economic clauses, the roles played by persons in the texts, details about commodities, and dates. The project is in its early stages, but they hope to identify aspects of the local economy, such as networks of exchange.

As one final example, consider the Critical Editions for Digital Analysis and Research project. This project seeks to demonstrate that the same computational strategies can be applied to very different text corpora. Specifically, the project will show that a single database environment can be used to create critical editions of the Gilgamesh story, Genesis chapter 1, and Shakespeare's *The Taming of the Shrew*. Each of these texts is attested by a wide range of source documents. There are dozens of Sumerian Gilgamesh tablets, many of which show variations on various levels. The transmission history of the book of Genesis can be studied by comparing the Dead Sea Scrolls, medieval Hebrew manuscripts, Septuagint manuscripts, and Latin texts, among others. The preserved editions of Shakespeare's *The Taming of the Shrew* show variation as well, from simple typesetting differences to more substantial fluctuations. This project is using OCHRE to model these three complex data sets, atomizing the texts down to the level of every Hebrew accent, every Sumerian sign, and every English punctuation. To my knowledge, this sort of revolutionary and extremely detailed approach to texts has not been attempted before. The user interface allows the researcher to compare any number of manuscripts in a corpus, to see exactly where they overlap and where they

---

14. The Research Computing Center of the University of Chicago maintains the server that runs the R statistics package. R is a language and programming environment rapidly gaining a large user-base in the humanities due to the ease of accessibility for nontechnical users and its useful prepacked libraries of functions. See https://cran.r-project.org.

15. See https://oi.uchicago.edu/research/projects/persepolis-fortification-archive.

diverge. In contrast to many critical editions where this detail is hidden and where the critical edition itself is a finalized work of scholarship, the Critical Editions for Digital Analysis and Research project will expose the underlying details and even allow the researcher to create their own customized critical edition.

The point of this brief overview is not to explain precisely how the OCHRE application works or to document the underlying data model. Instead, I wish only to illustrate the breadth and ambition of the research taking place in the same research database environment. Each project using OCHRE, in its own way, is responding to a grand challenge of digital research. OCHRE at large was built for ambitious, collaborative, grand projects looking for a digital tool that more closely parallels the nature of humanities research.

Conclusion

A paper such as this—one that resumes a specific scholarly discussion—in a volume such as this—a collection of papers of wide-ranging interests; such a paper requires a conclusion that distills the important points into a digestible summary. We find ourselves, as (digital) archaeologists ready to advance from the ad hoc use of business tools to the intentional application of digital tools built specifically for our research. Central in this discussion is the transition from programs like Excel, Access, and FileMaker to a data capture, curation, and analysis application built specifically for humanities research, even specifically for archaeological research. Yet many in the field remain frustrated by the difficulty of this transition. Geoff Carver and Matthias Lang (2013, 224) ask "why should something so useful and so obviously necessary be so difficult to implement? Why aren't archaeologists interested in benefiting from 'digital humanities'?" It has taken over a decade of use, testing, development, and expansion to create the current version of OCHRE. Most projects do not have the luxury of this amount of time. Regarding Carver and Long's final question, one hopes that digital tools created by and for archaeologists will convince more archaeologists to become digital archaeologists.

As an answer to the grand challenge of providing a digital tool to revolutionize the practice of digital archaeology, I have provided a rough sketch of the ways in which various projects at the University of Chicago and elsewhere around the world are using the OCHRE database environment. It's one thing to build a repository to centralize data, it's another thing entirely to build a research environment that captures and analyzes every detail of a site-based archaeological investigation in real time. As the examples above intend to demonstrate, this application is appropriate for a wide variety of research topics. How is it that OCHRE can accommodate such varying projects where other applications apply to a single project or topic? OCHRE is highly generalized, flexible, and customizable. It is not preconfigured with terminology or specific organizational structures. It's not even preconfigured for a specific type of research. It can store data about an entire region, sites therein, objects from sites, all the way down to the smallest botanical sample. OCHRE integrates an entire project, the result of which is to bring all aspects of the data to bear: faunal, pottery, GIS, chronology, phasing, imaging.

In their appraisal of the outcomes from a digital archaeology workshop they organized, Erin Walcek Averett, Jody Michael Gordon, and Derek Counts (2016, vii) offer the following,

> Originally, we hoped to come up with a range of best practices for mobile computing in the field—a manual of sorts—that could be used by newer projects interested in experimenting with digital methods, or even by established projects hoping to revise their digital workflows in order to increase their efficiency or, alternatively, reflect on their utility and ethical implications. Yet, what the workshop ultimately proved is that there are many ways to "do" digital archaeology, and that archaeology as a discipline is engaged in a process of discovering what digital archaeology should (and, perhaps, should not) be.

This conclusion is based in part on the fact that many digital tools are created with a narrow focus, so that the tool limits what can be done with it, thereby limiting what archaeology can be done digitally. A more generic tool imposes fewer constraints, allowing the archaeology to happen naturally as the archaeologist practices it.

While there are various intelligent tools incorporated in the application, OCHRE requires human interaction to organize the data. OCHRE provides analytical tools to help inspire creative analyses, but steers clear of the process of deskilling discussed above. The practice of using OCHRE (and even making customizations) is very closely related to the practice of doing research. Therefore, the experience of the researcher using OCHRE parallels the normal practice in that given field of research. As philologists, we parse verbs, analyze syntax, make epigraphic notes. These are all facilitated by OCHRE. As archaeologists, we record excavation activity, analyze periodization, consider deposit sequencing, and aggregate all types of data. These are all common activities in OCHRE.

Humanities research is rarely simple. A digital tool must be up to the task of responding to difficult problems, thereby not forcing the difficult problems into an "easy" solution. Scholars should be involved in defining the technological knowledge of their field, but digital archaeology is not fundamentally about becoming a builder and a maker of digital tools. It is about the application of tools and practices that enhance the incumbent archaeological process. The creation of the OCHRE database is not an archaeological act. The use of OCHRE on a minilaptop in the field to record the coordinates of small finds is an act of digital archaeology; but it is also an act whose performance directly parallels a practice that predates the digital era.[16]

If the world is data, we archaeologists are simply uncovering some small percentage of all existing data and recording only some small percentage of all possible data

---

16. Contra Allington, Brouillette, and Golumbia (2016). "For enthusiasts, Digital Humanities is 'open' and 'collaborative' and committed to making the 'traditional' humanities rethink 'outdated' tendencies: all Silicon Valley buzzwords that cast other approaches in a remarkably negative light, much as does the venture capitalist's contempt for 'incumbents.' Yet being taken seriously as a Digital Humanities scholar seems to require that one stake one's claim as a builder and maker, become adept at the management and visualization of data, and conceive of the study of literature as now fundamentally about the promotion of new technologies. We have presented these tendencies as signs that the Digital Humanities as social and institutional movement is a reactionary force in literary studies, pushing the discipline toward post-interpretative, non-suspicious, technocratic, conservative, managerial, lab-based practice."

based on the choices we make in recording and modeling. We lose a great deal of data simply due to the passage of time and the destructive process of deposition. Also, we are not able to excavate the full extent of a site, so we limit our potential data set by our minimal excavation exposure. Since we already lose a great deal of potential information, let us not further diminish our information by forcing it to fit into digital tools built for the business world. I picture the entire set of data from an excavation as a large lump of wet clay. If you force that clay into a small box, some of it necessarily is sheared off by the edge of the box and lost. Sure, the clay that made it into the box is nicely organized, but the sheared off clay—the data that do not fit neatly into a prescribed table of columns and rows—is lost forever. Because we are digging for data, we should demand digital tools that respect that data.

BIBLIOGRAPHY

Allington, Daniel, Sarah Brouillette, and David Golumbia. 2016. "Neoliberal Tools (and Archives): A Political History of Digital Humanities." *Los Angeles Review of Books*. https://lareviewofbooks.org/article/neoliberal-tools-archives-political-history-digital-humanities.

Awad, Elias M. 1968. *Business Data Processing*. 2nd ed. Englewood Cliffs, NJ: Prentice Hall.

Caraher, William. 2015. "Understanding Digital Archaeology." *Archaeology of the Mediterranean World*. https://mediterraneanworld.wordpress.com/2015/07/17/understanding-digital-archaeology.

———. 2016. "Slow Archaeology: Technology, Efficiency, and Archaeological Work." Pages 421–41 in *Mobilizing the Past for a Digital Future*. Edited by Erin Walcek Averett, Jody Michael Gordon, and Derek B. Counts. Grand Forks: Digital Press University of North Dakota.

Carver, Geoff, and Matthias Lang. 2013. "Reflections on the Rocky Road to E-Archaeology." Pages 224–36 in *Archaeology in the Digital Era: Papers from the Fortieth Annual Conference of Computer Applications and Quantitative Methods in Archaeology (CAA), Southampton, 26–29 March 2012*. Edited by Graeme Earl, Tim Sly, Angeliki Chrysanthi, Patricia Murrietta Flores, Constantinos Papadopoulos, Iza Romanowska, and David Wheatly. Amsterdam: Amsterdam University Press.

Costopoulos, Andre. 2016. "Digital Archaeology Is Here (and Has Been for a While)." *Frontiers in Digital Humanities* 3 (4). https://doi.org/10.3389/fdigh.2016.00004.

Gordon, Jody Michael, Erin Walcek Averett, and Derik B. Counts. 2016. "Mobile Computing in Archaeology: Exploring and Interpreting Current Practices." Pages 1–30 in *Mobilizing the Past for a Digital Future*. Edited by Erin Walcek Averett, Jody Michael Gordon, and Derek B. Counts. Grand Forks: Digital Press University of North Dakota.

Huggett, Jeremy. 2012. "What Lies Beneath: Lifting the Lid on Archaeological Computing." Pages 204–14 in *Thinking Beyond the Tool: Archaeological Computing and the Interpretative Process*. Edited by Angeliki Chrysanthi, Patricia Murrietta Flores, and Constantinos Papadopoulos. BARIS 2344. Oxford: Archaeopress.

———. 2013. "Disciplinary Issues: Challenging the Research and Practice of Computer Applications in Archaeology." Pages 13–24 in *Archaeology in the Digital Era: Papers from the Fortieth Annual Conference of Computer Applications and Quantitative Methods in Archaeology (CAA), Southampton, 26–29 March 2012*. Edited by Graeme Earl, Tim Sly, Angeliki Chrysanthi, Patricia Murrietta Flores, Constantinos Papadopoulos, Iza Romanowska, and David Wheatly. Amsterdam: Amsterdam University Press.

———. 2015a. "A Manifesto for an Introspective Digital Archaeology." *Open Archaeology* 1:86–95.

———. 2015b. "Challenging Digital Archaeology." *Open Archaeology* 1:79–85.

Kansa, Eric C. 2016. "Click Here to Save the Past." Pages 443–72 in *Mobilizing the Past for a Digital Future*. Edited by Erin Walcek Averett, Jody Michael Gordon, and Derek B. Counts. Grand Forks: Digital Press University of North Dakota.

Kersel, Morag M. 2016. "Response: Living a Semi-Digital Kinda Life." Pages 475–92 in *Mobilizing the Past for a Digital Future*. Edited by Erin Walcek Averett, Jody Michael Gordon, and Derek B. Counts. Grand Forks: Digital Press University of North Dakota.

Llobera, Marcos. 2011. "Archaeological Visualization: Towards an Archaeological Information Science (AISc)." *Journal of Archaeological Method and Theory* 18:193–223.

Mattessich, Richard. 1964. *Simulation of the Firm Through a Budget Computer Program*. Homewood, IL: Irwin.

Rabinowitz, Adam. 2016. "Mobilizing (Ourselves) for a Critical Digital Archaeology." Pages 493–520 in *Mobilizing the Past for a Digital Future*. Edited by Erin W. Averett, Jody Michael Gordon, and Derke B. Counts. Grand Forks: Digital Press University of North Dakota.

Roosevelt, Christopher H., Peter Cobb, Emanuel Moss, Brandon R. Olson, and Sinan Ünlüsoy. 2015. "Excavation Is Destruction Digitization: Advances in Archaeological Practice." *Journal of Field Archaeology* 40:325–46.

Schloen, David, and Sandra Schloen. 2014. "Beyond Gutenberg: Transcending the Document Paradigm in Digital Humanities." *Digital Humanities Quarterly* 8 (4).

Schloen, Sandra, and Miller. C. Prosser. forthcoming. *Database Computing for Scholarly Research: Case Studies Using the Online Cultural and Historical Research Environment*. Quantitative Methods in the Humanities and Social Sciences. New York: Springer.

Sobotkova, Adela, Shawn A. Ross, Brian Ballsun-Stanton, Andrew Fairbairn, Jessica Thompson, and Parker VanValkenburgh. 2016. "Measure Twice, Cut Once: Cooperative Deployment of a Generalized, Archaeology-Specific Field Data Collection System." Pages 337–71 in *Mobilizing the Past for a Digital Future*. Edited by Erin Walcek Averett, Jody Michael Gordon, and Derek B. Counts. Grand Forks: Digital Press University of North Dakota.

Walcek Averett, Erin, Jody Michael Gordon, and Derek B. Counts, eds. 2016. *Mobilizing the Past for a Digital Future*. Grand Forks: Digital Press University of North Dakota.

CHAPTER 21

Debriefing Enemy Combatants in Ancient Egypt

Donald B. Redford

IT HAS LONG BEEN OBSERVED that, while Egypt was protected from unwanted intrusion by the circumstances of its geographical location, through most of its history it enjoyed an ill-defined, but nonetheless real, sphere of influence in the lands adjacent to its borders. Different from an imperial structure, defined by extended and acknowledged boundaries, the sphere of influence constituted a region where pharaoh's fiat was not ignored or rejected. The chiefs within the sphere were said to be "on the water of the king," that is, loyal.[1] Sinuhe's advice to the Asiatic chief encapsulates the relationship: "let him (pharaoh) know your name, don't plot afar off against His Majesty. He will not fail to do good to a country which is loyal to him" (Sinuhe 73–75).[2]

In spite of the informal, amorphous structure of the sphere of influence, the acquisition of intelligence about what was going on in the territory was detailed and relevant. Pharaoh demanded the delivery of commodities and laborers, cooperation in political action, information on local personnel, freedom of movement for prospectors and the like.[3] The sphere of influence was not *terra incognita* and prospectors, messengers, runners, express messengers, and "bringers" traversed the area constantly.[4] The tone indicates to what extent the sphere of influence stood on intelligence and the ability to

---

It is a pleasure to offer this brief contribution as an appreciation of the first-rate scholarship of James K. Hoffmeier, my student, colleague, and friend.

1. Wolfhart Westindorf, "Auf jemandes Wasser sein" = "von ihm abhängig sein," *GM* 11 (1974): 47–48; Torben Holm-Rasmussen, "The Original Meaning of *ḥr mw*," *GM* 148 (1995): 53–62.

2. Roland Koch *Die Erzählung des Sinuhe*, Bibliotheca Aegyptiaca 17 (Brussells: Fondation égyptologique Reine Elisabeth, 1990), 39.

3. The best example of this system at work is the record of Amenemhet II for two unspecified regnal years.

4. Prospectors: *smnty*: Hannig 2:2212; Jean Yoyotte, "Les sementiou et l'exploitation des regions minières à l'Ancien Empire," *BSFE* 73 (1975): 44–55; H. G. Fischer "More about the *Smntjw*," *GM* 84 (1985): 24–32. Messengers: *ipwtyw*: Michel Valloggia, *Recherches sur les "messagers" (wpwtyw) dans les sources égyptiennes profanes* (Geneva: Droz, 1976), 67–73 and passim. Runners: *sin(w)*: *Wb.* 4:39:11–12; Hannig 2:2104; "let your bringers proceed, let your express messengers run; let them go forth to heaven, and speak to Re (himself)" (PT 1991; cf. 1532); "let your bringers proceed, let your express messengers haste and give orders to him with raised arm in the east" (PT 253; James K. Hoffmeier, *Sacred in the Vocabulary of Ancient Egypt: The Term DSR, with Special Reference to Dynasties I–XX*, OBO 59 [Fribourg: Universitätsverlag; Göttingen: Vandenhoeck & Ruprecht, 1985], 40–41); cf. Erik Hornung, *Der ägyptische Mythos von der Himmelskuh: Eine Ätiologie des Unvollkommenen*, OBO 46 (Fribourg: Universitätsverlag; Göttingen: Vandenhoeck & Ruprecht, 1982), 61–68. For "bringers": (the king is) "possessed of bringers, who dispatch work-orders" (PT 400); cf. PT 536; "let your bringers proceed, let your express messengers run, let your dispatchers be loosed, that they might speak to Re!" (PT 1539). Unless otherwise noted, all translations are the author's.

project (the royal) will.[5] Control of a region translated into the multiplicity of Egyptian emissaries who had free passage and who "searched out" the "roads."[6]

In fact, every carrier and king's scribe was required to have knowledge of transit corridors and optimal routes. Anastase I makes plain that such sequences of over-night stops were the common stock of international communication, and undoubtedly existed in writing.[7]

When, in imperial times, large bodies of troops had to pass through foreign parts, it would have been ludicrous to ignore established itineraries.[8] If any record of the passage of troops was made, it was confined to the "day-book of the king's house"; but the notation did not in any way indicate capture, much less destruction of an enemy town.[9] The toponym lists "raisonnée" of New Kingdom times, those of Thutmose III in particular, reflect known itineraries and cannot be used to reconstruct routes of march.[10] To interpret the presence of every town in the lists as a record of destruction pursuant to investment would involve a logistical nightmare for a force unskilled in siege warfare!

With the period of high empire, from the reign of Amenhotep III to the mid-Twentieth Dynasty, the scene changed with the addition of a military presence and an enhanced network of communication. On "march-abouts," *chevauché*, the king would plant his standard, establish camp, and expect locals to proffer tribute, and undoubtedly information.[11] When the royal progress was more important and the stay in any one spot longer, greater care would be taken to accommodate the king's needs. A "palace" ('ḥ) would be prepared in advance, "recko[ned there]in as suitable for a ʿrest stopʾ."[12] When pharaoh engaged in set-piece battles, which were relatively few, prisoners of war could be expected; and even as part of tax demands menials in

5. This is the reason messengers were considered dangerous; *pace* Yvan Koenig, "Les Textes d'envoûtement de Mirgissa," *RdE* 41 (1990): 107.

6. For free passage, see Elke Blumenthal, *Untersuchungen ägyptischen Königtum des Mittleren Reiches I* (Berlin: Akademie, 1970), 199: "His bringers are numerous in all lands, his emissaries carrying out what he wants." For those who searched out the roads, see Berlin 22820, 3–4; "I reached the western oasis, and I searched out all its roads."

7. For Anastase I, see Anast. i. 18.4–23.1; Hans-Werner Fischer-Elfert, *Die satirische Streitschrift des Papyrus Anastasi I*, Kleine ägyptische Texte (Wiesbaden: Harrassowitz, 1986), 159–97. Overnight stops: *sḏryt: Wb.* 4:392:12–13; Hannig 2:2413; Soldiers were well versed—sometimes not!—in their overnight stops: "what's the meaning of this, that there are no provisions at all? The overnight stopping-place/billet is afar off!" Anast. i. 17.8–18.1; the soldier on campaign "he doesn't even know where his overnight stop is!" Lansing 10.8–9

8. *Urk.* IV, 729:7; Lionel Casson, *Travel in the Ancient World* (Baltimore: Johns Hopkins University Press, 1994), 186–88. Cf. CT IV 81d "I am he that knows the roads of *Nu*. . . . I have gone to the overnight stop."

9. Donald B. Redford, *King Lists, Annals and Daybooks: A Contribution to the Study of the Egyptian Sense of History* (Mississauga: Benben, 1986), passim. A Term "day-book of the army" does not exist. The Ermant stela clinches the matter in favor of *royal* itineraries: *Urk.* IV, 1246: 16–17 "It was H. M. that opened its roads, striking its every trail for his army."

10. The sequence of place names, e.g., from Derʿa to Kerak (*Urk.* IV 785 nos. 91–101, the old "King's Highway"), the periplus of the Aegean (Elmar Edel, *Die Ortsnamenlisten aus dem Totentempel Amenophis III*, Bonner biblische Beiträge 25 [Bonn: Hanstein, 1966]), and the periplus of Cyprus (*KRI* V, 94 nos. 7–11) represent highways and ports of call.

11. *Ỉḥm*, "tent encampment": *Urk.* IV 671:3 "every place where H. M. arrived, turned into a tent encampment"; cf. 652:13–14, 656, 659, 1303:13.

12. *Urk* IV, 974:2; probably restore *st ḥmst: Wb.* 3:97:11.

high number were requisitioned.[13] In all cases information about the foreigners and intelligence on a broader scale was considered an absolute necessity. Places of origin and mother's name were carefully recorded, father's occasionally.[14] Whether under obligation to present themselves before pharaoh (Sinuhe, B73–74), or as captives taken before an army scribe, foreigners were regularly debriefed and assessed for loyalty.[15] In this regard snatches of questions, written in conjunction with the execration of foreigners, may preserve evidence of such interrogations. In an execration text, after the personal name and mother of a Nubian chief, comes the note: "it was said to him: 'Are you a dissident?'"[16] And again, in the case of a chieftainess in the same context the accompanying notice reads: "it was said to her: 'have [you] not made slaughter?'"[17] Of another chief: "It was said concerning him: 'does he have adherents?'"[18] And once more: of another cursed chieftain "it was said: '(he's) a calf!'"[19]

Clearly underlying these notices lies an intent to gain intelligence of foreigners who could prove helpful (or harmful) to the Egyptian state. While Thutmose III broadcast his far-flung conquests by purloining place name lists already in existence, Ramesses III took names right off the enemy ranks from the field of battle. No one told these prisoners of war to line up in alphabetical order from 𓄿 to 𓏭: they were interrogated and branded haphazardly, as they appeared before the army scribe.

13. For set-piece battles, see Donald B. Redford, *The Wars in Syria and Palestine of Thutmose III*, CHANE 16 (Leiden: Brill, 2003), 197–98. For prisoners of war, see Michael G. Hasel, *Domination and Resistance: Egyptian Military Activity in the Southern Levant 1300–1185 B.C.*, PAe 11 (Leiden: Brill, 1998), 66–74, 367. For tax demands, see Donald B. Redford, *Egypt and Canaan in the New Kingdom* (Beersheva: Ben-Gurion University, 1990), 37–39.

14. For place of origin and mother's name, see Georges Posener, *Princes et pays d'Asie et die Nubie* (Brussells: Fondation égyptologique Reine Élisabeth, 1940), 32–35; P. Bologna 1086. For father's name, see Kurt Sethe, *Die Ächtung feindlicher Fürsten Volker und Dinge auf Altägyptischen Tongefasscherben des Mittleren Reiches* (Berlin: de Gruyter, 1926), e 13.

15. Cf. Susanna C. Heinz, *Die Feldzugdarstellungen des Neuen Reiches: Eine Bildanalyse*, Österreichische Akademie der Wissenschaften Denkschriften der Gesamtakademie 18 (Vienna: Österreichischen Akademie der Wissenschaften, 2001), 308 (I. 19), showing Sea Peoples being branded and interrogated; Geoffrey T. Martin, *The Memphite Tomb of Horemheb, Commander-in-Chief of Tut'ankhamūn I: The Reliefs, Inscriptions, and Commentary* (London: Egypt Exploration Society, 1989), pls. 87, 88, 91, 93, 105.

16. Georges Posener, *Cinq figurines d'envoûtement* (Cairo: Institut français d'archéologie orientale, 1987), 28 (A7); cf. A8. The word is *ḏ'ysw*: Hannig 2:2819.

17. Posener, *Cinq figurines*, 29 (A9).

18. Ibid., 30 (A10).

19. Ibid., 30 (A11). I.e., "weak, compliant."

CHAPTER 22

Israelite Origins

Gary A. Rendsburg

HISTORIANS, ARCHAEOLOGISTS, AND BIBLICAL SCHOLARS continue to debate the topic of Israelite origins. The literature is so vast that one cannot possibly survey it all in the limited space afforded here. Suffice it to say that the two main positions are: (1) Israel originates as a desert or desert-fringe people, who came to settle in the central hill country of Canaan, a view that accords more or less with the picture portrayed in the Bible; and (2) the Israelites are indigenous Canaanites, who moved from the urban areas to smaller settlements in the hill country, where they created a somewhat distinctive culture.

The latter viewpoint has become more and more standard in recent years.[1] In this article, I will argue for the former position, though to repeat, space allows for a mere sketch only. Much of what I include below is well known, or at least has been stated by others before, so that the value of this article, to my mind, is the accumulation of data created by the converging lines of evidence.

I trust that the subject of this article will find favor in the eyes of our honoree, since he himself has discussed much of this material in his two books, *Israel in Egypt* and *Ancient Israel in Sinai*.[2] In fact, one of the first articles written by our honoree, now more than forty years ago, concerns tents, a topic to which we will return below.[3] As such, it is a distinct pleasure to publish this essay in this well-deserved Festschrift for James Hoffmeier, a friend and colleague for almost four decades now.

Yahweh of the Southland

The oldest biblical texts, consisting of archaic poetry, repeatedly connect Yahweh, the God of Israel, to the Southland, using a variety of geographical terms: Sinai, Se'ir, Edom, Paran, Teman, etc.[4]

---

1. See, e.g., Israel Finkelstein and Neil A. Silberman, *The Bible Unearthed: Archaeology's New Vision of Ancient Israel and the Origin of Its Sacred Texts* (New York: Free Press, 2001), 97–122; and William G. Dever, *Who Were the Early Israelites and Where Did They Come From?* (Grand Rapids: Eerdmans, 2003).

2. James K. Hoffmeier, *Israel in Egypt: The Evidence for the Authenticity of the Exodus Tradition* (New York: Oxford University Press, 1996); Hoffmeier, *Ancient Israel in Sinai: The Evidence for the Authenticity of the Wilderness Tradition* (New York: Oxford University Press, 2005).

3. James K. Hoffmeier, "Tents in Egypt and the Ancient Near East," *JSSEA* 7:3 (1977), 13–28. The findings of this article were incorporated into Hoffmeier, *Ancient Israel in Sinai*, 196–98. See further below, §4.

4. All translations are the author's.

Deuteronomy 33:2

YHWH, from Sinai he came forth,
And shined upon them from Seʿir.
He appeared from Mount Paran,
And approached from Rivevot-Qodesh.

Judges 5:4

YHWH, when you came forth from Seʿir,
When you marched forth from the highland of Edom.

Habakkuk 3:3

God comes from Teman,
And the Holy-one from Mount Paran.

Psalm 68:8–9

[8] O God, when you went out before your people,
   when you marched through the wasteland, Selah.
[9] The earth trembled, indeed, the sky poured, because of God, the one of Sinai;
   because of God, the God of Israel.

Were the Israelites indigenous Canaanites, it is hard to imagine that they would conceive of Yahweh as a deity associated with the Southland.

Shasu

Earlier echoes of the aforecited references may be heard in the mentions of *tꜣ šꜣśw ya-h-wa* "the land of the Shasu of Yahweh" and *tꜣ šꜣśw śa-ʿ-r-ir* "the land of the Shasu of Seʿir" in Egyptian topographical lists from Soleb and ʿAmarah (both in Nubia), dated to the New Kingdom period.[5] The term Shasu is the Egyptian designation for nomads, seminomads, denizens of the desert, dwellers on the desert-fringe, and so on, more or less equivalent to our word bedouin (derived from Arabic). The latter term, Seʿir, is one of the geographical designations that we saw above in the Bible, connected to Edom, to the south of Israel.[6] The former term most likely refers to worshipers of Yahweh somewhere in the general region, perhaps to be identified as proto-Israelites.

A further resonance occurs in P. Anastasi VI 4:11–5:5, dated to the reign of Merenptah, in which the frontier official Enana wrote to his superior: "We have

---

5. Hoffmeier, *Ancient Israel in Sinai*, 242–43; and Shmuel Aḥituv, "Nodedim ba-Negev bi-Mqorot Miṣrayim" (English title: "Nomads in the Desert in Egyptian Sources"), in *Ki Baruch Hu: Ancient Near Eastern, Biblical, and Judaic Studies in Honor of Baruch A. Levine*, ed. Robert Chazan, William W. Hallo, and Lawrence H. Schiffman (Winona Lake, IN: Eisenbrauns, 1999), 21*–27*.

6. The relevant passages are Gen 32:4; 36:8–9, 21; Num 24:18; Judg 5:4 (cited above); Ezek 35:15.

finished admitting the Shasu tribes of Edom at the fortress of Merenptah Hotephirmaat, life, prosperity, health, which is in Tjeku, to the pools of Per-Atum of Merenptah Hotephirmaat, which are in Tjeku, to keep them alive and to keep their flocks alive." This episode is strikingly similar to the migration of the Israelites in the book of Genesis, from southern Canaan, across the Sinai, with their flocks. Upon reaching Egypt, the Shasu of Edom are admitted into the country, and indeed are settled in Per-Atum in the eastern delta = Hebrew פִּתֹם "Pithom" (Exod 1:11), the city where also the Israelites were settled.

It would be too sleight-of-hand to simply replace "Edom" in P. Anastasi VI with the word "Israel," but given the close relationship between the two groups (see §3, immediately below), one sees in this Egyptian text the same trajectory recounted in the Bible.

For more on the Israelites as Shasu, see further below, §10, "'Israel' in the Merenptah Stele and on the Karnak Temple Reliefs."

Israel and Edom

The closeness of the two groups is reflected in manifold ways. First, as noted above, Egyptian topographical lists collocate "the land of the Shasu of Se'ir" and "the land of the Shasu of Yahweh." Second, as we learn from the Bible, the terms Se'ir and Edom are essentially synonymous: the former is used for the geographical region, while the latter is used for the people who inhabit the land (see the passages cited in n. 6 above). Third, the closeness of Edom and Israel is reflected in the foundation stories of the Bible through the twinness of the respective progenitors, Esau and Jacob. By contrast, other neighbors (such as Moab, Ammon, Aram, etc.) are more distantly related. Fourth, the closeness of the two groups is reflected by the incorporation into the book of Genesis of a sizable amount of genealogical detail (ch. 36), far unlike any information available for any other neighboring people (and see in particular 36:6–8, 31).

Tents

As indicated above, one of Hoffmeier's earliest articles (published in 1977; see above, n. 3) dealt with the topic of tents. Unbeknownst to him at the time, two additional relevant studies would appear either that year or the following year. Moreover, they were written by individuals who would become close colleagues as the years passed, namely, Kenneth Kitchen and Donald Wiseman.[7]

The purpose of all three of these studies was to overturn the rather bizarre suggestion of John Van Seters that references to tents in Genesis (12:8; 13:3; 13:5; etc.) signify a late date for the composition of the book, since, to his mind, tents did not become common in the land of Israel until the Arab migrations of the latter half of the

7. Kenneth A. Kitchen, *The Bible in Its World: The Bible and Archaeology Today* (Exeter: Paternoster, 1977), 58–59; and Donald J. Wiseman, "They Lived in Tents," in *Biblical and Near Eastern Studies: Essays in Honor of William Sanford Lasor*, ed. Gary Tuttle (Grand Rapids: Eerdmans, 1978), 195–200.

first millennium BCE. Hoffmeier, Kitchen, and Wiseman demonstrated clearly that tents were part of ancient Levantine society during the second millennium BCE, with the evidence ranging from Sinuhe (Twelfth Dynasty) to Thutmose III (Eighteenth Dynasty) to the Great Harris Papyrus of Ramesses III (Twentieth Dynasty).[8]

The entire subject of tents and tent imagery now has been thoroughly analyzed in the fine monograph by Michael Homan, *To Your Tents, O Israel* (2002); and I direct the reader to his excellent treatment for detailed discussion.[9] Here I would like to focus on one feature explored by Homan, but which to my mind did not receive sufficient emphasis and/or was interpreted differently.

I refer to the expression used in the title of the book and its various echoes in Samuel and Kings. As Homan observes, on numerous occasions the authors of the material dealing with monarchic Israel use the word "tents" with the connotation "home." During the time period of around 980 BCE through around 780 BCE (the approximate timeframe for these episodes), however, the Israelites were living in true houses, built of stone, as revealed in the archaeological record throughout Israel—and not in tents.[10]

And yet, the biblical text uses the following expressions:[11]

1. 2 Sam 18:18: "and all Israel had fled, each-man to his tents"—with reference to Absalom's supporters.

2. 2 Sam 19:9: "now Israel had fled, each-man to his tents"—upon the conclusion of David's mourning for Absalom.

3. 2 Sam 20:1: "each-man to his tents, O Israel"—spoken by Sheba, in his attempt to have the people defect from David.

4. 2 Sam 20:22: "and they dispersed from the city, each-man to his tents"—upon the end of the siege of Abel-Beth-Maacah.

5. 1 Kgs 8:66 (~ 2 Chr 7:10): "and they [sc. 'the people'] went to their tents"—upon the conclusion of Solomon's ceremony for the dedication of the temple.

6. 1 Kgs 12:16 (= 2 Chr 10:16): "to your tents, O Israel!"—spoken by the people of northern Israel, when they realize that there is no purpose in following Rehoboam.

7. 1 Kgs 12:16 (= 2 Chr 10:16): "and Israel went (each-man) to his tents"—the Israelites return to their homes, in light of the above.

8. 2 Kgs 14:12 (= 2 Chr 25:22): "and they fled, each-man to his tents"—with reference to the Judahites, routed by Israel, during the reign of Amaziah.

8. See the summary in Hoffmeier, *Ancient Israel in Sinai*, 196–98.

9. Michael M. Homan, *To Your Tents, O Israel! The Terminology, Function, Form, and Symbolism of Tents in the Hebrew Bible and the Ancient Near East*, CHANE 12 (Leiden: Brill, 2002).

10. B. S. J. Isserlin, *The Israelites* (London: Thames & Hudson, 1998), 122–24; and Philip J. King and Lawrence E. Stager, *Life in Biblical Israel*, Library of Ancient Israel (Louisville: Westminster John Knox, 2001), 21–23. For detailed information on more than two dozen sites, see Avraham Faust, *The Archaeology of Israelite Society in Iron Age II* (Winona Lake, IN: Eisenbrauns, 2002), 207–12, even if the data derive mainly from the eighth to seventh centuries BCE, due to the nature of the evidence.

11. See Homan, *To Your Tents, O Israel*, 17–19. I omit from Homan's registry the three instances from the book of Judges (7:8; 19:9; 20:8) and the one instance in 1 Samuel from premonarchic Israel (4:10). By this point in Israel's history, the people most likely were living in stone houses (see below, §6, on the elliptical sites), but my main focus here is on monarchic Israel, with well-established cities evident throughout the land.

Now, as I indicated above, during the period under consideration here, from early or late in David's reign (thus, ca. 980 BCE) through the reign of Amaziah (ca. 780 BCE), the Israelites were living in stone houses within well-developed cities. And yet the language persists with the tent imagery, especially when used as a functional semantic equivalency for "go home" or "they went home" or "they fled home."

The persistence of this idiom bespeaks a people who once upon a time lived in tents. The best analogy that I can conjure is the repeated use of "horse" within English idioms, into the twenty-first century: "hold your horses"; "stop horsing around"; "get off your high horse"; "I could eat a horse"; "a one-horse town"; "a dark-horse candidate"; "a horse of a different color"; "don't beat a dead horse"; "straight from the horse's mouth"; "wild horses couldn't drag me away"; "don't look a gift horse in the mouth"; "you can lead a horse to water, but you can't make him drink"; and so on.[12] These expressions reveal a people (to wit, Britons and Americans) for whom the horse was once an essential part of their cultural repertoire. Such is no longer the case in the mechanized age of the twentieth and twenty-first centuries, and yet the word "horse" (mainly as a noun, though in one case above, also as a verb) continues to inform the contemporary English language. Such was the case, I submit, with the word "tent" in ancient Hebrew. During the tenth, ninth, and eighth centuries BCE, and of course beyond, the vast majority of Israelites no longer lived in portable dwellings suitable for desert and desert-fringe lifestyle, and yet the word "tent" persevered in the key idiom examined above.[13]

Linguistic Terminology (a): Tents

Homan further observes that the Hebrew vocabulary is very rich in terms related to tents and to tent culture.[14] Items include: קֻבָּה "tent" (Num 25:8);[15] דֹּק "tent-curtain" (Isa 40:22); חֻפָּה "tent-canopy" (3×); שַׁפְרִיר "tent-canopy" (Jer 43:10); נָוֶה "tent-abode" (15×);[16] טִירָה "tent-encampment" (6×);[17] and חַוָּה "tent-encampment" (6×).[18] As indicated by the parenthetic comments, three of these lexemes are *hapax legomena*, while the others (except for נָוֶה) are infrequently attested. That said, as indicated in

12. Many of these expressions have a good English pedigree: http://mentalfloss.com/article/56850/origins-12-horse-related-idioms. For more detailed analysis, see *OED*, s.v. "horse."

13. Homan, *To Your Tents, O Israel*, 22, speaks more generally of "the fluidity of residential terminology," though as I hope to have demonstrated, there is more at stake in the linguistic usage.

14. Homan, *To Your Tents, O Israel*, 13–14.

15. See the Arabic cognate *qubba*.

16. It is not always easy to determine when the word means "tent-abode" and when the word means "pastureland." But of the thirty-one occurrences of the word, I count fifteen of them meaning "tent-abode" (Exod 15:13; 2 Sam 15:25; Isa 27:10; 32:18; 33:20; Jer 10:25; 31:23; 50:70; Ps 79:7; Prov 3:33; 21:20; 24:15; Job 5:3; 8:6; 18:15). In addition, I count only the singular form נָוֶה here, and not the plural form נְאוֹת, which may derive from a separate root, or in the very least would be formed irregularly from the singular. As to the second meaning, "pastureland," note the Mari Akkadian cognate *nawû*, used to refer to the land inhabited by the nonurban Amorites, along with the Safaitic cognate *nwy* "pastureland." The former is well known; while for the latter, see Ahmad Al-Jallad and Karolina Jaworska, *A Dictionary of the Safaitic Inscriptions*, Studies in Semitic Languages and Linguistics 98 (Leiden: Brill, 2019), 108.

17. Especially for Ishmaelites (Gen 25:16), Midianites (Num 31:10), and Qedemites (Ezek 25:4).

18. Always in conjunction with the "tent-encampments" of Jair in Transjordan (Num 32:41, etc.). Note the Arabic cognate *ḥiwā'*.

the footnotes, (1) these terms often are used in conjunction with those who continued to live in the desert and desert-fringe (Qedemites, etc.); and (2) several find cognates in Arabic and Mari Akkadian, with reference to nonurban society.

One item not included in Homan's treatment is the verb צ-ע-ן, a *hapax legomenon* in Isa 33:20. In this passage, the prophet envisions Jerusalem as an אֹהֶל בַּל־יִצְעָן "a tent not to be transported." While various cognates have been proposed, once again Arabic provides the best etymon: *ẓaʿana* "journey, depart, remove."[19]

Elliptical Sites

In his early work, Israel Finkelstein reached the brilliant conclusion that the numerous elliptical sites that dominate the central hill country in Iron Age I, dating mainly to the twelfth and eleventh centuries BCE, reflect the sedentarization of former desert nomads.[20] The layout of these settlements replicates the layout of bedouin encampments, with the use of stone buildings replacing the former tent structures. In both the standard bedouin encampment and the elliptical sites, the residences are placed on the perimeter, leaving the central portion as the courtyard for the sheltering of flocks.[21]

Key statements by Finkelstein include the following: "The elliptical site plan, where a series of broadrooms encompassed a large central courtyard, was adapted from the nomadic tent camp" (p. 337); "Most of the people who settled in the hill country in the Iron I period came from a background of pastoralism, and not *directly* from the urban Canaanite polity of the Late Bronze period. These people, who tended flocks but apparently did not herd camels, did not originate deep in the desert, but had lived on the fringes of the settled areas, or perhaps even in the midst of the sedentary dwellers" (p. 338; emphasis original). With this last phrase, Finkelstein leaves open the possibility that the pastoralists were resident in the central hill country prior to their construction of the elliptical site, though the larger picture—including the biblical material, per what I have written above—suggests the desert fringe, that is, the large swath of land that wraps around the arable land in Canaan, from the southwest

19. For the various cognates, see the discussion in Frederick E. Greenspahn, *Hapax Legomena in Biblical Hebrew: A Study of the Phenomenon and Its Treatment Since Antiquity with Special Reference to Verb Forms*, Society of Biblical Literature Dissertation Series 74 (Chico, CA: Scholars Press, 1984), 154. For the Arabic, see Edward William Lane, *Arabic-English Lexicon*, 8 vols. (London: Williams & Norgate, 1863–1893) 5:1911–12. See also Old South Arabian *ẓ-ʿ-n* "move, shift, decamp," listed in A. F. L. Beeston et al., *Sabaic Dictionary/Dictionnaire Sabéen* (Leuven: Peeters, 1982), 171; and Safaitic *ẓ-ʿ-n* "seek herbage or water," listed in Al-Jallad and Jaworska, *Dictionary of the Safaitic Inscriptions*, 143. The Akkadian, Ethiopic, and Aramaic cognates mean "load," clearly related, but semantically further afield. The Aramaic cognate ט-ע-ן passed into Hebrew with the meaning "load."

20. Israel Finkelstein, *The Archaeology of the Israelite Settlement* (Jerusalem: Israel Exploration Society, 1988), 238–50, 336–38. The page references embedded in the next paragraph refer to this book. The English book, which received wide attention when it was published, was based on the earlier Hebrew version: Israel Finkelstein, *Ha-ʾArkheʾologya šel Tequfat ha-Hitnaḥalut ve-ha-Šofṭim* (Jerusalem: Israel Exploration Society, 1986).

21. While Finkelstein's prose is illuminating, the clearest picture emerges from simply comparing the diagrams (both schematic plans and isometric reconstructions) of the archaeological findings and the photos and drawings of modern bedouin encampments; see the ample illustrations in Finkelstein, *Archaeology of the Israelite Settlement*, 239–49. The present writer continues to use these illustrations (along with his own photographs taken in the Negev from as early as 1975) in classroom teaching and public lecturing.

to the south to the southeast and even to the east, what I would call very generally "the Southland" (see above, §1, and see further below).

I must add here the following: If I understand his more recent work correctly, Finkelstein has moved away from his original conclusions regarding the significance of the elliptical sites.[22] While it is admirable for a scholar to alter his or her position in the light of new evidence, in the current case, I must say, the evidence endures, without change. The elliptical sites still bespeak the arrangement of the bedouin tent encampment, that fact remains.[23]

Linguistic Terminology (b): Desert

In an oft-overlooked comment, E. Y. Kutscher observed that Biblical Hebrew is rich in terminology "to denote the deserts":[24] מִדְבָּר "steppe, wilderness" (*passim*); עֲרָבָה "arid-land" (*passim*); יְשִׁימוֹן "wasteland" (13×);[25] מִדְבַּר שְׁמָמָה "desolate wilderness" (Jer 12:10, Joel 2:3); צִיָּה "desert" (16×); תֹּהוּ "wasteland" (Deut 32:10; Ps 107:40; Job 6:18); מְלֵחָה "barren-land" (lit. "salt-land") (Jer 17:6; Ps 107:34; Job 39:6); אֶרֶץ גְּזֵרָה "cut-off land" (Lev 16:22); אֶרֶץ תַּלְאֻבוֹת "land of drought" (Hos 13:5); חֲרֵרִים "scorched-places" (Jer 17:6); דֹּבֶר "steppe" (Isa 5:17; Mic 2:12); בָּתָה "desert-precipice" (Isa 5:6; 7:19).

Linguists continue to debate the observation made by the great Frank Boas in his pioneering linguistic-anthropological research concerning the many Inuit words for "snow."[26] Some go so far as to call this the Great Eskimo Snow Hoax or the Great Eskimo Vocabulary Hoax, but recent research by Igor Krupnick (Smithsonian Institution) appears to uphold the notion that the languages used in northern climes, such as those spoken by the Inuit and the Sami, indeed do contain numerous words for "snow" in its various manifestations.[27] In similar fashion, the lexeis of the Sami, Tofa, and other reindeer herders across northern Eurasia contain numerous words for "reindeer"; while the Omani camel herders who speak either Arabic and/or Mehri have similarly rich vocabularies for all manner of "camel" (classified by age, sex, traits, etc.).[28] I include this information here for those who may wish to claim that the rich Hebrew

22. See above, n. 1.

23. See the treatment by Thomas E. Levy and Augustin F. C. Hull, "Migrations, Ethnogenesis, and Settlement Dynamics: Israelites in Iron Age Canaan and Shuwa-Arabs in the Chad Basin," *Journal of Anthropological Archaeology* 21 (2002): 83–118, esp. pp. 91–100 (written by Levy).

24. E. Y. Kutscher, *A History of the Hebrew Language* (Jerusalem: Magnes; Leiden: Brill, 1982), 56, §82.

25. Including the general area of David's hiding places, for which see 1 Sam 23:19, 24; 26:1, 3.

26. For general introduction, see https://en.wikipedia.org/wiki/Eskimo_words_for_snow.

27. For a summary of the research see David Robson, "Are There Really 50 Eskimo Words for Snow?" *The New Scientist*, 18 December 2012; https://www.newscientist.com/article/mg21628962-800-are-there -really-50-eskimo-words-for-snow.

28. For reindeer, see K. David Harrison, *When Languages Die: The Extinction of the World's Languages and the Erosion of Human Knowledge* (New York: Oxford University Press, 2007), 27–29. Harrison's paradigm example is Tofa *chary* "'5-year-old male castrated rideable reindeer' (the most useful kind for riding)" (p. 27). For camels, see Domenyk Eades, Janet C. E. Watson, and Mohammed Ahmad al-Mahri, "Camel Culture and Camel Terminology among the Omani Bedouin," *Journal of Semitic Studies* 58 (2013): 169–86. Good examples (see p. 178) are Mehri *rgād* "female camel in beginning of pregnancy" vs. *madanay* "female camel in later stages of pregnancy" (with a similar distinction in the Omani Arabic dialect spoken by the herders). I am grateful to Aaron Rubin (Pennsylvania State University) for both of these references.

vocabulary for "desert" (see also above, §5, regarding "tent") is inconsequential to the present discussion.

Reuben and Simeon as the First Two Sons of Jacob

To the best of my knowledge, no one has noticed that the first two sons born to Jacob in the Genesis narrative, Reuben and Simeon, are the two southernmost, and thus most desert-like, of the tribes of Israel: the former in Transjordan, the latter in Cisjordan. Frank Moore Cross devoted a study to early Israelite traditions relevant to the territory of Reuben, and he came close to stating what I have just stated, though I am not sure if he ever makes the explicit comment.[29] Moreover, he did not address the matter of Simeon in Cisjordan.

The last we hear of Reuben, within the grand narrative of Genesis through Kings, is in Judg 5:16, where, quite tellingly, the tribe is associated with its flocks (עֲדָרִים) and sheepfolds (מִשְׁפְּתַיִם).[30]

Simeon disappears even earlier, in Judg 1 (vv. 3, 17), though already in this episode the tribe's individual identity is waning, as its destiny is allied with that of Judah. In the book of Joshua, there is a unique statement about Simeon, which does much to reveal its character. While all the tribes gain "cities and their settlements," including Simeon, only about Simeon do we read an additional statement with the word "settlements": וְכָל־הַחֲצֵרִים אֲשֶׁר סְבִיבוֹת הֶעָרִים הָאֵלֶּה "and all the settlements that surround these cities" (Josh 19:8).[31] This implies that the lifestyle of the Simeonites was more connected with unwalled, nonurban settlements (חֲצֵרִים) than that of other tribes.[32]

This is all rather obvious, of course, since the territories of Reuben and Simeon are on the desert fringe, without any large cities, and therefore the lifestyles of these two tribes was more connected to their flocks, sheepfolds, and unwalled settlements. And then the Bible loses track of Reuben and Simeon, not because they disappeared necessarily, but because the focus of the biblical material (prose, poetry, prophecy, etc.) becomes more and more focused on kingship, Jerusalem, temple, and such.[33]

But the Bible never lost track of the first-born and second-born status of Reuben and Simeon, respectively. These tribesmen retained their pastoral ways, even as most Israelites became more and more urbanized, and thus their eponymous ancestors are

---

29. Frank Moore Cross, "Reuben, First-Born of Jacob," *ZAW* 100 (1988): 46–65; revised as "Reuben, The Firstborn of Jacob: Sacral Traditions and Early Israelite History," in *From Epic to Canon: History and Literature in Ancient Israel* (Baltimore: Johns Hopkins University Press, 1998), 53–70. See also Avraham Faust, *Israel's Ethnogenesis: Settlement, Interaction, Expansion, and Resistance* (London: Equinox, 2006), 183.

30. True, the same word מִשְׁפְּתַיִם "sheepfolds" occurs in Gen 49:14, with reference to Issachar, but the usage there is metaphorical, as the son/tribe is compared to a donkey.

31. The only potential parallel to Josh 19:8 regarding Simeon is Josh 16:9 with reference to Ephraim and Manasseh, but the effect there is slightly different.

32. Most translations render חֲצֵרִים as "villages," though I prefer "settlements," with specific reference to unwalled settlements.

33. And ditto for the Northern Kingdom, based on the literary remains thereof that are preserved in the Bible, though with the focus on Dan, Bethel, Shechem, and Samaria (and not Jerusalem, of course).

accorded first and second position in the Jacob cycle (and in later rehearsals thereof, including, e.g., 2 Chr 2:1–2).

Some Lexical Features of Hebrew

Some years ago I commented to Anson Rainey that Hebrew shares some key lexemes with Transjordanian dialects and with Aramaic, in contrast to Phoenician. My examples included:

- ה-י-ה "be" (attested in Moabite and Aramaic; cf. Phoenician כ-ו-ן)
- ע-שׂ-ה "do" (attested in Moabite; cf. Phoenician פ-ע-ל)
- ה-ל-ך "go" (attested in Moabite; cf. Phoenician י-ל-ך)
- עִיר "city" (attested in Moabite; cf. Phoenician קרת)
- זָהָב "gold" (attested in Aramaic; also Arabic *dahab*; cf. Phoenician חרץ)
- שׁוֹר "bull, ox" (attested in Aramaic; cf. Phoenician אלף)
- לֹא "no, not" (attested in Moabite, Ammonite, Aramaic; cf. Phoenician בל)

From this oral communication, Rainey developed an entire theory about Hebrew as a "Transjordanian language" (his term).[34]

Rainey's proposal was met by a harsh rejoinder from the pens of Jo Ann Hackett and Na'ama Pat-El, who argued strongly that, notwithstanding the evidence garnered by Rainey, Hebrew remains a Canaanite dialect.[35] There is no doubt that the coauthors are correct, as it would be too extreme to remove Hebrew (and Moabite) from this classification.[36] That said, the data remain, and some explanation is required. Rainey may have reached too far, but a more reasoned approach was presented many years ago by H. L. Ginsberg, in a brilliant essay cited neither by Rainey nor by Hackett and Pat-El.[37] In said article, Ginsberg proposed to divide Canaanite (which includes Ugaritic in his schema) to a Phoenic group along the coast and a Hebraic group inland.

34. Anson. F. Rainey, "Redefining Hebrew: A Transjordanian Language," *Maarav* 14 (2007): 67–81; and Rainey, "Whence Came the Israelites and Their Language," *IEJ* 57 (2007): 41–64.

35. Jo Ann A. Hackett and Na'ama Pat-El, "On Canaanite and Historical Linguistics: A Rejoinder to Anson Rainey," *Maarav* 17 (2010) 173–88. For a response, see Leonid Kogan, "Postscript: On J. A. Hackett and N. Pat-El's (2010) criticism of Rainey's (2007) 'Transjordanian' hypothesis," in his book *Genealogical Classification of Semitic: The Lexical Isoglosses* (Berlin: de Gruyter, 2015), 369–75. I wrote almost the entirety of this section of my article before discovering Kogan's pages thereon, and I was very pleased to see considerable overlap, including his chart at the top of p. 372, with many of the same lexical items that I present above.

36. Though it is not clear that Rainey ever denied that Hebrew was a dialect of Canaanite, the claims of Hackett and Pat-El notwithstanding. For the record, nor did I ever suggest such, when I made the above-recorded observation to Rainey.

37. H. L. Ginsberg, "The Northwest Semitic Languages," in *The World History of the Jewish People, Vol. 2: The Patriarchs*, ed. Benjamin Mazar (New Brunswick: Rutgers University Press, 1970) 102–24, 293. As another indication of the overlap between my sketch here and Kogan's exceedingly comprehensive treatment, I note that he too refers to the Ginsberg essay throughout his book, indeed, with the same adjective that I use: "H. L. Ginsberg's brilliant summary description of NWS (1970)," for which see Kogan, *Genealogical Classification of Semitic*, 348.

To the former group are assigned Ugaritic, Phoenician, and Philistine; to the latter group are assigned Hebrew, Ammonite, Moabite, and Edomite.[38]

Remarkably Ginsberg wrote this article decades before the discovery of the Ekron dedicatory inscription, found at a major Philistine site, which indeed does share features with Phoenician.[39] I refer here specifically to the syntax in the opening phrase בת.בן.אכיש.בן.פדי "the temple (which) Ikaysu (~Achish) son of Padi built" (line 1), and to the use of the word אדתה "his lady" (line 3), both of which align with Phoenician, but not with Hebrew.[40]

By contrast, Hebrew, as all who have investigated the matter realize, is most closely aligned with Moabite (e.g., by use of אשר for the relative pronoun). If we had more Edomite material at our disposal, presumably we would be able to enlarge the picture. In sum, while Rainey overreached, there can be no doubt that Hebrew is more closely related to the Transjordanian dialects of Canaanite than it is to the coastal dialects. This linguistic evidence bespeaks a people with ties and origins to that region, and not to the major Canaanite urban centers.

10. "Israel" in the Merenptah Stele and on the Karnak Temple Reliefs

As is well known, the earliest reference to Israel in the archaeological record appears in the Merenptah Stele, dated to around 1210 BCE. In a wonderful piece of detective work, Frank Yurco revealed that the reliefs on the outer western wall of the Cour de la Cachette of the Karnak Temple provide a pictorial representation of the words inscribed on the Merenptah Stele.[41] This great discovery notwithstanding, Yurco identified the wrong scene as representing the Israelites. As a corrective to Yurco's work, Rainey demonstrated that the Israelites on the wall reliefs are the ones portrayed as Shasu, a conclusion which coheres perfectly with the information presented above, in §§2–3.[42]

11. Sidebar: Possible Reading of "Israel" on Berlin ÄM 21687

In 2001 Manfred Görg proposed to read the name "Israel" on a fragmentary stone relief in the Neues Museum (Berlin) bearing the accession number ÄM 21687.[43] Several scholars, including our own honoree, found the reading to be forced, but more recently Wolfgang Zwickel and Pieter van der Veen have confirmed both Görg's reading and

---

38. Ginsberg, "Northwest Semitic Languages," 108–11.

39. Seymour Gitin, Trude Dothan, and Joseph Naveh, "A Royal Dedicatory Inscription from Ekron," *IEJ* 47 (1997): 1–16.

40. Ibid, 12.

41. Frank J. Yurco, "Merenptah's Canaanite Campaign," *JARCE* 23 (1986): 189–215; and in a more popular version, Yurco, "3,200-Year-Old Picture of Israelites Found in Egypt," *BAR* 16.5 (Sept.–Oct. 1990): 20–38.

42. Anson F. Rainey, "Rainey's Challenge," *BAR* 17.6 (Nov.–Dec. 1991): 56–60, 93. A decade later the author returned to the subject within a longer treatment: Rainey, "Israel in Merenptah's Inscription and Reliefs," *IEJ* 51 (2001): 57–75.

43. Manfred Görg, "Israel in Hieroglyphen," *BN* 106 (2001): 21–27.

his interpretation.[44] This is not the place to enter into the debate, though I would note that the most recent treatment proposes a far more likely date for the inscription, to wit, the early thirteenth century BCE (as opposed to Görg's original suggestion of the Eighteenth Dynasty = fifteenth to fourteenth centuries BCE). Zwickel and van der Veen, moreover, situate the reference to Israel within the context of the nascent group's nomadic origins. To be perfectly honest, I do not follow their line of reasoning: which is to say, I do not see how, even if "Israel" is to be read in ÄM 21687, this bespeaks the people's nomadic origins. Naturally, I am happy to accept the authors' conclusion, as it coheres with my own analysis, though to repeat, I do not see the connection.

Regardless, this section, as its title above indicates, is only a sidebar comment, of no major consequence to the overall trajectory of the present article. My reason for mentioning ÄM 21687 here should be obvious: if the reading "Israel" is correct, clearly this datum demands attention in an article entitled "Israelite Origins."

12. The Mesopotamian Connection

The first ten sections of this article hopefully have demonstrated that Israel's origins are to be found in the orbit of desert-fringe seminomads who traversed the great Southland, which equals the area that today constitutes the Sinai of modern Egypt, the Negev of modern Israel, and the southern desert of modern Jordan.[45] Historical, linguistic, and archaeological lines of evidence converge to demonstrate the point.

The Bible, of course, speaks to this historical reconstruction, though there is also another origins story included in the corpus, to wit, the one associated with Mesopotamia. The historicity of the Genesis narrative aside, one must contend with the following elements, all of which must have meant something to the ancient Israelite consumers of the epic account: Abraham comes from the region of Ur and Harran; Jacob lives in Harran for twenty years; eleven of his sons, the progenitors of the tribes, are born in Harran; and so on.[46]

44. James K. Hoffmeier, "What Is the Biblical Date for the Exodus? A Response to Bryant Wood," *JETS* 50 (2007): 225–47, esp. pp. 241–42. Wolfgang Zwickel and Peter van der Veen, "The Earliest Reference to Israel and Its Possible Archaeological and Historical Background," *VT* 67 (2017): 129–40. See also Peter van der Veen, Christopher Theis, and Manfred Görg, "Israel in Canaan (Long) Before Pharaoh Merneptah? A Fresh Look at Berlin Statue Pedestal Relief 21687," *JAEI* 2.4 (2010): 15–25.

45. Naturally, there were no national borders in antiquity, so I am content to refer to this vast stretch of land as simply the Southland. Satellite photographs of the region are readily available on the internet, e.g., here: https://www.science.co.il/israel/images/satellite/f/Israel-STS094-728-10.jpg.

46. Ur, of course, equals modern-day Urfa, per local tradition, and not Ur in southern Mesopotamia, the famous city excavated by Leonard Woolley. See the series of articles published by Cyrus H. Gordon: "Abraham and the Merchants of Ura," *JNES* 17 (1958): 28–31; Gordon, "Abraham of Ur," in *Hebrew and Semitic Studies Presented to Godfrey Rolles Driver*, ed. D. Winton Thomas and W. D. McHardy (Oxford: Clarendon Press, 1963), 77–84; and Gordon, "Where Is Abraham's Ur?" *BAR* 3.2 (June 1977): 20–21, 52. This was common knowledge in the nineteenth century (see, e.g., George Bush, *Notes Critical and Practical on the Book of Genesis* [New York: Gould, Newman & Saxton, 1839], 189), until Woolley's excavations of the major Sumerian metropolis misdirected attention to the site in southern Iraq.

As an aside, note that the aforecited George Bush, the major American biblical scholar in the nineteenth century, is distantly related to the two scions of the presidential family bearing the same name. For a lively discourse on the scholar's life, see Shalom Goldman, *God's Sacred Tongue: Hebrew and the American*

We have far less material at our disposal either to confirm or deny the picture portrayed in the book of Genesis (with echoes in Josh 24:2–4 and Neh 9:7–8). The only potential evidence is the possibility of an ultimate connection between the tribe of Benjamin and the group called Banu-Yamina in the Mari archives dated to the eighteenth century BCE.[47] There is a more specific possible nexus between the city of Jericho in the territory of the former and the subgroup of the latter called Yariḫu.[48] Obviously, there are both temporal and geographical problems with this identification, as one must traverse seven centuries and eight hundred kilometers for the relationship to work. The temporal issue is less of a problem, since one can trace groups in the Near East over even larger spans of time.[49] As to the geographical issue, in order for the association to work, one must posit the movement of the Banu-Yamina, or some segment thereof, from the region of the middle Euphrates to southern Canaan sometime in the Late Bronze Age, to emerge as the tribe of Benjamin known from the Bible.[50]

Naturally, if this connection should be sustained, there is an irony at play, since Benjamin is the only tribal progenitor born in the land of Canaan (Gen 35:16–20), as opposed to all his brothers who were born in the land of Aram, according to the biblical account (Gen 29:32–30:24).[51] I know of no solution to this conundrum, other than to suggest the following: perhaps the biblical author wished to deny the connection to the older Banu-Yamina group, and therefore he went out of his way to ensure that Benjamin, of all the eponymous tribal ancestors, was the one born in the land of Canaan.

Conclusion

This last issue aside—and I do not mean to minimize its significance—the origins of core Israel are to be found among the Shasu or desert-fringe seminomads of the

---

Imagination (Chapel Hill: University of North Carolina Press, 2004), 199–207, 314–15. For his relationship to the two US presidents, see the sources cited by Goldman, *God's Sacred Tongue*, 315 n. 24.

47. For Abraham Malamat, notwithstanding all the other Mari-Israel interconnections he posited, there is "no connection between the two entities beyond the similarity of name" (Malamat, *Mari and the Early Israelite Experience*, Schweich Lectures 1984 [Oxford: Oxford University Press, 1989], 35); while for Daniel Fleming there is an ultimate connection between the two groups (Fleming, "Genesis in History and Tradition: The Syrian Background of Israel's Ancestors, Reprise," in *The Future of Biblical Archaeology: Reassessing Methodologies and Assumptions*, ed. James K. Hoffmeier and Alan R. Millard [Grand Rapids: Eerdmans, 2004], 193–232, esp. pp. 219–20).

48. See Michael Astour, "Benê-Iamina et Jéricho," *Semitica* 9 (1959): 5–20; and the summary statement by Jack M. Sasson, *Hebrew Origins: Historiography, History, Faith of Ancient Israel*, Chuen King Lecture Series 4 (Hong Kong: Chung Chi College, 2002), 53.

49. See, e.g., Michael Astour, *The Rabbeans: A Tribal Society on the Euphrates from Yaḫdun-Lim to Julius Caesar*, Syro-Mesopotamian Studies 2/1 (Malibu, CA: Undena, 1978).

50. For more general interconnections between Mari and the Bible, see the survey by Malamat, *Mari and the Early Israelite Experience*; and the programmatic essays by Jean-Marie Durand, "Réalités amorrites et traditions bibliques," *RA* 92 (1998): 3–39; and Jack M. Sasson, "About 'Mari and the Bible,'" *RA* 92 (1998): 97–123.

51. Though see also the list in Gen 35:23–26, which implies that Benjamin was born in Paddan-Aram. In addition, note that Judg 20 may retain some vague memory of a time when Benjamin was not part of Israel.

Southland.[52] Clearly, other elements joined up with the core group in order to form historical Israel (Dan, Asher, etc.), but the essential component of Israel, the one that created the ethos and the fabric of the national entity, were former denizens of the desert-fringe who abandoned their former (semi)nomadic ways to settle in the land of Canaan.[53] Anthropologists know well the process of sedentarization, and we should imagine that process during the twelfth century BCE when a group called Israel came to settle in the relatively open spaces of highland central Canaan.[54]

52. For a similar conclusion, see Shmuel Aḥituv, "The Origins of Ancient Israel—The Documentary Evidence," in *The Origin of Early Israel—Current Debate: Biblical, Historical and Archaeological Perspectives*, ed. Shmuel Aḥituv and Eliezer Oren, Beer-Sheva 12 (Beer-Sheva: Ben-Gurion University Press, 1998), 135–40.

53. For details about Dan and Asher in particular, see Gary A. Rendsburg, "The Early History of Israel," in *Crossing Boundaries and Linking Horizons: Studies in Honor of Michael C. Astour on His 80th Birthday*, ed. Gordon D. Young, Mark W. Chavalas, and Richard E. Averbeck (Bethesda, MD: CDL, 1997), 433–53, esp. pp. 447–50. The (semi)nomadic background might explain echoes of bedouin culture present in the Bible, even at a distance of three thousand years, as postulated by Clinton Bailey, "How Desert Culture Helps Us Understand the Bible," *BRev* 7.4 (1991): 14–21, 38. See also Bailey, *Bedouin Culture in the Bible* (New Haven: Yale University Press, 2018).

54. On sedentarization, see Levy and Hull, "Migrations, Ethnogenesis, and Settlement Dynamics."

CHAPTER 23

The Egyptian Background of the Joseph Story: Selected Issues Revisited

Nili Shupak

APPROXIMATELY TWO DECADES AGO, I published an article entitled "The Joseph Story: Legend or History?," in which I concluded that while the extant text in its final form is a tendentious political piece, the Egyptian features it exhibits indicate that it rests on a historical foundation that goes back to the New Kingdom period, primarily the fourteenth–twelfth centuries BCE.[1] Since then, numerous other studies have been conducted that require a renewed examination of this thesis. The present contribution takes a new look at the Egyptian background, focusing particularly on Gen 40–41 but also on other sections of Gen 43–46 in light of the current literature. Two questions will once again occupy our attention: Do the Egyptian features in the story enhance our understanding and aide us in reconstructing its evolution—perhaps even enabling us to pinpoint the historical context of its earliest stratum; and do these features reflect a specific Egyptian reality or are they timeless Egyptian generic shadings?

Starting with a survey of the present state of research into the Joseph story in general and the Egyptian features it displays in particular, I shall address the new Egyptian material published in recent years, summing up with some conclusions regarding the nature of these features and their implications for the understanding of the Joseph narrative and its formation.

The Joseph Story Today: Views and Achilles Heels

Contra the critical approach that developed in the nineteenth century that ascribed the Joseph story to the documents P, E, and J, the prevalent approach today regards the narrative as a single, homogenous unit—at least as a methodological starting point—written in a high literary style.[2] Contemporary scholarship thus focuses

I am pleased and honored to dedicate this article to my colleague, Jim Hoffmeier, as a token of gratitude and appreciation for his most significant contributions to the advancement of comparative study between Israel and ancient Egypt.

The manuscript for this contribution was submitted in early 2018. Literature after 2017 could not be included.

1. Nili Shupak, "The Joseph Story: Legend or History?" in *Texts, Temples, and Traditions: A Tribute to Menahem Haran*, ed. Michael V. Fox et al. (Winona Lake, IN: Eisenbrauns, 1996), 125*–33* [Hebrew].

2. For a comprehensive review of the controversial aspects of the critical method and the shift from a diachronic analysis of the story to a synchronic examination of the text as a whole, see Lindsay Wilson, *Joseph, Wise and Otherwise: The Intersection of Wisdom and Covenant in Genesis 37–50*, Paternoster Biblical Monographs (Carlisle: Paternoster, 2004), 38–44; Konrad Schmid, *Genesis and the Moses Story:*

primarily on its literary aspects—the genre to which it belongs and the motifs it contains.[3]

The importance of the Egyptian elements it manifests, frequently adduced in the past in support of the Joseph story's authenticity—has also waned in recent years. Most scholars now believe that the story contains very little credibly Egyptian material, the so-called Egyptian features being general in nature and rooted in vague memories, inserted in order to impart a sense of historical reality to the story.[4] Today, very few maintain that the Egyptian elements are authentic and point to a specific historical period.[5]

I shall relate to these two approaches:

1. The literary approach holds that the story is an exilic or postexilic narrative or "diaspora novella" about a courtier who rises to power in a foreign royal court, designed first and foremost to encourage the Israelites in exile. This view is based on inner and extrabiblical comparisons. Innerbiblical comparisons suggest that it closely resembles the accounts of Daniel and Mordechai and Esther in the Babylonian and Persian royal courts.[6] Extrabiblical comparisons cite mainly later Egyptian sources: the affinities

---

Israel's Dual Origins in the Hebrew Bible, trans. James D. Nogalski, Siphrut 3 (Winona Lake, IN: Eisenbrauns, 2010), 50–55; Schmid, "Exodus in the Pentateuch," in *The Book of Exodus: Composition, Reception and Interpretation*, ed. Thomas B. Dozeman, Craig A. Evans, and Joel N. Lohr, VTSup 154 (Leiden: Brill, 2014), 30–33 n. 13. For the Joseph story as a single unit, see George W. Coats, "The Joseph Story and Ancient Wisdom: A Reappraisal," *Catholic Biblical Quarterly* 35 (1973): 285–97; Wilson, *Joseph, Wise and Otherwise*, 42–48. For this approach in practice, see W. Lee Humphreys, *Joseph and His Family: A Literary Study* (Columbia: University of South Carolina Press, 1988); J. Robin King, "The Joseph Story and Divine Politics: A Comparative Study of a Biographic Formula from the Ancient Near East," *JBL* 106 (1987): 577–94; Susan Tower Hollis, "Out of Egypt: Did Israel's Exodus Include Tales?" in *Israel's Exodus in Transdisciplinary Perspective: Text, Archaeology and Geoscience*, ed. Thomas E. Levy, Thomas Schneider, and William H. C. Propp (New York: Springer , 2015), 209–22. In my opinion, the Joseph story began life as an autonomous pre-Priestly unit, only later becoming a chain linking the patriarchal narratives with the exodus, consisting primarily of Gen 37–50 (without 38 and 49): see Konrad Schmid, "Die Josephgeschichte im Pentateuch," in *Abschied von Jahwisten: Die Komposition der Hexateuch in der jüngsten Discussion*, ed. Jan Christian Gerz, Konrad Schmid, and Markus Witte, Beihefte zur Zeitschrift für die alttestamentliche Wissenschaft 315 (Berlin: de Gruyter, 2002), 83–118; Erhard Blum and Kristin Weingart, "The Joseph Story: Diaspora Novella or North-Israelite Narrative?," *ZAW* 129 (2017): 501–10.

3. The genres proposed include novella, miracle-story, didactic story, folktale, historiography, familial or political story, etc. See, e.g., James K. Hoffmeier, *Israel in Egypt: The Evidence for the Authenticity of the Exodus Tradition* (Oxford: Oxford University Press, 1996), 96–97; A. J. Soggin, "Notes on the Joseph Story," in *Understanding Poets and Prophets: Essays in Honour of George Wishart Anderson*, ed. A. Graeme Auld, JSOTSup 152 (Sheffield: JSOT, 1993), 338–39.

4. Humphreys, *Joseph and His Family*, 20–21; Soggin, "Notes on the Joseph Story," 339–44; Oren Biderman, "The Joseph Story (Genesis 37–50): Its Date, Context and Purpose" (PhD diss., Tel Aviv University, 2012), 120–96 [Hebrew]. Cf. Blum and Weingart ("Joseph Story," 502 n. 4), who question the usefulness of the story's Egyptian coloring for its dating.

5. The prevailing view today is that the Egyptian features are late, the dates proposed ranging from the seventh century BCE (see Donald B. Redford, *A Study of the Biblical Story of Joseph [Genesis 37–50]*, VTSup 20 [Leiden: Brill, 1970], 187–243; Redford, *Egypt, Canaan, and Israel in Ancient Times* [Princeton: Princeton University Press, 1992], 422–29; Bernd U. Schipper, "Gen 41:42 and the Egyptian Background to the Investiture of Joseph," *Revue Biblique* 118 [2011]: 331–38) through to the Hellenistic period (Soggin, "Notes on the Joseph Story," 340–44; Andreas Kunz, "Ägypten in der Perspective Israels am Beispiel der Josephsgeschichte [Gen 37–50]," *BZ* 47 [2003]: 206–29). An exceptional case is Kenneth A. Kitchen, *On the Reliability of the Old Testament* (Grand Rapids: Eerdmans, 2003), 349–50, 358–60, who believes the story reflects the Middle and New Kingdom periods, in which Semites occupied high positions.

6. See Arndt Meinhold, "Die Gattung der Josephgeschichte und des Estherbuches, Diasporanovelle I," *ZAW* 87 (1975): 306–24; Meinhold, "Die Gattung der Josephgeschichte und des Estherbuches, Diasporanovelle II," 88 (1976): 72–93; Kunz, "Ägypten in der Perspective Israels," 212–16; Soggin, "Notes on

between Joseph's economic reform and the motif of famine in Egypt and the Famine Stele (on Sehel Island) and the Canopus Decree, both from the Ptolemaic period; the Rosetta Stone, also from this period, in which the king's birthday celebrations are the setting of royal amnesties and executions, as in Gen 40:20; and the autobiographical inscriptions of Egyptian officials during the Twenty-second and Twenty-third dynasties (850–700 BCE) that attribute titles to their owners such as those Joseph attained.[7]

Previous scholars, however, noted that, rather than only emerging in a later period, the central motif in the story—the official who obtains high status in foreign royal court—is common throughout ancient Near Eastern biographies. The tales of famous heroes—the Egyptian Sinuhe, Idrimi king of Alalakh, Moses in Pharaoh's court, David's adventures prior to being enthroned—from the middle of the second millennium onward also belong to this genre.[8] Recently, Tawny Holm has drawn attention to the points of contact between the mid-second millennium Egyptian legends and the Daniel and Joseph narratives—the courtier who engages in rivalry, interprets dreams, is imprisoned and summoned from jail to give advice to the ruler or interpret dreams, foresees the future, displays magic skills, is praised by the king for his aid, and is rewarded or promoted.[9] Therefore, in and of itself, this motif is insufficient to

the Joseph Story," 338–39; Harald M. Wahl "Das Motiv des 'Aufstiegs' in der Hofgeschichte: am Beispiel von Joseph, Esther und Daniel," *ZAW* 112 (2000): 62–74; Thomas C. Römer, "La narration, une subversion: L'histoire de Joseph (Gn 37–50*) et les romans de la diaspora," in *Narrativity in Biblical and Related Texts*, ed. George J. Brooke and Jean-Daniel Kaestli, BETL 149 (Leuven: Leuven University Press, 2000), 23–24; Michael V. Fox, "Joseph and Wisdom," in *The Book of Genesis: Composition, Reception and Interpretation*, ed. Craig A. Evans, Joel N. Lohr, and David L. Petersen, VTSup 152 (Leiden: Brill, 2012), 248–49; Biderman, "Joseph Story," 197–228. Blum and Weingart ("Joseph Story," 501–21) dispute the interpretation of the Joseph story as a "diaspora novella," regarding it rather as a northern Israelite eighth-century BCE composition. Cf. Shupak, "Joseph Story," 132*–33*.

7. For the later parallels, see Kunz, "Ägypten in der Perspective Israels," 216–23. Although Kunz (ibid., 216 n. 13) adduces examples from Jansen-Winkeln, three of the eleven he cites do not form true parallels, the fourth also being uncertain: see Karl Jansen-Winkeln, *Ägyptische Biographien der 22. und 23. Dynastie*, ÄAT 8, 2 vols. (Wiesbaden: Harrassowitz, 1985), 2:330, 333 (×2), 354. Analogies to Joseph's titles and deeds can also be found, moreover, in official inscriptions from earlier periods, beginning from the Old Kingdom: see William A. Ward, "Egyptian Titles in Genesis 39–50," *BSac* 114 (1957): 52–55, 59; Shupak, "Joseph Story," 130* n. 16; Jozef Janssen, *De Traditioneele Egyptische Autobiografie vóór het Nieuwe Rijk* (Leiden: Brill, 1946), 16, 18, 49; Miriam Lichtheim, *Ancient Egyptian Autobiographies, Chiefly of the Middle Kingdom: A Study and an Anthology*, OBO 84 (Fribourg: Universitätsverlag; Göttingen: Vandenhoeck & Ruprecht, 1988), 46–47, 76, 78–79, 93, 96, 104, 107, 136, 139.

8. Thomas L. Thompson and Dorothy Irvin, "The Joseph and Moses Narratives," in *Israelite and Judaean History*, ed. John H. Hayes and J. Maxwell Miller (Philadelphia: Westminster, 1977), 180–91; Konrad von Rabenau, "Inductio in Tentationen—Joseph in Ägypten," in *Ägypten Bilder: Akten des Symposions zur Ägypten-Rezeption, Augst bei Basel, vom 9.–11. September 1993*, ed. Elisabeth Staehelin and Bertrand Jaeger, OBO 150 (Fribourg: Universitätsverlag; Göttingen: Vandenhoeck & Ruprecht, 1997), 45–46; King, "Joseph Story and Divine Politics," 577–94; Hollis, "Out of Egypt," 214–19; Michael Fieger and Sigrid Hodel-Hoenes, *Der Einzug in Ägypten: Ein Beitrag zur alttestamentlichen Josefsgeschichte*, Das Alte Testament im Dialog 1 (Bern: Lang, 2007), 253–57. Blum and Weingart ("Story of Joseph," 513–16, 521) have recently correctly noted that, while, like the Joseph narrative, the plot of the Story of Sinuhe, takes place in a foreign country no one assumes the existence of an Egyptian diaspora on this basis. This is a further confirmation that the Joseph story does not refer to a diaspora situation.

9. Tawny L. Holm, *Of Courtiers and Kings: The Biblical Daniel Narratives and Ancient Story-Collections*, Explorations in Ancient Near Eastern Civilizations (Winona Lake, IN: Eisenbrauns, 2013), 485–91. In contrast to other scholars who adduce parallels to the Joseph story principally from Mesopotamia and Persia, Holm stresses that the traditions relating to officials at the royal court were also widespread in Egypt. Among those she cites are King Cheops and the Magicians (Papyrus Westcar) and Neferti Prophecies from the second-millennium, Djoser and Imhotep, and The Second Tale of Setne (about Prince Khamwas

prove the story's late date. Likewise, if it was compiled during the exile in order to lift the people's spirits, we would expect it to be set in Babylon rather than Egypt.[10] The scholarly response that the Egyptian framework was chosen because the exiles feared the Babylonian authorities is untenable in light of their good relations. The Joseph narrative is also unusual in the favorable light in which it presents Egypt and Pharaoh, an attitude not found in any other biblical text. The famine motif similarly cannot be attributed solely to the Late period (ca. 650–330 BCE) or the Ptolemiaic period (ca. 330–30 BCE), as it occurs throughout the history of ancient Egypt. In the early biographies, high officials frequently boast of having opened their storehouses to the people during times of drought.[11] While the Famine Stele—which exhibits such close affinities with Joseph's reform (as I discussed at length in my previous article)— is now frequently thought to be a Ptolemaic piece of propaganda, it, too, contains archaisms attesting that it rests upon an early source. In other words, it may be a late reconstruction of an ancient document. [12] With respect to the Canopus Decree, even the scholar who appeals to it acknowledges that the Joseph model differs.[13] Similarly, the correspondences between the Joseph story and the second-century Rosetta Stone that records that on his birthday the king (Ptolemy V Epipanes) offered amnesties or ordered the execution of criminals and the frequent references to this custom during the Persian and Hellenistic periods do not necessarily imply a late date for the biblical text or later Egyptian influence on it. As James Hoffmeier observes, it is quite likely that, rather than a celebration of the royal physical birthday, the occasion marked was the anniversary of his accession. Known as early as the Old Kingdom and current during the Eighteenth Dynasty, this ceremony marked the king's divine birth as the son of Re, being accompanied by the pardoning of prisoners.[14]

---

and his son Si-Osiris), composed during the Hellenistic-Roman period. See also Adele Berlin, *Esther: Introduction and Commentary*, Mikra Leyisra'el (Tel Aviv: Am Oved; Jerusalem: Magnes, 2001), 24 [Hebrew], who maintains that the affinities between the Joseph and Mordechai stories indicate that the author of Esther drew on early traditions rather than the late date of the former; see also Michael Segal, "From Joseph to Daniel: The Literary Development of the Narrative in Daniel 2," *VT* 59 (2009): 142–43, who posits that Dan 2 rests upon the literary model of the Joseph story. See also Shemaryahu Talmon, "'Wisdom' in the Book of Esther," *VT* 13 (1963): 454–55.

10. See Bustenay Oded, *The Early History of the Babylonian Exile Eighth–Sixth B.C.E.* (Haifa: Pardes, 2010), 273 [Hebrew]. Biderman's claim ("Joseph Story," 264–67) that the intertextual contacts between the story of Jehoichin's release from prison and rise to power (2 Kgs 25:27–30) and the account of Joseph's appointment (Gen 41:40–43) demonstrate that the latter is an exilic novella is also untenable, the passage at the end of Kings almost certainly being added later by a later editor or redactor who employed the Joseph story as a model for evincing that David's lineage had not ceased, thereby giving hope to the Babylonian exiles that they would return home like Jacob's sons: see Michael J. Chan, "Joseph and Jehoiachin: On the Edge of Exodus," *ZAW* 125 (2013): 566–77.

11. See Nili Shupak, "A Fresh Look at the Dreams of the Officials and of Pharaoh in the Story of Joseph (Genesis 40–41) in the Light of Egyptian Dreams," *JANES* 30 (2005): 124–25 and n.77; Fieger and Hodel-Hoenes, *Der Einzug in Ägypten*, 160–63.

12. Shupak, "Fresh Look at the Dreams," 125–27. The most prominent motif common to the Joseph story and the Famine Stele is the seven-year famine. This being prevalent across the ancient Near East as a whole, its appearance in another Egyptian papyrus from the Persian period (see Günter Burkard, "Frühgeschichte und Römerzeit: P. Berlin 23071 VSO," *SAK* 17 [1990]: 107–33) does not attest to the late date of the Joseph story. For ancient Near Eastern references to the seven-year famine/drought motif, see Shupak, "Fresh Look at the Dreams," 126.

13. Kunz, "Ägypten in der Perspective Israels," 221.

14. Hoffmeier, *Israel in Egypt*, 89–91. For pardoning on the anniversary of the king's accession, see Stephen K. McDowell, "Crime and Punishment," *OEAE* 1:317. Although Redford (*Study of the Biblical*

2. The diminished significance attributed to the Egyptian features must also be treated cautiously. The most striking divergence between the Joseph story (from the end of Gen 37 onward) and the later books of Daniel and Esther lies in the fact that the former is set in Egypt. The Egyptian elements embedded in the story relate to diverse aspects—customs, daily practices, beliefs, and terminology—and are more numerous than in any other section of Genesis or perhaps in the biblical text as a whole. Their removal leaves us with a lifeless skeleton. We must thus ascertain whether these are late and generic features, as Redford and other recent scholars contend—arguing that the Joseph story is a late document composed at the very earliest during the Saitic period (seventh century BCE) or later, during the Persian or Hellenistic periods— or authentic features relating to a particular earlier historical timeframe.[15]

The subject being too broad to be exhaustively examined in the present context, I shall focus on those Egyptian features that, while having been addressed in research, have now been supplemented by new information (1) or have only recently been analyzed (2, 3, and 4).[16]

Egyptian Features

The Motif of Rewarding and Joseph's Appointment (Genesis 41:41–43)

This theme has been addressed latterly by Susanne Binder in a work that has received far less attention than it deserves.[17] Earlier scholars had already observed the correspondence between Joseph's appointment and the royal rewarding of officials favored by the king during the New Kingdom period.[18] Yet Binder adduces fresh relevant material that sheds new light on the question of the sources of the Joseph story, linking the

---

Story of Joseph, 205–6) ascribes this detail to the Saitic-Persian period, Ramesses IV (1152–1145 BCE) already recounts that in honor of his taking the throne he gave amnesties: see Bob Becking, *From David to Gedaliah: The Book of Kings as Story and History*, OBO 228 (Fribourg: Academic Press; Göttingen: Vandenhoeck & Ruprecht, 2007), 179–80; see also Fieger and Hodel-Hoenes, *Der Einzug in Ägypten*, 131–35.

15. See n. 5 above.

16. Dreams—a central motif in the Joseph story—also belong to the first group. In my 2005 article (Shupak "Fresh Look at the Dreams," 103–38), I noted the close correspondence between the ministers'/Pharaoh's dreams in the Joseph story and early Egyptian dreams—their type, structure, formulation, and mode of interpretation. Recent studies investigating the ancient Egyptian dreams now demand that the subject be revisited: see Scott B. Noegel, "On Puns and Divination: Egyptian Dream Exegesis from a Comparative Perspective," in *Through a Glass Darkly: Magic, Dreams and Prophecy in Ancient Egypt*, ed. Kasia Szpakowska (Swansea: Classical Press of Wales, 2006), 95–119; Noegel, *Nocturnal Ciphers: The Allusive Language of Dreams in the Ancient Near East*, American Oriental Series 89 (New Haven: American Oriental Society, 2007); Kasia Szpakowska, "Dream Interpretation in the Ramesside Age," in *Ramesside Studies in Honour of K. A. Kitchen*, ed. Mark Collier and Steven R. Snape (Bolton: Rusterford, 2011), 509–17. I hope to devote a separate paper to this issue.

17. Susanne Binder, "Joseph's Rewarding and Investiture (Genesis 41:41–43) and the Gold of Honour in New Kingdom Egypt," in *Egypt, Canaan and Israel: History, Imperialism, Ideology and Literature*, ed. Shay Bar, Dan'el Kahn, and J. J. Shirley, CHANE 52 (Leiden: Brill, 2011), 44–64; see also Binder, *The Gold of Honour in New Kingdom Egypt*, Australian Centre for Egyptology 8 (Oxford: Aris & Phillips, 2008).

18. Jozef Vergote, *Joseph en Égypte: Génèse chap. 37–50 à la lumière des études égyptologiques récentes* (Louvain: Publications Universitaires, 1959), 121–35; Redford, *Study of the Biblical Story of Joseph*, 208–13; Hoffmeier, *Israel in Egypt*, 91–2; Shupak, "Joseph Story," 127*–29*.

text to a specific time span in Egyptian history. The rewarding takes the form of various concrete gifts—fields, slaves, memorials, clothes, and jewelry. As in the Joseph story, however, the most prominent is a gold collar (*shebyu* [Eg. *šbyw*]), Binder asserting that this gift was only bestowed during the Eighteenth through Twentieth dynasties (1550–1100 BCE). Commemorated on steles, graves, and temple walls, the ceremony is represented as consisting of four stages: the official appears before the king, is crowned with a (gold) collar, exits the hall, and returns home, where he is greeted by his household. The affinities between the Egyptian and biblical accounts clearly attest that the Hebrew author was familiar with the New Kingdom Egyptian custom:

1. He associates the bestowal of a reward with an official appointment or promotion. Misreading the Egyptian text, earlier scholars such as Jozef Vergote, Donald Redford, and James Hoffmeier had argued that these constitute two separate genres relating to two different events. Binder, in contrast, reinforces Kenneth Kitchen's questioning of this view, and follows him citing two Amarna period examples in which an elevation and a reward of gold constitute part of the same ceremony.[19]

2. Unlike the other presents, the gift of gold was bestowed on members of the inner royal circle otherwise not in possession of any social standing or specific profession, being selected by the king himself. This detail closely matches the account of Joseph's rise to power from prisoner to royal consultant.

3. Although earlier scholars had noted the fact that, like those bestowed upon Joseph, the king's gifts included gold and clothes, Binder demonstrates that Egyptian royal rewards did not generally take the form of a signet ring. She thus conjectures that the ring symbolized Joseph's new position as "seal-bearer" (*ḥtmw bity*).[20]

4. Riding in the chariot: this element appears from the Amarna period onward up to the Nineteenth Dynasty, the recipient of the honor being carried in a chariot to his home, where his slaves and family greet him with calls, songs, dancing, and prostration. Although this detail had also been observed by earlier scholars, Binder argues that two obscure features in Gen 41:43 can be explained in light of a parallel in an Egyptian iconography: "And they shouted before him: "*abrēk* [אברך]' " is a form of bowing down,[21] and "he made him to ride him on *mirkebet hammišneh* [מרכבת המשנה]" refers to a "chariot for two" that

---

19. These relate to two officials named Huya and Tutu: see Kenneth A. Kitchen, review of *A Study of the Biblical Story of Joseph (Genesis 37–50)*, by Donald B. Redford, *Oriens Antiquus* 12 (1973): 240–41; Binder, "Joseph's Rewarding," 54–56. For a survey of the controversy, see Hoffmeier, *Israel in Egypt*, 91–92; Shupak, "Joseph Story," 128* n. 9.

20. The presentation of a signet ring symbolized the granting of authority to an official appointed to an important position. The Egyptian term *ḏbʿt* signified a signet ring up until the New Kingdom period, when it was replaced by *ḥtmt* "seal." Both terms found their way into biblical language.

21. Binder ("Joseph's Rewarding," 58) derives the term from the Hebrew noun "knee" (בֶּרֶךְ), reading it as an imperative: "Bow the knee!" Other scholars have offered further proposals in accordance with Egyptian, the most plausible being *ib-rk* "Take heed!" See Yoshiyuki Muchiki, *Egyptian Proper Names and Loanwords in North-West Semitic*, Society of Biblical Literature Dissertation Series 173 (Atlanta: Society of Biblical Literature, 1999), 236. The translation of biblical references herein follows the RSV, with slight modifications when necessary.

appears in descriptions from the New Kingdom period rather than a "second-ary chariot," as traditionally understood.[22]

The depiction of Joseph's appointment in Gen 41:41–43 thus corresponds to the reward ceremony documented in New Kingdom Egyptian inscriptions and iconography. The closest parallels to the association between the rewarding and appointment of an official and the riding in a chariot (an element that continues to occur in this ceremony up until the beginning of the Nineteenth Dynasty) come from the Amarna period. Binder thus suggests that the Egyptian features in the biblical passage may derive from this time frame or were inserted at a later point when this custom was still in practice. Irrespective of this issue, the author of the Joseph story was clearly acquainted with a well-known Egyptian praxis prevalent during the New Kingdom period.[23]

In light of the evidence Binder adduces, it is no longer tenable to assert that the account of Joseph's appointment must form part of a late biblical stratum on a par with the depiction of Daniel and Mordechai's rise to prominence. Nor is it on a par with the seventh-century extrabiblical sources such as Ashurbanipal's investiture of prince Neco as viceroy in Egypt or a Greek mercenary's appointment to a mayor by Psamtik I.[24]

The "Abomination of Egypt" (Genesis 43:32; 46:34; Exodus 8:22)

This phrase, which recurs several times in the Joseph story, also appearing in the account of Israel's bondage in Egypt, likewise reflects a number of authentically Egyptian beliefs and customs. It relates to forbidden foods in the ancient Egyptian society rather than later Israelite "kashrut" laws or impurity prohibitions practiced in Hellenistic-Roman Egypt, as some scholars contend.[25] Although late Egyptian and classical sources provide instructive information relating to this matter, it is present also in earlier texts from the New Kingdom period onward.[26] Ancient Egyptian society prohibited the eating of certain foods deemed to be *bwt* "abomination," these prohibitions generally relating to specific areas or regions.[27] Although observed meticulously

22. As per Fieger and Hodel-Hoenes, *Der Einzug in Ägypten*, 179.

23. This view finds support in other Egyptian elements in this episode, many of which date to the New Kingdom period: see Shupak, "Joseph Story," 126*–31*.

24. For Pharaoh Neco's investiture, see Redford, *Study of the Biblical Story of Joseph*, 225. For the Greek soldier's appointment, see Schipper, "Gen 41:42 and the Egyptian Background," 334–38. These two examples are from the seventh century BCE. For the disparities between the version in Ashurbanipal's annals and the biblical text, see Schipper, "Gen 41:42 and the Egyptian Background," 333–34. The Greek mercenary's investiture, which is accompanied solely by the gift of a gold collar, also differs from the Joseph story, which speaks of a gold collar, ring, clothes, and riding in a chariot.

25. See Nili Shupak, "'The Abomination of Egypt': New Light on an Old Problem," in *Marbeh Ḥokmah: Studies in the Bible and the Ancient Near East in Loving Memory of Victor Avigdor Hurovitz*, ed. Shamir Yona et al., 2 vols. (Winona Lake, IN: Eisenbrauns, 2015), 2:271*–94* [Hebrew]. Having discussed the issue therein at length, I shall merely summarize the findings below, focusing on the meaning of the expression in the Joseph story.

26. The classical authors who address various food prohibitions include the fifth-century BCE Herodotus (*Histories* 2), the first-century BCE Diodorus Siculus, Strabo, and Plutarch, and the third-century CE Porphyry. See Shupak, "Abomination of Egypt," 278*. The principal Egyptian texts from the Hellenistic-Roman period dealing with the subject are the "geographical texts" from the temples at Dendera, Edfu, and Kom Ombo: see ibid., n. 29.

27. These prohibitions included, e.g., six types of fish, pigs, cows, honey, and leeks.

by priests and high-ranking officials, including kings, they were not practiced by commoners. Inscriptions left behind by some kings show that they took pains to follow these rules. Piankhi, one of the Nubian rulers who sat on the pharaonic throne in the middle of the eighth century BCE, for example, adopting the local customs, states that the defeated lords of the delta were forbidden to enter his palace because "they were uncircumcised ['*m'w*] and were eaters of fish, which is an abomination in the king's house." Only king Namart was allowed entrance because "he was pure [*w'b*] and did not eat fish" (lines 150–151).[28] Ramesses IV makes a general declaration in this regard on the Abydos stele: "I never ate what I considered to be an abomination."[29]

Egyptian literary and iconographical sources evince that table manners in the land of the Nile were rigid and set, eating etiquette constituting a primary theme in the wisdom instructions from the end of the third millennium BCE onward. Violation or deviation was considered "an abomination to the *ka*":[30]

> If you are one of the guests
> At the table of one who is greater than you,
> Take what he gives, when it is set before you,
> Look at what is before you,
> Do not shoot many glances at him,
> For to annoy him is abomination to the *ka*.
> Do not speak to him until he calls,
> One does not know what may displease;
> Speak when he addresses you,
> Then your words will please his heart.
> The magnate, when he is behind the food,[31]
> Behaves as his *ka* commands him;
> He will give to whom he favors (Instruction of Ptaḥḥotep, P 119–137).[32]
> Do not eat in the presence of an official,
> And do not set to eating (or speaking) first.
> If you are sated with fraudulently chewing,
> Enjoy yourself with your saliva.
> Look at the bowl that is before you,[33]
> And let it serve your needs.[34] (Instruction of Amenemope, 23, 13–18).[35]

---

28. The translation follows *AEL* 3:80, with slight modifications.

29. See Mikhaïl Korostovtsev, "Stele de Ramsès IV," *BIFAO* 45 (1947): 158, 162.

30. The *ka* is an individual's double that accompanied him from birth to death. Here, it serves as the source of the decisions the host makes as the night wears on. The phrase "abomination of the *ka*," which also occurs in *Ptaḥḥotep* P160 and P189, relates to improper social conduct, being identical in meaning to the expression "abomination to god" that recurs in the eleventh-century BCE Instruction of Amenemope chs. 10, 13, 17. In the biblical text, the term 'ה תועבת' appearing only in Proverbs (twelve times) parallels both these, likewise pertaining to inappropriate social behavior.

31. In other words, stands before the food to serve.

32. *AEL* 1:65, with slight modifications.

33. In other words, be satisfied with what is given you.

34. See also: Instruction to Kagemni, 1, 3–11(*AEL* 1:59–60); Papyrus Insinger, 5,12–6,24 (*AEL* 3:189–90), etc.

35. *AEL* 2:160 with slight modifications.

Analysis of the illustrations depicting banquets and festivals common among the Egyptian elite demonstrates a fixed order of seating. At these repasts, women and men were separated, the only exception being spouses, who were allowed to sit side by side. At tables loaded with delicacies, the attendees were waited upon by young servants. These along with the entertainers (singers and dancers) could be non-Egyptians, but the participants in the banquets were always Egyptian. Eating with strangers was uncommon, only rare exceptions being made. Thus, for example, when Ramesses II's bride, Hattushili III's daughter, reached the Egyptian border, the Egyptian soldiers and royal entourage mingled together with the Hittite escort, all being described as "eating and drinking together with one heart like brothers without bothering one another."[36] In a Ramesside period letter from Deir el-Medina, a father reproves his rebellious son for having wandered far from his home in the delta region, reproaching him in particular for having made an alliance with the local Asiatics (ʿ3mw) affirmed by a joint meal of "bread on his (lit. your) blood."[37] Explicit reservations toward foreign foods appear in the cycles of stories about Setne (Khamwas), son of Ramesses II. These Hellenistic-Roman period tales, written in Demotic, recount the visit of a Nubian magician to the king's court. After amazing the audience with his magic skills, pharaoh ordered to have a room for him, and a meal of "abominable things [nbʿy] (according to the custom) of the Nubians."[38]

As we remarked above, Piankhi not only fastidiously kept the abomination laws but also gave Egyptian leaders as well as foreigners a cold welcome in his palace if they did not conform to the laws of purity, entry being refused to the rulers of Upper and Lower Egypt because they were uncircumcised and ate fish.[39]

These second-millennium to Third Intermediate period (mid-eighth century BCE) examples suffice to demonstrate that an invitation to a banquet or eating with foreigners held special significance in ancient Egyptian culture. This brief survey elucidates the picture painted in Gen 43:32, where Joseph, a top-ranking official in the royal court, behaves according to local upper-class norms, refraining from eating with foreigners: "They served him by himself, and them by themselves, and the Egyptians who ate with him by themselves, because the Egyptians could not eat with the Hebrews, for that is an abomination to the Egyptians" (Gen 43:32).

The food that Joseph as an Egyptian was prohibited from consuming appears to have been sheep, an unsurprising circumstance in light of the fact that rams represented two of the chief Egyptian creators gods—Khnum, depicted as a potter, and Amun, god of the air and wind—as well as other local gods. The iconographic and

---

36. Inscription from the Abu Simbel Temple, *KRI* 2:251, 1–5.

37. Egyptian: *wnm.k ʿḳw ḥr snf.k.* For this custom, see Jaroslav Černý, "Reference to Blood Brotherhood Among Semites in an Egyptian Text of the Ramesside Period," *JNES* 14 (1955): 161–63.

38. Setne II 3, 5–6. For the meaning of the *hapax legomenon nbʿy*, see F. L. Griffith, *Stories of the High Priests of Memphis: The Sethon of Herodotus and the Demotic Tales of Khamuas* (Oxford: Clarendon, 1900), 165; cf. Serge Sauneron, "L'Avis des Egyptiens sur la cuisine Soudanaise," *Kush* 7 (1959): 63, who maintains that the Egyptian loathing of foreigners also finds expression in the proscription of foreign food.

39. This evidence undermines Soggin's view ("Notes on the Joseph Story," 341) that Gen 43:32 reflects the postexilic period because there are no early Egyptian sources indicating that Egyptians did not eat with foreigners—such texts appearing for the first time in classical documents. Although this norm appears to have been practiced in Egypt, Egyptians who traveled outside the country did not hesitate to sit with non-Egyptians and taste local food: see the Story of Sinuhe, B 87–92 (*AEL* 1:227).

textual findings evince that Egyptians rarely ate sheep, certainly consuming it much less often than beef or goats meat. Of the dozens of scenes portraying the bringing of animals as offerings to the dead, only one contains a sheep, the latter also being absent from the lists of sacrifices offered to the gods and the pictures of loaded tribute tables so popular in Egyptian art.[40]

Despite their late date and the doubt cast upon their accuracy, the information provided by classical sources complements and confirms the picture we gain from the early Egyptian texts. This demonstrates that at least some Egyptians refrained from eating or sacrificing sheep(s)—mainly those in places in which the ram was worshiped as a god, and the upper class and priests, for whom its meat was taboo. Pasturing flocks was also regarded as a despicable task in Egypt, those who engaged in it belonging to the lowest social strata.

The early Egyptian sources, together with some classical ones, thus shed light on the distinctive phrase "abomination of Egypt," and elucidate its use in Gen 43 and 46. Joseph and his Egyptian entourage did not sit down to eat with his brothers because the latter were shepherds and ate sheep. Joseph's words to his brothers—"When Pharaoh calls you, and says, 'What is your occupation?' you shall say, 'Your servants have been keepers of livestock from our youth even until now, both we and our ancestors,' in order that you may dwell in the land of Goshen; for every shepherd is an abomination to the Egyptians" (Gen 46:33–34)—also become clearer against this backdrop. Fearing to represent his brothers as shepherds lest they be treated badly by the authorities and possibly even harmed, Joseph requests that they be given land in Goshen close to Egypt's northeastern border in order to put a good distance between them and the priests and ram worshipers. It also clarifies Moses's request of pharaoh in Exod 8:21–22 [Eng. 25–26]: "Then Pharaoh called Moses and Aaron, and said, 'Go, sacrifice to your God within the land.' But Moses said, 'It would not be right to do so; for we shall sacrifice to the LORD our God offerings abominable to the Egyptians. If we sacrifice offerings abominable to the Egyptians, will they not stone us?'" The Israelites could only sacrifice sheep to God outside the borders of Egypt, doing so within its confines bearing the risk of a violent reaction on the part of those who worshiped them and

40. See Bertha Porter and Rosalind L. B. Moss, *Topographical Bibliography of Ancient Egyptian Hiero-glyphic Texts, Reliefs, and Paintings, Volume 1: The Theben Necropolis; Part 1; Private Tombs* (Oxford: Oxford University Press, 1974), 463–70, esp. 467. Sheep are also absent from the offerings-to-the-dead lists in the Pyramid Texts (see Raymond O. Faulkner, *The Ancient Egyptian Pyramid Texts* [Oxford: Clarendon, 1969]) and Old and Middle Kingdom autobiographies published by Lichtheim (*Ancient Egyptian Autobiographies*). According to Darby, Ghalionngui, and Grivetti, "The sacrifice of sheep was relatively rare through much of Dynastical time." See William J. Darby, Paul Ghalionngui, and Louis Grivetti, *Food: Gift of Osiris*, 2 vols (London: Academic Press, 1977), 1:220. Support for this view can be found in Barta's comprehensive study of the lists of the sacrifices to the gods and the dead from the Early Dynastic through the Hellenistic-Roman period. See Winfried Barta, *Die altägyptische Opferliste, von der Frühzeit bis zur griechisch-römischen Epoche*, Münchner ägyptologische Studien 3 (Berlin: Hessling, 1963). Sheep do not occur in any of these, the noun ʾwt "flock" also only appearing once—in a list of offerings on a First Dynasty cylinder seal: see ibid., 6. In contrast, beef, geese, and sometimes pigeon and goat (2×) are frequently adduced, a finding that contravenes Englund's contention that sheep are cited in the sacrifices-to-the-gods lists: Gertie Englund, "Offerings," *OEAE* 2:567; see also Salima Ikram, *Choice Cuts: Meat Production in Ancient Egypt*, OLA 69 (Leuven: Peeters, 1995), 17 (who relates sheep and goats together). For the visual representations, see Madeleine Peter-Descrate, *Pain, bière et toutes bonnes choses . . . L'alimentation dans l'Éypte ancienne* (Monaco: Rocher, 2005), 303. These findings are supported by the dozens of illustrations of tribute-tablets in Egyptian texts and ancient Egyptian sites on the web.

forbade their slaughter. The identification of sheep as an "abomination" in the Joseph story thus attests to the Hebrew author's familiarity with Egyptian eating habits and table etiquette as evidenced in writings across the historical spectrum, including the New Kingdom period.

"Imaginary" Egyptian Features

Joseph's Two "Purificatory" Rites (Genesis 41:14; 43:30–31)

Genesis 41:14

> Then Pharaoh sent and called Joseph, and they brought him hastily out of the dungeon; and when he had shaved himself and changed his clothes, he came in before Pharaoh.

According to Lisbeth Fried, this verse depicts an Egyptian custom of shaving one's head and beard contra the Assyrian and Israelite practice of letting their hair grow long.[41] Joseph's shaved head thus appears to symbolize the fact that he was no longer a non-Egyptian but had been "naturalized." This claim of Fried may be supported by a parallel incident in the Story of Sinuhe, the Egyptian refugee who, after having spent many years abroad in northern Canaan, describes his home-returning in these words : "Years were removed from my body. I was shaved; my hair was combed. Thus, was my squalor returned to the foreign land, my dress to the Sand-farers. I was clothed in fine linen; I was anointed in oil. I slept on a bed. I had returned the sand to those who dwell in it, the tree-oil to those who grease themselves with it."[42] This detail in the Joseph story may thus indicate the Hebrew author's familiarity with the Egyptian royal court. However, Fried's suggestion that the shaving was related to ritual of purification goes one step too far.[43] Although she contends that, like the priests, Joseph was required to shave all the hair off his body when entering a temple because, Pharaoh being considered a god, his palace was a sacred place, to the best of my knowledge only one text expressly states that the impure were forbidden to enter the palace: the mid-eighth-century Piankhi's stele, which asserts that the rebellious delta rulers were denied entrance because "they were uncircumcised and were eaters of fish, which is an abomination in the king's house" (cf. above). Not only does this text not adduce shaving or the cutting of hair, but the visual representations of foreign delegations in Pharaoh's court always portray them in their native garb and hairstyle rather than with their heads and beards shaved as per Egyptian custom.[44]

---

41. Lisbeth S. Fried, "Why Did Joseph Shave?" *BAR* 33.4 (2007): 36–41, 74.

42. *AEL* 1:233.

43. Joseph's act may also be interpreted more straightforwardly, however, as cleaning himself up after a long period in jail: cf. the foreign woman taken in warfare, who must "shave her head and pare her nails" before her new husband can go into her (Deut 21:10–12).

44. For visual images of West Semites in Egyptian art, see further Phyllis Saretta, *Asiatics in Middle Kingdom Egypt: Perceptions and Reality*, Bloomsbury Egyptology (London: Bloomsbury, 2016), 43–108.

Genesis 43:30–31

When Joseph sees Benjamin, his younger brother, on his second meeting with his brothers, he finds it difficult to contain his emotions:

> Then Joseph made haste, for his heart yearned for his brother, and he was about to weep. So he entered his chamber and wept there. Then he washed his face and came out; and controlling himself he said, "Let food be served."

The phrase "washed his face" (*r-ḥ-ṣ pānîm*) not occurring elsewhere in the biblical text, Philip Yoo proposes that it may be a literal translation of the Egyptian *iʿj ḥr* that appears in Egyptian sources in the context of purification and resurrection in the world to come from the Old Kingdom Pyramid Texts through to the eighth century BCE.[45] Although acknowledging that ritual purification does not suit the Joseph story, Yoo argues that the Hebrew author adapted the Egyptian expression as a way of making Joseph appear more Egyptian.

This thesis is untenable for a number of reasons. The root *r-ḥ-ṣ* frequently used with objects relating to various bodily organs—hands, feet, flesh—in the biblical text, it thus merely being coincidental that "face" only occurs once. Joseph's act also makes good sense in light of the circumstances, its explanation not requiring an appeal to an Egyptian phrase: seeking to conceal his feelings from his brothers and his emotion at seeing his younger brother, when he can no longer restrain himself Joseph goes to a side chamber to weep, then washing his face so that his tears will not betray him.

In summary, I believe neither Fried's nor Yoo's proposals to be tenable, the biblical text in both cases being completely understandable in light of inner-biblical exegesis. The verses are better read in their plain sense rather than being dressed in Egyptian garb in order to support the theory that the Egyptian hues in the story come from the hand of a Hebrew writer who sought to strengthen Joseph's Egyptian attributes.

Conclusions

The two principal Egyptian elements discussed herein—Joseph's appointment to office and rise to power, and the phrase "abomination of Egypt"—reflect Egyptian customs and beliefs prevalent during the New Kingdom period (middle of the second millennium BCE through to the eleventh century BCE). While the distinctive aspects of Joseph's elevation—the combination of rewarding with investiture, and the riding in a chariot—belong to a specific timeframe in Egyptian history (Amarna period), the "abomination of Egypt" represents centuries-long tradition—abstention from eating certain foods is mentioned frequently in the classical sources as a typical Egyptian custom.[46] Thus even if prohibition from consuming sheep is known from Egyptian sources from the second millennium onward, unlike the account of Joseph's investiture

---

45. Philip Y. Yoo, "Why Does Joseph Wash His Face?" *JSOT* 38 (2013): 3–14.
46. The riding in a chariot is, however, also attested into the early Nineteenth Dynasty.

this cannot serve as a chronological peg for attributing the biblical story to a particular historical framework.

Although the Joseph story could *not* have been written down prior to the time when official writing became established in Israel—namely, with the emergence of the monarchy in the first millennium BCE—this does not preclude the possibility that it preserves authentic Egyptian traditions from the New Kingdom period. In its extant form, the story has passed through many transformations, reflecting a long editorial process. It may thus have commenced as an oral version whose origins go back to the end of the second millennium BCE, the Hebrew author being acquainted with the Egyptian traditions incorporating them years after the related events took place.[47] To this early stage belong the prominent Egyptian motifs and elements interwoven into the episode, such as Joseph's appointment and part of his titles, the patterns and formulation of the officials' and Pharaoh's dreams, Egyptian terms and names—*parʿōh, yěʾōr, ʾaḥû, ḥarṭummîm, ḥōrî, ṭabaʿat, šēš, ʾōn* (Heliopolis), *Ṣāpnat-paʿnēḥ*, and perhaps also the motif of the seven cows/ears of corn, and Joseph's burial in a coffin and lifespan of 110 years, which recall Egyptian mythology and beliefs regarding the dead.[48] Later editors and redactors inserted other elements, such as the "land of the Hebrews," *sāris*, the oath "by the life of Pharaoh," and the names *ʾOsnat* and *Pôṭipar/Pôṭiperaʿ*.[49]

The story thus contains "Egyptian fossils" from the New Kingdom period alongside later features from the Saitic (seventh century BCE) and Hellenistic (third–second centuries BCE) periods as noted by Redford and those following him.[50] Yet the later strata of the story should not negate the existence of earlier buried traditions, these being revealed in the case of the Joseph story via its comparison with ancient Egyptian culture and literature.[51]

47. For an excellent up-to-date survey of the relations between ancient Israel and Egypt and the Egyptian influence on the local inhabitants from the beginning of the eleventh century BCE through to the end of the eighth century BCE, see, Shirley Ben Dor Evian, "Israel and Egypt: The Never-Ending Story," *NEA* 80 (2017): 30–39.

48. While some scholars are wary of the conventional view that *ḥarṭummîm* were engaged in dream interpretation in ancient Egypt, all concur that the term is borrowed from Egyptian: see Muchiki, *Egyptian Proper Names*, 245. For a survey of the possible meanings of the name *Ṣāpnat-paʿnēḥ*, see ibid., 224–26. For the other Egyptian elements—patterns and formulation of dreams, high official's titles, terms and names, see Shupak, "Joseph Story," 128*–31*; Shupak, "Fresh Look at Dreams," 107–37; Shupak, "Funeral and Burial Customs in the Story of Joseph," *Beit Mikra* 55 (2010): 84–93 [Hebrew]. In my opinion, the core of the Joseph story is the autobiography of an official in the Egyptian royal court: see Shupak, "Joseph Story," esp. 131*–32* n. 24.

49. For the Egyptian origin of these names, see Muchiki, *Egyptian Proper Names*, 208–9, 221.

50. Inter alia, Redford (*Study of the Biblical Story of Joseph*, 46–65) bases his opinion on a linguistic analysis of the Joseph story that includes fifty-two late Hebrew terms evincing that the text belongs to the exilic or restoration period. As Kitchen (*Study of the Biblical Story of Joseph*, 477) and Biderman ("Joseph Story," 85–103) have shown, however, a significant number of these are not in fact late, Biderman identifying only eight certain examples and thirty possible ones. Even if we accept this view, thirty-eight of the five thousand three hundred words that make up the account constitute an insignificant proportion (0.7 percent). Whatever the case may be in this respect, the examples of late language may, as I have suggested above, be the result of later reworking or editing, a phenomenon known in the Egyptian manuscripts—e.g., later copies of the Instruction of Ptahhotep and the Story of Sinuhe exhibiting variations in vocabulary and grammar.

51. Cf. Binder, "Joseph's Rewarding," 60–61.

CHAPTER 24

Mighty Bull Appearing in Napata: Memorialization and Adaptation of the Bronze Age into the Iron Age World of the Kushite, Twenty-Fifth Dynasty of Egypt

Stuart Tyson Smith

THE NUBIAN PHARAOH PIANKHI'S first Horus name, "Mighty Bull appearing in Napata" illustrates the complexities inherent in the commemoration of the past by the Kushite, Twenty-fifth Dynasty of Egypt (ca. 747–656 BCE). The use of the title and its materialization in the form of monumental inscriptions and stelae mimics that of New Kingdom ruler Thutmose III (ca. 1479–1425 BCE), evoking a royal connection stretching back into the Bronze Age, while at the same time alluding to Amun's preeminent Nubian cult center at Napata instead of its Egyptian counterpart at Thebes (Eide et al. 1994, 47–118). Other aspects of Kushite material culture interwove elements imitated or adapted from styles stretching back as far as the Old Kingdom (ca. 2686–2160 BCE) with those from contemporary Egypt, while others drew upon traditional Nubian material culture and practices with roots in the Bronze Age Kerma culture (ca. 2400–1502 BCE), including the revival of the distinctively Nubian black-topped pottery style.

Some of the Egyptian Bronze Age influences, like both royal and private pyramid complexes, were most likely the consequence of the long history of interaction and entanglement between Egypt and Nubia, especially during the New Kingdom Empire (ca. 1502–1069 BCE). Other features were clearly strategically adopted as a means of legitimating the power and authority of Kushite royalty internally through appeals to polyvalent Nubian pasts and externally as restorers of order and true successors to Egyptian kingship, an ideology that itself resonated with the New Kingdom theology of *ma'at* and was expressed through art and architecture. A consideration of long-term social memory versus dislocation and shorter-term commemorations of the past, drawing on theories of Maurice Halbwachs, as applied to Egypt by Lynn Meskell and Jan Assmann (Halbwachs and Coser 1992; Meskell 2003; Assmann 2011), as well as inscribed versus incorporated memory (Connerton 1989) in Kushite society can help us better understand how the memory of the Bronze Age was incorporated materially in Iron Age Nubia and Egypt, as well as allowing for a more nuanced distinction between the conscious and unconscious remembrances of the past that underlay Kushite kingship and are reflected through broader material cultural expressions that resonate with contrasting Egyptian and indigenous pasts. I offer this study of Egypt's southern entanglements to Jim as I hope a fitting complement to his remarkable contribution to our understanding of Egypt's engagements to the north.

Background: The New Kingdom Empire and the Kushite Dynasty

Egypt's most profound engagement with Nubia, or Nubia's engagement with Egypt depending on one's perspective, straddles the Late Bronze Age and Iron Age. After the conquest of Thutmose I, Nubia was brought into an Egyptian empire that at one point stretched at least notionally from the Euphrates in Syria to the fifth cataract of the Nile in Nubia (Edwards 2004; Török 2009). The region from the first to second cataract was reoccupied/colonized, and the reach from the second to third cataract was newly colonized, with fortified temple-centered towns established at several sites (fig. 24.1). After five hundred years of colonial occupation, which included intermarriage and cultural entanglements between Egyptians and Nubians, the colony split away from Egypt after the Viceroy of Kush Panehesy revolted against the authority of Ramesses XI, the last pharaoh of the New Kingdom. Although it is often asserted that the colony was withdrawn or abandoned, the archaeological record suggests instead continuity, both for Panehesy himself, who was buried at the former colonial capital at Aniba, and colonial sites like Amara West and Tombos, which continued to be occupied into the Third Intermediate period (Smith and Buzon 2014a; Spencer 2014). Some two hundred years after the fall of the empire, a new polity emerged at Napata that consolidated control over all of Nubia and whose leaders eventually ruled as Egypt's Twenty-fifth Dynasty (Morkot 2000). Piankhi's conquest stela represents an eloquent expression of piety and restoration, doubtless aided by strong support from Thebes, but also informed by their long history of entanglement during the empire, still present in a monumental landscape and the living descendants of the multiethnic colonial communities that emerged over the course of empire.

Memory and Meaning in Egypt and Nubia

The Kushite use of the Bronze Age past in the Iron Age present, while strategic and to some extent revisionist and manipulative, was nevertheless grounded in the real, long-term memory of the colonial experience. In contrast, Meskell has argued that the historically layered landscape at Deir el Medina was characterized by extreme disjunction between the realities of the Bronze Age past and how those meanings were dramatically changed in the reuse of the site during the Greco-Roman period (Meskell 2003). Their commemorations, in the form of burials placed in the old settlement, layered a newly constituted past on a deeply palimpsest landscape in order to construct an entangled Egyptian/Hellenistic identity. She sees this disconnect between the past and its use in the present as a natural part of the dynamics of long-term social or cultural memory versus shorter-term memory by individuals, lasting only a generation or two.

Paul Connerton's (1989), distinction between inscribed versus incorporated commemorations helps to identify deliberate signaling versus more personal practices that might find origins and/or resonate with the Bronze Age. The practice of inscribed memory is deliberate and discursive. Statuary, stelae, and monuments like the great temple of Amun at Gebel Barkal and royal and private pyramid tombs created an enduring materialization that signaled specific messages about the history and identity of those who commissioned them. On the other hand, incorporated memory consists

Mediterranean Sea

Syro-Palestine

Nile Delta

Saqqara/Memphis

Red Sea

Abydos

Deir el-Medina   Thebes
Medinet Habu

Egypt

Aswan

— 1

Nubia (Kush)   Lower

Abu Simbel

2

Semna

Amara West   Upper

Thutmose I
Conquest Stela   3   Tombos

Kerma   Gebel Barkal/Napata   New Kingdom
Boundary Stela

Kawa

4

Nuri   5

Kurru

○ Site
□ Egyptian Temple-town
■ Egyptian Fortress
⟍ Cataract

6

FIGURE 24.1. Map.

of less publicly obvious practices that might have origins in the deeper past but are largely unconscious, akin to Pierre Bourdieu's notion of habitus (Bourdieu 1977). These two kinds of commemoration are not mutually exclusive, but are better seen on a continuum, with one or the other emphasized in specific social contexts and settings. Two images of the popular god Bes reflect these two contexts (fig. 24.2). Bes amulets found in a woman's Nubian-style burial at Tombos (ca. 1350 BCE) show how Egyptian deities came to be selectively adopted by Nubians at a personal level,

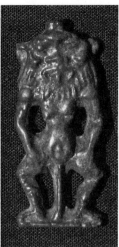

FIGURE 24.2. Bes.

while the monumental columns commissioned by Taharqa at Gebel Barkal's Mut temple inscribed a connection with the deity onto that sacred landscape that is also transformative, bringing Bes into an innovative, monumental context (ca. 690 BCE). Both inscribed and incorporated commemorations ultimately reflect choices made by individuals, constrained and perhaps guided, but not determined by habitus.

Meskell takes a skeptical view of the ability of ancient Egyptians to have maintained a long-term social memory of the past outside of the context of the state ideology (Meskell 2003). She rightly points out (as does Assmann 2011) that in order for the detailed knowledge of the past to be retained, there must be a sustained social context, one that she finds broadly lacking for Egypt, even among the elites, where short-term commemorations, lasting only a generation or two, were the norm. Moreover, the transmission of memory is subject to refreshing, revision, ignoring, and forgetting (following Halbwachs and Coser 1992; Meskell 2003; Küchler 1993). The latter in particular can lead to the transformation of social memories to varying degrees, like those described by Meskell that ultimately led to disjuncture at Deir el Medina. But while she makes a good case for that specific situation, her model of disarticulation may have a more limited application to Egypt and in our case Nubia.

The ancient Egyptians, and by extension Nubians, were clearly capable of maintaining the kind of long-term social memory envisioned in these discussions. As Meskell herself acknowledges, the veneration of personal and royal ancestors appears in a number of New Kingdom contexts, for example at Deir el Medina in the tomb of Inherkhau, but also a variety of others, including a household shrine at the Egyptian colony of Askut used through the mid-Eighteenth Dynasty that was dedicated to a Second Intermediate period ancestor named Meryka (Meskell 2003; Smith and Buzon 2014b; Smith 2003, 127–31). The cult of deceased kings and queens like Amenhotep I and Ahmose Nofretari were maintained both inside and outside of Deir el Medina over many generations, which is also the case for other "saintly" figures, like Prince Wajmose, a son of Thutmose I who had a chapel that was restored (and expanded?) under Amenthotep III with votive offerings dedicated there down to at

FIGURE 24.3. Amenirdis.

least the Ramesside period (Petrie and Spiegelberg 1897). Similarly, Heqaib of Aswan was an Old Kingdom nomarch whose cult place on Elephantine Island was active for around five centuries (Habachi, Haeny, and Junge 1985).

Archaeological evidence suggests that at least some of these commemorative monuments remained in use from the Bronze Age into the Iron Age, like the mortuary temples of Ramesses III and Seti I, providing at least some degree of continuity. Ramesses III's mortuary temple at Medinet Habu played a particularly important role during the Third Intermediate period as a religious administrative center and burial place for the powerful women who held the title "God's Wife (or Adoratrice) of Amun," an office that played a central role in the Kushite Dynasty (Aston 2003; Ayad 2009). The tomb of Amenirdis I and the other "God's Wives" were placed along the approach to the first pylon, explicitly tying the present to the past by reinscribing a sacred landscape (fig. 24.3). Amenirdis was the daughter of Kashta and sister of Pharaohs Piankhi and Shabaka. Three Nubian princesses (Amenirdis I, Shepenwepet II, and Amenirdis II) were installed in this office and buried at Medinet Habu. The office gained considerable political power under Amenirdis's predecessor, Shepenwepet I, a feature that continued through larger political transitions until the Persian conquest in 525 BCE (Ayad 2009). Stephen Quirke (1999; following Jansen-Winkeln 1994) notes the enhanced autonomy and prominence of women in the funerary realm from the late Ramesside into the Third Intermediate period, attributing this feature to Libyan influence. The placement of women in positions of power like the "God's Wife" under the Libyans would have also appealed to Nubians, reflected in the continuing prominence of the office during the Kushite Dynasty.

Similarly, the grand temples on the East Bank also maintained an inscribed memory of the New Kingdom past through inscriptions and reliefs that, while constantly added to, still bore the names and deeds of past kings. John Baines (1991) has argued that these monuments were themselves disarticulated from all but the highest priestly elite, but there is ample evidence of private piety through votive offerings (e.g., Pinch 1993; Dreyer 1986; Sadek 1987), and as Erik Hornung (1992, 34) points out, the power of image could transcend the written word, reaching beyond an elite, literate audience. The texts themselves could reach a wider audience through oral memory, recitations, and ritual performances, at a minimum in a temple setting during the many festivals that punctuated the year (Török 2009, 453; Smith 2003, 177–83; and cross-culturally Goody 1977, 156). Ramesses II's bombastic account of the battle of Kadesh, for example, was well known enough at the time for the Hittite king to complain of its accuracy (Liverani 2001, 217).

Egypt's strong scribal tradition could also provide a foundation for long-term cultural memory, whether in a more public or private context. Texts like the Immortality of Writers and Song of the Harper from the Tomb of King Intef praise the authors of "classic" works of Egyptian literature, going back to Imhotep in the Old Kingdom (*AEL* 1:175–78; Simpson 2003, 308, 332–33). Similarly, the popularity of literature set in the past, like the Story of Sinuhe, both in schools and at home (Simpson 2003, 54–66), suggests that the long-term social memory of the past was more common than Meskell would allow, at least among the literate. In line with this, individuals like Inherkhau tapped into this kind of collective social memory by commemorating not only their own ancestors but also a long line of kings stretching in his case back to Nephepetre Montuhotep, the founder of the Middle Kingdom who lived nearly a thousand years before. Royal documents and monuments like the Palermo Stone, Turin Canon, and Abydos king lists provided a similar memorialization of the deep past. The construction of both private and royal monuments within the Theban necropolis and also within the city of Thebes thus inscribed a sacred landscape with both subtle and explicit articulations between the past and present(s). That is not to say that this long-term social memory was transmitted without both subtle and potentially drastic transformations and manipulations for personal and/or ideological purposes, but it does allow for the possibility of a more genuine remembrance of the past in different social and political contexts.

Social Memory and the Kushite Dynasty

The early Third Intermediate period inscription of Nubian Queen Katimala at Semna implies the continuation of a scribal tradition and existence of some kind of successor state to the New Kingdom Empire, albeit factionalized (Darnell 2006). Placed upon a New Kingdom temple built in a Middle Kingdom fortress that memorialized deified Middle Kingdom king Senwosret III, this monumental inscription marks the beginning of the Kushite use of the past to legitimize royal power in the present. In a similar way, Piankhi's choice of Horus name "Mighty Bull appearing (crowned) in Napata" on his early (ca. 747 BCE) sandstone stela set up in Thutmose III's great temple to Amun at Gebel Barkal evokes a long-term social memory of the Bronze Age empire.

Commemorating his coronation by Amun, he explicitly connected his Iron Age reign to that of the earlier king, placing him symbolically in a long line of succession.

FIGURE 24.4. Montuemhet and Taharqa.

Nevertheless, it also represents a transformation or revision, in the substitution of Amun of Napata for Amun of Karnak. This could simply be a reference to his corona-tion naturally having taken place at Amun's southern center, reflecting a long-term cultural entanglement arising from the New Kingdom colonial encounter. But there may be a subtler message being sent here. During the New Kingdom, Napata enjoyed a parallel role to Karnak, extending to its symbolic importance in the coronation of kings, a feature revived under Kushite rule. Piankhi's adoption of Thutmose's titulary, including his Horus, Golden Horus, Nebty, and throne name, was not arbitrary, but can be seen as a clever paraphrase of the earlier text that could be still be read nearby on the large stela that Thutmose III had erected in the temple hundreds of years earlier (Eide et al. 1994, 55–62).

Piankhi and his successors also created ties between their new dynasty and Bronze Age Egypt through renovating and expanding older temples, and commissioning new temples and statuary, all of which drew upon New Kingdom and even older proto-types. As Edna Russmann (1989) pointed out some time ago, Kushite royal statuary was modeled on the strong physique of the Old Kingdom. This Kushite archaizing was not haphazard, but methodical and elegant, imitating but at the same time adapting styles from various periods in Egyptian history and creating new elements, like the use of a novel cap-crown. This archaizing style extended to the elite, seen in a statue of Montuemhet, powerful mayor of Thebes during the Twenty-fifth and Twenty-sixth Dynasties, whose pose and muscular appearance echoes that of Taharqa and is mod-eled on the same Old Kingdom private and royal prototypes (fig. 24.4).

In addition to construction at temples like Karnak in Egypt, the Kushite Pharaohs, most notably Taharqa, restored, embellished and expanded a series of New King-dom temples in Nubia, notably at Gebel Barkal/Napata and downstream at Kawa and

FIGURE 24.5. Barkal.

Kerma (fig. 24.5). That this was a commemorative act of restoration and expansion of older monuments was made explicit in their dedicatory inscriptions. In order to accomplish this act of commemoration, László Török (2002, 52) argues that the new rulers forged an alliance with Theban priests to support the emerging Kushite strategy of presenting themselves as the legitimate successors to the pharaohs of the New Kingdom. The transformation from descendants of a conquered people to legitimate successor was implemented through the "reinterpretation of ancient native concepts and by an increasing interest in the monuments of the Egyptian domination ... with the aim of articulating the present as the embodiment of the ideal continuity with an ideal past that was created from a selection of normative elements."

The result was an emphasis on the colonial past but tied to the Iron Age present in a way that legitimized the new dynasty's power at home and in Egypt (Smith 1998). These features included new iconography reviving the New Kingdom royal theology of *ma'at*, of restoring and maintaining a pious order in the face of chaos. Piankhi constantly alludes to this in his Victory Stela, contrasting his piety with the transgressions of his enemies against *ma'at* (Eide et al. 1994, 62–117). As in the New Kingdom, this theme was materialized by later kings though scenes of defeating/slaying foreigners and offering to Amun-Re and other deities. Some of these motifs were part of long-term continuities in Egypt, like the ritual slaying of enemies that lasted into the Greco-Roman period. Others do seem to harken back more specifically to a Kushite remembrance of the New Kingdom, like the motif of the king as a sphinx trampling enemies from the temple at Kawa, in this case not surprisingly all apparently Asiatic (Macadam 1949, pl. IX/b). Kawa's decoration also included scenes modeled after Old Kingdom representations from the mortuary complexes of Sahure, Neuserre, and Pepi II, while the scenes of defeating and trampling enemies were accompanied by a quotation from the Instruction of King Amenemhet, one of that group of Middle Kingdom texts that were still popular in the New Kingdom and apparently still had currency in the Third Intermediate period, in this case associating the Kushite domination of the north to Amenemhet's victories over the northlands (Török 2002, 46–128, pls. 14–16). Some of these features may represent a new use of the past inspired by their reconnection with Egypt, but at least some likely came as a result of the legacy of Nubia's colonial past—for example, an ostracon with part of the Teaching of Amenemhet, a school practice piece, was found in the Ramesside town at Amara West (Spencer 2014).

It is of course possible that these renovated monuments simply played a role the creation of a new, disjunctive past by the Kushite rulers, as was the case in Greco-Roman Thebes. The archaeological evidence for continuity of New Kingdom cults from the New Kingdom through Third Intermediate period in Nubia is equivocal, but this is in part because of the early date of most of the excavations. Strong continuities in the style of ceramics and other material culture through the Third Intermediate period has also created a tendency to push diagnostic markers toward the Ramesside period or Twenty-fifth Dynasty, creating an artificial "Dark Age" (Aston 1996). Recent archaeological work has established that the region was not abandoned, as previous models had posited, and that the colonial communities remained in place and were not somehow withdrawn (Smith and Buzon 2014a). It is at least plausible that cult activity continued at major centers of worship like Gebel Barkal, even if epigraphic activity and construction ceased, with the inscription of Katimala standing out as the exception and perhaps an indication of the survival of literacy and by extension memory into the period of the Kushite Dynasty. As Török points out, it is hard to imagine that the restorations of New Kingdom temples to their original cults could have taken place without tapping into local religious traditions that stretched back into the New Kingdom, thus providing the kind of sustained context required for the maintenance of social memory (as envisioned by Halbwachs and Coser 1992; Török 2002, 48–54).

Török makes the perceptive argument that this creation of an ideological underpinning of Kushite monarchy that evoked an Egyptian past served the interests of both

FIGURE 24.6. Pyramids.

sides, promoting reunification in Egypt with its emphasis on a strong monarchy and producing political power for the new Nubian pharaohs through the integration of indigenous traditions with Egyptian kingship ideology in Nubia (Török 2009; also Smith 1998). The restoration and expansion of New Kingdom temples projected continuity with an idealized past, and the reinterpretation of older monuments like the stela of Thutmose III from the great temple of Amun-Re at Gebel Barkal (at their capital Napata) provided important conduits for the "Egyptianization" of Napatan kingship. Török also points out that the correspondences between the localized iconography and epithets of deities in New Kingdom and Kushite monuments suggests real continuities with surviving religious traditions at the old Egyptian centers of worship, which themselves drew upon earlier Bronze Age native cults. This process was manifested in Lower Nubia most dramatically during the reign of Taharqa, whose ambitious building campaign recreated and elaborated upon the sacred geography of the New Kingdom.

The Kushite use of pyramids as the royal burial monument is another clear reference to the Bronze Age (Fig. 24.6). David O'Connor (1993) and others have seen this as inspired by the Old and Middle Kingdom royal tombs in Egypt, a new influence from the north adapted in an innovative context as the Kushite Dynasty gained control. However, this perspective fails to take into account the long tradition of pyramid building in Nubia during the empire (Török 1997, 118–21; Ambridge 2007; Smith 2007). Shortly after royal pyramids stopped being built, pyramids made of mud-brick and stone became the preeminent private monument for officials during the New Kingdom, with numerous examples built at the main northern and southern necropoleis of Saqqara (serving Memphis) and Thebes. Over a period of nearly five hundred years, colonial and indigenous officials built pyramids at a number of sites in both Upper and Lower Nubia, as far south as Tombos (Smith and Buzon 2017). The plan and scale of the Kushite royal pyramids, with their steep sides and small, attached axial chapels, match these private monuments, not their older royal counterparts in Egypt (Smith 2014). Thus, it is very likely that their use as a royal funerary monument reflects an allusion to the colonial era, not the creation of a fictive linkage to Egyptian kingship that might be characterized as dislocation. They created an inscribed commemoration of an Egyptian, colonial past for a largely internal audience in a similar way to the renewal of the New Kingdom cults, even though some elements of both might also reflect the kind of amalgamation envisioned by Török as well as a less self-conscious incorporated memory as adopted and adapted Egyptian features became Nubian.

Other elements were borrowed directly from Egypt. Some of these were contemporary, including new editions of funerary texts like the Book of the Dead. Others established new continuities with the Egyptian past. Taharqa modeled the underground complex of his pyramid tomb on the Bronze Age Osirion at Abydos, which remained in use during the Iron Age (Török 1997). This also reflects a subtle deployment of sacred knowledge revolving around Egyptian beliefs, but at the same time is novel in its realization. Other features were at the same time imitative in form but adaptive in use. In particular, ushabti figurines closely follow contemporary Egyptian styles in both form and inscription. However, they occur in unusually large numbers and were arrayed along the walls of the underground chambers in a practice very different from contemporary Egypt (Balanda 2014). These objects would have been on display during the funeral, at the same time signaling ties to Egypt and redefining Egyptian practices to suit a new blended or entangled Nubian theology.

Social Memory and Individual Commemoration in Kushite Society

Pyramids provide a point of intersection between royal and private practice, where long-term social memories of the Bronze Age were also deployed on a more individual level. I will use our work at Tombos as a case study to examine some of the complexities of the use of the past in the past, connected with a sense of place, in a private context. Tombos was established and colonized by Egyptians around 1450 BCE, although the colonial population quickly established biological ties to the indigenous population through intermarriage and/or other liaisons. In contradiction to models positing an Egyptian withdrawal at the end of the New Kingdom, Tombos continued as an important center throughout the Third Intermediate period and into the Twenty-fifth Dynasty, a pattern replicated by new excavations elsewhere in Nubia (Smith and Buzon 2014b; Binder, Spencer and Millet 2011).

Pyramids were built at Tombos through the Ramesside period and perhaps even into the Third Intermediate period, although confirming this will require further excavation. In any case, New Kingdom pyramid and other tombs either continued to be used or were reused during the Third Intermediate period, and new private pyramids were built in the Twenty-fifth Dynasty. One of the New Kingdom tombs contained the ninth or tenth millennium BCE burial of a horse about half way down its shaft (fig. 24.7). This is a practice attested in the New Kingdom, perhaps borrowed from the Hyksos, along with the horses themselves. Burials of whole chariot teams appear in the royal Kushite cemetery (Dunham 1950, 110–17). They were so important to the

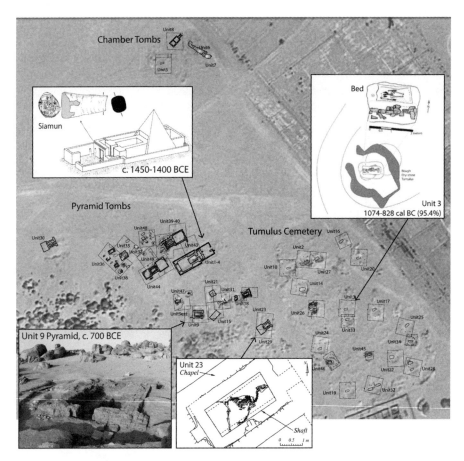

FIGURE 24.7. Tombos plan.

Kushite kings that Piankhi seems more offended that the rebels against his rule mistreated his horses. The practice would resonate with the strong emphasis on animal burial in earlier Kushite practice, and thus might represent the deeper memory of a Kushite past.

At the same time, Nubian-style tumuli were built in a separate part of the cemetery at Tombos starting in the late Ramesside period and continuing through the Twenty-fifth Dynasty. A similar pattern exists at the royal cemetery of el-Kurru, where both pyramids and tumuli occur. This suggests a complex process of commemoration in both the royal and private spheres, deploying competing or polyvalent commemorations of the Bronze Age with very different antecedents. The continuing practice of bed burial reflects a similar dynamic. Burial on a bed was common in the tumulus cemetery during the Napatan period, but also appears in the older part of the cemetery associated with new or reused mud-brick tombs. The placement of the deceased on a bed during the funeral would have signaled ties to a Nubian past (fig. 24.7). With only two exceptions, however, the bodies were extended and supine, sometimes mummified and sometimes placed in a wooden coffin in line with Egyptian practices. This juxtaposition would again signal a mixed message of both Egyptian and Nubian ancestral

FIGURE 24.8. Tombos beakers.

ties. Royal burials were also placed on beds, in spite of the otherwise strong signaling of Egyptian ties through the use of coffins and a variety of specialized Egyptian grave goods, all of which would have been on display during the funeral.

At a more quotidian level, the revival of a handmade pottery tradition also signaled ties to a deeper past. During the New Kingdom, Nubian style pottery never disappeared, but becomes muted, the ceramic assemblage dominated by Egyptian wheel-made wares. Handmade pottery reemerges as a strong component of the overall assemblage during the Third Intermediate period, including classic styles like polished blacktopped red ware. An example from Tombos combines Egyptian technology with Nubian decoration in a new vessel type (fig. 24.8). These tall beakers became extremely common in the Twenty-fifth Dynasty (Vila 1980). While not as refined as the famous Bronze Age Kerma style beakers, they would have signaled ties to earlier Kushite society and seem to have played a similar role in feasting during life and as part of the funeral assemblage after death. This particular example was one of a set of three, the other two with overall red polish. Curiously, all three were thrown on a wheel, in spite of their Nubian decorative treatment. They were found in a mud-brick tomb with the burial of a wealthy soldier who was mummified, placed in a coffin on top of a bed, again reflecting a dual consciousness and signaling of Egyptian and Nubian primordial ties.

Conclusions

A key prerequisite for long-term social memory is the existence of continuing traditions, something that we have evidence for in both Egypt and Nubia through continuities in scribal tradition, sacred landscapes and settlement. For a long time, the Third Intermediate period in Nubia was seen as a kind of dark age, but a closer consideration of the historical record and increasing archaeological evidence suggests strong continuities at New Kingdom colonial sites. Kushite archaism does appear to reflect, to some extent, a genuine remembrance and commemoration of colonial and even deeper Egyptian and Nubian pasts, albeit with adaptations and manipulation to suit their goals in a new Iron Age social and political milieu, in particular a sophisticated revision of cultural memory by the Kushite rulers to legitimate their political and social role as true successors of the Bronze Age New Kingdom pharaohs. At the same time, the adaptation of pharaonic kingship to a Nubian milieu served to reinforce the authority of Kushite rulers at home (Smith 1998). The emphasis on sophisticated adaptations of text and representation in the renovated and enlarged temples suggest the presence of a literate internal audience, as well as forms that were intelligible to nonliterate members of society participating in ritual activity and festivals.

While to a large degree strategic, the Kushite evocation of the Bronze Age past does not mirror the kind of dislocation and creation of new, ultimately fictive social memory that Meskell describes for Greco-Roman period Deir el Medina. At the same time, elements from the Bronze Age that evoked both a colonial (Egyptian) and deeper indigenous past (Kerman) were deployed in private contexts. In each case, royal and private, individuals made decisions about how to commemorate the past that ran on a continuum between inscribed and incorporated memory. In the end, cultural memory was created not by the collective, but by an accumulation of individual decisions about how to deploy the past in the present.

Acknowledgments

The joint UCSB-Purdue University project at Tombos is directed by myself and bio-archaeologist Michele Buzon. Principle funding has been provided by the National Geographic Society and National Science Foundation, with additional support from the Brennan and Schiff Giorgini Foundations and private donations. We appreciate the support of the Sudan National Corporation for Antiquities and Museums, in particular Dr. Abdelrahman Mohamed Ali, General Director, and Dr. El-Hassan Mohamed Ahmed, Director of Fieldwork and research collaborator. Personal thanks to Drs. Julie Anderson, Bruce Williams, David Edwards, Ali Osman M. Salih and the faculty of Archaeology at the University of Khartoum.

BIBLIOGRAPHY

Ambridge, Lindsay. 2007. "Inscribing the Napatan Landscape: Architecture." Pages 128–54 in *Negotiating the Past: Identity, Memory, and Landscape in Archaeological Research.* Edited by Norman Yoffee. Tuscon: University of Arizona Press.

Assmann, Jan. 2011. *Cultural Memory and Early Civilization: Writing, Remembrance, and Political Imagination.* New York: Cambridge University Press.

Aston, David A. 1996. *Egyptian Pottery of the Late New Kingdom and Third Intermediate Period (Twelfth–Seventh Centuries BC): Tentative Footsteps in a Forbidding Terrain.* Studien zur Archäologie und Geschichte Altägyptens 13. Heidelberg: Heidelberger Orientverlag.

———. 2003. "The Theban West Bank from the Twenty-fifth Dynasty to the Ptolemaic Period." Pages 138–66 in *The Theban Necropolis: Past, Present and Future*. Edited by Nigel Strudwick and John H. Taylor. London: British Museum Press.

Ayad, Mariam F. 2009. *God's Wife, God's Servant: The God's Wife of Amun (c. 740–525 BC)*. London: Routledge.

Baines, John. 1991. "Society, Morality, and Religious Practice." Pages 123–200 in *Religion in Ancient Egypt: Gods, Myths, and Personal Practice* .. Edited by Byron E. Schaefer. Ithaca: Cornell University Press.

Balanda, Brigitte. 2014. "Protecting the Mummy: A Reinterpretation of 'Shabtis' in Napatan Funerary Customs." Pages 655–62 in *The Fourth Cataract and Beyond: Proceedings of the Twelfth International Conference for Nubian Studies*. Edited by Julie R. Anderson and Derek A. Welsby. Leuven: Peeters.

Binder, Michaela, Neal Spencer, and Marie Millet. 2011. "Cemetery D at Amara West: The Ramesside Period and Beyond." *British Museum Studies in Ancient Egypt and Sudan* 16:47–99.

Bourdieu, Pierre. 1977. *Outline of a Theory of Practice*. Cambridge Studies in Social and Cultural Anthropology 16. Cambridge: Cambridge University Press.

Connerton, Paul. 1989. *How Societies Remember*. Cambridge: Cambridge University Press.

Darnell, John Coleman. 2006. *The Inscription of Queen Katimala at Semna: Textual Evidence for the Origins of the Napatan State*. YES 7. New Haven: Yale Egyptological Seminar.

Dreyer, Günter. 1986. *Der Tempel der Satet: Die Funde der Frühzeit und des alten Reiches*. Mainz: von Zabern.

Dunham, Dows. 1950. *The Royal Cemeteries of Kush, Vol. 1: El Kurru*. Cambridge: Harvard University Press.

Edwards, Dean N. 2004. *The Nubian Past: An Archaeology of the Sudan*. London: Routledge.

Eide, Tormod, Tomas Hagg, Richard Holton Pierce, and Lásló Török. 1994. *Fontes Historiae Nubiorum: Textual Sources for the History of the Middle Nile Region Between the Eighth Century BC and the Sixth Century AD*. 4 vols. Bergen: University of Bergen Department of Classics.

Goody, Jack. 1977. *The Domestication of the Savage Mind*. Themes in Social Sciences. Cambridge: Cambridge University Press.

Habachi, Labib, Gerhard Haeny, and Friedrich Junge. 1985. *The Sanctuary of Heqaib*. 2 vols. DAIK 33. Mainz: von Zabern.

Halbwachs, Maurice, and Lewis A. Coser. 1992. *On Collective Memory*. Chicago: University of Chicago Press.

Hornung, Erik. 1992. *Idea into Image: Essays on Ancient Egyptian Thought*. New York: Timken.

Jansen-Winkeln, Karl. 1994. "Der Beginn der libyschen Herrschaft in Ägypten." *BN* 71:78–97.

Küchler, Sharon. 1993. "Landscape as Memory: The Mapping of Process and Its Representation in Melanesian Society." Pages 85–106 in *Landscape, Politics and Perspectives*. Edited by Barbara Bender. Explorations in Anthropology. Providence: Berg.

Liverani, Mario. 2001. *International Relations in the Ancient Near East, 1600–1100 BC*. Studies in Diplomacy. New York: Palgrave Macmillan.

Macadam, Miles F. Laming. 1949. *The Temples of Kawa: Oxford University Excavations in Nubia*. Oxford: Oxford University Press.

Meskell, Lynn. 2003. "Memory's Materiality: Ancestral Presence, Commemorative Practice and Disjunctive Locales." Pages 34–55 in *Archaeologies of Memory*. Edited by Ruth van Dyke and Susan E. Alcock. Oxford: Blackwell.

Morkot, Robert G. 2000. *The Black Pharaohs: Egypt's Nubian Rulers*. London: Rubicon.

O'Connor, David. 1993. *Ancient Nubia: Egypt's Rival in Africa*. Philadelphia: University Museum, University of Pennsylvania.

Petrie, William M. Flinders, and Wilhelm Spiegelberg. 1897. *Six Temples at Thebes. 1896*. London: Quaritch.

Pinch, Geraldine. 1993. *Votive Offerings to Hathor*. Oxford: Griffith Institute, Ashmolean Museum.

Quirke, Stephen. 1999. "Women in Ancient Egypt: Temple Titles and Funerary Papyri." Pages 227–35 in *Studies on Ancient Egypt in Honour of H. S. Smith*. Edited by Anthony Leahy and W. J. Tait. Occasional Publications 13. London: Egypt Exploration Society.

Russmann, Edna R. 1989. *Egyptian Sculpture: Cairo and Luxor*. Austin: University of Texas Press.

Sadek, Ashraf I. 1987. *Popular Religion in Egypt During the New Kingdom*. HÄB 27. Hildesheim: Gerstenberg.

Simpson, William Kelly, ed. 2003. *The Literature of Ancient Egypt: An Anthology of Stories, Instructions, and Poetry*. New Haven: Yale University Press.

Smith, Stuart Tyson. 1998. "Nubia and Egypt: Interaction, Acculturation, and Secondary State Formation from the Third to First Millennium B.C." Pages 256–87 in *Studies in Culture Contact: Interaction, Culture Change, and Archaeology*. Center for Archaeological Investigations Occasional Paper 25. Edited by James G. Cusick. Carbondale: Southern Illinois University.

———. 2003. *Wretched Kush: Ethnic Identities and Boundaries in Egypt's Nubian Empire*. London: Routledge.

———. 2007. "Death and Tombos: Pyramids, Iron and the Rise of the Napatan Dynasty." *Sudan and Nubia* 11:2–14.

———. 2014. "Desert and River: Consumption and Colonial Entanglements in Roman and Late Antique Nubia." Pages 89–107 in *Inside and Out: Interactions Between Rome and the Peoples on the Arabian and Egyptian Frontiers in Late Antiquity*. Edited by Jitse H. F. Dijkstra and Greg Fisher. Late Antique History and Religion 8. Leuven: Peeters.

Smith, Stuart Tyson, and Michele R. Buzon. 2014a. "Colonial Entanglements: 'Egyptianization' in Egypt's Nubian Empire and the Nubian Dynasty." Pages 431–50 in *Proceedings of the Twelfth International Conference for Nubian Studies, 01.–06. August 2010*. Edited by Derek A. Welsby and Julie R. Anderson. Leuven: Peeters.

———. 2014b. "Identity, Commemoration and Remembrance in Colonial Encounters: Burials at Tombos During the Egyptian New Kingdom Empire and Its Aftermath." Pages 185–215 in *Remembering and Commemorating the Dead: Recent Contributions in Bioarchaeology and Mortuary Analysis from the Ancient Near East*. Edited by Benjamin Porter and Alex Boutin. Boulder: University Press of Colorado.

———. 2017. "Colonial Encounters at New Kingdom Tombos: Cultural Entanglements and Hybrid Identity." Pages 613–28 in *Nubia in the New Kingdom: Lived Experience, Pharaonic Control and Local Traditions*. Edited by Neal Spencer, Anna Stevens, and Michaela Binder. Leuven: Peeters.

Spencer, Neal. 2014. "Creating and Re-Shaping Egypt in Kush: Responses at Amara West." *JAEI* 6:42–61.

Török, László. 1997. *The Kingdom of Kush: Handbook of the Napatan-Meroitic Civilization*. HdO 31. Leiden: Brill.

———. 2002. *The Image of the Ordered World in Ancient Nubian Art: The Construction of the Kushite Mind, 800 BC–300 AD*. PÄe 18. Leiden: Brill.

———. 2009. *Between Two Worlds: The Frontier Region Between Ancient Nubia and Egypt, 3700 BC–AD 500*. PÄe 29. Leiden: Brill.

Vila, André. 1980. *La nécropole de Missiminia, I, Les sepultures napatéennes*. Paris: Centre National de la Recherche Scientifique.

CHAPTER 25

Hosea 1–3 as the Key to the Literary Structure and Message of the Book

Eric J. Tully

SOMETIMES AN AUTHOR uses a vivid story or motif so powerful that it captures the imagination and subsequently dominates one's view of the entire literary work. One thinks, for example, of the story of the Trojan Horse in Virgil's *Aeneid* or Rhett's dismissal of Scarlet at the end of *Gone with the Wind*. Even those who have never read the works still know these specific episodes and feel as though they have a sense of the whole. In the same way, the story of the prophet Hosea buying back his wife in the midst of her adultery encapsulates the subsequent fourteen chapters of oracles in the book. The introductory prophetic sign-act in Hos 1 and 3 not only hooks the reader's interest, it provides a powerful analogy and conceptual framework for thinking about rebellion, judgment, and reconciliation in YHWH's relationship with Israel.

However, the significance of Hos 1–3 as an introduction to the book goes beyond this conceptual conditioning. The three chapters are also key to the book in two additional ways. First, they forecast the three-fold pattern that organizes the macrostructure of the oracles in chapters 4–14. Second, they introduce the distinctive theological themes in the book that arise out of that structure.

Chapters 1–3 and the Macrostructure of the Book

The book of Hosea has a reputation for challenging interpreters with its obscure linguistic constructions and uncertain historical allusions. In addition, although its message is straightforward, the book has frequently defied attempts to discern a coherent macrostructure that gives shape to the literary work as a whole while logically connecting the various oracles from the prophet. Robert Chisholm writes that the book appears "to be a loose anthology of speeches rather than a tightly structured collection."[1] A number of commentaries on Hosea reflect this view by identifying the contents of successive units and subunits in the book without attempting to subordinate them to one another or to show how each section contributes to an overall,

---

I am grateful for the opportunity to offer this essay in honor of James Hoffmeier. Jim was my professor in my MDiv program at TEDS and then a friend and colleague in the department. He has been a model to me of rigorous, top-level scholarship combined with faithful conviction, church ministry, and love for his family and students. I have always appreciated his humorous comments and his wisdom in faculty meetings.

1. Robert B. Chisholm, *Handbook on the Prophets: Isaiah, Jeremiah, Lamentations, Ezekiel, Daniel, Minor Prophets* (Grand Rapids: Baker Academic, 2002), 336.

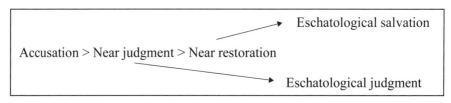

FIGURE 25.1. Periods of judgment and restoration.

progressive argument.[2] I argue, along with other recent commentators, that the book of Hosea does have a sophisticated macrostructure, anticipated three times in a threefold pattern in chapters 1–3.[3]

Preexilic prophets typically speak on behalf of YHWH in reference to five time periods relative to their own point of standing (see fig. 25.1). First, they speak about the past and describe the ways that Israel, Judah, or another nation has broken the covenant and sinned against YHWH. Second, they predict that in the near future—that is, within history—YHWH will judge that nation by depriving it of his good gifts or destroying it by means of conquest and/or exile. Third, they predict that following that judgment, YHWH will restore the nation within history by bringing them back from exile or reversing the predicted consequences. Fourth, they draw upon temporal judgment and extend it to announce eschatological judgment when YHWH will secure permanent victory over his enemies. Finally, they draw upon the imagery of temporal restoration and extend it to a time when God will permanently and totally redeem his people, both spiritually and physically. He will be vindicated, his people will know him in blessing and restored relationship, and the nations will stream to Jerusalem to worship him. While all five of these phases are evident in a book like Isaiah, other prophets speak only to some of them.

The first three chapters of Hosea are structured according to the first, second, and fifth of these phases: accusation, temporal judgment in the near future, and ultimate reconciliation in the indeterminate, eschatological future.[4] This three-phase pattern is found in the introduction to the sign-act (1:2–2:3 [1:2–2:1]), in the application of the sign-act to the relationship between YHWH and Israel (2:4–25 [2:2–23]), and in the recapitulation and extension of the sign-act (3:1–5).[5] This pattern in the introductory

2. See, e.g., James L. Mays, *Hosea: A Commentary*, OTL (London: SCM, 1969); Hans Walter Wolff, *Hosea: A Commentary on the Book of the Prophet Hosea*, Hermeneia (Philadelphia: Fortress, 1974); Thomas E. McComiskey, "Hosea," in *The Minor Prophets: An Exegetical and Expository Commentary* (Grand Rapids: Baker Academic, 2009), 1–237; A. A. Macintosh, *A Critical and Exegetical Commentary on Hosea*, International Critical Commentary 28 (Edinburgh: T&T Clark, 2014).

3. See, e.g., Francis I. Andersen and David Noel Freedman, *Hosea*, AB 24 (New York: Doubleday, 1980); Douglas K. Stuart, *Hosea–Jonah*, Word Biblical Commentary 31 (Waco, TX: Word, 1987); Duane A. Garrett, *Hosea, Joel: An Exegetical and Theological Exposition of Holy Scripture*, NAC 19A (Nashville: Broadman & Holman, 1997); J. Andrew Dearman, *The Book of Hosea*, NICOT (Grand Rapids: Eerdmans, 2010). See also Eric J. Tully, *Hosea: A Handbook on the Hebrew Text*, Baylor Handbook on the Hebrew Bible (Waco, TX: Baylor University Press, 2018).

4. The prophet likely deals only with these three phases because he is speaking to the Northern Kingdom, which did not see temporal restoration from exile (third phase). He does not address the fourth phase, eschatological judgment, because his primary interest is in the reconciliation of Israel to God.

5. Where Hebrew and English versification differ, Hebrew verse numbers are given first and then English in square brackets.

	Accusation (past)	Temporal judgment (near future)	Ultimate reconciliation (eschatological future)
Sign-act 1:2–2:3 [1:2–2:1];	**1:2–3**	**1:4–9**	**2:1–3 [1:10–2:1]**
Application of sign-act (2:4–25 [2:2–23])	**2:4–10 [2:2–8]**	**2:11–15 [2:9–13]**	**2:16–25 [2:14–23]**
Sign-act (3:1–5)	**3:1 (Gomer and Israel)**	**3:2–4 (Gomer and Israel)**	**3:5 (Israel)**
First set of oracles	**4:1–8:14**	**9:1–10:15**	**11:1–11**
Climax of the book	**11:1–4**	**11:5–7**	**11:8–11**
Second set of oracles	**12:1–15 [11:12–12:14]**	**13:1–14:1 [13:1–16]**	**14:2–9 [1–8]**

FIGURE 25.2. The three-phase structural pattern in Hosea.

chapters anticipates and provides an interpretive guide for the oracles in chapters 4–14, which are arranged in parallel structural panels. The prophet moves from accusation to temporal judgment to ultimate reconciliation in 4:1–11:11 and again in 12:1–14:9 [11:12–14:8]. In addition, the three-phase pattern structures chapter 11, which is the climax of the book. See figure 25.2. The book is structured as shown in figure 25.3[6]

Previous scholars have observed the interaction between accusation/judgment and restoration in the book. In a series of four articles, Charles Silva argues for six cycles in the book, each of which progresses from judgment to restoration.[7] J. Andrew Dearman also identifies repeating units that move from judgment to salvation in chapters 4–14, but in two larger sections. YHWH makes his case once in 4:1–11:11 and a second time in 11:12–14:8.[8]

My own analysis of the book generally confirms the work of Silva and Dearman in terms of the progression from judgment to salvation. However, I differ from them at significant points. First, Silva's short cycles reveal the pattern in smaller units throughout the book, including in chapters 1–3. However, his divisions sometimes unnaturally

6. This image is adapted from my book, *Hosea: A Handbook on the Hebrew Text*, 4.

7. Charles H. Silva, "Literary Features in the Book of Hosea," *BSac* 164 (2007): 34–48; Silva, "The Literary Structure of Hosea 1–3," *BSac* 164 (2007) 181–97; Silva, "The Literary Structure of Hosea 4–8," *BSac* 164 (2007) 291–306; Silva, "The Literary Structure of Hosea 9–14," *BSac* 164 (2007) 435–53. He outlines the book as follows:

Prologue: Superscription (1:1)
I. Hosea's Marriage and Family (1:2–3:5)
    a. Cycle A (1:2–2:1)
    b. Cycle B (2:2–23)
    c. Cycle C (3:1–5)
II. Hosea's Prophetic Oracles (4:1–14:8)
a. Cycle D (4:1–6:3)
b. Cycle E (6:4–11:11)
c. Cycle F (11:12–14:8)
Epilogue: Wisdom Saying (14:9) (English versification)

8. Dearman, *Book of Hosea*, vi–vii. Dearman uses English versification.

		1:1 :Superscription		
	Sign-act:	Gomer and Israel are two adulterous wives, but there is hope (1:2–2:3 [1:2–2:1]		
Application of the Sign-Act to Israel	Accusation	She goes to adulterous lovers for gifts (בִּיר) (2:4–10) [2:2–8]	Accusation (ריב): idols, political schemes and manipulative worship (4:1–8:14) • Introduction to YHWH's case (4:1–3) • The wicked priest and the illegitimate cult (4:4–19) • Israel does not truly seek YHWH (5:1–15) • Call to return to YHWH (rejected) (6:1–3) • Israel and Judah are entrenched in covenant violations (6:4–7:2) • Israel is like an oven and a cake (7:3–10) • Israel is like a dove and a bow (7:11–16) • Israel has rejected the good (8:1–3) • Summation: idols, political schemes and manipulative worship (8:4–14)	Accusation (ריב): Israel is not like their father Jacob (12:1–15 [11:12–12:14])
Application of the Sign-Act to Israel	Temporary judgment	He will take away her gifts and leave her desolate (2:11–15) [2:9–13]	YHWH will destroy Israel's food, children, cult sites, and the nation itself (9:1–10:15) • YHWH will destroy their hope: no food (9:1–9) • YHWH will destroy their hope: no children (9:10–17) • YHWH will destroy their cult sites (10:1–8) • YHWH will destroy the nation itself (10:9–15)	YHWH has become Israel's enemy (13:1–14:1 [13:1–16])
	Ultimate reconciliation	He will put away her lovers and establish a new relationship (2:16–25) [2:14–23]	YHWH's resolve and Israel's repentance will lead to relationship (11:1–11)	Relationship will be restored through repentance (14:2–9 [14:1–8])
	Sign-act:	Gomer and Israel are two wives, awaiting full reconciliation (3:1–5)		
				14:10 [14:9]: Postscript

FIGURE 25.3. The macrostructure of Hosea.

divide discrete poems that have an internal coherence, and he does not recognize the large macro units in chapters 4–14.[9] On the other hand, Dearman discerns the progression from judgment to restoration in the large macro units in chapters 4–14. They each see part of the structure. Second, both Silva and Dearman understand the pattern to be two parts: accusation/judgment and restoration. They merge the retrospective accusation of Israel's sin and the prospective judgment, yet these are separate in the text. I argue that the pattern consists of three distinct parts in each case: Israel's failings in the past, future consequences, and final restoration. I also divide subunits differently, see the three-phase pattern at work in chapter 11, and note additional lexical correspondences between sections.

The book of Hosea does not contain many formal features that introduce or conclude units. This results in a "blurring of the edges of individual units of speech" and creates difficulty in discerning the structure.[10] As a result, the primary way we discern the units and overall structure is by topic: internal coherence and distinction from the adjacent unit. Douglas Stuart writes, "the unity of a passage is evident . . . in subject matter, theological categories, tone, and general logic—things which by their nature cannot be quantified."[11]

Prophetic Sign-Act (1:2–2:3 [1:2–2:1] and 3:1–5)

Following the superscription in 1:1, the book begins in 1:2–2:3 [1:2–2:1] with YHWH's instruction to Hosea to marry an אֵשֶׁת זְנוּנִים ("a wife of fornication") and יַלְדֵי זְנוּנִים ("children of fornication").[12] YHWH is explicit that this is to function as a sign-act to illustrate Israel's covenant unfaithfulness to him. This is the first accusation panel (1:2–3). The focus of this unit is on the meaning of the names of the three children, all of which portend temporal judgment (1:4–9). The first name, "Jezreel" (יִזְרְעֶאל), announces bloodshed upon Israel, the second, "Not Pitied" (לֹא רֻחָמָה), proclaims that YHWH will no longer show mercy, and the third, "Not My People" (לֹא עַמִּי), signals a break in the covenant relationship.

Hosea frequently juxtaposes oracles of judgment and oracles of restoration without an explicit transition. Suddenly pivoting to a statement of hope, in 2:1–3 [1:10–2:1], he announces that the Israelites and Judahites will be reconstituted as a people.[13] In addition, their names will be reversed. In the great day of "Jezreel" (2:2) (יִזְרְעֶאל

---

9. E.g., 11:1–11 is a discrete unit that begins with accusation, progresses to judgment, and concludes with a declaration of future restoration. As a unit, it speaks to YHWH's determination to redeem Israel in spite of her determination to rebel. All eleven verses constitute an oracle of deliverance. In Silva's understanding, however, 11:8–11 become the restoration component of Cycle E (6:4–11:11), which destroys the internal integrity of the poem.

10. Mays, *Hosea*, 5.

11. Stuart, *Hosea–Jonah*, 89.

12. The statement that the children were also characterized by זְנוּנִים likely foreshadows the role that their names play in Hosea's message. The statement is anticipatory: Hosea will have children, and they will be symbols of Israel, which is promiscuous. See Andersen and Freedman, *Hosea*, 168. Unless otherwise noted, all translations are mine.

13. The statement וְעָלוּ מִן־הָאָרֶץ likely is a metaphor for sprouting like a plant (repopulation) rather than return from exile, since it is uncommon to use אֶרֶץ to refer to foreign nations, see Garrett, *Hosea, Joel*, 73; Macintosh, *Critical and Exegetical Commentary on Hosea*, 33.

1:11]]), "Not My People" (לֹא עַמִּי) will become "My People" (עַמִּי) and "Not Pitied" (לֹא רֻחָמָה) will become "Pitied" (2:1] 2:3) (רֻחָמָה]).

Thus 1:2–2:3 [1:2–2:1] is a discrete unit, indicated by YHWH's address to Hosea regarding the sign-act, reference to Israel in the third-person, and the significance of the children's names as prophetic symbols. This first unit is distinct from the next one (beginning in 2:4 [2:2]), which begins with the announcement of a רִיב ("case") and addresses the "children" (the people of Israel) directly with second-person plural verbs and pronouns.

Following 2:4–2:25 [2:2–23], the sign-act is revisited in 3:1–5. This unit concludes the first three introductory chapters by presenting Hosea's relationship with Gomer more vividly as a representation of YHWH's relationship with Israel.[14] Chapter 3 is also organized according to the three phases that form the book's structure. The accusation comes in 3:1, when YHWH reviews the sin of Gomer ("loved by another and commits adultery") and that of Israel ("though they turn to other gods"). Hosea 3:2–4 announce temporary judgment. Although Hosea will hire Gomer back (3:2), he will abstain from sexual intercourse from her for many days (3:3; יָמִים רַבִּים).[15] In the same way, YHWH will distance himself from his people for many days (3:4; יָמִים רַבִּים).[16] In 3:5, Hosea predicts that in the end, there will be ultimate reconciliation. The eschatological locus of this statement is indicated by the preposition אַחַר ("after"), the reference to "David their king" (דָּוִד מַלְכָּם), and especially the expression אַחֲרִית הַיָּמִים ("latter days").

The Application of the Sign-Act to Israel (2:4–25 [2:2–23])

In 2:4–25 [2:2–23], the prophet applies the sign-act to Israel in more detail. He begins with family language such as "mother" (2:4 [2]), "children" (2:6 [4]), "lovers" (2:9 [7]), and "husband" (2:9 [7]). As the unit progresses, however, it becomes increasingly clear that the oracle applies to YHWH and Israel, not to Hosea and Gomer. He refers to killing her (2:5 [3]) and having no mercy on her children (2:6 [4]). Because the people (third-person plural) used his gifts for Baal (2:10 [8]), his response will be to put an end to her religious festivities (2:13 [11]) and to destroy her crops (2:14 [12]). Beginning in 2:15 [13], the speaker is explicitly YHWH (see also 2:18 [16], 22 [20], 23 [21], 25 [23]). Thus, the oracle is not part of the sign-act, but the sign-act is in the background, bringing all of its social, moral, and emotional associations to bear. The unit consists of three distinct movements: accusation of past sins in 2:4–10 [2:2–8], announcement

14. In 3:1, the כְּ preposition explicitly compares the two, as does the כִּי conjunction at the beginning of 3:4.

15. Hosea says to Gomer לֹא תִזְנִי ("you must not fornicate") and לֹא תִהְיִי לְאִישׁ ("you must not belong to a man") and then וְגַם־אֲנִי אֵלַיִךְ ("and also I will be [so] toward you"). The question is whether Hosea's final statement is in contrast or continuity to his first two statements. I understand it as continuity, based on the parallel statement regarding YHWH/Israel in the next verse. Just as Gomer is forbidden from sexual relations with a man, Hosea is going to abstain from sexual relations with her as well. This is an extension of the sign-act; YHWH will also make a temporary break in his relationship with Israel (3:4).

16. In 3:4, the list of things that Israel must do without alternates between legitimate and illegitimate items related to their worship of YHWH. Just as Gomer will cease for a time from both illegitimate (lovers) and legitimate (husband) sexual partners, Israel will be without both illegitimate and legitimate means of worship.

of temporary judgment (2:11–15 [2:9–13], and the promise of ultimate reconciliation (2:16–25 [2:14–23]).

The first subunit, 2:4–10 [2:2–8], is set apart from the preceding subunit (1:2–2:3 [1:2–2:1]) by the use of the root רִיב√, which occurs only in 2:4; 4:1, 4; and 12:3 in the book. Each of these three occurrences (combining 4:1, 4) initiates an accusation phase in the overall structure (see fig. 24.3 above). YHWH describes the unfaithfulness of Israel throughout the section. The leadership is characterized by her "fornications" (זְנוּנֶיהָ) and "adulteries" (נַאֲפוּפֶיהָ) in 2:4 [2] and in 2:7 [5].[17] The people are character-ized by fornication (זְנוּנִים) as well (2:6 [4], 9 [7]). While it is true that the threat of consequences is found in 2:4b–5 [2b–3], 8–9 [6–7], the main point of this is to under-score her guilt.[18]

The second subunit, 2:11–15 [9–13], forecasts temporary judgment. The word "therefore" (לָכֵן) in 2:11 signals the transition from actions to consequences.[19] This unit is set apart by the predominance of first-person *yiqtol* and irrealis *qatal* verbs that, in the context, refer to the future rather than the past.[20] YHWH states that he will remove all of the good gifts that he had given to her: the grain, wine, wool, and flax (2:11 [9]), the covering of her lewdness (2:12 [10]), her rejoicing and festivals (2:13 [11]), and her crops (2:14 [12]). In a biting play on words, he states that he will "snatch away" (נצל√) the gifts, and that no one will be able to rescue (נצל√) her from his judgment.[21]

The final subunit in 2:4–25 [2:2–23] concerns ultimate reconciliation in 2:16–25 [14–23]. In 2:16 [14] there is a sudden change of topic when YHWH announces that he will coax her back into relationship with him with the verb פתה√ ("entice") and the collocation דבר + עַל + לֵב√ ("to coax").[22] He signals the transition with another use of "therefore" (לָכֵן). Whereas the preceding section referred to the future with *yiqtol* and irrealis *qatal* verbs, here he signals an eschatological horizon with the expression בַּיּוֹם־הַהוּא ("in that day"; 2:18 [16], 20 [18], 23 [21]). The promises in this section cancel or reverse the threats in the former section. Her children were killed by wild animals (2:14 [12]), now he will make a covenant with the animals (2:20 [18]). He had destroyed her vineyards (2:14 [12]), now he will give her new ones (2:17 [15]).

2:4–25 [2–23] forms the core of the introduction to the book and serves two primary functions. First, the passage applies the sign-act to the nation and goes into greater detail concerning Israel's infidelity to the covenant and YHWH's response. These details are

---

17. Garrett argues that the "mother" is a reference to the leadership and institutions of the nation, who have led the people to be unfaithful; Garrett, *Hosea, Joel*, 39. The children of fornication (זְנוּנִים) are then the common people who have learned from their "mother" and will therefore share the same punishment; Macintosh, *Critical and Exegetical Commentary on Hosea*, 46.

18. 2:5 [3] states that she should put away her adultery *lest* (פֶּן) he strip her naked. Likewise, YHWH will hedge up her way (2:8 [6]) in order to frustrate her consistent unfaithfulness.

19. The word לָכֵן ("therefore") also occurs previously in 2:8 [6]. The significance of the word in 2:11 [9], however, is its use in conjunction with a sharp change in topic to a list of judgment oracles.

20. See 2:11a, 11b, 12, 13, 14a, 14b, 15 [2:9a, 9b, 10, 11, 12a, 12b, 13]. Except for the *wayyiqtol*, verbs in Hebrew express aspect, not tense. However, the imperfective viewpoint aspect of the *yiqtol* and the irrealis use of the *qatal* are most commonly used in nonpast situations.

21. The verb נצל√ means "to take something without consent." Thus in 2:11 [9] it refers to his taking back the gifts even though she does not want to give them up, and in 2:12 [10] it refers to the inability to deliver her from YHWH without his consent.

22. For the latter expression, see Gen 34:3; 50:21; Judg 19:3; Ruth 2:13; Isa 40:2.

then greatly expanded again in chapters 4–14. Thus, they serve as a transition between the sign-act and the extended treatment in Hosea's oracles. The passage's second function is to establish the pattern of YHWH's response, which will form the structure of the rest of the book to follow. Israel's sin will lead to inescapable judgment in the short term but, following that judgment, YHWH will reconcile the nation to himself.

YHWH's First Case: Accusation (4:1–8:14)

The units and subunits in chapters 4–14 are complex and sometimes mix elements of past accusation and future judgment or restoration. What must be identified in each case is the overall point of the unit. The goal is to avoid reductionism on the one hand, and the fragmentation of units on the other.

YHWH's first case against Israel begins with accusation in 4:1–8:14. The prophet introduces the case in 4:1–3 with the word ריב√ (cf. 2:4; 4:1; 12:3, which introduce the primary accusation panels of the structure). In the remainder of the lengthy unit, he describes the various ways that Israel's unfaithfulness to YHWH is manifested: cultic idolatry, manipulative worship, and trust in foreign political and military alliances. In 4:4–19, he addresses the illegitimate and unorthodox cult. The first eleven verses attack the priesthood directly.[23] I understand the priest addressed with singular forms in 4:4–6 to be a general address to the priesthood, rather than a specific individual.[24] In 4:12–19, the focus broadens from the priesthood to the cult and worship as a whole. This segment is marked off by an *inclusio* of the word רוּחַ in 4:12 and 4:19, which refers to the *Zeitgeist* or the "spirit of the age" that creates the philosophical and social foundation for their rebellion.

The third subunit is found in 5:1–15. It opens with a plural imperative addressed to the priests, and then expands to the broader leadership. The theme that dominates this unit is the failure to seek YHWH. They do not return to God (5:4), they seek (בקשׁ√) YHWH, but will not find him (5:6); they persist in going after what is worthless (5:11). Therefore, YHWH will go to his place until they seek (בקשׁ√; שׁחר√) him.

In 6:1–3, there is a brief interlude in which Hosea issues a call to repentance.[25] Yet, as this call is juxtaposed to a description of Israel's determined covenant violations in 6:4–7:2, it only serves to intensify the incrimination. Ironically, Israel appears to be faithful through their fastidious observance of cultic stipulations, but they reject true

23. At the end of 4:4, the MT reads עַמְּךָ כִּמְרִיבֵי כֹהֵן. I revocalize עמך to עִמֶּךְ ("with you"). כמריבי is either the noun מְרִיבָה ("my contention") with a 1cs suffix or the noun רִיב with a suffix, preceded by כִּי and an enclitic מ, see Willibald Kuhnigk, *Nordwestsemitische Studien Zum Hoseabuch*, Biblica et Orientalia, Sacra Scriptura Antiquitatibus Orientalibus Illustrata 27 (Rome: Biblical Institute Press, 1974), 30–31; Stuart, *Hosea–Jonah*, 72. The last word, כֹּהֵן is a vocative.

24. The "children" in 4:6 are not the biological children of the priest, but rather those who depend upon the priesthood for truth and leadership, but have been led astray.

25. Some see this as a false or half-hearted repentance by the people, see David Allan Hubbard, *Hosea: An Introduction and Commentary*, Tyndale Old Testament Commentary (Downers Grove, IL: InterVarsity Press, 2009), 125; Mays, *Hosea*, 94. However, the first-person plural verbs and pronouns are more likely Hosea appealing to the people. He includes himself for rhetorical effect: he is one of them and knows what must be done.

knowledge of God (6:4–6). This is shown in their transgression of ethical stipulations: they are characterized by murder, theft and evil deeds (6:7–7:2).[26]

The next two units each contain two metaphors, which give shape to their contents. The first (7:3–10) uses imagery of baking and cakes. Hosea first compares Israel to an oven that is operated by an incompetent baker. Their sin heats up and breaks out like flames (7:4, 6, 7). The imagery shifts in 7:8–10 when Israel is compared to a cake that is not baked properly. It is mixed with the peoples, a reference to attempted foreign alliances (7:8a). As a result, it will be ruined and inedible (7:8b). The next subunit, 7:11–16, compares Israel to a dove and a faulty bow. Just as a dove flies from place to place without sense, (7:11–12), the bow is incapable of hitting its target (7:14–16).

A short subunit, 8:1–3, announces invasion as a response to Israel's rejection of YHWH. This anticipates Hosea's "closing statement" in 8:4–14. Here Hosea revisits all three evidences of covenant unfaithfulness presented in the previous subunits. They are guilty of political schemes (8:4, 8–10), idolatry (8:5), and the appearance of ortho-dox cultic ritual without true commitment (8:11–13). Hosea concludes that because Israel has forgotten his maker, YHWH will destroy his cities and strongholds (8:14). This anticipates the next major unit, which focuses on the temporal punishment that YHWH will bring upon Israel.

4:1–8:14 contains both accusations of sin and predictions of judgment, but the for-mer dominate the section, while the latter intensify the sense of Israel's guilt. Several key words in 4:1–8:14 are mostly restricted to those passages identified as accusation panels in chapters 1–3, including eleven out of twelve occurrences of verb זנה√ ("for-nicate"; 1:2; 2:7[5]; 3:3; 4:10, 12, 13, 14, 14, 15, 18; 5:3; 9:1), five out of five occurrences of זְנוּנִים ("fornication"; 1:2; 2:4[2], 6[4]; 4:12; 5:4), and five out of five occurrences of נאף√ ("commit adultery"; 3:1; 4:2, 13, 14; 7:4).

YHWH's First Case: Temporary Judgment (9:1–10:15)

Having described Israel's infidelity to YHWH and his covenant in 4:1–8:14, Hosea transitions to a new unit that announces the consequences for that infidelity. The sub-units are distinguished by change in topic, as well as change in speaker. The speakers alternate: YHWH (8:4–14), Hosea (9:1–9), YHWH (9:10–17), and Hosea 10:1–8.[27] Each subunit begins with a brief historical retrospective of Israel's guilt before announcing the consequence for those actions. In 9:1, Israel fornicated, so threshing floor and wine vat will not feed them (9:2). In 9:10, Israel went to Baal-Peor, so Ephraim's glory will fly away (9:11–12). In 10:1, they improved their altars, so now they must bear their guilt (10:2). In 10:9a, they sinned from the days of Gibeah, so now war will overtake them

---

26. Here, Hosea returns again to the theme of the evil priesthood (6:8–10); cf. 4:4–19.

27. The distinctions are not absolute. E.g., in 9:10–17 YHWH is clearly the speaker in most of the pas-sage, referring to the past when he saw their fathers in the wilderness (9:10), threatening to bereave them (9:12), and announcing that he will drive them out of his house (9:15). However, it seems as though the prophet interjects in 9:14 ("Give to them, YHWH, what will you give to them?") and in 9:17 ("My God will reject them"). This is common in the prophets. Because the prophet speaks for YHWH, the two voices are often indistinguishable.

in Gibeah (10:9b).[28] Thus, there is a mix of accusation and judgment, but in this unit the accusations legitimate the judgments, which are the focus.[29]

In 9:1–9, he states that he will take away their food. There are several links to the temporary judgment panel in 2:11–15 [2:9–13] including the word אֶתְנַן/אֶתְנָה ("pay of a prostitute), a technical, uncommon word, which appears only in 2:14 [12] and in 9:1. In 9:10–17, he will kill their offspring. This section is characterized by three pseudosorites in 9:11, 12, and 16, which illustrate that chasing after fertility will only lead to a lack of fertility.[30] In 10:1–8 he will destroy their cult sites.[31] Previously, Israel's "glory" (כְּבוֹדָם) was their offspring (9:11); in 10:5 it is their calf-idol (כְּבוֹדוֹ). Both will be destroyed. The final subunit (10:9–15) announces the destruction of the nation itself. The first-person voice (YHWH) uses three historical allusions to make the connection between past sin and necessary judgment: the nation's sin in the days of Gibeah, YHWH's past "training" of Israel like a calf, and the destruction of Beth-arbel by Shalman.[32]

YHWH's First Case: Ultimate Reconciliation (11:1–11)

In the previous unit (9:1–10:15), Hosea systematically dismantles Israel's hope in her "lovers" (cf. 2:7 [5]). She had turned to idolatry, political alliances, and manipulative ritual to build wealth and gain security, but the result would be the opposite of what she had hoped. YHWH would destroy the things that she sought so desperately. However, although her false hopes will fail her, that does not mean that there is no hope at all.

Like 3:1–5, chapter 11 is another key text in the book, which is itself also structured according to the three-phase pattern: accusation (11:1–4), temporary judgment (11:5–7), and ultimate reconciliation (11:8–11). In 11:1–4, YHWH states that Israel has been wayward from the beginning, alluding to the exodus from Egypt and her immediate turn

28. Andersen and Freedman support this division of subunits based on various historical retrospectives. They view each subunit as a different perspective on the "Spiritual History of Israel," *Hosea*, xii. However, while each subunit briefly reviews a specific rebellion, the segment is focused on the correspondent judgment that will inevitably come as a result.

29. This is in contrast to the mix of accusation and judgment in 4:1–8:14 where the judgment intensified the accusation.

30. A pseudosorites is a rhetorical device in which the speaker states that something will not happen, but even if it does happen, it will be no benefit anyway, Michael Patrick O'Connor, "The Pseudosorites: A Type of Paradox in Hebrew Verse," in *Directions in Biblical Hebrew Poetry*, ed. Elaine B. Follis, JSOTSup 40 (Sheffield: JSOT Press, 1987), 161–72; Richard D. Patterson, "An Overlooked Scriptural Paradox: The Pseudosorites," *JETS* 53 (2010): 19–36. The logic of 9:11 suggests that there will be no conception, but even if there is conception there will be no gestation, and even if there is gestation, there will be no birth. A second pseudosorites appears in 9:11–12, when YHWH states that they will not give birth, but even if they raise children, YHWH will bereave them. The third states that they will not bear fruit (offspring), but even if they do, YHWH will put their children to death.

31. Note the similarity with 3:3–4, which is the temporary judgment panel in 3:1–5. There YHWH states that Israel will be without king, prince, sacrifice, pillar, ephod, or household gods—i.e., both legitimate and illegitimate means of relating to him.

32. The third allusion has defied identification by modern scholars; however, Hosea's audience must have understood the reference. For the major options, see Macintosh, *Critical and Exegetical Commentary on Hosea*, 429. André Lemaire suggests, based on the new Moabite inscription (eighth century), that שלמן is Salamanu of Moab, "Éssai d'interprétation historique d'une nouvelle inscription monumentale moabite," *CRAIBL* 149 (2005): 95–108.

to idolatry.[33] Hosea 11:5–7 predicts judgment in the near future: the coming captivity (11:5), destruction (11:6), and estrangement from YHWH (11:7). However, although Israel deserves judgment, YHWH is conflicted and will not allow that to be the last word (11:8–11). He will not destroy her completely but will reconcile her to himself, bringing her back from captivity in Egypt and Assyria (11:11).[34]

YHWH's Second Case: Accusation (12:1–15 [11:12–12:14])

The units comprising 12:1–14:9 [11:12–14:8] form one final progression through the three-phase pattern of accusation, temporary judgment, and ultimate reconciliation. The units are shorter than those in the previous panels in 4:1–11:11, and also more personal and emotionally raw in their tone. They lead to the final prediction in 14:5–9 [4–8] that, in the future, YHWH and Israel will be fully reconciled, and Israel will once again enjoy his good gifts.

As mentioned above, 12:2 contains the final occurrence of the word רִיב in the book, indicating the beginning of a new accusation panel that corresponds to 2:4–10 [2:2–8] and 4:1–8:14. Hosea organizes the unit around two allusions to Jacob the patriarch (12:3–7 [2–6] and 12:13–14 [12–13]). In the first allusion, Hosea uses Jacob as an example of a schemer who was known for doing wrong for his own interest, but then finally submitted to YHWH (12:5b–6 [4b–5]). Like Jacob, the people of Israel are schemers who attempt to strengthen themselves. Unlike him, however, they have yet to turn to God (12:7 [6]). In the second allusion, Hosea subtly recalls Jacob's scheming for a wife and his own sheep (12:13 [12]). Yet, in the end, Jacob was a part of YHWH's redemptive plan (12:14 [13]). Jacob is then a foil for Israel: If even he finally recognized YHWH as the covenant God, when will Israel do so?

YHWH's Second Case: Temporary Judgment (13:1–14:1 [13:1–16])

In 13:1–14:1 [13:1–16], the prophet again begins with a historical retrospective. Ephraim incurred guilt through Baal, and then increased the sin of idolatry (13:1–2). In the rest of the passage, he predicts ferocious judgment in the near future. There are two interlocking themes in the unit. The first theme is that YHWH is the only possible savior. In 13:4, he states this explicitly: "you did not know a god besides me, and there is no savior except me." He says in 13:9 that he is their "helper" (עֵזֶר) and mentions his own possible role in saving them from Sheol and death (13:14).[35]

---

33. In my view, the apparently obscure 11:2 is an allusion to the Baal-Peor incident (cf. 9:10; Num 25:3–5 as well as references in Deut 4:3 and Ps 106:28). This is suggested by the lexemes in 11:2, including √קרא, √זבח, and בַּעַל. This makes sense of the chronology of 11:1–2: (1) called Israel, (2) led them out of Egypt, (3) they were seduced at Baal-Peor, (4) which led to idolatry. For the reading of the Hebrew at 11:2, see Tully, *Hosea: A Handbook on the Hebrew Text*, 269–70.

34. The use of יוֹנָה ("dove") is a reversal of 7:11. In that chapter, Israel was going to Assyria like doves rather than trusting in YHWH. Now they will return from Assyria like doves.

35. Although YHWH is a possible savior, the context suggests that he will *not* do so. In my view, the first two rhetorical questions in 13:14 assume a negative answer. Therefore, the last phrase in the verse, נֹחַם יִסָּתֵר מֵעֵינָי should be understood in a natural way. YHWH's compassion is "hidden" and therefore inevitable.

The second theme describes the terrible judgment that awaits them. Although YHWH should have been their savior, he has instead become their enemy. They will be like mist, dew, chaff, and smoke that passes away quickly (13:3). YHWH will be like a lion, leopard, and bear to them, and will kill them (13:7–9). In response to their request for a king (13:10; נָתַן√), YHWH will give (נָתַן√) them a king—the king of Assyria (13:11).[36] YHWH announces that he will devastate their land and wealth (13:15), before finally killing them (14:1 [13:16]).

YHWH's Second Case: Ultimate Reconciliation (14:2–9 [1–8])

That 14:2 [1] begins a new unit is evident from the series of four imperatives, combined with the shift in topic from judgment oracle (14:1 [13:16]) to a call to repentance. Hosea, referring to YHWH in the third-person, calls on Israel to "return" (שׁוּבָה), "take" words (קְחוּ), "return" (שׁוּבוּ), and "say" (אִמְרוּ) (14:2–3 [1–2]). Hosea is giving Israel (and now, the reader) a script: they must commit themselves to YHWH (14:3b [2b]) and reject Assyria and idols as their objects of trust (14:4 [3]).[37] Whereas the call to repentance in 6:1–3 is immediately followed by a description of Israel's rebellion, here the call is followed by YHWH's promise to heal them (14:5 [4]). This will lead to agricultural renewal, conveyed with vivid images of natural flourishing (14:6–8 [5–7]), an echo of 2:23–25a [21–23a].

Chapters 1–3 and Key Themes in the Book

In addition to establishing the structural pattern that organizes the oracles in the book of Hosea, the first three chapters also introduce Hosea's distinctive message by anticipating three key themes: Israel's and YHWH's resolve, knowledge and memory, and the relationship between blessing and fidelity.

The first theme centers on Israel's resolve to be faithless and YHWH's corresponding resolve to restore and reconcile her to himself. In 2:7 [5], she states, with intentionality and awareness of her motives, that she will go after her lovers. But in chapter 3, there is no hint of a condition in YHWH's statement that the Israelites will return and seek YHWH and will experience his goodness in the latter days (3:5). This two-sided determination appears in the main body of the book in both accusation and reconciliation. In 5:4, the prophet states that "their deeds do not permit them to return"—they are compelled to certain actions by a "spirit of fornication" (רוּחַ זְנוּנִים). In 11:7, Hosea states that they are "bent" (תְלוּאִים) on apostasy. Yet, YHWH is even more determined to save. His unequivocal statement that he will not "execute his burning anger" (11:9) and the whole of chapter 11 paves the way for chapter 14 where, without any explicit

---

36. The verb in the clause אֶתֶּן־לְךָ מֶלֶךְ בְּאַפִּי is often translated as past tense (compare the rendering of the Septuagint and Syriac Peshitta). McComiskey interprets the verb as present tense, suggesting that this is a reference to the general failure of the monarchy, "Hosea," 221. It is Garrett's suggestion that this is an ironic statement oriented toward the future, announcing submission to the king of Assyria in exile, *Hosea, Joel*, 261.

37. Assyria is likely a metonymy for any nation to which they would go for help, rather than to YHWH.

statement that Israel has repented, the reconciliation with YHWH and its attendant blessing are lavishly described.

The second theme involves knowledge (and ignorance) and memory (and forgetting). The book contains numerous occurrences of ידע√ ("know"), בין√ ("understand"), זכר√ ("remember") and שׁכח√ ("forget") in both verbal and nominal forms. The first of these comes in 2:10 [8] when YHWH states, "she did not know that I gave her the grain, the wine, and the oil." Knowledge first implies an accurate understanding of reality, which leads to skillful actions and therefore to success. Because Israel does not know the true source of blessing, she has erred. This anticipates a fuller exploration of knowledge in the remainder of the book. Israel has forsaken YHWH for fornication and wine, which take away understanding (4:10). Furthermore, when she began to experience the consequences of her infidelity, she did not understand what foreigners were doing to her (7:9) or that it was YHWH who had healed (11:3). Yet when the days of punishment come, then she will know (9:7).

Knowledge, an accurate assessment of reality, is also used to describe its natural conclusion: commitment to YHWH. In 2:22 [20], YHWH states that when Israel is fully reconciled to him, then she will know him (2:20). Yet, for now, Israel does not know YHWH; this is the basis of the accusation (4:1). Israel has rejected knowledge and forgotten (שׁכח√) the law of her God (4:6). The people are without understanding (4:14) (לֹא־יָבִין), led astray by a spirit of fornication so that they do not know God (4:12, 19; 5:4). Hosea appeals to his audience, "Let us strive to know YHWH" (6:3), but he is rejected. YHWH desires knowledge of God and covenant faithfulness (חֶסֶד) rather than burnt offerings (6:6). Israel has forgotten his maker (8:14).

This theme of knowledge also depicts YHWH's interaction with Israel: he knows their sins and remembers their evil (5:3; 7:2), and makes known certain judgment (5:9). Now, he will remember their iniquity and punish their sins (8:13; 9:9). The majority of the knowledge theme occurs within and contributes to accusation and temporal judgment within the structure.

The third and final theme considers the relationship between blessing and fidelity. This is perhaps the most significant theme in the book and constitutes Hosea's primary distinctive contribution among the prophetic books. Blessing, including material and agricultural abundance as well as security, is first of all the motivation for Israel's apostasy. In 2:7 [5], Israel explicitly states that she is adulterous and goes after other lovers,[38] abandoning YHWH, because she believes they will give her bread, water, wool, flax, oil, and drink. When that fails, she decides to return to her first husband (אִישִׁי הָרִאשׁוֹן) for he was able to offer more. Thus, there is a competition between YHWH and competing lovers over who will more competently "deliver the goods" and provide blessing. Hosea condemns this attitude, mostly in accusation panels, in the remainder of the book in 5:13; 7:14b; 9:1–2; 10:1; 13:6. In each case, Israel is motivated to worship false gods, attempt political alliances, and pursue illegitimate cult practices in order to bolster their material wealth and security.

YHWH's response to Israel's infidelity, ironically, is to take back his blessings: both material wealth (2:11 [9], 14 [12]) and national security (2:12 [10]). This consequence,

---

38. The *piel* participle מְאַהֲבַי is used exclusively in the Old Testament of illegitimate lovers (see Jer 30:14; Ezek 16:33–37; Ezek 23:5, 9, 22).

raised in chapter 2, is explored in detail in chapters 4–14. As a result of their spiritual adultery, YHWH will cause the land to languish and will remove the animals (4:3). They will eat without satisfaction and fornicate without bearing offspring (4:10). He will take away material blessings of grain (7:7), offspring (9:14) and agriculture (10:4, 8; 13:15), and will have their pregnant women ripped open (13:16). He will also remove their land and security (7:8; 9:15; 13:15b). The prophet also uses imagery of agriculture and childbirth to make various points (10:11, 13; 13:13).

However, eventually YHWH will bring Israel back to himself and they will be reconciled. This results in blessing from YHWH as the gifts connected to the covenant relationship flow freely once again. In 2:20a [18a], YHWH promises to establish a covenant between Israel and nature, which suggests that nature will once again benefit Israel. Furthermore, YHWH will reestablish peace and security (2:20b [18b]). The unit closes with a restarting of the natural and agricultural mechanisms that produce wealth and flourishing.[39] The verb ענה√ here (five times in 2:21–22 [19–20]) means something like "activate," as YHWH starts a chain reaction that once again delivers his gifts to Israel.

The relationship between blessing and allegiance is also seen by tracing the adjective טוֹב ("good") throughout the book. In 2:9, Israel decides that she will return to her first husband because it was better (טוֹב) for her. And the promise of eschatological hope in 3:5 states that Israel will come to YHWH and his goodness (טוּב) in the latter days. These occurrences of the word in the first three chapters anticipate its use in the main structural panels. In the first accusation panel (4:1–8:14), Israel's pursuit of goodness is wrong-headed. In 4:13, she makes idolatrous sacrifices under trees because their shade is "good" (טוֹב). In 8:3 the prophet states that Israel has rejected "the good" (טוֹב), a metonymy for YHWH. In the judgment panel, Israel will lose what she has because she took the "good" (טוֹב) covenantal gifts that YHWH had given and used them to further her idolatrous pursuits (10:1). However, in the end, Israel's prayer will be that YHWH would accept what is good (טוֹב), a reference to her final repentance and submission (14:3).

The book ends in a gentle, intimate dialogue between Ephraim and YHWH in 14:9 [8].[40] Ephraim and YHWH speak in alternating poetic lines. Ephraim rejects idols once and for all. YHWH states that he will answer (ענה√) and look after him. This recalls 2:23 [21], which is in the reconciliation phase of 2:4–25 [2–23]. Ephraim then announces that he is an evergreen tree, flourishing, because he is now rightly related to YHWH. YHWH concludes the verse by acknowledging that he is the source of all good gifts.

---

39. The verb ענה√ is used to describe action and response. In 2:11 [9], YHWH responds to Israel's sin by stopping her agriculture and taking away its products. In 2:17 [15], Israel answers (ענה√) his wooing. In 2:23–24 [21–22], YHWH in turn responds by answering (ענה√) nature so that it delivers for Israel again.

40. See A. S. van der Woude, "Bemerkungen zu einigen umstrittenen Stellen im Zwoelfpropheten-buch," in *Melanges bibliques et orientaux en l'honneur de M. Henri Cazelles*, ed. André Caquot and Matthias Delcor, AOAT 212 (Kevelaer: Butzon & Bercker, 1981) 483–85. For a more detailed discussion, see Tully, *Hosea: A Handbook on the Hebrew Text*, 350–52. Gordis gives example of Biblical Hebrew poetry in which the identity of the speaker is not explicit, Robert Gordis, "Quotations in Biblical, Oriental, and Rabbinic Literature," in *Poets, Prophets, and Sages: Essays in Biblical Interpretation* (Bloomington: Indiana University Press, 1971) 104–59.

The book ends with a postscript (14:10 [9]), filled with wisdom language, which concludes that success comes from following YHWH. One may be a tempted to believe that full fidelity to YHWH may hamper wealth and blessing by cutting off other avenues to the "good life" (such as other deities or political solutions). Yet the opposite is true. The choice is not between YHWH and blessing. The choice is between YHWH *and* blessing, or rebellion against YHWH *and* failure and death. YHWH is the way to truth, and a life of flourishing.

CHAPTER 26

The Egyptian Fortress Commander:
A Career Check Based on Selected Middle and
New Kingdom Examples

Carola Vogel

Introduction

Little is known about the daily life of the minor ranking military and administrative garrison members stationed in both the Middle Kingdom fortresses and the New Kingdom fortress-towns. However, whereas the minor ranking officers do not occur frequently in the official records, the situation looks better for the high-ranking personal including the commanding level.

This paper seeks to shed light on those officials whom we know, either by their titles or their tasks, that they commanded a *mnnw-* or *ḥtm-*fortress. Selected biographies will be examined to show the variety and importance of the commandants' duties, their careers and their close relationship to the royal court.

An examination of titles and functions of fortress commandants requires an investigation of the term "fortress" itself. Only by knowing the expressions used by the ancient Egyptians to differentiate between various types of fortresses are we able to approach the question of their overseers. From the earliest evidence onward the term *mnnw* seems the primary expression to be assigned to sites whose military character was predominant.[1] Deriving from the verbal root *mn* "to last, to withstand" this assignment was well chosen to meet a fortress's most important task, to endure against possible attacks.

Besides the term *mnnw* further expressions were chosen to distinguish different types of fortresses and fortress-towns.[2] However, over time *mnnw-*fortresses, as well as other fortified sites, seem to have varied in architecture and nature. Whereas *mnnw-*towns of New Kingdom Nubia seem to have been rather civil than military settlements, their Libyan Nineteenth Dynasty namesakes were not. Therefore, although

---

It is with great pleasure to dedicate this short article to my estimated colleague James K. Hoffmeier, with whom I share a deep interest in Egypt's ancient fortifications.

1. See Carola Vogel, *Ägyptische Festungen und Garnisonen bis zum Ende des Mittleren Reiches*, HÄB 46 (Hildesheim: Gestenberg, 2004), 21–22; Ellen Fowles Morris, *The Architecture of Imperialism: Military Bases and the Evolution of Foreign Policy in Egypt's New Kingdom*, PÄe 22 (Leiden: Brill, 2005), 809–14; Claire Somaglino, "La toponymie égyptienne en territoires conquis: Les noms-programmes des menenou," in *Du Sinaï au Soudan: Itinéraires d'une égyptologue; Mélanges offerts au Professeur Dominique Valbelle*, ed. Nathalie Favry, Orient et méditerranée 23 (Paris: de Boccard, 2017), 229–42.

2. For a compilation of the most common terms as well as a list of the known fortresses from the beginnings up to the New Kingdom, see Franck Monnier, *Les forteresses égyptiennes du Prédynastique au Nouvel Empire*, Collection Connaisance de l'Égypte Ancienne 11 (Brussels: Safran, 2010), 190–94.

it is obvious that the Egyptians distinguished different fortress-types textually and archaeology from each other, it remains difficult to categorize these differences. As an in-depth discussion of all known types of fortresses can't be offered here, this paper will concentrate on two crucial types of fortresses and their commandants respectively, the already mentioned *mnnw*-fortresses as well as the so-called *ḥtm*-installations.[3] The latter is known from the mid-Eighteenth Dynasty onward and characterizes a new type of border fort.[4] The following paragraphs present selected examples from the Middle and New Kingdom in chronological order.

Middle Kingdom Examples

The first commanders chosen are known from textual sources found at the Second Cataract. Here, in the neighborhood of the Egyptian Middle Kingdom fortresses, a large number of rock inscriptions refer to soldiers garrisoned within them.[5] They sometimes contain important hints about their titles and duties. In the first two examples given here we are informed about two "overseers of the army," the first a great, the second a regular one who were both in command (*tjez*) of the fortress at Semna-West.

Found in close proximity to the fortress, the inscriptions record Nile Levels, dated to the late Twelfth and early Thirteenth Dynasties. They belong to a group of Middle Kingdom inscriptions originally carved in a rock face below the fortress, which already collapsed before the New Kingdom.[6] The inscriptions were cut off and rescued for the floods of Lake Nasser to be finally moved to the garden of the National Museum in Khartoum in 1968.[7]

Example 1 (FSN, no. 504) naming the commander Rs-snb (reign of Amenemhat IV)

1. *rꜣ nj ḥꜥpj nj rnpt-sp 7(?) ḥr ḥm nj nj-sw.t bj.tj (Mꜣꜥ-ḫrw-Rꜥ) ꜥnḫ ḏt*
2. *r nḥḥ ḫft wnn ḥtmw bj.tj jmj-rꜣ mšꜥ wr*
3. *Rs-snb ḥr ṯz m mnn.w Sḫm-(Ḫꜥj-kꜣ.w-Rꜥ)-mꜣꜥ-ḫrw*

3. The fortified sites and neighboring wells along the Ways of Horus, as represented and labeled in the famous battle reliefs of Seti I in Karnak, were designated by a wide variety of architectural terms, remarkably absent the term *mnnw*. Instead we find: *ḥtm* (= "border fort," only Tjaru/Tell el-Hebua I), *mktr/mkdr* (= "migdol," adopted from the Semitic word for tower), *nḫt* (= "stronghold"), *at* (= "dwelling"), *bḫn* (="fortified structure?"), or *dmi* (= "town/settlement") plus their individual names. Further expressions are: *swnw* ("tower"), *inb* ("wall"), *sbty, ṯsmt, wrsht, tshkr, itḥ, wmt, snb, snbt,* and *ṯꜣrt*.

4. So far, there are only six sites attested that we know were labeled *ḥtm*-fortresses: Senmet, Elephantine, the *ḥtm* at the highland of Coptos (Wadi Hammamat), Tjaru (Tell el-Hebua I), Tjeku (Tell el-Retabeh), and *ḥtm* of the Sea.

5. An extensive study of the corpus was carried out and consequently published by Fritz Hintze, Walter Friedrich Reineke, and Adelheid Burkhardt, *Felsinschriften aus dem sudanesischen Nubien*, Publikation der Nubien-Expedition 1961–1963 (Berlin: Akademie, 1989), henceforth *FSN*.

6. *FSN*, 148.

7. For information on both the current state of conservation of the rescued blocks and their traceable epigraphic evidence, see Elsa Yvanez, *Rock Inscriptions from Semna and Kumma: Epigraphic Study* (Khartoum, Section Française de la Direction des Antiquités du Soudan, 2010). Yvanez was able to discover *FSN*, no. 509 among the fragments, but could not track down the remains of *FSN*, no. 504. http://www.sfdas.com /IMG/pdf/rock-inscrip28e2.pdf.

FIGURE 26.1. FSN, no. 509 [=SNM 34370] naming Rn-snb (perhaps the successor of Rz-snb, reign of Imenemhat-Sobekhotep = Sobekhotep II.

1. Nile level of year 7(?) under the majesty of the king of Upper and Lower Egypt Maa-kheru-ra (=Amenemhat IV), may he live forever,
2. and ever according when the royal sealer, the great overseer of the army,
3. Res-seneb was in command of the fortress of Sekhem-kha-kau-ra-maa-kheru (= Senusret III, justified, is powerful; the Egyptian name for the fortress of Semna-West).[8]

Example 2 (FSN, no. 509 [=SNM 34370]) naming Rn-snb (perhaps the successor of Rz-snb, reign of Imenemhat-Sobekhotep = Sobekhotep II, fig. 26.1)

1. *r₃ nj ḥ'pj nj rnpt-sp 3*
2. *ḥr ḥm nj nj-sw.t bj.tj (Sḫm-R'-ḫwj-t₃.wj)* (Imenemhat-Sobekhotep = Sobekhotep II) *dj 'nḫ dt*
3. *ḫft wnn ḫtmw bj.tj jmj-r₃ mš' Rn-snb*
4. *ḥr tz m mnn.w Sḫm-(Ḫj-k₃.w-R')-m₃'-ḥrw*

1. Nile level of year 3,
2. under the majesty of the king of Upper and Lower Egypt, "Imenemhat-Sobekhotep," who may be given life forever.
3. When the royal seal-bearer, the overseer of the army, Ren-Seneb,
4. was in command of the fortress of "Semna-West."[9]

8. Unless otherwise noted, all translations are the author's.
9. This man is also known from a rock inscription at Aswan. See William M. Flinders Petrie, *A Season in Egypt, 1887* (London: Field & Tuer, 1888), 160, where he is meanwhile promoted to a great overseer of the army.

To gain a better understanding of the two officials from Semna-West a third man shall be introduced who—almost at the same time—also was in charge of a fortress at the Second Cataract.

The inscription naming this individual derives from a Nile level record at Askut and contains the information that this fortress was headed by an official called Sobek's son Ib, who commanded the fortress "Senusret, true of voice" in year 3 of Amenemhat V, Sekhem-ka-Ra.

***Example 3: Rock Inscription Askut 1 (reign of king Sekhem-ka-Ra, year 3)*[10]**

1. *r3 nj ḥʿpj rnpt-sp 3 ḥr ḥm nj*
2. *nj-sw.t bj.tj (Sḫm-k3-Rʿ) ʿnḫ ḏt r nḥḥ*
3. *ḫft wnn šmsw nj ḥq3 Sbk z3 ʾIb*
4. *ḥr ṯz m mnn.w jrj.n*
5. *Snwsrt m3ʿ-ḫrw*

1. Nile level of year 3 under the majesty of
2. the king of Upper and Lower Egypt, Sekhem-ka-Ra (= Amenemhat V), may he live forever and ever,
3. at the time, when the follower/guard of the ruler, Sobek's son Ib
4. was commanding the fortress (= Askut),[11] which
5. Senusret, true of voice, built.

By comparing the three records, the question occurs why Semna-West was commanded by a high-ranking (great) overseer of the army, whereas Askut was headed by a military official whose title, *šmsw nj ḥq3*, reflects proximity to the king, but was clearly of lower rank. In my view this phenomenon can be explained by the different size and significance of the two fortresses. As discussed elsewhere, due to the large number of barracks attested for Semna-West, this fortress must have housed at least five hundred to seven hundred men.[12] On the other hand, Askut, whose main purpose was to protect an enormous granary, possessed just a few barracks that hardly provided more space than for approximately eighty men.

Excursus: The Military Career of Hui-ui-sobek

The military grade of a "follower/guard of the ruler" and his subsequent role at Askut can be better judged by investigating the *cursus honorum* of the famous Twelfth

10. Stuart Tyson Smith, *Askut in Nubia: The Economics and Ideology of Egyptian Imperialism in the Second Millennium B.C.*, Studies in Egyptology (London: Kegan Paul, 1995), 27.
11. I do not follow the translation of Liszka and Kraemer here, who consider this follower as an official under the command of an anonymous superior, see Kate Liszka and Bryan Kraemer, "Evidence for Administration of the Nubian Fortresses in the Late Middle Kingdom: P. Ramesseum 18," *Journal of Egyptian History* 9 (2016): 192: "One inscription from Askut dating to Dynasty 13 notes that the commandant of the fortress held the title *šmsw n ḥk3 ḥr ṯsw m mnnw*, 'šmsw of the Ruler Commanding the Fortress.'"
12. Cf. Vogel, *Ägyptische Festungen und Garnisonen*, 131–132, 259.

dynasty official Hui-ui-Sobek. We know that he started his military career as a simple warrior under Senusret III and ended up as a great city commandant in the reign of Amenemhat III.[13] The second step in his career is of particular interest to us, as it was then that Senusret III promoted him from a regular warrior (*ḥȝwtj*) exercising with seven men in the residence to a follower/guard of the ruler supervising a unit of sixty men. In fact, sixty soldiers was a common size of a unit under command of a "follower/guard of the ruler," this fit well with the supposed number of soldiers garrisoned at Askut during the time of its commander Ib.

In light of this, it seems most likely that, at least in the Middle Kingdom, fortress-commanders were elected according to their latest military rank, to be more precise: the number of subordinates under their command in their former position had to correlate with the size of the garrison they were assumed to head.

It remains unclear if the command of a fortress was considered the perfect choice for soldiers at the end of their active military service in the field—something worth thinking about, as this practice is a well-known phenomenon in various armies until today.

All three fortress-commanders introduced so far bear military titles and, in addition, are termed as *tjezu*. This is the common expression for (fortress) commanders up to the early New Kingdom when the fortresses at the First Cataract and at Buhen were still under the command of *tjezu*-officials who in addition bore the title *zȝ nj-swt*. As proven by the different-sized garrisons, the term *tjezu* is hardly more than a job description and does not say anything about the position of its holder, as the true status of a fortress commandant depends on the size of the garrison he was in charge of.

New Kingdom Examples

In the New Kingdom, a new title occurs in the context of the commanding level of a fortress, the title *idenu*, which seem to replace the former *tjezu*-title—as its holders take care of the *mnnw*-fortress-towns after the Egyptian reconquest and reorganization of Nubia.

The title *idenu*, often explained as deputy, should better be translated with "representative." Officials referred to as *idenu* should not consequently be considered the second man of the fortress. On the contrary, most often they were the number one even in those cases were the fortress-town was headed by two officials, as, for instance, is known for sites like Faras and Soleb. For those and other fortress-towns a subdivision in military and administrative responsibilities is attested by the simultaneous existence of an *idenu* and a *khati-a* governor/mayor.

From the hierarchy reflected in the representations in the tomb of the viceroy Huy I at Thebes (TT 40, reign of Tutankhamun), it becomes clear that in such cases the military commanders were of higher rank than their administrative counterparts, a phenomenon also well-attested for early modern fortresses.[14]

13. Wolfram Grajetzki, *Die höchsten Beamten der ägyptischen Zentralverwaltung zur Zeit des Mittleren Reiches: Prosopographie, Titel und Titelreihen, Achet*, rev. ed., Schriften zur Ägyptologie A2 (Berlin: Achet, 2003), 199–200.

14. Ingeborg Müller, *Die Verwaltung Nubiens im Neuen Reich*, Meroitica 18 (Wiesbaden: Harrassowitz, 2013), 39.

Up to here we have only discussed officials in command of a *mnnw*-fortress. From the time of Thutmose III onward a further term occurs, which refers to a new type of fortification specifically attested in border regions and reflecting tasks resulting from those locations. This term is *ḥtm*, sealing off or locking in.[15]

Whereas New Kingdom *mnnw*-fortresses were under the command of military official termed *idenu*, *ḥtm*-fortresses were—in the majority of the known cases—headed by an *imi-ra*.[16] The most important *ḥtm*-fortress known to us is the fortress of Tjaru (Tell el-Hebua I) at Egypt's northeastern border. At Tjaru, administrative and military duties sometimes overlapped. This might explain why occasionally officials like Nebi under Thutmose IV could even possess both functions, thus they were governors and commandants of the fortress. Nebi's military qualification obviously derives from his experience as a *heri pedschet*, troop commandant, a title frequently attested for fortress commanders in the New Kingdom.[17]

A man whom we know bore both titles, *idenu* of a *mnnw*-fortress and *imi-ra* of a *ḥtm*-fortress, is an official named Penniut. His career leads us back to Nubia.

The Career of Penniut

Till recently, Penniut was primarily recognized as one of the officials present at the promotion of Huy I to viceroy of Kush in his Theban tomb no. 40. Here, Penniut is referred to as the deputy commander of the Tutankhamun *mnnw*-fortress of Faras. As already mentioned above, he is shown in front of his colleague "The *khati-a* from Faras" and hence of higher rank.

New evidence for Penniut as a fortress commandant comes from a stela that was discovered in 1997 by soldiers of the modern Egyptian army stationed at an outpost near Kurkur oasis. Its unique text was published by John Darnell in 2003 and has been subsequently discussed by various scholars.[18] It sheds new light on border patrols and the men involved. The main authority mentioned on the stela is our official Penniut arguing with a *medjay* who failed to fulfill his tasks.

According to the inscription, an anonymous *medjay*-man accused of neglecting his duty defends himself impressively against Penniut by complaining about the inhumanly long distance of approximately forty-two kilometres he has to patrol along the "Western Wall (of the Pharaoh)": "How great are they, the four *jtrw* (ca. 42 km) which I make daily; five times going up (the *gebel*), and five times going down (the *gebel*) so do not let me be replaced by another" (after Darnell 2003).

The vivid discussion between the unnamed *medjay* and his superior documents the human side of Egypt's observation procedures and their subsequent limits. For us of utmost interest is the string of titles Penniut bears on this stela: *imj-rȝ šnwtj Pȝ-n-njwt*, "Overseer of the double granary, Penniut," *ḥȝtj-ʿ m dwȝ(w)t-nfrt Pȝ-n-njwt*, "governor

---

15. Morris, *Architecture of Imperialism*, 804–9.

16. For an exception of the rule, see pAnastasi V = pBM EA 10244 (Miscellanies), 25.2, 26.1 where an official named May is referred to as an *idenu nj Tjeku* (reign of Seti II).

17. Gun Björkman, "Neby, the Mayor of Tjaru in the Reign of Tuthmosis IV," *JARCE* 11 (1974): 43–51.

18. John Coleman Darnell, "A Stela of the Reign of Tutankhamun from the Region of Kurkur Oasis," *SAK* 31 (2003): 73–91.

in Duatnefret, Penniut," *jdnw n(j) Wȝwȝt Pȝ-n-njwt*, "Deputy Commander/Representative of Wawat, Penniut," *sš Pȝ-n-njwt* "Scribe, Penniut," and finally as the title preceding Penniut's speech to the *medjay* the title *imi-rȝ ḫtm*, "fortress commander, Penniut."

I agree with Darnell that the choice of "fortress commander" here suggests that it is in this capacity that Penniut speaks to the *medjay*.[19] Bearing Penniut's position in the tomb of Huy in mind, Darnell favors the idea that the anonymous fortress headed by him must have been Faras.[20] He suggests that Penniut was promoted from the deputy commander of the Tutankhamun *mnnw*-fortress of Faras to its commander. Kate Liszka and others—including myself—rather doubt this interpretation as Faras is not known as a *ḫtm*-fortress at any time.[21] The walled town "Satisfying-the-gods" was termed a *mnnw*-fortress exclusively. The only sites for which the term *ḫtm* is attested in the south are Senmet and Elephantine, both situated at the First Cataract.

In light of this, it seems much more likely to assume that Penniut headed the fortress of Senmet and that it was from this spot that he had to control the western desert including being responsible for medjay units up to Kurkur oasis. This assumption is supported by the representation of Khnum, lord of Senmet in the lunette of the stela. The precise location of Senmet, which was known as a *mnnw*-fortress in the Middle Kingdom, as was Elephantine, is unknown. As I discussed elsewhere, I disagree with its old identification with the island of Biggeh and rather suggest that Senmet was situated in the plain of Shallal at the end of the fortification wall bypassing the First Cataract.[22] Penniut's superior, Huj, viceroy of Kush was holder of the title "overseer of the southern countries." Whereas a couple of colleagues in the north who were bearing the title "overseer of the northern countries" simultaneously were commanders of the most important fortress in their supervised region, hence Tjaru, this pattern is not attested for their southern counterparts.

Apart from the four officials introduced, numerous other commanders would be worth mention. However, at least one further man should be named whose career as a fortress commander at Egypt's Libyan border will broaden our understanding tremendously—not only with respect to Egypt's northwestern border. It is the official Neb-Re who was in command of the *dmj*, i.e., the *mnnw*-fortress at Zawyet Umm el-Rakham.[23] Zawyet Umm el-Rakham, a major fortress-town established next to the modern city of Mersa Matrouh under Ramesses II, has been excavated by the University of Liverpool since 1994 and belonged to a complex system of new fortress-towns stretching along the edge of the western delta and along the Marmarican coast, Kom Firin, and Kom el-Hisn. Presently, the fort is considered as Egypt's farthest western outpost. Material found at the site has produced a wealth of information on both its local tasks and its role within a larger network to gain control along the Marmarican coast in response to a changing relationship with the "Libyans" in the thirteenth

19. Ibid., 79.
20. Ibid., 80.
21. Kate Liszka, "'We Have Come to Serve Pharaoh:' A Survey of the Medjay and Pangrave as an Ethnic Group and as Mercenaries from c. 2300 BCE Until c. 1050" (PhD diss., University of Pennsylvania, 2012), 361–63.
22. Vogel, *Ägyptische Festungen und Garnisonen*, 175–78.
23. Steven R. Snape, *The Complete Cities of Ancient Egypt* (London: Thames & Hudson, 2014), 220.

century BCE.[24] Among the amazing finds at Zawyet Umm el-Rakham, the monuments belonging to an official called Neb-Re deserve special mention. Unfortunately, the rich amount of textual sources referring to his career has not been published yet—but should be shortly by Steven Snape and Glenn Godenho.[25] However, what can be said now is still impressive. Neb-Re belongs to the few officials with evidence for the Gold of Honor under Ramesses II.[26] Among them—perhaps three—officials were rewarded for service in the armed forces. From Neb-Re's statues we learn that he rose from the first charioteer of the king and elite soldier to become head of the garrison at the Libyan border. Among his titles we find "Chief of *medjau* in the foreign land of Libya." This information is of special value as we recall that Penniut, as commandant of a *ḥtm*-fortress, was a superior of a *medjay* who failed to fulfill his tasks. Moreover, Neb-Re is propagandistically referred to as "One who brings an end to the transgressors of his boundary."[27] He proudly claims that it was his responsibility to take care of the supply of grain for his troops by organizing local cultivation and import via the sea by *menesh*-ships. This information is just one of many to come. Neb-Re's titles show the significance of the tasks an Egyptian fortress commandant had to execute. His sensitive job at Egypt's border required special skills and absolute loyalty to the king. It becomes pretty clear that the king relied on his overseers, who had to observe every single action conducted by the fortress-commandants installed in sensitive border regions carefully to ensure that Egypt's economic and political, as well as military interests were guaranteed. For the south it seems obvious that the commandants' primary task, the transhipment of the Nubian gold, which was temporarily stored within the forts, required special attention. With respect to *Zawyet Umm el-Rakham* it looks as if Neb-Re did not meet his master's expectations. At an unknown point in time he became a victim of *damnatio memoriae*.[28]

24. Steven R. Snape, "Vor der Kaserne: External Supply and Self-Sufficiency at Zawiyet Umm el-Rakham," in *Cities and Urbanism in Ancient Egypt: Papers from a Workshop in November 2006 at the Austrian Academy of Sciences*, ed. Manfed Bietak, Ernst Czerny, Irene Forstner-Müller; Denkschriften der Gesamtakademie 60 (Vienna: Österreichische Akademie der Wissenschaften, 2010), 271–88.

25. Steven R. Snape and Glenn Godenho, *Zawyet Umm el-Rakham II: The Monuments of Neb-Re*, forthcoming.

26. Susanne Binder, *The Gold of Honour in New Kingdom Egypt*, Australian Centre for Egyptology Studies 8 (Oxford: Aris & Phillips, 2008), 248, 320–21 = No. 132.

27. Bruce Routledge, *Archaeology and State Theory: Subjects and Objects of Power* (London: Bloomsbury, 2014), 24.

28. Steven R. Snape, "Interesting Times for Neb Re," *Ancient Egypt* 2.2 (2001): 12–16.

CHAPTER 27

Mud-Bricks as a Dating Tool in Egyptian Archaeology

Kei Yamamoto and Pearce Paul Creasman

JAMES K. HOFFMEIER, who has contributed greatly to bridging Egyptology and biblical archaeology, has written extensively on the interpretations of the exodus narrative in the Old Testament.[1] While definitive archaeological evidence for its historicity is still lacking, Hoffmeier has pointed out the numerous descriptions in the exodus that fit the political, social, and cultural pictures of that time. For example, the theme of "hard labor in mortar and brick" (Exod 1:14) reflects the ubiquitous use of, and thus the great demand for, mud-bricks in Egyptian architecture. Having investigated many archaeological sites, from Karnak in Upper Egypt to Tell el-Borg in Sinai, Hoffmeier himself has surveyed, unearthed, and recorded innumerable bricks throughout his distinguished career. In appreciation for his achievement, the present study reviews the issues surrounding the use of bricks as a dating tool in Egyptian archaeology.[2]

Introduction

Since their introduction in the Predynastic period, sun-dried bricks quickly became one of the most common construction materials in ancient Egyptian architecture.[3] Being relatively easy and cheap to manufacture and well-suited for the generally rainless climate of Egypt, mud-bricks were used extensively in construction of houses, granaries, palaces, forts, enclosure walls, chapels, and tombs. Brickworks also formed the cores of some pyramids and foundations of monumental stone temples. They were even employed in construction ramps that were dismantled after the buildings were completed. In rural areas, Egyptians have continued using mud-bricks until well into the twentieth century CE, although fired bricks and "white bricks" offer more durable

---

1. James K. Hoffmeier, *Israel in Egypt: The Evidence for the Authenticity of the Exodus Tradition* (New York and Oxford: Oxford University Press, 1997), passim; Hoffmeier, "Out of Egypt: The Archaeological Context of the Exodus," *BAR* 33.1 (2007) 33–41, 77.

2. Model bricks, usually placed in foundation deposits, are excluded from the present discussion. For these bricks, which are normally smaller than regular architectural bricks, see James M. Weinstein, "Foundation Deposits in Ancient Egypt" (Ph.D. diss., University of Pennsylvania, 1973), 419–21.

3. Marek Chłodnicki, "Beginnings of Mud Brick Architecture in Egypt: A Case Study from Kom C at Tell el Farkha," in *Egypt at Its Origins 4: Proceedings of the Fourth International Conference "Origin of the State. Predynastic and Early Dynastic Egypt," New York, 26th–30th July 2011*, ed. Matthew Douglas Adams, OLA 252 (Leuven: Peeters, 2016), 21–32.

and equally affordable alternatives today.[4] Due to the diverse and enduring usage of mud-bricks, archaeologists working in Egypt and its sphere of influence often encounter this versatile construction material at their sites, regardless of their geographical settings or chronological contexts.

Essentially, mud-bricks are simple, rectangular blocks of compacted soil that have been formed with brick molds (usually made of wood in ancient Egypt) and left out in the sun to dry and harden. If encountered out of archaeological contexts, therefore, they usually cannot be dated easily. Bricks exhibit certain variations in physical properties, and many scholars have variously used and misused these attributes to assign dates to the monuments under investigation.

In 1885, for example, William M. Flinders Petrie surveyed a massive enclosure wall at the western delta site of Naukratis and dated this "Great Temenos" to the Twenty-sixth Dynasty because its bricks were comparable in size (41.4 × 21.1 cm) to the bricks he observed at the nearby site of Kom Firin, which he believed to date from the same dynasty. Petrie claimed that the bricks employed in a Ptolemaic gateway at Kom Firin were notably smaller (37.6 × 18.3 cm), even more so than those of the Thirtieth Dynasty structures found at yet another site, Saft el-Henna, in the southeast delta.[5] He thus implicitly assumed a progressive reduction of brick sizes from the Late period to the Ptolemaic period in this region. Unfortunately, his methodology was erroneous in multiple ways. First, Petrie who did not work at Kom Firin, could not have known the exact history of this complex site and that it was occupied almost continuously from the Ramesside period to the seventh century CE. Second, both brick formats mentioned by Petrie fall within the acceptable ranges from many periods other than Late and Ptolemaic periods respectively. Based on the associated artifacts that can be dated more reliably, Brian Muhs has redated the Great Temenos of Naukratis to the Ptolemaic period despite the use of relatively large brick size.[6]

Gustave Jéquier, writing in 1924, might have been the first to reject the chronological value of the mud-brick size, stating "il est impossible, d'après les mensurations précises des briques, de determiner l'âge d'un monument."[7] Jéquier's opinion, echoed by A. J. Spencer, Barry Kemp, Dieter Arnold, and other experts, still holds true in general.[8] Yet, the reality is that many Egyptologists continue to try dating architectural features based primarily on the brick types.[9] For example, some archaeologists working in Luxor agree that they can distinguish New Kingdom and Late period brickworks on this basis, at least locally. If mud-bricks can indeed be used as a dating tool, at what

4. Another reason for the modern decrease in mud-brick architecture is the regulation against the loss of fertile mud that can be used in agriculture instead. The so-called white bricks, colloquially also termed Amarna bricks, are technically blocks of porous stone consisting mostly of fossilized marine organisms.

5. William M. Flinders Petrie, *Naukratis 1: 1884–1885*, Memoir of the Egypt Exploration Fund 3 (London: Trübner, 1886), 26.

6. Brian Muhs, "The Great Temenos of Naukratis," *JARCE* 31 (1994): 103–4.

7. Gustave Jéquier, *Manuel d'archéologie égyptienne: Les éléments de l'architecture*, Manuel d'archeologie egyptienne 1 (Paris: Picard, 1924), 14–15.

8. Dieter Arnold, *The Encyclopedia of Ancient Egyptian Architecture* (Princeton: Princeton University Press, 2003), 36; Barry Kemp, "Soil (Including Mud-Brick Architecture)," in *Ancient Egyptian Materials and Technology*, ed. Paul T. Nicholson and Ian Shaw (Cambridge: Cambridge University Press, 2000), 85; A. J. Spencer, *Brick Architecture in Ancient Egypt* (Warminster: Aris & Phillips, 1979), 147.

9. Maury E. Morgenstein and Carol A. Redmount, "Mudbrick Typology, Sources, and Sedimentological Composition: A Case Study from Tell el-Muqdam, Egyptian Delta," *JARCE* 35 (1998): 130.

spatial and temporal scope is it possible, and to what degree of reliability? What other evidence can be used to substantiate these suggested dates?

Stamped Bricks

Not surprisingly, the most reliable dates of mud-bricks come from the inscriptional evidence. Ancient Egyptian bricks were occasionally stamped with royal names or the names of institutions that incorporated royal names, and those bricks can normally be dated to the reigns of respective kings, even if they are found out of archaeological contexts. For example, an unprovenanced brick in a museum could be dated to the Twenty-first Dynasty, because it bears the title and name of Menkheperre, a man who is known to have served as the high priest of Amun in Thebes and acted as a de facto ruler of southern Egypt between the reigns of Smendes I and Psusennes I.[10]

The current evidence suggests that Egyptians started stamping bricks in the reign of Ahmose.[11] Also as early as that reign, bricks could be stamped for other members of the royal family and court officials.[12] If the nonroyal individuals are historically well-known figures, such as viziers and treasurers, then the bricks bearing their names can be dated just as securely as the royal inscribed bricks. Because the brick stamping practice started in the beginning of the Eighteenth Dynasty, this method of dating bricks based on inscriptions cannot be applied to earlier specimens.[13] On the other hand, almost all stamped bricks, even those with illegible or undatable inscriptions, can be assigned to the New Kingdom or later. Stamped bricks were reportedly observed on large Middle Kingdom nonroyal memorial chapels in North Abydos, but these chapels most likely had been repaired and reused in the New Kingdom or the Late period.[14]

At some sites, archaeologists have recorded different stamp types that can be correlated with the structures built in different phases of a king's reign. Among numerous buildings commissioned by Amenhotep III at Malqata, for example, more than ten different types of stamps were identified. According to William C. Hayes, his brick stamp types I, II, and V (all naming Amenhotep III) were found at the Main Palace

10. Joachim Śliwa, "An Unpublished Stamped Brick of Menkheperre, High Priest of Amun," *Studies in Ancient Art and Civilization* 2 (1992): 23–26.

11. Stephen P. Harvey, "The Cults of King Ahmose at Abydos" (PhD diss., University of Pennsylvania, 1998), 190–91, fig. 34; Spencer, *Brick Architecture*, 144, pl. 21.

12. Harvey, "Cults of King Ahmose," 191–92, 198–99, fig. 34.

13. A single brick bearing the owner's name, roughly inscribed with a finger (Manchester 5176), was found at the Old Kingdom tomb of Nefermaat in Meydum, but this exceptional example belongs to a separate category, as the name was not stamped. William M. Flinders Petrie, Ernest J. H. Mackay, and Gerald A. Wainwright, *Meydum and Memphis (3)*, British School of Archaeology in Egypt and Egyptian Research Account (London: British School of Archaeology in Egypt, 1910), 4, pl. 20 (2); Spencer, *Brick Architecture*, 146, pl. 38.

14. David O'Connor, "The 'Cenotaphs' of the Middle Kingdom at Abydos," in *Mélanges Gamal Eddin Mokhtar*, ed. Paule Posener-Kriéger, 2 vols., Bibliothèque d'étude 97 (Cairo: Institut français d'archéologie orientale, 1985), 2:175; William Kelly Simpson, *Inscribed Material from the Pennsylvania-Yale Excavations at Abydos*, Publications of the Pennsylvania-Yale Expedition to Egypt 6 (New Haven: Peabody Museum of Natural History of Yale University; Philadelphia: University of Pennsylvania Museum of Archaeology and Anthropology, 1995), 79, fig. 145. For repair and reuse, see Kei Yamamoto, "A Middle Kingdom Pottery Assemblage from North Abydos" (PhD diss., University of Toronto, 2009), 15–16.

from an early phase of the site, while types VIII and IX (both mentioning "Temple of Amun in the House of Rejoicing") were found at the Temple of Amun from a late phase of Malqata.[15]

Bricks with different types of stamps can appear even within a single monument, and their distribution, combined with other data, has been employed to reconstruct its architectural phases. At the memorial temple of Ahmose at South Abydos, for example, archaeologists could infer that some parts of the main temple were constructed in the later years of Ahmose's reign because they employed bricks that either use an orthography characteristic of that time or mention the royal treasurer Neferperet who is attested from the end of the reign elsewhere.[16]

It is important to recognize that a stamped inscription designates the destination, not the source, of the mud-bricks.[17] In other words, the stamps indicate the building where the mud-bricks were intended to be used, not where they were produced. In this light, it must be questioned whether stamps naming an earlier king were ever manufactured posthumously, for example, if the bricks were meant to be used in restoration or renovation of an older royal cult temple.[18] The present authors are not aware of any evidence of such a scenario and it may be difficult to detect, but more research is needed before rejecting its possibility.

Conversely, if a structure was found to be built with bricks bearing an earlier king's name, archaeologists would normally conclude that the bricks were reused from an earlier construction. For example, many mud-bricks with the cartouche of Thutmose IV were found incorporated into the masonry of the Temple of Millions of Years of Tausret on the Theban West Bank. In this case, the bricks were undoubtedly brought from the adjacent temple of Thutmose IV built in the Eighteenth Dynasty and repurposed for the Nineteenth Dynasty Tausret temple.[19]

Nonroyal individuals could also appropriate bricks from royal monuments. For example, brick structures above the tomb of Djehutymes (TT 32) at el-Khokha from the reign of Ramesses II incorporate many reused bricks bearing the stamp of Hatshepsut (the estimated dimensions of a complete brick being about 40 × 19 × 13 cm) and a few others inscribed with the names of Thutmose IV (?), Amenhotep IV or Horemheb, Ramesses II, and possibly Merenptah.[20] The presence of the last two royal names indicate that some of these brick features postdate Djehutymes.

Another limitation to the use of stamped bricks in dating architectural remains is their rarity. Even at monuments where stamped mud-bricks were employed, the

15. William C. Hayes, "Inscriptions from the Palace of Amenhotep III," *JNES* 10 (1951): 232–43, figs. 24, 30; M. A. Leahy, *Excavations at Malkata and the Birket Habu 1971–1974: The Inscriptions*, Egyptology Today 2.4 (Warminster: Aris & Phillips, 1978), 46.

16. Harvey, "Cults of King Ahmose," 190–209, fig. 36.

17. Hayes, "Inscriptions from the Palace," 163.

18. Objects inscribed with the name of a prominent past rulers include the post-Eighteenth Dynasty scarab seals bearing the name of Menkheperre (Thutmose III). Bertrand Jaeger, *Essai de classification et datation des scarabées Menkhéperrê*, OBO.SA 2 (Göttingen: Vandenhoeck & Ruprecht; Fribourg: Presses Universitaire, 1982), 184–253.

19. Pearce Paul Creasman et al., "The Tausret Temple Project: 2014 Season: University of Arizona Egyptian Expedition," *Ostracon* 25 (2014): 5 n. 7.

20. Ernő Gaál, *Stamped Bricks from TT 32*, Studia Aegyptiaca 15 (Budapest: Chaire d'Égyptologie, 1993), 47–52.

majority of the bricks were left plain and uninscribed. At the temple of Thutmose III in Thebes, for example, the archaeologists estimated that only 25–30 percent of the bricks bear stamp impressions.[21] The rest of this article, therefore, will assess the usefulness of these regular unstamped bricks as a dating tool.

Brick Sizes

Undoubtedly, the most commonly documented and published attribute of ancient Egyptian mud-bricks is the size, because, to quote Kemp, "measuring ancient bricks is perhaps the most obvious thing to do with them."[22] Field archaeologists always need to measure the length, width, and height of bricks as they draw the plans and profiles of the architecture that they excavate or survey, so the relevant data are readily available. It is up to the individual scholars to decide in how much detail they publish those data within their limited number of pages. Some provide the range of brick dimensions, others only give the average (sometimes specified as mean, median, or mode), and yet others merely let the scaled architectural illustrations speak for themselves. It has been suggested that the brick sizes should ideally be recorded and published to the nearest millimeter, but considering the restricted time in the field and the inevitable unevenness of the artifacts, data to the nearest half-centimeter would probably represent the archaeological reality more accurately.[23]

Brick sizes can vary within a site, a monument, or even a feature. Even if one assumes that they were recorded with perfect accuracy, there are several factors that contribute to variation in brick dimensions, including: (1) brick mold; (2) shrinkage rate; (3) manufacturing technique and location; and (4) later damages. First, and perhaps most obviously, brick molds of different sizes yield mud-bricks of different sizes. Each brick maker might have used only one mold at a time, but if broken, it would have to be repaired or replaced by a new one, potentially with different internal dimensions. If two or more brick makers worked as a team or in a workshop, then the size of their molds might not have matched exactly. Second, the internal dimensions of molds do not equate with the size of the final products because mud-bricks always shrink by about 30 percent as they dry.[24] The actual shrinkage rate is determined by the composition of the mud. The difference between alluvial soil and desert marl, the clay-silt-sand ratio, the amount and type of other inclusions, and the proportion of water all affect how much the bricks would shrink while drying. The precise recipe of the mud and temper mixture would have varied slightly each time, and the quantity of water would have decreased gradually due to continuous percolation and evaporation. Third, ethnographic comparison suggests that brick makers would have jiggled the mold to free the newly formed bricks, and this manufacturing process could create

21. Myriam Seco Álvarez and Augustín Gamarra Campuzano, "Thutmosis III Temple of Millions of Years and the Mud Brick Marks: Conservation and First Conclusions," in *Non-Textual Marking Systems in Ancient Egypt (and Elsewhere)*, ed. Julia Budka, Frank Kammerzell, and Sławomir Rzepka, Lingua Aegyptia 16 (Hamburg: Widmaier, 2015), 65.

22. Kemp, "Soil (Including Mud-Brick Architecture)," 84.

23. Spencer, *Brick Architecture*, 147, says to the nearest millimeter. Kemp, "Soil (Including Mud-Brick Architecture)," 84, says half-centimeter is more common.

24. Spencer, *Brick Architecture*, 3.

some unevenness in the final products.[25] The new bricks would have been left to dry on a relatively flat land, but any roughness in the terrain would have shaped the bottom side of the bricks accordingly, resulting in an uneven height. Fourth, the bricks would naturally chip and erode during and after construction. Given the complex combination of factors affecting the brick sizes, one or two centimeters of differences should not be considered major discrepancies even among the bricks made by the same brick maker, using the same mold, and from the same batch of mud. Instead, archaeologists must look at a broader pattern through ancient Egyptian history.

In general, Early Dynastic Egyptians exclusively used very small format bricks, their average length and width being about 24 × 12 cm and almost never exceeding 30 × 15 cm.[26] For example, the funerary enclosures from the time of Aha at North Abydos were made of bricks measuring 22–24 × 11–13 × 8–9 cm, which are normal sizes for all Early Dynastic monuments at that site.[27] At Elephantine, the First and Second Dynasty structures were built with bricks that are only slightly larger (24–28 × 10–14 × 6–10 cm).[28]

The use of these small bricks continued in the Old Kingdom. For example, the brick sizes were commonly 26–28 × 14 × 8 cm at the Fourth Dynasty workmen's village in Giza.[29] At the same time, there was also emergence and increased usage of larger brick formats.[30] In the most extreme case, two radically different formats of bricks were used at a single Old Kingdom mastaba at Quesna, probably dating to late Third or early Fourth Dynasty. The core of the mastaba was made of very small bricks (23 × 15 × 11 cm), while the sides were made of astonishingly large bricks (50 × 30 × 15 cm).[31] At the Fifth Dynasty pyramid complex of Raneferef in Abusir, archaeologists recorded a moderately wide spectrum of brick sizes, ranging from about 25 × 11 × 7 cm to 36–40 × 18–19 × 11.5–12 cm.[32]

By the Middle Kingdom, the smallest bricks (under 25 cm in length) disappeared almost completely, but otherwise the range of brick formats remained wide.[33] Since this period, the bricks tended to cluster into two main formats: large (about 40 cm long) and smaller (about 33 cm long). At the town of Kahun associated with pyramid complex of Senwosret II, for example, the two most commonly encountered formats are 40–43 × 20–23 × 12–14 cm and 32–35 × 15–16.5 × 9–11 cm.[34] Intriguingly,

25. Kemp, "Soil (Including Mud-Brick Architecture)," 84.

26. Kemp, "Soil (Including Mud-Brick Architecture)," 87; Spencer, *Brick Architecture*, 10–25, 59, 83, 104, 147, pl. 41.

27. Laurel Bestock, *The Development of Royal Funerary Cult at Abydos: Two Funerary Enclosures from the Reign of Aha*, Menes 6 (Wiesbaden: Harrassowitz, 2009), 66.

28. Martin Ziermann, *Elephantine 16: Befestigungsanlagen und Stadtentwicklung in der Frühzeit und im frühen Alten Reich*, Archäologische Veröffentlichungen 87 (Mainz: von Zabern, 1993), 140, 142.

29. Ashraf Abd el-Aziz, "Gallery 3.4 Excavations," in *Giza Reports, Vol. 1: Project History, Survey, Ceramics, and Main Street and Gallery 3.4 Operations*, ed. Mark Lehner and Wilma Wetterstrom (Boston: Ancient Egypt Research Associates, 2007), 202; Abd el-Aziz, "Main Street Excavations," in Lehner and Wetterstrom, *Giza Reports, Vol. 1*, 113.

30. Spencer, *Brick Architecture*, 25–37, 59–61, 94, 104, pl. 41.

31. Joanne Rowland, "A New Era at Quesna," *Egyptian Archaeology* 38 (2011): 11–12.

32. Jaromír Krejčí, "Mudbrick Masonry," in *Abusir 9: The Pyramid Complex of Raneferef: The Archaeology*, ed. Miroslav Verner, Excavations of the Czech Institute of Egyptology (Prague: Czech Institute of Egyptology, 2006), 113–37.

33. Spencer, *Brick Architecture*, 37–43, 61–63, 83–84, 94, 104–6.

34. Felix Arnold, "Baukonstruktion in der Stadt Kahun: zu den Aufzeichnungen Ludwig Borchardts," in *Structure and Significance: Thoughts on Ancient Egyptian Architecture*, ed. Péter Jánosi, Denkschriften der Gesamtakademie 33 (Vienna: Österreichischen Akademie der Wissenschaften, 2005), 80.

these dimensions are close to, although slightly smaller than, the two brick lengths mentioned in a papyrus document from Kahun: six palms (45.0 cm) and five palms (37.5 cm).[35] The application of the two different brick formats and its chronological implications will be discussed further below.

Egyptians continued to use bricks of wide-ranging sizes (normally 25–45 cm long) throughout the New Kingdom, Third Intermediate period, and Late period.[36] Among the Theban private tombs where bricks could be measured, those dating from the original Eighteenth Dynasty and post-Amarna period brickworks (n = 50) had the range of 26 × 11 × 5 cm to 41 × 19 × 12.5 cm (mean average of 32.9 × 15.2 × 9.2 cm), while those from the original Ramesside period (n = 42) had the range of 27 × 12 × 8.5 cm to 40 × 20 × 14 cm (mean average of 33.1 × 15.5 × 9.0 cm).[37] One may conclude, therefore, that there was no statistically significant difference in brick formats between the Eighteenth Dynasty and Ramesside period nonroyal tombs in this area.

In the Third Intermediate and Late periods, very large bricks (45–47 cm long) were sometimes used for temple enclosure walls in the delta.[38] On the other hand, at Late period private tombs in the Theban west bank, including earlier tombs that were reused in the Late period (n = 8), the attested dimensions varied from 26 × 12 × 7.5 cm to 34 × 15 × 11 cm (mean average of 30.3 × 14.2 × 8.9 cm), thus slightly smaller than the New Kingdom ones in general.[39] Since this range falls completely within the wider New Kingdom range, however, bricks cannot be dated to the Late period based on their sizes alone.

In the Ptolemaic period, the largest bricks (over 42 cm long) nearly disappeared, and large bricks (about 38–42 cm long) were generally restricted to massive temple enclosure walls, such as the abovementioned temenos at Naukratis where Petrie observed the 41.4 × 21.1 cm bricks.[40] Meanwhile, other brick sizes continued as before.[41] Archaeologists working at Medinet Madi have reported that the temple at this site was built with mud-bricks "of Ptolemaic proportions (36 × 15 × 12 cm)."[42] While the statement is not wrong in a sense that the dimensions are within the normal range for the Ptolemaic period, it is somewhat misleading since this format can date from almost any period in the pharaonic era.

In the Roman period, Egyptians resumed the use of very small bricks, not unlike the Early Dynastic ones in size. According to an ethnographic research conducted in the

35. Arnold, "Baukonstruktion in der Stadt Kahun," n. 10; Francis Llewellyn Griffith, *The Petrie Papyri: Hieratic Papyri from Kahun and Gurob (Principally of the Middle Kingdom)*, 2 vols. (London: Quaritch, 1898), 59, pl. 23 (3.1A recto); Kemp, "Soil (Including Mud-Brick Architecture)," 87.

36. Spencer, *Brick Architecture*, 44–53, 64–77, 84–89, 94–98, 106–9.

37. Friederike Kampp, *Die thebanische Nekropole: zum Wandel des Grabgedankens von der 18. bis zur 20. Dynastie*, Theben 13 (Mainz: von Zabern, 1996), 134–38.

38. Rosanna Pirelli, "Once More on Undulating Walls in Ancient Egypt: Mythological Reasons or Technical Requirements?" in *Egyptological Studies for Claudio Barocas*, ed. Rosanna Pirelli, Serie egittologica1 (Naples: Istituto Universitario Orientale, 1999), 58; Spencer, *Brick Architecture*, 70–72, 76.

39. Kampp, *Die thebanische Nekropole*, 134–38.

40. Farouk Gomaà, Rentate Müller-Wollermann, and Wolfgang Schenkel, *Mittelägypten zwischen Samalūṭ und dem Gabal Abū Ṣīr: Beiträge zur historischen Topographie der pharaonischen Zeit*, BTAVO B 69 (Wiesbaden: Reichert, 1991), 247; Pirelli, "Once More on Undulating Walls in Ancient Egypt," 60.

41. Spencer, *Brick Architecture*, 53–58, 77–82, 89–93, 98–103, 109–10.

42. Edda Bresciani and Rosario Pintaudi, "The Discovery of a New Temple at Medinet Madi," *Egyptian Archaeology* 15 (1999): 18.

Qena region, some modern brick makers specified the ideal brick format as 24 × 12 × 9 cm, which is identical to some of the Early Dynastic and Roman brick sizes.[43] The use of fired bricks also became increasingly common from the Roman period onward.

As can be seen from the summary above, the pharaonic brick formats evolved over time. However, the change was not unilinear, and there were potentially great variations within each dynasty. Moreover, there was a considerable overlap in brick sizes between different periods. As a result, most brick sizes (30–40 cm long) can date from any time between the Old Kingdom and the Ptolemaic period. Even small bricks (under 25 cm long) do not always date from the periods before or after that timespan. At Kahun, for example, Petrie found a wooden brick mold (Manchester 51), whose internal dimensions are 28.8 × 14.6 × 8.4 cm.[44] This mold, presumably of Middle Kingdom date, probably produced bricks of about 20 × 10 × 6 cm after shrinkage.[45] Similar small bricks (about 20–24 × 10–11 cm) were used at the Late period chapel of Khonsuirdis on the west bank of Thebes.[46] Bricks, therefore, cannot be dated automatically to a specific period based on their sizes.

Some readers may be surprised by the lack of standardization, especially among the large "royal" bricks, since some of the state-sponsored brickworks clearly followed the royal cubit (about 52.4 cm) system.[47] If the whole building was to be built according to cubits, it would be sensible to manufacture bricks that would fit that scheme. The reality, however, is that even royal constructions frequently deviated from the actual round multiples of 52.4 cm. In other words, the ancient Egyptian cubit was a very loosely defined or applied unit, especially in comparison to the strictly standardized units of measurement found in the modern world. Elke Roik has proposed that many New Kingdom brick sizes derive from another unit of length, called *nebi*, and the target size was 4 × 2 × 1 palms (about 32 × 16 × 8 cm) in this system.[48] Be that as it may, brick sizes still often deviated significantly from that hypothetical ideal size throughout the New Kingdom. In fact, despite their ability to achieve remarkably precise architecture, ancient Egyptians tended to demonstrate little concern for the concept of standardized measurements, not only in length but also in other units such as weight and volume.[49]

There were other reasons for producing bricks of different sizes. In some constructions, bricks of intentionally varied dimensions were used within a feature. At Kom

43. Maria Correas-Amador, "A Survey of the Mud-Brick Buildings of Qena," *Egyptian Archaeology* 38 (2011): 15.

44. Rosalie David, *The Pyramid Builders of Ancient Egypt: A Modern Investigation of Pharaoh's Workforce* (London: Routledge; Kegan Paul, 1986), 149, pl. 18; William M. Flinders Petrie, *Kahun, Gurob and Hawara* (London: Kegan Paul, Trench, Trübner, 1890) 26, pl. 9 (23). http://www.museum.manchester.ac.uk/collection.

45. One possibility is that this mold is a model that was originally placed in a foundation deposit. Alternatively, the brick mold from Kahun dates from the Early Dynastic period, as some tombs of that period have been found outside the Middle Kingdom town. Petrie does not specify the archaeological context of the mold.

46. Richard H. Wilkinson, "The Tausret Temple Project: 2009 Season," *Ostracon* 20 (2009): 8.

47. Spencer, *Brick Architecture*, 149–50.

48. Elke Roik, "Der Lehmziegel: Schlüssel zum altägyptischen Längenmaßsystem," *GM* 179 (2000): 51–67; Roik, "Die zwei Längenmaßsysteme in Deir el Medine," *GM* 166 (1998): 65–75.

49. Leslie Anne Warden, "The Organization and Oversight of Potters in the Old Kingdom," in *Abusir and Saqqara in the Year 2010*, ed. Miroslav Bárta, Filip Coppens, and Jaromír Krejčí, 2 vols. (Prague: Czech Institute of Egyptology, Faculty of Arts, Charles University in Prague, 2011), 2:800–19.

el-Samak, for example, a combination of two clearly different formats ($35 \times 17 \times$ 10 cm; $31 \times 15 \times 9.5$ cm) were used in a single construction phase to adjust the brick-works to the desired wall dimensions.[50]

Nonetheless, there are circumstances in which archaeologists can use brick sizes to reconstruct the site history to some extent. As mentioned above, pharaonic bricks tended to cluster into two format categories, especially in the Middle Kingdom, and the two brick types had different general purposes. Large bricks (about 37–43 cm long) were usually used in state-sponsored constructions, such as royal tombs and temples. Smaller format bricks (about 32–35 cm long) were more often used in nonroyal build-ings, such as private memorial chapels and domestic architecture.[51] At South Abydos, for example, the mortuary temple of Senwosret III employed bricks measuring about $42 \times 21 \times 14$ cm, and the initial phase of the associated town used bricks measur-ing about $39 \times 19 \times 12$ cm, because both were state-sponsored projects aimed at the creation of a royal cult complex. In contrast, the later phase of the same settlement, including newly added walls, were built with more varied smaller bricks of about $32–34 \times 14–15 \times 8–9$ cm, because these modifications were of mainly private initia-tives.[52] A similar pattern could be observed at the town of Kahun built in association of the pyramid complex of Senwosret II.[53] At these sites, therefore, the features made of smaller format bricks could be identified as being later than those made of large bricks. It must be stressed, however, that the brick sizes changed in these cases because the ownership of the towns shifted from royal to nonroyal, not because of the chronologi-cal differences as such.

At Malqata, Hayes felt that "as a general rule the bricks from the later buildings tend to be somewhat larger than those from earlier stages of construction. Thus, the brick size most frequently encountered in the Palace of the King (with stamp Type I) is $32 \times 14.5 \times 8$ cm.; while that found in the Temple of Amūn (with stamp Type IX) is $38 \times 18 \times 12$ cm."[54] More recent studies demonstrate that the reality was more complicated. The Waseda University mission to Malqata in the 1980s detected three different formats (about $30 \times 14 \times 8$ cm; $36 \times 17 \times 9$ cm; $40 \times 18 \times 9$ cm) at the Main Palace (Hayes's "Palace of the King") alone.[55] The medium format was the most common, while the small format was used on some walls. The large format was used almost exclusively at the palace entrance area. At the Amun Temple of the same site, the archaeologists again identified three brick formats but of slightly different

50. Yasutada Watanabe, *Studies on the Palace of Malqata: Investigations at the Palace of Malqata, 1985–1988* (Tokyo: Chuo Koron Bijutsu, 1993), 2, 7.

51. Somers Clarke and Reginald Engelbach, *Ancient Egyptian Construction and Architecture* (London: Oxford University Press, 1930; repr. New York: Dover, 1990), 209–10.

52. Josef Wegner, "Excavations at the Town of *Enduring-Are-the-Places-of-Khakaure-Maa-Kheru-in-Abydos*: A Preliminary Report on the 1994 and 1997 Seasons," *JARCE* 35 (1998): 9–10. The apotropaic birth brick found at the same site, the only archaeologically attested example of its kind, measured 35×17 cm. Wegner, "A Decorated Birth-Brick from South Abydos: New Evidence on Childbirth and Birth Magic in the Middle Kingdom," in *Archaism and Innovation: Studies in the Culture of Middle Kingdom Egypt*, ed. David P. Silverman, William Kelly Simpson, and Josef Wegner (New Haven: Department of Near Eastern Languages and Civilizations, Yale University; Philadelphia: University of Pennsylvania Museum of Archaeology and Anthropology, 2009), 449.

53. Arnold, "Baukonstruktion in der Stadt Kahun," 82–83.

54. Hayes, "Inscriptions from the Palace of Amenhotep III," 234.

55. Watanabe, *Studies on the Palace of Malqata*, 169.

dimensions (about 32 × 16 × 9 cm; 38 × 18 × 12 cm; 44 × 23 × 6 cm) from those at the palace.[56] The large format was used mostly for the pavement, the medium one (which almost corresponds to the large format at the palace) was used for the enclosure wall, and the small one was used for the temple building itself. The current investigation of the temple by the Joint Expedition of the Metropolitan Museum of Art Expedition and the Ancient Egyptian Heritage and Archaeology Fund has observed even smaller bricks (under 30 cm long) being used in the features that were added later, probably at the time of the third Sed Festival of Amenhotep III.[57]

Within the same archaeological site and even within a single reign, therefore, the brick sizes varied widely. The change did not necessarily follow the chronological sequence, and it certainly was not unilinear. Instead, it depended on the individual brick suppliers and the nature of features being built. The difference in brick formats can reflect a development of the monuments, but such conclusion always must be supported by other pieces of evidence such as architectural phases and associated artifacts.

Raw Materials

The raw material is potentially significant to the study of mud-brick industry, although it is often described less thoroughly in archaeological reports than the brick size. The main ingredient is most commonly alluvial mud found naturally on the banks of the Nile or a lake, but bricks made primarily of calcareous marl (*tafla*) found in the desert wadi beds are also known. At some sites, such as the workmen's village in Amarna, both types were used concurrently.[58] Each soil type contains mineral grains of various degrees of coarseness, which can be sorted into clay, silt, sand, and sometimes gravel. The variations in clay-silt-sand proportion can be visualized in a series of segmented bar charts or a ternary diagram.[59]

To complicate the matter, brick makers often added some sand to the mud mixture, so the amount of sand in the brick does not represent the environment from which the mud was collected. Another inclusion that was commonly added is chopped straw (*tibn*) or chaff. Hoffmeier would remind the readers that this is illustrated in the exodus narrative, in which Egyptians demanded Hebrew labors to produce the same quota of bricks even after they stopped supplying straw (Exod 5:7–8, 5:18).[60] The sand and straw were added intentionally to prevent bricks from cracking while they dried and shrank, thus improving the strength of the final products.[61] Contrary to the impression given in the exodus that the chopped straw was absolutely essential for brick production, a modern observation suggests that sand is a perfectly acceptable substitute.[62]

56. Watanabe, *Studies on the Palace of Malqata*, 190–91.

57. Catharine Roehrig, pers. comm.

58. Charles A. I. French, "A Sediments Analysis of Mud Brick and Natural Features at el-Amarna," in *Amarna Reports 1*, ed. Barry J. Kemp, Occasional Publications 1 (London: Egypt Exploration Society, 1984), 191; Kemp, "Soil (Including Mud-Brick Architecture)," 81.

59. For a bar chart, see French, "Sediments Analysis of Mud Brick," fig. 14.2. For a ternary diagram, see Tessa Dickinson, "Messages in Mud: Analysing Mud-Bricks from HK27C," *Nekhen News* 26 (2014): 26.

60. Hoffmeier, *Israel in Egypt*, 115; Hoffmeier, "Out of Egypt," 34.

61. Kemp, "Soil (Including Mud-Brick Architecture)," 82; Spencer, *Brick Architecture*, 3.

62. Clarke and Engelbach, *Ancient Egyptian Construction and Architecture*, 209.

The differences in the main ingredient (alluvial mud as opposed to marl clay) and the variable amount of added sand (mainly quartz particles) naturally result in different colors. Many archaeologists verbally describe brick colors in their publications, but surprisingly few express them with standardized Munsell soil colors.[63] In general, bricks made of alluvium tend to be brownish gray, while those made of marl tend to be more olive or cream-colored. Increase in sand content usually results in a paler, more yellowish color. Colors of mud-bricks are also influenced by the smoothness and moistness of the bricks as well as the amount of soluble salt that sometimes effloresces to their surface.

Like the brick size, the brick composition rarely indicates the absolute date of the monument, but it can sometimes reveal different phases of the brickwork. For example, a geological compositional analysis of the enclosure of Khasekhemwy in Hierakonpolis suggests that an early stage of the Second Dynasty monument was constructed with bricks that were 12 percent clay, 42 percent silt, and 46 percent sand, mixed with many microartifacts, in contrast to the higher-quality bricks of the late phase that were 13 percent clay, 48 percent silt, and 39 percent sand, mixed with ash and more organic content.[64] The difference was interpreted as an indication of a better-organized workforce in the latter part of the reign.

Yet, at the pyramid complex of Raneferef in Abusir, bricks of the exact same dimensions but different geological compositions were identified in restoration works and partition walls from a late phase of the monument. This compositional variation might derive from the fact that some of these bricks were made from a freshly collected batch of mud, while others were manufactured from crushed older bricks mixed with more sand and *tafla* but using the same mold.[65] The interpretation is corroborated by the discovery of later mud-mixing depressions on top of an earlier dismantled enclosure wall.[66]

In some other cases, however, differences in geological compositions of bricks, as characterized by clay-silt-sand ratio, might be related more to cultural rather than chronological factors. At another cemetery in Hierakonpolis, for example, the soil grain sizes of bricks collected from Nubian C-Group tumuli dating from the early Middle Kingdom were contrasted against those from Egyptian vaulted tomb chapels of the Second Intermediate period. The former could be divided into two groups, one very sandy and another siltier, while the latter fell between the two Nubian types in terms of grain coarseness and contained larger amount of chaff, which is typical of Egyptian bricks. The compositional variation here could be due to the chronological differences, but it could be influenced equally by the manufacturers' personal or cultural preference or simply their access to natural and human resources.[67] More samples are needed to assess these possibilities.

63. Virginia L. Emery and Maury Morgenstein, "Portable EDXRF Analysis of a Mud Brick Necropolis Enclosure: Evidence of Work Organization, El Hibeh, Middle Egypt," *Journal of Archaeological Science* 34 (2007): 113–14; French, "Sediments Analysis of Mud Brick," 192–98; Morgenstein and Redmount, "Mud-brick Typology, Sources, and Sedimentological Composition," 138–39; Kemp, "Soil (Including Mud-Brick Architecture)," 81.

64. Tessa Dickinson, "Making the Bricks Speak: Compositional Analysis at the Fort," *Nekhen News* 24 (2012): 23.

65. Krejčí, "Mudbrick Masonry," 134–35.

66. Jaromír Krejčí, "Eine Lehmziegelwerkstatt aus dem Alten Reich in Abusir," *GM* 148 (1995): 63–69.

67. Dickinson, "Messages in Mud," 26–27. A similar lack of correlation between brick composition and construction purposes was observed in Amarna. French, "Sediments Analysis of Mud Brick," 201.

The geological variation of the raw material can be analyzed and characterized in terms of not only soil grain coarseness but also mineral types and chemical compositions. At a Late period settlement site in Tell el-Muqdam, a field laboratory was set up to examine the geochemical and physical properties of bricks, which were thus classified into five types. The distribution of the brick types in domestic structures showed some correspondence with construction history of the site.[68]

Geochemical differences, however, do not always reflect chronological differences. At el-Hiba, for example, a portable XRF was used to characterize the chemical variations of bricks used in a cemetery enclosure and two distinct brick types were identified based mainly on the amount of certain elements such as strontium, rubidium, and iron.[69] When the two brick types were plotted on the architectural plan, it became clear that one type was used in the northwestern portion of the enclosure and the other type was used in the southeastern portion. The archaeologists inferred from this distribution pattern that the builders of the enclosure were divided into two teams and that they collected their raw material from two different locations.[70] Assuming that the two halves of the enclosure were built as a single project, one must conclude that the different brick types do not have a strong chronological implication in this case.

In addition to mud and tempering agents, such as sand and straw, some other inclusions often got mixed in either intentionally or accidentally. These items might include small artifacts, bones and shells, charcoal and other plant remains, and gravels. They can reveal information about either where the raw materials were collected or where the bricks were produced.[71]

Because ancient pottery evolved over time, ceramicists can often use it to date different strata of archaeological sites. Similarly, potsherds embedded in mud-bricks can be dated if they are large enough and chronologically diagnostic based on their shapes or surface treatments. In such cases, the date of the latest pottery should be considered the *terminus post quem* of the brick. In North Abydos, for example, a thick mud-brick tumble layer was encountered below Middle Kingdom nonroyal memorial chapels.[72] With the aim to date the bricks in the stratum, some sample bricks were gently crushed and wet-sieved to retrieve the potsherds in them. Most fragments were nondiagnostic body sherds, but because some of the rim and base sherds could be dated to the Middle Kingdom, the bricks that contained those sherds also could not be any earlier than that date. Moreover, since a layer of wind-blown sand separated this tumble layer from the nonroyal chapels also of Middle Kingdom date standing above, it was possible to reconstruct a relatively quick succession of events at this site—brick production and supply, construction of many brickworks, dismantling of those structures and massive deposition of the brick debris, temporary abandonment, and construction of the later chapels—all within the same period.

Botanical and faunal remains have been extracted from mud-bricks through wet-sieving and flotation to study the paleoenvironment. For example, the pollens

68. Morgenstein and Redmount, "Mudbrick Typology, Sources, and Sedimentological Composition," 145.

69. Emery and Morgenstein, "Portable EDXRF Analysis," 113.

70. Emery and Morgenstein, "Portable EDXRF Analysis," 115.

71. Mark Lehner, Mohsen Kamel, and Aana Tavares, *Giza Plateau Mapping Project, Season 2005: Preliminary Report*, Giza Occasional Papers 2 (Boston: Ancient Egypt Research Associates, 2006), 44.

72. Yamamoto, "Middle Kingdom Pottery Assemblage," 55–56, fig. 20.

embedded in bricks from the Khufu cemetery and the mortuary temple of Menkaure in Giza were analyzed to examine the plant diversity in the Fourth Dynasty.[73] In Abusir, scientists found that the mollusks mixed in the Old Kingdom mud features were species that prefer slow-flowing or stagnant waters, suggesting that the mud was collected from Abusir Lake rather than the Nile.[74] To the authors' knowledge, however, these organic remains from bricks have not been used for dating purpose, although there is a clear potential to do so. For instance, charred seeds and grains are especially suited for radiocarbon dating. Although the methodology is inherently limited in precision, it would be useful for dating the bricks broadly, for example to distinguish an Old Kingdom brick from a New Kingdom one.

Evidence from various archaeological sites in Egypt suggests that the raw material alone is not chronologically diagnostic. Bricks made of different materials were used within the same reign, and bricks from different periods could have very similar geochemical compositions. Like the brick size, however, a change in the brick material within a site could indicate a change in the brick supplier, which sometimes corresponded to a different phase of the monument. In such cases, the diachronic development could be linked to the raw materials, but only if they are supported by other pieces of evidence.

Archaeological and Historical Contexts

The possible dates of certain brick types always must be considered in conjunction with their contexts. The importance of architectural history has been discussed already in the previous sections. Other kinds of contextual evidence that can corroborate the chronological implication of brick types include archaeological stratigraphy and associated artifacts.

Kemp once observed that some remnants of an enclosure wall in Kom Ombo exhibit "a positive resemblance to early town enclosure walls at Tell Edfu, Elephantine and El-Kab, which date to the period between the Old Kingdom and First Intermediate period. All share also an approximately similar brick size in their construction."[75] He also noticed some other wall fragments made of similar bricks were erected on roughly the same elevation level and tentatively concluded that "they would seem, therefore, to derive from a common archaeological horizon." As discussed already, these statements by themselves constitute a weak argument. After admitting that "on their own brick sizes are a dangerous form of dating evidence," however, Kemp convincingly supported his late Old Kingdom–First Intermediate period dating of

73. Sekkina Ayyad, Knut Krzywinski, and Richard Pierce, "Mudbrick as a Bearer of Agricultural Information: An Archaeopalynological Study," *Norwegian Archaeological Review* 24 (1991): 77–96.

74. Miroslav Bárta, "In Mud Forgotten: Old Kingdom Palaeoecological Evidence from Abusir," *Studia Quaternaria* 30 (2013): 76–77; Martin Odler, Veronika Dulíková, and Lucie Juříčková, "Molluscs from the Stone and Mud-Brick Tombs in Abusir (Egypt) and the Provenance of So-Called 'Nile-Mud,'" *Interdisciplinaria Archaeologica: Natural Sciences in Archaeology* 4 (2013): 9–22.

75. Barry J. Kemp, "Kom Ombo: Evidence for an Early Town," in Posener-Kriéger, *Mélanges Gamal Eddin Mokhtar*, 2:43–4.

these brickworks by extensively illustrating the corpus of ceramics that were found in the same contexts.[76]

Similarly, Horst Jaritz tentatively dated a substantial mud-brick wall between Aswan and Konosso to the Middle Kingdom based on the observation that the bricks of exactly same format were recorded for the Middle Kingdom city wall at Elephantine. He also noted that the same finger markings were found on bricks from several other Middle Kingdom sites. In this case, Jaritz strengthened his suggestion with not only ceramic evidence (unfortunately not illustrated) but also textual evidence— a nearby rock inscription of Hepu commemorating the official's inspection of Lower Nubian fortress in the reign of Senwosret II.[77]

Fired Bricks

Although the present study is mainly about unfired mud-bricks, a few remarks will be made about red/fired bricks. As noted above, baked bricks became increasingly common from the Roman period onward, and consequently they tend to be associated with those later eras. Pharaonic Egyptians, however, also used red bricks sporadically. For example, the Middle Kingdom fortresses in Nubia were sometimes paved with fired slabs of square format, probably because of their resistance to wear and dampness.[78] Another important example comes from an Eighteenth Dynasty fort at Tell el-Borg, where many years of excavation by Hoffmeier has revealed a moat lined with baked bricks.[79] Measuring 33–36 × 14–16 × 5–7 cm (35 × 15 × 6 cm on average), these bricks were produced locally out of the same material as the regular sun-dried bricks, and they were fired at the expense of much fuel required in order to waterproof the defensive fosse. Djehutymes and Nebsumenu, Nineteenth Dynasty officials who built their tombs at el-Khokha (TT 32 and TT 183), were probably among the "pioneers" in the use of fired bricks (about 33 × 15 × 7 cm and 28 × 21 × 4.5 cm, respectively) in nonroyal funerary architecture.[80] After the New Kingdom, red bricks became a more common construction material, and archaeologists must remember that their usage is not always chronologically diagnostic of Roman and later periods.[81]

Red bricks, like pottery vessels and other fired ceramics, can be dated with the thermoluminescence dating technique. As with radiocarbon dating, this method does not provide as precise dates as one might like in Egyptology, but it is effective enough to obtain a broad range of dates for the bricks in question.

---

76. Kemp, "Kom Ombo," 51–53, figs. 8–13.

77. Horst Jaritz, "The Investigation of the Ancient Wall Extending from Aswan to Philae: Second Preliminary Report," *MDAIK* 49 (1993): 112–14.

78. Kemp, "Soil (Including Mud-Brick Architecture)," 79; Spencer, *Brick Architecture*, 140.

79. Thomas W. Davis, and James K. Hoffmeier, "Excursus II: Fired Bricks at Tell el-Borg," in *Tell el-Borg I: The "Dwelling of the Lion" on the Ways of Horus*, ed. James K. Hoffmeier, Excavations in North Sinai (Winona Lake, IN: Eisenbrauns, 2014), 198–201.

80. Gaál, *Stamped Bricks from TT 32*, 19–46.

81. Spencer, *Brick Architecture*, 140–41; Ursula Verhoeven, "Eine technologische Rarität: Das Brennen von Ziegeln in der Grabdekoration des Mittleren und Neuen Reiches," *MDAIK* 43 (1987): 263.

Conclusion

Bricks can help dating a monument and reconstructing the site history, if used judiciously. Although less common and restricted temporally, inscribed bricks obviously provide more concrete evidence unless they are reused in later monuments. On the other hand, contrary to the widespread notion, brick sizes and compositions are often less reliable means to date architecture. In some cases, brick types indeed reflect different architectural phases. To support the chronological implication, however, it is vital to find additional pieces of evidence, such as stratigraphic contexts and associated artifacts. Few studies have made use of embedded artifacts and organic remains to date bricks so far, but analyses of the ceramics and plants extracted from ancient mud-bricks may open new avenues of research.

The last two decades have witnessed increasing awareness and progress in the conservation and restoration of ancient Egyptian mud-brick architecture. Edward Johnson's recent article, for example, reviews the current state of theories and practices of ancient brick conservation in the Memphite region.[82] Ongoing discussions revolve around topics, such as what kind of materials to use and approaches to take, whether to make new bricks that imitate the old ones or to prioritize their durability, and how to ensure the restorations are harmonious with but distinguishable from the original. To tackle the last issue, some projects have chosen to inscribe the new bricks so that future archaeologists can easily differentiate ancient masonry from modern one. At Abydos, for example, the conservators working with the American (Penn-Yale-Institute of Fine Arts) and German (Deutsches Archäologisches Institut) expeditions stamp the newly formed mud-bricks with the letters "PYIFA" and "DAI," respectively.[83] In the light of what the present article has emphasized, this is a highly recommended practice and should be followed by all.

Although it has been long recognized that the mud-bricks were an essential component of ancient Egyptian architecture throughout the pharaonic era, and despite numerous publications written on brick vaults and other masonry techniques, the bricks themselves still deserve more detailed research. This situation may improve soon, as some in-depth analyses of bricks and their usage are under way at some important sites like Giza.[84] It is hoped that similarly rigorous recording, analysis, and publication of mud-bricks will be conducted throughout Egypt.

82. Edward Johnson, "Survey of the State of Mudbrick Conservation in and Around Giza and the Memphite Necropolis," *ASAE* 86 (2015): 229–73.

83. David O'Connor et al., "The Funerary Cult Enclosure of Khasekhemwy at Abydos: Preserving an Ancient Mud-Brick Royal Monument," *Preserving Egypt's Cultural Heritage: The Conservation Work of the American Research Center in Egypt*, ed. Randi Danforth (Cairo: American Research Center in Egypt, 2010), 16.

84. Lehner, Kamel, and Tavares, *Giza Plateau Mapping Project, Season 2005*, 44.

CHAPTER 28

The God 'El of Ramesses II's Stela from Sheikh S'ad (the "Job Stone")

K. Lawson Younger Jr.

IN 1886, GOTTLIEB SCHUMACHER INVESTIGATED the so-called *saḥrat Ayyūb* "the stone of Job," located in a mosque at Sheikh S'ad (ancient Qarnaim) in the Bashan.[1] Although badly eroded, it was soon ascertained to be an important monument set up by Ramesses II during one of his campaigns into northern Transjordan.[2] This was the first time that an Egyptian royal stela had been identified in the Levant. Since then, other Egyptian stelae have been found, a number in the region of the Ḥaurān or the south Syrian context.[3] The stela, being found in a mosque, is obviously not in its original context, but in a secondary setting linked to the tradition about Job.

What is preserved of it measures 2.11 m in height, although it is divided into halves by an intentional break that was done for the purposes of transport, though not for a great distance.[4] It contains a badly deteriorated relief showing a winged sun at the top and a scene of Ramesses II offering Ma'at (the goddess of truth) in the form of a small statue on a *nb*-sign to a Canaanite deity who is depicted *en face* with horns protruding from an *atef*-crown (see fig. 28.1).

The Egyptian king is depicted on the right side, facing left, wearing the *ḫprš* ("the Blue Crown"). Above him is the cartouche with the name of Ramesses ⊙⟨𓍿⟩. To the left of the cartouche, more or less centered, is an inscription in Egyptian group writing in two vertical columns. The reading of the text (Erman's original drawing in fig. 28.1 does not correctly show the *r* in the first word) and my transliteration of the signs are:[5]

It is a great pleasure to offer this modest essay in honor of my longtime friend and colleague, James K. Hoffmeier, who has contributed so much to constructive understandings in the disciplines of Egyptology, archaeology and biblical studies. It is my hope that this essay will bring together these three disciplines in an integrated fashion as well as Jim would have done it.

1. Gottlieb Schumacher, *Across the Jordan* (London: Watt, 1889), 191; Schumacher, "Der Hiobstein, Sachrat Eijub im Hauran," *ZDPV* 14 (1891): 142–47, esp. p. 142. According to ancient local tradition, this was the stone against which Job leaned when the reports of devastation came to him.

2. Adolf Erman, "Der Hiobstein," *ZDPV* 15 (1892): 205–11.

3. Stefan J. Wimmer, "A New Stela of Ramesses II in Jordan in the Context of Egyptian Royal Stelae in the Levant," paper presented at the Third International Congress on the Archaeology of the Ancient Near East, Paris, 18 April 2002; https://core.ac.uk/download/pdf/12174504.pdf.

4. Bedřich Hrozný, "Discoveries in the Land of Job: Relics of Hittite and Greek Art," *Illustrated London News*, 25 June (1927): 1162–63.

5. *KRI* 2:223 (no. 61).

(1) *'a₂ - r ku - –n - 'a₂* (2) *ḏa - pu₃ - –n* (male deity determinative).[6]

The first Egyptologist who attempted to read the inscription was Adolf Erman, who initially read the inscription as *i-kʾ-ᵉn-i-ḏʾ-pʾ-ᵉn*.[7] However, he soon after corrected the reading to *i-rʾ-kʾ-n-i-ḏʾ-n* and suggested the meaning "(the god) Arkan of the North."[8] However, it is clear that the initial word (*'a₂ - r*) should be understood as 'El.[9] Johannes C. de Moor concluded: "The god who is represented on the left side of the stele is without any doubt Ilu/El." This is because, in addition to the reading of the name 'El in the hieroglyphics, the headdress worn by the Canaanite deity on the stela is "identical with that of Ilu in Ugarit" (as depicted on a statue, RS 88.070).[10] However, although there are some similarities, the crowns are most certainly not "identical." Far closer in comparison is the bronze and gold statue of the god 'El (RS 23.393).[11] On the head of this metal statue is "a Syrian version of the Egyptian *atef* headdress" with lateral horns (unfortunately now missing) that were fastened on two mortises above the ears.[12] Thus, it is correct to say that what is preserved in the relief of the deity on the Sheikh Sʿad Stela is very consistent with known depictions of 'El. Jean Yoyotte has suggested that the deity pictured on the upper left side of the Tell Keswē Stela of

6. Although the last sign is not clear and could be the determinative for a god 𓀭 or a goddess 𓁦, there can be little doubt that the former is the correct reading for the following reasons: the apparent masculine form of the first word, "El"; and all references to a deity connected with Ṣapunu are masculine.

7. Erman, "Der Hiobstein," 208–10. This reading is reflected in the drawing in fig. 28.1 above.

8. Adolf Erman, "Das Denkmal Ramses' II. im Ostjordanland," *ZÄS* 31 (1893): 100–101. Other earlier contributions include: Hugo Gressmann, *Altorientalische Bilder zum Alten Testament*, 2nd ed. (Berlin: de Gruyter, 1927), pl. 45, see also pp. 35–36; Albrecht Alt, "Das Institut im Jahre 1932," *Palästinajahrbuch* 29 (1933): 19–20; William F. Albright, "The Jordan Valley in the Bronze Age," *Annual of the American School for Oriental Research* 6 (1926): 13–74; Albright, "Baal-Zephon," in *Festschrift Alfred Bertholet zum 80. Geburtstag: Gewidmet von Kollegen und Freuenden*, ed. Walter Baumgartner (Tübingen: Mohr, 1950), 1–14, esp. p. 8 n. 4; Bertha Porter and Rosalind L. B. Moss, *Topographical Bibliography of Ancient Egyptian Hieroglyphic Texts, Reliefs and Paintings* (Oxford: Griffith Institute, Ashmolean Museum, 1952), 383; and Stig I. L. Norin, *Er spaltete das Meer: Die Auszugsüberlieferung Psalmen und Kult des alten Israel*, Coniectanea Biblica: Old Testament 9 (Lund: Gleerup, 1977), 49–51.

9. Raphael Giveon, "Two Egyptian Documents Concerning Bashan from the Time of Ramses II, I. the Job-Stone," *RSO* 40 (1965): 197–200, esp. p. 198; *KRI* 2:223 (no. 61); James E. Hoch, *Semitic Words in Egyptian Texts of the New Kingdom and Third Intermediate Period* (Princeton: Princeton University Press, 1994), 323–34, no. 466. Only Rainer Stadelmann has suggested a different reading (see below).

10. De Moor claims that this headdress is "identical with that of Ilu in Ugarit." See Johannes C. de Moor, *Rise of Yahwism: The Roots of Israelite Monotheism*, BETL 91 (Leuven: Leuven University, 1990), 126. For the statue of 'Ilu at Ugarit that de Moor is comparing (RS 88.070), see Marguerite Yon and Jacqueline Gachet, "Une statuette du dieu El à Ougarit," *Syria* 66 (1989): 349; Yon et al., "Fouilles de la 48e campagne (1988) à Ras Shamra-Ougarit," *Syria* 67 (1990): 4–5; Yon, "El, le père des dieux," *Monuments et Mémoires de la Fondation Eugène Piot* 71 (1991): 1–19. Mark S. Smith, *The Early History of God: Yahweh and the Other Deities in Ancient Israel* (San Francisco: Harper, 1990), 31 n. 44.

11. Marguerite Yon, *The City of Ugarit at Tell Ras Shamra* (Winona Lake, IN: Eisenbrauns, 2006), 133 (photo on p. 132, no. 14). See also Claude F. A. Schaeffer, "Résumé de la XXIIIᵉ campagne de fouille à Ras Shamra–Ugarit, 1960," *AAS* 11–12 (1961–1962): 187–96.

12. Yon, *City of Ugarit*, 133.

FIGURE 28.1. Erman's drawing of the Sheikh S'ad Stela. Source: Adolf Erman, "Der Hiob-stein," *ZDPV* 15 (1892).

Ramesses II may be the god 'El (based on the dress worn by the deity).[13] However, in my opinion, this seems far from certain.

In any case, there is now complete agreement that the final word ($\underline{d}a$ - pu_3 - $-n$) should be interpreted as ṣapun "Ṣapunu," even though the writing here on the "Job Stone" is slightly different from the usual rendering ($\underline{d}a$ - pu_2 - na = ṣapuna).[14] The root ṣpn in the West Semitic languages can refer to a city (toponym), a mountain, a region, or a god. In Ugaritic, Old Aramaic, Phoenician, and epigraphic Hebrew, there is no attestation for ṣpn with the meaning "north."[15] The meaning "north" is only attested in Biblical Hebrew.[16] Thus, in the case of our stela, at least initially, it might seem to be a reference to Mount Ṣapunu, particularly known in the Ugaritic literature (see further

13. He states: "Inversement, la divinité de gauche vers qui le roi est tourné serait le dieu supérieur, normalement habillé long: le soleil (Shamash) ou encore El, 'le créateur des créatures.' Le dieu qui suit le roi serait Seth-Ba'al." See Jean Yoyotte, "La stèle de Ramsès II à Keswé et sa signification historique," *Bulletin de la Société française d'égyptologie* 144 (1999): 44–58, esp. p. 46. For the relief on the stela, see Ahmed Ferzat Taraqji, "Nouvelles découvertes sur les relations avec l'Egypte à Tell Sakka et à Keswé, dans la région de Damas," *Bulletin de la Societé française d'égyptologie* 144 (1999): 27–43, esp. p. 42, fig. 13. See further, Kenneth A. Kitchen, "Notes on a Stela of Ramesses II from near Damascus," *GM* 173 (1999): 133–38.

14. Hoch, *Semitic Words in Egyptian Texts*, 384, no. 576. There are other instances where 𓈋𓃀 has the value of pu_3 (see p. 507). I will not use the transliteration "Zaphon," except in quotes from other scholars.

15. *DULAT*, 788, s.v. "ṣpn"; *DNWSI*, 972–73, s.v. "ṣpn₂."

16. *HALOT*, 1046–47, s.v. "צָפוֹן."

discussion below). [17] There was a *b'l ṣpn* "Baal Ṣapunu," who was a very well-known deity in the Levant and in ancient Egypt.[18] In fact, the Ras Shamra stela pictures a Levantine deity with a caption that contains this name, as well as "the *ḥtp di nsw* offering formula: '[*Ḥtp di nsw n B'l*] Ṣaphon, the great god, that he might give....'"[19] Raphael Giveon argued that since there are occurrences of Ṣapunu, Baal Ṣapunu, 'El Ṣapunu in Ugarit and in Egypt, in addition to the Bashan, "the god of the Job Stone cannot be described as a local deity 'Ortsgottheit' nor as 'quelque varieté amoréenne d'Astarte.'"[20]

The crux of the inscription, however, is the second word. Giveon suggested that the hieroglyphs are reflecting: "*il kn ṣpn* El kan Zaphon, that is 'El establishes Zaphon,'" understanding *kn* as a verbal form of *kûn* (כּוּן).[21] Of course, the expression "El kan Zaphon" brings to mind the biblical phrase: אֵל עֶלְיוֹן קֹנֵה שָׁמַיִם וָאָרֶץ "El 'Elyōn, creator of heaven and earth"; along with a number of other attestations, in particular, the Phoenician inscription of Azatiwada from Karatepe which reads: *'lqn'rṣ* "El creator of earth."[22] However, Giveon maintains that there is no possibility of a change between *k* and *q* in the Egyptian writing.[23] This he felt eliminates the possibility of the hieroglyphics standing for the verbal root *qny/qnh*. Yet, he cites a toponym *ykn'm* that occurs in various administrative lists from Ugarit that is the biblical toponym "Yoqne'am" (יָקְנְעָם, Josh 12:22, etc.), and states:

The parallel employ of the two verb stems with *q* and *k* in Biblical expressions extolling Yahwe as creator and founder of the earth and the parallel formation

17. Jebel Aqra' (1,729 m; 5,671 ft) is 40 km north of Ugarit. It was known in antiquity as Ṣapunu (Mount Casius to the Greeks). See *DULAT*, 788, s.v. "*ṣpn*." For a full discussion of the vocalization and etymology (although with an unnecessary discounting of this Ramesses II stela from consideration), see Nicolas Wyatt, "The Significance of Ṣpn in West Semitic Thought: A Contribution to the History of a Mythological Motif," in *Ugarit: Ein ostmediterranes Kulturzentrum im Alten Orient*, ed. Manfried Dietrich and Oswald Loretz, ALASP 7 (Münster: Ugarit-Verlag, 1995), 213–17; repr. in Wyatt, *The Mythic Mind: Essays on Cosmology and Religion in Ugaritic and Old Testament Literature*, BibleWorld (London: Equinox, 2005), 102–24. His table summarizing the etymological discussion is more lucid in the reprint on pp. 115–16. Earlier and with problems, Cecilia Grave, "The Etymology of Northwest Semitic *ṣapānu*," *UF* 12 (1980): 221–29. See also Klaus Koch, "Ḥazzi-Ṣafôn-Kasion: Die Geschichte eines Berges und seiner Gottheiten," in *Religionsgeschichtliche Beziehungen zwischen Kleinasien, Nordsyrien und dem Alten Testament: Internationales Symposion Hamburg 17.–21. März 1990*, ed. Bernd Janowski, Klaus Koch, and Gernot Wilhelm, OBO 129 (Fribourg: Universitätsverlag; Göttingen: Vandenhoeck & Ruprecht, 1993), 171–223.

18. *KTU* 1.47:5 = RS 1.017:5. The first line of this text reads: *il ṣpn* "the gods [*ilû*] of Ṣapunu," being a heading for the list. That *il* is plural is demonstrated by *dbḥ ṣpn* (*KTU* 1.148:1 = RS 24.643:1) which is clearly a heading and *KTU* 1.91:3 = RS 19.015:3. See Dennis Pardee, *Ritual and Cult at Ugarit*, WAW 10 (Atlanta: Society of Biblical Literature, 2002), 23 n. 3. Also Koch, "Ḥazzi-Ṣafôn-Kasion," 187.

19. Quotation from Hoch, *Semitic Words in Egyptian Texts*, 384. For the Ras Shamra stela, see F.-A. Schaeffer, "Les fouilles de Minet-el-Beida et de Ras Shamra," *Syria* (1931): pl. 6.

20. Giveon is treating *il ṣpn* as a separate deity ("Two Egyptian Documents," 198). However, this phrase should be understood as "the gods of Ṣapunu" (see note 18 above). Ibid., 199–200. The former ("Ortsgottheit") was suggested by Hermann Ranke in Hugo Gressman et al., *Altorientalische Texte und Bilder zum Alten Testament*, 2nd ed. (Leipzig: de Gruyter, 1926), 26; the latter ("quelque varieté amoréenne d'Astarte") was suggested by Louis-Hugues Vincent, *Canaan d'après l'exploration récente* (Paris: Gabalda, 1907), 451 n. 1. Unless otherwise noted, all translations are the author's.

21. Giveon, "Two Egyptian Documents," 198. See also, Norin, *Er spaltete das Meer*, 49–51.

22. *KAI* 26 iii.18. Note no word dividers. See discussion below.

23. Giveon, "Two Egyptian Documents," 198.

of the toponyms Yokne'am/Yoqne'am shows the affinity of the two. Kan Zaphon is, thus, a variant of Qone Zaphon as an epithet of El.[24]

However, James Hoch pointed out a problem in Giveon's analysis: he did not account for the *'a₂* following *ku - –n*. He rightly pointed out that if the verbal root were *kwn* (כּוּן), there should not be an *aleph*; and furthermore, one would expect either a causative (Š-stem or H-stem) or else D-stem (which would be a *polel* form with a reduplication of the third radical in a II-*w* verb).[25] Hence, the verbal root cannot be *kwn*.

A few years after Giveon made his proposal, Rainer Stadelmann made a very different suggestion.[26] He speculated that the Sheikh S'ad inscription should yield the reading: "Ba'l Alijan auf der Spitze des Ṣāpān."[27] Edward Lipiński has followed this, translating "Mightest Ba'al on top of the Ṣaphon."[28] However, Stadelmann's proposal was based solely on his analysis of the inscription through a photograph and his speculation *on what the text ought to read*.[29] This is a highly hypothetical restoration, which Stadelmann rightly declared, and was intended only as a suggestion. Moreover, the crown worn by the deity on the stela seems to best match that worn by 'El (see above). Therefore, there is little chance that this reading is correct.

Hoch's solution to the crux is to posit that *ku - –n - 'a₂* should be understood as the root *kl'*, namely a G participle *kōli'a* with the meaning of "guardian." The root *kl'* occurs in a number of Semitic languages: in Biblical Hebrew, כלא means "to detain, restrain, shut up, withhold"; in Aramaic, in the G-stem: כלי / כלא "hold back, restrain, to ward off"; in the D-stem: "impede, detain, force"; as a noun: כלאי "guard-house"; in Syriac, (*k'lā*) "to ward off, guard, detain"; in Arabic, (*kala'a*) "to protect, guard, preserve, keep safe"; and in Akkadian, *kalû* "to detain."[30] Hoch states: "If the derivation is correct, then perhaps this is a lexical isogloss from Aramaic, which would not be unlikely given the location of the stele in Bashan."[31] Thus, Hoch would see the composite deity name as: *Il(u)—kōli'a—ṣa-pa-nu* "'Ēl Guardian(?) of Ṣaphon."[32] I would point out that *kl'* was originally a III-*y* verb (*kly*), which, like some other III-*y* verbs in Aramaic, come to be written with an *aleph*.[33]

24. Ibid.

25. Hoch, *Semitic Words in Egyptian Texts*, 323. This point was also made earlier by de Moor, *Rise of Yahwism*, 126 n. 118. See also *KRI* 2:134.

26. Rainer Stadelmann, *Syrisch-palästinensische Gottheiten in Ägypten*, PAe 5 (Leiden: Brill, 1967), 44–46. Stadelmann was apparently unaware of Giveon's work.

27. Ibid., 46. Stadelmann did not give the complete transliteration of the inscription, only a discussion of his proposal. However, Helck supplies a transliteration: "*ba-'a-l 'á-l[i]-[ja]-n [ḥrj-tp] sá-pá-n[a]*" (brackets should be around [*ba-'a-l*] since it is not in the text). See Wolfgang Helck, *Die Beziehungen Ägyptens zu Vorderasien im 3. und 2. Jahrtausend v. Chr.*, 2nd ed., ÄA 5 (Wiesbaden: Harrassowitz, 1971), 449 n. 28.

28. Edward Lipiński, *On the Skirts of Canaan in the Iron Age: Historical and Topographical Researches*, OLA 153 (Leuven: Peeters, 2006), 234–36.

29. Kitchen (*KRI* 2:223 n. a) refers in the critical apparatus of his edition to a squeeze used by Erman.

30. For Biblical Hebrew, see *HALOT*, 475, s.v. "כלא." For Aramaic, see CAL s.v. "*kl*"; for the D-stem, see Morris Jastrow, *A Dictionary of the Targumim, the Talmud Babli and Yerushalmi, and the Midrashic Literature with an Index of Scriptural Quotations* (London: Luzac; New York: Putnam, 1903), 638.

31. Hoch, *Semitic Words in Egyptian Texts*, 324.

32. Ibid., 572.

33. See Stanislav Segert, *Altaramäische Grammatik mit Bibliographie, Chrestomathie und Glossar* (Leipzig: Enzyklopädie, 1975), 297, §5.7.8.1.3.

Hoch himself recognizes the tentativeness of his proposal, giving the entry a level of certainty rating of [3], that is, "questionable." And there are problems with his proposal. First, *kl'* in Aramaic really means "detain, restrain, hold back."[34] Thus, "guardian" as a meaning in this early period is very doubtful. Second, understanding the writing /–n/ as /l/ is very difficult. Concerning the representation of /l/, Hoch states:

> /L/ is quite well attested, and is most often rendered by Egyptian *r*, and considerably less often by *n* {i.e., –n} or the combination *n* + *r*, {i.e., –n + r} which specifically represented [*l*]. Again the use of Egyptian *r* for /l/ tends to suggest that the Egyptian articulation of *r* was "tapped" rather than "trilled."[35]

Surveying all the examples in Hoch's impressive volume, a very large percentage of the time, –n is followed by *r* when *l* is the consonant that is being represented. Most of the examples of –n representing *l* without a following *r* are variants of instances where –n is followed by *r*. I cannot find an example of –n being *l* when it is followed by *'a₂*. Therefore, it would seem more likely that –n here should be seen as representing *n*.

Giveon rejected a derivation from *qny* "to create, beget." However, Giveon's conclusion in the above quote ("Kan Zaphon is, thus, a variant of Qone Zaphon as an epithet of El") contradicts his argument.[36] Thus, while it is rare, Semitic /q/ can be rendered by Egyptian *k*. Hoch acknowledges that this is a possibility.[37] If *ku* here represents *qu*, then one could understand *ku - –n - 'a₂* as *kuni*, thus reflecting *qōnē* (with *aleph* serving to note the correct vowel of the open syllable with the III-*y* verb). Granting its rarity, this is still the most likely solution.

There is, in fact, an analogy. In 1953, Heinrich Otten published the Canaanite "Myth of Elkunirša and Ašertu" that was discovered at Ḫattusa (modern Boğazköy).[38] Harry Hoffner states: "This myth has not been found so far among the Late Bronze West Semitic myths at Ugarit, but the characters and plot leave no doubt that it was an authentic 'Canaanite' myth."[39] The Hittite text of Elkunirsa and Ashertu represents the result of creative adaptation, which probably took place in north Syria and may reflect the spread of the Elkunirsa cult to the Hittite Empire, or at least to its southern periphery.

Briefly, in the myth (the beginning of the tablet is broken), the younger, more virile storm god (translated by Hoffner as "Ba'al," though the reading is ᵈU) is propositioned by the god Elkunirsa's wife, Ashertu (Semitic: "Asherah"). The storm god goes to the tent of the god Elkunirsa at the headwaters of the Mala River (i.e., the Euphrates).[40]

---

34. CAL s.v. "*kl'*." It is clear that this is its primary nuance in Aramaic. There is no derived noun in any stage of the language that means "guardian."

35. Hoch, *Semitic Words in Egyptian Texts*, 407.

36. Giveon, "Two Egyptian Documents," 198.

37. Hoch thinks that Giveon was "probably right" in rejecting *q* being rendered by *k*, although he acknowledges that this is a possibility (*Semitic Words in Egyptian Texts*, 323).

38. Heinrich Otten, "Ein kanaanäischer Mythus aus Boğazköy," *MIO* 1 (1953): 125–50. Emmanuel Laroche, "Textes mythologiques hittites en transcription: Deuxième Partie: mythologie d'origine étrangère," *RHA* 26/82 (1968): 139–44. For translations, see Albrecht Goetze, "El, Ashertu and the Storm-god," *Ancient Near Eastern Texts*, ed. James B. Pritchard, 3rd ed. (Princeton: Princeton University Press), 519; Harry A. Hoffner Jr., *Hittite Myths*, ed. Gary Beckman, 2nd ed., WAW 2 (Atlanta: Scholars Press, 1998), 90–92; Gary Beckman, "Elkunirša and Ašertu," *COS* 1:149.

39. Hoffner, *Hittite Myths*, 90.

40. The use of the term "tent" may also point "to a nomadic cultural setting" (Wolfgang Röllig, "El-Creator-of-Earth," *DDD*, col. 534). Singer argued that the setting for the myth is not the Levantine

He relates to him Ashertu's proposition, his refusal and her threat. The storm god addresses Elkunirsa as "my father." Elkunirsa advises the storm god to "threaten/ injure/sleep with" her and "humble her."[41]

So, the storm god (Baal) goes to Ashertu and says to her: "I have killed your 77 [children]; your 88 I have killed." After lamenting for "seven" years, Ashertu went to her husband Elkunirsa. After the two slept together, Elkunirsa tells his wife: "Come [take] Baal as your [prisoner(?)], and do to him as you wish." The storm god's sister, Anat-Astarte (Hittite uses the Akkadogram *IŠTAR*), overhears their plan and, being in the form of an owl, she flies to warn her brother. The text is interrupted by a long break. When it resumes, Baal is being treated for injuries (§§6–11).

The god, "Elkunirsa" (written: [d]*El-ku-ni-ir-ša*), is the well-known West Semitic god 'El, who bears the epithet *qn 'rṣ* "creator/possessor of earth."[42] At present, it is the earliest known attestation of this West Semitic divine epithet. Gary Beckman has posited that the Hittite translator misunderstood the Semitic phrase as a simple divine name, which he rendered as Elkunirsa.[43] Within this Hittite myth, the entire phrase does appear to be functioning as a single divine name. Nevertheless, Matthew McAffee has recently done an extensive evaluation of the name and has concluded that "one can make good sense of this name only if it is analyzed from a Canaanite grammatical perspective. The phonological and grammatical processes that would have occurred in a Semitic-Hittite transfer can be plausibly elucidated."[44] The entrance of the deity into Hittite mythology would have occurred at a point after the Canaanite shift /ā/ > /ō/, that is, at some point after the fourteenth century.[45] Singer questioned whether the *u*-vowel of [d]*El-ku-ni-ir-sa* was evidence of the Canaanite shift.[46] However, Ilya Yakubovich notes "The vocalization of the second syllable in Hitt. *El-ku-ni-ir-ša-* and Palm. *'lqwnr'* reflects the characteristic 'Canaanite shift' *ā > ō and indicates

coast but the upper and middle Euphrates. See Itamar Singer, "The Origins of the 'Canaanite' Myth of Elkunirša and Ašertu Reconsidered," in *Tabularia Hethaeorum: Hethitologische Beiträge; Silvin Košak zum 65. Geburtstag*, ed. Detlev Groddek and Marina Zorman, DBH 25 (Wiesbaden: Harrassowitz, 2007), 632–42. While Elkunirsa's dwelling is located at the headwaters of the Mala River (i.e., the Euphrates), the evidence for the middle Euphrates is based on a fragmentary toponym. His argument is based primarily on the identifications of the two conjurers (*hukmatalleš*): a man of Amurru and a man of Ana[...] (KUB 12.61 III 7′–11′). The first can be understood as a reference to an "Amorite"; but the second is uncertain, since the toponym is only partially preserved.

41. Singer states: "The *Glossenkeil* imperative *šaššumai*, which is a *hapax legomenon*, must be related to Hittite *šeš*- 'to sleep (with),' as conveyed in early translations. Despite the fact that later translations have preferred to interpret the term as a non-sexual humiliation ('threaten,' 'reprimand,' 'to make sorry,' etc.; for refs. see *CHD*, Š/2:310f.), I still feel that a vulgar sense (e.g., 'lay her!') makes more sense in this context" ("Origins of the 'Canaanite' Myth," 632 n. 10).

42. In this instance, the Hittite *s* (/š/) corresponds to Semitic /ṣ/. For all the occurrences of the name, see Ben H. L. van Gessel, *Onomasticon of the Hittite Pantheon*, 2 vols., HdO 33 (Leiden: Brill, 1998), 1:63.

43. Beckman *COS* 1:149. There can be no doubt that the relationship of the Hittite to the West Semitic original is complicated. Hoffner demonstrated that in the Hittite translation there are traces of the forms of West Semitic poetry, specifically the so-called *parallelismus membrorum*. At least once (§5) this may have led to a mistranslation: "cup" (Sumerogram GAL) and "owl" (Hittite *hapupi*) are not the expected synonyms. Hoffner proposed that West Semitic *kôs* which can mean either "cup" or a variety of owl (Lev 11:17, Ps 102:7) was misunderstood by the Hittite translator as "cup." See Harry A. Hoffner Jr., "The Elkunirša Myth Reconsidered," *RHA* 23 (1965): 5–16.

44. Matthew McAffee, "A Grammatical Analysis of Hittite [d]*El-ku-ni-ir-sa* in Light of West Semitic," *UF* 44 (2013): 201–16, esp. p. 213.

45. Ibid., 208–9.

46. Singer, "Origins of the 'Canaanite' Myth," 636.

TABLE 28.1. Occurrences of the deity (’l)qn’rṣ.

	Reading	Text
1.	ᵈEl-ku-ni-ir-sa	Myth of Elkunirsa and Ashertu (7×) (thirteenth century BCE)
2.	ᵈKu-ni-ir-sa	Hittite Offering List (KUB 36.38 rev. 8)
3.	’lqn’rṣ	Karatepe, Phoenician (no word dividers) ‖ HL = Iya/Ea (ca. 700 BCE)
4.	’lqn<r>’rṣ	Incirli Trilingual (no word dividers) (Phoenician: back, line 14)
5.	⁽³⁾[’] ’l’qn’rṣ	Jerusalem (eighth–seventh century BCE) (no word dividers, though there are in the first two lines)
6.	’l ‘lywn qnh šmym w’rṣ	Gen 14:19, 22 = Yahweh
7.	’lqwnr‘	Palmyra (first century CE) = Poseidon
8.	’lqnr‘	Palmyra, four times (exact date unknown)
9.	’lqn’rṣ	Leptis Magna, Neo-Punic (second century CE)
10.	[K]όνναρος and Conna[ri]	Connarus/Konnaros, Greek and Latin inscriptions at Baalbeq
11.	*does not contain reading*	Ḥaṭrā (Wadi Tharthar in northern Iraq). *KAI* 244:3 was misread and does not contain a deity (see below).

that both forms represent early assimilated borrowings from Canaanite *’il qōnē ’arṣ, ‘El-Creator-of-Earth.’”[47] Moreover, the *u*-vowel in the Ramesses II inscription above is taken by Egyptologists as evidence of the Canaanite shift.[48] Thus, the Hittite and Egyptian evidence combine to testify to this phenomenon. Moreover, the /k/ for /q/ is really not surprising in Hittite.[49] Consequently, the writing *kuni* reflects *qōnē*, just like the Egyptian rendering *kuni* in the Ramesses II stela reflects this word.

In fact, there is a long history of the use of this phrase as an epithet. At some point, the entire phrase itself became, in fact, a divine name. Table 28.1 is a list of other possible occurrences.

A few comments are necessary.[50] In the case of number 2, a misunderstanding probably occurred in the writing ᵈKu-ni-ir-ša "creator of earth" in the offering list of KUB 36.38 rev. 8 where it seems that the first component of the divine name (’El) was replaced by the divine determinative DINGIR.[51]

One of the more important passages is found in number 3, the curse formula of the Karatepe Phoenician and hieroglyphic Luwian bilingual, where ’l qn ’rṣ is equated with Iya/Ea.[52] The readings are as follows:

47. Ilya Yakubovich, "The West Semitic God El in Anatolian Hieroglyphic Transmission," in *Pax Hethitica: Studies on the Hittites and their Neighbours in Honour of Itamar Singer*, ed. Yoram Cohen, Amir Gilan, and Jared L. Miller, Studien zu den Boğazköy-Texten 51 (Wiesbaden: Harrassowitz, 2010), 385–98, esp. p. 394.

48. Hoch, *Semitic Words in Egyptian Texts*, 324 n. 43.

49. McAffee, "Grammatical Analysis of Hittite ᵈEl-ku-ni-ir-sa," 208.

50. One should also note the Hebrew personal name אלקנה (1 Sam 1:1, etc.): "El created." A meaning of "El possessed" is doubtful based on analogy of other personal names with the component *qnh*.

51. Singer, "Origins of the 'Canaanite' Myth," 636 n. 40.

52. Space does not permit an investigation here of the possible links with the role of Iya/Ea with the Hurrian theogony in the Kumarbi Cycle.

1. KARATEPE (Hu. = Lower Gate) §73 (Hawkins, *CHLI*, 1:58; *CHLI* 2:pl. 86)
   wa/i-ta ‖ *ARHA* | MANUS(-)*i-ti-tu* CAELUM (DEUS)TONITRUS-*hu-za-sá*
   CAELUM (DEUS)SOL-*za-sá* (DEUS)*i-ia-sá* OMNIS-*MI-zi-ha* DEUS-*ní-zi*
   á-pa | REX-*hi-sá* | *á-pa-há* "REX"-*na* | *á-pa-há-wa/i* | CAPUT-*ti-na*
   May Tarhunza of Heaven, Sun of Heaven, Iya/Ea, and all the gods annihilate
   that kingdom, and that king, and that man![53]

2. KARATEPE (Ho. = Upper Gate) §73 (Hawkins, *CHLI*, 1:58; *CHLI*, 2:pl. 105)
   | *wa/i-ta* | *ARHA* | "*69"(-)*i-ti-tu* (DEUS)*i-ia-sá* | "CAELUM" (DEUS)
   TONITRUS-*hu-za-sá-'* | "CAELUM" (DEUS)SOL-ʿza`-sá* | OMNIS-MI-*zi-
   há-wa/i* DEUS-*ní-zi* | *á-pa-sá* REX-*ta-hi-sa* | *á-pa-há-'* | "REX"-*ti-na* | *á-pa-
   há-wa/i* CAPUT-*ti-na*
   May Iya/Ea, Tarhunza of Heaven, Sun of Heaven, and all the gods annihilate
   that kingdom, and that king, and that man!

3. Karatepe (Phoenician A = North Gate)[54]—no word dividers in the text
   wmḥ bʿl šmm wʾl qn ʾrṣ [(19)]*wšmš ʿlm wkl dr bn ʾlm ʾyt hmmlkt hʾ wʾyt hmlk hʾ wʾyt*
   IV [(1)]*ʾdm hʾ ʾš ʾdm šm*
   ʾps [(2)]*šm ʾztwd ykn lʿlm km* [(3)]*šmš wyrḥ*
   then shall Baal Shamem and El, creator of the earth, and Shemesh, the eternal,
   and the whole group of the children of the gods erase that kingdom, and that
   king, and that man who is a man of renown.
   Only may the name of Azatiwada be forever like the name of the sun/Shemesh
   and the moon/Yariḥ!

The two Luwian versions of KARATEPE list the same triad: Tarhunza of Heaven, Sun
of Heaven, and Iya/Ea, though in a different order. Iya/Ea is listed last on the Lower
Gate inscription and first on the Upper Gate inscription. In the case of the Phoenician
(which is only preserved on the North Upper Gate), "El, creator/possessor of the earth"
(= Iya/Ea) is in the second or middle position. All this "suggests that the relative order
of gods in the curse formula is not hierarchical."[55] Obviously, the other deities match:
Tarhunza of the heaven with Baal, and Sun of heaven with Shemesh. The equation
of El with Ea/Enki has some antiquity since it appears to be reflected at Mari.[56] The
mythological profiles of the deities closely correspond, though there are differences.[57]

   Interestingly, there is now another example of this same triad from the same general
context.[58] In number 4, the recently published Incirli Trilingual Inscription contains

53. Hawkins *CHLI* 1:58 translates: "May celestial Tarhunzas, the celestial Sun, Ea and all the gods
delete that kingdom and that king and that man!"
54. Röllig, *CHLI* 2:50–51. Not preserved on the Lower South Gate (Phoenician B).
55. Yakubovich, "West Semitic God El," 391. Note that he has accidentally switched the gates in this
statement in his article.
56. W. G. Lambert, *Ancient Mesopotamian Religion and Mythology: Selected Essays*, ed. Andrew R.
George and Takayoshi M. Oshima, Orientalische Religionen in der Antike 15 (Tübingen: Mohr Siebeck,
2016), 78–79.
57. Manfred Weippert, "Elemente phönikischer und kilikischer Religion in den Inschriften vom Karatepe," *XVII. Deutscher Orientalistentag: Vom 21. bis 27. Juli 1968 in Würzburg; Vorträge*, ed. Wolfgang
Voigt, Zeitschrift der Deutschen Morgenländischen Gesellschaft Supplement 1 (Wiesbaden: Steiner, 1969),
191–217, esp. pp. 208–9. Edward Lipiński, "Éa, Kothar et El," *UF* 20 (1988): 137–43, esp. p. 143.
58. Since the inscription mentions Tiglath-pileser III, Awariku and Matiʿ-ʾel of Arpad, it dates to
ca. 740–730 BCE.

in its Phoenician version the triad in slightly different order: [...] ´*šmš wbʿl ˈšmm w'lqn{r}<>rṣ* "Shemesh and Baalshamem and ʾEl creator of earth" (Incirli Phoenician: back, line 14).[59] While not well preserved, the photographs show clearly *'lqn'rṣ*. The writing of the name is very interesting in that an initial *resh* has been reworked into a large size *aleph*. Stephen Kaufman comments on the line: "The scribe first wrote *reš* without *'alep*, no doubt much as the divine name was pronounced, then revised the *reš* into an oversized *'alep* and continued."[60]

Number 5 is, so far, the southernmost of the attestations. In Jerusalem in 1971, an ostracon was discovered that contained three lines of text.[61] It dates archaeologically and paleographically to the end of the eighth or beginning of the seventh century. The first two lines contain personal names and the third line, which is separated from the other two by some extra space, reads: [*'l*]*qn'rṣ* with no word dividers, although there are in the first two lines. While concerns have been expressed about the lack of a final mater on *qn*, the evidence from Incirli and the Neo-Punic attestation (number 8) demonstrate that this writing (*qn 'rṣ*) must have become a frozen, fixed form.[62] Again, the lack of word dividers may reinforce this understanding.

Regarding number 6, the biblical phrases, אֵל עֶלְיוֹן קֹנֵה שָׁמַיִם וָאָרֶץ "El ʿElyōn, creator/possessor of heaven and earth" (Gen 14:19), and יהוה אֵל עֶלְיוֹן קֹנֵה שָׁמַיִם וָאָרֶץ "Yahweh, ʾEl ʿElyōn, creator/possessor of heaven and earth" (14:22), are clearly bringing together different traditions and investing new meaning/significance. The phrase is always *'l qn 'rṣ* or its linguistic equivalent; *'lyn* never occurs in conjunction with the phrase.

At this point, the Sefire treaties are enlightening. In Sefire I A 10c–12b, the second set of deity witnesses to the treaty are listed. The first two are listed separately (10c–11a), the rest are syntactically listed in pairs (11b–12):

[*wqdm hdd zy ḥ*][(11)]*lb*
wqdm sbt
wqdm 'l w'lyn
wqdm šmy[*n w'rq*]
[*wqdm mṣ*][(12)]*lh wm'ynn*
wqdm ywm wlylh

59. Stephen A. Kaufman, "The Phoenician Inscription of the Incirli Trilingual: A Tentative Reconstruction and Translation," *MAARAV* 14 (2007): 7–26. There are also Assyrian and Hieroglyphic Luwian versions of the text.

60. Ibid.

61. N. Avigad, "Excavations in the Jewish Quarter of the Old City of Jerusalem, 1971 (Third Preliminary Report)," *IEJ* 22 (1972): 193–200, pl. 42B; Patrick D. Miller Jr., "*El*, The Creator of Earth," *BASOR* 239 (1980): 43–46.

62. Johannes Renz and Wolfgang Röllig, *Handbuch der althebräischen Epigraphik* (Darmstadt: Wissenschaftliche Buchgesellschaft, 1995), 198 n. c; F. W. Dobbs-Allsop et al., *Hebrew Inscriptions: Texts from the Biblical Period of the Monarchy with Concordance* (New Haven: Yale University Press, 2005), 242 (although they explain this as assimilation: *qnh 'rṣ > qn 'rṣ*). Aḥituv explains: "The orthography in this ostracon, without the final *h* of the participle, shows that the title was read as one vocable, קנארץ, *qônē'ereṣ*. For the elision of the *h*, cf. the interchanging forms of the name חזאל/חזהאל." See Shmuel Aḥituv, *Echoes from the Past: Hebrew and Cognate Inscriptions from the Biblical Period*, Carta Handbook (Jerusalem: Carta, 2008), 42. For the Neo-Punic, see Johannes Friedrich and Wolfgang Röllig, *Phönizisch-punische Grammatik*, 3rd ed., rev. Maria Giulia Amadasi Guzzo, AnOr 55 (Rome: Pontifical Biblical Istitute, 1999), 115.

[and before Hadad of Ḥ]a[(11)]lab (Aleppo),
and before the Sebettu,
and before ʾEl and ʿElyān,
and before Heav[en and Earth (Arqu?)],
[and before (the) Ab]yss [(12)]and (the) Springs,
and before Day and Night.

In the Levantine tradition, *ʾl* (ʾEl) and *ʿlyn* (ʿElyān) are separate deities joined by the conjunction *w*.[63] *ʾl* (ʾEl) is not a heavenly deity, but an earthly, chthonic deity; *ʿlyn* (ʿElyān) is heavenly (obviously from the very etymology of the name). Although the Sefire text is fragmentary at this point, the next set of deities are *šmy[n]* (divine Heaven) and [*wʾrq*] (divine Earth). The two sets form a chiasm:

(A) *ʾl* (ʾEl) : (B) *ʿlyn* (ʿElyān)
(B′) *šmy[n]* (Heaven) : (A′) [*wʾrq*] (Earth).

Removing קֹנֵה temporarily for discussion and adding a conjunction, one has in Hebrew this same chiasm in Gen 14:19: אֵל וֶעֱלְיוֹן שָׁמַיִם וָאָרֶץ. Employing *ʾl qn ʾrṣ*, the use of קֹנֵה produces the unique formulation: אֵל עֶלְיוֹן קֹנֵה שָׁמַיִם וָאָרֶץ. Using the divine name Yahweh in Gen 14:22 brings everything under the one Sovereign, joining the chthonic and celestial.[64]

Numbers 7–8 are occurrences in Aramaic found at Palmyra from the first century CE or later.[65] Of course, the *ṣ* is reflected in the ʿ; and there is no *aleph*, reflecting the actual way that the divine name was pronounced.

From the second century CE and later come numbers 9–10: a Neo-Punic inscription from Libyan Leptis Magna (*KAI* 129:1) containing the reading: *lʾdn lʾlqnʾrṣ* "To the lord, to *ʾElqōnēʾarṣ*."[66] And from the early Roman Empire, there is also a Greek and a Latin inscription from the temple of Bacchus in Baalbeq/Heliopolis, which mention Konnaros ([K]όνναρος) and Connarus (Conna[ri]), respectively. Clearly, [K]όνναρος derived from Aramaic *ʾlqwnrʿ* / *ʾlqnrʿ*.[67]

Number 11 is an inscription from Ḥaṭrā (located in the Wadi Tharthar in northern Iraq). It has been cited in the past as evidence for the phrase "creator of earth," although the deity in view is Baalshamin. In the original publication and in earlier editions of *KAI* 244:3, the reading was *bʿ<l>šmwn qnh dy rʿh* and translated "BʿLŠMJN,

63. Contra Eric E. Elnes and Patrick D. Miller, "Elyon," *DDD*, cols. 560–71, esp. cols. 562–63; also John Day, *Yahweh and the Gods and Goddesses of Canaan*, JSOTSup 265 (Sheffield: Sheffield Academic, 2002), 21.

64. The Old Greek and Syriac omit יהוה.

65. Harald Ingholt, *Recueil des tessères de Palmyre*, Bibliothèque archéologique et historique 58 (Paris: Geuthner, 1955), 32; J. Cantineau, "Tadmorea. No. 31: Un Poséidon palmyrénien," *Syria* 19 (1938): 78–89, esp. pp. 78–79; Giorgio Levi Della Vida, "El ʿElyon in Genesis 14:18–20," *JBL* 63 (1944): 1–9, esp. p. 8.

66. Giorgio Levi Della Vida and Maria Giulia Amadasi Guzzo, *Iscrizioni puniche della Tripolitania (1927–1967)*, Monografie di archeologia libica 22 (Rome: Bretschneider, 1987), 45–47; Alain Cadotte, *La romanisation des dieux: L'interpretatio romana en Afrique du Nord sous le Haut-Empire*, Relgions in the Graeco-Roman World 158 (Leiden: Brill, 2007), 314–15.

67. Jean-Paul Rey-Coquais, "Connaros le puissant," *Syria* 55 (1978): 361–70; Julien Aliquot, *La vie religieuse au Liban sous l'Empire romain*, Bibliothèque archéologique et historique 189 (Beirut: Institut français du proche-orient, 2009).

Schöpfer der Erde" (*KAI* 2:298).[68] This has been corrected in *KAI*⁵ to read *lṭb bʿšmyn qnh wzʿh mn qmwhy*. Healey gives the exact same reading and translates: "Baalshamin 'will remove' his possessions and his offspring from before him."[69] Even so, some scholars continue to cite the old reading, which should be discarded.[70]

Based on the above survey of the evidence, it seems that *ʾlqnʾrṣ* was originally the name of the deity (*ʾl*) combined with the epithet *qnʾrṣ*. Later, the entire phrase was reckoned as a divine name. Thus, the Egyptian writing *ʾlqnʾṣpn* on the so-called Job Stone is probably the name of the deity (*ʾl*) combined with the epithet *qnʾṣpn*. Whether this became a divine name in its own right, only further discoveries can say.

It is very likely not fortuitous that both the Egyptian and Hittite utilize the syllable *ku* as the rendering of *qu*. In other words, both non-Semitic languages render the verbal form with the same syllable, reflecting the Semitic *qō*.[71] Therefore, the deity on the Ramesses II stela from Sheikh Sʿad should be understood as *ʾl qnʾ ṣpn* = *ʾEl qōnē ṣapunu* "El creator/possessor of Ṣapunu."[72] Other scholars have translated the Egyptian this way, though without philological discussion of the issues in the Egyptian group writing.[73]

The root *qny* is widely attested throughout the West Semitic languages. It is commonly glossed as "to acquire, possess" or "to make, create, beget."[74] There is significant debate among scholars about the etymology and the interrelationships of these meanings. Obviously, the appropriate meaning is determined by the individual context. I am translating the lexeme in the form here *qōnē* as "creator" (1) because of the

68. For the original publication, see André Caquot, "Nouvelles inscriptions araméennes de Hatra," *Syria* 29 (1952): 89–118, esp. p. 102; Caquot, "Nouvelles inscriptions araméennes de Hatra (V)," *Syria* 40 (1963): 1–16, esp. p. 15.

69. John F. Healey, *Aramaic Inscriptions and Documents of the Roman Period*, Textbook of Syrian Semitic Inscriptions 4 (Oxford: Oxford University Press, 2009), 282–84.

70. See, e.g., Aḥituv who is still citing the early edition of *KAI*. Aḥituv, *Echoes from the Past*, 42.

71. Kitchen gives the translation "El who . . . s Zaphon." He discusses the possibility that the second word should be understood as *kuni*, writing for *qōnē*, with *k* for *q* and *aleph* for the semivocalic *y*. But because Egyptian very rarely transcribes West Semitic *q* by a *k*, he hesitates to endorse it. In my opinion, he too quickly dismisses the analogy of Hittite Elkunirsa (*RITA*, 133–35).

72. It should be pointed out that de Moor interpreted this deity's name correctly. However, his conclusion is utter conjecture and should be discounted. He argued that "The Job-stele implies that according to the local mythology El had dispossessed Baal on his mountain Zaphon. Accordingly, the Bashan where the stone was erected had apparently been re-named 'Zaphon.' . . . This usurpation of Baal's mountain would seem to be an extremely important new datum. It means that the El of the Job-stele is not the weak, old god who is on the verge of surrendering his position to Baal of Zaphon. . . . Here in Bashan, however, El appears to have taken over the mountain of Baal, Mt. Zaphon. So he is an intolerant kind of El, an El who sought to oust Baal." Johannes C. De Moor, "Ugarit and Israelite Origins," in *Congress Volume: Paris 1992*, ed. J. A. Emerton, VTSup 61 (Leiden: Brill, 1995) 205–38, esp. pp. 217–18. He then conjectured that Yahweh assumed the role of El and that the Israelites' origins must be seen as coming out of the Bashan region (219–38).

73. Recently Kottsieper has stated: "Wahrscheinlich dürfte hinter dem *Il-kuni-Zapun* in der Stele von Tell Sheikh Saʿd trotz der bedenkenswerten Einwände von Giveon und Hoch das Epitheton 'der Besitzer des Zaphon' stehen." See Ingo Kottsieper, "El"; https://www.bibelwissenschaft.de/de/stichwort/17172. Yoyotte translates "El qui a crée(?) Saphon." See Yoyotte, "La stele de Ramsès II à Keswé," 46 n. 4; and 53. Cornelius simply gives de Moor's and Giveon's interpretations as options. See Izak Cornelius, *The Iconography of the Canaanite Gods Reshef and Baʿal: Late Bronze and Iron Age I Periods (c 1500–1000 BCE)*, OBO 140 (Fribourg: University Press; Göttingen: Vandenhoeck & Ruprecht, 1994), 145. For the stela see fig. 34.

74. *DNWSI*, 1015–16; *HALOT*, 1111–13; *DULAT*, 706.

parallel with Iya/Ea in the Karatepe inscription; (2) because of the development of the ascription "Yahweh, maker of heaven and earth" where the participial form *'ōśēh* replaces the participle *qōnēh* of Gen 14:19, implying a procreative nuance (Pss 115:15; 124:8; 134:4; 146:6; 121:2); and (3) because of the personal name אלקנה.[75]

While there were at least three different traditions at Ugarit about the location of the residence of the deity 'El, it is clear that as the highest god of the Ugaritic pantheon his abode was not located in heaven, but on earth.[76] There is one tradition, however, that Herbert Niehr has coined a "mittelsyrische Tradition," which was conveyed in the Rapi'uma texts (*KTU* 1.20–22).[77] Unfortunately, these are fragmentary and difficult.[78] Nonetheless, it seems clear that 'El invites a group of deities to a banquet in his palace (*KTU* 1.20 II; 21 I; 22 II). This banquet at the invitation of El is located in the *bt . ikl . bpr' bṣq* [.] *birt . lbnn*, "in the banquet house, on the summit, in the heart of Lebanon" (1.22 I:24–25).[79] Regrettably, the information given here cannot be narrowed down too much geographically. However, perhaps one can suggest that a reference might be to the highest elevation of the Anti-Lebanon range, i.e., Mt. Hermon, which is considered in some ancient texts as a seat of the deities.[80]

Niehr has suggested that this middle Syrian tradition came to Ugarit through the immigration of a dynasty, originally based in the southeast of Ugarit. It is also possible that the tradition came some other way. But, in *KTU* 1.108:1–3, the deity Rāpi'u, the ancestor of the royal dynasty of Ugarit, exercised his rule (*yṯb/tpẓ*) as king of the underworld (*mlk 'lm*) in 'Aštārōt (עַשְׁתָּרֹת) and 'Edreî (אֶדְרֶעִי), that is, at the foot of Mt. Hermon.[81] 'Aštārōt (Tell Aštara) is only four to five kilometers southwest of

---

75. For (2), see Norman C. Habel, "'Yahweh, Maker of Heaven and Earth': A Study in Tradition Criticism," *JBL* 91 (1972): 321–37.

76. Herbert Niehr, "Die Wohnsitze des Gottes El nach den Mythen aus Ugarit: Ein Beitrag zu ihrer Lokalisierung," in *Das biblische Weltbild und seine altorientalischen Kontexte*, ed. Bernd Janowski und Beate Ego, FAT 32 (Tübingen: Mohr, 2001), 325–60.

77. Ibid., 339–40.

78. Wayne T. Pitard, "A New Edition of the 'Rāpi'ūma' Texts: *KTU* 1.20–22," *BASOR* 285 (1992): 33–77; Theodore J. Lewis, "Toward a Literary Translation of the Rapiuma Texts," in *Ugarit, Religion and Culture: Proceedings of the International Colloquium on Ugarit, Religion and Culture, Edinburgh, July 1994; Essays Presented in Honour of Professor John C. L. Gibson*, ed. Nicolas Wyatt, Wilfred G. E. Watson, and Jeffrey B. Lloyd, Ugaritisch-biblische Literatur 12 (Münster: Ugarit-Verlag, 1996), 115–49.

79. Lewis, "Toward a Literary Translation of the Rapiuma Texts," 127, 131.

80. Edward Lipiński, "El's Abode: Mythological Traditions Related to Mount Hermon and to the Mountains of Armenia," *Orientalia Lovaniensa Periodica* 2 (1971): 13–69, esp. 15–41; Manfred Weippert, "Libanon," *Reallexikon der Assyriologie*, ed. Erich Ebeling et al. (Berlin: de Gruyter, 1980–1983) 6:641–50, esp. pp. 648–49.

81. Pardee states: "The similarity between biblical *'dr'y* and Ugaritic *hdr'y* is too great to be passed off (though accepting this aspect of Margalit's much broader theory of Rephaism does not imply nor necessitate the acceptance of the entirety of the theory)." See Dennis Pardee, "A New Datum for the Meaning of the Divine Name Milkashtart," in *Ascribe to the Lord: Biblical and Other Essays in Memory of Peter C. Craigie*, ed. Lyle Eslinger and Glen Taylor, JSOTSup 67 (Sheffield: JSOT Press, 1988), 55–68, esp. p. 64 n. 26. Margulis, who was the first to connect these two Ugaritic toponyms and the biblical cities, states "As for the orthography *hdr'y* (OT Edrei, modern Der'a), I suggest that we are confronted either with variant phonetic realizations of the initial (prosthetic?) phoneme or with a scribal error ({Ugaritic *h* [four horizontal wedges] / *i* [four horizontal wedges + small vertical under the four]})." See B. Margulis, "A Ugaritic Psalm (RŠ 24.252)," *JBL* 89 (1970): 292–303, esp. 293–94. 'Edreî (אֶדְרֶעִי) = *hdr'y* ("Haddu-the-Shepherd)" (de Moor, "Ugarit and Israelite Origins," 213). *DULAT*, 335 (but there are no grounds for calling it a mythical place). See W. H. Van Soldt, "The Topography and the Geographical Horizon of the City-State of Ugarit," in *Ugarit and the Bible*, ed. George J. Brooke, Adrian Curtis, and John F. Healy, Ugaritisch-biblische

Sheikh Sʿad (ancient Qarnaim). According to Niehr, with the arrival of a new dynasty from an area southeast of Ugarit, the Ugaritic tradition of the Bashan ancestors of the royal family (*rapiʾūma*) and a location of the god ʾEl on Mount Hermon was incorporated into the Ugaritic tradition. Thus, while ʾEl entertains the *rapiʾūma* on Mt. Hermon, it is unclear whether ʾEl has a palace there that he inhabits only temporarily, or whether this is an independent tradition of a residence of ʾEl, comparable to the Anatolian and northern Syrian traditions. What is striking here is the ʾEl, who is "creator/possessor of earth" is a chthonic deity; and Qarnaim and ʿAštārōt are in the region of the *rapiʾūma/rapaʾūma*, along with the deity Milku (according to the Ugaritic texts).[82] Like Baal on Mt. Ṣapunu, ʾEl in this tradition (as in the other two traditions at Ugarit) has his residence on a mountain.[83]

In the case of the stela of Ramesses II, what is the meaning of the phrase *ʾl qn ṣpn*? As already noted above, there is an inherent difficult with the root *qny*. However, there is also the matter of the interpretation of *ṣpn*. Thus, there are a number of possible ways that *ṣpn* might be understood:

1. A reference to the divine mountain, in particular Mt. Ṣapunu, north of Ugarit (modern Jebel al-Aqraʿ, ancient Mt. Hazzi, classical Mt. Cassius): "'El creator/possessor of Mt. Ṣapunu (modern Jebel al-Aqraʿ)."

2. A reference to the deity, Ṣapunu: "'El creator/possessor of (the god) Ṣapunu."

3. A reference to the divine mountain par excellence (i.e., a general term for a divine abode), wherever it is located (i.e., a figurative transfer of the reference). For example, in Ps 48:3, Mount Zion is designated "the summit of Ṣapôn" (יַרְכְּתֵי צָפוֹן) (see NJPS).[84]

The second and third options seem unlikely.[85] There may be a fourth option. One of the Ugaritic god-lists has the heading *il ṣpn* "the gods of Ṣapunu" (*KTU* 1.47:1 = RS 1.017:1) which is paralleled by the heading of another text *dbḥ ṣpn* "the offerings (for the gods) of Ṣapunu" (*KTU* 1.148:1 = RS 24.643:1).[86] A number of times in the Ugaritic texts ʾIlu/ʾEl is designated *qnyt ilm* "creator/begetter of the gods" (*KTU* 1.4 I:22; III:26, 30, 35; IV:32; 1.8 II:2). Thus, it may be that the stela of Ramesses II's *ʾl qnʾ ṣpn* should be understood as "'El, the creator/begetter of (the gods of Mt.) Ṣapunu," (i.e., all the deities of that divine mountain). However, until more textual data is discovered, it will remain an open question.

Literatur II (Münster: Ugarit-Verlag, 1994), 362–82, esp. p. 371; Schmuel Aḥituv, *Canaanite Toponyms in Ancient Egyptian Documents* (Jerusalem: Magnes, 1984), 90, s.v. EDREʿI (1) אֶדְרֶעִי.

82. Gregorio del Olmo Lete, "Bašan o el 'infierno' cananeo," *SEL* 5 (1988): 51–60.

83. For Baal, see Michael B. Hundley, *Gods in Dwellings: Temples and Divine Presence in the Ancient Near East*, WAW Supplement 3 (Atlanta: Society of Biblical Literature, 2013), 354–55. For ʾEl, see Niehr, "Die Wohnsitze des Gottes El," 327–39.

84. This is really more related to the transferal of Baal Sapan to other lands. See Mark S. Smith, *Where the Gods Are: Spatial Dimensions of Anthropomorphism in the Biblical World*, ABRL (New Haven: Yale University Press, 2016), 88. Perhaps too, the similarity in sound made a natural wordplay (צָפוֹן : צִיּוֹן).

85. The second option does not make much sense and the third option seems to be a later development in the Hebrew Bible that I am not sure would work for a site like Sheikh Šʿad.

86. Pardee, *Ritual and Cult at Ugarit*, 23 n. 3.

Even though it is poorly preserved, the significance of the relief on this stela of Ramesses II cannot be overstated. The scene depicts the royal presentation of the goddess Maʿat, an important ritual particularly of the Ramesside period. This ritual "could be thought of as an archetypal offering, a supreme offering into which all other offerings are subsumed."[87] She was the food of the deities, "the basic sustenance of the gods."[88] The presentation of Maʿat was also a potent expression of the legitimacy of the king, who is most frequently shown wearing the *ḫprš* "Blue Crown" (as Ramesses II wears on the stela's relief). Emily Teeter observes: "The presentation of Maat is a potent visible symbol that the king is capable of literally upholding the tenets of Maat by which the state is governed."[89] Consequently, this relief depicts the legitimate king, Ramesses II, who governs his lands through the maintenance of Maʿat, offering the very sustenance of the gods as a supreme offering to a Canaanite deity, "ʾEl creator of (the gods of) Ṣapunu," perhaps in this deity's shrine, which may have been located in the ancient city of Qarnaim, or at nearby ʿAštārōt, in the region renowned for its connections with the *rapiʾūma*.[90]

87. Emily Teeter, *The Presentation of Maat: Ritual and Legitimacy in Ancient Egypt*, SAOC 57; Chicago: Oriental Institute of the University of Chicago, 1997), 82.

88. Ibid.

89. Ibid., 83.

90. The original setting for the stela is, unfortunately, unknown. However, it would make sense that such a stela would be placed in the shrine of the deity to whom the offering is being made. Yoyotte states: "L'exécution consécratoire de ce geste symbolique devant le lointain Créateur du monde sémitique dans la zone où la route vers le nord passe par les montagnes du Hawrân revêt une haute importance politique." ("La stele de Ramsès II à Keswé," 54).